Machine-Learning-Assisted Intelligent Processing and Optimization of Complex Systems

Machine-Learning-Assisted Intelligent Processing and Optimization of Complex Systems

Editors

Xiong Luo
Manman Yuan

Basel • Beijing • Wuhan • Barcelona • Belgrade • Novi Sad • Cluj • Manchester

Editors

Xiong Luo
School of Computer and
Communication Engineering
University of Science and
Technology Beijing
Beijing
China

Manman Yuan
School of Computer Science
Inner Mongolia University
Hohhot
China

Editorial Office
MDPI
St. Alban-Anlage 66
4052 Basel, Switzerland

This is a reprint of articles from the Special Issue published online in the open access journal *Processes* (ISSN 2227-9717) (available at: www.mdpi.com/journal/processes/special_issues/Machine_Learning_Intelligent).

For citation purposes, cite each article independently as indicated on the article page online and as indicated below:

Lastname, A.A.; Lastname, B.B. Article Title. *Journal Name* **Year**, *Volume Number*, Page Range.

ISBN 978-3-0365-9059-2 (Hbk)
ISBN 978-3-0365-9058-5 (PDF)
doi.org/10.3390/books978-3-0365-9058-5

© 2023 by the authors. Articles in this book are Open Access and distributed under the Creative Commons Attribution (CC BY) license. The book as a whole is distributed by MDPI under the terms and conditions of the Creative Commons Attribution-NonCommercial-NoDerivs (CC BY-NC-ND) license.

Contents

About the Editors vii

Preface ix

Xiong Luo and Manman Yuan
Special Issue on "Machine-Learning-Assisted Intelligent Processing and Optimization of Complex Systems"
Reprinted from: *Processes* 2023, 11, 2595, doi:10.3390/pr11092595 1

Ruixuan Li, Hangxin Wei, Jingyuan Wang, Bo Li, Xue Zheng and Wei Bai
An Artificial Intelligence Method for Flowback Control of Hydraulic Fracturing Fluid in Oil and Gas Wells
Reprinted from: *Processes* 2023, 11, 1773, doi:10.3390/pr11061773 5

Ana Corceiro, Khadijeh Alibabaei, Eduardo Assunção, Pedro D. Gaspar and Nuno Pereira
Methods for Detecting and Classifying Weeds, Diseases and Fruits Using AI to Improve the Sustainability of Agricultural Crops: A Review
Reprinted from: *Processes* 2023, 11, 1263, doi:10.3390/pr11041263 22

Yangshuo Liu, Jianshe Kang, Liang Wen, Yunjie Bai, Chiming Guo and Weibo Yu
Fault Diagnosis Algorithm of Gearboxes Based on GWO-SCE Adaptive Multi-Threshold Segmentation and Subdomain Adaptation
Reprinted from: *Processes* 2023, 11, 556, doi:10.3390/pr11020556 62

Joel Alves, Tânia M. Lima and Pedro D. Gaspar
Is Industry 5.0 a Human-Centred Approach? A Systematic Review
Reprinted from: *Processes* 2023, 11, 193, doi:10.3390/pr11010193 92

Zhiqiang Yin, Lin Shi, Yang Yuan, Xinxin Tan and Shoukun Xu
A Study on a Knowledge Graph Construction Method of Safety Reports for Process Industries
Reprinted from: *Processes* 2023, 11, 146, doi:10.3390/pr11010146 107

Zuojun Dai, Ying Zhou, Hui Tian and Nan Ma
Task-Offloading and Resource Allocation Strategy in Multidomain Cooperation for IIoT
Reprinted from: *Processes* 2023, 11, 132, doi:10.3390/pr11010132 129

Nitisha Sharma, Mohindra Singh Thakur, Raj Kumar, Mohammad Abdul Malik, Ahmad Aziz Alahmadi and Mamdooh Alwetaishi et al.
Assessing Waste Marble Powder Impact on Concrete Flexural Strength Using Gaussian Process, SVM, and ANFIS
Reprinted from: *Processes* 2022, 10, 2745, doi:10.3390/pr10122745 146

Takahiro Ishigami, Motoki Irikura and Takahiro Tsukahara
Applicability of Convolutional Neural Network for Estimation of Turbulent Diffusion Distance from Source Point
Reprinted from: *Processes* 2022, 10, 2545, doi:10.3390/pr10122545 170

Yang Hong, Yuexia Zhang and Shaoshuai Fan
Research on Discrete Artificial Bee Colony Cache Strategy of UAV Edge Network
Reprinted from: *Processes* 2022, 10, 1838, doi:10.3390/pr10091838 183

Sadaf Waziry, Ahmad Bilal Wardak, Jawad Rasheed, Raed M. Shubair and Amani Yahyaoui
Intelligent Facemask Coverage Detector in a World of Chaos
Reprinted from: *Processes* 2022, 10, 1710, doi:10.3390/pr10091710 199

Ana P. Proença, Pedro Dinis Gaspar and Tânia M. Lima
Lean Optimization Techniques for Improvement of Production Flows and Logistics Management: The Case Study of a Fruits Distribution Center
Reprinted from: *Processes* **2022**, *10*, 1384, doi:10.3390/pr10071384 211

Moussa Tembely, Damien C. Vadillo, Ali Dolatabadi and Arthur Soucemarianadin
A Machine Learning Approach for Predicting the Maximum Spreading Factor of Droplets upon Impact on Surfaces with Various Wettabilities
Reprinted from: *Processes* **2022**, *10*, 1141, doi:10.3390/pr10061141 233

Xi Yang, Kaiwen Yang, Tianxu Cui, Min Chen and Liyan He
A Study of Text Vectorization Method Combining Topic Model and Transfer Learning
Reprinted from: *Processes* **2022**, *10*, 350, doi:10.3390/pr10020350 247

Siqiao Tan, Yu Liang, Ruowen Zheng, Hongjie Yuan, Zhengbing Zhang and Chenfeng Long
Dynamic Prediction of *Chilo suppressalis* Occurrence in Rice Based on Deep Learning
Reprinted from: *Processes* **2021**, *9*, 2166, doi:10.3390/pr9122166 263

About the Editors

Xiong Luo

Xiong Luo received a PhD degree in computer applied technology from Central South University, Changsha, China, in 2004. From 2005 to 2006, he worked as a Postdoctoral Fellow at the Tsinghua University, China. From 2012 to 2013, he worked as a Visiting Scholar at the Arizona State University, Tempe, AZ, USA. He is currently a Professor at the School of Computer and Communication Engineering, University of Science and Technology Beijing, Beijing, China. His current research interests include computational intelligence, data analytics, and machine learning. He co-edited two books published in Taylor & Francis and MDPI AG. Moreover, he has published more than 160 peer-reviewed papers in international journals and conferences, including *IEEE Transactions on Industrial Informatics, IEEE Transactions on Multimedia, IEEE Transactions on Image Processing, Processes, IEEE SMC*, and *IEEE IJCNN*. Among his published papers, there are 12 ESI Top 1% Highly Cited Papers and 2 ESI Top 0.1% Highly Cited Papers. He also received the Best Paper Award from the China Institute of Communications and IEEE Communications Society at the IEEE/CIC International Conference on Communications in China in 2019 and the IEEE Best Young Investigator Paper Award from the IEEE Control Systems Society—Beijing Chapter in 2002. Prof. Xiong Luo is an IEEE Senior Member.

Manman Yuan

Manman Yuan received a PhD degree in software engineering from the University of Science and Technology Beijing, Beijing, China, in 2020. From 2020 to 2022, she worked as a Postdoctoral Fellow at the University of Science and Technology Beijing, Beijing, China. From 2018 to 2019, she worked as a Visiting Scholar at the Humboldt–Universitat zu Berlin, Berlin, Germany. She is currently a Professor at the School of Computer Science, Inner Mongolia University, Hohhot, China. Her current research interests include complex networks, neuromorphic computing, and machine learning.

Preface

With the rapid development of the Internet of Things (IoT) and cloud computing in the past few years, a huge amount of data is being collected for various applications. Studies show that the modern world is increasingly dependent on data processing technologies. The collected data can be applied to effectively address a wide range of engineering and commercial demands. However, intelligent processing of this data is an enormous challenge that frequently confronts formidable obstacles. The main drawbacks of conventional data processing techniques originate in their limitations in extracting useful information from massive amounts of data. A feasible approach to efficient and intelligent processing is employing machine learning techniques. This approach involves gathering data from various sources, including networks, databases, applications, and sensors monitoring user activities. Appropriate algorithms are then utilized to analyze the collected data and extract useful information with reasonable performance.

Various systems with a huge amount of data and interconnected variables have been developed in communities and enterprises. Generally, conventional methods encounter significant limitations in processing and handling this amount of data, as well as complex processing algorithms. Furthermore, real-time monitoring and modifications are essential prerequisites for optimizing complex systems, achieving appropriate responses to changing circumstances, and obtaining accurate results based on reliable data. In order to continually enhance performance and enable automated and intelligent system optimization, machine learning models have been widely employed for data analysis, processing data streams in real time, and automatically adapting the system to changing conditions. This approach is also applicable to system optimization in various fields, including brain computing, smart cities, and smart businesses.

In summary, machine learning-assisted intelligent processing and optimization of complex systems have a great potential to significantly enhance the performance of processes, thereby affecting applications and industries. It should be indicated that machine learning techniques can learn from data and have a significant impact on the development of AI-driven systems.

As the Special Issue's Guest Editor, I would like to thank the authors of the papers for their excellent contributions and the reviewers for their insightful comments, which have helped to improve the work continuously. I would also like to express my gratitude to the MDPI Publications office personnel for their help with this endeavor. A special thank you to Dr. Luo Xiong, Managing Editor of the Special Issue, for his superb performance and important support throughout our collaboration.

Xiong Luo and Manman Yuan
Editors

Editorial

Special Issue on "Machine-Learning-Assisted Intelligent Processing and Optimization of Complex Systems"

Xiong Luo [1,2,3,*,†] and Manman Yuan [4,†]

1. School of Computer and Communication Engineering, University of Science and Technology Beijing, Beijing 100083, China
2. Shunde Innovation School, University of Science and Technology Beijing, Foshan 528399, China
3. Beijing Key Laboratory of Knowledge Engineering for Materials Science, Beijing 100083, China
4. School of Computer Science, Inner Mongolia University, Hohhot 010021, China; yuanman@imu.edu.cn
* Correspondence: xluo@ustb.edu.cn
† These authors contributed equally to this work.

1. Introduction

Complex systems and their various characteristics have been widely considered in economic and industrial systems. With the growth of studies in the field of artificial intelligence (AI), traditional methods that relied on prior knowledge and experiences cannot satisfy the accuracy and speed requirements of current complex systems in diversified environments.

Due to the increasing popularity of big data and AI technologies, these have become crucial types of monitoring data in fields such as finance, industry, and medicine. People can predict future trends, monitor irregularities, and categorize collected data by analyzing raw data from complex networks. For instance, according to Corceiro et al. [1], new developments have been studied in deep learning models and approaches to identify and categorize weeds, in order to enhance crops' sustainability. Although many complex systems cannot be directly observed, their internal relations and optimization can be constructed by analyzing the relevant data, which is crucial for controlling the corresponding complex systems. Thus, the processing and optimization of complex systems from big data has become a prominent and challenging issue.

Learning is the most fundamental property of any intelligent system, and machine learning (ML) is emerging as one of the most profound research areas in AI, which focuses on acquiring, transferring, regenerating, and utilizing potential information from complex systems. However, ML faces challenges when analyzing systems with strong uncertainty, randomness, redundancy, or imperfect characteristic information. In this context, Alves et al. [2] underline that human centricity should strengthen human beings and industrial operators to enhance their proficiencies and merits in collaborating or cooperating with digital devices. Focusing on ML as the critical problem in processing and optimization, this dissertation systematically discusses important and unsolved topics, including intelligent processing, system identification and optimization, malware detection and classification, intelligent modeling algorithms, etc.

Considering the data-driven capabilities and assisted-intelligent processing for complex systems, ML could revolutionize various applications and industries, which is crucial in AI-driven systems. The ultimate objective of such assistance is to execute an environmentally friendly procedure, prosperously yielding economic and health benefits.

The current Special Issue on "Machine-Learning-Assisted Intelligent Processing and Optimization for Complex Systems" (https://www.mdpi.com/journal/processes/special_issues/Machine_Learning_Intelligent, accessed on 20 May 2023) compiles new research by prominent scholars in the fields of modeling, ML, intelligent processing, and optimization of some relevant complex systems. Therefore, it provides innovative and illustrative examples, potential applications, and possible solutions to enhance the mentioned systems.

2. Intelligent Processing of Complex System

Some articles utilize ML approaches to solve practical problems from complex systems. Yin et al. [3] proposed a novel framework to effectively extract industrial safety knowledge, which summarizes the knowledge concept entities of machine and model description languages by combining the asset management shell. Dai et al. [4] presented a task-offloading and resource-allocating technique in multidomain cooperation (TARMC) for the industrial Internet of Things (IIoT) in response to the non-uniform distribution of task allocation between different cluster domain networks and the stability of conventional industrial wireless network architecture. The results indicate the superior performance of the Gaussian process technique, due to its lower error bandwidth.

In order to locate the source of gas leaks in several engineering areas, Ishigami et al. [5] investigated the practical applicability of adopting a convolutional neural network (CNN) to predict the location of gas leaks based on captured infrared images. The study found that a single learner trained with a sufficient number of images achieved an inference precision higher than 85%. Considering the problem of fault diagnosis accuracy, Liu et al. [6] integrated adaptive multi-threshold segmentation with a subdomain adaptation to propose a deep transfer fault diagnosis technique, exhibiting a higher diagnostic accuracy than and superiority to other diagnostic methods. ML methods were proposed to assess flexural strength by Li et al. [7]. Compared to other methods, the results illustrated the lower error bandwidth of the Gaussian process technique, which results in superior performance.

The striped rice stem borer (SRSB), *Chilo suppressalis*, has significantly alleviated the yield and quality of rice in China. Proper and precise forecasting of the rice pest population may assist in determining a pest control approach. Tan et al. [8] utilized weather parameters and time series of relevant pests to apply multiple linear regression (MLR), gradient boosting decision tree (GBDT), and deep auto-regressive (DeepAR) models to dynamically predict the SRSB population incidence within the crop season from 2000 to 2020 in the Hunan Province, China, and the results can achieve the most accurate dynamic forecasting.

3. Controlling of Complex Systems

Additionally, another article demonstrates the combination of ML methods and control strategies from the perspective of intelligent control. Hydraulic fracturing is crucial to improve oil and gas production. Nevertheless, traditional approaches cannot directly control the nozzle diameter, leading to 'sand production' in the flowback fluid, thus influencing the hydraulic fracturing application. The nozzle should be appropriately adjusted to prevent 'sand production' in the flowback fluid. A new augmented residual deep learning (DL) neural network (AU-RES) was presented by Sharma et al. [9] in order to detect the features of multiple one-dimensional time series signals and efficiently forecast the nozzle diameter.

4. Optimization of Complex Systems

Many studies verify particular processes to enhance the efficiency of particular models by extracting more information from specific environments. With the growth of Internet cloud technology, the data scale is extending. Conventional processing approaches cannot solve the problem of data extraction from big data. Thus, ML-assisted intelligent processing should be employed for extracting data to solve optimization problems in complex systems. The relevant works will be presented in the following.

Hong et al. [10] presented the discrete artificial bee colony cache strategy of UENs (DABCCSU). The simulations indicated that the precision of DABCCSU in content popularity forecasting exceeded 90%, attaining an excellent forecasting impact. Text data is essential data that immediately describes semantic data. Therefore, Yang et al. [11] demonstrated that topic-modeling- and transfer-learning-based text vectorization (TTTV) obtain superior outcomes when computing the similarity of texts with a similar topic, indicating that it can more precisely distinguish whether the two particular texts' contents belong to a similar topic.

The drop effect on a dry substrate can be observed in natural and industrial processes. In contrast to the conventional method through scaling rules and analytical models, Tembely et al. [12] proposed a data-driven technique to estimate the maximum spreading parameter via supervised ML approaches. This research facilitates the establishment of a general model to adjust the droplet effect, which can optimize various industrial systems.

Moreover, one article deals with the relationship between COVID-19 risk and the rate of wearing masks in public places. The prevalence of COVID-19 worldwide has resulted in a universal safety disaster associated with economic outcomes. As per the World Health Organization (WHO), the mentioned destructive crisis can be alleviated by utilizing facemasks in public locations. Nevertheless, COVID-19 can be prevented only by proper nose and mouth coverage. An automatic mask-wearing system is required for these situations, in accordance with the work of Waziry et al. [13], whose experimental work indicated the superiority of InceptionV3 and EfficientNetB2 to other approaches, achieving a total precision of about 98.40%.

Regarding the economic effects of complex systems with ML assistance, optimization approaches have been utilized to enhance production flows, cold storage management, and fruit center distribution. Proença et al. [14] optimized the production rules and management logistics to improve productivity, energy efficiency, human resources distribution, and food quality, while alleviating food waste.

5. Conclusions

We believe that the articles in this Special Issue reveal several advantages in intelligent processing and optimization for complex systems based on ML assistance. Expertise in ML, as well as numerical analysis and applications of complex networks, should be demanded for in pursuing research in this field. We hope that this issue promotes integration among different communities, as artificial intelligence becomes increasingly indispensable.

Finally, we sincerely thank all the authors, editorial staff, and reviewers for their enthusiastic effort and valuable contributions to this Special Issue.

Author Contributions: Writing—original draft preparation, X.L. and M.Y.; writing—review and editing, X.L. and M.Y. All authors have read and agreed to the published version of the manuscript.

Funding: This work was partly funded by the Beijing Natural Science Foundation under Grant L211020.

Conflicts of Interest: The authors declare no conflict of interest.

References

1. Corceiro, A.; Alibabaei, K.; Assunção, E.; Gaspar, P.D.; Pereira, N. Methods for Detecting and Classifying Weeds, Diseases and Fruits Using AI to Improve the Sustainability of Agricultural Crops: A Review. *Processes* **2023**, *11*, 1263. [CrossRef]
2. Alves, J.; Lima, T.M.; Gaspar, P.D. Is Industry 5.0 a Human-Centred Approach? A Systematic Review. *Processes* **2023**, *11*, 193. [CrossRef]
3. Yin, Z.; Shi, L.; Yuan, Y.; Tan, X.; Xu, S. A study on a knowledge graph construction method of safety reports for process industries. *Processes* **2023**, *11*, 146. [CrossRef]
4. Dai, Z.; Zhou, Y.; Tian, H.; Ma, N. Task-Offloading and Resource Allocation Strategy in Multidomain Cooperation for IIoT. *Processes* **2023**, *11*, 132. [CrossRef]
5. Ishigami, T.; Irikura, M.; Tsukahara, T. Applicability of Convolutional Neural Network for Estimation of Turbulent Diffusion Distance from Source Point. *Processes* **2022**, *10*, 2545. [CrossRef]
6. Liu, Y.; Kang, J.; Wen, L.; Bai, Y.; Guo, C.; Yu, W. Fault diagnosis algorithm of gearboxes based on GWO-SCE adaptive multi-threshold segmentation and subdomain adaptation. *Processes* **2023**, *11*, 556. [CrossRef]
7. Li, R.; Wei, H.; Wang, J.; Li, B.; Zheng, X.; Bai, W. An Artificial Intelligence Method for Flowback Control of Hydraulic Fracturing Fluid in Oil and Gas Wells. *Processes* **2023**, *11*, 1773. [CrossRef]
8. Tan, S.; Liang, Y.; Zheng, R.; Yuan, H.; Zhang, Z.; Long, C. Dynamic Prediction of *Chilo suppressalis* Occurrence in Rice Based on Deep Learning. *Processes* **2021**, *9*, 2166. [CrossRef]
9. Sharma, N.; Thakur, M.S.; Malik, M.A.; Alahmadi, A.A.; Alwetaishi, M.; Alzaed, A.N. Assessing Waste Marble Powder Impact on Concrete Flexural Strength Using Gaussian Process, SVM, and ANFIS. *Processes* **2022**, *10*, 2745. [CrossRef]

10. Hong, Y.; Zhang, Y.; Fan, S. Research on Discrete Artificial Bee Colony Cache Strategy of UAV Edge Network. *Processes* **2022**, *10*, 1838. [CrossRef]
11. Yang, X.; Yang, K.; Cui, T.; Chen, M.; He, L. A Study of Text Vectorization Method Combining Topic Model and Transfer Learning. *Processes* **2022**, *10*, 350. [CrossRef]
12. Tembely, M.; Vadillo, D.C.; Dolatabadi, A.; Soucemarianadin, A. A Machine Learning Approach for Predicting the Maximum Spreading Factor of Droplets upon Impact on Surfaces with Various Wettabilities. *Processes* **2022**, *10*, 1141. [CrossRef]
13. Waziry, S.; Wardak, A.B.; Rasheed, J.; Shubair, M.; Yahyaoui, A. Intelligent Facemask Coverage Detector in a World of Chaos. *Processes* **2022**, *10*, 1710. [CrossRef]
14. Proença, A.P.; Gaspar, P.D.; Lima, T.M. Lean Optimization Techniques for Improvement of Production Flows and Logistics Management: The Case Study of a Fruits Distribution Center. *Processes* **2022**, *10*, 1384. [CrossRef]

Disclaimer/Publisher's Note: The statements, opinions and data contained in all publications are solely those of the individual author(s) and contributor(s) and not of MDPI and/or the editor(s). MDPI and/or the editor(s) disclaim responsibility for any injury to people or property resulting from any ideas, methods, instructions or products referred to in the content.

Article

An Artificial Intelligence Method for Flowback Control of Hydraulic Fracturing Fluid in Oil and Gas Wells

Ruixuan Li, Hangxin Wei *, Jingyuan Wang, Bo Li, Xue Zheng and Wei Bai

Mechanical Engineering College, Xian ShiYou University, Xi'an 710065, China; liruixuan106@163.com (R.L.); m15191764635@163.com (J.W.); libo@xsyu.edu.cn (B.L.); 19893318643@163.com (X.Z.); 17391826659@163.com (W.B.)
* Correspondence: weihangxin@xsyu.edu.cn; Tel.: +86-152-9118-4063

Citation: Li, R.; Wei, H.; Wang, J.; Li, B.; Zheng, X.; Bai, W. An Artificial Intelligence Method for Flowback Control of Hydraulic Fracturing Fluid in Oil and Gas Wells. *Processes* **2023**, *11*, 1773. https://doi.org/10.3390/pr11061773

Academic Editor: Xiong Luo

Received: 18 May 2023
Revised: 2 June 2023
Accepted: 5 June 2023
Published: 10 June 2023

Copyright: © 2023 by the authors. Licensee MDPI, Basel, Switzerland. This article is an open access article distributed under the terms and conditions of the Creative Commons Attribution (CC BY) license (https://creativecommons.org/licenses/by/4.0/).

Abstract: Hydraulic fracturing is one of the main ways to increase oil and gas production. However, with existing methods, the diameter of the nozzle cannot be easily adjusted. This therefore results in 'sand production' in flowback fluid, affecting the application of hydraulic fracturing. This is because it is difficult to identify the one-dimensional series signal of fracturing fluid collected on site. In order to avoid 'sand production' in the flowback fluid, the nozzle should be properly controlled. Aiming to address this problem, a novel augmented residual deep learning neural network (AU-RES) is proposed that can identify the characteristics of multiple one-dimensional time series signals and effectively predict the diameter of the nozzle. The AU-RES network includes three parts: signal conversion layer, residual and convolutional layer, fully connected layer (including regression layer). Firstly, a spatial conversion algorithm for multiple one-dimensional time series signals is proposed, which can transform the one-dimensional time series signals into images in high dimensional space. Secondly, the features of the images are extracted and identified by the residual network. Thirdly, the network hyperparameters are optimized to improve the prediction accuracy of the network. Simulations and experiments performed on the field data samples show that the RMSE and LOSS when training the AU-RES network are 0.131 and 0.00021, respectively, and the prediction error of the test samples is 0.1689. In the gas field experiments, fracturing fluid sand production could be controlled, thus demonstrating the validity and reliability of the AU-RES network. By using the AU-RES neural network, sand particles will not be present in the flowback of fracturing fluid, thus improving the efficiency of hydraulic fracturing and reducing the cost of hydraulic fracturing. In addition, the AU-RES network can also be used in other similar situations.

Keywords: artificial intelligence; deep learning neural network; process control; hydraulic fracture

1. Introduction

Artificial intelligence has become a research hotspot, and will come to be widely used in various industries [1,2], especially in the oil and gas industry [3–6]. In the process of oil and gas recovery, hydraulic fracturing technology is widely used to increase production. In the context of hydraulic fracturing technology, flowback control of the fracturing fluid is an aspect belonging to process control, and is achieved by controlling the opening or closing of the nozzle at the wellhead according to the downhole fluid parameters. This results in the diameter of the nozzle being adjusted. In this way, no sand is produced in the fracturing fluid. However, conventional control methods are inefficient and sand particles in the formation can easily be discharged with the flowback of fracturing fluid, resulting in a 'sand production' problem. Therefore, the introduction of artificial intelligence technology into the flowback control process of fracturing fluid is necessary, as it will be able to solve this problem.

When considering the use of artificial intelligence in the flowback control of fracturing fluid, research has been performed evaluating a number of different methods, including fuzzy control [3], shallow artificial neural network control [7], deep artificial neural network control [8–10] (such as CNN, LetNet, VGG16, Alexnet), and so on. However, because the flowback control of fracturing fluid is characterized by strong nonlinearity, and some of the downhole parameters are difficult to obtain, it is necessary to use the deep learning neural network, which can achieve good results. The conventional deep neural networks, i.e., the CNN, LetNet, VGG16, Alexnet networks, are often used in image classification. Although they can output a continuous value if their last layer (the activation function Softmax) can be substituted by a regression layer, the accuracy will be low. Therefore, these neural networks should be modified to adapt their prediction of continuous values [11] such as the nozzle diameter. In essence, the fracturing fluid flowback control identifies multiple one-dimensional signals in oil and gas wells using a deep learning neural network, then performs high-level feature transformation, and outputs a continuous signal (nozzle diameter). Therefore, its structure is similar to that of the long short-term memory (LSTM) network [12,13] and certain kinds of temporal convolutional network (TCN) [14].

To date, LSTM, TCN and other similar methods have been studied by many researchers. Hu Xiaodong [7] proposed a shale gas production prediction model with a fitting function neural network. The model, consisting of a fitting function, LSTM and a DNN neural network, predicts the parameters according to time domain signals. Zhang Lei et al. [12] proposed a time-domain convolutional neural network TCN model to solve the problem of time-domain signal prediction. Sagheer A [13] proposed a kind of deep LSTM recurrent network for predicting production. BAI S J et al. [14] evaluated convolutional networks and recurrent networks for time sequence signal modeling. In addition, they proposed a combination of convolutional networks with recurrent networks. Gu Jianwei [15] introduced an LSTM network to predict oil production. Huang R J [16] used an LSTM network to forecast the production performance of a carbonate reservoir. Wang J [17] studied a hybrid network of CNN and LSTM to forecast the production of fractured wells, overcoming the shortcomings of the traditional method, which relies on personal experience. In essence, LSTM is used to predict future values according to historical data. However, for the control of the flowback of fracturing fluid (or nozzle diameter prediction), it is necessary to determine the current value (nozzle diameter) according to multiple kinds of current signal and the historical signal. Therefore, the above methods still present challenges in terms of processing these unstructured data and processing multiple one-dimensional time series signals, such as those related to the flowback of fracturing fluid. In addition, the inclusion of a CNN layer in LSTM or TCN results in degradation when the training epoch increases. Therefore, the accuracy of the LSTM or TCN network will decrease.

From the above discussion, it is clear that the neural networks described above cannot be directly applied in the flowback control of fracturing fluid, due to the complexity of the fracturing flowback process. In this case, the nozzle diameter needs to be predicted based on multiple one-dimensional time series signals. In addition, it is necessary to consider not only the dynamical factors affecting the nozzle diameter, but also the static factors affecting the nozzle diameter. Therefore, an augmented residual deep learning neural network (AU-RES) structure is proposed to control the fracturing flowback process. Firstly, the spatial transformation of multiple one-dimensional time series signals of fracturing flowback is carried out. Then, the conventional residual neural network structure [18] is modified to form a new AU-RES neural network to control the flowback of fracturing fluid. Next, the AU-RES neural network is used to identify and judge the input signal, and outputs a nozzle diameter. Finally, the performance of the AU-RES network is verified by simulation and experiment.

2. Problem Description and Solution

2.1. Problem Description

The principle of fracturing flowback control is shown in Figure 1a, and includes two steps. First step: the fracturing fluid containing sand is firstly injected underground at high pressure from the ground surface. The high-pressure fluid creates cracks in the rock. Sand particles in the fluid support cracking, so that oil or gas from the rock will permeate into the well. Second step: after a crack or fracture has been formed in the rock, the fracturing fluid needs to flow back to the surface. Fracturing fluid flows through the well via the oil tube, and then flows out through the surface nozzle. During this process, the sand needs to remain in the fracture, otherwise it will close again. In order to prevent sand in the fracture from flowing out of the well, it is necessary to control the ground nozzle. Therefore, methods for determining an optimal nozzle diameter constitute a core problem of fracturing flowback control.

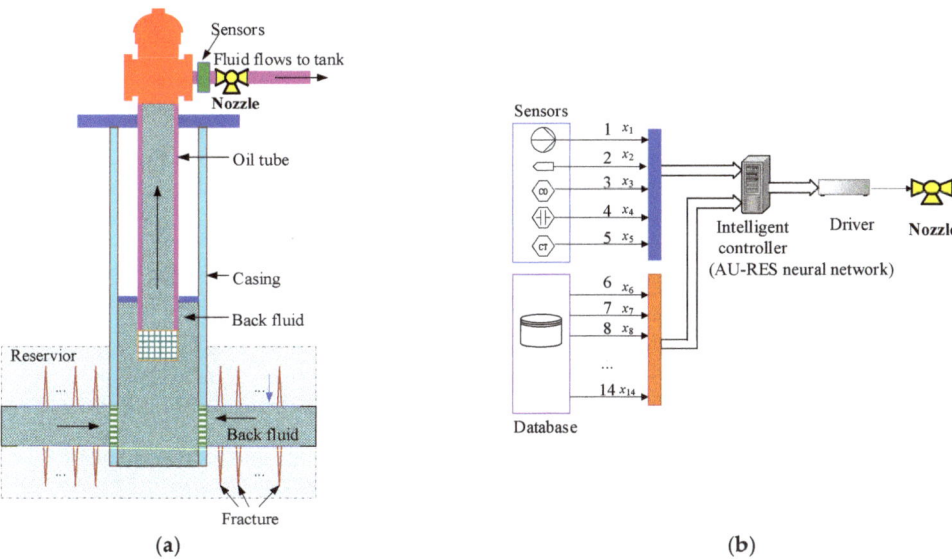

Figure 1. Principle of hydraulic fracturing and intelligent control scheme. 1—Fluid pressure; 2—flow rate; 3—viscosity; 4—temperature; 5—sand rate; 6—pressure in reservoir; 7—permeability; 8—porosity; 9—Poisson's ratio of rock; 10—fracture length; 11—fracture height; 12—inner diameter of oil tube; 13—inner diameter of casing; 14—depth of gas well. (**a**) Principle of hydraulic fracturing. (**b**) Intelligent control scheme.

In the past, the method for determining the diameter of the nozzle usually involved analyzing the hydrodynamic formula of flowback fluid, on the basis of which an approximate solution for the nozzle diameter was obtained. For example, in Figure 1a, when the diameter of the nozzle changes, the inlet pressure (at the left side of the nozzle) p_d will also change. In addition, the fluid in the oil tube transmits the p_d to the bottom well. Therefore, the pressure p_r at the bottom well will also change. p_d is the inlet pressure of the nozzle, which reflects the fluid pressure in the oil tube before the nozzle. p_r is the formation pressure, which reflects whether the fracturing particles can leave the rock fractures (cracks). The pressure p_d and p_r can be written as:

$$p_d(t) = \varphi(d, p_o, t) \tag{1}$$

$$p_r(t) = f(p_d, t, x_1, x_2, x_3, \ldots, x_n) \tag{2}$$

In Equations (1) and (2), t is time. $x_1, x_2, x_3, \ldots, x_n$ parameters related to the flowback fluid in the oil tube. d is the nozzle diameter. Po is the outlet pressure of the nozzle (at the right side of the nozzle). Because φ ( ) and f ( ) are nonlinear functions and Equations (1) and (2) involve multiple hydrodynamic differential equations, it is difficult to obtain a precise solution. The prediction error of the nozzle diameter using the traditional method is large. Therefore, a problem to be solved is to predict the nozzle diameter according to the nonlinear function relationship in the variable $x_1 \sim x_n$ simulation Equations (1) and (2).

2.2. Solution

In order to solve the problem of the large error when predicting the nozzle diameter using traditional methods, a new artificial intelligence method is proposed for predicting nozzle diameter. The scheme is shown in Figure 1b. The intelligent controller in Figure 1b is the deep learning neural network. In this paper, we introduce a novel augmented residual deep learning neural network (AU-RES) that is able to identify time series signals of flowback fluid on the basis of the characteristics of fracturing flowback fluid signals, thus allowing accurate prediction of the nozzle diameter.

The principle of Figure 1b is as follows: firstly, fracturing fluid flowback parameters are collected and fed into the AU-RES neural network. Secondly, the AU-RES neural network extracts the features of the input data ($x_1 \sim x_{14}$) and recognizes it according to the self-learning algorithm. Thirdly, the AU-RES neural network outputs the diameter of the nozzle. Because AU-RES neural networks can simulate the complex nonlinear functional relationships in Equations (1) and (2), when trained with field data, the neural networks can learn from the experience of the operator. Therefore the AU-RES neural network can achieve good control effect.

In Figure 1b, $x_1 \sim x_5$ change over time. Therefore, they need to be collected with sensors. x_1 is the oil pressure in the flowback fluid. x_2 is the casing pressure. x_3 is the flow rate. x_4 is viscosity. x_5 is the temperature of the flowback fluid. The signals for $x_6 \sim x_{14}$ generally do not change with time. Therefore, they can be obtained from the database. x_6 is the pressure of the formation. x_7 is permeability. x_8 is porosity. x_9 is crack half-length. x_{10} is crack height. x_{11} is the Poisson's ratio of the rock. x_{12} is the inner diameter of the casing. x_{13} is the inner diameter of the oil tube. x_{14} is the depth of the oil/gas well.

Focusing on the characteristics $x_1 \sim x_{14}$, the AU-RES neural network was designed as shown in Figure 2. The input data for the AU-RES neural network are the time series signals, and the output is the diameter of the nozzle. The network includes a signal conversion layer, a residual connection layer, and a fully connected layer (including regression layer). The function of the signal conversion layer is to transform the one-dimensional time series signals into a two-dimensional image so that the neural network can identify it better. For the first layer, $x_1 \sim x_{14}$ are time series signals, as shown in Figure 1. These signals are input into the signal conversion layer. The function of the residual connection layer is to extract the high-level features from the inputted images to identify the different time series signals. In order to distinguish the differences in time series signals, the sublayers Stem, Incept-A, Incept-B, Incept-C, and Incept-D are used, which have different convolutional nodes. The function of convolution is to extract information from the input image. The role of pooling is to perform feature selection, thereby reducing the number of features, and thus the number of parameters. In this paper, the residual connection layer is transferred directly from the Res-incept-V2 neural network, which absorbs the transfer learning neural network [19]. The fully connected layer transforms the high-level features (matrices) into large one-dimensional vectors that can identify images and output a continuous value (i.e., nozzle diameter). The regression layer must be located at the end of the AU-RES neural network. Because the AU-RES neural network outputs a continuous value, it is a regression problem, rather than a classification problem.

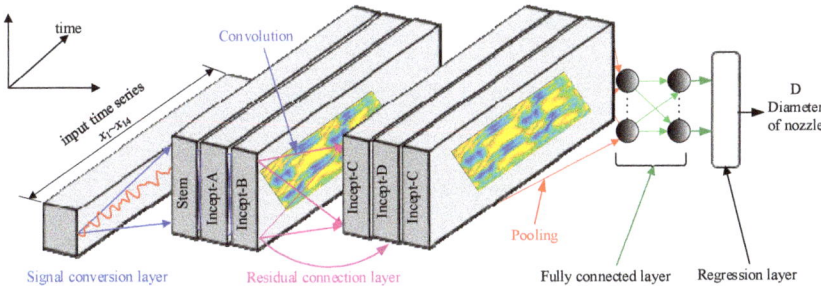

Figure 2. Structure of AU-RES neural network.

3. Algorithm of AU-RES Neural Network

3.1. Signal Conversion in the Time Domain

The data collected in Figure 1b include $x_1 \sim x_{14}$. However, in practice, these data have different effects on nozzle diameter. $x_1 \sim x_5$ denote real-time data collected during fracturing fluid flowback. These data change frequently, and are the main factor affecting nozzle diameter, while $x_6 \sim x_{14}$ are data measured off-line, and are generally stored in the database. They rarely change, and are minor factors affecting the nozzle diameter. In addition, there are other parameters, but because these parameters have very little influence on nozzle diameter, they are ignored, and their influence is implied in the weight of the AU-RES neural network. Therefore, the data transformation algorithm is designed according to the characteristics of these data.

We can define one-dimensional time series signals $x_1 = [x_{11}, x_{12}, \ldots, x_{1M}]$, $x_2 = [x_{21}, x_{22}, \ldots, x_{2M}]$, $\ldots$, $x_5 = [x_{51}, x_{52}, \ldots, x_{5M}]$, where $x_1 \sim x_5$ are shown in Figure 1b. M is the sample number. Therefore, they can be written as:

$$x_i = [x_{i1}, x_{i2}, \ldots, x_{iM}], i = 1 \sim 5 \tag{3}$$

We can also define another one-dimensional signal, as follows:

$$\tilde{x}_j = [x_j, x_j, x_j] \; j = 6 \sim 14 \tag{4}$$

In Equation (4), we want to extend $x_6 \sim x_{14}$ in Figure 1b as vectors, so that variations in nozzle diameter can be reflected.

Definition 1. *We define a multi-variant time series and non-time series signal:*

$$X = [x_1, x_2, x_3, x_4, x_5, x_1, x_2, x_3, x_4, x_5, \tilde{x}_6, \tilde{x}_7, \ldots, \tilde{x}_{14}] \tag{5}$$

where $x_1 \sim x_5$ are time series signals, and $\tilde{x}_6 \sim \tilde{x}_{14}$ is a single data point, in which $x_1 \sim x_5 \in R^M$, $\tilde{x}_6 \sim \tilde{x}_{14} \in R^3$. Therefore, X is a column vector and $X \in R^{10M+27}$, and we merge all the data in Figure 2 to X. When M = 28, the length of X is 307. Because the signals $x_1 \sim x_5$ contain noise, we need to filter the signals, as shown in Figure 3. In Figure 3, the input signals include $x_1 \sim x_5$ and $\tilde{x}_6 \sim \tilde{x}_{14}$. The process of data merging is shown in Figure 4. Since the amplitude of the input signals are inconsistent, it needs to be normalized to convert its amplitude to [0–1]. The normalization equation is:

$$\hat{X}_i = (X_i - X_{\min})/(X_{\max} - X_{\min}) \tag{6}$$

where X_i is the ith element of X. $\hat{X}_i$ is the normalized result. The normalized data can meet the requirement of neural network. In the next module, all the components of $\hat{X}_i$ are combined to form a column vector with dimensions of 10M + 27. Finally, a matrix, namely a two-dimensional image, is formed by the algorithm presented as Equation (8).

Definition 2. *We also define a dataset:*

$$D = \{(X^1,Y^1), (X^2,Y^2), \ldots, (X^N,Y^N)\} \tag{7}$$

D is taken as the training sample and testing sample for the AU-RES network. Y is the diameter of the nozzle, which is a continuous number. Therefore, the task of the AU-RES network is to find the map between the time series signal X and the nozzle diameter. Note that this is a regression problem, which is different from the problem of time series classification.

Next, we create a mapping relationship, X→I, which converts X into a two-dimensional matrix (image) using the following equation:

$$I = \begin{bmatrix} \cos(X_1 + X_1) & \cos(X_1 + X_2) & \cos(X_1 + X_{10M+27}) \\ \cos(X_2 + X_1) & \cos(X_2 + X_2) & \cos(X_2 + X_{10M+27}) \\ \cos(X_{10M+27} + X_1) & \cos(X_{10M+27} + X_2) & \cos(X_{10M+27} + X_{10M+27}) \end{bmatrix} \tag{8}$$

where $I \in R^{(10M+27) \times (10M+27)}$, which is similar to the GAF transformation [20–23].

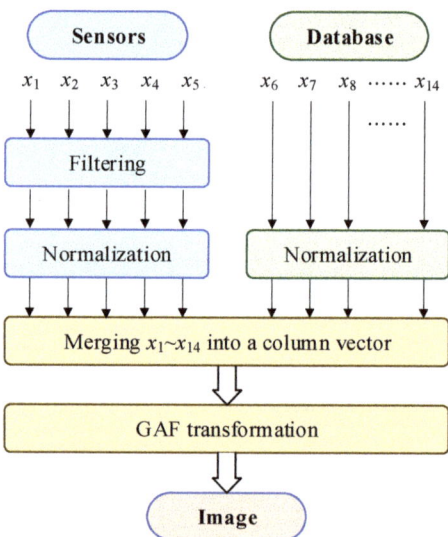

Figure 3. Algorithm of data conversion.

The matrix I can be drawn as an image, as shown in Figure 4. Figure 4a is a clear image that includes many square lattices. Every lattice reflects the relationship between x_i and x_j. Therefore, this image can represent the characteristics of $x_1\sim x_{14}$. The blue color (dark color) represents low signal amplitude (the lowest value is 0), and the yellow color (bright color) represents high signal amplitude (the highest value is 1). Therefore, the color of the image reflects the distribution of the original signal amplitude. In order to improve the generalization ability of the neural network, it is necessary to convert clear images into fuzzy images. Therefore, Figure 4a is blurred, and the fuzzy image is shown at Figure 4b.

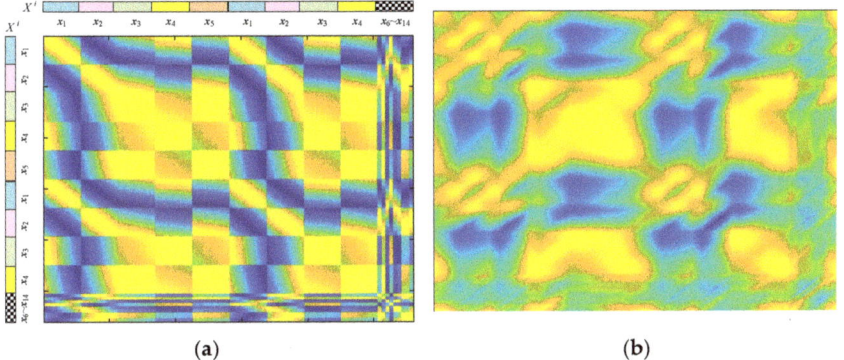

Figure 4. The image converted by the GAF transformation. (**a**) Clear image. (**b**) Blurred and fuzzy image.

3.2. Residual Neural Network

In the course of our research, we compared different networks, such as Lenet, Alexnet, VGG16, residual network Inception V2, etc., and we found that the residual network [24–26] had the best performance, so the residual network was used to predict the nozzle diameter. The residual network was proposed by Kaiming HE [18,24], and consists of different residual modules; the basic residual module is shown in Figure 5.

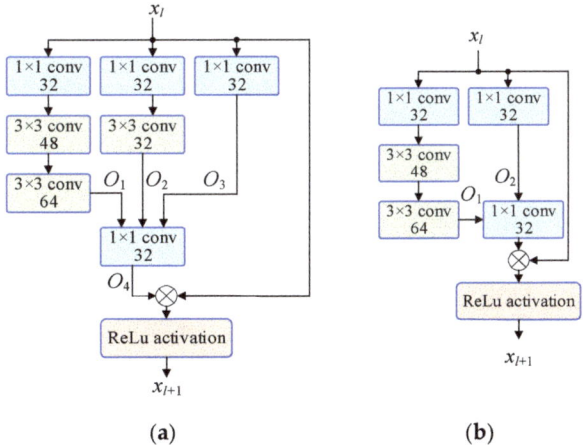

Figure 5. *Cont.*

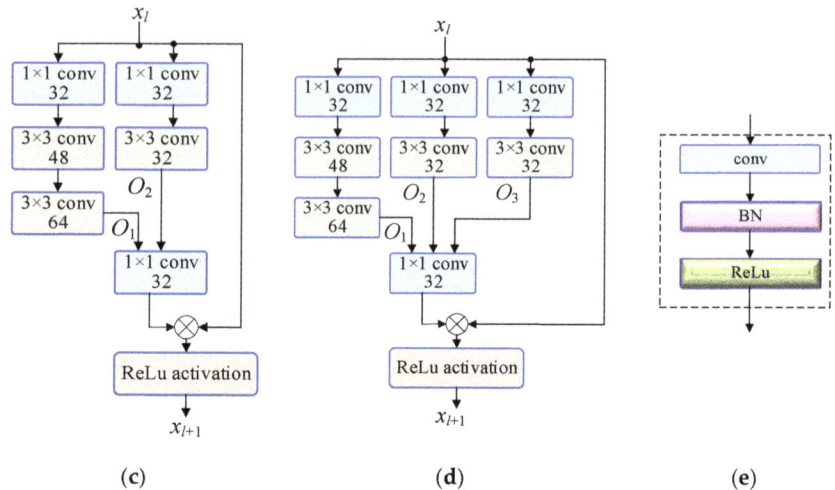

Figure 5. The basic residual modules. (**a**) Incept-A. (**b**) Incept-B. (**c**) Incept-C. (**d**) Incept-D. (**e**) Inner structure of $i \times i$ conv in Incept-A~Incept_D (i = 1,3).

In Figure 5, it can be seen that the residual neural network includes 4 kinds of residual module, with each module having a different function. Different module combinations are designed in the residual network to sense different visual fields in the image, that is, to extract different features of the image. In addition, there is a phenomenon in deep learning neural networks whereby if the number of network layers is small, the training error will be large, but if the number of network layers is too large, a "degradation" phenomenon can easily occur, that is, the network accuracy will decrease instead of increasing. Therefore, a direct channel is added to the residual network, the main purpose of which is to retain the image information (after many convolutional layers have been transformed, the original information of the image may disappear, resulting in network degradation). By employing this setting, the residual network can not only obtain higher precision, but the degradation phenomenon can also be avoided.

Figure 5a shows the residual module of Incept-A, which has 4 channels to convert the input signal. From left to right, in the first channel, the image is converted through 1×1, 3×3, and 3×3 convolutional layers. Where '1×1 conv 32' means the kernel size is 1×1, and the depth is 32. Every 'conv' includes a convolutional layer, a batch normalization (BN) layer and an activation function (ReLu), as is shown in Figure 5e. Similarly, in the second channel, the image is converted through 1×1 and 3×3 convolutional layers. In the third channel, the image is converted through a 1×1 convolutional layer. The first layer, the second layer and the third layer are all connected to a 1×1 convolutional layer. This layer plays the role of changing the image dimensions so that the dimensions are the same as those of the fourth channel. If the input image is 64×64, the output O_1 is 60×60, the output O_2 of the second channel on the left is 62×62, and the output O_3 of the third channel on the left is 64×64, since the dimensions of the three images are inconsistent, it is necessary to perform a transformation in the 1×1 convolutional layer to obtain an output image with dimensions of 64×64. The fourth channel is the direct channel of the image, which reflects the 'identity mapping'. This channel is very important for the residual neural network, and can reserve the information in the image during signal conversion. Therefore, network degradation during training can be avoided, and the precision of the network can be improved. Because of the existence of the identity mapping layer, the error of image recognition can be reduced.

In the same way, Figure 5b shows Incept-B, which consists of three channels. Figure 5c shows Incept-C, which consists of three channels. In addition, Figure 5d shows Incept-D, which consists of four channels. These modules contain different numbers of convolutional layers. Compared with Incept-A and Incept-D, the third channel on the left of Incept-A has only one convolutional layer, while the third channel on the left of Incept-D has two convolutional layers. Therefore, the output O_3 of Incept-A is different from that of Incept-D.

3.3. AU-RES Neural Network

Based on the structure of the residual network, we added a data feature transformation layer and a fully connected layer to form a new AU-RES neural network. The structure of the AU-RES neural network is shown in Figure 6. Layer 1 is the signal conversion layer in Figure 2. It can convert multiple one-dimensional time series signals into a two-dimensional image. Layer 2 is the residual connection layer in Figure 2, which can extract the high-level features of the input image. In layer 2, the 'stem' includes 12 convolutional layers, 12 batch normalization layers, 12 activation functions (ReLu), a max-polling layer, and an average-pooling layer. Since the structure of 'stem' in layer 2 is the same as that of Res-Inception-V2, the detailed structure of the 'stem' is not drawn here. Layer 3 is the fully connected layer, and the last part is the regression layer, which outpus a value for nozzle diameter.

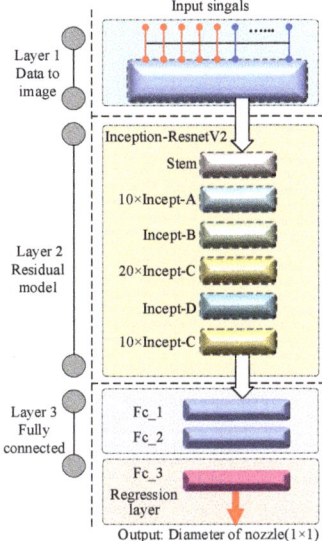

Figure 6. Structure of AU-RES neural networks.

3.4. Loss Function

Since the AU-RES network outputs continuous values, the mean square error MSE is used as the loss function, as follows:

$$Loss(\hat{Y}_t, Y_t) = \frac{1}{n}\sum_{i=1}^{n}(\hat{Y}_t^i - Y_t^i)^2 \qquad (9)$$

where $\hat{Y}_t$ is the expected output. Y_t is the actual output. n is the number of training samples. Loss reflects the difference between the actual output and the expected output.

3.5. Training Algorithm

The training algorithm is shown in Figure 7, and can be described as follows:

Step 1: Data are collected on site. Then, unreasonable data are filtered out and deleted. Finally, samples are made using the processed data. The input to the residual model in the AU-RES neural network is the two-dimensional image of the data transformation, including flow, pressure, and temperature. In addition, the output of the AU-RES neural network is the label (Y in Equation (6)).

Step 2: The finite element difference method is used to calculate the downhole fluid dynamics model, supplementing the simulated sample.

Step 3: The neural network hyperparameters and initial values are set.

Step 4: 80% of samples are selected as the training set to train the neural network.

Step 5: Whether the AU-RES neural network training process converges is observed.

Step 6: 20% of the sample set is used as the test set to study the influence of different hyperparameters on the prediction accuracy and optimize the AU-RES neural network structure. Here, we introduce an index of prediction error E for AU-RES.

$$E = \sqrt{\|y^e - y^a\|_2} \tag{10}$$

where $\| \|_2$ represents the norm of Euclidean space vectors.

Step 7: Training process finished.

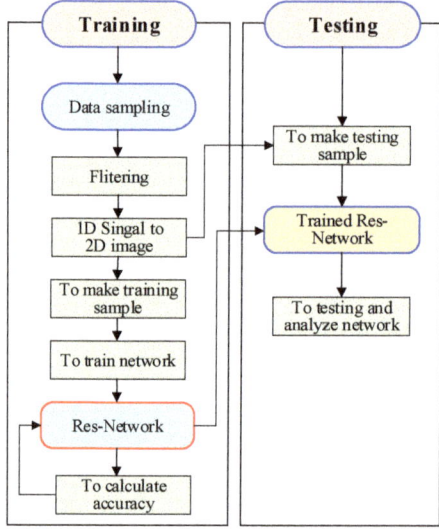

Figure 7. Training algorithm.

4. Simulation and Experiment

4.1. Training Sample

Training samples for the AU-RES network come in two types: samples collected on site, and simulated samples calculated using the finite element difference method. The flow rate, fluid pressure, fluid temperature, fluid viscosity, and sand content in the fluid are collected at 1 min intervals at the gas well site. When the AU-RES neural network is trained, the training sample is input to the AU-RES neural network, and the label is added to the output end of the neural network. Here, the label is nozzle diameter (Y^i in Equation (6)).

These samples (one-dimensional time series signals) are transformed into images in the signal conversion layer. Images are shown in Figure 8 that correspond to nozzle diameters from 3 mm to 13 mm. In Figure 8, the blue color (dark color) represents low signal amplitude (the lowest value is 0), and the yellow color (bright color) represents high signal amplitude (the highest value is 1). Different color distributions in the image represent changes in the amplitude of the input one-dimensional time series signals. Therefore, the overall color of the image reflects the nozzle diameter corresponding to the time series signal.

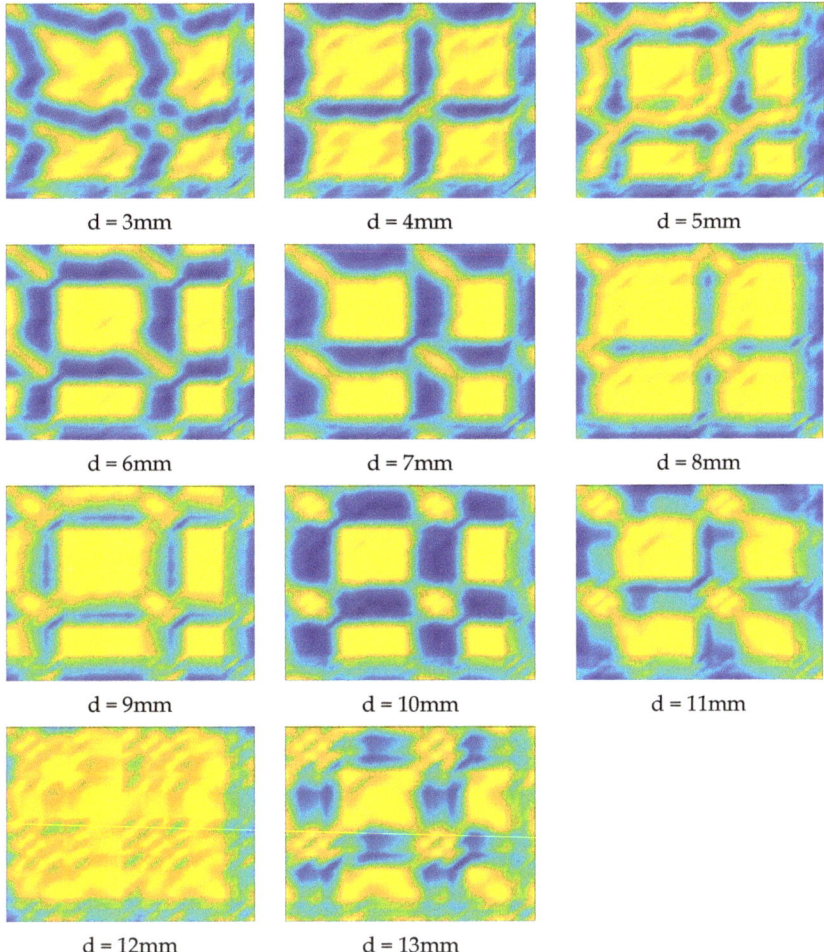

Figure 8. Images transformed by the signal conversion layer in the AU-RES network.

4.2. Training Process

The training samples are input into the AU-RES neural network to train the AU-RES neural network. The parameters corresponding to node number and convolutional kernels in the convolutional layer and the pooling layer in the AU-RES network are the same as those of Res-Inception-V2. The initial bias value of each node in the convolutional layer is set as [0.001, 0.001, ... , 0.001], the weight as [0, 0, ... , 0], and the initial learning rate is 0.0001. The parameter update method for the AU-RES neural network is Adam. When training the neural network, the computer configuration was as follows: the CPU was an AMD Ryzon 3 3100, and the memory (RAM) size was 24 GB. The computer graphics card was an NVIDIA GeForce GTX 1050Ti. It took 26 h to train the AU-RES neural network. However, the testing time was only 0.20 s. Therefore, the AU-RES neural network can be used in engineering applications. The AU-RES neural network was trained for 150 epochs, and its convergence was observed, as shown in Figure 9. Figure 9a represents the training RMSE, which reflects the Root Mean Square Error between the actual output and the expected output of the training sample. Figure 9b represents the training loss, which reflects the loss function in Equation (8) between the actual output and the expected output of the training sample. When training the AU-RES neural network, loss can often be used to calculate the gradient and update the weight value of each node. As can be seen from Figure 9, after 150 epochs of training, the RMSE value converges stably to 0.131, and the loss value converges to 0.00021, which indicates that the AU-RES neural network parameters have reached their optimal values. The AU-RES neural network training process is concluded.

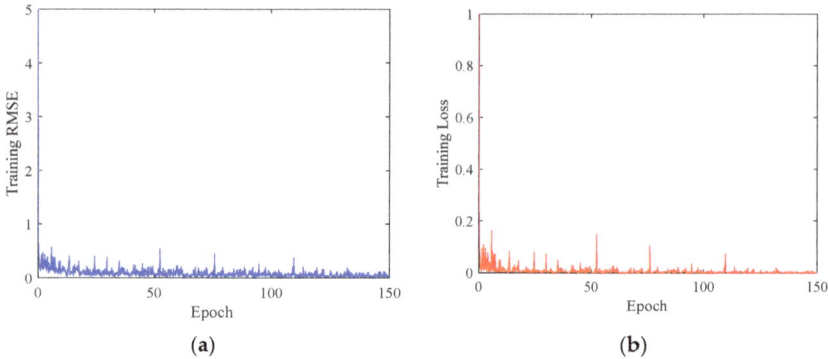

Figure 9. AU-RES neural network training process. (**a**) Training RMSE. (**b**) Training Loss.

4.3. The Influence of Hyperparameters on AU-RES Network Performance

AU-RES neural network hyperparameters include internal node number, convolution kernel size, learning rate, and gradient update method. In this paper, since the number of nodes and the convolutional kernel of the convolutional layer are the same as those of the residual network Res-Inception-V2, these parameters are fixed. When training the AU-RES network, the change in network performance was observed when changing the learning rate, gradient update method, and the number of nodes in the fully connected layer.

After changing the learning rate of the AU-RES neural network, we observed the change in the performance of the network, with results as shown in Table 1. As can be seen from Table 1, the AU-RES neural network performance was best when the learning rate was 0.0001.

Table 1. The effect of using different learning rates on the performance of the neural network.

Number	Learning Rate	Loss	E
1	0.001	0.0512	0.4601
2	0.0001	0.00021	0.1689
3	0.00001	0.0020	0.2015

The gradient update method is changed, with Sgdm, Adam and RMSprop being employed, respectively. The test error of the different methods after network training was observed, with results as shown in Table 2. It can be seen that when the Adam method was adopted, the test sample prediction error E was the lowest, which means that the accuracy of the network was the highest.

Table 2. The effect of update method of hyperparameters on the performance of the neural network.

Number	Gradient Updating Methods	Loss	E
1	Adam	0.00021	0.1689
2	RMSprop	0.00137	0.3358
3	Sgdm	divergence	divergence

4.4. The Influence of the Fully Connected Layer on AU-RES Network Performance

The number of nodes in the fully connected layer can be changed, and the corresponding changes in AU-RES network performance can be observed, as shown in Figure 10. The fully connected layer of the AU-RES network is divided into three layers, among which the number of nodes in the third layer must be consistent with the dimensions of the output signal. Since the output of the AU-RES network is a one-dimensional continuous value, the number of nodes in the third layer (i.e., the regression layer) network can only be 1. However, we can change the number of nodes in layer 1 and layer 2 to find the best fully connected layer structure. Here, the number of nodes is adjusted from 16 to 64. If the number of nodes is too great, the computing speed will decrease, and overfitting will occur. As can be seen from Figure 10, the RMSE reaches its lowest value of 0.1605 when fc_1 = 24 and fc_2 = 32. Therefore, the performance of the AU-RES neural network is the best.

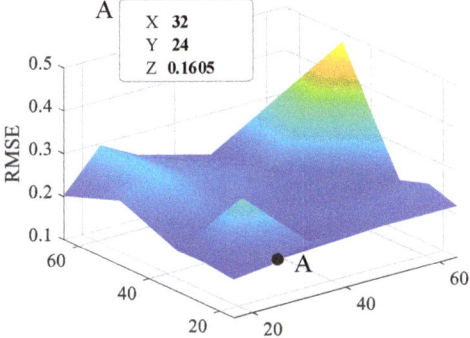

Figure 10. The effect of the number of fully connected layer in the performance of neural network.

4.5. Comparison of AU-RES Network with Other Networks

The AU-RES neural network was compared with other deep learning neural networks, and the simulation results are shown in Figure 11. In the past, the experience control method has often been used for fracturing flowback control, but there were no artificial intelligence methods available. Therefore, there are no articles comparing their results. In this paper, we only compared the results of the AU-RES neural network with those of other deep learning neural networks. The selected deep learning neural networks include LetNet5, AlexNet, VGG16, etc. When training the networks, the learning rate of the networks was 0.0001, and the hyperparameter update method was Adam. The number of epochs for neural network training was 150. Then, the same test sample was input into different neural networks, and the output of each neural network was observed, as shown in Figure 11 and Table 3. As these deep learning neural networks are often used for image recognition, the RegressionLayer for the final layer needs to be changed to ClassficationLayer, so that the networks can output continuous values.

In Figure 11, the blue line 'TestLabel' is the output label of the neural network, which is equivalent to the expected output of the neural network. The orange line 'LeNet5' represents the actual output of LeNet5 neural network. The green line 'AlexNet' represents the actual output of the AlexNet neural network, the black line 'VGG16' represents the actual output of the VGG16 neural network, and the purple line 'AU-RES' represents the actual output of the AU-RES neural network proposed in this paper. The values of these curves range from 3 to 13. If a curve is far from the blue line, it has a large error. As can be seen from Figure 11, the LeNet5 network exhibited the largest error. The reason for this is that the network has a simple structure and can only recognize the characters 0–9, so it has difficulty recognizing complex continuous one-dimensional time series signals. AlexNet is a mature transfer learning neural network with increased network depth, so its recognition accuracy is higher than LeNet5 network. VGG16 is a deeper neural network, so its recognition accuracy is further improved. The AU-RES network studied in this paper is an augmented residual neural network. Because the data transformation layer is added and the residual layer and the fully connected layer are improved, the prediction accuracy is the highest. The total error of the output signal of the AU-RES neural network is 0.1689, which indicates the superiority of the AU-RES neural network.

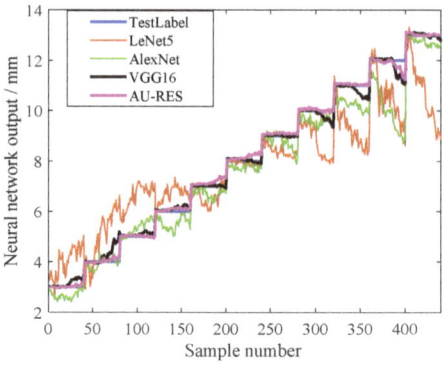

Figure 11. Comparison of the AU-RES network with other networks.

Table 3. Performance of the different neural networks.

Number	Network	RMSE	Loss	E
1	LeNet5	0.183	0.0065	2.1032
2	AlexNet	0.162	0.0013	0.8875
3	VGG16	0.157	0.0010	0.8023
4	AU-RES	0.131	0.00021	0.1689

4.6. Experiment

On the basis of the AU-RES neural network algorithm studied in this paper, control software was developed. We installed the software on an intelligent controller, so as to produce a prototype of the intelligent control device for fracturing fluid flowback. The prototype of the intelligent control device is shown in Figure 12.

Figure 12. Intelligent controller prototype for fracturing fluid flowback.

The prototype was applied to a gas field experiment. During the experiment, the main parameters of the fracturing fluid in the oil tube were collected once an hour, and the results are shown in Table 4. In Table 4, the data in the first column represent time, and the data in the second to fourth columns correspond to the main fracturing fluid parameters in the oil tube, and the data in the seventh column indicate the nozzle diameter predicted by the AU-RES neural network. Through the experiment, it was found that there was no sand present in the fracturing fluid, indicating that the AU-RES neural network was able to correctly predict the diameter of the nozzle, and the experiment was successful.

Table 4. The main data collected during the experiment.

Time Hour:Minute	Oil Pressure MPa	Casing Pressure MPa	Flow Rate m^3/h	Viscosity mPas	Temperature °C	Nozzle Diameter mm
6:00	3.5	4.1	4.50	1	39	6
7:00	3.5	4.1	4.50	1	39	6
8:00	3.5	4.1	4.50	1	39	6
9:00	3.5	4.1	4.50	1	39	6
10:00	3.0	3.8	3.85	1	39	6
11:00	3.0	3.8	3.85	1	39	6
12:00	3.0	3.8	3.85	1	39	6
13:00	3.0	3.4	3.85	1	38	6
14:00	2.6	3.4	3.18	1	38	6
15:00	2.6	3.4	3.18	1	38	6
16:00	2.6	3.4	3.18	1	38	6
17:00	2.6	3.4	3.18	1	38	6

When training the AU-RES neural network, it is necessary to collect a lot of data from the oil and gas field. This is a potential limitation or challenges for the application of the AU-RES neural network. Sometimes, these data are difficult to obtain due to data privacy. However, the AU-RES neural network is often used in industrial enterprises. Because they have a lot of data, they are able to easily train the AU-RES neural network.

5. Conclusions

Through the research of this paper, the following conclusions can be drawn:

In the process of hydraulic fracturing flowback control, it is difficult for traditional methods to achieve good results due to a variety of nonlinear and uncertain factors, leading to the problem of 'sand production'. An artificial intelligence method consisting of the AU-RES neural network can solve this problem well, and the field experiment results were good.

The AU-RES neural network was based on an existing residual network, adding a signal conversion layer to transform one-dimensional time series signals into two-dimensional images that can better adapt to the characteristics of the residual network, thus improving the prediction accuracy.

In the AU-RES neural network, the performance of the neural network can be improved by optimizing the hyperparameters (learning rate, gradient update method, number of nodes in the fully connected layer, etc.) After optimization, the learning rate was 0.0001. The gradient update method used was 'Adam'. The fully connected layer had 3 sublayers, i.e., Fc_1, Fc_2 and Fc_3, among which Fc_1 had 24 nodes and had Fc_2 32 nodes. The RMSE and loss of AU-RES network training were 0.131 and 0.00021, respectively, and the prediction error of the test samples was 0.1689.

The AU-RES neural network can effectively predict multiple one-dimensional time series signals and explore their signal features. It can be applied not only to tight gas fracturing fluid flowback control, but also to other industries, where one-dimensional timing signals need to be identified and predicted. Therefore, this study provides a theoretical basis for the application of artificial intelligence technology in various industries.

With the development of new materials and new processes, hydraulic fracturing flowback technology has developed rapidly. The use of new nanomaterials, new proppants, new hydraulic fracturing flowback design models, and artificial intelligence to control the flowback process have greatly improved the efficiency and quality of hydraulic fracturing flowback.

Author Contributions: Conceptualization, H.W.; writing—original draft preparation, R.L.; software, J.W.; funding acquisition, B.L.; formal analysis, X.Z.; data curation, W.B. All authors have read and agreed to the published version of the manuscript.

Funding: This research was funded by the Natural Science Basic Research Program of Shaanxi, grant number 2021JM-405, Xi'an Science and Technology Plan, grant number 22GXFW0103, and supported by the Postgraduate Innovation and Practice Ability Development Fund of Xi'an Shiyou University, grant number YCS23114171.

Acknowledgments: Oil and gas field companies provided field data for this article. The authors express their gratitude to them.

Conflicts of Interest: The authors of this article declare that there are no known competing financial interest or personal relationship that could influence the work presented in this article.

References

1. Aloysius, N.; Geetha, M. A review on deep convolutional neural networks. In Proceedings of the 2017 IEEE International Conference on Communication and Signal Processing, ICCSP 2017, Chennai, Tamilnadu, India, 6–8 April 2017; pp. 588–592.
2. Sharma, N.; Jain, V.; Mishra, A. An analysis of convolutional neural networks for image classification. *Procedia Comput. Sci.* **2018**, *132*, 377–384. [CrossRef]
3. Lin, B.; Guo, J. Discussion on current application of artificial intelligence in petroleum industry. *Pet. Sci. Bull.* **2019**, *4*, 403–413. [CrossRef]
4. Zhang, S.; Chen, Z. Status and prospect of artificial intelligence application in fracturing technology. *Pet. Drill. Tech.* **2023**, *51*, 69–77.
5. Hui, G.; Chen, S.; He, Y.; Wang, H.; Gu, F. Machine learning-based production forecast for shale gas in unconventional reservoirs via integration of geological and operational factors. *J. Nat. Gas Sci. Eng.* **2021**, *94*, 104045. [CrossRef]
6. Liu, W.; Liu, W.D.; Gu, J.W. Forecasting oil production using ensemble empirical model decomposition based Long Short-Term Memory neural network. *J. Pet. Sci. Eng.* **2020**, *189*, 107013. [CrossRef]
7. Hu, X.; Tu, Z.; Luo, Y.; Zhou, F.; Li, Y.; Liu, J.; Yi, P. Shale gas well productivity prediction model with fitted function-neural network cooperation. *Pet. Sci. Bull.* **2022**, *3*, 94–405. [CrossRef]
8. Zhou, L.; Yu, W. Improved Convolutional Neural Image Recognition Algorithm based on LeNet-5. *J. Comput. Netw. Commun.* **2022**, *2022*, 2022. [CrossRef]
9. Su, J.; Wang, H. Fine-Tuning and Efficient VGG16 Transfer Learning Fault Diagnosis Method for Rolling Bearing. *Mech. Mach. Sci.* **2023**, *117*, 453–461.
10. Zhang, C.; Zhang, H.; Tian, F.; Zhou, Y.; Zhao, S.; Du, X. Research on sheep face recognition algorithm based on improved AlexNet model. *Neural Comput. Applic.* **2023**, *35*, 1–10. [CrossRef]
11. Fawaz, H.I.; Lucas, B.; Forestier, G.; Pelletier, C.; Schmidt, D.F.; Weber, J.; Webb, G.I.; Idoumghar, L.; Muller, P.-A.; Petitjean, F. InceptionTime: Finding AlexNet for time series classification. *Data Min. Knowl. Discov.* **2020**, *34*, 1936–1962. [CrossRef]
12. Zhang, L.; Dou, H.; Wang, T.; Wang, H.; Peng, Y.; Zhang, J.; Liu, Z.; Mi, L.; Jiang, L. A production prediction method of single well in water flooding oilfield based on integrated temporal convolutional network model. *Pet. Explor. Dev.* **2022**, *49*, 996–1004. [CrossRef]
13. Sagheer, A.; Kotb, M. Time series forecasting of petroleum production using deep LSTM recurrent networks. *Neurocomputing* **2019**, *323*, 203–213. [CrossRef]
14. Bai, S.; Kolter, J.Z.; Koltun, V. An empirical evaluation of generic convolutional and recurrent networks for sequence modeling. *arXiv* **2018**, arXiv:1803.01271.
15. Gu, J.W.; Zhou, M.; Li, Z.T.; Jia, X.; Liang, Y. A data mining-based method for oil well production prediction with long and short-term memory network model. *Spec. Oil Gas Reserv.* **2019**, *26*, 77–81+131.
16. Huang, R.; Wei, C.; Wang, B.; Yang, J.; Xu, X.; Wu, S.; Huang, S. Well performance prediction based on Long Short-Term Memory (LSTM) neural network. *J. Pet. Sci. Eng.* **2022**, *208*, 109686. [CrossRef]
17. Wang, J.; Qiang, X.; Ren, Z.; Wang, H.; Wang, Y.; Wang, S. Time-Series Well Performance Prediction Based on Convolutional and Long Short-Term Memory Neural Network Model. *Energies* **2023**, *16*, 499. [CrossRef]
18. He, K.; Zhang, X.; Ren, S.; Sun, J. Deep Residual Learning for Image Recognition. In Proceedings of the IEEE Computer Society Conference on Computer Vision and Pattern Recognition, Las Vegas, NV, USA, 27–30 June 2016.
19. Alom, M.Z.; Taha, T.M.; Yakopcic, C.; Westberg, S.; Sidike, P.; Nasrin, M.S.; Van Esesn, B.C.; Awwal, A.A.S.; Asari, V.K. The history began from alexnet: A comprehensive survey on deep learning approaches. *arXiv* **2018**, arXiv:1803.01164.

20. Lyu, C.; Huo, Z.; Cheng, X.; Jiang, J.; Alimasi, A.; Liu, H. Distributed Optical Fiber Sensing Intrusion Pattern Recognition Based on GAF and CNN. *J. Light. Technol.* **2020**, *38*, 4174–4182. [CrossRef]
21. Wang, Z.; Oates, T. Encoding time series as images for visual inspection and classification using tiled convolutional neural networks. In Proceedings of the 29th AAAI Conference on Artificial Intelligence, Austin, Texas, USA, 25–30 January 2015; AI Access Foundation: El Segundo, CA, USA, 2015.
22. Yang, C.L.; Chen, Z.X.; Yang, C.Y. Sensor classification using convolutional neural network by encoding multivariate time series as two-dimensional colored images. *Sensors* **2020**, *20*, 168. [CrossRef]
23. Gu, Y.; Wu, K.; Li, C. Rolling bearing fault diagnosis based on Gram angle field and transfer deep residual neural network. *J. Vib. Shock* **2022**, *41*, 228–237.
24. He, K.; Zhang, X.; Ren, S.; Sun, J. Identity mappings in deep residual networks. In Proceedings of the 21st ACM Conference on Computer and Communications Security, Scottsdale, AZ, USA, 3–7 November 2014.
25. Veit, A.; Wilber, M.J.; Belongie, S. Residual networks behave like ensembles of relatively shallow networks. *Adv. Neural Inf. Process. Syst.* **2016**, 550–558. [CrossRef]
26. Yuan, D.-R.; Zhang, Y.; Tang, Y.-J.; Li, B.-Y.; Xie, B.-L. Multiscale Residual Attention Network and Its Facial Expression Recognition Algorithm. *J. Chin. Comput. Syst.* **2022**, *11*, 1–9.

Disclaimer/Publisher's Note: The statements, opinions and data contained in all publications are solely those of the individual author(s) and contributor(s) and not of MDPI and/or the editor(s). MDPI and/or the editor(s) disclaim responsibility for any injury to people or property resulting from any ideas, methods, instructions or products referred to in the content.

Review

Methods for Detecting and Classifying Weeds, Diseases and Fruits Using AI to Improve the Sustainability of Agricultural Crops: A Review

Ana Corceiro [1], Khadijeh Alibabaei [2], Eduardo Assunção [1,3,4], Pedro D. Gaspar [1,3,4,*] and Nuno Pereira [4]

[1] Department of Electromechanical Engineering, University of Beira Interior, Rua Marquês d'Ávila e Bolama, 6201-001 Covilhã, Portugal; ana.corceiro@ubi.pt (A.C.); eduardo.assuncao@ubi.pt (E.A.)
[2] Steinbuch Centre for Computing, Zirkel 2, D-76131 Karlsruhe, Germany; khadijeh.alibabaei@kit.edu
[3] C-MAST Center for Mechanical and Aerospace Science and Technologies, University of Beira Interior, 6201-001 Covilhã, Portugal
[4] Department of Computer Science, Instituto de Telecomunicações, University of Beira Interior, 6201-001 Covilhã, Portugal; nuno.pereira@ubi.pt
* Correspondence: dinis@ubi.pt

Citation: Corceiro, A.; Alibabaei, K.; Assunção, E.; Gaspar, P.D.; Pereira, N. Methods for Detecting and Classifying Weeds, Diseases and Fruits Using AI to Improve the Sustainability of Agricultural Crops: A Review. *Processes* **2023**, *11*, 1263. https://doi.org/10.3390/pr11041263

Academic Editor: Xiong Luo

Received: 20 March 2023
Revised: 3 April 2023
Accepted: 11 April 2023
Published: 19 April 2023

Copyright: © 2023 by the authors. Licensee MDPI, Basel, Switzerland. This article is an open access article distributed under the terms and conditions of the Creative Commons Attribution (CC BY) license (https://creativecommons.org/licenses/by/4.0/).

Abstract: The rapid growth of the world's population has put significant pressure on agriculture to meet the increasing demand for food. In this context, agriculture faces multiple challenges, one of which is weed management. While herbicides have traditionally been used to control weed growth, their excessive and random use can lead to environmental pollution and herbicide resistance. To address these challenges, in the agricultural industry, deep learning models have become a possible tool for decision-making by using massive amounts of information collected from smart farm sensors. However, agriculture's varied environments pose a challenge to testing and adopting new technology effectively. This study reviews recent advances in deep learning models and methods for detecting and classifying weeds to improve the sustainability of agricultural crops. The study compares performance metrics such as recall, accuracy, F1-Score, and precision, and highlights the adoption of novel techniques, such as attention mechanisms, single-stage detection models, and new lightweight models, which can enhance the model's performance. The use of deep learning methods in weed detection and classification has shown great potential in improving crop yields and reducing adverse environmental impacts of agriculture. The reduction in herbicide use can prevent pollution of water, food, land, and the ecosystem and avoid the resistance of weeds to chemicals. This can help mitigate and adapt to climate change by minimizing agriculture's environmental impact and improving the sustainability of the agricultural sector. In addition to discussing recent advances, this study also highlights the challenges faced in adopting new technology in agriculture and proposes novel techniques to enhance the performance of deep learning models. The study provides valuable insights into the latest advances and challenges in process systems engineering and technology for agricultural activities.

Keywords: weed detection; deep learning; weed classification; support decision-making algorithm; fruit detection; disease detection; CNN; performance metrics; agriculture

1. Introduction

The world population began growing rapidly during the industrial revolution, mainly due to medical advances and increases in agricultural productivity. Currently, it is estimated that the population increases dramatically, by an average of 80 million per year. With any type of projection, there is a degree of uncertainty; however, the United Nations predicts that there will be 8.1 billion people on the planet by 2025 [1–3].

In this era, the highest rates of population growth occur mainly in developing countries reflecting their higher fertility rates and an increase in longevity. Furthermore, urbanization has been increasing, and by 2050 over 70% of the world's population will live in urban areas, dependent on food produced by others [2].

Given the increasing demand for food, the level of production should increase by 70% [1,3]. However, agriculture faces tremendous challenges including climate change, drought, pests, weeds, diseases, pollution, soil deterioration, pump irrigation costs, rising groundwater, the switch from a fuel-based to a bio-based transition economy, and finally, the decreasing availability of freshwater as demand rises [4].

According to [4], weeds directly compete with fruit or vegetable crops for water, growing space, nutrients, and sunlight, leaving the crops susceptible to insects and diseases, which results in productivity losses of 34% on average.

Water is one of the most important resources in crop growth. Amongst other issues, weeds can steal water from the field and prevent crop growth. Furthermore, climate change is directly connected with the changes in average global temperature. This contributes to the reduction of available water and, therefore, producers need to adopt water-saving practices, and keep the fields free of weeds [5].

One of the most essential factors in agricultural yield is weed management, and hand weeding is the oldest method. However, it has a high labor cost, and is inefficient and time-consuming. Mechanical weeding techniques are far more effective and labor-saving than hand weeding; however, they can easily cause crop damage [4].

One of the solutions for weed control is the application of herbicides. Although these chemicals can eliminate weeds efficiently, they can also pollute water supplies or food. Thus, to neutralize these problems, many European nations have started to restrict the use of pesticides in farming [6].

Due to these problems, weed management must become more environmentally friendly. Precision agricultural technology needs to be used to minimize the negative effects of herbicides on the environment and to optimize their usage [7,8].

Precision agriculture (PA) is the most favorable key to these problems. Using a variety of cutting-edge information, communication, and data analysis approaches, PA is a management strategy that aids in improving crop output while minimizing water and fertilizer losses, as well as enabling a better environmental impact [9].

The development of decision-making algorithms has placed a lot of emphasis on artificial intelligence (AI). AI includes any method that allows robots to learn from experience, adjust to new inputs, and emulate human behavior [10]. The sub-field of artificial intelligence known as machine learning (ML) employs computational algorithms to transform data from the real world into usable models and decision-making guidance. Finally, deep learning (DL) is a section of machine learning [11].

Remote sensing has been used frequently to map weed patches in agricultural fields for Site-Specific Weed Management (SSWM). Weeds can be identified or separated from cultivated plants based on their distinctive spectral signatures. Over the past few years, picture categorization using machine learning methods has proven to be very accurate and effective for weed mapping [9].

Convolution Neural Networks (CNNs) are now the most widely used deep learning method for the agriculture industry. Convolutional neural networks belong to a class of deep neural networks, usually employed to analyze visual imagery [12].

It is expected that these technologies will change agribusiness since they allow for decision-making in days rather than weeks. Additionally, they guarantee a significant drop in expenses and an increase in productivity [13].

In conclusion, to identify new approaches, difficulties, and potential fixes for employing deep learning in agriculture, this study will evaluate published studies. The objective of this paper is to give an overview of current work and to point out difficulties in the collection and preparation of data for deep learning models; to review the current DL model methods used in agriculture; to emphasize the challenges in model training; to evaluate the novel edge devices utilized to implement the trained models, as well as the difficulties involved in using them in the real world. This review will not cover vegetation recognition methods based on radar/microwave sensors.

The remainder of this paper is structured as follows. Materials and methods, including information about the eligibility of the articles reviewed, are presented in Section 2. Section 3 gives an overview of deep learning as well as a review of the papers. The major challenges in this research are detailed in Section 4, while Section 5 concludes the article.

2. Materials and Methods

Since the evolution of weeds and the uncontrolled use of herbicides are hot and rising topics of the present times, a comprehensive literature review was conducted to collect, verify, analyze, and describe the scientific facts on the goals, difficulties, and constraints of weed detection and categorization, while putting people at the center of productive processes and systems.

As a result, the purpose of this systematic review is to research the philosophies of and approaches to deep learning in agriculture for purposes of detection and classification, with a focus directed to the problem of weeds.

Finally, this study was carried out using a four-phase flow diagram and PRISMA's standards, also known as a systematic review and meta-analysis statement.

2.1. Focus Questions

Deep learning emerges as a complement to agricultural production as a resource centered on the human being, where fruit and vegetable production is prioritized, to maintain productive and sustainable performance in respect of the supply of healthy foods [10].

This technique, due to its benefits, including strong feature extraction ability and excellent identification accuracy, is commonly employed in image recognition.

Future prospects for food generation are to reduce the number of plants that emerge by themselves in regions where the population maintains their crops. However, the objective is to do this sustainably and efficiently, contributing to the reduction of the uncontrolled use of herbicides.

That said, it is important to research and evaluate the deep learning approaches, introducing and evaluating the ideas and philosophies behind weeds, their detection, and classification, to achieve a sustainable and resilient system, especially for the worker. This led us to our research questions:

(1) What types of models can be applied for deep learning for detection or classification in agriculture?
(2) Which model is better for detection and/or classification?
(3) What type of metrics can be used to evaluate the model?

2.2. Sources of Information and Methods Used to Obtain Data

Initial data screening and collection for this systematic literature review article began in September 2022, and for the bibliographic study, three electronic databases, Science Direct, ResearchGate, and Google Scholar, were employed. Pre-determined keywords connected to the study's main emphasis were utilized for the database search: weed detection and weed classification. The keywords were chosen to be comprehensive and not to condition or restrict the study.

Therefore, all information and data that would be pertinent to the inquiry were included. The screening titles' keywords included "deep learning" together with one of the following keywords: "agriculture", "weeds", "precision agriculture", "weeds detection", "weeds classification", and "crop classification". The language search was always conducted in English.

2.3. Eligibility Criteria

In this analysis, the evolution of distinct strategies for weed, disease, and fruit detection and classification are explored, as well as their classification employing performance metrics. Based on article titles and abstracts, the writers initially performed a preliminary selection and exclusion process. For eligibility, the following inclusion and exclusion criteria were used. Only research published in English with text available, including research articles and review articles, was included. Furthermore, given the recent development of the technologies for weed detection and classification under consideration here, a study period between 2015 and 2022 was chosen.

In addition to these inclusion factors, articles should describe and explore at least one of the two focus subjects of the study: artificial intelligence and weeds detection/classification. Moreover, other features were added such as results, sustainability, and the algorithms associated with deep learning for detection or classification. Additionally, some of the other applications include the detection of plant and leaf diseases and detection and classification of fruits or vegetables were introduced. Articles before 2015, with a non-exclusive focus on classification or detection, and those not considering deep learning were excluded. The following aspects were considered while analyzing the articles:

- The process used to gather the dataset and the difficulties encountered when using it to train the model.
- The performance of the models and the DL models/architectures employed in the paper.
- The measures that were used for the model's evaluation.
- The model's inference time (if specified), as this is a crucial factor in the use of the model in real-time applications.
- The examination of the model's failure prediction.
- Whether the trained model was deployed using a low-cost device developed by the authors.

3. Review of Extracted Research

3.1. Principal Findings

To perform this review, a four-phase flow diagram PRISMA were applied. Thus, the procedure employs four phases, of which the first is the identification of the papers. The second phase is the screening. Following this, the eligibility is considered, and the number of papers is determined.

This literature research obtained an aggregate of 175 articles: 35 from Science Direct, 53 from ResearchGate, and 87 from Google Scholar. Of these articles, 12 were not available for full-text reading and 59 were duplicates or triplicates among the three databases, and for that reason were excluded.

Thus, when the non-eligible articles were excluded, 104 articles remained. Upon reviewing the titles and abstracts of the papers, 62 papers were eliminated in the following stage, leaving 42 articles. The 42 publications were then subjected to a full-text analysis to determine their eligibility, during which 9 were disqualified since they did not match the current study's objectives (Figure 1).

This literature study comprised analysis of the remaining 33 publications.

Dates and numbers of papers were the focus of the first examination. As can be seen in Figure 2, despite the publications' recent publication dates (from 2015 to 2022), there has been a marked increase in research into the notion of deep learning for weed categorization and detection.

The second study goal was to validate the genre of recently themed articles that were being written and distributed. Among the 33 articles, four dealt with plant diseases, four with fruit detection, fourteen with weed detection, and eleven with weed categorization. This is represented in Figure 3.

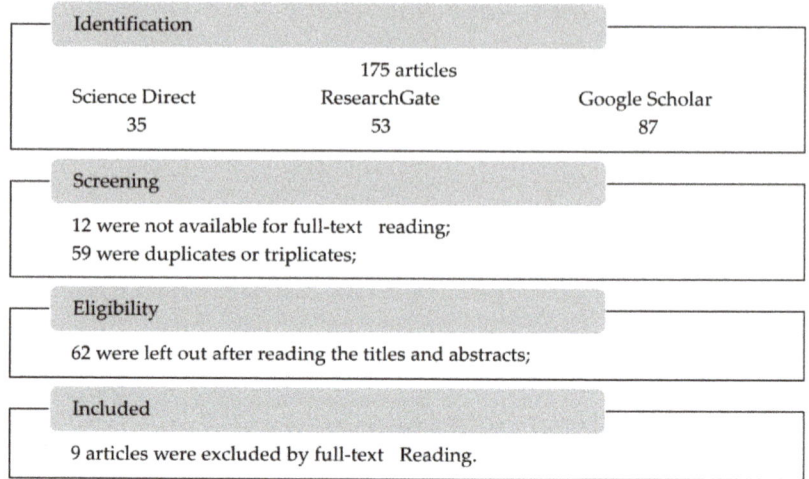

Figure 1. Diagram created using PRISMA that shows the systematic research's findings.

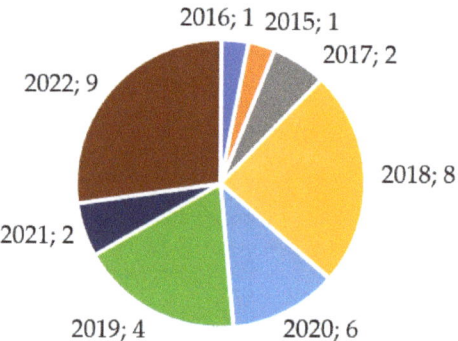

Figure 2. Number of articles published by year (Year; Number of publications).

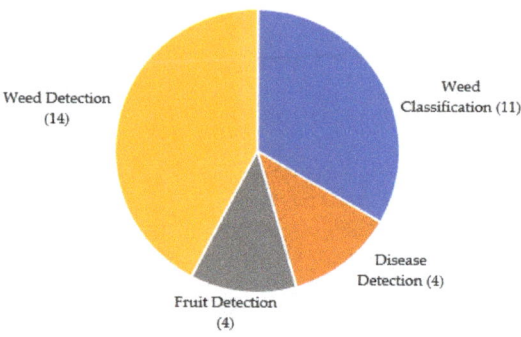

Figure 3. Papers published by application area.

3.2. An Overview of Deep Learning

The brain's neural networks in humans served as an inspiration for DL models. The phrase "deep" refers to how many covert levels the data is converted through. To produce predictions, the models pass the input across a deep network with several layers, each of which employs a hierarchy to extract certain characteristics from the data at various sizes or resolutions and combine them into a higher-level feature [11]. DL models are broken down into three categories: reinforcement learning, unsupervised learning, and supervised learning. The process of learning a function using labelled training data is known as supervised learning. In supervised learning, each pair of data in the dataset represents the intended output value and an input item. The purpose of reinforcement learning (RL) is to determine how an agent should behave in each environment to maximize rewards.

A model of supervised learning is the CNN model, created primarily for segmentation, classification, and detection.

Convolutional layers, pooling layers, nonlinear operations, and fully linked layers make up a CNN model. A convolutional layer is a method for obtaining characteristics from inputs and has a series of kernels, the parameters of which must be learned. The dot product between each kernel entry and each point in the input is calculated as each kernel is moved over the input's height and width [11].

A nonlinear activation function is utilized to include nonlinear characteristics in the model after each convolutional layer. Rectified Linear Units (ReLU) are the most popular activation function in DL models since they are state-of-the-art. Between two convolutional layers, a pooling layer is typically employed to decrease the number of parameters and prevent overfitting [11]. The subsequent layers are made up of completely interconnected layers that use the features that the preceding layer retrieved to provide class probabilities or scores. All the neurons in these layers are linked to this layer [11].

3.2.1. Segmentation by CNN

CNN models can also be used to complete the segmentation task. Segmentation is the division of an image into groups of pixels and the assignment of a class to each group. DeepLab, Mask R-CNN, and Fully Convolutional Networks (FCN) are DL models for segmentation [11].

3.2.2. Detection by CNN

The CNN model may also be used for object detection. You Only Look Once (YOLO), Single Shot Multi-box Detector (SSD), and LedNet are examples of single-stage detectors. Current object detection algorithms come in two varieties. Two-stage detectors include R-CNN, Fast R-CNN, and Faster R-CNN, for instance. The first stage of the two-stage detector establishes regions of interest using the Region Proposal Network (RPN). The suggested regions are then put to the test for item classification using bounding box regression and convolutional layers. In contrast, bounding boxes and object categorization are instantly provided by a single feed-forward convolutional network in single-stage detectors [11].

3.2.3. Classification by CNN

Regression or classification problems can be resolved using the CNN model. When performing classification or regression tasks, the last layer of the model is chosen as a completely connected layer with a SoftMax activation function, and as a fully connected layer, frequently with a linear function. AlexNet, GoogleNet, VGG, and ResNet are among the most often used CNN designs for classification, along with more contemporary, lighter models such as MobileNet and EfficientNet [11].

3.2.4. Vegetation Index

In precision agricultural applications involving remote sensing, vegetation indices (VIs) are frequently utilized. In both qualitative and quantitative vegetation analysis, they are regarded as being particularly useful for tracking the development and health of crops. Vegetation indices are based on the vegetation's ability to absorb electromagnetic radiation [13]. There are modifications in the mathematics of electromagnetic spectrum scattering and absorption in various bands depending on the type of vegetation. and these parameters can be determined using data from either each individual shot or after the creation of orthophotos showing the whole crop. Several factors, including plant biochemical and physical characteristics, ambient factors, soil background characteristics, and moisture content impact the reflectance in different bands. Differences in reflectance can provide accurate temporal and geographical information on the crops being monitored [13].

There are two primary categories for vegetation indices: vegetation indices created on hyperspectral or multispectral data and those based on information from the visible spectrum [13]. The capacity to identify bands of radiation of green (G), healthy vegetation has been greatly enhanced by the development of simple vegetation indicators that can integrate RGB (Red-Green-Blue) data with various spectral bands, such as NIR (Near-infrared), and RE (Red Edge) [13].

The Ratio Vegetation Index (RVI), and Normalized Difference Vegetation Index (NDVI), which are based on the NIR and bands of radiation of Red (R) channels of radiation, are intended to give more pronounced contrast between the plant and the soil. The RVI, shown in Equation (1), is one of the multispectral plant indices, which highlights the difference between soil and vegetation. It is also susceptible to the visual characteristics of the ground. The NDVI, shown in Equation (2), is a development of RVI and is determined by the visible and near-infrared light reflected from the vegetation. It is the most well-known and often used vegetation index. It provides a simple way to monitor the development and health of many agricultural crops, since unhealthy or sparse vegetation reflects more visible light and less near-infrared radiation [13].

The ratio of NIR to RE radiation is normalized by the Normalized Difference Red Edge (NDRE), shown in Equation (3). The Green Normalized Difference Vegetation Index (GNDVI) with NIR and Green (G) bands, is shown in Equation (4).

The most used indices when analyzing the VIs generated from RGB photos are Excess Greenness Index (ExG) and Normalized Difference Index (NDI). ExG is predicated on the idea that plants exhibit a superior level of greenness, and that soil is the only background component. It is determined by the doubling the radiation in G channels minus the radiation in Red (R) and Blue radiation (B) channels, as shown in Equation (5). The NDI was suggested to use just green and red channels to differentiate plants from background pictures of dirt and debris, as shown in Equation (6). Table 1 provides a selection of the most used vegetation indices [13].

Table 1. Most applied vegetation indices.

Vegetation Index	Abbreviation	Formula	N°
Vegetation Indices derived from multispectral information			
Ratio Vegetation Index	RVI	$\frac{NIR}{R}$	(1)
Normalized Difference Vegetation Index	NDVI	$\frac{NIR-R}{R+NIR}$	(2)
Normalized Difference Red Edge Index	NDRE	$\frac{NIR-RE}{RE+NIR}$	(3)
Green Normalized Difference Vegetation Index	GNDVI	$\frac{NIR-G}{NIR+G}$	(4)
RGB-based Vegetation Indices			
Excess Greenness Index	ExG	$2 \cdot G-R-B$	(5)
Normalized Difference Index	NDI	$\frac{G-R}{G+R}$	(6)

3.2.5. Data Acquisition

A large amount of labelled data is necessary for DL-based weed identification and classification approaches. In the first step, it is important to acquire a useful quantity of data for further analysis. Image acquisition can be defined as the act of obtaining an image from different sources. Hardware systems such as cameras, encoders, and sensors can be used for this. Different images can be captured depending on the type of camera, and the type of sensor embedded. The sensors' job is to take pictures with great temporal and spatial resolution, which can help with identifying a variety of vegetation-related characteristics [14]. Different types of sensors deployed on a range of platforms are used to capture various modalities of data. These pictures can be captured through unmanned aerial vehicles (UAV), field robots (FR), all-terrain vehicles (ATV), micro aerial vehicles (MAV), cameras, satellite images, and public datasets [7].

Datasets can also be obtained from free internet sources, such as the Broadleaf Dataset, DeepWeed [15], Oilseed image, and Sugar Beets [16]. Each type of sensor can monitor many aspects of the plant, including its color, texture, and geometric shape. Some sensors can measure specific wavelengths of radiation. The information gathered by these sensors may be further processed to track critical agricultural properties during the various growth stages, including soil moisture, plant biomass, and vegetation health [13].

Nowadays, for agriculture, there are four types of sensors entrenched in cameras: hyperspectral, multispectral, RGB, and thermal sensors. Visible light sensors are the most popular sensors for PA applications. They are economical, easy to use, and can capture high resolution photographs. In addition, the information obtained needs straightforward processing [13].

RGB sensors are frequently adjusted to obtain information on radiation in other bands, most commonly the Infrared (IR) or RE band. This is created by changing one of the original optical filters for one that allows the perception of NIR [13].

In addition to collecting data using wavelengths that are visible, multispectral devices also gather data using wavelengths that are invisible to the human eye, such as near-infrared radiation, short-wave infrared radiation (SWIR), and others [3].

Hyperspectral sensors analyze a wide spectrum of light instead of just assigning primary colors to each pixel, using wavelengths with a range of 400 to 1100 nm in steps of 1 nm. Both multispectral and hyperspectral sensors can obtain data regarding the vegetation's spectral absorption and reflection on numerous bands [13].

Thermal infrared sensors detect the temperature of the materials and produce pictures using this information instead of their visible properties. Thermal cameras employ infrared sensors and an optical lens to collect infrared energy. In these cases, warmer items are frequently shown as yellow and cooler ones as blue. However, this type of sensor is used for very specific applications, for example, irrigation management [13]. Other types of sensors, described in the literature, can be employed in addition to the ones indicated above, such as light detection and range (LiDAR) sensors. These devices are also known as "distance sensors", and when used in conjunction with other sensors they could be used by vehicles (such as robots) to navigate in the field [13].

3.2.6. Performance Metrics

The quality or efficiency of the model is assessed using measurement techniques referred to as performance metrics or evaluation metrics. With the help of these performance indicators, how well the simulation processed the given data can be assessed. It is feasible to improve the performance of the model by changing the hyper-parameters [17]. The most used metrics to determine the excellence of the model are shown in Table 2.

Table 2. Principal performance metrics used to evaluate the models.

Performance Metric	Formula	N°
Precision	$\frac{TP}{TP+FP}$	(7)
Recall	$\frac{TP}{TP+FN}$	(8)
True Negative Rate	$\frac{TN}{TN+FP}$	(9)
F1-Score	$2\frac{P \cdot R}{P+R}$	(10)
Kappa Coefficient	$\frac{P_a - P_r}{1 - P_r}$	(11)
Normalized mutual information	$\frac{I(X,Y)}{\sqrt{H(X) \cdot H(Y)}}$	(12)

The confusion matrix is a tabular representation of the ground-truth labels and model predictions [18]. In the matrix, columns correspond to the predicted values, and rows specify the actual values. Both ground truth and predicted values have two possible classes, positive or negative. An assessment factor is represented by each cell in the confusion matrix: True Positive (TP) denotes the number of positive class samples that the model correctly predicted; True Negative (TN) is the number of negative class samples that the model properly predicted; False Positive (FP) is the number of negative class samples that the model erroneously predicted, while False Negative (FN) denotes the number of positive class samples that the model incorrectly predicted [7,19].

Accuracy (ACC) corresponds to a percentage of correctly predicted events divided by all predicted events; this means that it is the degree of closeness to the true value [7].

Precision (P) is the degree to which an instrument or process will repeat the same value. It is the number of TP values, from all relevant findings, divided by the total number of TP and false positives (FP), as shown in Equation (7) [7,17].

Recall (R), Positive Rate (TPR) or sensitivity, is fundamentally the percent of real positives compared to all the ground truth's positives. It is the number of TP values, divided by the sum of TP and FN values, as shown in Equation (8) [17,20].

Specificity or True Negative Rate (TNR) is a test's capacity accurate to identify negative results. It is the number of TN values, divided by the sum of TN and FP values, as shown in Equation (9) [19,20].

The F1-score is the harmonic mean between recall and precision. It is the fraction given by the multiple of P and R divided by the sum of P and R, multiplied by two, as shown in Equation (10) [19,20].

The Kappa Coefficient (k) measures the degree to which the projected values and the real values accord [7]. Cohen's Kappa is calculated as the probability of agreement (Pa) minus the chance of random agreement (Pr) and then divided by one minus the probability of random agreement, as shown in Equation (11), [7].

The area under the receiver operating characteristic curve (AU-ROC or AUC) represents a graph displaying a classification model's effectiveness at different threshold levels. The sensitivity and false-positive rate (FPR) are shown on a probability curve called the ROC. The AUC calculates the performance across the thresholds and provides an aggregate measure [21].

Intersection over union (IoU) is a metric used to estimate how well a predicted mask or bounding boxes match the ground truth data, by dividing the area of overlap by the area they cover as a union [17].

Mean Intersection over Union (mIoU) is the dataset's average IoU for each class of an item [7].

Normalized mutual information (NMI) is the accepted metric for assessing clustering outcomes [15]. This statistic may be used to trade off the number of clusters vs the quality of the clustering. Using two random variables (X and Y), the NMI is determined by Equation (12). In this equation, H is entropy, and I is the mutual information metric. This measurement is done by contrasting the labels assigned to the clusters with actual labels [15]. Table 2 provides a selection of the most used performance metrics [7,11].

3.3. Brief Review of Papers

3.3.1. Disease Detection

Crop diseases reduce agriculture production and compromise global food security. A deep learning system that clearly identifies the specific timing and location of crop damage, leading to the spraying of herbicides only in affected areas can contribute to the moderation of resource use and environmental impacts [11].

Disease Detection in Individual Fruits

Afonso et al. [22] intended to categorize blackleg-diseased or healthy potato plants using deep learning techniques. An industrial RGB camera was employed to capture color pictures. Two deep convolutional neural networks (ResNet18 e ResNet50) were trained with RGB images with diseased and healthy plants. A model that had already been trained on the ImageNet dataset was employed to transfer learning for network weight initialization, and the Adam optimizer for weight optimization. Both networks were trained with a mini-batch size of 12 over a period of 100 epochs. The network ResNet18 was experimentally superior, with 94% of the images classified correctly. In contrast, only 82% of the ResNet50 classifications were correct. Precision was 85% and recall was 83% for the healthy class. The classifier used a rectified linear unit (RELU) activation to redefine the fully connected (FC) layer after linearly aggregating the output of the FC layer into a vector of size. The final network layer included a two-class linear classifier that enabled our binary classification utilizing logarithmic SoftMax activation (healthy versus blackleg).

Assunção et al. [23] presented a deep convolutional network to operate on mobile devices to categorize three peach disorders and healthy peach fruits (healthy, rot, mildew, and scab). In this research, the authors used transfer learning, data augmentation, and CNN MobileNetV2, which was trained on the ImageNet dataset to evaluate the outcomes of the disease classification in our comparatively small dataset of peach fruit disorders. The peach dataset was arranged with RGB images stored in the open website platform Forestry Images, Appizêzere, PlantVillage, University of Georgia, as well as from the Pacific Northwest Pest Management Handbooks, Utah State University. The ImageNet dataset was used to train the model initially (source task). Scab disease had the highest F1-score of 1.00, followed by the Rot and Mildew classes, each of which had a 0.96 F1-score. The classification for the Healthy class was an 0.94 F1-Score. The average F1-score for the model's overall performance was 0.96. No disease class was incorrectly classified by the model, which is crucial for disease study for control and infection. These successes highlight the promise of CNN for classifying fruit diseases with little training data. The model was also made to work with portable electronics.

According to Azgomi et al. [24], a low-cost method was created for the diagnosis of apple disease in four different types, scab, bitter rot, black rot, and healthy fruits. The investigation employed a multi-layer perceptron (MLP) neural network. This technique was called Apple Diseases Detection Neural Network (ADD-NN). The images were captured with a digital camera. For picture clustering, the k-means technique was utilized in the study. Semi-automatic support vector machine (SVM) classification was carried out. After that, the disease was found by analyzing the attributes of the chosen clusters. A neural network was employed to enhance the procedure, make it completely automatic, and test the viability of increasing the created system's accuracy. Furthermore, the network was trained with the Levenberg–Marquardt algorithm. The accuracy of the procedure using various architectures for the neural network trained with 60% of the data was then evaluated. The implementation of a two-layer formation with eight neurons in the first layer and eight in the second layer produced a maximum accuracy of 73.7%, according to the data. Figure 4 presents an input of an apple fruit, with both healthy and infected parts. After processing, the affected area is shown as orange in the middle picture, and the healthy area is then painted in yellow and the affected area in black, in the right-hand photo.

Disease Detection in Areas of Crops

Table 3 describes the features of research works in the field of disease detection.

In Kerkech et al. [25], the method proposed used a deep learning segmentation algorithm on UAV photos to identify the mildew disease in vines. The data was collected utilizing a UAV equipped with two MAPIR Survey2 camera sensors, comprising an infrared sensor and a RGB sensor configured for automated lighting. The SegNet architecture was used to divide visible and infrared pictures into four classes: symptomatic vine, ground, shadow, and healthy. When a symptom is seen in both the RGB and infrared pictures, it is considered that the disease has been discovered, and this was named "Fusion AND". In the second scenario, referred to as "fusion by the union", the symptom is declared identified if it is visible in either the infrared or RGB picture and is denoted by the sign "fusion OR". The model trained with RGB images outperformed the model trained with infrared images, with an accuracy of 85.13% and 78.72%, respectively. Moreover, the model fusion OR outpaced the fusion AND with an accuracy of 92.23% and 82.80%, in that order. For visible and infrared photos, SegNet's runtime on a UAV image was estimated to be 140 s. Less than 2 s are required for the merging of the two segmented pictures.

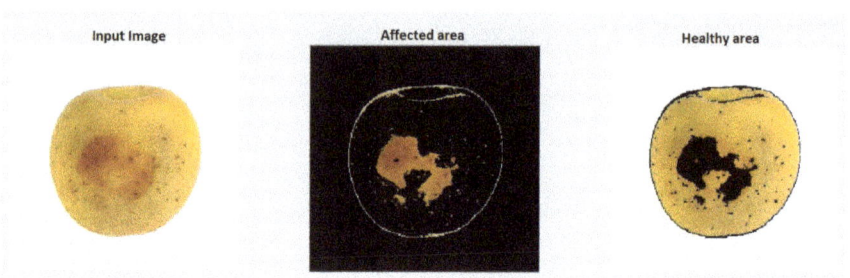

Figure 4. Example of the input fruit, showing the separated infected and healthy parts [24].

Figure 5 shows an example of segmentation by SegNet, and the fusion compared with the ground truth (GT). The first set of images (a–h) does not show examples of the symptom class, so it is healthy; it can be shown that the visible and infrared estimates and the fusion are similar. However, in the second set (i–p), it can be observed that the ground truth in both spectra, which depicts a region that is almost entirely polluted by mildew, is the same except for the distinct color code.

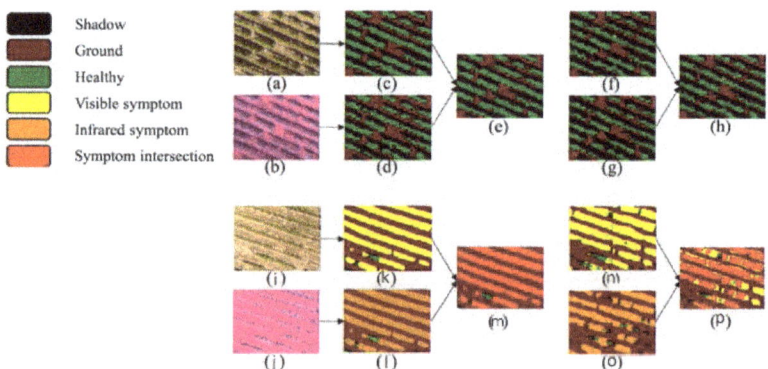

Figure 5. An illustration of segmenting and fusing a healthy region. Images in the following order: (**a**) visible image, (**b**) infrared image, (**c**) visible GT, (**d**) infrared GT, (**e**) fusion GT, (**f**) visible SegNet estimate, (**g**) infrared SegNet estimation, and (**h**) fusion of segmentation findings. An example of segmenting and fusing a mold-infested region. For example, (**i**) stands for visible image, (**j**) for infrared image, (**k**) for visible ground truth, (**l**) for infrared ground truth, (**m**) for fusion ground truth, (**n**) for visible segmentation net estimation, (**o**) for infrared segmentation net estimation, and (**p**) fusion of segmentation results (adapted from [25]).

Table 3. Feature descriptions of publications in the field of "Disease Detection".

References	Application	Data Used	Model Used	Metric Used	Model Performance
Afonso et al. [22]	Classify diseased potato plants.	RGB camera.	Deep CNN: ResNet18, ResNet50.	Precision Recall	The findings of this study demonstrate that a CNN, more especially ResNet18, may function as a reliable detector for potatoes infected with the blackleg disease in the field. The detection performance can also be anticipated to increase with larger datasets and data augmentation.
Assunção et al. [23]	Detect peach disease.	Six datasets from [23].	CNN	F1-score	No disease class is incorrectly classified by the model. These successes highlight the promise of CNN for classifying fruit diseases with little training data. The model is also made to work with portable electronics.
Azgomi et al. [24]	Detect apple disease.	Digital camera.	MLP ANN	Accuracy	The results showed a maximum accuracy of 73.7% for the implementation of a two-layer structure with eight neurons in the first layer and eight neurons in the second layer.
Kerkech et al. [25]	Detect Esca disease in grapevine.	UAV system with an RGB sensor.	CNN: SegNet.	Accuracy	In comparison to the model trained using infrared pictures, the RGB pictures gave better performance. One of the research's flaws is the small size of the training sample, which negatively impacted how well the deep learning segmentation worked.

3.3.2. Weed Detection

In addition to disease, weeds are seen as a common danger to food production. The technologies described in this study may be used to power weed-detecting and weed-eating robots [11].

Weed Detection in Individual Plants

In accord with Sujaritha et al. [26], fuzzy real-time classifiers were used to find weeds in sugar cane fields. Using a Raspberry Pi microcontroller and appropriate input/output subsystems including two different cameras, motors with power supplies, and tiny light sources, a robotic prototype was created for weed detection. During the movement of the robot, a divergence in the established course might occur due to obstacles in the field. An automatic image classification system was constructed, and it used a fuzzy real-time classification method and extracted leaf textures.

Among nine distinct weed species, the proposed robot prototype accurately recognizes the sugarcane crop. With a processing time of 0.02 s, the system identified weeds with an accuracy of 92.9%.

Milioto et al. [27] developed a new methodology for crop-weed classification using data taken with a 4-channel RGB and NIR camera, which depends on a modified encoder-decoder CNN. Three separate inputs were used to train the networks: RGB, RGB and near-infrared (NIR) images, and 14 channels including vegetation indices RGB, Excess Green (ExG), Excess Red (ExR), Color Index of Vegetation Extraction (CIVE), and Normalized Difference Index (NDI). To supplement the CNN with additional inputs, the authors first computed various vegetation indices and alternative interpretations that are often employed in plant categorization.

The authors found that the model performed better when additional channels were added to the input to the CNN. The network using RGB was 15% quicker to converge to 95% of the final accuracy than the network using the NIR channel. In terms of object-wise performance, the model achieved an accuracy of 94.74%, a precision of 98.16% for weeds, and 95.09% for crops. For recall, the system accomplished 94.79% for weeds and 94.17% for crops. The intersection over the union was 80.8%.

Lottes et al. [28] designed a sequential model encoder-decoder FCN for weed identification in sugar beet fields. The dataset was collected using a field robot, namely, BoniRob, with a 4-channel RGB+NIR camera. The processing model used 3D convolution to analyze five images in a series, creating a sequence code that was then used to learn sequential information about the weeds in the five images in a series. With the help of an addition known as the sequential module, it was possible to use picture sequences to implicitly encode local geometry. Even if the optical appearance or development stage of the plant changes between training and test time, this combination improves generalization performance.

The results indicated that, in comparison to the encoder-decoder FCN, the encoder-decoder with a sequential model raised the module's F1-score by around 11 to 14%. The suggested model outperformed encoder-decoder FCN without a sequential model, with an F1-score of 92.3.

Ma et al. [29] proposed an image segmentation procedure with SegNet for rice seedlings and weeds at the seedling stage in the paddy field based on fully convolutional networks (FCN). The model was then compared with another model, namely, U-Net. In this study, RGB color images were captured in seedling rice paddy fields. SegNet was developed using a symmetric structure for encoding and decoding, which was utilized to extract multiscale features and increase feature extraction accuracy. This AI method can directly extract the characteristics from the original RGB photos as well as categorize and identify the pixels in paddy field photographs that belong to the rice, background, and weeds. The primary goal of this study was to evaluate how well the suggested strategy performed in comparison to a U-Net model.

The proposed method worked effectively in classifying the pixels in pictures of weeds and shaped rice seedlings found in paddy areas. The U-Net and FCN techniques had an average accuracy rate of 89.5% and 70.8%, respectively. Figure 6 shows the experimental results for the FCN based on SegNet and U-Net compared with the original and ground truth images; blue represents rice, brown represents weeds, and the grey scale is the background.

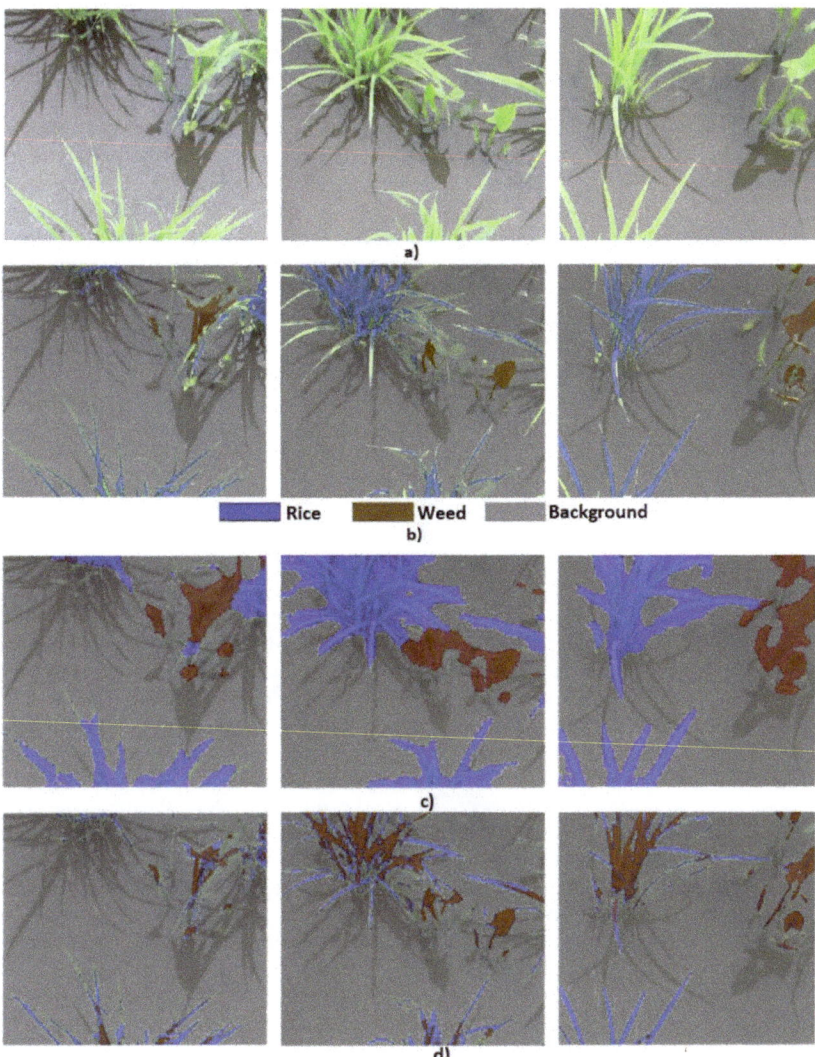

Figure 6. Results of the proposed model. (**a**) Original images; (**b**) Ground truth images; (**c**) Output by FCN; (**d**) Output by U-Net [29].

Ferreira et al. [15] analyze the performance of unsupervised deep clustering algorithms in real weeds datasets (Grass-Broadleaf dataset, and DeepWeeds), for the identification of weeds in a soybean field. Deep Clustering for Unsupervised Learning of Visual Features, and Joint Unsupervised Learning of Deep Representations and Image Clusters (JULE) are two contemporary unsupervised deep clustering techniques (DeepCluster).

The DeepCluster model was built using AlexNet and VGG16 as a baseline to obtain features, and K-means were implemented as the clustering algorithm.

Analyzing the two clustering algorithms evaluated, JULE performed more poorly than DeepCluster, in terms of the normalized mutual information (NMI), and accuracy. In JULE, for the first dataset, the results of MNI and ACC were 0.28% and 65.6%, respectively, for 80 clusters. In the second dataset, the results of MNI and ACC were 0.08% and 25.9%, respectively, for 160 clusters. On the other hand, in DeepCluster for the first dataset, the results of MNI and ACC were 0.41% and 87%, respectively, for 160 clusters. For the second dataset, the results of MNI and ACC were 0.26% and 51.6%, respectively, for 320 clusters.

In Wang et al. [16], pixel-wise semantic segmentation of weed and crop was examined using an encoder-decoder deep learning network. The two datasets used in the study, specifically, sugar beet and oilseed, were collected under quite varied illumination conditions. Three picture improvement techniques, Histogram Equalization (HE), Auto Contrast, and Deep Photo Enhancer, were examined to lessen the impacts of the various lighting situations. To improve the input to the network, several input representations, including different color space transformations and color indices, were compared. The models were trained with YCrCb and YCgCb color spaces and vegetation indices such as NDI, NDVI, ExG, ExR, ExGR, CIVE, VEG, and MExG. The results demonstrated that while the inclusion of NIR information significantly increased segmentation accuracy, images without NIR information did not improve segmentation results, demonstrating the value of NIR for accurate segmentation in low light conditions. The segmentation results for weed detection obtained by applying deep networks and image enhancement techniques in this work were encouraging. The model trained using NIR pictures attained a mIoU of 87.13% for the sugar beetroot dataset. For the oilseeds' dataset, the models were trained with RGB images only, and outperformed the other models with a mIoU of 88.91%. The best accuracy was 96.12%.

Kamath et al. [30] applied semantic segmentation models, namely, UNet, PSPNet, and SegNet in paddy crops and two types of weeds. The paddy field image collection was compiled from RGB photographs from two separate sources using two digital cameras. Two datasets were then created; only weed plants were included in Dataset-1, whereas paddy crop and photos of weeds were included in Dataset-2. A segmentation architecture using the ResNet-50 base model was built in PSPNet. A feature map for PSPNet was produced from the base network. On these pooled feature maps, convolution was used before feature maps were upscaled and concatenated. The use of a final convolution layer results in segmented outputs. The encoder-decoder framework used by the UNet design was constructed using the ResNet-50 base model. This model used skip connections which are additional connections that join down sampling layers with up sampling layers. The rebuilding of segmentation boundaries with the aid of skip connection after down sampling results in a more accurate output image. The VGG16 network and the encoder network used by the SegNet model are topologically identical. Each encoder layer has a matching decoder layer, and then each pixel receives class probabilities from a multi-class SoftMax classifier.

Using the playment.io program, photos were annotated, and each pixel was labelled to a categorization from one of four categories: Background 0, Broadleaved weed-1, Sedges-2, and Paddy-3. PSPNet outperformed SegNet and UNet in terms of effectiveness. The mean IoU for PSPNet was 0.72 and, the frequency weighted IoU was 0.93, whereas for SegNet and UNet, the mIoU values were 0.82 and 0.60, respectively. Finally, the frequency weighted IoU values were 0.74 and 0.38, respectively. Figure 7 represents the results of the proposed model using PSPNet; the images of the first row correspond to the original images, the second row represents the predicted output, and the last one is the ground truth image. The first line relates to the paddy, and the second characterizes the broadleaved weed. After that, the third shows the broadleaved weed (blue) and paddy (yellow), and the fourth, the sedge weeds. Sedge weeds were difficult to identify, whereas broadleaved weeds and paddy were clearly identified. This loss could be explained by how sedges and paddy are alike.

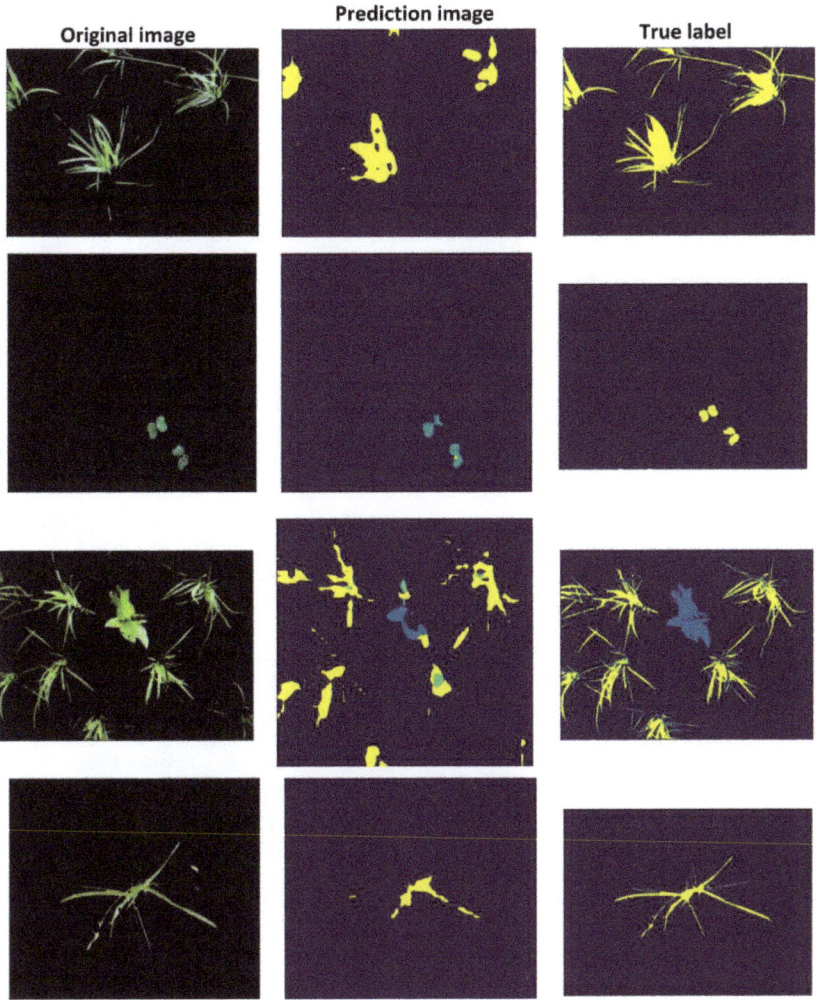

Figure 7. The results of PSPNet, the images of the first row, correspond to the original images, while the second row represents the predicted output, and the last is the ground truth image. The first line is the paddy, the second one is the broadleaved weed, the third one is the broadleaved weed (blue) and paddy (yellow), and the last, is the sedge weed, (adapted from [30]).

Mu et al. [31] developed a project to identify weeds in photos of cropping regions using a network model based on Faster R-CNN. Beyond that, another model combining the first one with Feature Pyramid Network (FPN) was developed for improved recognition accuracy. Images from the V2 Plant Seedlings dataset were used; this file includes photos in different weather conditions. The Otsu technique was applied to transform the obtained greyscale pictures into binary images to segregate the plants. Clear photos of the plants were obtained after processing. The convolutional features are shared using the Faster R-CNN deep learning network model, and feature extraction is done by fusing the ResNeXt network with FPN, to improve the model's weed identification detection accuracy. The experimental results show that the Faster R-CNN-FPN deep network model obtained greater recognition accuracy by employing the ResNeXt feature extraction network and combining it with the FPN network. Both models achieved good results; however, the prototype with FPN reached an accuracy of 95.61%, a recall of 87.26%, an F1-value of 91.24, an IoU of 93.7, and a detection time of 330ms. The model without FPN achieved the following results for the same metrics, 92.4%, 85.2%, 88.65%, 89.6%, and 319 ms.

Assunção et al. [32] explored the optimization of the weed-specific semantic segmentation model at model DeeplabV3 with a MobileNetV2 backbone, as well as its impacts on segmentation performance and inference time. In this study, the experiments were conducted with DM = 1.0 and DM = 0.5. The OS hyperparameter is the ratio of the size of the encoder's final output feature map to the size of the input image. Values of 8, 16, and 32 were chosen for OS to explore the trade-off between accuracy and inference time since this hyperparameter affects segmentation accuracy and inference time. There are three sections to this piece. There were two datasets utilized in the first one. To train and test the models, the Crop Weed Field Image Dataset (CWFID) dataset, which includes crops (carrots) and weeds, was employed. The second section of the process utilized crop and weed photos for the model's training and validation. By choosing several model hyperparameters and using model quantization, the model was optimized both before and after training. The primary goal is to extract the characteristics of the input image.

To obtain the performance necessary for the application, the depth multiplier (DM) and output stride (OS) hyperparameters of the MobilinetV2 were modified (i.e., light weight and fast inference time). The checkpoint files were then transformed into a frozen graph using a TMG framework tool (script). Finally, using the TensorRT class converter, the frozen graph was modified (optimized) to operate on the Tensorflow Real-Time (TensorRT) engine.

The semantic segmentation model was utilized in the most recent test of the robotic orchard rover created by Veiros et al. (2022). In this study, the accuracy and viability of a computer-vision framework were evaluated using a system for spraying pesticide on weeds. A Raspberry Pi v2 camera module with an 8-megapixel Sony IMX219 sensor was used to take the video pictures. The actuators that the Jetson Nano device controls are the herbicide container, pressure motor, a DC motor that applies pressure to it, manipulator motor, a stepper motor that moves the axis of the Cartesian manipulator, nozzle relay, a relay that opens and closes the spray valve, and spray nozzle.

According to the study results of the second test, segmentation performance mean intersection over union (mIOU) declined by 14.7% when employing a model hyperparameter DM of 0.5 and the TensorRT framework compared to a DM of 1.0 and no TensorRT. The model with the best segmentation performance has a 75% mIOU for OS = 8 and DM = 1.0. The model with a DM of 0.5 and OS of 32 had the lowest performance, which was 64% mIOU.

In addition, with the CWFID and weeds dataset, the outcomes were also contrasted with the initial segmentation work. The test with OS = 8 and DM = 1.0 achieved a mIOU of 75%, and an OS = 32 and DM = 0.5 accomplished a mIOU of 64%. Figure 8 displays the relevant segmentation quality outcomes. Different hyperparameters for DM and OS caused variations in segmentation performance (quality).

In Figure 9, a version of non-weeds segmentation is in the upper-left corner. The subsequent pictures display the input weed picture along with the associated segmentation outcomes (output). In the middle of each segmented region are the green dots that represent the weeds' center of gravity. The findings demonstrate the method's viability and outstanding spraying precision. Given that the trade-off between segmentation accuracy and inference time can be managed via the hyperparameters DM and OS, DeepLabV3 has shown to be an incredibly flexible model for segmentation tasks. Weed spraying in real-time was also precise and practical. The system correctly positioned the nozzle at all target weeds and sprayed the spray, as seen in the video demonstration. This outcome demonstrates the possibility of improvements for creating compact models with high predictive accuracy.

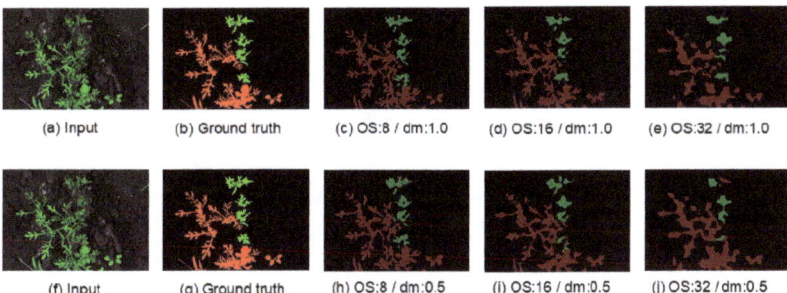

Figure 8. CWFID and weeds dataset qualitative segmentation results. Except for input and ground truth, the labels of each sub-image indicate the optimization that was applied to the model to produce the segmentation [32]. (**a**) Input; (**b**) Ground truth; (**c**) OS:8/dm:1.0; (**d**) OS:16/dm:1.0; (**e**) OS:32/dm:1.0; (**f**) Input; (**g**) Ground truth; (**h**) OS:8/dm:0.5; (**i**) OS:16/dm:0.5; (**j**) OS:32/dm:0.5.

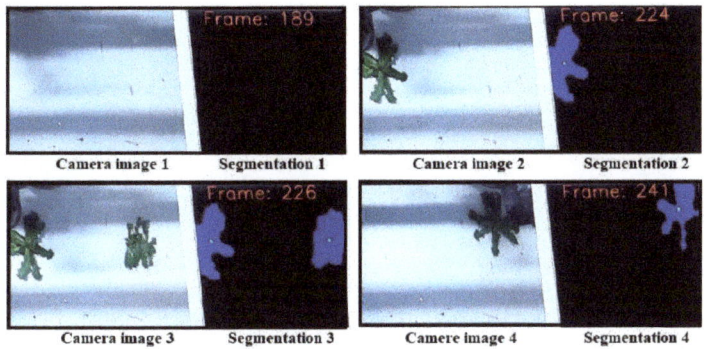

Figure 9. Segmentation of weeds as result of the application in real time [32].

Weed Detection in Areas of Crops

Peña et al. [33] created a study to evaluate the effectiveness and constraints of remotely sensed imagery captured by visible and multispectral cameras in an unmanned aerial vehicle (UAV), for early weed seedling detection. The objectives of the work were: to choose the best sensor for enhancing vegetation (weed and crop) and bare soil class discrimination as affected by the vegetation index applied; to design and test an algorithm object-based image analysis (OBIA) technique for crop and weed patch detection; and to determine the best arrangement of the UAV flight for the altitude, the type of sensor (visible-light + near-infrared multispectral cameras vs. visible-light), and the date of flight.

The OBIA procedure combined object-based characteristics such as spectral values, position, and orientation, as well as hierarchical relationships between analysis levels. As a result, the system was designed to identify crop rows with high accuracy using a dynamic and self-adaptive classification process and to label plants outside of crop rows as weeds.

The maximum weed detection accuracy, up to 91%, was found in the color-infrared pictures taken at 40 m and on date 2 (50 days after seeding), when plants had 5–6 true leaves. The images taken earlier than date 2 performed significantly better than the ones taken subsequently at this flight level. With a higher flight altitude, the multispectral camera had superior accuracy, while the visible light camera had higher accuracy at lower altitudes. The errors are due to the higher altitudes as a consequence of the spectral mixture between bare soil elements and sunflowers that occurred at the perimeters of the crop-rows. Figure 10 shows a comparison of results. The first line (A) presents on-ground photographs, while the second line (B) shows manual categorization of observed data. The third line

(C) shows the image classification achieved by the OBIA algorithm. The model results were divided into four types: the number of correct frames (1); underestimated weeds (2), namely, frames with weed infestations in which the OBIA system spotted some weed plants but missed others; false negative frames (3), with weed-infested frames in which no weeds were detected; and false positive frames (4), in which weeds were overestimated.

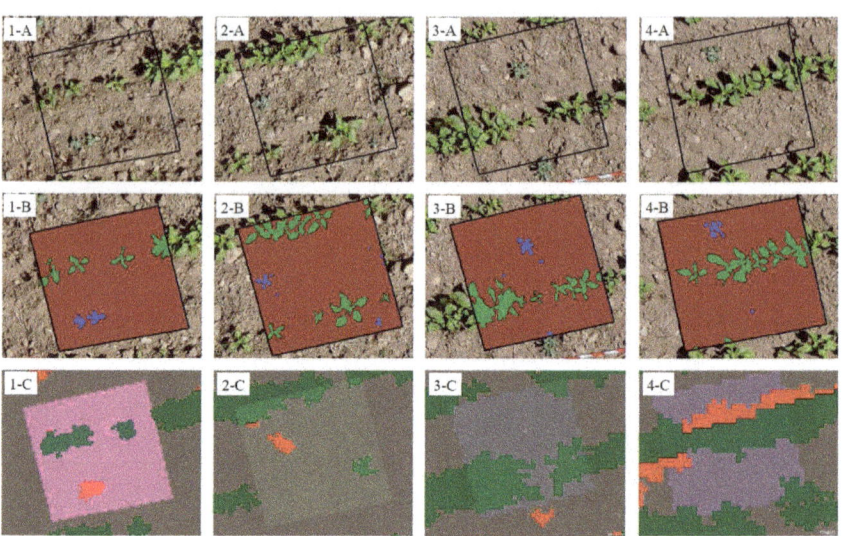

Figure 10. Example of the four sample frames' outcomes. (**A**) On-ground images; (**B**) manual classification of observed data; and (**C**) image classification conducted by the OBIA algorithm. (**1**) Correct categorization; (**2**) underestimation of weeds; (**3**) negative errors; (**4**) false positive errors [33].

Huang et al. [34] used photos from a UAV Phantom 4 to create an accurate weed cover map in rice fields, to detect weeds and rice crops. The Fully Convolutional Network (FCN) approach was proposed for preparing a weed map of the captured images. In the training phase, the image-label pairings from the training set that correlates pixel-to-pixel are fed into the FCN network. The network converts the input picture into an output image of the same size, and the output image is applied to calculate the loss as an objective function together with the ground truth label (GT label).

According to the investigational results, the performance of the FCN technology was very effective. The general accuracy of the system reached 0.935, its weed detection accuracy reached 0.883, and an IoU 0.752, indicating that this algorithm can provide specific weed cover maps for the UAV images under consideration. In Figure 11, it is possible to observe the results of the FCN with different pre-trained CNNs. In (a), the real UAV images are presented; (b) is the ground truth representation; and images from (c) to (e) show results obtained by FCN-AlexNet, FCN-VGG16, and FCN-GoogLeNet, respectively.

Bah et al. [35] developed a completely automated learning technique for weed detection in bean and spinach fields using UAV photos utilizing ResNet18 with a selection of unsupervised training datasets. This algorithm created super-pixels based on k-mean clustering.

A simple linear iterative clustering (SLIC) algorithm was used to construct a marker and define the plant rows after the Hough transform was used to determine the rate of plant rows on the skeleton. Super pixels were produced by this technique using k-mean clustering.

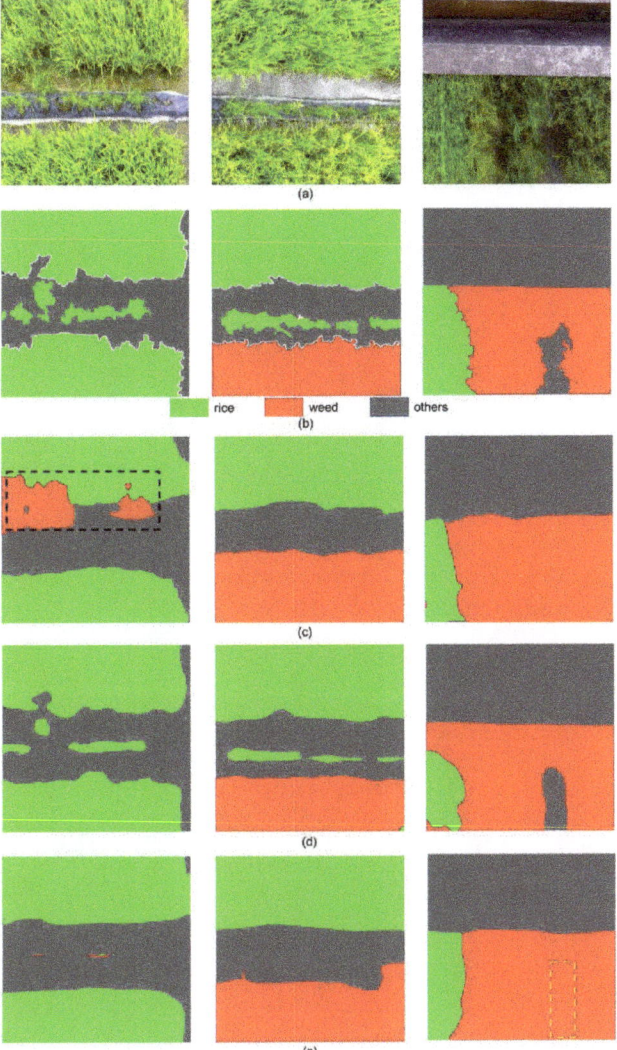

Figure 11. Classification results of the FCN with distinct pre-trained CNNs. (**a**) Real UAV image; (**b**) Ground truth results; (**c–e**) Results acquired by FCN-AlexNet, FCN-VGG16 and FCN-GoogLeNet, respectively [34].

Other models, namely, SVM and RF, were used to compare the model's performance. ResNet18 performs better overall than SVM and RF in supervised and unsupervised learning techniques. The model achieved an accuracy of 0.945 and a kappa coefficient of 0.912. Figure 12 shows two examples of image classification with models produced by unsupervised data in spinach fields at the top (a,b), and bean fields at the bottom (c,d). The samples acquired using a sliding window, without a crop line or any background details, are shown on the left (a,c). The weeds found after applying crop line and background information are shown on the right in red (b,d). The plants are designated as being crops, weeds, or ambiguous decisions by the red, blue, and white dots, respectively.

Figure 12. Examples of unmanned aerial vehicle (UAV) picture categorization using unsupervised data models in spinach, and bean fields. (**a**) Sample of a spinach field acquired using a sliding window, without a crop line or any background details; (**b**) Sample from spinach field acquired after applying crop line and background information; (**c**) Sample of a been field acquired using a sliding window, without a crop line or any background details; (**d**) Sample from been field acquired after applying crop line and background information. Crops are represented in blue, weeds in red, and uncertain decisions in white [35].

In line with Osorio et al. [8], three different weed estimation methods were proposed based on deep learning image processing and multispectral images captured by a drone. An NDVI index was used in conjunction with these techniques. The first technique uses histograms of oriented gradients (HOG) as a feature descriptor and is based on SVM. The ground and other aspects that are unrelated to vegetation are covered by a mask that is created by NDVI. These objects' characteristics are retrieved using HOG and are then used as inputs by a support vector machine that has already been trained. The SVM determines whether the identified items fall into the lettuce class. The second approach employed a CNN based on YOLOv3 for object detection. An algorithm removes crop samples from the image using model's bounding box coordinates after it has been trained to recognize the crop. After that, a green filter binarizes the picture, turning the pixels that do not have any vegetation into black and the ones that the green filter accepts into white. Finally, vegetation that does not match the crop is highlighted, making it easier to calculate the percentage of weeds in each image. The last method was to apply masks on the CNN, to obtain an instance segmentation for each crop. RCNN extracts 2000 areas from the picture using the "selective search for object recognition" method. They feed data into the Inception V2 CNN in this case, and it extracts characteristics used by an SVM to categorize the item into the appropriate category. Centered on the metrics that were used, the F1-scores for crop detection using this approach were 88%, 94%, and 94%, respectively. The accuracy was 79%, 89%, and 89%. The sensitivity was 83%, 98%, and 91%. The specificity was 0%, 91%, and 98%. Finally, the precision was 95%, 91%, and 94%.

Considering the version of the YOLO model used, it is important to say that there are currently more up-to-date versions. YOLOv4 is an advanced real-time object detection model that was introduced as an improvement over the previous versions of YOLO. Developed by a team at the University of Washington, YOLOv4 boasts a significantly improved performance in terms of accuracy and speed compared to its predecessors. It includes a new architecture that incorporates spatial pyramid pooling and a backbone network based on CSPDarknet53. This architecture allows for more efficient use of computing resources, resulting in faster processing times and improved accuracy. Additionally, YOLOv4 uses a combination of anchor boxes and dynamic anchor assignment to improve object detection accuracy and reduce false positives. Another notable feature of YOLOv4 is its use of a modified loss function that includes a term to penalize incorrect classifications of small objects. This leads to better performance on small object detection tasks [36].

YOLOv5 is a state-of-the-art object detection and image segmentation model introduced by Ultralytics in 2020. It builds on the success of previous YOLO models and introduces several new features and improvements. One of the key innovations in YOLOv5 is its use of a new, more efficient architecture based on a single stage detection pipeline. This pipeline uses a feature extraction network combined with a detection head, which allows for faster processing times and improved accuracy. Additionally, YOLOv5 introduces a range of new anchor-free object detection methods, including the use of center points, corner points, and grids [36].

YOLOv8 is an advanced object detection and image segmentation model that was developed by Ultralytics. It is an improvement over previous YOLO versions and has gained popularity among computer vision researchers and practitioners due to its high accuracy, speed, and versatility. One of the main strengths of YOLOv8 is its speed, which enables it to process large datasets quickly. Additionally, its accuracy has been improved through a more optimized network architecture, a revised anchor box design, and a modified loss function. This results in fewer false positives and false negatives, leading to better overall performance. Overall, YOLOv8 is an excellent tool for computer vision applications and offers many advantages over previous models. Its speed, accuracy, and versatility make it an ideal choice for a broad range of tasks, including object detection, image segmentation, and image classification [37].

Islam et al. [14] used three types of approaches, namely, KNN, RF, and SVM to detect weeds in crops. The images were acquired from an RGB camera coupled in a UAV, in an Australian chilli farm, and then pre-processed using image processing methods. Red, green, and blue bands' reflectance was extracted, and from there, the authors deduced vegetation indicators such as the normalized red band, normalized green band, and normalized blue band. The pre-processed pictures' features were extracted using MATLAB, which was also utilized to simulate machine learning-based methods. The experimental findings show that RF outperformed the other classifiers. In light of this, it is clear that RF and SVM are effective classifiers for weed detection in UAV photos. RF, KNN, and SVM each had accuracy results of 0.963, 0.628, and 0.94. Recall and specificity were 0.951 and 0.887, 0.621 and 0.819, and 0.911 and 0.890 with RF, KNN, and SVM, respectively. With RF, KNN, and SVM, respectively, the accuracy, false positive rate (FPR), and kappa coefficient were 0.949, 0.057, and 0.878; 0.624, 0.180, and 0.364; and 0.908, 0.08, and 0.825.

Table 4 describes the feature of research works in the field of Weed Detection.

3.3.3. Weed Classification

Another crucial component of agricultural management is the categorization of species (such as insects, birds, and plants). The conventional human method of classifying species takes time and calls for subject-matter experts. Deep learning can analyze real-world data to provide quicker, more accurate solutions [11].

Weed Classification in Individual Plants

According to Dyrmann et al. [38], a convolutional neural network was developed to recognize plant species in color images. The images originated from six different datasets namely, Dyrmann and Christiansen (2014), Robo Weed Support (2015), Aarhus University—Department of Agroecology and SEGES (2015), Kim Andersen and Henrik Midtiby, Søgaard (2005), Minervini, Scharr, Fischbach, and Tsaftaris (2014). The six datasets include all pictures taken during lighting-controlled events and photographs taken on mobile devices while out in the field during varying lighting circumstances.

Table 4. Feature descriptions of publications in the field of "Weed Detection".

References	Application	Data Used	Model Used	Metric Used	Model Performance
Sujaritha et al. [26]	Weeds in sugar cane fields' detection.	Two digital cameras.	Fuzzy real time classifier.	Accuracy	The prototype distinguished between nine different weed species with greater precision and a shorter processing time. The field obstructions provoked the robot to deviate from the planned path while it is moving.
Milioto et al. [27]	Crop-weed sugar beet detection (VIs added to the input).	4-channel RGB and NIR camera.	Mask R-CNN.	Accuracy IoU Precision Recall	By including a new channel at its input, the model's performance improved. Compared to the NIR channel network, the RGB channel network converges 15% more quickly to the final accuracy of 95%.
Lottes et al. [28]	Crop and weed detection in the sugar field.	FR with a 4-channel RGB+NIR camera.	Encoder–Decoder FCN: DenseNet.	F1-score	The suggested model was able to robustly identify crops in all growth phases and outperformed encoder-decoder FCN without a sequential model, RF, and vanilla FCN with an F1-score of 92.3.
Ma et al. [29]	Detection of weeds and rice seedlings.	RGB images.	FCN: SegNet.	Accuracy	The suggested technique successfully classified the pixels in images of weeds and distinctively shaped rice seedlings discovered in paddy regions. The SegNet approach produced a good accuracy classification.
Ferreira et al. [15]	Detection of weeds in a soybean field (unsupervised clustering).	Two datasets from [15].	JULE; DeepCluster.	Accuracy NMI	Performance-wise, DeepCluster outperformed JULE. The outcomes from these datasets point to a viable use of clustering and unsupervised learning for agricultural issues.
Wang et al. [16]	Detection of crops of sugar, weeds, and oilseeds.	Two datasets from [16].	Encoder-decoder CNN.	Accuracy IoU	The outcomes show how useful NIR information is for exact segmentation in low-light settings. The accuracy of segmentation was greatly increased by the addition of NIR data.
Kamath et al. [30]	Weed detection in paddy crops.	Digital camera.	PSPNet, UNet, and SegNet.	IoU	In terms of efficiency, PSPNet fared better than SegNet and UNet. The frequency weighted IoU falls between 80% and 90%, with the mean IoU lying between 70% and 80%.

Table 4. *Cont.*

References	Application	Data Used	Model Used	Metric Used	Model Performance
Mu et al. [31]	Weed identification in maize, sugar beet, and wheat crops.	Dataset: V2 Plant Seedlings, from [31].	FPN; Faster R-CNN: ResNeXt.	Accuracy Recall F1-Score IoU	The experimental findings demonstrate that by merging the ResNeXt feature extraction network with the FPN network, the Faster R-CNN-FPN deep network model achieves a higher recognition accuracy.
Assunção et al. [32]	Weed detection using semantic segmentation.	Five datasets from [32].	TMG DeepLabV3 MobilenetV2.	mIOU	Given that the trade-off between segmentation accuracy and inference time can be managed via the hyperparameters OS and DM, DeepLabV3 has been shown to be an incredibly flexible model for segmentation tasks.
Peña et al. [33]	Weed seedlings in sunflower field detection.	Visible-light and multispectral cameras in a UAV.	OBIA.	Accuracy	While the visible light camera performed better at lower flight altitudes, the multispectral camera proved more accurate at higher altitudes. The spectrum mixing of flowers and bare soil components caused some mistakes in the higher elevations.
Huang et al. [34]	Weed cover maps to detect weeds and crops in rice fields.	UAV with a digital camera.	FCN.	Accuracy IoU	The FCN technology performed well in terms of efficiency and accuracy for weed identification. Since FCN is a supervised algorithm, it necessitates a lot of manual labelling effort because it needs a large amount of labelled pictures for training and updating.
Bah et al. [35]	Weed detection in bean and spinach fields.	Drone with a digital camera.	CNN: Resnet18.	Accuracy	Given the disparities between supervised and unsupervised labelling's accuracy, the unsupervised one may be a preferable option for weed detection, especially when crop rows are widely spaced.
Osorio et al. [8]	Weed detection in lettuce crops (VIs added to the input).	Mavic Pro with a multispectral camera.	SVM+ HOG; Mask R-CNN; YOLOv3.	F1-Score Accuracy Precision Recall Specificity	The HOG-SVM approach was shown to work quite well, and given that it requires less processing power, it is an excellent choice for IoT systems. As compared to the other two, the YOLO approach overestimates the high values of weed coverage.
Islam et al. [14]	Weed detection.	RGB camera coupled in a UAV.	RF; KNN; SVM.	Accuracy Recall Precision FPR Kappa	The experimental results indicate that RF outperformed the other classifiers. The efficiency of RF and SVM as classifiers for weed detection from UAV pictures is noteworthy.

To identify green pixels, a straightforward excessive green segmentation was employed. After that, batch normalization makes sure that the inputs to layers always fall within the same range. The network's activation function (ReLu) adds non-linear decision boundaries. Max pooling is a procedure that shrinks a feature map's spatial extent and gives the network translation invariance. In this study, the network's layering was decided upon by assessing the network's filtering power and coverage.

The training was ended after 18 epochs to get the maximum accuracy feasible without over-fitting the network. With an average accuracy of 86.2%, the network's categorization accuracy varied from 33% to 98%. With accuracy rates of 98%, 98%, and 97%, respectively, Thale Cress (*A. thaliana*), Sugar Beet (*B. vulgaris*), and Barley (*H. vulgare* L.) were frequently accurately diagnosed. However, Broadleaved Grasses (*Poaceae*), Field Pansy (*Viola arvensis*), and Veronica (*Veronica*) were frequently misclassified. Just 46%, 33%, and 50% of these three species received the proper classification. Overall, the classes with the greatest number of species also had the greatest categorization accuracy. As a result, classes with fewer picture samples made a smaller total loss.

Andrea et al. [39] demonstrated the creation of an algorithm capable of classifying and segmenting images. It uses a convolutional neural network (CNN) to separate weeds from maize plants in real-time. This discrimination was performed using four types of CNN, namely, AlexNet, LeNet, sNet, and cNet. A multispectral camera was used to acquire RGB and NIR images for segmentation and classification. A dataset created during the segmentation phase was used to train the CNN. Each of the four CNN models was trained using the same dataset and solver of type Adam after being selected.

The most successful algorithms offer great potential for real-time autonomous systems for categorizing weeds and plants. The network that produced the best results was the cNET of 16 filters. It had a training accuracy of 97.23% and used a dataset of 44,580 segmented pictures from both classes.

Gao et al. [40] proposed a hyperspectral NIR snapshot camera for classifying weeds and maize by measuring the spectral reflectance of an interest zone (ROI). The aim of this work was to identify the relevant spectral wavelengths and key features for classification, investigate the viability of weed and maize classification using a near infrared (NIR) snapshot mosaic hyperspectral camera, and provide the best parameters for a random forest (RF) model construction. In that work, 185 features were retrieved using vegetation indices (VIs), specifically, NDVI and RVI.

According to the findings, the ideal random forest model with 30 crucial spectral properties can successfully identify the weeds *Convolvulus arvensis*, *Rumex*, and *Cirsium arvense*, as well as the crops *Zea mays*. It was demonstrated that *Z. mays* can be identified with 100% recall (sensitivity) and 94% precision (positive predictive values). The model accomplished precision and F1 scores of 0.940 and 0.969, 0.959 and 0.866, 0.703 and 0.697, and 0.659 and 0.698, for crop *Zea mays* and weeds *Convolvulus arvensis*, *Rumex* and *Cirsium arvense*, respectively.

Bakhshipour and Jafari [41], using shape characteristics, utilized a Support Vector Machine (SVM) and an artificial neural network (ANN) classifier to categorize four different species of weeds and a sugar beet crop. Pictures were captured by using a weed robot with a camera, providing RGB images. Multi-layer feed-forward perceptron ANN was created using the Levenberg–Marquardt (LM) back-propagation learning method and two hidden layers. Principal Component Analysis (PCA) was employed as a feature selection method to reduce the initial 31 feature expressions into four components. The PCA values were then employed in SVM.

Both ANN and SVM correctly classified the sugar plants, with an accuracy of 93.33% and 96.67%, respectively. Compared to the sugar beet crop, the weeds were correctly identified by ANN and SVM 92.50% and 93.33% of the time, respectively. With an overall accuracy of 92.92% and 95%, respectively, both ANN and SVM were able to detect the shape-based patterns and categorize the weeds quite well. The results of the SBWD algorithm at various levels are shown in Figure 13. The initial RGB image is shown in (a); (b) shows the EXG method for segmenting plants; (c) demonstrates the image created using morphological techniques (noise removal, area thresholding for removing small plants, and edge erosion for removing touching overlaps); (d) shows the SBWD algorithm for segmenting sugar beets; (e) shows the subtraction of the result of greenness from image (c) from image (b) showing the weeds; and, finally (f) displays the result of the SBWD algorithm showing weeds, sugar beet, and false negatives; red pixels indicate weeds, green pixels indicate sugar beet plants, and yellow pixels show areas that were incorrectly identified as undesirable objects.

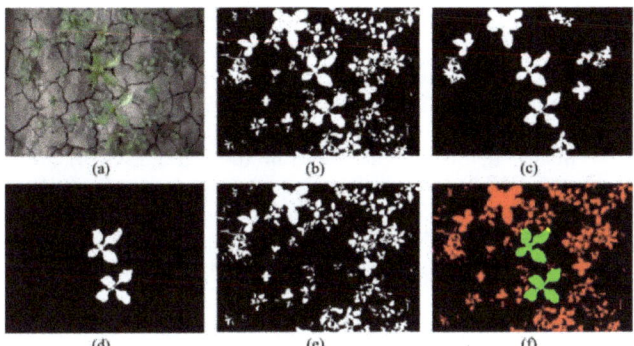

Figure 13. Results from steps of the SBWD algorithm: (**a**) initial RGB image; (**b**) segmented plants using EXG method; (**c**) the result after morphological filtering of small objects; (**d**) segmented sugar beets with SBWD algorithm; (**e**) subtraction of image (**c**) from image (**b**) showing the weeds; (**f**) result of SBWD algorithm showing weeds, sugar beet and false negatives [41].

Sa et al. [42] performed weed and sugar beet classification using a CNN with multispectral images collected by a MAV. These images were converted to SegNet format. The information gathered from this field was divided into photographs with only crops, pure weeds, or a combination of crops and weeds. For improved class balance, the frequency of appearance (FoA) for every single class is modified depending on the training dataset. With changing input channel sizes and training settings, the authors trained six distinct models, assessed them quantitatively using AUC and F1-scores as metrics, and then compared the results.

The learning rate for the training model was set to 0.001, the batch size was 6, the weight delay rate was 0.005, and the maximum iterations were 640 epochs. This model was able to achieve an average accuracy of 80% using the test data, with an average F1-score of 0.8. However, spatiotemporal inconsistencies were found in the model due to limitations in the training dataset.

Yang et al. [43] investigated deep learning techniques for hyperspectral image classification. The authors designed and developed four deep learning models: a two-dimensional CNN (2-D-CNN); a three-dimensional CNN (3-D-CNN); a region-based 2-dimensional CNN (R-2-D-CNN); a region-based 3-dimensional CNN (R-3-D-CNN). The objective was that a 2-D-CNN worked in the spatial context, while a 3-D-CNN worked in both spectral and spatial factors of the hyperspectral images retrieved from six datasets, viz., Botswana Scene, Indian Pines Scene, Salinas Scene, Pavia Center Scene, Kennedy Space Center, and Pavia University Scene.

The patch and feature extraction and the label identification steps make up the 2-D-CNN model. The primary distinction is that the 3-D-CNN model contains an additional reordering step. The D hyperspectral bands are rearranged in this phase in ascending order. A multiscale deep neural network is used by the R-2-D-CNN model to fuse numerous shrinking patches into multilevel instances, which are then used to make predictions. The primary distinction is that the 3-D-CNN model makes use of 3-D convolution operators whereas the R-2-D-CNN model do so use their 2-D equivalents.

An effective hyperspectral image classification process should consider both the spectral factor and the spatial factor since both have an impact on the class label prediction of a pixel. With this knowledge, the proposed deep learning models, namely the R-2-D-CNN and the R-3-D-CNN, achieved better results. The best results of the first network, in one of the datasets, were 99.67% and 99.89%, which correspond to values of average accuracy of each class (AA), and overall accuracy of all classes (OA), respectively. In the second model, the best results were 99.87% and 99.97%, for the same metrics.

Yashwanth et al. [44] implemented an image Classification System using the Deep Learning function. KERAS API in combination with the Tensorflow backend has been used in Python. Images of nine different crops and their respective weeds have been collected (wheat-*Parthenium*; Soybean-*Amaranthus Spinosus*; Maize-*Dactyloctenium Aegyptium*; Brinjal-*Datura Fatuosa*; Castor-*Portulaca Oleracea*; Sunflower-*Cyperus Rotundus*; Sugarcane-*Convolvulus Arvensis*; Paddy-*Chloris Barbata*; Paddy-*Echinochloa colona*. In the first stage, images that will be used to train the neural network are pre-processed. The input layer stores the image's pixels in the form of arrays. The "ReLU" activation function is used in the next step to obtain the image's corrected feature map. To accomplish edge detection, pooling is employed. The matrix gets flattened after using this flattened function. The thick layer receives this feeding. The object in the image is recognized by a completely linked layer.

The model was tested using nine different types of crops and the corresponding weeds, and the highest accuracy was found to be 96.3%. The provided photos were correctly categorized as either plants or weeds.

Jin et al. [45] created an algorithm for robotic weed eradication in vegetable farms based on deep learning and image processing. Images were captured in the field using a digital camera. Bounding boxes were drawn on the vegetable in the input photos as a manual annotation. In CenterNet, each item is represented by a single point, and object centers are predicted using a heatmap. Estimated centers are obtained from the heatmap's peak values using a Gaussian kernel and an FCN. Using a Gaussian kernel and focal loss, each ground truth key point is transformed into a smaller key-point heatmap to train the network. A color index was established and assessed using Genetic Algorithms (GAs) in accordance with Bayesian classification error to extract weeds from the background.

The trained CenterNet earned an F1-score of 0.953, an accuracy of 95.6%, and a recall of 95.0.

In El-Kenawy et al. [46], a new methodology based on metaheuristic optimization and machine learning was proposed, which aims to classify weeds based on wheat images acquired by a drone. Three models were proposed, specifically, artificial neural networks (NNs), support vector machines (SVMs), and the K-nearest neighbors' algorithm (KNN). The ANN was trained across a public dataset, through transfer learning and feature extraction. According to AlexNet, a binary optimizer is further suggested to improve the feature selection procedure and choose the optimal collection of features. A collection of assessment criteria is used to evaluate the efficacy of the feature selection algorithm to analyze the performance of the suggested technique. The suggested model used two more different types of machine learning models, namely, SVM and KNN, to improve the parameters. This classifier is improved by a brand-new optimization approach that combines grey wolf (GWO) and sine cosine optimizers (SCA). These suggested classifiers contribute to a creation of a hybrid algorithm.

The results demonstrate that the recommended technique works better than other alternatives and enhances classification accuracy, with a detection accuracy of 97.70%, an F1-score of 98.60%, a specificity of 95.20%, and a sensitivity of 98.40%.

Sunil et al. [47] analyzed the performance of a deep learning model for weed detection in photos with non-uniform and uniform backgrounds. Four Canon digital cameras were used to capture the weed and crop shots, namely, Palmer amaranth, horseweed, redroot pigweed, waterhemp, ragweed, and kochia, and crop species of sugar beets and canola. Weed classification models were developed using deep learning architectures, namely,

Convolutional Neural Network (CNN) based on a Residual Network (ResNet50), and Visual Group Geometry (VGG16). The uniform background scenario data, non-uniform background scenario data, and combined-datasets scenarios created after combining both scenarios' data were trained using the ResNet50, and VGG16.

With an average f1-score of 82.75% and 75%, respectively, the VGG16 and ResNet50 models built from non-uniform backdrop pictures performed well on the uniform background. The performance of the VGG16 and ResNet50 models, which were built using uniform backdrop photos, did not fare as well, with average f1-scores of 77.5% and 68.4%, respectively, on non-uniform background images. The f1-score value of 92% to 99% was achieved by a model that was trained using fused information from two background circumstances.

Sunil et al. [48] compared the classification models of Support Vector Machine (SVM) and deep learning-based Visual Group Geometry 16 (VGG16) utilizing RGB picture texture information to categorize weeds and crop species. Six crop species as well as four weeds (horseweed, kochia, ragweed, and waterhemp) were classified using the SVM and VGG16 deep learning classifiers (the crop species were black bean, canola, corn, flax, soybean, and sugar beets). Gray-level co-occurrence matrix (GLCM) features and local binary pattern (LBP) features are two different categories of texture characteristics that were retrieved from the grayscale picture. After this, a machine learning classifier was built by operating a SVM and VGG16.

All SVM model classifiers have fallen short in comparison to the VGG16 model classifiers. The findings showed that the VGG16 model classifier's average F1 results varied from 93% to 97.5%, while the average F1-score results of SVM ranged from 83% to 94%. In the VGG16 Weeds-Corn classifier, the corn class achieved a F1-score value of 100%.

Table 5 summarizes the features of research works in the field of weed classification.

3.3.4. Fruit Detection

Fruit quality detection is a technique for automatically evaluating the quality of fruits based on several aspects of a picture, such as color, size, texture, and form, among others. The main element preventing adverse health issues in people is fruit quality. In the food business and agriculture specifically, automatic detection is crucial.

Fruit Detection in Individual Plants

Mao et al. [49] proposed a Real-Time Fruit Detection model (RTFD), a simple method for edge CPU devices that can identify fruit, specifically strawberries and tomatoes. The PicoDet-S model-based RTFD enhances the efficiency of real-time detection for edge CPU computing devices by enhancing the model's structure, loss function, and activation function. Two datasets were used with pictures taken in different conditions; the tomato dataset was compiled using the publicly accessible Laboro Tomato dataset, while the strawberry dataset was acquired from the publicly available StrawDI dataset. The technical path was divided into two objectives: model training, and model quantization and deployment. In the first, the RTFD model's performance was improved using the CIoU bounding box loss function, the ACON-C activation function, and the three-layer LC-PAN architecture.

The RTFD model was quantitatively trained for fruit detection. After being transformed into a Paddle Lite model and integrated into a testing Android smartphone app, the RTFD model performed extremely accurately in terms of real-time detection.

It is anticipated that edge computing will successfully implement the idea of redesigning the model structure, loss function, and activation function, as well as training by quantization, to expedite the detection of deep neural networks. The proposed RTFD has enormous potential for intelligent picking machines. For the strawberry and tomato datasets, PicoDet-S has an average accuracy of 94.2% and 76.8%, respectively. It is anticipated that edge computing will successfully implement the idea of redesigning the model structure, loss function, and activation function, as well as training by quantization, to expedite the detection using deep neural networks. The proposed RTFD has enormous potential for intelligent picking machines.

Table 5. Feature descriptions of publications in the field of "Weed classification".

References	Application	Data Used	Model Used	Metric Used	Model Performance
Dyrmann et al. [38]	Weed classification in 22 different crops.	Six databases from [38].	CNN.	Accuracy	In general, the classes with the highest number of species also had the greatest categorization accuracy. As a result, classes with fewer picture samples made a smaller total loss. The network's classification precision varied from 33% to 98%, with an average precision of 86.2%.
Andrea et al. [39]	Image segmentation and classification of weeds in maize fields.	Multispectral camera to acquire RGB and NIR images.	CNN: LeNet, AlexNet, cNet, and sNet.	Accuracy	Based on its accuracy and processing speed, the network cNET provided the greatest training outcomes.
Gao et al. [40]	Weed and maize classification (VIs added to the input).	Hyperspectral snapshot camera sensor.	RF.	Precision Recall F1-score	The RF model that was used to create classifiers using various spectral feature combinations performed well. Vegetation indices are useful techniques for developing important aspects for the categorization of crops and weeds.
Bakhshipour and Jafari. [41]	Classification of sugar beet crop and weeds.	RGB camera.	SVM; ANN.	Accuracy	Both ANN and SVM properly identified the effectiveness of sugar plants and weeds.
Sa et al. [42]	Classification of sugar beet and weeds.	Multispectral images collected by a MAV.	CNN.	Accuracy F1-score	Most of the weeds were classified well. Due to restrictions in the dataset the model was trained on, certain spatiotemporal discrepancies were identified.
Yang et al. [43]	Classification of weeds in crops and landscapes.	Six datasets from [13].	CNN: 2-D-CNN, 3-D-CNN, R-2-D-CNN, R-3-D-CNN.	Accuracy	For most of the data sets, the suggested R-3-D-CNN model performs better than most of the current models and can also converge more quickly. Nevertheless, compared to conventional machine learning techniques, these models need more training samples.
Yashwanth et al. [44]	Image classification of weeds in nine different crops.	Digital camera.	Keras API; TensorFlow.	Accuracy	The model was tested using nine different types of crops and the corresponding weeds, and the greatest accuracy was determined to be 96.3%. All the provided photos were correctly categorized as either plants or weeds.

Table 5. Cont.

References	Application	Data Used	Model Used	Metric Used	Model Performance
Jin et al. [45]	Weed identification in cabbage fields.	Digital camera.	CNN: CenterNet.	Precision Recall F1-score	The recommended approach has application value for the sustainable development of the vegetable sector and is suited for ground-based weed detection in vegetable agricultural land under diverse circumstances, lighting, and complicated backdrops, as well as various growth phases.
El-Kenawy et al. [46]	Weed classification in wheat crops.	Images captured by a drone.	NN; SVM; KNN; GWO; SCA.	Accuracy F1-score Recall Specificity	The research shown that the suggested strategy outperforms existing methods and improves classification accuracy, with a detection accuracy of 97.70%, an F1-score of 98.60%, a specificity of 95.20%, and a sensitivity of 98.40%.
G C et al. [47]	Weed classification in sugar beets.	Four Canon digital cameras.	CNN: VGG16, ResNet50.	F1-Score	The VGG16 and ResNet50 models, which were created using non-uniform backdrop photos, performed well on the uniform background, with average f1-scores of 82.75% and 75%, respectively. Employing non-uniform backgrounds led to poorer results. The model that was trained using combined datasets from two background scenarios performed better than any.
Zhang et al. [48]	Weed classification in black bean, canola, corn, flax, soybean, and sugar beets.	RGB camera.	SVM; VGG16.	F1-score	All SVM model classifiers have failed in comparison to the VGG16 model classifiers. The results demonstrated that the range of the VGG16 model classifier's average F1-scores was between 93% and 97.5%. The range of SVM average F1 scores was 83 to 94 percent. In the VGG16 Weeds-Corn classifier, the corn class scored 100% F1.

Figure 14 shows the results of strawberry and tomato detection. The picture contains varied colored borders that reflect separate categories. The blue arrows serve as suggestive indication symbols, and the blue circles highlight regions of faulty or missing detections. The red, orange/yellow, and light blue correspond, respectively, to mature strawberries, half-mature strawberries, and immature strawberries.

Figure 14. The impact of RTFD model detection on the tomato and strawberry datasets. The blue circles denote locations of inaccurate or missing detections, while the blue arrows act as suggestive indicator symbols. The red, orange/yellow, and light blue corresponded, respectively to mature strawberries, half-mature strawberries, and immature strawberries [49].

In line with Pereira et al. [50], six grape types that predominate in the Douro Region were automatically identified and classified using a methodology based on the AlexNet architecture and transfer learning scheme. Two natural vineyard image datasets, taken in various parts of Douro, were called Douro Red Grape Variety (DRGV), and GRGV_2018. For picture managing, different image processing (IP) methods were applied, such as independent components filter (ICFs), leaf segmentation algorithm (LSA) with four-corners-in-one, leaf patch extraction (LPE), LPE with ICF, LPE with canny edge detector (CED), and LPE with Gray-scale morphology processing (GMP). These new datasets, with pre-processed and augmentation pictures were then trained in the AlexNet CNN.

The suggested method, four-corners-in-one, supplemented by the leaf segmentation algorithm (LSA), revealed success in reaching the best classification accuracy in the set of performed experiments. With a testing accuracy of 77.30%, the experimental results indicated the suggested classifier to be trustworthy. The algorithm took roughly 6.1 ms to identify the grape variety in a picture.

Fruit Detection in Areas of Crops

Santos et al. [51] estimated grape wine production from RGB photos including deep learning algorithms and computer vision models. Pictures were taken of five distinct grape varietals, using a Canon camera and a smartphone. Mask R-CNN, YOLOv2, and YOLOv3 models from deep learning (DL) were trained to recognize and separate grapes in the photos. After that, spatial registration was carried out using the Structure from Motion (SfM) image processing technique, incorporating the information produced by the CNN-based stage. To prevent counting the same clusters across many photos, the clusters found in distinct images were removed using the CV model's outputs in the final phase.

While the Mask R-CNN outperformed YOLOv2 and YOLOv3 in terms of object detection, the YOLO model outperformed it in terms of detection time. Using YOLOv3, the poorest performance was attained. With an intersection over union (IoU) of 0.300, Mask R-CNN achieved an average accuracy of 0.805, a precision of 0.907, a recall of 0.873, and an F1-score of 0.890. YOLOv2 achieved an average accuracy of 0.675, a precision of 0.893, a recall of 0.728, and an F1-score of 0.802. In last place, YOLOv3 achieved an average accuracy of 0.566, a precision of 0.901, and a recall of 0.597, and an F1-score of 0.718.

Figure 15 shows an example of the detection of the five grape varieties with the three neural networks employed, viz., Mask R-CNN, YOLOv2, and YOLOv3, as well as the ground truth images. In the image it is possible to observe several object identification results, where the color does not indicate correlation. In this example, it is possible to observe the difference between the models and better understand visually the results from performance metrics.

Figure 15. Example of object detection results produced by the three neural networks, namely, Mask R-CNN, YOLOv2, and YOLOv3, compared to the ground truth images, for the five grape varieties in the study. The same color does not mean correspondence [51].

In Assunção et al. [52], for a real-time peach fruit identification application, a tensor processing unit (TPU) accelerator was created with a Raspberry Pi target device, to give a lightweight and hardware aware MobileDet detector model. Three fruit peach cultivars— Royal Time, Sweet Dream, and Catherine—were combined into one picture dataset. A RGB camera was used to capture the pictures. The following components make up the hardware platform (edge device) utilized to execute inferences: a Raspberry Pi 4 microcontroller development kit; a Raspberry Pi Camera Module 2, a Coral TPU accelerator, a DC-to-DC converter, and three Li-ion batteries. As a detector, the single-shot detector (SSD) model was applied. The backbones underwent SSD modifications. In this paper, a MobileNet CNN was used as the basis for the SSD model in experiments to look at the trade-off between detection accuracy and inference time. MobileNetV1, MobileNetV2, MobileNet EdgeTPU, and MobileDet were the backbones that were utilized.

In comparison to the other models, SSD MobileDet excelled, achieving an average precision of 88.2% on the target TPU device, according to the data. The model with the least performance degradation (drop) was SSD MobileNet Edge TPU, which had a decrease of 0.5%; the model with the most impact, SSD MobileNetV2, experienced a drop of 1.5%. SSD MobileNetV1 has the smallest latency at 47.6 ms (average). The authors have contributed to the field by expanding the applications of accelerators (the TPU) for edge devices in precision agriculture. Figure 16 shows an example of detection samples of the three cultivars, with Catherine at the left, Sweet Dream in the middle, and Royal Time at the right.

Table 6 summarizes the features of research work in the field of fruit detection.

Table 6. Feature descriptions of publications in the field of "Fruit Detection".

References	Application	Data Used	Model Used	Metric Used	Model Performance
Mao et al. [49]	Identify tomatoes and strawberries.	Two datasets: StrawDI; Laboro Tomato, from [21].	PicoDet-S.	Accuracy	The proposed RTFD has enormous potential for intelligent picking machines, and it is anticipated that edge computing will successfully implement the idea of redesigning the model structure, loss function, and activation function, as well as training by quantization to expedite the detection of deep neural networks.
Pereira et al. [50]	Identify and classify grapes.	Two datasets: DRGV And DRGV_2018, from [23].	LSA; CED; GMP; LPE; ICF; and CNN: AlexNet.	Accuracy	With a testing accuracy of 77.30%, the experimental findings proved the suggested classifier's trustworthiness. The algorithm took roughly 6.1 ms to identify the grape variety in a picture.
Santos et al. [51]	Identify grapes and estimate grape wine yield.	RGB camera.	Mask R-CNN; YOLOv2; YOLOv3.	Precision Recall F1-score	The YOLO model beat the Mask R-CNN in terms of detection time, while the Mask R-CNN outperformed YOLOv2 and YOLOv3 in terms of object detection. Using YOLOv3, the poorest performance was attained.
Assunção et al. [52]	Identify peaches.	RGB camera.	MobileDet; MobileNet Edge TPU; MobileNetV2; MobileNetV1.	Precision	The model performed at 19.84 frames per second (FPS) with an average precision (AP) of 88.2% and a 640 × 480 picture size. According to the results, the TPU accelerator can be a great replacement for processing at the cutting edge in precision agriculture.

Figure 16. Detection sample for the Catherine peach cultivar (**left**), Sweet Dream peach cultivar (**middle**), and Royal Time peach cultivar (**right**), (adapted from [52]).

4. Discussion

According to the research analyzed here, the following conclusions of each study as well as specific challenges can be indicated.

In ref. [8], the authors employed three models, namely, SVM-HOG, Mask R-CNN, and YOLOv3. Images were captured by a multispectral camera and used the following performance metrics: F1-Score, accuracy, specificity, precision, and recall. The HOG-SVM approach was shown to work quite well, and given that it requires less processing power, it is an excellent choice for IoT systems.

In ref. [14], the authors used three models, namely, RF, KNN, and SVM. Images were captured by a RGB camera and used the following performance metrics: accuracy, k, FPR, precision, and recall. The findings of this study indicate that RF outperformed the other classifiers. Furthermore, the efficiency of RF and SVM as classifiers for weed detection from UAV pictures is noteworthy.

Another model was employed in ref. [15], with JULE and DeepCluster. In this study, images were taken from two datasets, and the authors choose accuracy and normalized mutual information. The model achieved better performance with DeepCluster. Furthermore, the outcomes from these datasets point to a viable use of clustering and unsupervised learning for agricultural issues.

In ref. [16], an encoder-decoder CNN was employed, with pictures from two datasets, and working with accuracy and IoU to evaluate the model. The results demonstrate the effectiveness of NIR information for precise segmentation under low lighting conditions, while VIs without NIR information did not improve the segmentation results.

In ref. [22], the authors employed a deep CNN, with pictures from a RGB camera, and used the following performance metrics: precision and recall. The findings of this study demonstrate that a CNN, more especially ResNet18, may function as a reliable detector for potatoes infected with the blackleg disease in the field. However, with larger datasets and data augmentation, the performance can be increased.

In ref. [23], a CNN was used, with pictures from five datasets, and an F1-Score was applied as a performance metric. The findings of this study demonstrate that the CNN did not classify any disease incorrectly.

A MLP with an ANN model was developed in ref. [24], pictures were taken with a digital camera, and the model was evaluated in terms of accuracy. The implementation of a two-layer structure with eight neurons in the first layer and eight neurons in the second layer produced a maximum accuracy of 73.7%.

In ref. [25], a CNN was employed, with accuracy as a performance metric. Images were captured by a RGB sensor. The findings of this study demonstrate that the model trained with RGB photos performed better than the model trained with infrared images. The limited size of the training sample is one of the research study's weaknesses.

A fuzzy real time classifier was created in ref. [26], and two digital cameras were utilized, while accuracy was used for classifying the model. The prototype distinguished weed species with greater precision and a shorter processing time. However, the field obstructions provoked the robot to diverge from the planned path while it was moving.

A Mask R-CNN was applied in ref. [27], with RGB and NIR images; the model was evaluated through accuracy, IoU, precision, and recall. The model achieved better performance by adding an extra channel at the input of the model.

In ref. [28], an encoder- decoder CNN was evaluated, and the authors used RGB and NIR images, with the F1-Score as a classification metric. The suggested model was able to robustly identify crops in all growth phases and outperformed encoder-decoder FCN.

An FCN with RGB images was developed in ref. [29]. Once again, accuracy was used as a metric. The suggested technique successfully classified the pixels in images of weeds.

Four different models of the CNN were utilized in ref. [30], a digital camera was used, and this model was evaluated by IoU. The results showed that in terms of efficiency, PSPNet fared better than SegNet and UNet.

In ref. [31], two models were studied, FPN, and Faster R-CNN, where images were from a dataset, and accuracy, recall, F1-Score, and IoU were used as metrics. The experimental results show that the Faster R-CNN-FPN deep network model obtains greater recognition accuracy by employing the ResNeXt feature extraction network and combining the FPN network.

In ref. [32], five datasets were used in the following models: TMG, DeepLabv3, and MobileNetv2. The results show that the trade-off between segmentation accuracy and inference time can be managed via the hyperparameters OS and DM. DeepLabV3 has shown itself to be an incredibly flexible model for segmentation tasks.

In ref. [33], an OBIA model was used, with images from a visible-light and multi-spectral camera. Accuracy was used to evaluate the system. The findings of this study demonstrate that the multispectral camera was more accurate at higher flight altitudes, whereas the visible light one was better at lower altitudes. However, the spectrum mixing of flowers and bare soil components caused some mistakes at higher elevations.

In ref. [34], the authors employed an FCN, with pictures from a digital camera, and used the performance metrics of accuracy and IoU. The findings of this study demonstrate that the FCN technology performed well in terms of accuracy and efficiency for weed identification. On the other hand, it necessitates a great deal of manual labelling effort because it needs a large number of labelled pictures for training and updating.

In ref. [35], a CNN was developed, images were taken from a digital camera, and the authors used accuracy as a metric. In terms of adaptability and flexibility, this method is attractive since a model may be simply trained on a dataset. On the other hand, it necessitates a great deal of manual labelling.

In ref. [38], the authors used six datasets in a CNN, the model was evaluated using accuracy. The model achieved an accuracy of 86.2%. However, classes with fewer picture samples made a smaller total loss.

Different models of CNN were employed in ref. [39]. Images were taken by RGB and NIR cameras, and, once again, accuracy was used as the key metric. Based on its accuracy and processing speed, the network cNET provided the greatest training outcomes.

An RF model was developed in ref. [40]; the authors used hyperspectral images, and evaluated the model using precision, recall, and F1-Score. The results showed that the RF model performed well, and the vegetation indices are also useful techniques for developing important aspects of the categorization of weeds and crops.

In ref. [41], a SVM and an ANN were created with RGB images, using accuracy as a performance metric. The results showed that both models properly identified weeds and sugar plants.

In ref. [42], a CNN was designed, multispectral images were used, and the model was evaluated using accuracy, and F1-Score. The results showed that most of the weeds were classified well. However, spatiotemporal inconsistencies were found in the model due to limitations in the training dataset.

Four models of CNN were employed in ref. [43], and six datasets were used, as well as accuracy as a performance metric. The results showed that the proposed R-3-D-CNN model frequently outperforms existing models for most of the data sets and can also converge more quickly. However, these models require more training samples.

In ref. [44], a model with Keras API, and Tensorflow was implemented, and a digital camera was used to take the pictures. Accuracy was the evaluation metric. The crops and weeds were correctly detected, achieving the greatest accuracy.

In ref. [45], genetic algorithms were implemented with CenterNet. A digital camera was used as well as, and precision, recall, and F1-Score were applied to evaluate the model. The suggested method is suitable for ground-based weed identification in vegetable agricultural land under various conditions, illumination, complex backgrounds, as well as various growth stages.

In ref. [46], three models were developed, NN, SVM, and KNN, and these versions were evaluated with the genetic algorithms, GWO, and SCA. The research showed that the proposed technique performs better than other methods and increases classification accuracy.

A CNN model was implemented with CGG16, and ResNet50 in ref. [47]. Four digital cameras were used to take the images, and the model was evaluated by F1-score. The results showed that the model that was trained using combined datasets from two background scenarios performed best. Furthermore, the models which were built using non-uniform backdrop pictures behaved well on the uniform background. Those trained on a uniform background functioned poorly

In ref. [48], the researchers created a model with SVM, and VGG16, where RGB images were applied. The results showed that the VGG16 model classifiers outperformed all SVM model classifiers.

A Mask R-CNN, with a YOLOv2, and YOLOv3 were employed in ref. [51]. In this model, RGB images were used, and authors utilized precision, recall, and F1-Score to evaluate the model. The results showed that the YOLO model beat the Mask R-CNN in terms of detection time, while the Mask R-CNN outperformed YOLOv2 and YOLOv3 in terms of object detection.

A picoDet-S CNN model was engaged in ref. [49]. Two datasets were used, and accuracy was the performance metric. The proposed RTFD has enormous potential for intelligent picking machines, and it is anticipated that edge computing will successfully implement the idea of redesigning the model structure, loss function, and activation function, as well as training by quantization to expedite the detection of deep neural networks.

In ref. [50], a CNN model with optimizing algorithms was developed. Two datasets were used, as the accuracy as a performance metric. The results demonstrate that the model classifiers are trustworthy with an accuracy of 77.30%.

In ref. [52], a MobileNet with TPU model was employed, the research used RGB images, and the model was evaluated using precision as a performance metric. According to the results, the TPU accelerator can be a great replacement for processing at the cutting edge in precision agriculture.

The papers under examination highlight the following difficulties. The most critical point involves the datasets. Even with transfer learning and data augmentation, training the model may still need a substantial quantity of data, and an insufficient dataset for training the model might result in substantial failures [22,25,43]. Datasets with more samples will be able to perform better. Furthermore, the quality of the datasets is also a problem; images with bad quality will perform worst [42]. As a result, the first and most crucial phase is gathering real field data and photos under various circumstances.

Agricultural image datasets are also more complex due to outdoor conditions, the fact that the object of interest typically occupies a very small and off-center portion of the image, the similarity between objects and background, the obstruction of the object by leaves and branches, the presence of multiple objects in one image, and a variety of other factors. The dataset must, however, accurately reflect the condition of the environment for it to be useful in the actual world [49,51,52]. Furthermore, datasets with LED pictures will have a low accuracy [38]. Data augmentation may also be useful in some circumstances, such as fluctuating illuminance.

Another important challenge is the large amount of data that needs to be labelled. This task is expensive and time-consuming. Moreover, some tasks can only be carried out by experts in the industry, such as tasks involving plant diseases. Supervised learning needs a huge number of labelled images, for training and updating the models [34,35].

Data augmentation and transfer learning, as observed in multiple works, are approaches to avoid labelling a huge dataset, although labelling a small dataset still takes time. Unsupervised and semi-supervised learning techniques can be very beneficial but still require further research [12].

The performance of the model is impacted by the type of input [23,24,27,28,33]. The model's performance is affected by background removal from images [46], using various color spaces and vegetation indices as input [27], and crop detection at various growth stages [45]. The altitude when images are taken is also important for the input [33]. Finding the ideal input set for a given activity is therefore difficult.

In addition, field obstructions are a problem for the use of field robots. When robots find some obstacle in their path, they diverge from the planned path [26]. To solve this problem, instead of robots, drones can be applied. Another solution is that farmers can have the field clean and plain.

Accuracy and inference time must be traded off when selecting a model for a task. The model can be selected based on the application. In the field of agriculture, no setting is exactly comparable to another, and each environment and problem has its unique dataset; therefore, the DL model could not be relevant in all situations. The model performance could suffer because of the variations in the visual quality of the photos in the training and test datasets [38]. Retraining the already learned model using a tiny dataset from the new environment is one technique to get around the problem [11].

Moreover, the performance of these models depends on the choice of hyperparameters, loss functions, and optimization algorithms. Algorithms such as Bayesian optimization can help to find the right hyperparameters [11,23].

The models' capacity to be applied in real-time presents another difficulty. Most deep learning models need to be trained on many parameters, and once trained, the model's inference is not made in real time. Time inference is crucial in some applications, such as employing a robot for harvesting. However, there are still several issues with implementation on devices such as smartphones that must be considered, including memory usage and performance. Deep Learning models may now be used in practical and real-world applications because of the emergence of edge devices such as the Raspberry Pi and Jetson Nano, lightweight categorization models such as MobileNet, and cloud computing. The model size may be compressed, and the detection speed increased using the quantization approach [11,23].

5. Conclusions

The manuscript discusses the use of deep learning in agriculture and biodiversity and identifies certain difficulties in the field. It is suggested that reduced herbicide administration, minimal pesticide use, organic farming, suitable crop rotations, small-scale fields, and preservation of natural gaps between agroecosystems may contribute to more sustainable agriculture and the development of biodiversity in agricultural systems.

Additionally, the latest IoT technologies in conjunction with the most recent biodiversity algorithms and Artificial Intelligence models can be used to detect, classify, and eradicate specific weed species, as well as locate and identify fruits and vegetables, detect diseases, and boost ecosystem productivity without resorting to activities that harm the environment. Deep learning is already employed in several aspects of agriculture, but its application is still far from widespread. The most popular deep learning model in agriculture is the CNN. The adoption of novel techniques, such as attention mechanisms, new lightweight models, and single-stage detection models, can enhance the model's performance. Performance metrics include accuracy, precision, recall, and F1-Score, and usually, precision, recall, and F1-Score are used together. The type of data that researchers employed the most is pre-existing datasets and from cameras.

In the future, crop management decision-support models for farmers may be created or enhanced to recommend the best course of action. Digital tools could be added that can instantly categorize weeds. The implementation of new sustainable practices backed by deep learning models and biodiversity monitoring will aid in managing the farm more efficiently and with less human labor.

Author Contributions: Conceptualization, P.D.G. and K.A.; methodology, A.C., E.A. and K.A.; validation, E.A., K.A. and N.P.; formal analysis, A.C., P.D.G., E.A., K.A. and N.P.; investigation, A.C. and K.A.; resources, A.C., E.A. and K.A.; data curation, E.A., K.A. and N.P.; writing—original draft preparation, A.C., E.A., K.A. and N.P.; writing—review and editing, P.D.G.; supervision, P.D.G.; project administration, P.D.G.; funding acquisition, P.D.G. All authors have read and agreed to the published version of the manuscript.

Funding: The work is supported by the R&D Project BioDAgro—Sistema operacional inteligente de informação e suporte á decisão em AgroBiodiversidade, project PD20-00011, promoted by Fundação La Caixa and Fundação para a Ciência e a Tecnologia, taking place at the C-MAST—Centre for Mechanical and Aerospace Sciences and Technology, Department of Electromechanical Engineering of the University of Beira Interior, Covilhã, Portugal.

Data Availability Statement: Not applicable.

Acknowledgments: P.D.G. acknowledges Fundação para a Ciência e a Tecnologia (FCT—MCTES) for its financial support via the project UIDB/00151/2020 (C-MAST).

Conflicts of Interest: The authors declare no conflict of interest.

References

1. Tripathi, A.D.; Mishra, R.; Maurya, K.K.; Singh, R.B.; Wilson, D.W. Estimates for World Population and Global Food Availability for Global Health. In *The Role of Functional Food Security in Global Health*; Elsevier: Amsterdam, The Netherlands, 2019; pp. 3–24. [CrossRef]
2. United Nations. Population. Available online: https://www.un.org/en/global-issues/population (accessed on 8 November 2022).
3. European Commission. *A Farm to Fork Strategy for a Fair, Healthy and Environmentally Friendly Food System. Communication from the Commission to the European Parliament, the Council, the European Economic and Social Committee and the Committee of the Regions. COM/2020/381 Final. Document 52020DC0381*; European Commission: Bruxels, Belgium, 2020.
4. Wang, A.; Zhang, W.; Wei, X. A review on weed detection using ground-based machine vision and image processing techniques. *Comput. Electron. Agric.* **2019**, *158*, 226–240. [CrossRef]
5. United Nations. Water. Available online: https://www.un.org/en/global-issues/water (accessed on 8 November 2022).
6. Wato, M.A.T. The Agricultural Water Pollution and Its Minimization Strategies—A Review J. *Resour. Dev. Manag.* **2020**, *64*, 10–22. [CrossRef]
7. Hasan, A.S.M.M.; Sohel, F.; Diepeveen, D.; Laga, H.; Jones, M.G.K. A survey of deep learning techniques for weed detection from images Comput. *Electron. Agric.* **2021**, *184*, 106067. [CrossRef]
8. Osorio, K.; Puerto, A.; Pedraza, C.; Jamaica, D.; Rodríguez, L. A Deep Learning Approach for Weed Detection in Lettuce Crops Using Multispectral Images. *AgriEngineering* **2020**, *2*, 471–488. [CrossRef]
9. Sishodia, R.P.; Ray, R.L.; Singh, S.K. Applications of Remote Sensing in Precision Agriculture: A Review. *Remote Sens.* **2020**, *12*, 3136. [CrossRef]
10. Littman, L.M.; Ajunwa, I.; Berger, G.; Boutilier, C.; Currie, M.; Doshi-Velez, F.; Hadfield, G.; Horowitz, M.C.; Isbell, C.; Kitano, H.; et al. *Gathering Strength, Gathering Storms: The One Hundred Year Study on Artificial Intelligence (AI100) 2021 Study Panel Report*; Stanford University: Stanford, CA, USA, 2021; Available online: http://ai100.stanford.edu/2021-report (accessed on 6 November 2022).
11. Alibabaei, K.; Gaspar, P.D.; Lima, T.M.; Campos, R.M.; Girão, I.; Monteiro,, J.; Lopes, C.M. A review of the challenges of using deep learning algorithms to support decision-making in agricultural activities. *Remote Sens.* **2022**, *14*, 638.
12. Espejo-Garcia, B.; Mylonas, N.; Athanasakos, L.; Fountas, S. Improving weeds identification with a repository of agricultural pre-trained deep neural networks. *Comput. Electron. Agric.* **2020**, *175*, 105593. [CrossRef]
13. Tsouros, D.C.; Bibi, S.; Sarigiannidis, P.G. A review on UAV-based applications for precision agriculture. *Information* **2019**, *10*, 349. [CrossRef]
14. Islam, N.; Rashid, M.M.; Wibowo, S.; Xu, C.Y.; Morshed, A.; Wasimi, S.A.; Moore, S.; Rahman, S.M. Early Weed Detection Using Image Processing and Machine Learning Techniques in an Australian Chilli Farm. *Agriculture* **2021**, *11*, 387. [CrossRef]

15. Ferreira, A.D.S.; Freitas, D.M.; da Silva, G.G.; Pistori, H.; Folhes, M.T. Unsupervised deep learning and semi-automatic data labeling in weed discrimination. *Comput. Electron. Agric.* **2019**, *165*, 104963. [CrossRef]
16. Wang, A.; Xu, Y.; Wei, X.; Cui, B. Semantic Segmentation of Crop and Weed using an Encoder-Decoder Network and Image Enhancement Method under Uncontrolled Outdoor Illumination. *IEEE Access* **2020**, *8*, 81724–81734. [CrossRef]
17. Kamilaris, A.; Prenafeta-Boldú, F.X. Deep learning in agriculture: A survey. *Comput. Electron. Agric.* **2018**, *147*, 70–90. [CrossRef]
18. Sunasra, M. Performance Metrics for Classification Problems in Machine Learning. *Medium*. 11 November 2017. Available online: https://medium.com/@MohammedS/performance-metrics-for-classification-problems-in-machine-learning-part-i-b085d432082b (accessed on 6 December 2022).
19. Javatpoint. Performance Metrics in Machine Learning. Available online: https://www.javatpoint.com/performance-metrics-in-machine-learning (accessed on 6 December 2022).
20. Swift, A.; Heale, R.; Twycross, A. What are sensitivity and specificity? *Evid. Based Nurs.* **2020**, *23*, 2–4. [CrossRef] [PubMed]
21. Rushikanjaria. Classification Model Performance Evaluation Using AUC-ROC and CAP Curves. *Geek Culture*. 5 July 2021. Available online: https://medium.com/geekculture/classification-model-performance-evaluation-using-auc-roc-and-cap-curves-66a1b3fc0480 (accessed on 7 December 2022).
22. Afonso, M.; Blok, P.M.; Polder, G.; van der Wolf, J.M.; Kamp, J. Blackleg detection in potato plants using convolutional neural networks. *IFAC-Pap.* **2019**, *52*, 6–11. [CrossRef]
23. Assuncao, E.; Diniz, C.; Gaspar, P.D.; Proenca, H. Decision-making support system for fruit diseases classification using Deep Learning. In Proceedings of the 2020 International Conference on Decision Aid Sciences and Application (DASA), Sakheer, Bahrain, 8–9 November 2020; pp. 652–656. [CrossRef]
24. Azgomi, H.; Haredasht, F.R.; Motlagh, M.R.S. Diagnosis of some apple fruit diseases by using image processing and artificial neural network. *Food Control* **2023**, *145*, 109484. [CrossRef]
25. Kerkech, M.; Hafiane, A.; Canals, R. Vine disease detection in UAV multispectral images using optimized image registration and deep learning segmentation approach. *Comput. Electron. Agric.* **2020**, *174*, 105446. [CrossRef]
26. Sujaritha, M.; Annadurai, S.; Satheeshkumar, J.; Sharan, S.K.; Mahesh, L. Weed detecting robot in sugarcane fields using fuzzy real time classifier. *Comput. Electron. Agric.* **2017**, *134*, 160–171. [CrossRef]
27. Milioto, A.; Lottes, P.; Stachniss, C. Real-time Semantic Segmentation of Crop and Weed for Precision Agriculture Robots Leveraging Background Knowledge in CNNs. *arXiv* **2018**, arXiv:1709.06764.
28. Lottes, P.; Behley, J.; Milioto, A.; Stachniss, C. Fully Convolutional Networks with Sequential Information for Robust Crop and Weed Detection in Precision Farming. *IEEE Robot. Autom. Lett.* **2018**, *3*, 2870–2877. [CrossRef]
29. Ma, X.; Deng, X.; Qi, L.; Jiang, Y.; Li, H.; Wang, Y.; Xing, X. Fully convolutional network for rice seedling and weed image segmentation at the seedling stage in paddy fields. *PLoS ONE* **2019**, *14*, e0215676. [CrossRef]
30. Kamath, R.; Balachandra, M.; Vardhan, A.; Maheshwari, U. Classification of paddy crop and weeds using semantic segmentation. *Cogent Eng.* **2022**, *9*, 2018791. [CrossRef]
31. Mu, Y.; Feng, R.; Ni, R.; Li, J.; Luo, T.; Liu, T.; Li, X.; Gong, H.; Guo, Y.; Sun, Y.; et al. A Faster R-CNN-Based Model for the Identification of Weed Seedling. *Agronomy* **2022**, *12*, 2867. [CrossRef]
32. Assunção, E.; Gaspar, P.D.; Mesquita, R.; Simões, M.P.; Alibabaei, K.; Veiros, A.; Proença, H. Real-Time Weed Control Application Using a Jetson Nano Edge Device and a Spray Mechanism. *Remote Sens.* **2022**, *14*, 4217. [CrossRef]
33. Peña, J.; Torres-Sánchez, J.; Serrano-Pérez, A.; de Castro, A.; López-Granados, F. Quantifying Efficacy and Limits of Unmanned Aerial Vehicle (UAV) Technology for Weed Seedling Detection as Affected by Sensor Resolution. *Sensors* **2015**, *15*, 5609–5626. [CrossRef]
34. Huang, H.; Deng, J.; Lan, Y.; Yang, A.; Deng, X.; Zhang, L. A fully convolutional network for weed mapping of unmanned aerial vehicle (UAV) imagery. *PLoS ONE* **2018**, *13*, e0196302. [CrossRef]
35. Bah, M.; Hafiane, A.; Canals, R. Deep Learning with Unsupervised Data Labeling for Weed Detection in Line Crops in UAV Images. *Remote Sens.* **2018**, *10*, 1690. [CrossRef]
36. Jiang, P.; Ergu, D.; Liu, F.; Cai, Y.; Ma, B. A Review of Yolo Algorithm Developments. *Procedia Comput. Sci.* **2022**, *199*, 1066–1073. [CrossRef]
37. BioD'Agro. E 3.3 Arquitetura, Desenvolvimento e Testagem do Algoritmo de Análise de Dados. *BioD'Agro Project Report*. March 2023. Available online: https://biodagro.wearespaceway.com/biblioteca-e-eventos/entreg%C3%A1veis (accessed on 13 April 2023). (In Portuguese)
38. Dyrmann, M.; Karstoft, H.; Midtiby, H.S. Plant species classification using deep convolutional neural network. *Biosyst. Eng.* **2016**, *151*, 72–80. [CrossRef]
39. Andrea, C.-C.; Daniel, B.B.M.; Misael, J.B.J. Precise weed and maize classification through convolutional neuronal networks. In Proceedings of the 2017 IEEE Second Ecuador Technical Chapters Meeting (ETCM), Salinas, Ecuador, 16–20 October 2017; pp. 1–6. [CrossRef]
40. Gao, J.; Nuyttens, D.; Lootens, P.; He, Y.; Pieters, J.G. Recognising weeds in a maize crop using a random forest machine-learning algorithm and near-infrared snapshot mosaic hyperspectral imagery. *Biosyst. Eng.* **2018**, *170*, 39–50. [CrossRef]
41. Bakhshipour, A.; Jafari, A. Evaluation of support vector machine and artificial neural networks in weed detection using shape features. *Comput. Electron. Agric.* **2018**, *145*, 153–160. [CrossRef]
42. Sa, I.; Chen, Z.; Popović, M.; Khanna, R.; Liebisch, F.; Nieto, J.; Siegwart, R. weedNet: Dense Semantic Weed Classification Using Multispectral Images and MAV for Smart Farming. *IEEE Robot. Autom. Lett.* **2018**, *3*, 588–595. [CrossRef]

43. Yang, X.; Ye, Y.; Li, X.; Lau, R.Y.K.; Zhang, X.; Huang, X. Hyperspectral image classification with deep learning models. *IEEE Trans. Geosci. Remote Sens.* **2018**, *56*, 5408–5423. [CrossRef]
44. Yashwanth, M.; Chandra, M.L.; Pallavi, K.; Showkat, D.; Kumar, P.S. Agriculture Automation using Deep Learning Methods Implemented using Keras. In Proceedings of the 2020 IEEE International Conference for Innovation in Technology (INOCON), Bangluru, India, 6–8 November 2020; pp. 1–6. [CrossRef]
45. Jin, X.; Che, J.; Chen, Y. Weed Identification Using Deep Learning and Image Processing in Vegetable Plantation. *IEEE Access* **2021**, *9*, 10940–10950. [CrossRef]
46. El-Kenawy, E.S.M.; Khodadadi, N.; Mirjalili, S.; Makarovskikh, T.; Abotaleb, M.; Karim, F.K.; Alkahtani, H.K.; Abdelhamid, A.A.; Eid, M.M.; Horiuchi, T.; et al. Metaheuristic Optimization for Improving Weed Detection in Wheat Images Captured by Drones. *Mathematics* **2022**, *10*, 4421. [CrossRef]
47. Sunil, G.C.; Koparan, C.; Ahmed, M.R.; Zhang, Y.; Howatt, K.; Sun, X. A study on deep learning algorithm performance on weed and crop species identification under different image background. *Artif. Intell. Agric.* **2022**, *6*, 242–256. [CrossRef]
48. Sunil, G.C.; Zhang, Y.; Koparan, C.; Ahmed, M.R.; Howatt, K.; Sun, X. Weed and crop species classification using computer vision and deep learning technologies in greenhouse conditions. *J. Agric. Food Res.* **2022**, *9*, 100325. [CrossRef]
49. Mao, D.; Sun, H.; Li, X.; Yu, X.; Wu, J.; Zhang, Q. Real-time fruit detection using deep neural networks on CPU (RTFD): An edge AI application. *Comput. Electron. Agric.* **2022**, *204*, 107517. [CrossRef]
50. Pereira, C.S.; Morais, R.; Reis, M.J.C.S. Deep Learning Techniques for Grape Plant Species Identification in Natural Images. *Sensors* **2019**, *19*, 4850. [CrossRef] [PubMed]
51. Santos, T.T.; de Souza, L.L.; dos Santos, A.A.; Avila, S. Grape detection, segmentation, and tracking using deep neural networks and three-dimensional association. *Comput. Electron. Agric.* **2020**, *170*, 105247. [CrossRef]
52. Assunção, E.; Gaspar, P.D.; Alibabaei, K.; Simões, M.P.; Proença, H.; Soares, V.N.; Caldeira, J.M. Real-Time Image Detection for Edge Devices: A Peach Fruit Detection Application. *Future Internet* **2022**, *14*, 323. [CrossRef]

Disclaimer/Publisher's Note: The statements, opinions and data contained in all publications are solely those of the individual author(s) and contributor(s) and not of MDPI and/or the editor(s). MDPI and/or the editor(s) disclaim responsibility for any injury to people or property resulting from any ideas, methods, instructions or products referred to in the content.

Article

Fault Diagnosis Algorithm of Gearboxes Based on GWO-SCE Adaptive Multi-Threshold Segmentation and Subdomain Adaptation

Yangshuo Liu [1], Jianshe Kang [1], Liang Wen [1], Yunjie Bai [2], Chiming Guo [1] and Weibo Yu [1,*]

[1] Army Engineering University of PLA, Shijiazhuang 050003, China
[2] 66029 Unit of the Chinese People's Liberation Army, Xilinguole Meng 011200, China
* Correspondence: 13393231566@163.com

Abstract: The data distribution of the vibration signal under different speed conditions of the gearbox is different, which leads to reduced accuracy of fault diagnosis. In this regard, this paper proposes a deep transfer fault diagnosis algorithm combining adaptive multi-threshold segmentation and subdomain adaptation. First of all, in the data acquisition stage, a non-contact, easy-to-arrange, and low-cost sound pressure sensor is used to collect equipment signals, which effectively solves the problems of contact installation limitations and increasingly strict layout requirements faced by traditional vibration signal-based methods. The continuous wavelet transform (CWT) is then used to convert the original vibration signal of the device into time–frequency image samples. Further, to highlight the target fault characteristics of the samples, the gray wolf optimization algorithm (GWO) is combined with symmetric cross entropy (SCE) to perform adaptive multi-threshold segmentation on the image samples. A convolutional neural network (CNN) is then used to extract the common features of the source domain samples and the target domain samples. Additionally, the local maximum mean discrepancy (LMMD) is introduced into the parameter space of the deep fully connected layer of the network to align the sub-field edge distribution of deep features so as to reduce the distribution difference of sub-class fault features under different working conditions and improve the diagnostic accuracy of the model. Finally, to verify the effectiveness of the proposed diagnosis method, a fault preset experiment of the gearbox under variable speed conditions is carried out. The results show that compared to other diagnostic methods, the method in this paper has higher diagnostic accuracy and superiority.

Keywords: acoustic signal; fault diagnosis; adaptive multi-threshold segmentation; subdomain adaptation; variable speed condition; local maximum mean discrepancy

Citation: Liu, Y.; Kang, J.; Wen, L.; Bai, Y.; Guo, C.; Yu, W. Fault Diagnosis Algorithm of Gearboxes Based on GWO-SCE Adaptive Multi-Threshold Segmentation and Subdomain Adaptation. *Processes* **2023**, *11*, 556. https://doi.org/10.3390/pr11020556

Academic Editor: Xiong Luo

Received: 14 September 2022
Revised: 8 October 2022
Accepted: 21 October 2022
Published: 11 February 2023

Copyright: © 2023 by the authors. Licensee MDPI, Basel, Switzerland. This article is an open access article distributed under the terms and conditions of the Creative Commons Attribution (CC BY) license (https:// creativecommons.org/licenses/by/ 4.0/).

1. Introduction

Due to the rapid development of industrial intelligence, data monitoring and deep intelligence algorithms are widely used in equipment health monitoring, especially in fault diagnosis [1–3]. The process of fault diagnosis mainly includes data acquisition, data preprocessing, feature extraction, and classifier diagnosis. At present, in terms of data acquisition, most of the fault diagnosis models use the vibration signal of the equipment as the original training sample. Mariela Cerrada et al. [4] realized gearbox fault diagnosis by extracting the time and frequency features from the vibration signal of the spur gearbox and combining them with the genetic algorithm and the random forest classifier. Wen et al. [5] designed a novel convolutional network, which took the vibration datasets of motor bearings, self-priming centrifugal pumps, and axial piston hydraulic pumps as the original input and then used the deep learning ability of the network to achieve fault diagnosis of different equipment. Hou et al. [6] proposed a novel feature selection method that can eliminate redundant and invalid interference information in the vibration signal of the bearing and ensure the best feature subset with low computational complexity. Although the vibration signal can directly reflect vibration excitation during operation of the equipment, in the process of data acquisition there are disadvantages, such as high requirements for the placement of the vibration sensor, the ease with which it may fall off, and high installation cost. As a non-destructive testing technology, the acoustic signal method can collect data without affecting the installation of the sensor and has the advantages of low consumption cost and easy layout while acquiring equipment fault signals. Adam Glowacz [7] analyzed the fault acoustic signal of a single-phase asynchronous motor and developed and implemented a method of acoustic signal feature extraction, with the fault diagnosis of the motor bearing finally realized through the KNN classifier. Yao et al. [8] proposed a novel fault diagnosis algorithm for planetary gearboxes based on acoustic signals, and the proposed comprehensive characteristic parameters can significantly improve the accuracy of fault diagnosis compared to single characteristic parameters. Wail M. Adaileh [9] proposed an experimental study on the detection of engine faults using acoustic signals through analysis of the domain parameters, such as RMS amplitude, peak amplitude, and energy for condition monitoring, and fault diagnosis of internal combustion engines.

In terms of data preprocessing and feature extraction, because of the rapid development of deep networks in recent years, their powerful deep self-learning capabilities have been widely used. More and more studies use raw 1D fault signals or simple 2D time–frequency transformed images as training samples. Gao et al. [10] used the continuous wavelet transform (CWT) of complex Morlet wavelets to obtain the time–frequency characteristics of the vibration signal through joint time–frequency analysis and obtained the input of the deep network through normalization. Wang et al. [11] used short-time Fourier transform (STFT) to transform the raw vibration signal of the device to obtain the corresponding time–frequency map. The features of the time–frequency map are then adaptively extracted using a convolutional neural network (CNN). Gu et al. [12] proposed a hybrid fault diagnosis method for rolling bearings based on CWT and CNN, which is suitable for small sample diagnosis. Zhang et al. [13] used STFT transform theory to obtain input images, introduced a scaled exponential linear unit (SELU) function in the network to avoid excessive 'dead' nodes during training, and used hierarchical regularization to obtain better training results. Although the diagnosis method of time–frequency images combined with a deep network has obtained good diagnosis results, the single signal time–frequency conversion cannot effectively highlight the fault characteristics of the sample. In this regard, some scholars have introduced the theory of threshold segmentation in image preprocessing, trying to highlight the edge factors of different key components in image samples. Threshold segmentation is a method of processing an image into a high-contrast, easy-to-recognize image with a suitable pixel value as a boundary. Therefore, it can effectively distinguish the target interest boundary in time–frequency image samples. Rakoth Kandan Sambandam et al. [14] combined the dragonfly optimization algorithm and the threshold segmentation algorithm to obtain the global optimal solution of segmentation by effectively exploring the solution space. Shan et al. [15] segmented massive infrared images based on chroma-saturated luminance space to distinguish defective device images and extracted defective device regions from the images. Finally, the improved residual network is trained for fault feature learning through an online mining method. Manikanta Prahlad Manda et al. [16] effectively calculated the threshold for image segmentation based on the concept of one-dimensional histogram approximation, and finally verified the excellent performance of the method on various infrared images. The above research results show that the threshold segmentation algorithm can effectively improve the boundaries of different components in image samples, thereby improving the accuracy of classification.

In the classification stage of fault diagnosis, in recent years, fault diagnosis algorithms based on deep learning have shown they can adaptively learn and mine the deep-level features of data and achieve better diagnosis results than traditional feature engineering [17,18]. However, most of the deep learning diagnosis algorithms currently assume that the training data and the test data have the same probability distribution, which is often untenable in the actual industrial environment where the operating environment is changeable and the working conditions are complex. For example, changes in operating conditions, such as equipment speed, load, normal aging, and deepening damage to faulty parts, will lead to real-time changes in the distribution of data. At this point, when a new data stream is entered, the diagnostic accuracy of the model trained on the historical data will decrease. In recent years, the concept of transfer learning has been put forward to solve the above-mentioned limitations in the fault diagnosis of industrial equipment and has been widely used. The basic problem is how to solve new fields (target domain). Obviously, a certain similarity between the source domain and the target domain is a major premise of transfer learning. Therefore, the main work of transfer learning is to reduce the feature difference between the data in the source domain and the target domain and improve the transferability between the data so as to achieve the purpose of knowledge transfer and reduce the amount of data participation in the target domain [19–21]. In addition, transfer learning takes full advantage of deep learning in expressing high-dimensional abstract features of data. Deep learning methods represented by deep networks map two sets of data with similar but different distributions into a high-dimensional shared feature space and use transfer methods to minimize inter-domain differences when the edge distribution of the data becomes clearer [22]. Among them, domain adaptation, as one of the subdomains of transfer learning, mainly solves the problem of knowledge transfer between two domains with the same feature space and label space (isomorphic domain) through distance measurement. The metrics for distance measurement include maximum mean difference (MMD), KL divergence, and Wasserstein distance, among others. Yang et al. [23] used conditional domain adversarial (CDA) domain adaptive networks and joint maximum mean deviation standard (JMMD) to align the source and target domains, effectively realizing cross-domain diagnosis under different operating conditions. Xiao et al. [24] used convolutional neural networks to extract multi-level features of the device's original vibration signal. Further, the maximum mean difference (MMD) can be added during the training of the network to impose constraints on the parameters of the CNN, thereby reducing the distribution differences in the characteristics of the source and target domain data. Zhu et al. [25] used the Kuhn–Munkres algorithm to improve the calculation process of the Wasserstein distance, which can better learn transferable features between labeled and un-labeled signals from different forms of devices. Finally, the effectiveness of the proposed method is verified under different mechanical parts and transmission scenarios. The above research shows that transfer methods, such as domain adaptation based on the distance metric method, can effectively reduce the feature difference between the source domain and the target domain and realize the knowledge transfer between the same or similar types of devices, which solves the above-mentioned key constraint of constant data distribution in practical industrial environments. However, in practice, the data in different domains not only have significant differences in marginal distributions, but also in conditional distributions. By aligning the marginal distribution of data in different domains, the invariant eigenvectors of the domain can be learned. However, if the differences in conditional distribution between different domain data are not taken into account, the optimal cross-domain classification hyperplane will be difficult to obtain. In response, Wang et al. [26] built a subdomain adaptive transfer learning network by stacking two convolutional building blocks to extract transferable features from raw data. Pseudo-label learning is then modified and the target subdomain of each class is constructed, which reduces the marginal and conditional distribution deviations and improves the classification performance and generalization of the network. Tian et al. [27] used a multi-branch network structure to respectively match the feature space distribution of each source domain and target domain in order to align the subdomain distributions in the same category of different domains and diagnose the device status. Wang et al. [28] proposed a joint subdomain adaptive network (JSAN) that reduces the difference between two domains by jointly local maximum mean disparity, improving the diagnostic accuracy. The above study shows that the conditional distribution difference between subdomains is also an important factor to be considered in domain adaptive diagnosis.

Inspired by the above research, we propose a gearbox acoustic signal fault diagnosis algorithm based on adaptive multi-threshold segmentation and subdomain adaptation to solve the problem of cross-domain adaptive fault diagnosis under the condition of variable gearbox speed. The main innovations in this article are as follows:

(1) Signal monitoring using acoustic sensors makes it easier to collect fault signals from gearbox equipment without contact.

(2) The combination of a gray wolf optimization algorithm (GWO) and symmetric cross entropy (SCE) can realize the adaptive multi-threshold segmentation of CWT time–frequency map samples of the gearbox, thereby enhancing the boundary of target fault characteristics.

(3) We design a subdomain adaptive network model based on a CNN structure and add the local maximum mean discrepancy (LMMD) metric criterion to the fully connected layer parameter space in the deep network. At the same time, the differences in the data distribution of sub-categories within the domain are considered before the difference is eliminated.

Finally, we verify the effectiveness and superiority of the method with the dataset from the gearbox variable speed experiment. The rest of the paper is organized as follows: Section 2 introduces the relevant theories in detail. Section 3 discusses the proposed fault diagnosis model and diagnosis process. Section 4 provides the process of preparing gearbox fault data, and the results of the fault diagnosis experiment are analyzed and discussed. Finally, the conclusions of this paper are elaborated in Section 5.

2. Methodology

2.1. Transfer Learning

Transfer learning is a new type of deep learning whose goal is to extract similar components (transfer components) between different but related domains so as to transfer knowledge from one domain to another. Among them, the original data domain and the target interest domain are called the source domain and the target domain, respectively [29,30]. To facilitate the description, the concepts of domain and task are first introduced. A domain Ω consists of two parts, a d-dimensional feature space χ and a marginal probability distribution $P(X)$, where X is a set of n samples, and each sample corresponds to a feature vector in the space χ, that is $X = \{x_1, x_2, \cdots, x_n\} \subset \chi$. Therefore, a domain can be represented by $\Omega = \{\chi, P(X)\}$. Further introduce the concept of tasks, a task Υ consists of a label space φ and a class prediction function $f(\cdot)$. When given a feature vector, the class prediction function $f(\cdot)$ can predict its corresponding class label $f(x)$. From the probabilistic point of view, the label category can be denoted as $P(y|x)$, so the task can be denoted as $\Upsilon = \{\varphi, P(Y|X)\}$. After the source domain Ω_S and learning task Υ_S, target domain Ω_T and learning task Υ_T are determined separately, $\Omega_S \neq \Omega_T$ or $\Upsilon_S \neq \Upsilon_T$, that is, the distribution of the source domain and the target domain is different, transfer learning will use the tasks and knowledge of the source domain to help improve the computational performance of the target prediction function $f(\cdot)$ for the target domain data (see Figure 1) [31,32].

2.2. Subdomain Adaptation

Usually, in the transfer learning fault diagnosis of mechanical equipment, the data of the source domain and the target domain can be the data of the same equipment under different working conditions, or the data of the same model of different equipment. The tasks to be solved in both domains are the same, that is, both domains have the same fault category and classification tasks. Such transfer tasks are called domain adaptation and they are an important branch of transfer learning (see Figure 2) [33]. This paper intends to implement migration diagnosis under different rotational speed conditions on the same rotating mechanical equipment, that is, the feature space dimension and fault label space of the source domain and target domain data are the same. Most of the current diagnosis algorithms only consider the alignment of the global marginal distribution between the source domain and the target domain. However, the lack of distinguishing the conditional distributions between the same subclass of faults will lead to a decrease in the accuracy of transfer fault diagnosis (as shown in Figure 3a). On this basis, the concept of subdomain adaptation is further proposed, that is, when the global distribution of the source domain data and the target domain data is roughly the same, the conditional distribution between the subdomain fault data is further aligned [34]. This will reduce the distribution difference of sub-type fault data under different working conditions of the equipment, thereby improving the accuracy of fault diagnosis (as shown in Figure 3b).

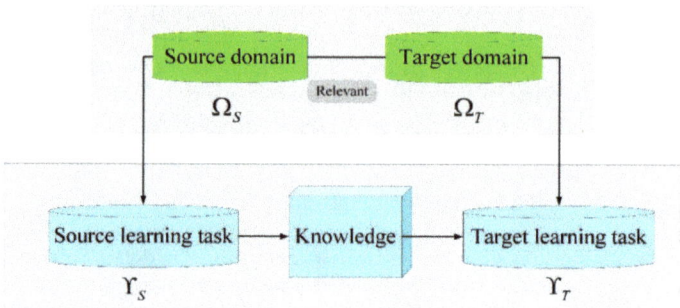

Figure 1. Schematic diagram of transfer learning.

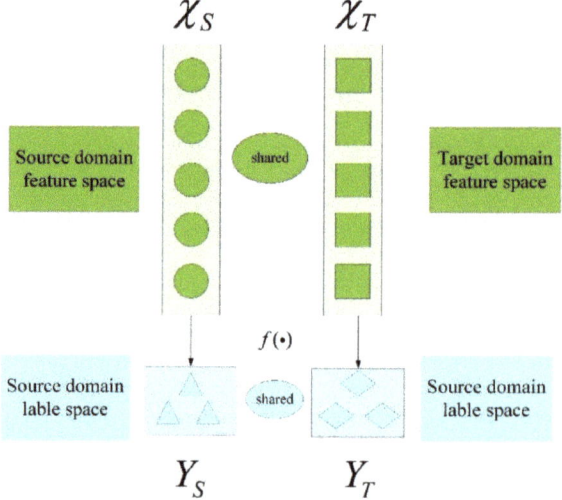

Figure 2. Domain Adaptive Schematic.

2.3. Continuous Wavelet Transform (CWT)

CWT has good localized analysis ability and multi-resolution analysis ability for equipment fault signals and has the characteristic of window adaptation compared to time–frequency conversion methods such as STFT. It uses a limited length wavelet base with an attenuation effect and locates the time node at which the signal frequency component appears via telescopic transformation and translation of the wavelet. For a series of time series, the wavelet function can move in the time dimension and compare the window signals at different positions one by one to obtain the wavelet coefficients. The larger the wavelet coefficients, the better the fitting degree of the wavelet and the signal. In the calculation, the convolution of the wavelet function and the window signal are used as the wavelet coefficient under the window. Therefore, the length of the window and the length of the wavelet are the same. In the frequency domain, the length and frequency of the wavelet are changed by stretching or compressing the length of the wavelet to realize the wavelet coefficients at different frequencies. Correspondingly, the window length also varies with the wavelet length. Combining the wavelet coefficients at different frequencies, the wavelet coefficient map of the time–frequency transform is obtained. The specific calculation process is as follows [35].

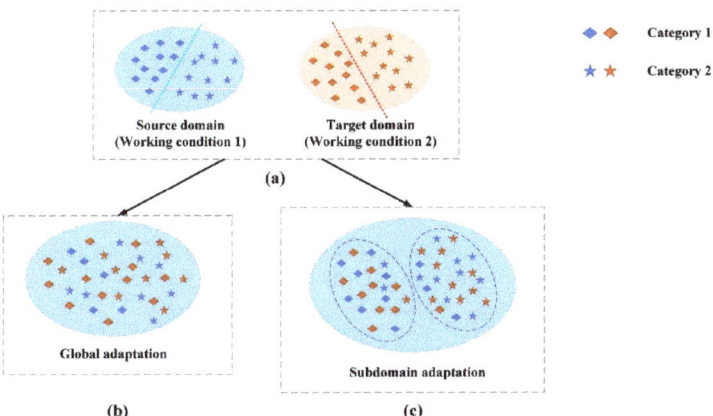

Figure 3. Subdomain adaptation schematic: (**a**) source and target domain conditions; (**b**) global adaptation; (**c**) subdomain adaptation.

Assuming that both the input signal $x(t)$ and the wavelet basis function $\psi(t)$ satisfy $x(t) \in L^2(R)$, $\psi(t) \in L^2(R)$, and $L^2(R)$ represents a square-integrable real number space, the continuous wavelet transform of the input signal $x(t)$ can be expressed as [36]:

$$\mathrm{WT}_x(a,\tau) = \frac{1}{\sqrt{a}} \int x(t) \cdot \overline{\psi(\frac{t-\tau}{a})} dt = \langle x(t), \psi_{a\tau}(t) \rangle \tag{1}$$

$$\psi_{a\tau}(t) = \frac{1}{\sqrt{a}} \psi(\frac{t-\tau}{a}) \tag{2}$$

In the formula, a and τ respectively represent the scale parameter and displacement parameter in the wavelet transformation. Further, the displacement and scale expansion of the wavelet base in the transformation process are represented by $\psi_{a\tau}(t)$. $\overline{\psi(t)}$ represents the complex conjugate value of $\psi(t)$, and the symbol $\langle x, y \rangle$ represents the inner product operation. The frequency domain form of wavelet transform can be expressed as,

$$\mathrm{WT}_x(a,\tau) = \frac{\sqrt{a}}{2\pi} \int x^*(v) \cdot \overline{\psi^*(a,v)} \cdot e^{jvt} dv \tag{3}$$

In the formula, $x^*(v)$ represents the Fourier transform of the signal $x(t)$; $\overline{\psi^*(a,v)}$ represents the complex conjugate value of the Fourier transform of the wavelet basis function $\psi(t)$.

2.4. Adaptive Multi-Threshold Segmentation

2.4.1. Symmetric Cross Entropy (SCE)

Cross-entropy is used in Shannon information theory to measure the difference between two probability distributions. Suppose $\mu(x)$ and $\sigma(x)$ are two distributions distributed on the probability space Ω, then the cross-entropy of $\mu(x)$ to $\sigma(x)$ is defined as [37]:

$$M(x) = \sum_{x \in \Omega} \mu(x) \log \frac{\mu(x)}{\sigma(x)} \tag{4}$$

where μ refers to the correct distribution and σ refers to the approximate estimated distribution. Cross entropy is used to estimate the distance difference between distributions.

However, considering that it does not have distance symmetry, Brink et al. [38] developed the concept of symmetric cross entropy (SCE). SCE essentially adds the forward Kullback divergence and the backward Kullback divergence, which makes the cross entropy symmetrical and thus allows it to become a real distance measure. The expression of symmetric cross entropy is:

$$D(x) = \sum_{i=0}^{x} h_i (i \ln \frac{i}{\mu(x)} + \mu(x) \ln \frac{\mu(x)}{i}) + \sum_{i=t+1}^{L-1} h_i (i \ln \frac{i}{\sigma(x)} + \sigma(x) \ln \frac{\sigma(x)}{i}) \quad (5)$$

On this basis, image adaptive multi-threshold segmentation is carried out with SCE as the standard. Even if Formula (5) takes the minimum value of x to be the optimal threshold,

$$x^* = \operatorname{argmin}(0 \leq x \leq L-1)\{D(x)\} \quad (6)$$

Generalizing at most thresholds is performed to find a set of thresholds $(x_0, \cdots, x_n)$ that minimize the entropy value.

$$x(1, \cdots, n)^* = \operatorname{argmin}\{D_0 + D_1 + \cdots + D_n\} \quad (7)$$

2.4.2. Gray Wolf Optimization Algorithm (GWO)

The gray wolf optimization algorithm (GWO) is a swarm intelligence optimization algorithm that was proposed by Mirjalili et al. from Griffith University in Australia in 2014 [39]. The algorithm is inspired by the hunting activities of gray wolves and has the characteristics of few parameters, strong convergence performance, and easy implementation. In recent years, the GWO algorithm has been widely and successfully applied in parameter optimization, image classification, and other fields. The algorithm divides the wolves into four levels (α, β, δ, and ω) according to the hierarchy of the wolf society, as shown in Figure 4.

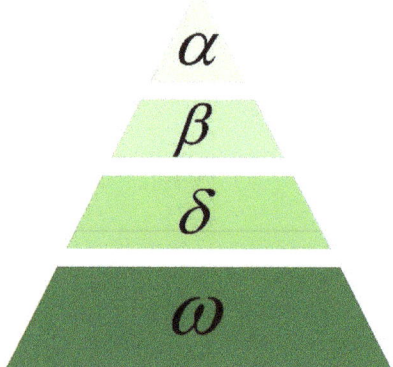

Figure 4. Subdomain adaptation schematic.

The three gray wolves closest to the prey are named α, β and δ in order from near to far, corresponding to the optimal solution, the second optimal solution and the third optimal solution of the fitness function respectively; the remaining gray wolves are named uniformly as ω, corresponding to other candidate solutions. α, β and δ guide ω to search for prey, ω update location around α, β and δ. The entire hunting optimization process is shown in Figure 5, which mainly includes:

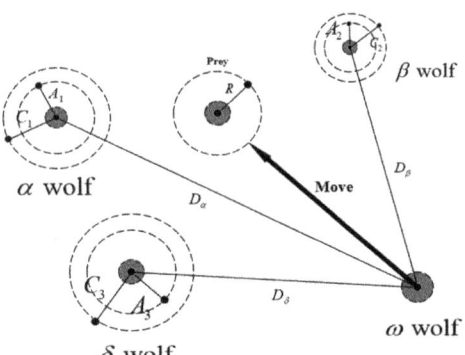

Figure 5. The hunting optimization process diagram of gray wolves.

(1) Surrounding the prey. The behavior of surrounding the prey can be represented by the following computational procedure [40]:

$$\begin{cases} \vec{D} = \left| \vec{C} \cdot \vec{X_p}(t) - \vec{X}(t) \right| \\ \vec{X}(t+1) = \vec{X_p}(t) - \vec{A} \cdot \vec{D} \end{cases} \quad (8)$$

In the formula, $\vec{D}$ represents the distance between the prey and the gray wolf, $\vec{A}$ and $\vec{C}$ are the coefficient vectors, $\vec{X_p}$ and $\vec{X}$ represent the position vector of the prey and the gray wolf, respectively, and t is the current number of iterations.

(2) Attacking and searching for prey. Since the locations of the wolves in relation to the prey is unknown, the location update of ω during the hunting process is guided by α, β and δ. The behavior of attacking prey can be described as:

$$\begin{cases} \vec{D_\alpha} = \left| \vec{C_1} \cdot \vec{X_\alpha} - \vec{X} \right| \\ \vec{D_\beta} = \left| \vec{C_2} \cdot \vec{X_\beta} - \vec{X} \right| \\ \vec{D_\delta} = \left| \vec{C_3} \cdot \vec{X_\delta} - \vec{X} \right| \end{cases} \quad (9)$$

In the formula, $\vec{D_\alpha}$, $\vec{D_\beta}$, $\vec{D_\delta}$ represent the distances from ω to α, β and δ respectively, $\vec{C}$ is a random number with a value of [0, 1], $\vec{D_\alpha}$, $\vec{D_\beta}$, $\vec{D_\alpha}$ and $\vec{D_\delta}$ represent the current location of α, β, δ and ω:

$$\begin{cases} \vec{X_1} = \vec{X_\alpha}(t) - \vec{A_1} \cdot (\vec{D_\alpha}) \\ \vec{X_2} = \vec{X_\beta}(t) - \vec{A_2} \cdot (\vec{D_\beta}) \\ \vec{X_3} = \vec{X_\delta}(t) - \vec{A_3} \cdot (\vec{D_\delta}) \end{cases} \quad (10)$$

$$\vec{X}(t+1) = \frac{\vec{X_1} + \vec{X_2} + \vec{X_3}}{3} \quad (11)$$

ω moves to α, β and δ according to the direction and step size specified in Formula (10), and Formula (5) represents the final position of ω. α, β and δ predict the location of the prey, ω randomly update the location around the prey. When the prey stops moving, the gray wolf completes the hunting behavior by attacking the prey.

2.4.3. Adaptive Multi-Threshold Segmentation Based on GWO-SCE

Due to the differences between different picture samples, especially in the time–frequency pictures with changing working conditions, it is more difficult to highlight the fault features. Therefore, the intelligent optimization algorithm can be used to optimize the threshold value to achieve the effect of adaptively obtaining the best threshold value. According to the SCE threshold segmentation principle in Section 2.4.1, to obtain the final threshold, it is necessary to find the corresponding minimum entropy value. Therefore, choose $H(x)$ as the optimized fitness function:

$$H(x) = x(1, \cdots, n)^* = \mathrm{argmin}\{D_0 + D_1 + \cdots + D_n\} \tag{12}$$

$H(x)$ represents the image cross entropy at different thresholds, and the optimization goal of the algorithm is to find an optimal set of thresholds so that the corresponding $H(x)$ values are minimized. When the GWO algorithm iteration is over, it is considered that $H(x)$ gets the smallest optimization value and that the fault feature boundary in the image has been effectively highlighted. When the threshold number changes from 1 to 4, the corresponding optimal fitness function values are constantly getting smaller: 1.0343×10^6, 4.9×10^5, 2.54×10^5, 1.78×10^5, respectively. When the threshold number is 4, the value of $H(x)$ is the smallest and the segmentation effect is the best.

Further, to verify the effectiveness of the GWO-SCE adaptive multi-threshold segmentation method, we take the Lena image as an example (Figure 6a) and set the number of threshold segmentations to 1, 2, 3, and 4, respectively, with the optimization boundary set to [0, 255] (because the pixel value of the image ranges from 0 to 255). The number of wolves is set to 50, and the maximum number of iterations is set to 100. The experimental results are shown in Figure 6b–e.

It can be concluded from the experimental results in Figure 6 that the algorithm quickly achieved convergence and reached the minimum value of the fitness function at the 100th iteration, which indicates that the GWO-SCE algorithm has effective optimization ability. When the threshold number changes from 1 to 4, the corresponding optimal fitness function values are constantly getting smaller: 1.0343×10^6, 4.9×10^5, 2.54×10^5, 1.78×10^5, respectively. According to the entropy value theorem, the smaller the entropy value, the more information the image contains. Therefore, after optimization, the key information and features in the image are effectively highlighted and segmented, which is very useful for the learning and application of transferable features of image samples using deep networks.

2.5. Convolutional Neural Network (CNN)

The convolutional neural network is a unique neural network structure that was discovered when the neurons for local perception and direction selection were studied in the brains of cats. It is also a commonly used network in deep learning. It has strong feature learning ability, can effectively avoid the loss of local information, and performs well in the field of image classification. Its basic structure consists of an input layer, a convolutional layer, a pooling layer, a fully connected layer, and an output layer, as shown in Figure 7 [41,42].

Among them, the calculation formula of the convolutional layer is:

$$y_z^j = f\left(\sum_{x \in X} y_x^{j-1} \cdot K_{xz}^j + b_z^l\right) \tag{13}$$

where X represents the input image set, z represents the z-th output image, j represents the number of layers of the neural network, y_x^{j-1} represents the input of the j-th layer, y_z^j represents the output of the j-th layer, K_{xz}^j represents the convolution kernel, b_z^l represents the bias, $f(\cdot)$ represents the activation function.

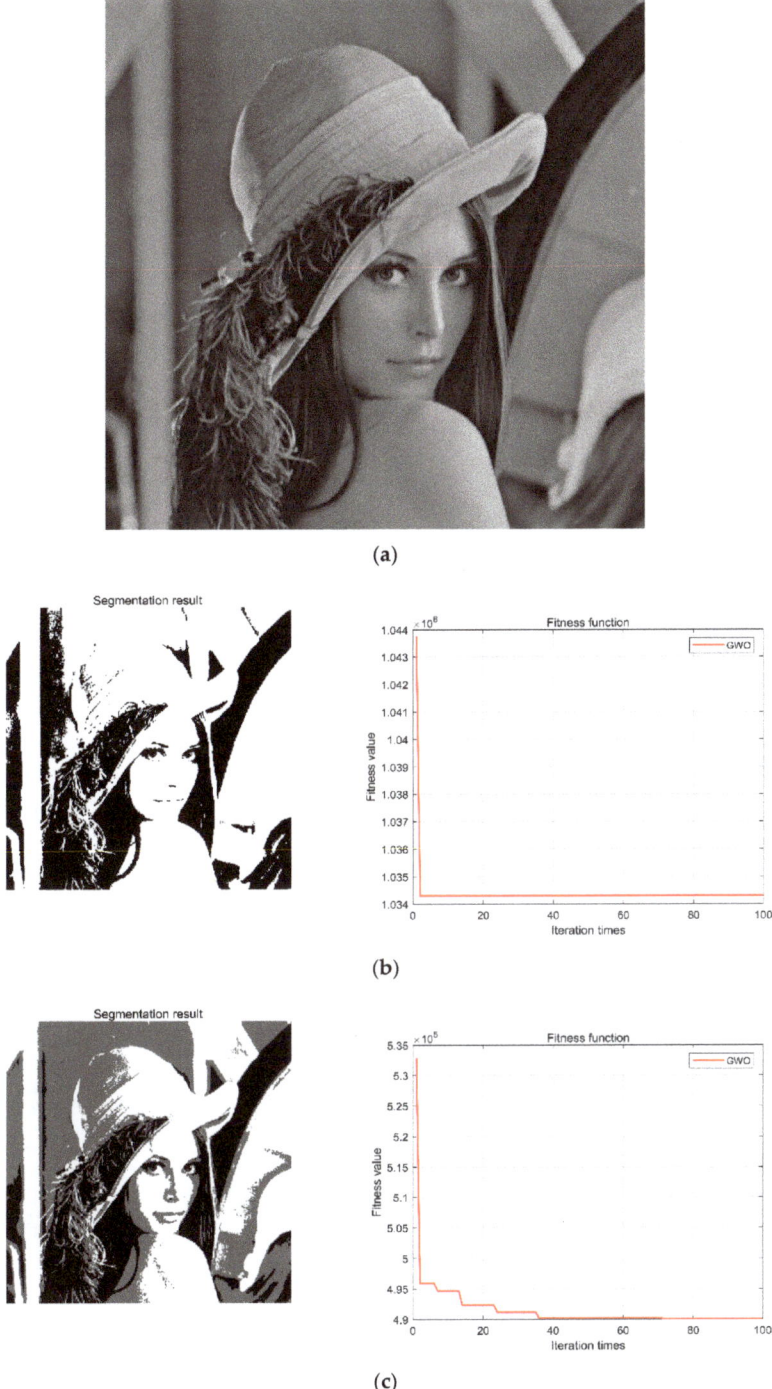

(a)

(b)

(c)

Figure 6. *Cont.*

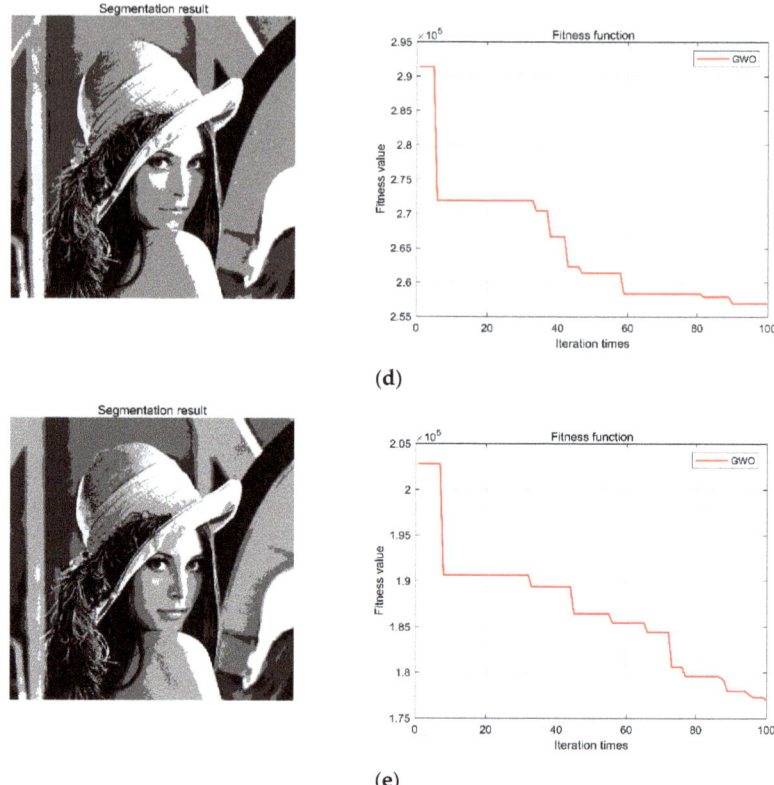

(d)

(e)

Figure 6. Adaptive multi-threshold segmentation results of the Lena image. (**a**) Lena image; (**b**) single threshold segmentation and GWO iteration results; (**c**) two threshold segmentations and GWO iteration results; (**d**) three threshold segmentations and GWO iteration results; (**e**) four threshold segmentations and GWO iteration results.

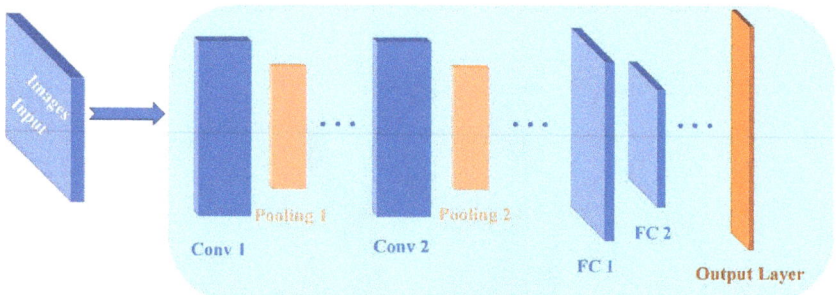

Figure 7. Basic structure diagram of a CNN.

In the pooling layer, the max pooling function or the average pooling function is used for feature mapping, thereby reducing the dimension of the feature map and the amount of training calculations; however, this does not change the number of feature maps. The calculation formula of the pooling layer is:

$$y_k = f(w_k down(y_{mn}) + b_k) \tag{14}$$

where y_k represents the k-th output image, y_{mn} represents the feature map with output size $m \times n$, w_k represents the weight connection coefficient, b_k represents the bias, and down (·) represents the pooling function.

In a deep network, being fully connected means that neurons in each layer establish a weighted relationship with neurons in the previous layer.

The number of input images for the fully connected layer is l and the size is $m \times n$.

First, the input l image matrices are expanded in columns and then connected end to end according to the output order of the previous layer. Thus, it is spliced into $l \times m \times n$, a one-dimensional feature column vector that is finally mapped to the corresponding category of the output layer. The mapping expression between the fully connected layer and the output layer is:

$$y_g = f(w_g x + b_g) \tag{15}$$

where y_g represents the g-th value of the output layer, x represents the feature vector, w_g represents the weight connection coefficient (weight value), b_g represents the bias, and the activation function is generally the Softmax function. Finally, the output of the fully connected layer is divided into corresponding categories through the Softmax function [43,44].

2.6. Maximum Mean Difference (MMD)

The maximum difference in means is based on a nuclear two-sample test that rejects or accepts the null hypothesis $p = q$ for the observed sample, which is defined as a nonparametric distance measure in the reproducing kernel Hilbert space (RKHS) that measures the difference in the distributions of two datasets. In recent years, MMD has been widely used in the field of domain adaptation to perform cross-domain adaptation of features through minimization of the MMD distance between the source domain Ω_S and target domain Ω_T. The square of the MMD distance between the source dataset and target domain dataset is defined as [45,46]:

$$\begin{aligned} D_H^2(\Omega_S, \Omega_T) &= \left\| \frac{1}{n_s} \sum_{i=1}^{n_s} \phi(X_i^s) - \frac{1}{n_t} \sum_{j=1}^{n_t} \phi(X_i^t) \right\|_H^2 \\ &= \frac{1}{n_s^2} \sum_{i=1}^{n_s} \sum_{j=1}^{n_s} K(X_i^s, X_j^s) + \frac{1}{n_t^2} \sum_{i=1}^{n_s} \sum_{j=1}^{n_s} K(X_i^t, X_j^t) - \frac{2}{n_s n_t} \sum_{i=1}^{n_s} \sum_{j=1}^{n_t} K(X_i^s, X_j^t) \end{aligned} \tag{16}$$

where H is the RKHS and $\phi : \Omega_S, \Omega_T \to H$ and $K(\cdot, \cdot)$ are Gaussian kernel functions.

$$K(\Omega_s, \Omega_T) = \exp(-\|\Omega_s - \Omega_T\|/2\delta^2) \tag{17}$$

In the formula, δ is the bandwidth of the kernel function, which can take multiple different values to calculate the MMD and superimpose its calculation results to form the so-called multi-core MMD.

3. CNN-Based Subdomain Adaptive Fault Diagnosis

Aiming at the inconsistency of characteristic distribution of fault state signal data collected under the different operating conditions of gearboxes, a subdomain adaptive depth transfer diagnosis method is proposed. The method mainly consists of two parts: transfer fault feature extraction and subdomain adaptation. Self-designed CNNs can be used to extract common features of samples; the subdomain adaptation uses the adaptive layer to learn the transfer knowledge, uses the local maximum mean discrepancy (LMMD) metric for conditional distribution difference calculation, and aligns the subdomains to achieve gearbox transfer learning for different operating conditions.

3.1. Subdomain Adaptive Deep Network Model

Based on quantitative research on feature transferability in deep convolutional networks, the general feature extraction layer mainly extracts the general features of the source domain data and the target domain data, and the difference between the two domains is mainly reflected in the fully connected layer (adaptive layer). Based on this theory, the subdomain adaptive network model proposed in this paper is shown in Figure 8. The number of layers and the network parameter settings are shown in Table 1.

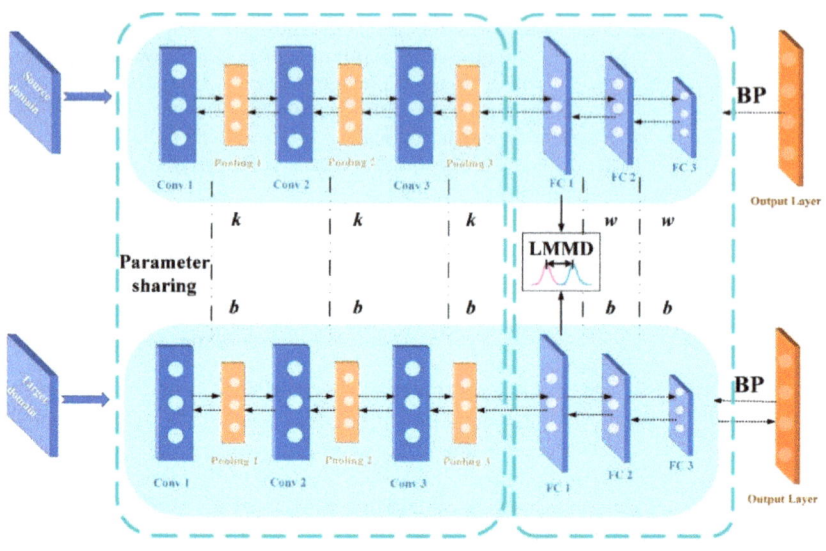

Figure 8. Subdomain adaptive network model.

Table 1. Subdomain adaptive network structure and parameter settings.

Layers	Tied Parameters	Activation Functions	Output Size
Input	/	/	$224 \times 224 \times 1$
Conv1	Kernels: $3 \times 3 \times 16$, Bias: 16×1	ReLU	$222 \times 222 \times 16$
Pool1	S: 2×2	/	$111 \times 111 \times 16$
Conv1	Kernels: $3 \times 3 \times 32$, Bias: 32×1	ReLU	$109 \times 109 \times 32$
Pool2	S: 2×2	/	$55 \times 55 \times 32$
Conv1	Kernels: $3 \times 3 \times 64$, Bias: 64×1	ReLU	$53 \times 53 \times 64$
Pool3	S: 2×2	/	$27 \times 27 \times 64$
Flatten	/	/	729×64
FC1	Weights: 7×1, Bias: 512×1	ReLU	512×1
FC2	Weights: 512×128, Bias: 128×1	ReLU	128×1
FC3/Classification	Weights: 128×7, Bias: 7×1	Softmax	7×1

After the CWT time–frequency map samples of different speeds are put into the network, the convolutional layer extracts and learns the general features of the image. Further, the first layer of the fully connected network is set as the adaptive layer, and the LMMD metric is used for subdomain adaptation. Finally, a Softmax classifier performs fault diagnosis on the target domain's work–case dataset. The objective function f optimized during training is:

$$F = \min_f \frac{1}{n_s} \sum_{i=1}^{n_s} J(f(X_i^s), Y_i^s) + \lambda \mu \sum_{l \in L} \hat{d}_l(p, q) \tag{18}$$

In the formula, $J(\cdot, \cdot)$ is the cross entropy loss function, $\hat{d}_l(\cdot, \cdot)$ is the subdomain adaptation function, and the total number of adaptive layers is denoted by L. In this paper, the LMMD metric is added to the first fully connected layer, thus $L = 1$. As a nonparametric distance estimation between two distributions, MMD is mainly used to measure the difference between the source domain distribution and the target domain distribution; for the subdomain adaptation problem, LMMD needs to be introduced:

$$\hat{d}_H(p,q) = \frac{1}{C}\sum_{c=1}^{C} \left\| \sum \omega_i^{sc} \phi(X_i^s) - \sum \omega_j^{tc} \phi(X_j^t) \right\|_H^2 \tag{19}$$

In the formula, ω_i^{sc} and ω_j^{tc} are the weights of X_i^s and X_j^t belonging to the c-th class, respectively, which can be expressed as:

$$\omega_i^c = \frac{y_{ic}}{\sum_{(X_j,Y_j)\in D} y_{jc}} \tag{20}$$

In the formula, y_{ic} is the c-th label of the input vector Y_i. Further, the ground-truth labels are used to calculate the weights of samples in the source domain. For the samples in the target domain, the deep neural network uses the learned probability distribution to represent the probability that the sample is recognized as a certain category. The weights of the target domain are therefore calculated using the predicted labels of the network. In implementing the adaptation process of deep network layers, the activation factor u^l needs to be known. Given domains subject to probability distributions p and q, respectively, the network will generate activations for $\{u_i^{sl}\}_{i=1}^{n_s}$ and $\{u_j^{tl}\}_{j=1}^{n_t}$ in the adaptive layer. Therefore, the subdomain adaptation function is:

$$\hat{d}_l(p,q) = \frac{1}{C}\sum_{c=1}^{C}\sum_{i=1}^{n_s}\sum_{j=1}^{n_s} \omega_i^{sc}\omega_j^{sc} K(u_i^{sl}, u_j^{sl}) + \sum_{i=1}^{n_t}\sum_{j=1}^{n_t} \omega_i^{tc}\omega_j^{tc} K(u_i^{tl}, u_j^{tl}) - 2\sum_{i=1}^{n_s}\sum_{j=1}^{n_t} \omega_i^{sc}\omega_j^{tc} K(u_i^{sl}, u_j^{tl}) \tag{21}$$

In the formula, u^l is the activation factor of the l-th layer ($l \in L = \{1, 2, \cdots, |L|\}$). In the network training process, the objective function that needs to be finally optimized is:

$$F = \min_f \frac{1}{n_s}\sum_{i=1}^{n_s} J(f(X_i^s), Y_i^s) + \lambda\mu \sum_{l\in L} \frac{1}{C}\sum_{c=1}^{C} \left\{ \sum_{i=1}^{n_s}\sum_{j=1}^{n_s} \omega_i^{sc}\omega_j^{sc} K(u_i^{sl}, u_j^{sl}) + \sum_{i=1}^{n_t}\sum_{j=1}^{n_t} \omega_i^{tc}\omega_j^{tc} K(u_i^{tl}, u_j^{tl}) - 2\sum_{i=1}^{n_s}\sum_{j=1}^{n_t} \omega_i^{sc}\omega_j^{tc} K(u_i^{sl}, u_j^{tl}) \right\} \tag{22}$$

3.2. Fault Diagnosis Algorithm Flow

The complete adaptive diagnosis algorithm flow from this paper is shown in Figure 9.

(1) Carry out the fault preset experiment and perform acoustic signal acquisition under the variable speed conditions of the gearbox while preprocessing the data to obtain digital samples.

(2) Perform CWT conversion on the signal to obtain two-dimensional time–frequency image samples.

(3) Adaptive multi-threshold segmentation is performed on the image samples to obtain the source domain sample and target domain sample required for the input of the network model.

(4) The source domain sample and target domain sample are entered into the subdomain adaptive network model for training and diagnosis, and the diagnosis results of the gear box target's working condition data are obtained.

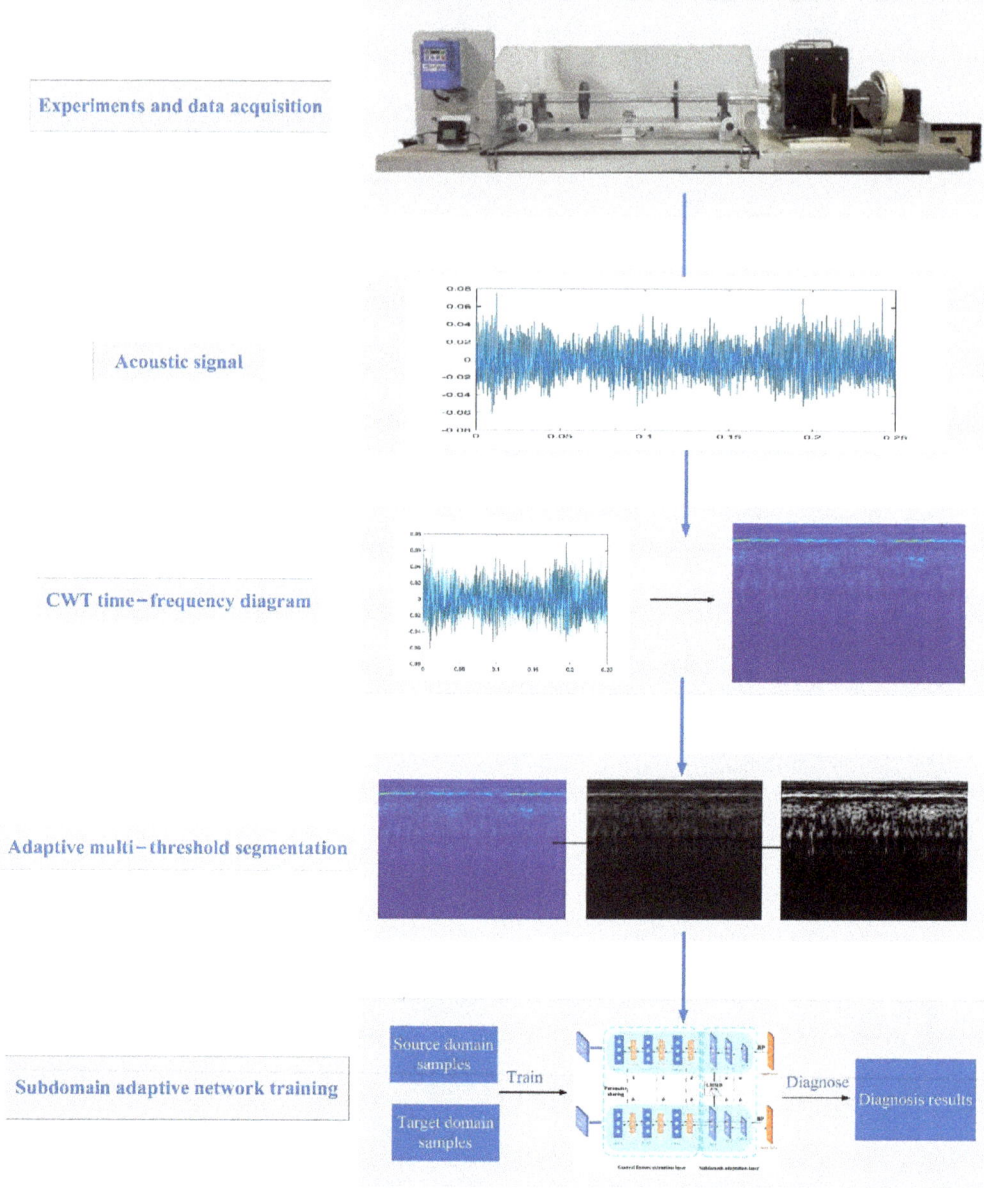

Figure 9. Fault diagnosis strategy flowchart.

4. Case Study

4.1. Data Preparation

In this paper, the gear and bearing fault preset experiments are carried out with the help of a mechanical fault comprehensive simulation test bench. The experimental object is a secondary spur gearbox (as shown in Figure 10), and the collected acoustic signal data are used as the follow-up analysis object. The composition of the test bench includes power and control parts, a bearing fault simulation part, a gearbox fault simulation part, and a data acquisition part. This paper mainly conducts the pre-fault experiment on the gearbox part of the test bench. This part is mainly composed of a secondary reduction spur gear box (which can realize the preset faults of gears, bearings, and composite cases), magnetic powder brakes (providing loads), and magnetic powder brake controllers (controlling load changes).

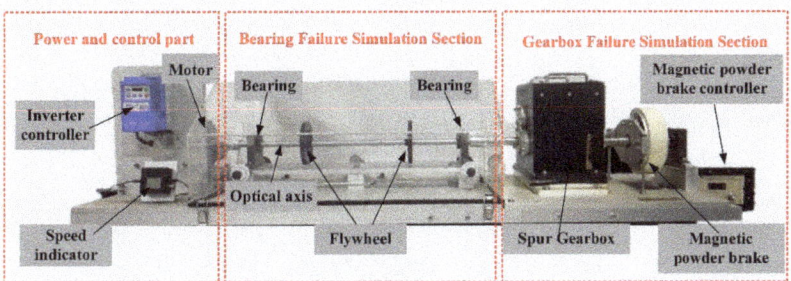

Figure 10. Comprehensive fault simulation test bench.

The perspective view and internal structure diagram of the secondary reduction spur gear box are shown in Figure 11a,b. The number of teeth on the gears, from high-speed to low-speed shafts, are: 41, 79, 36, and 90, respectively. The preset faulty gear is gear 3, and the faulty bearing is located at the ER-16K bearing at the end cap in Figure 11b. The size parameters are shown in Table 2. Figure 11c shows the sound pressure sensor used in the experiment; the sensor is a YSV5001 high-precision ICP sound pressure sensor, which is mainly composed of an electret head and an ICP preamplifier, and its related performance indicators are shown in Table 3. These indicators meet the requirements of IEC61672 and GB/T3661 primary indicators. Figure 11d shows the process of acoustic signal acquisition, and the part marked in red in the figure is the sound pressure sensor.

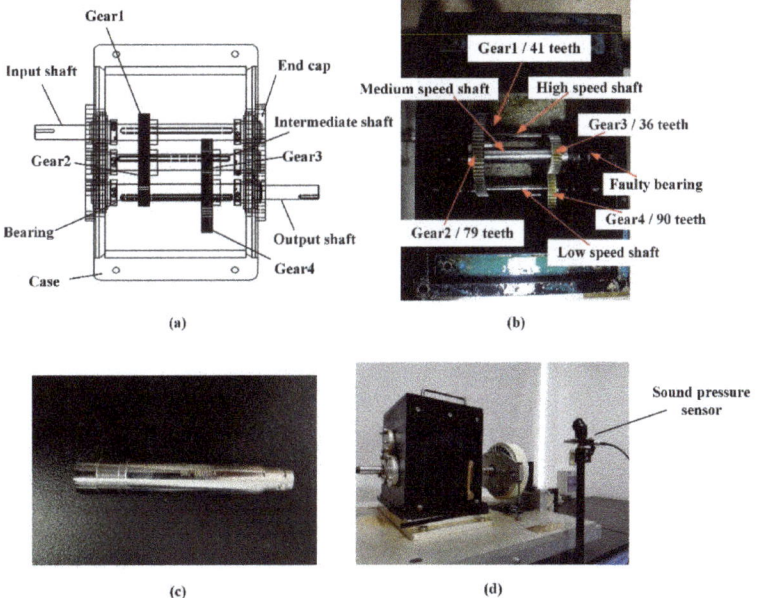

Figure 11. (a) Perspective view of the gearbox; (b) internal structure of the gearbox; (c) sound pressure sensor; (d) view of signal acquisition.

Table 2. Structural parameters of the ER-16K bearing.

Number of Rolling Elements	Rolling Body Diameter/inch	Pitch Diameter/Inch	Contact Angle/°
8	0.3125	1.516	0

Table 3. Related technical indexes of the sound pressure sensor.

Indicator	Model	Pole Size/mm	Polar Head Range/dB	Output Impedance/GΩ	Power Supply/mA	Frequency Response/Hz
Type	YSV5001	12.7	20~146	<110	2~20	20~20 K

During the experiment, motor speed was controlled by the motor inverter controller or the MotorControl motor control software. MotorControl can change the motor speed by controlling the motor frequency conversion controller to realize the constant speed and continuous variable speed of the motor. The data acquisition system consists of a sound pressure sensor and VQ-USB4/LF data acquisition board. The board consists of the data acquisition board itself and VibraQuest Pro signal analysis software. VibraQuest Pro is a versatile data acquisition and condition detection system that records signal data in real-time from data acquisition boards. Figure 12 shows the signal acquisition system and software used in the experiment.

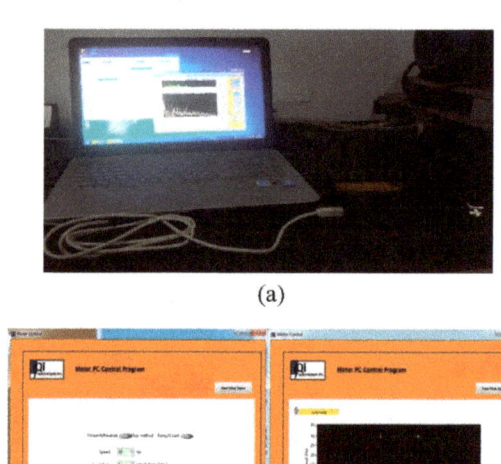

(a)

(b)

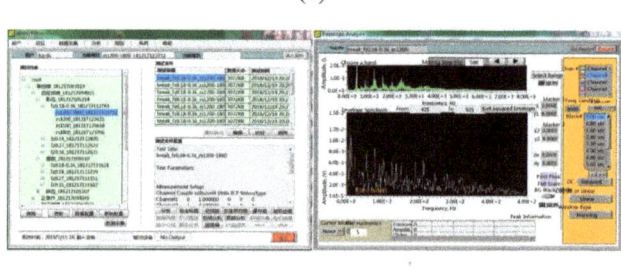

(c)

Figure 12. (a) Data collection systems; (b) motor control software; (c) VibraQuest Pro software.

In the preset fault experiment in this paper, the fault types for gear settings include a missing tooth fault, broken tooth fault, and wear fault. The failure types for bearing settings include an inner ring failure, outer ring failure, and single ball failure. The fault is processed by pre-processing a deep groove with a width of 0.5 mm on the bearing outer ring, inner ring, and ball body. The relevant components corresponding to the six fault conditions are shown in Figure 13. Table 4 details the relevant information of the seven states of the gearbox under a single working condition.

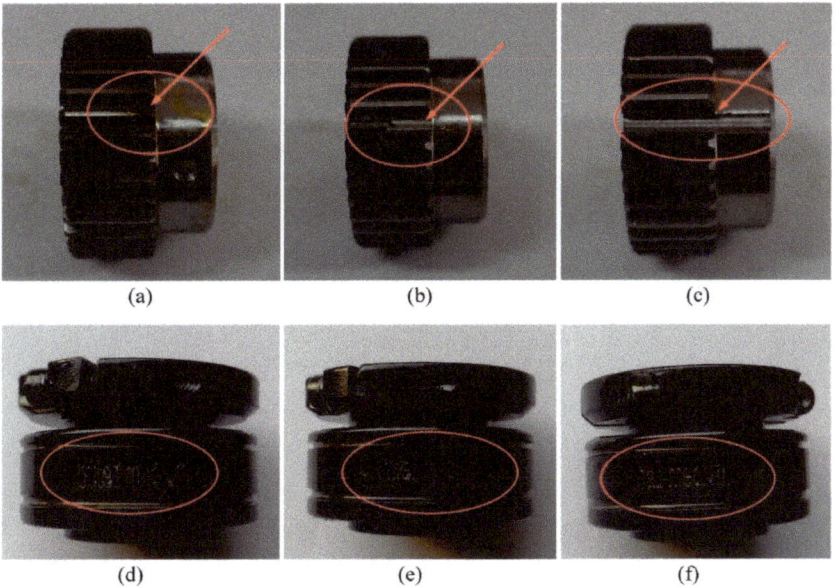

Figure 13. (**a**) Missing gear; (**b**) broken gear; (**c**) uniform worn gear; (**d**) bearing outer fault; (**e**) bearing inner fault; (**f**) bearing rolling ball fault.

Table 4. Gear and bearing fault status types.

Fault Code	Fault Type
F1	Missing gear
F2	Broken gear
F3	Uniform worn gear
F4	Bearing inner fault
F5	Bearing outer fault
F6	Bearing rolling ball fault
F7	Health

In the experiment, the combined working conditions of different rotational speeds are set, and the acoustic signals of the normal state and the six fault states of the gearbox with different working conditions are collected respectively. In each experiment, the signal acquisition time was 48 s and the procedure was repeated 10 times. The design of the combined working conditions of different loads and speeds is shown in Table 4. A total of 5000 sampling points were used as a vibration sequence sample and 120 samples were taken for each set of fault data. Further, according to the working condition design in Table 5, we created six transfer learning tasks, namely $A \rightarrow B$, $A \rightarrow C$, $A \rightarrow D$, $B \rightarrow C$, $B \rightarrow D$, $C \rightarrow D$. The transfer task $A \rightarrow B$ indicates that the data of working condition A are the source domain, and the data of working condition B are the target domain.

Table 5. Design of the experimental conditions.

Condition Code	Rotating Speed/rpm	Load Current/N·m	Number of Source Domain Samples	Number of Target Domain Samples
A	1200 (constant)	5	120	120
B	1500 (constant)	5	120	120
C	1800 (constant)	5	120	120
D	1200~1800 (even speed change)	5	120	120

Further, we use CWT to convert the one-dimensional acoustic signal into a $m*n*3$—dimensional RGB color time–frequency map with three channels (m and n are the length and width of the image, respectively, and three represents the number of primary color channels). To reduce the amount of computation, the RGB images are converted into $m*n$—dimensional grayscale images. The adaptive multi-threshold segmentation method from Section 2.4 is used to perform adaptive threshold segmentation on the gray image samples. The specific processing process is shown in Figure 14. Due to limited article space, only the sample preparation process for the F5 fault signals under condition A (1200 rpm and 5 Nm) is listed here. The results of the experiments at different thresholds are shown in Figure 15.

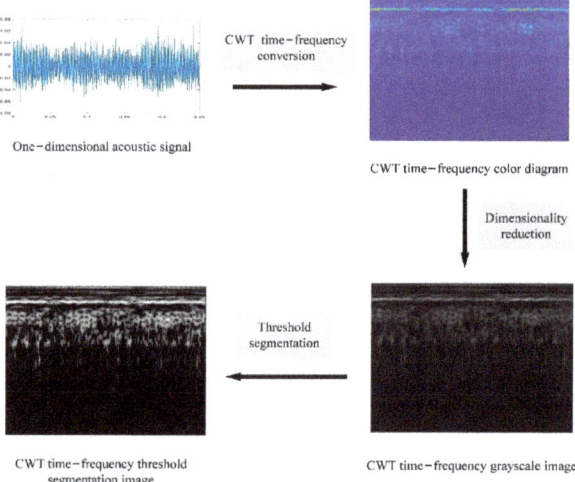

Figure 14. Processing of image samples.

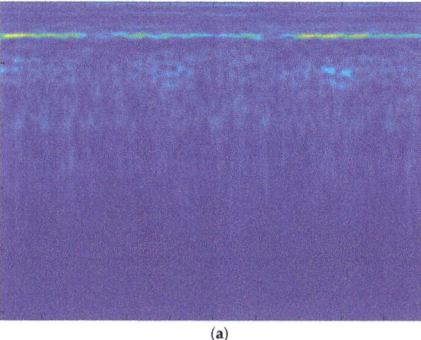

(a)

Figure 15. *Cont.*

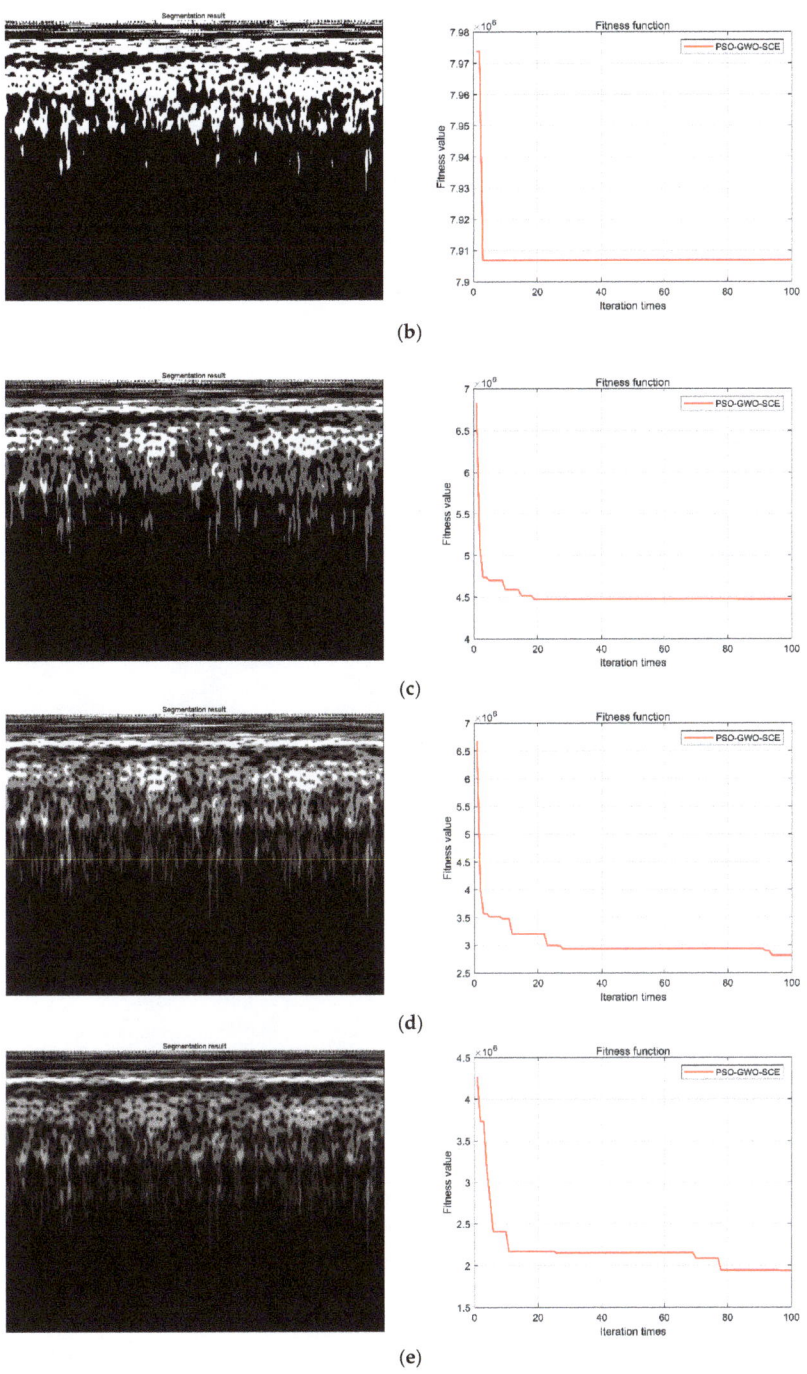

Figure 15. Adaptive multi-threshold segmentation results of the F5 CWT image: (**a**) F5 CWT image; (**b**) single threshold segmentation and GWO iteration results; (**c**) two threshold segmentations and GWO iteration results; (**d**) three threshold segmentations and GWO iteration results; (**e**) four threshold segmentations and GWO iteration results.

From the experiment results in Figure 15, it can be seen that compared to the original CWT time–frequency map, the boundary of the image feature components after threshold segmentation is well highlighted, and with the increase in threshold number, the types and levels of components are also clearer. The corresponding fitness function values become smaller, with values of 7.907×10^6, 4.49×10^6, 2.75×10^6, 1.88×10^6, respectively. That is, when the threshold number is four, the cross entropy of the image reaches the minimum value and the fault classification feature information contained in the image is the greatest. In addition, after the threshold number exceeds five, the calculation amount and calculation time of sample processing become longer. Therefore, combined with the diagnostic effect and timeliness, the number of threshold segments is selected as four.

Further, the threshold segmentation results of the seven types of fault signal are shown in Figure 16. Due to limited article space, we have only listed the processing results of case A (1200 rpm and 5 Nm). Finally, 120 grayscale samples were obtained from the data of each fault type under the four speed conditions.

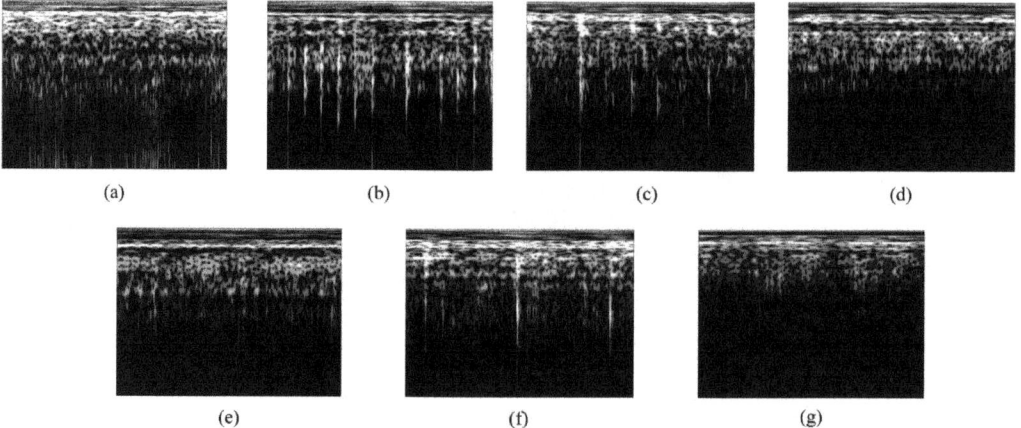

Figure 16. Threshold segmentation processing results for different types of fault signals under case A: (**a**) F1 fault; (**b**) F2 fault; (**c**) F3 fault; (**d**) F4 fault; (**e**) F5 fault; (**f**) F6 fault; and (**g**) F7 fault.

4.2. Experimental Results

The source domain samples and target domain samples are entered into the subdomain adaptive network for training, and the parameter settings of the network during the training process are shown in Table 6. The average value of 10 fault diagnosis results is shown in Table 7. Figure 17 shows the network training and loss function curves for different transfer tasks.

Table 6. Network hyperparameter settings.

Parameter	Value
Batch size	42
Learn rate	1×10^5
Weight decay	0.9

From the above experimental results, in different transfer tasks, the proposed subdomain diagnosis fault algorithm can obtain high diagnosis accuracy, and the average diagnosis accuracy of the target domain reaches more than 99.84%. This shows that the characteristic knowledge between fault data under different rotational speed conditions has been transferred well, which proves the superiority of the algorithm in this paper. To further verify the fault features learned from the deep parameter space of the network, the effectiveness of cross-domain feature learning for subdomain adaptation was assessed. Using t-distributed stochastic neighbor embedding (t-SNE), the visualization is performed by mapping high-level feature representations from raw feature space to 2D space [47]. The visualized results are shown in Figure 18.

Table 7. Fault diagnosis results.

Transfer Task	Source Domain Training Accuracy/%	Target Domain Test Accuracy/%
$A \rightarrow B$	99.81	99.96
$A \rightarrow C$	99.90	99.92
$A \rightarrow D$	99.79	99.89
$B \rightarrow C$	99.88	99.92
$B \rightarrow D$	99.92	99.95
$C \rightarrow D$	99.75	99.84

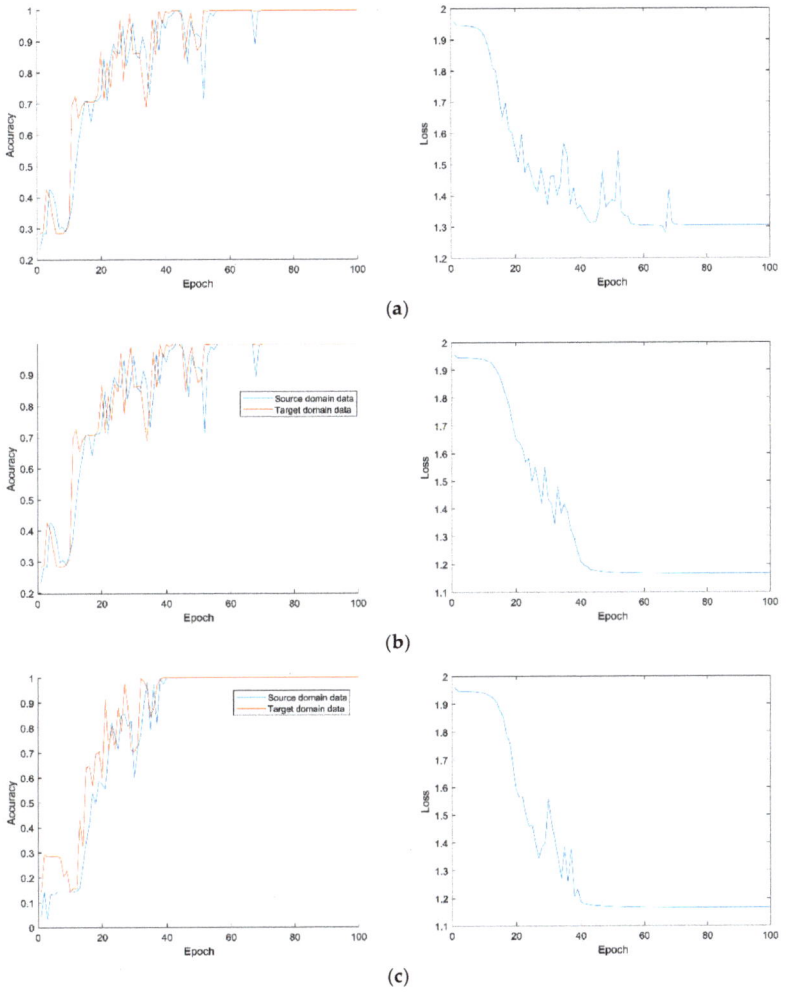

Figure 17. *Cont.*

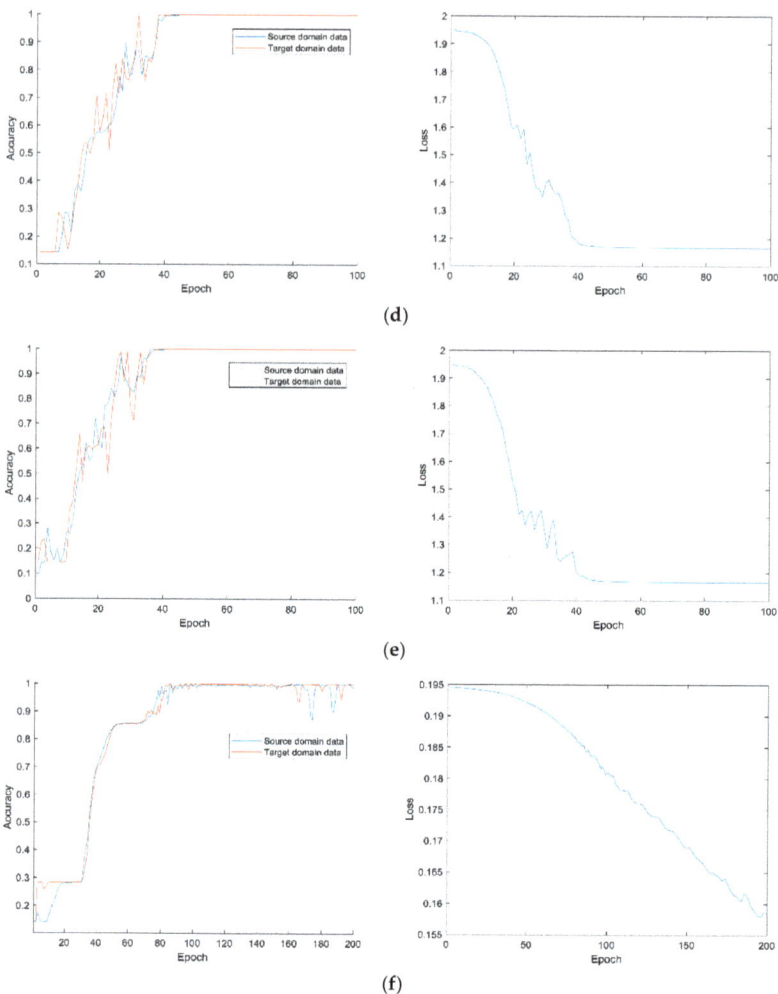

Figure 17. Network training and loss function curves under different transfer tasks: (**a**) transfer task $A \rightarrow B$; (**b**) transfer task $A \rightarrow C$; (**c**) transfer task $A \rightarrow D$; (**d**) transfer task $B \rightarrow C$; (**e**) transfer task $B \rightarrow D$; (**f**) transfer task $C \rightarrow D$.

The left column of Figure 18 illustrates that, without subdomain adaptive training, different types of data in the source domain are better classified but data obfuscation occurs in the target domain. The data distribution difference between the source domain and the target domain has not been effectively adapted to the domain, indicating that the knowledge of fault features is not transferred between domains. This resulted in a large number of diagnostic misjudgments. Observing the column on the right side of Figure 18 leads to the conclusion that, after the data is adaptively trained on subdomains, the fault features of the source and target domains are projected to the same region after deep learning and transfer. It can be observed that not only are the classification characteristics of the source domain data well distinguished, but the classification characteristics of the target domain are also consistent with the distribution of the source domain, a high-precision distinction. Therefore, the accuracy and effect of fault diagnosis have been greatly improved.

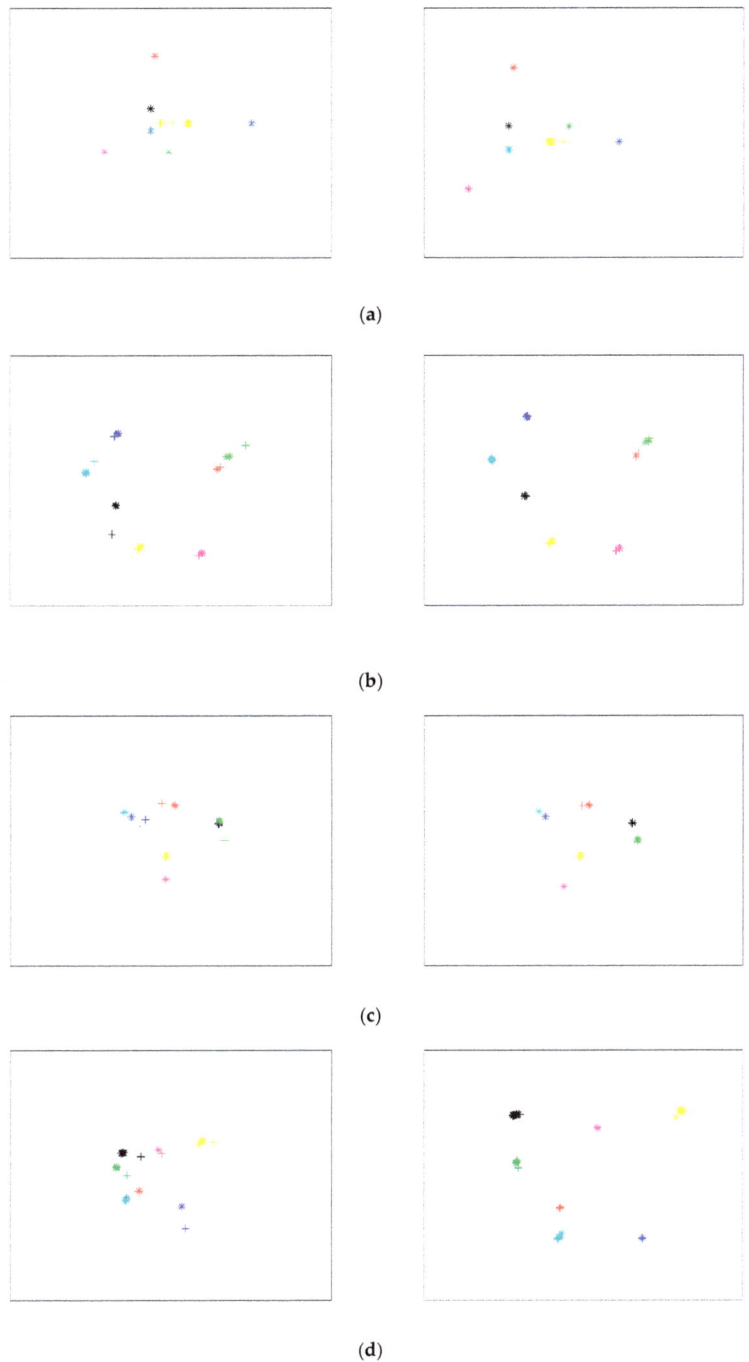

Figure 18. *Cont.*

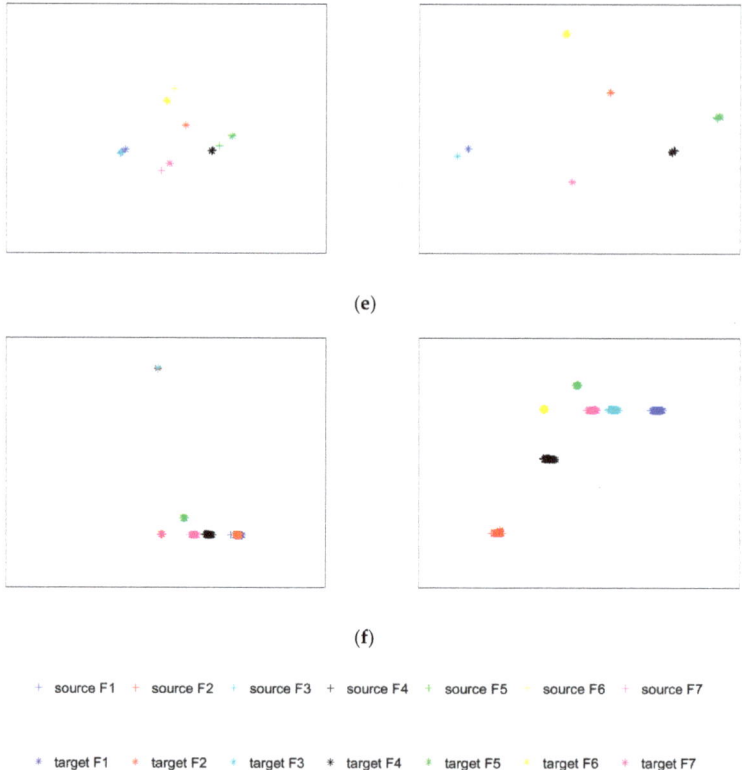

(e)

(f)

+ source F1 + source F2 + source F3 + source F4 + source F5 + source F6 + source F7

* target F1 * target F2 * target F3 * target F4 * target F5 * target F6 * target F7

Figure 18. Visualization of fully connected layer transfer features: (**a**) transfer task $A \to B$; (**b**) transfer task $A \to C$; (**c**) transfer task $A \to D$; (**d**) transfer task $B \to C$; (**e**) transfer task $B \to D$; (**f**) transfer task $C \to D$.

4.3. Small Sample Performance Analysis

To verify the diagnosis effect of the proposed fault diagnosis algorithm under the small sample diagnosis condition, the sample sizes for the source domain and target domain data in the transfer task were set to 40, 60, 80, 100, and 120, respectively. The average of ten experimental results is shown in Table 8 and Figure 19.

From the experimental results in Figure 19, it can be clearly concluded that the proposed fault diagnosis algorithm does not experience a large decline in diagnostic accuracy when the sample size drops sharply. On the contrary, because of the powerful feature learning ability of the deep network and the adaptive component training in the fully connected layer, the effective features in the sample can be learned and applied, and the failure accuracy rate can be maintained above 59%. At the same time, the fluctuation of diagnostic accuracy indicates that, in fault diagnosis based on deep networks, the accuracy of fault diagnosis can be improved by increasing the sample size.

4.4. Method Performance Comparison Analysis

To further verify the effectiveness of the diagnostic algorithm proposed in this paper, other diagnostic models are used for comparative analysis. Model 1 is the traditional machine learning classifier support vector machine (SVM, G1) [48]. Model 2 is the network model used in this paper but the samples are not segmented by a GWO-SCE adaptive multi-threshold, and only the CWT time–frequency transform (G2) is performed [49]. Model 3 replaces the domain distance measurement criterion with MMD (G3) [25]. Model 4 replaces the domain distance measurement criterion with the Wasserstein metric (G4) [50]. Model 5 is a domain adversarial neural network (DANN) that employs a domain discriminator to adversarially train the model to learn domain-invariant features (G5) across source and target domains. The method in this paper is denoted by G6. The average of ten experimental results is shown in Table 9 and Figure 20, where the training sample size was 120.

Table 8. Diagnostic performance of the algorithm with different sample sizes.

Transfer Task	Sample Size	Target Domain Test Accuracy/%
$A \to B$	120	99.96
	100	92.29
	80	82.19
	60	80.36
	40	73.35
$A \to C$	120	99.92
	100	94.62
	80	89.54
	60	76.35
	40	71.62
$A \to D$	120	99.89
	100	96.33
	80	84.66
	60	76.95
	40	69.18
$B \to C$	120	99.92
	100	89.55
	80	85.49
	60	65.95
	40	59.54
$B \to D$	120	99.95
	100	91.44
	80	85.85
	60	74.55
	40	72.62
$C \to D$	120	99.84
	100	92.62
	80	86.29
	60	76.55
	40	63.54

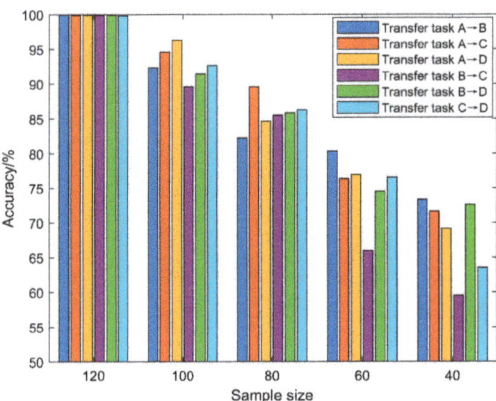

Figure 19. Diagnostic performance graph of the algorithm under different sample sizes.

Table 9. Diagnostic performance under different diagnostic methods.

Transfer Task	Method	Target Domain Test Accuracy/%
$A \to B$	G1	52.97
	G2	86.97
	G3	90.56
	G4	91.09
	G5	94.22
	G6	99.96
$A \to C$	G1	51.57
	G2	85.11
	G3	91.92
	G4	91.93
	G5	95.64
	G6	99.92
$A \to D$	G1	50.68
	G2	87.55
	G3	91.94
	G4	90.32
	G5	95.01
	G6	99.89
$B \to C$	G1	52.82
	G2	87.80
	G3	91.87
	G4	90.97
	G5	96.31
	G6	99.92
$B \to D$	G1	50.62
	G2	87.04
	G3	91.60
	G4	90.28
	G5	94.52
	G6	99.95
$C \to D$	G1	53.12
	G2	84.27
	G3	90.84
	G4	91.83
	G5	93.85
	G6	99.84

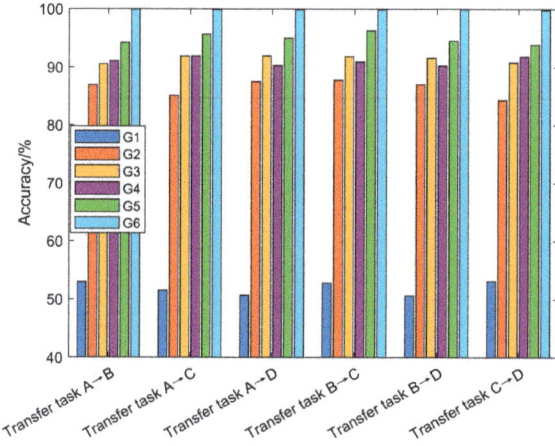

Figure 20. Diagnostic performance graph under different diagnostic methods.

The following conclusions can be drawn from the above experimental results: (1) As a machine learning method, SVM cannot learn the deep-level features of image samples and cannot maintain high diagnostic accuracy when the data distribution of samples changes. (2) The CWT time–frequency map without threshold segmentation is used in the training process of the G2 model, and the diagnosis result is lower than that of the G6 model. This shows that GWO-SCE adaptive multi-threshold segmentation can better highlight the fault feature boundary of image samples, which can greatly improve the accuracy of fault diagnosis. (3) The MMD and Wasserstein metric criteria are used in the G3 and G4 models, respectively, and the conditional distribution between sub-type faults in the field is not considered, thus the diagnostic accuracy is lower than that of the G6 model. (4) The domain adversarial training of the G5 model also only considers the reduction of inter-domain differences, while ignoring the elimination of intra-domain differences. Therefore, the fault diagnosis effect of the G5 model is also weaker than that of the G6 model. In summary, the fault diagnosis algorithm proposed in this paper has outstanding effectiveness and superiority in the face of fault diagnosis problems under cross-domain variable working conditions.

5. Conclusions

The role of fault diagnosis theory in the health management of equipment is increasing. Aiming at the cross-domain fault diagnosis of gearboxes under variable speed conditions, this paper proposes a fault diagnosis algorithm for gearboxes based on GWO-SCE threshold segmentation and subdomain adaptation. Through experimental verification, the following conclusions are drawn.

(1) This paper uses the sound pressure sensor's advantages of no contact, easy placement, and low cost to acoustically collect the fault signal of a gearbox, which effectively solves the problems of traditional vibration acceleration sensors, such as the limitation of contact-based installation and increasingly strict layout requirements.

(2) The adaptive multi-threshold segmentation method based on GWO-SCE can segment and highlight the effective fault components in CWT time–frequency images, which greatly helps the deep network learn the fault feature of the samples and then transfer them.

(3) The subdomain adaptive network adds the LMMD metric in the depth parameter space, which not only reduces the data distribution difference between the source and target domains, but also considers the conditional distribution between sub-class fault data. The experimental results of fault diagnosis show that the network model can complete the cross-domain transfer diagnosis under the condition of variable gearbox speed with high diagnostic accuracy.

As a fault diagnosis algorithm combining time–frequency analysis and a deep network, this research method can provide theoretical support and reference for equipment health management technology represented by fault diagnosis. In the future, seeking more effective time–frequency analysis technology, a greater number of targeted domain distance metrics, and network structures with stronger learning ability should be the direction of further research.

Author Contributions: Writing—original draft preparation, Y.L.; supervision, J.K.; data curation, L.W.; data curation, Y.B.; writing—review & editing, C.G.; writing—review & editing, project administration, W.Y. All authors have read and agreed to the published version of the manuscript.

Funding: This research was funded by [the Natural Science Foundation of China] grant number [No. 71871220].

Institutional Review Board Statement: Not applicable.

Informed Consent Statement: Not applicable.

Data Availability Statement: Not applicable.

Conflicts of Interest: The authors of this article declare that there are no known competing financial interest or personal relationships that could influence the work of this article.

References

1. Chen, X.; Zhang, B.; Gao, D. Bearing fault diagnosis base on multi-scale CNN and LSTM model. *J. Intell. Manuf.* **2021**, *32*, 971–987. [CrossRef]
2. Wang, X.; Mao, D.; Li, X. Bearing fault diagnosis based on vibro-acoustic data fusion and 1D-CNN network. *Measurement* **2021**, *173*, 108518. [CrossRef]
3. Han, T.; Zhang, L.; Yin, Z.; Tan, A.C.C. Rolling bearing fault diagnosis with combined convolutional neural networks and support vector machine. *Measurement* **2021**, *177*, 109022. [CrossRef]
4. Cerrada, M.; Zurita, G.; Cabrera, D.; Sánchez, R.-V.; Artés, M.; Li, C. Fault diagnosis in spur gears based on genetic algorithm and random forest. *Mech. Syst. Signal Process.* **2016**, *70–71*, 87–103. [CrossRef]
5. Wen, L.; Li, X.; Gao, L.; Zhang, Y. A New Convolutional Neural Network-Based Data-Driven Fault Diagnosis Method. *IEEE Trans. Ind. Electron.* **2018**, *65*, 5990–5998. [CrossRef]
6. Hui, K.H.; Ooi, C.S.; Lim, M.H.; Leong, M.S.; Al-Obaidi, S.M. An improved wrapper-based feature selection method for machinery fault diagnosis. *PLoS ONE* **2017**, *12*, e0189143. [CrossRef] [PubMed]
7. Glowacz, A. Fault diagnosis of single-phase induction motor based on acoustic signals. *Mech. Syst. Signal Process.* **2019**, *117*, 65–80. [CrossRef]
8. Yao, J.; Liu, C.; Song, K.; Feng, C.; Jiang, D. Fault diagnosis of planetary gearbox based on acoustic signals. *Appl. Acoust.* **2021**, *181*, 108151. [CrossRef]
9. Adaileh, W.M. Engine fault diagnosis using acoustic signals. *Appl. Mech. Mater.* **2013**, *295–298*, 2013–2020. [CrossRef]
10. Gao, D.; Zhu, Y.; Wang, X.; Yan, K.; Hong, J. A Fault Diagnosis Method of Rolling Bearing Based on Complex Morlet CWT and CNN. In Proceedings of the—2018 Prognostics and System Health Management Conference, PHM-Chongqing 2018, Chongqing, China, 26–28 October 2018; Institute of Electrical and Electronics Engineers Inc.: Manhattan, NY, USA, 2019; pp. 1101–1105.
11. Wang, L.H.; Zhao, X.P.; Wu, J.X.; Xie, Y.Y.; Zhang, Y.H. Motor Fault Diagnosis Based on Short-time Fourier Transform and Convolutional Neural Network. *Chin. J. Mech. Eng.* **2017**, *30*, 1357–1368. [CrossRef]
12. Suman, S.; Chatterjee, D.; Mohanty, R. Comparison of PSO and GWO Techniques for SHEPWM Inverters. In Proceedings of the 2020 International Conference on Computer, Electrical & Communication Engineering (ICCECE), Kolkata, India, 17–18 January 2020.
13. Zhang, Y.; Xing, K.; Bai, R.; Sun, D.; Meng, Z. An enhanced convolutional neural network for bearing fault diagnosis based on time–frequency image. *Measurement* **2020**, *157*, 107667. [CrossRef]
14. Sambandam, R.K.; Jayaraman, S. Self-adaptive dragonfly based optimal thresholding for multilevel segmentation of digital images. *J. King Saud Univ. Comput. Inf. Sci.* **2018**, *30*, 449–461. [CrossRef]
15. Rongrong, S.; Zhenyu, M.; Hong, Y.; Zhenxing, L.; Gongming, Q.; Chengyu, G.; Yang, L.; Kun, Y. Fault Diagnosis Method of Distribution Equipment Based on Hybrid Model of Robot and Deep Learning. *J. Robot.* **2022**, *2022*, 9742815. [CrossRef]
16. Verdejo, H.; Pino, V.; Kliemann, W.; Becker, C.; Delpiano, J. Implementation of particle swarm optimization (PSO) algorithm for tuning of power system stabilizers in multimachine electric power systems. *Energies* **2020**, *13*, 2093. [CrossRef]
17. Tang, S.; Yuan, S.; Zhu, Y. Data Preprocessing Techniques in Convolutional Neural Network Based on Fault Diagnosis towards Rotating Machinery. *IEEE Access* **2020**, *8*, 149487–149496. [CrossRef]
18. Tang, S.; Yuan, S.; Zhu, Y. Convolutional Neural Network in Intelligent Fault Diagnosis toward Rotatory Machinery. *IEEE Access* **2020**, *8*, 86510–86519. [CrossRef]
19. Shao, S.; McAleer, S.; Yan, R.; Baldi, P. Highly Accurate Machine Fault Diagnosis Using Deep Transfer Learning. *IEEE Trans. Ind. Inf.* **2019**, *15*, 2446–2455. [CrossRef]
20. Li, C.; Zhang, S.; Qin, Y.; Estupinan, E. A systematic review of deep transfer learning for machinery fault diagnosis. *Neurocomputing* **2020**, *407*, 121–135. [CrossRef]
21. Yang, B.; Lei, Y.; Jia, F.; Xing, S. An intelligent fault diagnosis approach based on transfer learning from laboratory bearings to locomotive bearings. *Mech. Syst. Signal Process.* **2019**, *122*, 692–706. [CrossRef]
22. Qian, W.; Li, S.; Yi, P.; Zhang, K. A novel transfer learning method for robust fault diagnosis of rotating machines under variable working conditions. *Measurement* **2019**, *138*, 514–525. [CrossRef]
23. Yang, X.; Chi, F.; Shao, S.; Zhang, Q. Bearing Fault Diagnosis under Variable Working Conditions Based on Deep Residual Shrinkage Networks and Transfer Learning. *J. Sens.* **2021**, *2021*, 5714240. [CrossRef]
24. Xiao, D.; Huang, Y.; Zhao, L.; Qin, C.; Shi, H.; Liu, C. Domain Adaptive Motor Fault Diagnosis Using Deep Transfer Learning. *IEEE Access* **2019**, *7*, 80937–80949. [CrossRef]
25. Zhu, Z.; Wang, L.; Peng, G.; Li, S. WDA: An improved wasserstein distance-based transfer learning fault diagnosis method. *Sensors* **2021**, *21*, 4394. [CrossRef] [PubMed]
26. Li, F.; Guo, W.; Deng, X.; Wang, J.; Ge, L.; Guan, X. A Hybrid Shuffled Frog Leaping Algorithm and Its Performance Assessment in Multi-Dimensional Symmetric Function. *Symmetry* **2022**, *14*, 131. [CrossRef]
27. Yan, B.; Han, G. Effective Feature Extraction via Stacked Sparse Autoencoder to Improve Intrusion Detection System. *IEEE Access* **2018**, *6*, 41238–41248. [CrossRef]
28. Sun, W.; Shao, S.; Zhao, R.; Yan, R.; Zhang, X.; Chen, X. A sparse auto-encoder-based deep neural network approach for induction motor faults classification. *Measurement* **2016**, *89*, 171–178. [CrossRef]
29. Weiss, K.; Khoshgoftaar, T.M.; Wang, D.D. A survey of transfer learning. *J. Big Data* **2016**, *3*, 1345–1459. [CrossRef]

30. Tan, C.; Sun, F.; Kong, T.; Zhang, W.; Yang, C.; Liu, C. A Survey on Deep Transfer Learning. In *Lecture Notes in Computer Science*; LNCS; Springer: Berlin/Heidelberg, Germany, 2018; Volume 11141, pp. 270–279.
31. Cheng, C.; Zhou, B.; Ma, G.; Wu, D.; Yuan, Y. Wasserstein distance based deep adversarial transfer learning for intelligent fault diagnosis with unlabeled or insufficient labeled data. *Neurocomputing* **2020**, *409*, 35–45. [CrossRef]
32. Tong, Z.; Li, W.; Zhang, B.; Jiang, F.; Zhou, G. Bearing Fault Diagnosis under Variable Working Conditions Based on Domain Adaptation Using Feature Transfer Learning. *IEEE Access* **2018**, *6*, 76187–76197. [CrossRef]
33. Li, X.; Zhang, W.; Ding, Q.; Sun, J.-Q. Multi-Layer domain adaptation method for rolling bearing fault diagnosis. *Signal Process.* **2019**, *157*, 180–197. [CrossRef]
34. Zhao, K.; Jiang, H.; Wang, K.; Pei, Z. Joint distribution adaptation network with adversarial learning for rolling bearing fault diagnosis. *Knowl. Based Syst.* **2021**, *222*, 106974. [CrossRef]
35. Cheng, Y.; Lin, M.; Wu, J.; Zhu, H.; Shao, X. Intelligent fault diagnosis of rotating machinery based on continuous wavelet transform-local binary convolutional neural network. *Knowl. Based Syst.* **2021**, *216*, 106796. [CrossRef]
36. Zhang, X.; Liu, Z.; Wang, J.; Wang, J. Time–frequency analysis for bearing fault diagnosis using multiple Q-factor Gabor wavelets. *ISA Trans.* **2019**, *87*, 225–234. [CrossRef] [PubMed]
37. Kumar, A.; Gandhi, C.; Zhou, Y.; Tang, H.; Xiang, J. Fault diagnosis of rolling element bearing based on symmetric cross entropy of neutrosophic sets. *Measurement* **2020**, *152*, 107318. [CrossRef]
38. Kumar, A.; Gandhi, C.P.; Zhou, Y.; Kumar, R.; Xiang, J. Variational mode decomposition based symmetric single valued neutrosophic cross entropy measure for the identification of bearing defects in a centrifugal pump. *Appl. Acoust.* **2020**, *165*, 107294. [CrossRef]
39. Fu, W.; Tan, J.; Zhang, X.; Chen, T.; Wang, K. Blind Parameter Identification of MAR Model and Mutation Hybrid GWO-SCA Optimized SVM for Fault Diagnosis of Rotating Machinery. *Complexity* **2019**, *2019*, 3264969. [CrossRef]
40. Dong, Z.; Zheng, J.; Huang, S.; Pan, H.; Liu, Q. Time-shift multi-scaleweighted permutation entropy and GWO-SVM based fault diagnosis approach for rolling bearing. *Entropy* **2019**, *21*, 621. [CrossRef]
41. Wang, H.; Xu, J.; Yan, R.; Sun, C.; Chen, X. Intelligent bearing fault diagnosis using multi-head attention-based CNN. *Procedia Manuf.* **2020**, *49*, 112–118. [CrossRef]
42. Huang, D.; Li, S.; Qin, N.; Zhang, Y. Fault Diagnosis of High-Speed Train Bogie Based on the Improved-CEEMDAN and 1-D CNN Algorithms. *IEEE Trans. Instrum. Meas.* **2021**, *70*, 20317712. [CrossRef]
43. Wang, Z.; Liu, Q.; Chen, H.; Chu, X. A deformable CNN-DLSTM based transfer learning method for fault diagnosis of rolling bearing under multiple working conditions. *Int. J. Prod. Res.* **2021**, *59*, 4811–4825. [CrossRef]
44. Song, X.; Cong, Y.; Song, Y.; Chen, Y.; Liang, P. A bearing fault diagnosis model based on CNN with wide convolution kernels. *J. Ambient Intell. Humaniz. Comput.* **2021**, *13*, 4041–4056. [CrossRef]
45. Yang, B.; Lei, Y.; Jia, F.; Li, N.; Du, Z. A Polynomial Kernel Induced Distance Metric to Improve Deep Transfer Learning for Fault Diagnosis of Machines. *IEEE Trans. Ind. Electron.* **2020**, *67*, 9747–9757. [CrossRef]
46. Lu, W.; Liang, B.; Cheng, Y.; Meng, D.; Yang, J.; Zhang, T. Deep Model Based Domain Adaptation for Fault Diagnosis. *IEEE Trans. Ind. Electron.* **2017**, *64*, 2296–2305. [CrossRef]
47. He, W.; He, Y.; Li, B.; Zhang, C. Analog circuit fault diagnosis via joint cross-wavelet singular entropy and parametric t-SNE. *Entropy* **2018**, *20*, 604. [CrossRef]
48. Ren, L.; Lv, W.; Jiang, S.; Xiao, Y. Fault Diagnosis Using a Joint Model Based on Sparse Representation and SVM. *IEEE Trans. Instrum. Meas.* **2016**, *65*, 2313–2320. [CrossRef]
49. Lu, N.; Xiao, H.; Sun, Y.; Han, M.; Wang, Y. A new method for intelligent fault diagnosis of machines based on unsupervised domain adaptation. *Neurocomputing* **2021**, *427*, 96–109. [CrossRef]
50. Li, Y.; Song, Y.; Jia, L.; Gao, S.; Li, Q.; Qiu, M. Intelligent Fault Diagnosis by Fusing Domain Adversarial Training and Maximum Mean Discrepancy via Ensemble Learning. *EEE Trans. Ind. Inform.* **2021**, *17*, 2833–2841. [CrossRef]

Disclaimer/Publisher's Note: The statements, opinions and data contained in all publications are solely those of the individual author(s) and contributor(s) and not of MDPI and/or the editor(s). MDPI and/or the editor(s) disclaim responsibility for any injury to people or property resulting from any ideas, methods, instructions or products referred to in the content.

Review

Is Industry 5.0 a Human-Centred Approach? A Systematic Review

Joel Alves [1,2], Tânia M. Lima [1,2] and Pedro D. Gaspar [1,2,*]

1. Electromechanical Engineering Department, University of Beira Interior, Calçada Fonte do Lameiro, 6201-001 Covilha, Portugal
2. C-MAST—Center for Mechanical and Aerospace Science and Technologies, Calçada Fonte do Lameiro, 6201-001 Covilha, Portugal
* Correspondence: dinis@ubi.pt

Abstract: Industry 5.0 presents itself as a strategy that puts the human factor at the centre of production, where the well-being of the worker is prioritized, as well as more sustainable and resilient production systems. For human centricity, it is necessary to empower human beings and, respectively, industrial operators, to improve their individual skills and competences in collaboration or cooperation with digital technologies. This research's main purpose and distinguishing point are to determine whether Industry 5.0 is truly human-oriented and how human centricity can be created with Industry 5.0 technologies. For that, this systematic literature review article analyses and clarifies the concepts and ideologies of Industry 5.0 and its respective technologies (Artificial Intelligence, Robotics, Human-robot collaboration, Digitalization), as well as the strategies of human centricity, with the aim of achieving sustainable and resilient systems, especially for the worker.

Keywords: Industry 5.0; human-centricity; human-centred; I5.0 technologies; artificial intelligence; robotics; cyber-physical systems; digitalization

Citation: Alves, J.; Lima, T.M.; Gaspar, P.D. Is Industry 5.0 a Human-Centred Approach? A Systematic Review. *Processes* 2023, *11*, 193. https://doi.org/10.3390/pr11010193

Academic Editor: Xiong Luo

Received: 13 December 2022
Revised: 3 January 2023
Accepted: 4 January 2023
Published: 7 January 2023

Copyright: © 2023 by the authors. Licensee MDPI, Basel, Switzerland. This article is an open access article distributed under the terms and conditions of the Creative Commons Attribution (CC BY) license (https://creativecommons.org/licenses/by/4.0/).

1. Introduction

The 4th industrial revolution and the concept of Industry 4.0 presented itself as a fourth technological wave, with an overwhelming impact on digital systems [1]. Industry 4.0 promotes high production efficiency and quality levels, and it is oriented toward innovation and industrial technology development [1,2]. Furthermore, Industry 4.0 has a techno-economic vision, i.e., for economic development through technological advances, and, therefore, at the industrial level, innovative technologies are used to improve value chains and cope with changing economic transformations [1]. However, although Industry 4.0 has not been fully implemented and integrated globally, companies and industries are faced with the arrival of the 5th Industrial Revolution, which will involve autonomous manufacturing, but with human intelligence [3,4]. When industries started their involvement and adaptation to Industry 4.0, the 5th Industrial Revolution and the concept and ideology of Industry 5.0 emerged [3]. It can thus be said that Industry 5.0 is a prolongation and chronological extension of Industry 4.0 [1]. Industry 4.0 has limitations with regard to industrial sustainability and workers' well-being, as it focuses on the efficiency and flexibility of production through digitalization and technologies [2,3].

Industry 5.0 aims to address the human challenges of Industry 4.0 as a human-centric solution [2], placing the worker's well-being at the centre of the production process [3]. The ideology of Industry 5.0 emerged in 2020, after discussions and sharing of ideas in two virtual workshops, and officially in January 2021, with its formal publication in the European Commission (EC) document [3,5]. The focus of the EC document is to foster transformation and drive change in companies and industries to make them more sustainable and human-centric [5,6]. Industry 5.0 is in parallel with European societal goals, i.e., in addition to job creation and resilient development, industrial sustainability needs to be ensured by respecting the limits of our planet and the well-being of industrial workers [7].

Thus, while Industry 4.0 is an approach centred on technological digitalization, Industry 5.0 is an approach centred on humans through three core pillars: resilience, sustainability, and human centricity [8]. Industry 5.0 intends to capture the value of innovative digital technologies [8] and their human-machine interaction. Currently, the operator works alongside and with the assistance of machines in smart industrial environments [6]. The EC, with the introduction of Industry 5.0 within industry, aims to make workplaces more inclusive, as well as more resilient and sustainable ways of working [8].

In this article, a systematic review was conducted to clarify and assess the concept, ideology, and proposals of Industry 5.0. It is also intended to analyse the main concerns and challenges of human-centricity in future industrial environments and how Industry 5.0 technologies can help and boost the operator of the future. Hence, the study started with data analysis and relevant information on the theme. This information is divided into three lines of investigation: the first line of research is Industry 5.0 definition, ideas, and concepts; the second line of research is the analysis of the Technologies of Industry 5.0; and, finally, the third line of research focuses on Human Centricity. The discussion is also performed in stages: Industry 5.0 from an industrial perspective and in society; the centralization of the human being with Industry 5.0 technologies; the Industry 5.0 operator; and, finally, some challenges, limitations, and the future research agenda are raised. Thus, it is possible to determine whether Industry 5.0 is truly human-oriented and how human centricity can be created with Industry 5.0 technologies.

2. Materials and Methods

As Industry 5.0 and Human-centricity are hot and rising topics of the present times, in this work, a Systematic Literature Review (SLR) was conducted to collect, verify, analyse, and detail the available scientific data on the ideals, constructs, challenges, and limitations of Industry 5.0 as a strategy that places the human being at the centre of productive processes and systems. Thus, this SLR aims to establish a literature review process that allows the identification and interpretation of recent literature on the ideologies and strategies of Industry 5.0, with a focus directed to the centralization of the human being and especially to the operator in the industries. To perform this systematic review article, a four-phase flow diagram and the guidelines for Systematic Review and Meta-Analysis Statement, commonly known as PRISMA, were applied [9,10].

2.1. Focus Questions

Industry 4.0 turned out to be more technology oriented than human being oriented, neglecting the human factor in productive systems. Therefore, Industry 5.0 emerges as a complement and transitional ideology from a technological Industry 4.0 to an industry centred on the human being, where the worker's well-being is prioritized, but maintaining productive performance. The future perspectives for human-centricity are to empower humans and human operators by enhancing their individual capabilities and skills, i.e., human factors, and to achieve the balance and fullness of human-machine collaboration, i.e., to improve human-robot interaction in dynamic and complex industrial systems. Therefore, it is important to study and analyse the human-centricity strategies, introducing and evaluating the concepts and ideologies of Industry 5.0, Human Factors, and Industry 5.0 Technologies to achieve a sustainable and resilient system, especially for the worker, which leads to the research questions:

(1) Is Industry 5.0 truly human-centric oriented?
(2) How can we create human-centricity with Industry 5.0 technologies?

2.2. Information Sources and Data Collection Process

For this SLR article, the initial data collection and screening were processed in November 2022, and three electronic databases were used for the bibliographic research, namely,

Science Direct, Scopus, and Web of Science. For the database search, pre-determined keywords were used that are related to the principal focus of the study: Industry 5.0 and Human-centricity. Furthermore, Boolean operators were used to carry out this SLR. As previously stated, being a "fresh research" theme, the keywords were chosen to be comprehensive research and not to condition or restrict the study. Hence, potentially relevant data and information for the investigation would not be left out. Thus, the established search equation was ((("Industry 5.0") AND (("Human-centric") OR ("Human-centered") OR ("Human-centred"))), and it was used in the advanced search of Science Direct and Web of Science. After that, the syntax was adapted for the Scopus database: TITLE-ABS-KEY ((("Industry 5.0") AND (("Human-centric") OR ("Human-centered") OR ("Human-centred") OR ("Human centered"))). The language search was conducted in English and without any time restriction.

2.3. Eligibility Criteria

In this review, we analysed studies that present data about the ideologies of Industry 5.0 and strategies for human-centricity, especially for the factories of the future. The authors first conducted the preliminary selection and exclusion based on paper titles and abstracts. The screening process was performed by three authors. The following inclusion/exclusion criteria were employed for eligibility: only studies with full text available, published in English, including research articles, review articles, and conference papers that present and explore at least one of the two focus subjects of the study: Industry 5.0 and Human-centricity. In addition to these inclusion factors, others were added, such as sustainability, resilience, and technologies, when associated with Industry 5.0 and Human-centricity. Articles with an exclusive focus on technological advancement without human-centricity or articles that only suggested Industry 5.0 as a future perspective were excluded.

2.4. Principle Findings

This systematic literature search identified a total of 227 articles: 126 from Science Direct, 60 from Scopus, and 40 from Web of Science. Of these articles, 18 were not available for full-text reading and 52 were duplicates or triplicates, and because of that, they were excluded. Thus, a total of 157 articles remained after the exclusion of repeated articles. In the next phase, exclusion was performed by reading the titles and abstracts of the articles, excluding 85 and leaving only 72 articles. The next was to analyse the eligibility of these 72 articles by full-text reading, where 15 were excluded for not meeting the purpose of the current study. The remaining 57 articles were analysed and included in this systematic literature review (see Figure 1).

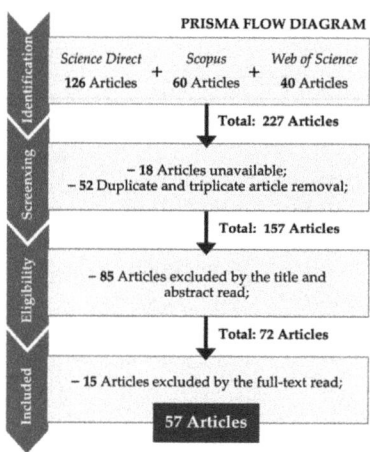

Figure 1. PRISMA flow diagram displaying the results of the systematic research.

The first analysis performed in this review article focused on the publication dates, location, and article type of the articles eligible and included in the study. Although no time restriction was applied in the search, the publication dates of the articles are very recent (from 2019 to 2023), which demonstrates the growing research on the concepts of Industry 5.0 and Human-centricity; specifically, there were a high number of publications in the year 2022 (Figure 2). The second analysis was to check the type of articles that were being produced and published on this recent theme. Of the 57 articles selected to be included in this review study, the majority are research articles, i.e., 36 articles, followed by 14 conference papers. In this short period of time, six reviews on different topics and aspects of Industry 5.0 have already been conducted (Figure 3).

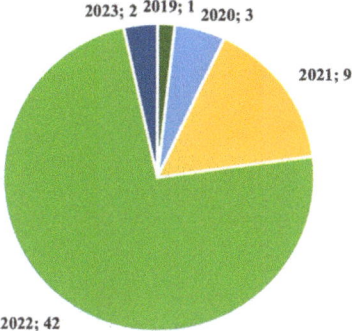

Figure 2. Number of articles published by year (Year; Number of publications).

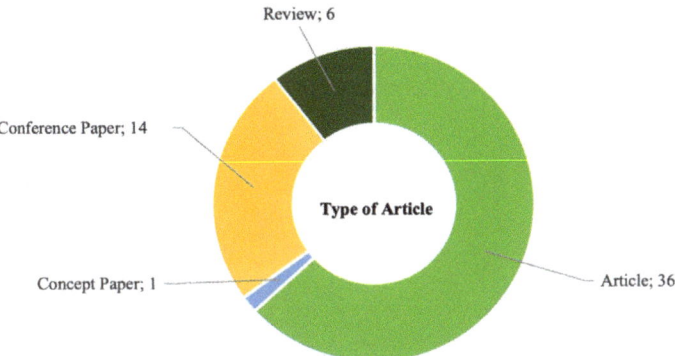

Figure 3. Type of articles.

Another feature evaluated was the occurrence of publications by location, as represented in Figure 4. To this end, the location of the first author or the respective affiliation was chosen for all articles included in the review to follow a homogeneous process. The countries with the highest number of published articles were Italy and Germany, followed by China, Sweden, and New Zealand. These are countries with a high degree of industrial development and, therefore, with a high potential for research and innovation.

In addition to these initial analyses and evaluations, the main keywords were verified, as well as their main relationships and interconnections. To this end, software named VOSviewer 1.6.17 was used to generate maps from the database information. VOSviewer is a free and easy-to-use program that is designed to construct and visualize bibliometric maps. This software can be applied in two ways: (1) to construct author or journal maps based on co-citation data or (2) to construct keyword maps based on co-occurrence data. VOSviewer allows bibliometric maps to be examined in detail through various functionalities, such as zooming, scrolling, and searching [11]. In the case of this review article, a VOSviewer Map was created through the occurrence of the keywords. The software analysed the articles included and eligible for the study and created a map with the keywords that have a higher occurrence (Figure 5).

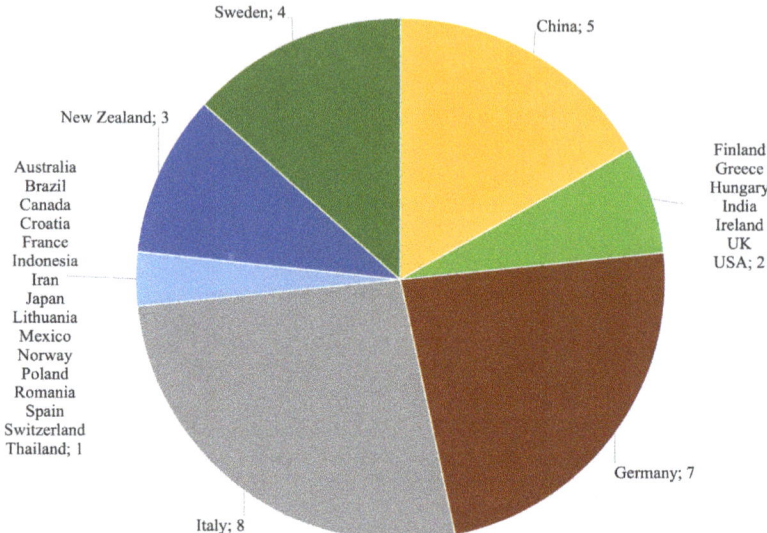

Figure 4. Graphic representation of the number of articles published by location (Country; Number of publications).

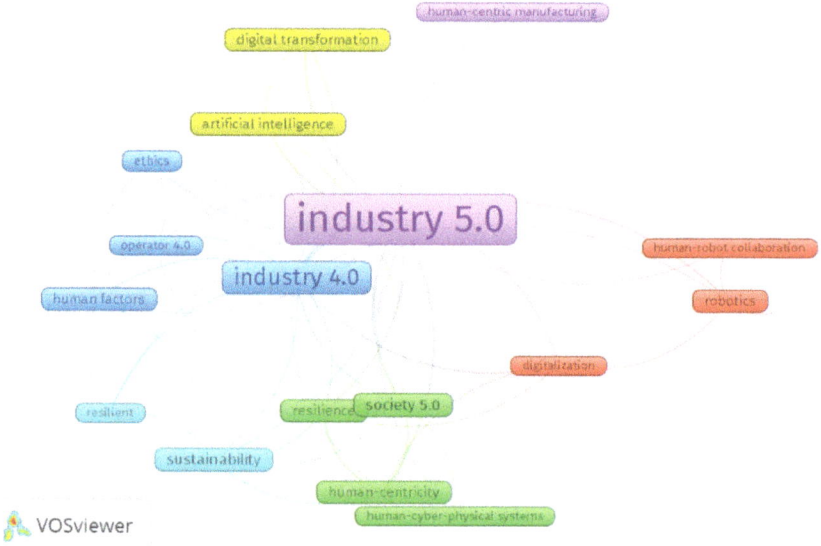

Figure 5. VOSviewer map of the keywords with high occurrence.

The keywords that had high occurrence were Industry 5.0, Industry 4.0, Robotics, Sustainability, Resilience, Digital Transformation, and Human-centricity, which are interconnected and linked to another, such as human-centric manufacturing, human-robot collaboration, ethics, human-cyber-physical systems, society 5.0, human factors, resilient, among others. They are organized by six clusters, as represented in Figure 5 through different colours: Industry 5.0 as purple, Industry 4.0 as blue, Robotics as red, Digital transformation as yellow, Sustainability as turquoise, and, finally, Human-centricity as green. To guide the article toward data analysis and relevant information to answer the research questions, the results and discussion of the theme will be divided into three lines of investigation, grouping some of these clusters. The first line of research will be Industry 5.0 (including Industry 4.0, Human Factors, Resilient, and Sustainability); the second line of research will analyse the Technologies of Industry 5.0 (incorporating Digital transformation, Artificial Intelligence, Robotics, Human-robot collaboration, Digitalization); and, finally, the third line of research will focus on Human Centricity (including Resilience, Society 5.0, Human-centric manufacturing).

3. Review of Extracted Research

3.1. Industry 5.0—Concept, Ideology, and Proposals

The concept of Industry 5.0 was coined by the European Commission for the need to integrate European priorities with respect to social and environmental issues and drive companies and industries to evolve and become more sustainable, resilient, and human-centric [3,5]. Despite this concept, some research publications reveal that the concept of Industry 5.0 had been introduced by Michael Rada in social media in 2015, subsequently investigated by many researchers, and, finally, legitimized by the EC in 2021, so that the 2030 goals for the European Union could be achieved [12–14]. Industry 5.0 is an ideology of future industrial evolution aimed at using the creativity of human beings operating in combination with efficient, intelligent, and accurate systems [15]. These changes at the industrial level and in relation to technological innovations require rethinking the role of industries and their positioning and role in society [3].

With the recent COVID-19 pandemic crisis, it was possible to highlight the vulnerability of companies and industries to economic, technological, and social adversities. It was then necessary to reconsider the existing working approaches and methodologies, improving industries in terms of resistance and resilience, as well as sustainability and human factor centricity [16,17]. Furthermore, the turning point and starting point for the transition from Industry 4.0 to 5.0 focuses on changing the relationship between humans and intelligent systems [18]. While Industry 4.0 was only about automating processes with smart digital technologies with the aim of improving efficiency and optimizing industrial processes, neglecting the human factor, Industry 5.0 focuses on the synergy and pairing of humans and machines, where human desire and intention will prevail [19].

However, the concept of Industry 5.0 is evolving, and, therefore, there are diverse definitions elaborated by various industry practitioners and researchers [15]. The most consensual definition among researchers meets the one defined by the EC, whose industrial future is dependent on the consideration and weighting of human-centred, sustainable, and resilient production systems [18].

Focusing on sustainability, Industry 5.0 may be the first to be human-driven, which is based on the principle of industrial recycling, i.e., the 6R's policy: Recognize, Reconsider, Realize, Reduce, Reuse, and Recycle, so that it is possible to prevent waste and, at the same time, create/produce customized products with high quality [15]. However, there is a controversy associated with the ideology of Industry 5.0, i.e., how this strategy might contribute to sustainable development [20]. On the contrary, Industry 5.0 can be associated with the goal of bringing humans back into factories, where human and machines are paired and work in full collaboration in order to increase the efficiency of the production process through human cognitive capabilities (creativity and knowledge) and interconnecting them with the workflows of intelligent systems [15,18,19]. It is a similar perspective, in which professionals in industries and companies, information technicians, and researchers are required to focus and concentrate on human factors in the implementation of new technological systems of Industry 5.0 [15,18].

On the technological side, Industry 5.0 can be considered the era of the socially smart factory, or "Social Smart Industry", whose social business networks converge with people for seamless communication, namely, cyber-physical production systems interconnected with the human factor synergistically [15,18,21]. Additionally, Industry 5.0 is a human-centric solution, with humans and technologies, such as collaborative robots, working together hand in hand. Machines will be used for work-intensive or repetitive tasks, while humans will oversee personalization and critical thinking [15]. Another concept defines Industry 5.0 as a symmetric innovation that will be used for the next generation of global governance, whose goal is to create safe outputs for production by segregating automation systems [15].

Industry 5.0 involves again humans in global industrial environments and intends to empower them through the incorporation of innovative technologies. The main idea of this strategy is the convergence of several aspects of human centrality, systems resilience, and sustainability, through industrial harmonization between machines and humans [18]. However, the ideologies and concepts of Industry 5.0 are open, evolving, and expansive, but always based on the three fundamental pillars described above. Thus, the goal of Industry 5.0 is to place the well-being of workers at the centre of production processes, maintaining a balance between humans and machine systems, and aggregating the ideals of resilience and sustainable development at ecological, economic, and social levels.

3.2. Industry 5.0 Technologies

Industry 4.0 has led to rapid technological advances and high industrial performance [22]. In parallel, the concept of Industry 5.0 has flourished, with the intention to integrate physical and virtual spaces through human-centricity with technology, namely, the application of Internet of Things (IoT), robots, and augmented reality to achieve a smart industry and society of digital innovation [23]. Interactivity between humans and machines is considered one of the key differences between Industry 4.0 and 5.0, as when this interaction increases, there is an empowerment of operators' expression in how products and services are personalized, creating synergistic relationships between technological and social systems [22,23].

Industry 5.0 requires human beings to undergo a socio-technical evolution, i.e., a paradigm shift in the role of the operator as the central focus of manufacturing and production systems through intelligent strategies and approaches underpinned by advanced information and communication technologies [22]. Industry 5.0 ideology can be applied to cyber-physical production systems (CPPS), from their conceptualization, learning, and integration [24], and including a human perspective [25], to data interoperability and information sharing [26] using 5G and 6G networks [27]; automatic identification and traceability (Auto-ID) systems [28]; Artificial Intelligence (AI)-based systems for work assistance, organization, and supervision [29]; industrial simulation [30]; user application of Augmented Reality systems [31,32]; and also collaborative robots or cobots to achieve intelligent manufacturing systems [33,34].

The introduction of robotics in production systems can increase productivity, but also increase the well-being of workers, as well as improve the health and safety conditions of workplaces [35,36]. Robots and their human-robot collaborative environments leverage individual and technological capabilities together, making it possible to overcome limitations in the execution of awkward, repetitive, and potentially harmful tasks and operations, improving the workplace, as well as the repeatability and reliability of processes [35]. Thus, collaborative robots support and reduce low-value-added operations for operators, while workers' potential is harnessed for advanced operations and tasks that require greater sensitivity, mental processes, rapid self-adaptation [22,35], customization, and critical thinking [31]. In scenarios of cooperative or collaborative sharing of workspaces between humans and robots, it is necessary to assess human factors before, during, and after the whole human-robot interaction, so that analysis and evaluation of working conditions can be done [31].

A particularity of the use of robots is the development of the Digital Twin (DT), which represents a high-fidelity, virtual, physical entity with real-time communication [30,37]. These DT systems are technological advances identified for Industry 5.0 that, together with simulation systems, allow production optimization and, at the same time, perform operational safety tests [38]. Moreover, although DTs are technological models focused on connectivity and modelling of production systems [37], they can be used to combat educational inequality by providing learning and training through tele-operability [39], and they can be included in educational systems [38]. Interactive productive systems with robots can also be used to create training and learning environments [40].

With the introduction of Industry 5.0 and human-centric production systems, human-robot interactions raise questions regarding safety [41] and ethical issues [29]. Safety requirements are higher, and, therefore, safety strategies need to be adopted to achieve higher degrees of reliability and production flexibility through dynamic and synergistic measures (from both human and robotic perspectives) [41]. Ethical issues concern the use of autonomous intelligent systems, such as robots and artificial intelligence, and should have been taken into consideration from the very beginning of the design processes of new digital production systems [29,42].

However, companies and industries must put human beings at the centre of production processes by developing and applying reliable technologies that provide better working environments and improved well-being for workers [43]. Thus, it is important to retain and apply the organizational memory of past experiences and operators so that successful experiences can be reused [44], making it essential to understand the experience and knowledge of operators during work operations [43].

For companies and industries to achieve the ideologies and benefits of Industry 5.0, they would need to draw on and make use of Industry 4.0 digital technologies, such as cyber-physical systems; big data technologies; and human-machine interaction technologies, such as artificial intelligence, digital twins, and collaborative robots [28]. The European Commission has identified six guidelines to be considered as Industry 5.0 technologies: individualized human-machine interaction, intelligent bio-inspired technologies, simulation and digital twins, data transmission, storage and analysis technologies, artificial intelligence, and technologies for ecological autonomy [28].

3.3. Human-Centricity in Future Industrial Environments

Prior to digitalization and automation, human beings were responsible for ensuring manual jobs, including repetitive and physically demanding operations. However, with the adoption of digital technologies, humans were considered a weak point within the industry, as they were prone to errors and defects; therefore, they were gradually replaced by technology [45]. In contrast, the human factor is a central resource in most companies and industries; hence, the shift to a human-centred strategy, where human needs and interests are placed at the centre of production processes [3]. It evolves from a technology-centred approach to a human-centred approach, where human beings will use the power and precision of technology as a resource that can be adaptable to the needs and diversity of industrial workers. Thus, the flexibility and creativity of operators can be preserved and empower them to overcome the adversities and limitations imposed by technology [3,45].

Industry focused on worker well-being is prioritized and ensured by developing technologies that create rewarding and motivating work environments that match users' needs [46], but mainly industries with safe and inclusive work environments that focus on workers' physical and mental health, well-being, autonomy, privacy, and dignity [3].

Other strategies to improve operator well-being include providing a diversity of work schedule times; job rotation; considering the demands of getting the job done and the needs and qualifications of operators; and ergonomic workplace exposure [43]. On the contrary, human-centeredness can be accomplished by involving all production system stakeholders in the processes of conception, design, and innovation [46,47]; in system planning and control processes [48]; and in product and process design [49]. The application of lean management tools to put humans at the centre of production processes has also been studied [50], such as the application of human centricity in the SMED tool (H-SMED) [51].

In the future, industrial workers need to shift from technological to socio-technological productive systems and, consequently, continue to acquire, upgrade, and retrain their knowledge, skills, and qualifications to create better career opportunities, balance work and personal life, and enhance job development and polarization [3,52]. In parallel with sustainable, resilient, and human-centred transformation, the operators of the future need to be prepared and trained, so that they can take an active role in production systems and promote the success of the industrial digital transformation [53]. Industry 5.0 will have a major impact on the collaboration between humans and smart technologies, as well as on the technological and social management of future production systems; therefore, continuous training is needed to ensure future skilled labour through the development of multifaceted human skills and digital education [54].

4. Discussion

4.1. Industry 5.0—Industrial Perspective and in Society

To boost the development of individual well-being and sustainable economic growth, Industry 5.0 has emerged with the aim of making production human-centric, putting the well-being of the worker at the centre of industrial smart production processes [55,56]. The fifth industrial revolution associated with Industry 5.0 determines the joint work between operators and machines to increase the productivity and efficiency of companies and industries [57]. Operationalizing and putting into practice Industry 5.0 is a future ideology, as industries are still in the implementation phase of Industry 4.0. However, it can be said that the two will coexist, that is, the technological development of Industry 4.0 will be made with the ideologies of I5.0 regarding human centering.

Industry 5.0 is also characterized by high precision and low-cost mass customization [34], introducing sustainable and resilient thinking in a digital transformation with human-centricity and bio-economic ideals for a future society, Society 5.0 [58]. Society and Industry 5.0 require companies and industries capable of establishing active relationships between humans and digital technologies that target workers, becoming socially automated [59]. There are numerous definitions and concepts for Industry 5.0, and their interpretation can distinguish key points that differentiate them. Most of them focus on the socio-technological era, while there are others that focus only on industrial transformation [18].

4.2. Human Centricity with Industry 5.0 Technologies

Human-centred production systems are a recent and controversial topic in need of clarification and discussion. However, the concept draws on ongoing human-focused research, such as Ergonomics, Operator 4.0, and Human-Robot Collaboration [56]. Industrial production and manufacturing will move towards Industry 5.0, which will be supported by collaborative robots [60], artificial intelligence, and cognitive computing technologies [57]. Human-Robot Interaction is a technological enabler for the transfer from digital system-centric to operator-centric production, in a digital production environment that considers human and robotic characteristics equally [36]. For the interaction to be beneficial and provide advantages for production systems, it is necessary to optimize the use of available resources, both humans and robots [36]. Another advantage of using these collaborative systems is the reduction of stressful and repetitive operations that can expose the worker to potential health and safety risks, without the need to invest in other expensive and sophisticated digital equipment [35]. Augmented Reality can be used to enhance human and robot cognitive capabilities by integrating humans into production systems in real time and dynamically [41]. Moreover, the evaluation of the impact of Human-Robot Interaction is difficult to elaborate and restrictive because classical tools are based on kinematic and static aspects, omitting relevant information. Therefore, alternatives for Human-Robot Interaction assessment have been currently studied and used through computational and sensor systems that allow for a more complex, advanced, and dynamic analysis [31].

To achieve social, environmental, and economic sustainability and resilience in companies and industries, engineering education will have to be reviewed and redesigned to train future engineers with technological, data, and knowledge fluency to make industries more resilient, sustainable, and human-centric in the era of Industry 5.0 [61]. The future workforce should have the experience and knowledge to distinguish and understand the different production systems to make the most appropriate decisions among the different ways of working: only human effort, only technological effort, or a collaboration between the two. Thus, engineering education should focus on human-technology interaction, especially on the different forms of communication and collaboration with future cyber-physical systems [61]. In addition, human-assisted learning strategies can be applied to monitor and control automated additive manufacturing systems, as well as manufacturing error detection systems [62,63].

4.3. Operator of Industry 5.0

The ideology of Industry 4.0 by automated and highly efficient production systems has put workers' welfare in the background. As a consequence, it can be said that in Industry 4.0, the human factor is neglected. In contrast, the Industry 5.0 operator should strategically use technology to improve the work environment's quality. Thus, this idea meets the centrality of the human being in production processes, where technology supports the human being. Hence, a synergistic effect is achieved regarding the interaction of humans and robots, where the human factor can collaborate, integrate, and deal with new digital technologies [45]. In parallel with the introduction of Industry 5.0, the concept of the Operator 5.0 has also emerged, representing the Operator 4.0 of the future, that is, more resilient against the adversities encountered in digital industrial environments, the Resilient Operator 5.0 [64]. The Operator 5.0 can be divided according to its purpose, i.e., a self-resilient operator that has evolved in the face of its inherent weaknesses and adversities, and an operator focused on system resilience, i.e., resilient human-machine systems [15]. However, it is essential to understand the complexity of future industrial production systems that are highly volatile and imply more complex and multi-faceted decision making for the worker. Therefore, the operators of the future must be empowered with human-centric technology and adequate education to be able to remain in control of production and manufacturing systems [53]. As such, it becomes important to empower workers of different ages and with different biographies, as they are the focus of human workforce sustainability [53], especially employed ageing workers who are associated with high-intensity work [65].

4.4. Challenges, Limitations, and Future Agenda

In relation to the research process, the limitations of this study are related to the limited number of real industrial cases of application of concepts and ideologies of Industry 5.0. Moreover, given the actuality, urgency, and emergency of the human centricity theme, it would be important not to restrict the scientific data of the research exclusively to English. Thus, as future research perspectives, it would be crucial to use publications in different languages to provide new and valuable insights in this study. On the contrary, a challenge for the future will be to conduct studies in laboratory settings to accelerate the research process. However, it should be noted that these experiments may lead to results that are out of touch with reality.

In moving towards human-centric production and manufacturing, there are several challenges, limitations, and opportunities from social, technological, and ethical perspectives. Regarding the ethical concerns, already in Industry 4.0, ethical issues were arising. However, just as Industry 5.0 follows on from and co-exists in parallel with Industry 4.0, ethical problems also overlap. In this case, of even greater relevance due to human centralization, the human being is placed in a position where ethical issues are more pertinent. In industrial and automated environments with digital technologies, ethical, health, and safety issues are very important, and, because of that, a hot topic for future studies exists.

Shifting from a strategy of high industrial performance (Industry 4.0) to a strategy of human centricity (Industry 5.0), there will have to be a balanced equilibrium between performance, technologies (digitalization), and human well-being. Despite human limitations, there is a window of opportunity for improvement and development, namely, leveraging human-machine interactions and developing human skills and capabilities for this new human-digital era. One of the challenges centres on acceptance and trust in technology, as for human-centric work environments, the technologies to be used need to be reliable, intelligent, and friendly to work with, while always maintaining privacy boundaries. Robot-Human Interaction becomes a limitation and a challenge for the future, as there is a need for collaborative and cooperative technologies that help the operator and do not replace him, and that is customizable according to each operator's individual characteristics and skills. In addition, these systems need to be transparent, i.e., share all the information and data they use for their functioning in performing tasks and operations and their decision making.

On the contrary, there are opportunities that can be achieved when overcoming some challenges imposed by the era of human centricity, such as changes in work dynamics, both at the team level and interaction with technologies, and the capacity and acceptance for lifelong learning, for a constant and evolutionary adaptation of human beings to emerging technological advances. Another major limitation of conducting studies in industrial environments is the difficulty of openness and acceptance of operators and top management to new ideas and technologies.

As a future research agenda, it is necessary to act and create real and achievable strategies and methodologies to put the human factor at the centre of production, without neglecting the human factor and implementing the ideologies of Industry 5.0. It is perhaps too early to speak of Industry 6.0 when Industry 5.0 is in its early stages of development. It is important to note that one of the pillars of Industry 5.0, according to the European Commission, is sustainability, which encompasses the environmental/ecological aspects regarding the limits of our planet. However, if Industry 5.0 is human-oriented, will Industry 6.0 be devoted to the environmental-oriented? For now, the goal of Industry 5.0 is to place the well-being of workers at the centre of industries and companies, maintaining a balance between human-machine systems and developing a resilient and sustainable work environment at ecological, economic, and social levels. Figure 6 shows our vision of a schematic representation of how the human factor, i.e., Operator 5.0, is placed in the control of production systems, where the well-being of the workers is a high priority. Furthermore, the centralization of the human being through the aid of digital and robotic technologies in sustainable and resilient smart factories in the age of Industry 5.0 is represented.

Figure 6. Schematic representation of the human-centricity at the control of smart factories in the era of Industry 5.0.

5. Conclusions

Industry 5.0 follows Industry 4.0 with the ideology of placing the human being at the centre of industrial production processes. Thus, the transformation will occur from production systems oriented towards technological advance and high productivity to production systems oriented towards the human being and high customization. As such, the human being is no longer commanded by technology and becomes its controller, using it to his advantage. However, the concept of Industry 5.0 is not yet fully accepted by companies and industries, but it is driven by researchers because, nowadays, the industrial reality faces challenges still inherent to Industry 4.0 and the digitalization era. Thus, up to this point, the idea of the concept of Industry 5.0 is the centralization of humans in production systems, but the studies carried out focus a lot on technological advances and the development of technologies for this purpose. It can be concluded that there are not many studies that prove this human centralization, but research has been done in the sense of applying digital technologies for human benefit in industrial environments. It can be concluded, then, that research involving the ideologies and concepts of Industry 5.0 is human-oriented, specifically to increase the well-being, health, and safety of humans.

Moreover, it could be said that the digital technologies of Industry 4.0 will be applied and used as Industry 5.0 technologies, only empowering and manipulating them to create value for the human factor. With the introduction of Industry 5.0 in smart manufacturing systems, the operator will also have to evolve into a resilient and digital operator, always taking into consideration the existing human capital in today's industrial reality, specifically the ageing workforce.

Author Contributions: Conceptualization, J.A.; methodology, J.A.; validation, T.M.L. and P.D.G.; formal analysis, T.M.L. and P.D.G.; investigation, J.A.; data curation, J.A.; writing—original draft preparation, J.A.; writing—review and editing, T.M.L. and P.D.G.; visualization, J.A.; supervision, T.M.L. and P.D.G.; funding acquisition, J.A., T.M.L. and P.D.G. All authors have read and agreed to the published version of the manuscript.

Funding: This research was funded by Fundação para a Ciência e Tecnologia (FCT), grant number UI/BD/151478/2021.

Data Availability Statement: No new data were created or analysed in this study. Data sharing is not applicable to this article.

Acknowledgments: The authors would like to thank the support provided by the Center for Mechanical and Aerospace Science and Technologies (C-MAST) under project UIDB/00151/2020.

Conflicts of Interest: The authors declare no conflict of interest.

References

1. Moller, D.P.F.; Vakilzadian, H.; Haas, R.E. From Industry 4.0 towards Industry 5.0. In Proceedings of the IEEE International Conference on Electro Information Technology, Mankato, MN, USA, 19–21 May 2022; pp. 61–68. [CrossRef]
2. Huang, S.; Wang, B.; Li, X.; Zheng, P.; Mourtzis, D.; Wang, L. Industry 5.0 and Society 5.0—Comparison, complementation and co-evolution. *J. Manuf. Syst.* **2022**, *64*, 424–428. [CrossRef]
3. Xu, X.; Lu, Y.; Vogel-Heuser, B.; Wang, L. Industry 4.0 and Industry 5.0—Inception, conception and perception. *J. Manuf. Syst.* **2021**, *61*, 530–535. [CrossRef]
4. Mourtzis, D.; Angelopoulos, J.; Panopoulos, N. A Literature Review of the Challenges and Opportunities of the Transition from Industry 4.0 to Society 5.0. *Energies* **2022**, *15*, 6276. [CrossRef]
5. Breque, M.; De Nul, L.; Petrides, A. *Industry 5.0—Towards a Sustainable, Human-Centric and Resilient European Industry*; European Commission: Brussels, Belgium, 2021. [CrossRef]
6. Grabowska, S.; Saniuk, S.; Gajdzik, B. Industry 5.0: Improving humanization and sustainability of Industry 4.0. *Scientometrics* **2022**, *127*, 3117–3144. [CrossRef] [PubMed]
7. Saniuk, S.; Grabowska, S.; Straka, M. Identification of Social and Economic Expectations: Contextual Reasons for the Transformation Process of Industry 4.0 into the Industry 5.0 Concept. *Sustainability* **2022**, *14*, 1391. [CrossRef]
8. Ivanov, D. The Industry 5.0 framework: Viability-based integration of the resilience, sustainability, and human-centricity perspectives. *Int. J. Prod. Res.* **2022**. [CrossRef]

9. Liberati, A.; Altman, D.G.; Tetzlaff, J.; Mulrow, C.; Gøtzsche, P.C.; Ioannidis, J.P.A.; Clarke, M.; Devereaux, P.J.; Kleijnen, J.; Moher, D. The PRISMA Statement for Reporting Systematic Reviews and Meta-Analyses of Studies That Evaluate Health Care Interventions: Explanation and Elaboration. *PLoS Med.* **2009**, *6*, e1000100. [CrossRef] [PubMed]
10. Snyder, H. Literature review as a research methodology: An overview and guidelines. *J. Bus. Res.* **2019**, *104*, 333–339. [CrossRef]
11. Van Eck, N.J.; Waltman, L. Software survey: VOSviewer, a computer program for bibliometric mapping. *Scientometrics* **2010**, *84*, 523–538. [CrossRef] [PubMed]
12. Borchardt, M.; Pereira, G.M.; Milan, G.S.; Scavarda, A.R.; Nogueira, E.O.; Poltosi, L.A. Industry 5.0 Beyond Technology: An Analysis Through the Lens of Business and Operations Management Literature. *Organizacija* **2022**, *55*, 305–321. [CrossRef]
13. Di Nardo, M.; Yu, H. Special Issue "Industry 5.0: The Prelude to the Sixth Industrial Revolution". *Appl. Syst. Innov.* **2021**, *4*, 45. [CrossRef]
14. Madsen, D.; Berg, T. An Exploratory Bibliometric Analysis of the Birth and Emergence of Industry 5.0. *Appl. Syst. Innov.* **2021**, *4*, 87. [CrossRef]
15. Maddikunta, P.K.R.; Pham, Q.-V.; Prabadevi, B.; Deepa, N.; Dev, K.; Gadekallu, T.R.; Ruby, R.; Liyanage, M. Industry 5.0: A survey on enabling technologies and potential applications. *J. Ind. Inf. Integr.* **2021**, *26*, 100257. [CrossRef]
16. Madhavan, M.; Wangtueai, S.; Sharafuddin, M.A.; Chaichana, T. The Precipitative Effects of Pandemic on Open Innovation of SMEs: A Scientometrics and Systematic Review of Industry 4.0 and Industry 5.0. *J. Open Innov. Technol. Mark. Complex.* **2022**, *8*, 152. [CrossRef]
17. Martins, Y.S.; Domingues, J.P.T.; Poltronieri, C.F.; Leite, L.R. The emergence of Industry 5.0: A bibliometric analysis. In Proceedings of the International Conference on Quality Engineering and Management, Braga, Portugal, 14–15 July 2022; pp. 837–852.
18. Leng, J.; Sha, W.; Wang, B.; Zheng, P.; Zhuang, C.; Liu, Q.; Wuest, T.; Mourtzis, D.; Wang, L. Industry 5.0: Prospect and retrospect. *J. Manuf. Syst.* **2022**, *65*, 279–295. [CrossRef]
19. Nahavandi, S. Industry 5.0—A Human-Centric Solution. *Sustainability* **2019**, *11*, 4371. [CrossRef]
20. Ghobakhloo, M.; Iranmanesh, M.; Mubarak, M.F.; Mubarik, M.; Rejeb, A.; Nilashi, M. Identifying industry 5.0 contributions to sustainable development: A strategy roadmap for delivering sustainability values. *Sustain. Prod. Consum.* **2022**, *33*, 716–737. [CrossRef]
21. Longo, F.; Padovano, A.; Umbrello, S. Value-Oriented and Ethical Technology Engineering in Industry 5.0: A Human-Centric Perspective for the Design of the Factory of the Future. *Appl. Sci.* **2020**, *10*, 4182. [CrossRef]
22. Prassida, G.F.; Asfari, U. A conceptual model for the acceptance of collaborative robots in industry 5.0. *Procedia Comput. Sci.* **2022**, *197*, 61–67. [CrossRef]
23. Aslam, F.; Aimin, W.; Li, M.; Ur Rehman, K. Innovation in the Era of IoT and Industry 5.0: Absolute Innovation Management (AIM) Framework. *Information* **2020**, *11*, 124. [CrossRef]
24. Bitsch, G. Conceptions of Man in Human-Centric Cyber-Physical Production Systems. *Procedia CIRP* **2022**, *107*, 1439–1443. [CrossRef]
25. Wang, B.; Zheng, P.; Yin, Y.; Shih, A.; Wang, L. Toward human-centric smart manufacturing: A human-cyber-physical systems (HCPS) perspective. *J. Manuf. Syst.* **2022**, *63*, 471–490. [CrossRef]
26. Khan, A.A.; Abonyi, J. Information sharing in supply chains—Interoperability in an era of circular economy. *Clean. Logist. Supply Chain* **2022**, *5*, 100074. [CrossRef]
27. Maier, M.; Ebrahimzadeh, A.; Beniiche, A.; Rostami, S. The Art of 6G (TAO 6G): How to wire Society 5.0 [Invited]. *J. Opt. Commun. Netw.* **2021**, *14*, A101–A112. [CrossRef]
28. Fraga-Lamas, P.; Varela-Barbeito, J.; Fernandez-Carames, T.M. Next Generation Auto-Identification and Traceability Technologies for Industry 5.0: A Methodology and Practical Use Case for the Shipbuilding Industry. *IEEE Access* **2021**, *9*, 140700–140730. [CrossRef]
29. Kaasinen, E.; Anttila, A.-H.; Heikkilä, P.; Laarni, J.; Koskinen, H.; Väätänen, A. Smooth and Resilient Human–Machine Teamwork as an Industry 5.0 Design Challenge. *Sustainability* **2022**, *14*, 2773. [CrossRef]
30. Turner, C.J.; Garn, W. Next generation DES simulation: A research agenda for human centric manufacturing systems. *J. Ind. Inf. Integr.* **2022**, *28*, 100354. [CrossRef]
31. Coronado, E.; Kiyokawa, T.; Ricardez, G.A.G.; Ramirez-Alpizar, I.G.; Venture, G.; Yamanobe, N. Evaluating quality in human-robot interaction: A systematic search and classification of performance and human-centered factors, measures and metrics towards an industry 5.0. *J. Manuf. Syst.* **2022**, *63*, 392–410. [CrossRef]
32. Kolaei, A.Z.; Hedayati, E.; Khanzadi, M.; Amiri, G.G. Challenges and opportunities of augmented reality during the construction phase. *Autom. Constr.* **2022**, *143*, 104586. [CrossRef]
33. Doyle-Kent, M.; Kopacek, P. Adoption of Collaborative Robotics in Industry 5.0. An Irish industry case study. *IFAC-PapersOnLine* **2021**, *54*, 413–418. [CrossRef]
34. Mourtzis, D.; Angelopoulos, J.; Papadokostakis, M.; Panopoulos, N. Design for 3D Printing of a Robotic Arm Tool Changer under the framework of Industry 5.0. *Procedia CIRP Mater. Asp. Manuf. Process.* **2022**, *115*, 178–183. [CrossRef]
35. Colla, V.; Matino, R.; Schröder, A.; Schivalocchi, M.; Romaniello, L. Human-Centered Robotic Development in the Steel Shop: Improving Health, Safety and Digital Skills at the Workplace. *Metals* **2021**, *11*, 647. [CrossRef]

36. Nourmohammadi, A.; Fathi, M.; Ng, A.H. Balancing and scheduling assembly lines with human-robot collaboration tasks. *Comput. Oper. Res.* **2021**, *140*, 105674. [CrossRef]
37. Montini, E.; Cutrona, V.; Bonomi, N.; Landolfi, G.; Bettoni, A.; Rocco, P.; Carpanzano, E. An IIoT Platform For Human-Aware Factory Digital Twins. *Procedia CIRP* **2022**, *107*, 661–667. [CrossRef]
38. Eriksson, K.; Alsaleh, A.; Behzad Far, S.; Stjern, D. Applying Digital Twin Technology in Higher Education: An Automation Line Case Study. *Adv. Transdiscipl. Eng.* **2022**, *21*, 461–472. [CrossRef]
39. Kaarlela, T.; Arnarson, H.; Pitkäaho, T.; Shu, B.; Solvang, B.; Pieskä, S. Common Educational Teleoperation Platform for Robotics Utilizing Digital Twins. *Machines* **2022**, *10*, 577. [CrossRef]
40. Pozo, E.; Patel, N.; Schrödel, F. Collaborative Robotic Environment for Educational Training in Industry 5.0 Using an Open Lab Approach. *IFAC-PapersOnLine* **2022**, *55*, 314–319. [CrossRef]
41. Li, C.; Zheng, P.; Yin, Y.; Pang, Y.M.; Huo, S. An AR-assisted Deep Reinforcement Learning-based approach towards mutual-cognitive safe human-robot interaction. *Robot. Comput. Manuf.* **2023**, *80*, 102471. [CrossRef]
42. Ciobanu, A.C.; Meșniță, G. AI Ethics for Industry 5.0—From Principles to Practice. In Proceedings of the Workshop of I-ESA'22, Valencia, Spain, 23–24 March 2022.
43. Khamaisi, R.K.; Brunzini, A.; Grandi, F.; Peruzzini, M.; Pellicciari, M. UX assessment strategy to identify potential stressful conditions for workers. *Robot. Comput. Manuf.* **2022**, *78*, 102403. [CrossRef]
44. Melendez, S.; Sima, X.; Coudert, T.; Geneste, L.; de Valroger, A. An experience feedback process for learning from collaboration experiences. *Comput. Ind.* **2022**, *141*, 103693. [CrossRef]
45. Wan, P.K.; Leirmo, T.L. Human-centric zero-defect manufacturing: State-of-the-art review, perspectives, and challenges. *Comput. Ind.* **2023**, *144*, 103792. [CrossRef]
46. Orso, V.; Ziviani, R.; Bacchiega, G.; Bondani, G.; Spagnolli, A.; Gamberini, L. Employee-centric innovation: Integrating participatory design and video-analysis to foster the transition to Industry 5.0. *Comput. Ind. Eng.* **2022**, *173*, 108661. [CrossRef]
47. Wang, L. A futuristic perspective on human-centric assembly. *J. Manuf. Syst.* **2021**, *62*, 199–201. [CrossRef]
48. Rannertshauser, P.; Kessler, M.; Arlinghaus, J.C. Human-centricity in the design of production planning and control systems: Human-centricity in the and control control systems: Systems: Human-centricity in A the approach towards Industry Human-centricity in design control A first approach towards tow. *IFAC PapersOnLine* **2022**, *55*, 2641–2646. [CrossRef]
49. Brunzini, A.; Peruzzini, M.; Grandi, F.; Khamaisi, R.K.; Pellicciari, M. A Preliminary Experimental Study on the Workers' Workload Assessment to Design Industrial Products and Processes. *Appl. Sci.* **2021**, *11*, 12066. [CrossRef]
50. Mladineo, M.; Cubic, M.; Gjeldum, N.; Crnjacizic, M. Human-centric approach of the Lean management as an enabler of Industry 5.0 in SMEs. In Proceedings of the International Conference Mechanical Technologies and Structural Materials, Split, Croatia, 23–24 September 2021; pp. 111–117.
51. Fonda, E.; Meneghetti, A. The Human-Centric SMED. *Sustainability* **2022**, *14*, 514. [CrossRef]
52. Kolade, O.; Owoseni, A. Employment 5.0: The work of the future and the future of work. *Technol. Soc.* **2022**, *71*, 102086. [CrossRef]
53. Brauner, P.; Ziefle, M. Beyond playful learning—Serious games for the human-centric digital transformation of production and a design process model. *Technol. Soc.* **2022**, *71*, 102140. [CrossRef]
54. Eriksson, K.; Chirumalla, K.; Myrelid, P.; Ericsson, M.; Granlund, A.; Håkansson, L.; Johansson, D. Experiences in Running a Professional Course on Digitally-Enabled Production in Collaboration Between Three Swedish Universities. *Adv. Transdiscipl. Eng.* **2022**, *21*, 653–664. [CrossRef]
55. Carayannis, E.G.; Dezi, L.; Gregori, G.; Calo, E. Smart Environments and Techno-centric and Human-Centric Innovations for Industry and Society 5.0: A Quintuple Helix Innovation System View Towards Smart, Sustainable, and Inclusive Solutions. *J. Knowl. Econ.* **2021**, *13*, 926–955. [CrossRef]
56. Lu, Y.; Zheng, H.; Chand, S.; Xia, W.; Liu, Z.; Xu, X.; Wang, L.; Qin, J.; Bao, J. Outlook on human-centric manufacturing towards Industry 5.0. *J. Manuf. Syst.* **2022**, *62*, 612–627. [CrossRef]
57. Adel, A. Future of industry 5.0 in society: Human-centric solutions, challenges and prospective research areas. *J. Cloud Comput.* **2022**, *11*, 40. [CrossRef]
58. Chaudhari, P.; Utgikar, R.; Kelkar, B.; Borse, P. A Novel Approach: Bioeconomy Industry 5.0 Enhanced version. In Proceedings of the IEEE Pune Section International Conference, Pune, India, 16–19 December 2021; IEEE: New York, NY, USA, 2021; pp. 1–6. [CrossRef]
59. Del Giudice, M.; Scuotto, V.; Orlando, B.; Mustilli, M. Toward the human-centered approach. A revised model of individual acceptance of AI. *Hum. Resour. Manag. Rev.* **2021**, *33*, 100856. [CrossRef]
60. Doyle Kent, M.; Kopacek, P. Do We Need Synchronization of the Human and Robotics to Make Industry 5.0 a Success Story? In *ISPR 2020: Digital Conversion on the Way to Industry 4.0*; Lecture Notes in Mechanical Engineering; Springer: Cham, Switzerland, 2020; pp. 302–311. [CrossRef]
61. Broo, D.G.; Kaynak, O.; Sait, S.M. Rethinking engineering education at the age of industry 5.0. *J. Ind. Inf. Integr.* **2021**, *25*, 100311. [CrossRef]
62. Li, Y.; Mu, H.; Polden, J.; Li, H.; Wang, L.; Xia, C.; Pan, Z. Towards intelligent monitoring system in wire arc additive manufacturing: A surface anomaly detector on a small dataset. *Int. J. Adv. Manuf. Technol.* **2022**, *120*, 5225–5242. [CrossRef]

63. Xia, C.; Pan, Z.; Li, Y.; Chen, J.; Li, H. Vision-based melt pool monitoring for wire-arc additive manufacturing using deep learning method. *Int. J. Adv. Manuf. Technol.* **2022**, *120*, 551–562. [CrossRef]
64. Romero, D.; Stahre, J. Towards the Resilient Operator 5.0: The Future of Work in Smart Resilient Manufacturing Systems. *Procedia CIRP* **2021**, *104*, 1089–1094. [CrossRef]
65. Battini, D.; Berti, N.; Finco, S.; Zennaro, I.; Das, A. Towards industry 5.0: A multi-objective job rotation model for an inclusive workforce. *Int. J. Prod. Econ.* **2022**, *250*, 108619. [CrossRef]

Disclaimer/Publisher's Note: The statements, opinions and data contained in all publications are solely those of the individual author(s) and contributor(s) and not of MDPI and/or the editor(s). MDPI and/or the editor(s) disclaim responsibility for any injury to people or property resulting from any ideas, methods, instructions or products referred to in the content.

Article

A Study on a Knowledge Graph Construction Method of Safety Reports for Process Industries

Zhiqiang Yin [1,†], Lin Shi [1,†], Yang Yuan [1,†], Xinxin Tan [2,†] and Shoukun Xu [1,*,†]

1 Big Data Research Laboratory of Process Industry, Computer and Artificial Intelligence, Alibaba Cloud Big Data College, Changzhou University, Changzhou 213000, China
2 College of Microelectronics and Control Engineering, Changzhou University, Changzhou 213000, China
* Correspondence: xsk@cczu.edu.cn
† Current address: School of Computer and Artificial Intelligence, Changzhou University, Changzhou 213000, China.

Abstract: There are some representative reports in industrial safety engineering, such as the Hazard and Operability Analysis and Pre-Hazard Analysis; however, a large amount of industrial safety knowledge in the report has not been fully explored. In order to reuse and release the value of industrial safety knowledge, this paper constructs a new industrial safety knowledge extraction framework. The framework combines the asset management shell to summarize the knowledge concept entities of machine description language and model description language. According to the safety report template, the framework also constructs a new industrial safety knowledge-mapping standard structure. Specifically, firstly, considering that the knowledge structure of safety reports is different in different processes of the process industry, this paper innovatively proposes a general industrial safety knowledge-mapping standard structure, which provides a practical solution for the integration of industrial knowledge representation problems in different processes. Secondly, based on the research progress of named entities, this paper presents an industrial named entity extraction method (INERM) for the process industry. This method designs an entity weight model to calculate the entity weight of each sentence, and adds part-of-speech weight to improve the entity extraction algorithm, which alleviates the problem that the existing entity extraction methods cannot reasonably use the semantic information and context of word. Finally, we construct a triple of industrial safety knowledge based on the rules and store it in Neo4j. In this paper, four semantic-type templates and five semantic relation templates are constructed based on the new industrial safety knowledge map standardization construction process of the process industry. The comparative experiments show that the accuracy of the INERM on the test set is improved by 17 percentage points on average compared with other key entity extraction algorithms. A total of 1329 entities are constructed in the directional application example of the fluid transportation process, which provides a large number of references for the safety of the fluid transportation process and is more conducive to improving the safety guarantee of the fluid transport process.

Keywords: knowledge graph; knowledge structuring; entity extraction methods; asset administration shell; process industry entity relationship networks

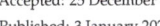

Citation: Yin, Z.; Shi, L.; Yuan, Y.; Tan, X.; Xu, S. A Study on a Knowledge Graph Construction Method of Safety Reports for Process Industries. *Processes* **2023**, *11*, 146. https://doi.org/10.3390/pr11010146

Academic Editor: Xiong Luo

Received: 24 November 2022
Revised: 25 December 2022
Accepted: 25 December 2022
Published: 3 January 2023

Copyright: © 2023 by the authors. Licensee MDPI, Basel, Switzerland. This article is an open access article distributed under the terms and conditions of the Creative Commons Attribution (CC BY) license (https://creativecommons.org/licenses/by/4.0/).

1. Introduction

At present, many risk analysis methods are popular in the industry, such as the Hazard and Operability Analysis (HAZOP), which can provide safety analysis decisions for any process in the industry. HAZOP can predict the spread of dangerous events through the potential deviation in nodes in the system and propose effective solutions. The analysis results are eventually recorded in the HAZOP report in the form of text [1]. For example, a prior risk analysis (PHA) can analyze the types, distribution, occurrence conditions, and possible accident consequences of various risk factors in the project before carrying out a project activity, such as involving, construction, production, or maintenance [2]. It is stored in a security report as text. The common characteristics of these risk analysis methods make the industrial safety report contain a wealth of safety knowledge systems. However, the existing industrial safety reports have the following shortcomings:

(1) Industrial safety reporting is an expert-driven engineering design in the form of brainstorming [3]. It relies on the experience and real-time judgment of experts, which makes the analysis time-consuming and laborious, and it may not be comprehensive. The current methods such as HAZOP and FMEA, given human limitations, are not providing confidence that these will lead to a complete inventory of all the significant possibilities [4].

(2) For the same process, various HAZOP reports appear in the analysis strategies of different expert teams [5], making the industrial safety knowledge extraction process more difficult.

The core of the above problem is that human factors cannot be excluded. In each stage and step, various human factors will harm the quality of learning [6]. Previously, some studies attempted to reuse industrial safety knowledge in a computer-aided manner. In 2013, Nicola Paltrinieri designed a tool to support the identification and assessment of atypical potential accident scenarios related to the considered material, equipment, and site [7]. Manuel Rodríguez introduced a tool for the semi-automatic HAZOP study of process units. The diagnostic system used an expert system to predict behavior modeled using d diagrams [8]. Faisal I. Khan developed an expert system for automating HAZOP (HAZard and operability) studies [9]. With the rise of artificial intelligence, some studies focused on introducing natural language processing technology into HAZOP reports mining semantic information and industrial safety knowledge. In recent years, research at the safety reporting level was applied by some scholars due to the rise of natural language processing techniques. Hu proposed a fault diagnosis method that combines HAZOP with a dynamic Bayesian network inference to reveal early deviations in the causal chain of faults [10], which is important for emergency decision making. Feng (2021) used a deep learning approach to classify the consequences reported by HAZOP according to the severity of consequences [11]. Wang et al. designed a variety of novel active learning algorithms to construct entity recognition models and mine industrial safety knowledge in HAZOP reports, which is of great significance for improving industrial safety. Zeng (2021) conducted a comprehensive analysis of the causal factors of a chemical park or enterprise explosion [12], extracted the entities and relationships in chemical safety knowledge, stored them in Neo4j, and presented them in a visualized form. The knowledge-mapping technology in the chemical safety field provides ideas for the follow-up. Wang proposed HAZOP-based industrial safety knowledge mapping [13], which developed a standardized framework for safety reports through deconstruction and generalization [14] and realized the integration, sharing, and reuse of industrial safety report knowledge. The aforementioned studies are mainly aimed at alleviating the problem of this paper and lack in-depth research on the issue. In this study, the new knowledge graph connecting data science and engineering design inspires [15–18], and we propose a new industrial safety knowledge graph integrating matter of fact, which is based on industrial safety reports and can improve the effective comprehensiveness of safety reports. First, because the knowledge structure of different processes in different process industries is different [19], for example, the "low-low interlock" of the oil and gas inlet process and the "open valve" of the vaporization process are different, we analyze and summarize and creatively develop a general safety knowledge standardization framework for industrial safety report extraction in a top-down manner. The safety knowledge standardization framework contains safety knowledge ontology and safety knowledge relations, which can standardize the safety reports of different processes and unify the representation and integration of different types of safety knowledge as a practice to broaden the research field of industrial safety engineering design. Secondly, considering the specificity of the text, a novel and reliable information extraction model (INERM) based on deep learning and data science is selectively conceived in safety report text, and the INERM consists of four modules: BERT, with a powerful linguistic representation and feature extraction capability to extract semantic features [20], and a bidirectional long- and short-term memory network (BiLSTM) to obtain the INERM extracts the industrial safety knowledge. Finally, the industrial safety knowledge triad is constructed and stored in a Neo4j-based graphical database.

The INERM can extract industrial safety knowledge from safety reports based on a standardized framework of safety knowledge. We take potential safety knowledge in fluid transportation processes as an example to construct a knowledge graph of fluid transportation safety, which can integrate, share, and reuse safety knowledge and also inspire other researchers. Our main contributions are as follows:

(1) Inspired by the new knowledge graph connecting data science and engineering design [15], we propose a new industrial knowledge graph structure with safety reports as the carrier, which can enhance the value of industrial safety knowledge and improve the knowledge reuse and efficiency of safety reports;

(2) A standardized framework of industrial safety knowledge based on the idea of an asset management shell to provide digital representation for assets is proposed. Our work is about discovering this atomized asset-based representation of the concept, or how assets are accurately represented in the knowledge-mapping domain, and practicing this asset representation application in the oil and gas transportation process. It can provide a structured representation scheme for different safety reports to represent industrial safety knowledge in a unified way with different expressions to achieve the expressibility of industrial safety knowledge;

(3) Through the BERT-BILSTM-CRF-TFIDF model and formulating dynamic data update rules based on the characteristics of the industrial safety knowledge in this paper, industrial safety knowledge can be extracted effectively, which provides a structured and logically feasible solution for the process industrial safety knowledge extraction;

(4) The application of industrial knowledge-mapping orientation for the fluid transportation process is carried out, which can effectively reduce the safety hazards of the gathering and transportation process, optimize the safety decision awareness, and strengthen industrial safety.

2. Related Work

In this paper, we combine safety reports, asset administration shells, and knowledge graphs together, so we carry out the related research work on safety reports, asset administration shells, and knowledge graphs, respectively.

2.1. Knowledge Graph

Applying knowledge graph technology to the industrial domain requires first realizing the formal representation of domain knowledge, i.e., realizing a machine-understandable knowledge representation under multimodal data requirements [21]. In the direction of the formal representation of industrial domain knowledge, the key technical means involved contain the predicate logic knowledge representation method [22], the framework-based knowledge representation method [23], the semantic network-based knowledge representation method [24], and the ontology-based knowledge representation method [25]. The current representative works on ontology-based knowledge representation methods in the industrial domain include the following: for product design process knowledge and manufacturing process knowledge, Chhim et al. developed ontologies that unite the two types of knowledge and tried to apply them to the knowledge reuse process; for process design knowledge [16], Guo et al. considered the process knowledge characteristics and domain scope [25] and proposed a logical architecture of process knowledge management based on ontology; for the whole life cycle knowledge of the manufacturing domain, Liu et al. [26] proposed a multi-level and multidimensional knowledge expression model based on ontology to realize the structured and dimensional representation of manufacturing domain knowledge; and for collaborative design knowledge, Bock et al. explored the method of combining ontology and model-based technology for collaborative design [27].

It can be seen that the current ontology-based knowledge representation methods in industrial fields have gained extensive research, and the research scope involves the creation of multidimensional ontologies for design processes and manufacturing processes, which provides a basis for the subsequent automatic construction of knowledge graphs.

In the process of practical application in enterprises, the ontologies constructed by existing scholars can be used as the basis to improve the efficiency of enterprise knowledge ontology construction. However, the ontologies constructed in the existing studies are often not highly detailed, and the application process needs to be expanded according to the actual enterprise needs. Huang et al. (2022) designed a KG-based automatic knowledge base construction method for the machining domain, which overcomes the disadvantages of the traditional method of being time-consuming, and constructed a knowledge-mapping-driven method for optimizing equipment resource allocation [28], which improved equipment utilization as well as equipment machining flexibility, while integrated knowledge reuse also reduced the cost of optimally allocating manufacturing resources required for machining tasks [29]. Wang proposed the industrial safety knowledge graph with HAZOP as the carrier and developed a standardized framework for safety reporting through deconstruction and generalization [13], realizing the integration, sharing, and reuse of industrial safety reporting knowledge. Wang analyzed report text mining based on the harm and operability of active learning [30].

The above-mentioned work began to apply knowledge graph technology to the industrial field, but the research rarely involved a large amount of knowledge reuse of industrial safety reports, so knowledge graph technology could not be used from a safety perspective. We have designed an industrial safety knowledge graph construction technology with safety reports as the carrier, which can effectively enhance the value of industrial safety knowledge, improve the knowledge reuse and efficiency of safety reports, and can also escort industrial safety.

2.2. Safety Report

The industrial safety report emerged to predict the propagation of hazard events through potential deviations in nodes in the system and to propose effective solutions. This core feature is more logical and, as an industry-recognized report template, it can be a powerful aid to the structuring of industrial safety knowledge. The main presentation forms of industrial safety reports are [31] the Job Hazard Analysis (JHA), Failure-Type Effects (FMEA), PHA, Event Tree (ET), Accident Tree (AT), Operating Conditions Hazard Evaluation Method (OCHE), HAZOP, Quantitative Risk Assessment (QRA), Layer of Protection Analysis (LOPA), risk-based risk assessment-based equipment inspection techniques (RBI), safety integrity-level analysis (SIL), and failure assumption method (WI). Safety reporting is an analytical process of reverse reasoning whose main purpose is to explore systematically and in an organized manner whether there are hazards in process equipment or facilities [32] and which provides the necessary decisions to eliminate and reduce the hazards in the process and mitigate the consequences of accidents. Currently, safety reports have achieved great success in various process industries widely used in various processes and have achieved excellent performance [33]. For example, in the natural gas boosting process, q Yang et al. (2021) analyzed the main hazards and causes of the generation of piston gas compressors in a safety report PHA environment, which improved the staff's ability to prevent hazards [34]. Most of the improved quantitative and semi-quantitative methods are based on the LOPA, using the LOPA as a database to solve the problem of overly conservative traditional safety reports [35]. Li used the HAZOP analysis method to analyze the preliminary design of a natural gas distribution field station as an example [36]. Lu et al. introduced the phenol hydrogenation reaction of a company's 100-ton-per-year cyclohexanone unit, selected the unit reactor to produce cyclohexanone with higher risk, and used the LOPA to conduct a further analysis to quantify the frequency to determine whether some protection is sufficient [37]. Based on the current abundant and important industrial safety report templates, we innovatively design a common expression structure so that the knowledge of safety reports can be effectively utilized and knowledge reuse and expressible work can be realized.

2.3. Asset Administration Shell

An asset administration shell (AAS) is intended to be a standardized digital representation of assets. According to its goals, it has the potential to integrate all data generated during the PLM process into one data model and to provide a universally valid interface for all PLM phases [38]. The asset administration shell, as a component of Industry 4.0, has the three-layer concept of RAMI4.0 for communication, information, and functionality.

RAMI4.0 integrates the key elements of I4.0 components into a structured and hierarchical model; the AAS is a virtualized, digital, and active representation of I4.0 components. The "inventory" is considered a catalog of data that represents the meta-information of the assets and is an important component of the virtual representation. In addition to the meta-information, the "inventory" also includes the connection relationships between the management shell and the assets, as well as information related to security capabilities [39].

The IEC/TS 62832-1 standard defines the concept of an asset class to describe a set of assets with common characteristics in a digital factory, each specific asset being directly or indirectly derived from an asset class. The structure of the asset class consists of two parts, the leader and body, where the leader contains the identification information of the asset class and the body mainly contains the identification information of the asset class. In the asset class, the specification of the definition of data elements shall follow the principles defined in IEC 61360 for the characteristic data structure. These property data structures have been fixed in the form of a database called the Common Data Dictionary (CDD) and used as the base data model [39], together with the lists of equipment characteristics (LOPs) in the IEC 61987 series of standards to form the Property Database reference system for assets, which becomes the enabling technical framework for building an AAS. Drawing on the idea that the AAS takes the standardized digital representation of assets as its main theme, our work is to discover the conceptual expression of this asset-based atomization. This article will demonstrate how assets are accurately expressed in the field of knowledge mapping and how assets are applied in the process of oil and gas transportation.

3. Methods

In the following section, we describe the process of developing industrial safety knowledge in the form of safety reports. First, because the safety reports of different processes in the process industry contain different knowledge, we innovatively build a general industrial knowledge standardization framework at the "conceptual layer" to structure the safety reports of different processes and represent the industrial safety knowledge of different processes in a unified manner. Then, considering the specificity of safety texts, we combine data science to conceive an artificial intelligence-based INERM model, which can extract industrial safety knowledge from safety reports based on the industrial safety knowledge standardization framework, called the "extraction layer". The quality of the conceptual layer and the extraction layer will directly affect the quality of the knowledge graph, which is the focus of this paper. Finally, in the "storage layer", we construct industrial safety knowledge triads based on the extraction results of the "extraction layer" and store them in the graph database. The overall structure is shown in Figure 1.

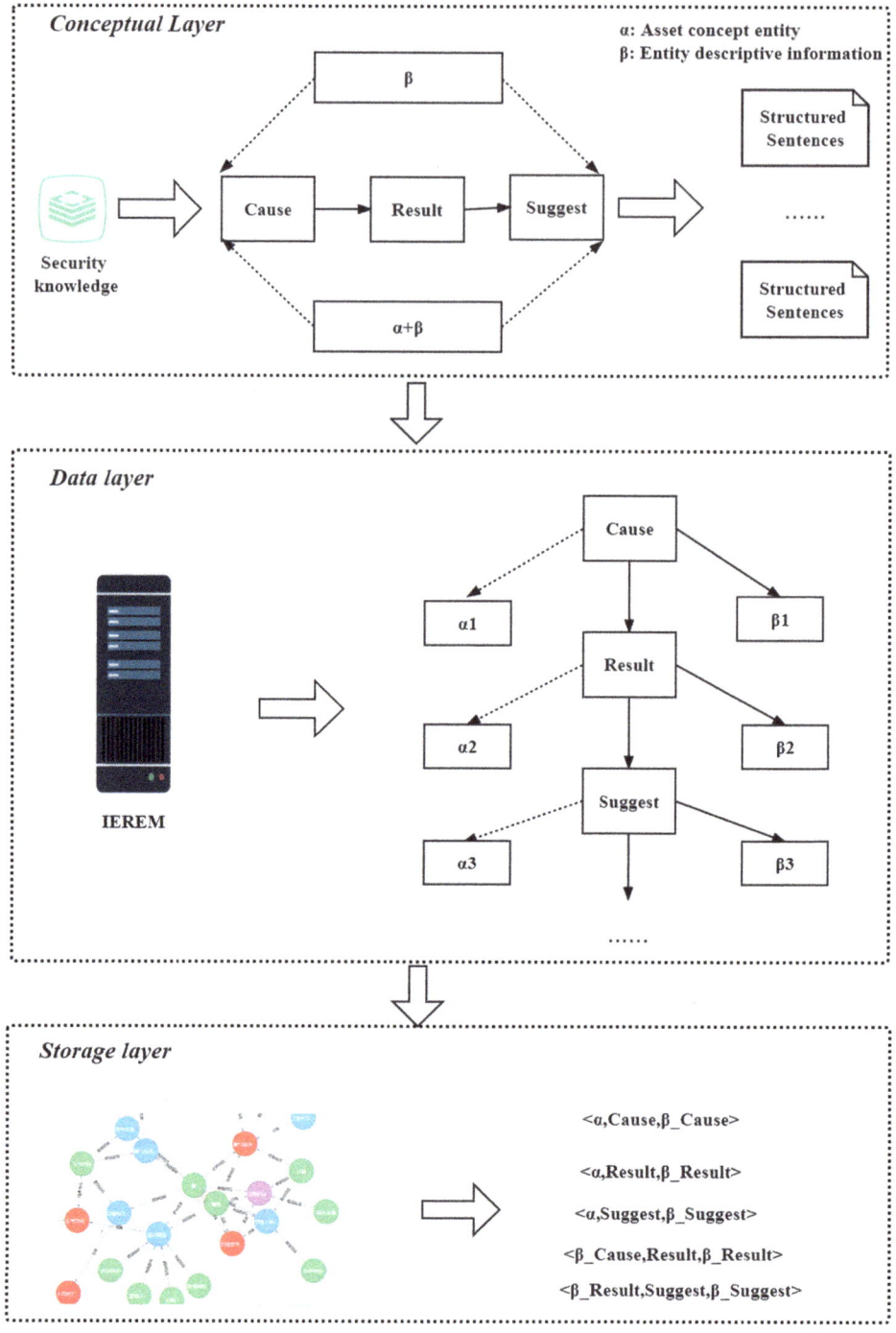

Figure 1. Industrial safety knowledge development process.

3.1. Conceptual Layer

Safety reports contain different knowledge for different processes in the process industry, such as fans and compressors in the fluid transport industry, and even within the same process, as safety experts have different focuses [40]. Therefore, the design of industrial safety knowledge entities and their relationships faces a great challenge. To address this difficulty, we propose a process industry safety knowledge standardization framework to standardize the safety knowledge information of different processes and to represent the industrial safety knowledge of different processes uniformly. In addition, we design a generic process industrial safety knowledge expression relationship.

Due to the existence of a large number of obscure and difficult professional terms in the safety report, it is impossible to adopt methods such as clustering and merging to describe the industrial safety knowledge ontology. Therefore, we try to use the main structure of the safety report as a breakthrough. Inspired by the international standard IEC 61882 [41], we use a top-down approach to systematically parse safety reports. First, we decompose safety reports into various hazard event processes, then decompose them into generic structures, and finally obtain an industrial safety knowledge ontology.

We decompose the safety report into a set of entities $E_{ISK} = \{C, R, S\}$. The E_{ISK} is briefly described as follows:

(1) C: Cause entity, which is derived from the abnormal causes in HAZOP and the formation causes in PHA, such as "transport system failure" and "flow control valve FVC closed", "coil blockage".

(2) R: Resulting entity, derived from consequences in HAZOP, consequences in JHA, event description in LOPA, consequences in PHA, e.g., "liquid crude oil without vaporization flows into the transport system", "crude oil in the vaporizer will boil".

(3) S: Recommended entities, derived from the recommended measures in HAZOP, recommendations in LOPA, control measures in JHA, and preventive measures in PHA, e.g., "Clean the coils" and "Shut down the FCV linkage".

The diagram category EL is appropriately divided into string (E_{ss}) and inverse tree (E_{rt}), positive tree (E_{pt}), and tie tree (E_{bt}) according to the differences between entities in E_{ISK}, as shown in Equation (1).

$$EL \in \{E_{ss}, E_{rt}, E_{pt}, E_{bt}\} \quad (1)$$

Among them, E_{ss} is the simplest EL, which contains only a single causal chain of relations. For E_{rt}, different causes produce the same result, and it is a very tricky problem to analyze E_{rt} by exhausting all the causes. In the E_{pt} structure, each result generates multiple suggestions, which creates more obstacles for subsequent work. E_{bt} is the most complex, integrating E_{ss}, E_{rt}, and E_{pt}. In general, industrial processes are closely connected, and if one process fails, it will affect the others. Therefore, E_{bt} has also gained the attention of industry professionals as a key structure in the field of process industry safety. Equations (2)–(5) are their definitions.

$$E_{ss} = \{C, R, S\} \quad (2)$$

$$E_{rt} = \{\sum_i^n C_i, R, S\} \quad (3)$$

$$E_{pt} = \{C, \sum_i^n R_i, \sum_i^n S_i\} \quad (4)$$

$$E_{bt} = \{\sum_i^n C_i, \sum_i^n R_i, \sum_i^n S_i\} \quad (5)$$

Furthermore, we denote each entity in each EL in the form of "$\alpha + \beta$", where α denotes the asset concept entity corresponding to the asset in the asset management shell (an asset is an "object of value to an organization"), and β denotes the descriptive information of the concept entity, e.g., the "failure" of the "supply system failure". "failure" is the descriptive information about the "failure" of the concept entity "feed system". α and β, as a general framework of basic knowledge, can be used to represent safety reports and form industrial safety knowledge ontologies (E_{ISKG}) from them. We transition the possible pitfalls of such a corpus by treating assets as possible components of entities, as shown in Equation (6).

$$\begin{cases} E_{\alpha,\beta} = E_{ss}(\alpha,\beta) \cup E_{rt}(\alpha,\beta) \cup E_{pt}(\alpha,\beta) \cup E_{bt}(\alpha,\beta) \\ E_{\beta} = E_{ss}(\beta) \cup E_{rt}(\beta) \cup E_{pt}(\beta) \cup E_{bt}(\beta) \\ E_{ISKG} = E_{\alpha,\beta} \cup E_{\beta} \end{cases} \quad (6)$$

$$E_{ss}(\alpha,\beta) = \{C(\alpha,\beta), \sum_{i}^{n} R_i(\alpha,\beta), S(\alpha,\beta)\} \quad (7)$$

$$E_{ss}(\beta) = \{C(\beta), \sum_{i}^{n} R_i(\beta), S(\beta)\} \quad (8)$$

The general framework of industrial safety knowledge constructed in this paper differs from the general knowledge graph in that there is no general sense of the relationship between industrial safety knowledge in safety reports. For example, "the main character of the movie Drunken Fist is Jackie Chan", "Drunken Fist", and "Jackie Chan" have the relationship of "main character", but in the industrial field, "Drunken Fist" and "Jackie Chan" have the relationship of "main character". However, in the industrial field, the "carburetor overload", there is no relationship. Therefore, to overcome this obstacle, it is necessary to step out of the traditional shackles. The nature of safety reporting leads us to the following discussions:

(1) Industrial safety knowledge relationships aim to connect industrial safety knowledge into an organic whole. Safety reports usually have potential categories, such as PHA with multiple categories consisting of risk factors, consequences, formation causes, and preventive measures. Safety report as the carrier of the relationship can be equated to the key elements in the industrial safety report template collection V: cause, result, and recommendation;

(2) Safety reports take time toward the implementation of safety measures for prevention, and their own characteristics of the order of execution in terms of the causes and consequences of events make the execution more logical.

Therefore, we follow the execution logic of safety reports in a novel way by using industrial safety knowledge attributes as relations e_{ISK} of ISK, with the relation links shown in Equations (9) and (10).

$$e_{ISK}(\alpha,\beta) = \{C(\alpha,\beta) \rightarrow R(\alpha,\beta) \rightarrow S(\alpha,\beta)\} \quad (9)$$

$$e_{ISK}(\beta) = \{C(\beta) \rightarrow R(\beta) \rightarrow S(\beta)\} \quad (10)$$

In summary, we have completed the construction of the conceptual layer of the industrial safety knowledge ontology in this section; studied how the knowledge categories, including those specific to industrial safety reports, are transformed into relationships; and proposed a novel unified structure of industrial safety knowledge that enables the reuse and structured representation of industrial safety reports for different processes. The unified structure of industrial safety knowledge is an industrial safety engineering design practice, which expands the perspective of industrial safety engineering design and provides ideas for academic researchers. We also believe that it can help realize the intelligent and automated expression of knowledge in the field of industrial safety.

3.2. Extraction Layer

The general structure of the knowledge graph is a triadic structure of entities through relationships to another entity. The extraction layer should address both entity extraction and relationship extraction. Because the industrial safety knowledge relationships are already identified in the conceptual layer, this section focuses on how to perform the extraction of entities. The current security report text mainly has the following characteristics:

(1) A wide variety of long entities. For example, "safety switch installation set machinery", "compressed gas regulation system", "gas mains and gas cabinet water of gas cabinet";

(2) Diversified entity nesting. For example, "gas main pipe of gas cabinet and gas cabinet water", "overflow pipe of gas washing tower", "water jacket or steam ladle constitutes a closed system";

(3) Plenty of technical terms, such as "valve diversion" and "opening degree";

(4) Even in the same process industry scenario, different experts usually have different semantic expressions for the same incident. For example, statements are inverted ("low flow initiates FAL"), and subjects are omitted ("no crude oil inflow"), so the text is more diverse.

It is worth noting that in the unified structure of industrial safety knowledge (ISKG), safety reports such as ISKG(α, β) (ISKG with α and β content) or ISKG(β) (ISKG with β content), α and β are intertwined, e.g., "The Roots blower pumped negative pressure, allowing air to enter the system and mix with semi-water gas". How to extract entities from security reports with such characteristics is a problem worth considering. Therefore, inspired by the new knowledge graph connecting data science and engineering design, we design an advanced industrial safety information extraction model, INERM, which is a named entity information extraction model with a mixture of multilayer neural network and machine learning. We will describe the extraction layer from three aspects: security report dataset, INERM, and experiment.

3.2.1. Safety Report Dataset

First, we extract unstructured data from professional websites, such as China Industrial Safety Network, China ChemNet, Oil and Gas Storage and Transportation Network, and Aerospace Cloud Network, and search websites, such as Baidu Encyclopedia, Wikipedia, and Baidu Library. We preprocess them to obtain the original text of safety reports and collect 12,948 safety reports from the original text by data cleaning and segmentation operations and rule-based methods.

BIO is a classical and common annotation method in the field of named entities: B means the word is at the beginning of an entity (Begin), I means inside (Inside), and O means outside (Outside). A group of BI can form an entity (Single), another expansion B_x expresses the beginning of entity category x, I_x expresses the end of entity category X, O indicates that it does not belong to any type. We adopted the BIO annotation method to label 8000 security descriptive sentences with different relationships. Our definition of entity categories is shown in Table 1. Finally, we split the security description corpus sentences into 80% training sets, 10% verification sets, and 10% test sets.

Table 1. Entity Label.

Label Name	Label Head	Label Tail
Assert	B_assert	I_assert
Cause	B_cause	I_cause
Result	B_result	I_result
Suggest	B_suggest	I_suggest

3.2.2. INERM

Bidirectional encoder representations for transformers (BERT) is a transformer's bidirectional encoder designed to pre-train deep bidirectional representations from an unlabeled text by conditional computation common in left and right contexts. For a more accurate logical structure of $R(\alpha, \beta)$ in security reports, NEST sentence prediction (NSP) can predict better. However, the coexistence of multiple entities in safety report information often leads to the problem of correct linkage of entities. For example, "equipment and piping are not observed in manufacturing, inspection, and maintenance, and are inherently defective", where there are multiple causal entities and only one factor, "defective", leading to undesirable consequences, while "Inspection and maintenance are not observed" will not lead to adverse consequences. To solve, we provide a more natural way of thinking: calculate the entity weight of each entity based on the entity contribution weight model of BERT-biLSTM-CRF, then improve the Term Frequency-Inverse Document Frequency (TFIDF) algorithm by combining the entity weight of each candidate key entity, and finally retrieve and extract the key entity.

In conclusion, INERM is mainly composed of BERT, bidirectional long short-term memory (BiLSTM), conditional random field (CRF), and TFIDF. BERT extends and enriches semantic features. BiLSTM is used to obtain context information and information from the long-distance-dependent encoder. CRF can calibrate the order and relationship between labels to obtain the global optimal prediction sequence. TFIDF extracts key entities through statistical features. Figure 2 shows the overall framework, where the input to INERM is the security report description and the output is the corresponding entity. First, token embedding (sentence embedding and position embedding) generated by the security report description is trantokensmitted to BERT, Then, BERT converts the joint embedding into semantic vectors containing semantic features and passes them to BiLSTM. Next, the BiLSTM uses a pair of bidirectional LSTM to encode the semantic vector to obtain a context vector with context characteristics. Finally, CRF calibrates the order and relationship between tags, the entity link rules constrain the output of entities, and TFIDF decodes the context vector to output the entity sequence with the maximum probability. A detailed description of each module follows.

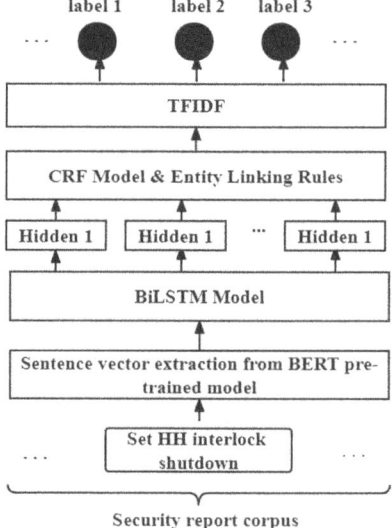

Figure 2. Overall structure diagram of INERM.

BERT

Language model pre-training can effectively improve many natural language processing tasks [42], where the BERT pre-training model is based on a bidirectional multilayer transformer model, and the transformer model is based on encoder–decoder and attention mechanisms [43]. The BERT model removes the limitation of self-attentiveness of the unilateral context (above or below) through the bidirectional self-attentiveness mechanism [44]. Applying the BERT pre-training model achieved better results in several natural language processing tasks.

In this paper, we use the model BERT, which is constructed as follows. First, the joint embedding $\mathbf{e} = \{e_0, e_1, \ldots, e_n\}$ of word embedding and location embedding is passed to the multi-headed attention layer. The attention distribution $\mathbf{a} = \{a_0, a_1, \ldots, a_n\}$ is obtained by the formulae of the multi-headed self-attentive layers q, k, v. Then, the vector e and the vector a are normalized to obtain $IN(\mathbf{e}, \mathbf{a})$, and $IN(\mathbf{e}, \mathbf{a})$ is transferred to the feedforward neural network (FFN) to obtain a deeper representation of the vector $\mathbf{f} = \{f_0, f_1, \ldots, f_n\}$. Finally, the vector $\mathbf{f}$ and the vector $IN(\mathbf{a}, \mathbf{c})$ are layer normalized once more to obtain the output vector $IN(\mathbf{a}, \mathbf{c}, \mathbf{f})$. The multi-headed sub-attention layer is the core of BERT, which solves the problem of long-range dependence on RNNs. The self-attention of BERT is shown in Equation (11).

$$Attention = \mathbf{V} * softmax(\frac{\mathbf{Q} \cdot \mathbf{K}^T}{\sqrt{d_k}}) \tag{11}$$

where $\mathbf{Q} = \{Q_0, Q_1, \ldots, Q_n\}$ is the query vector, $\mathbf{K} = \{K_0, K_1, \ldots, K_n\}$ is the key vector, $\mathbf{V} = \{V_0, V_1, \ldots, V_n\}$ is the value vector. $\mathbf{Q}$, $\mathbf{K}$, and $\mathbf{V}$ are obtained by linear mapping of the different weights W of the vector $\mathbf{E}$, which have the same dimension. It is worth noting that where d_K is the dimensionality of K. In addition, we apply the Chinese BERT pre-training model released by Google on GitHub, which is trained using the Chinese Wikipedia corpus. The specific parameters of the model are introduced as shown in Table 2.

Table 2. Chinese BERT model parameter.

Model Parameter	Value
Number of layers	14
H	768
A	14
max_seq	40

In this paper, we extract the output of the last 4 layers of the pre-trained BERT model to calculate the sentence vector. Assuming that a_{ij} is the output of the penultimate i layer of the pre-trained model with time step j (0 < i < 5, 0 < j < 41), the sentence vector is computed as follows. First, calculate the average A_i of the output of each layer:

$$A_i = mean(a_{ij}) \tag{12}$$

The entity vector $\mathbf{B}$ is the merge of the mean of the four layers.

$$B = concat(A_1, A_2, A_3, A_4) \tag{13}$$

That is, if the input text is a sequence of text tweens containing more than 3 entities, the final output $\mathbf{B}$ is a two-dimensional matrix, $B \in R^{l \times (4*H)}$, where l is the text length and H is the BERT model output vector dimension 768.

BiLSTM

BiLSTM is a special recurrent neural network that has been used as a tool for processing long time-series data and consists of the following three main parts. The first part is the information transfer part, where the input value x_t is a coefficient of m_t in the interval [0, 1], which is a mapping of the sigmoid function of x_t based on the output value h_{t-1}. If m_t is 1, the whole x_t will be retained. If m_t is 0, the whole x_t will be discarded as shown in Equation (14). Then comes the information addition part. First, the hyperbolic tangent (tanh) generalization is performed on h_{t-1} and x_t simultaneously to generate the candidate vector c_t^*; then, the sigmoid functionalization is performed on h_{t-1} and x_t simultaneously to generate the weights W to regulate the update of c_t^*; finally, the superimposed state vectors c_{t-1} and c_t^* to update C_t, as shown in Equation (15). The third part simultaneously sigmoid functionalizes h_{t-1} and x_t to generate weights k_t, k_t interacting with the functionalized C_t to obtain h_t, as shown in Equation (16). These operations give the LSTM the ability to memorize and retain only important features, which can alleviate the problems of poor long-term dependence, gradient disappearance, and gradient explosion [13].

$$m_t = sigmoid(\omega_f \cdot [x_t, h_{t-1}] + b_f) \tag{14}$$

$$\begin{cases} s_t = sigmoid(\omega_f \cdot [x_t, h_{t-1}] + b_i) \\ C_t^* = tanh(\omega \cdot [x_t, h_{t-1}] + b_c) \\ C_t = m_t \cdot C_{t-1} + s_t^* \end{cases} \tag{15}$$

$$\begin{cases} k_t = sigmoid(\omega_k \cdot [x_t, h_{t-1}] + b_k) \\ h_t = k_t \cdot tanh(C_t) \end{cases} \tag{16}$$

The entity weight recognition model proposed in this paper is namely a sequence-labeling model for textual entity sequences.

Among them, LSTM solves the problem that the standard RNN model disappears when the time lag between the relative input event and the target signal is greater than 5–10 discrete time steps ([44]) and has a wide range of applications in sequence-labeling-related tasks. The entity contribution recognition in this paper is a sequence-labeling task, and its processing of the current time-step semantic data requires both previous and subsequent semantic information, compared to standard RNN, LSTM cells add input gates, output gates, forgetting gates, a single LSTM cell as shown in Figure 3.

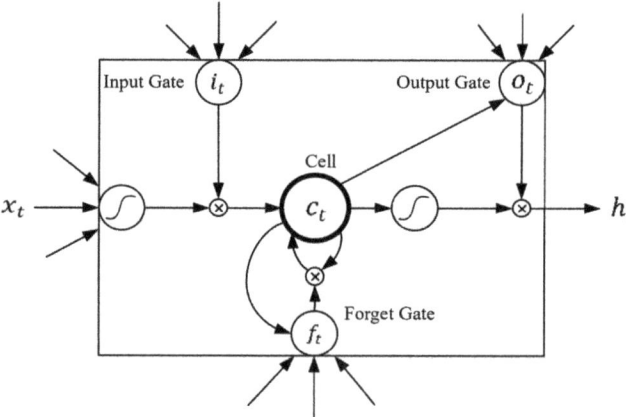

Figure 3. Single LSTM cells: O_t is output gate, C_t is cell, i_t is forget gate, f_t is forget gate.

Assuming that the input sequence is x_t, which x_t is the sequence of text vectors containing entities obtained by the BERT pre-training model, the LSTM cells are represented as follows:

$$\begin{cases} s_t = \sigma(W_{xi}x_t + W_{hi}h_{t-1} + W_{ci}c_{t-1} + b_t) \\ m_t = \sigma(W_{xf}x_t + W_{hf}h_{t-1} + W_{cf}c_{t-1} + b_f) \\ c_t = m_t c_{t-1} + s_t tanh(W_{xc}x_t + W_{hc}h_{t-1} + b_c) \\ o_t = \sigma(W_{xo}x_t + W_{ho}h_{t-1} + W_{co}c_t + b_o) \\ h_t = o_t tanh(c_t) \end{cases} \qquad (17)$$

where s_t is the input gate, m_t is the forgetting gate, c_t is the cell state, o_t is the output gate, h_t is the hidden layer, σ is the activation function, W is the weight parameter, b is the bias parameter, and W as well as b are the parameters to be trained in the model. The network structure is shown in Figure 4.

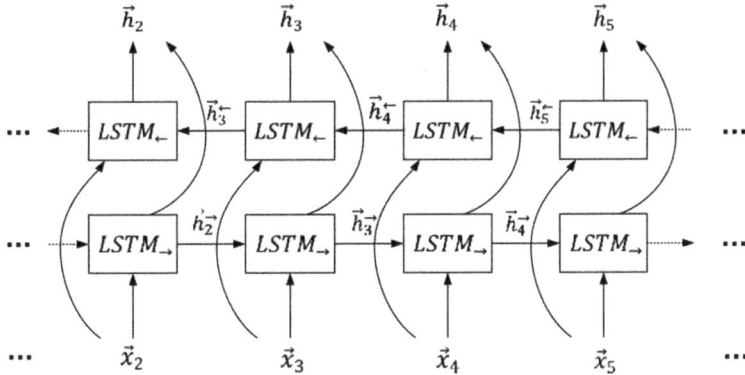

Figure 4. BILSTLM Network Structure.

The BiLSTM is a superposition of a forward LSTM and a backward LSTM, and the output equation of a single-layer BiLSTM is as follows:

$$y_t = \sigma(W_{\overrightarrow{h_t}y}\overrightarrow{h_t} + W_{\overleftarrow{h_t}y}\overleftarrow{h_t} + b_y) \qquad (18)$$

$\overrightarrow{h_t}$ is the output of the hidden layer with forward LSTM time step t in BiLSTM, and $\overleftarrow{h_t}$ is the output of the hidden layer with backward LSTM time step t.

CRF

BiLSTM treats each label as an independent existence and focuses more on the maximum probability of the labels without considering the dependency relationship between labels, which leads to confusing prediction information. INERM introduces CRF as a decoder to solve the above problem. CRF can calibrate the order and relationship between labels to obtain the globally optimal prediction sequence. The maximum likelihood estimation loss function of CRF is shown in Equation (19). It should be noted that after obtaining the entity label, the entity link rule constraint is performed, and the specific constraint is seen in the storage layer (Section 3.3).

$$Loss(i, o', o) = log \sum_{o'} e_{s(i,o')} - s(i, o) \qquad (19)$$

where $i = i_0, i_1, \ldots, i_n$ is the input sequence, $i' = i'_0, i'_1, \ldots, i'_n$ is the sequence of predicted entities, $o = o_0, o_1, \ldots, o_n$ is the actual entity sequence, and $s(i, o)$ is the sum of the firing and transition fractions.

BERT-BiLSTM-CRF-Based Entity Weight Calculation Model

The structure of the BERT-BiLSTM-CRF-based entity vector weight calculation model, i.e., the entity identification model. The entity vector weight calculation model based on BERT-BiLSTM-CRF is the entity identification model. The sentence vector sequence preprocessed by BERT is input to the BiLSTM model, and the output is the hidden vector H. The output of the hidden layer of the BiLSTM model enters the CRF to correct the entity labels at each time step, and then the classification is performed by the classifier to complete the entity identification. The selected classifier is a softmax classifier with the following equation:

$$p(c|H) = softmax(WH) \tag{20}$$

where W hidden layer output, H classifier parameters. Suppose the final trained BiLSTM model is a function g, the BERT Chinese model is a function f, and the input text sequence is x_i, then the probabilities of entity categories sen_{xi} (key entities (category 0), minor entities (category 1), and common entities (category 2)) in the model text sequence are calculated by sentence vectors as follows:

$$\{sen_{xi}\} = argmax(softmax(g(f\{x_i\}))) \tag{21}$$

where arguments of the maxima (argmax) is the function to determine the position of the maximum value.

TFIDF

TFIDF is a common method to extract keywords by statistical features. Among them are TF Term Frequency, which is used to quantify the ability of a word to summarize the subject content of a text, and IDF, which refers to Inverse Document Frequency, which is used to quantify the ability of a word to distinguish different categories of texts. In this paper, we add sentence weights and external corpus to improve the TFIDF algorithm.

TF Calculation The traditional TF calculation only takes the number of occurrences of a candidate word in a sentence as the ability of the word to summarize the text topic content, ignoring the semantic and contextual information, and thus cannot correctly represent the ability of the word to summarize the text topic content. In this paper, we propose the TF value algorithm for adding sentence weights, and the TF value for the t_i entity in the jth sentence is calculated as follows:

$$TF_{t_i,j} = \frac{\sum_i pos_{j,t_i,l}}{\sum_k n_{j,t_k}} \tag{22}$$

where n_{j,t_k} is the number of occurrences of t_k entity in the jth sentence, $\sum_k n_{j,t_k}$ to balance the effect of sentence length; entity t_k in the lth occurrence of the jth sentence.

The sentence contribution weight that $pos_{j,t_i,l}$ is introduced as follows. Firstly, the probability that an entity in a sentence belongs to each type is calculated by the entity contribution weight calculation model, then the entity type is the class with the highest probability. Because different entity types correspond to different entity contribution weights, we use the parameter ϱ to control the effect of type on the sentence contribution weight.

$$pos_{j,t_i,l} = \begin{cases} 1 + \varrho, sen_{ti} == 2(The\ key\ entity) \\ 1, sen_{ti} == 1(Secondary\ key\ entity) \\ 1 - \varrho, sen_{ti} == 0(General\ entity) \end{cases} \tag{23}$$

Calculation of IDF values by applying external corpus The traditional IDF value is calculated as the log value of the ratio of the number of texts with candidate words to the total number of texts, which ignores the distribution of candidate words among different topics, e.g., the word "accident" occurs in almost all of the safety report corpus. In this paper, we apply the external corpus value algorithm, i.e., in the process of IDF value calculation, the external general corpus is added to the safety report sentence corpus, and the corpus for calculating IDF value is the set of external general corpus and safety report corpus, and the formula for calculating IDF value of t_i words in the jth sentence is as follows:

$$IDF_{t_i} = log\frac{|D \cup d|}{|d : t_i \in D or t_i \in d|} \quad (24)$$

where D denotes the set of security report sentences and d denotes the set of external corpus sentences, where $|D \cup d|$ shows the total number of sentences in the original corpus and the external corpus merged set, $|d : t_i \in D or t_i \in d|$ the number of sentences with t_i words occurring in the corpus and the external corpus set.

TFIDF value calculation The TFIDF value is the product of the TF value and the IDF value, and the TFIDF value for the t_i entity in the jth sentence is calculated as follows:

$$TFIDF_{t_i,j} = TF_{t_i,j} * IDF_{t_i} \quad (25)$$

Experimental results The metrics precision (P), recall (R), and F1-score (F1) are used to evaluate the extraction performance of INERM. P: P in this paper refers to how many of the keywords extracted by the algorithm are correct and are calculated. The expression is as follows:

$$P = \frac{m}{n_{all}} \quad (26)$$

R: R in this paper refers to how many correct keywords are extracted by the algorithm in a sentence and are calculated. The expression is as follows:

$$R = \frac{m}{n_{self}} \quad (27)$$

m is the number of correct key entities extracted, n_{all} is the number of key entities extracted, and n_{self} is the number of keywords in the text itself. F: The F-value is the weighted summed average of the precision rate P and the recall rate R, calculated as follows:

$$F = \frac{2*P*R}{P+R} \quad (28)$$

In this paper, we determine the sentence contribution weight parameter ϱ experimentally, compare the model results of choosing different ϱ on the training set, and select the best ϱ value. Considering that most of the key entities of each sentence in the product development knowledge corpus are 2–4, the algorithm selects the first 4 as the key entities for each sentence. The performance of the algorithm corresponding to different ϱ values on the training set is shown in Table 3. When the ϱ value in the table is 0.6, the accuracy of the model on the test set and the verification set is on average 8 percentage points higher than other values. Therefore, the ϱ value selected is 0.6.

Table 3. The results of the evaluation experiments.

	P		R		F	
ϱ	Test	val	Test	val	Test	val
0.30	0.57393	0.54143	0.53154	0.56123	0.52810	0.55123
0.60	0.66390	0.63425	0.68422	0.63674	0.67423	0.65689
0.90	0.59304	0.52316	0.56381	0.55316	0.59019	0.55316

The keyword extraction algorithm proposed is used to verify the algorithm. Considering that there are different kinds of key entities in each sentence of the industrial safety report corpus, the total number of key entities is 1–4. For each sentence algorithm, 1–4 different types of key entities can be extracted. It should be noted that the common hyperparameters for all neural networks are the same in both evaluation and comparison experiments. For example, we use the Adam optimizer with a learning rate of 10^{-3}, the ReLU activation function, and train 30 epochs on the validation set and the test set for all models. In order to confirm the extraction effect of INERM, this paper conducts a comparative experiment on different algorithms to predict all entities on the test set. The comparison results are shown in Table 4. The results show that INERM has a strong extraction performance. The results show that INERM is feasible in the task of industrial safety knowledge extraction.

In the table, the F score of the INERM predicted entity in the test set is 67.5%. From the overall comparison experiment results, the accuracy of the existing models on the test set is far less than 67.5%. In addition, the overall performance of all models in P, R, and F scores is far less than that of the INERM model. In the comparison of the F value, INERM is 19 percentage points higher than BERT, 21.4 percentage points higher than BiLSTM, and 15 percentage points higher than the most classic combination model BERT-BiLSTM-CRF. The results show that INERM has a strong entity extraction performance and also prove the feasibility of INERM in the field of industrial safety. We believe that it can make an important contribution to the task of industrial safety knowledge extraction.

Table 4. Comparison of various algorithm models on the test set.

Model	P	R	F
TextRank	0.36624	0.43152	0.39621
TFIDF	0.38817	0.45732	0.41992
INERM	0.57511	0.63612	0.59231
BERT	0.35612	0.50232	0.43225
BERT+BiLSTM	0.37485	0.52622	0.42421
BiLSTM	0.42991	0.47892	0.40892
BiLSTM+CRF	0.41329	0.52340	0.38021
BERT+BiLSTM+CRF	0.44892	0.52301	0.45289

3.3. Storage Layer

We show the industrial safety knowledge graph triad constructed by the relationship between industrial entities and settings in the form of Equation (29). Where the set $< n_h, e, n_t >$ of the industrial safety knowledge-mapping triad consists of node head n_h and node tail n_t, which are both industrial safety entities, and two nodes are connected with an edge e, which denotes the relationship located between the two entities. Specifically, each industrial safety report node description is taken as input. By extracting the entities (α and β) in the input, element relationships are embedded between α and β in turn. Considering the possibility of multiple C and S, the triples about R are first constructed from both ends of the input, and then the triples about C and S are constructed.

$$ISKG = \{< n_h, e, n_t > | n_h, n_t \in E_{ISK}; e \in e_{ISK}\} \quad (29)$$

We import the industrial safety knowledge-mapping triad into the Neo4j graph database (Miller, 2013; Zhe Huang et al., 2020; W. Huang et al., 2020; Kim et al., 2021) to complete the non-normative industrial safety knowledge mapping. It is worth noting that the results recorded in the industrial safety reports are standardized and accurate with multiple analyses by expert groups, and even though the words are very close to each other literally, each word still has a unique meaning, such as "process pipeline" and "pipeline". In addition, due to the complexity of the process, some entities and relationships are redundant. Therefore, to address the above issues, we adopt a set of regular entity linking rules as follows:

(1) Multiple logical words of the same kind of entities are linked as one entity, and each iteration is merged into the entity library. For example, if "gas main pipe of the gas cabinet", "gas cabinet", and "gas main pipe" are all asset entities, at this time, due to the

logical word "of", you can consider "gas master of the gas cabinet" as the same asset entity. Similar logical words are "on, attributed to, attached to, attributed to, in... on, contains... in";

(2) The larger the length of the entity, the higher the priority of the association. The larger the length of an entity that has been linked to the entity library, the clearer the meaning of the entity and the more representative of a key entity, such as "ammonia production key equipment nitrogen and hydrogen compressor", which is more representative of "ammonia production key equipment" than "ammonia production key equipment". For example, "ammonia production critical equipment nitrogen and hydrogen compressor" is a class of entities compared to "ammonia production critical equipment". Therefore, when linking entities, it is preferred to associate entities with greater length to the entity library;

(3) If there is only one key entity in a sentence, the key entity is linked to the entity library first;

(4) When there are multiple concurrent entities in a sentence, the entities should be split and linked to the corresponding entities. For example, "Carbon is a kind of flammable material, which is prone to spontaneous combustion under the conditions of high temperature and superheat accidental mechanical impact, airflow impact, electrical short circuit, external fire and static spark", where "airflow impact", "high temperature and superheat", "accidental mechanical impact", and other causes may lead to the result of "carbon spontaneous combustion", so it should be split into multiple cause entities, respectively associated to the "carbon spontaneous combustion". Therefore, it should be split into multiple cause entities and linked to the resulting entity of "carbon self-ignition";

(5) For an entity extracted from INERM, if its degree of repetition with the entity in the entity library is greater than 80%, it is considered to belong to the corresponding entity in the entity library. In this paper, all kinds of industrial safety entities are composed of asset entities and descriptive language. If the asset entities are the same and the repetition of descriptive language is 80%, they are considered to be the same entity.

It should be noted that this entity linking rule is also used in the extraction layer (CRF).

4. Case Study

In this study, we have studied fluid transportation processes in the industry. Due to the danger and complexity of the gathering process, the safety production of the gathering process has become the focus of attention of society. In the process of oilfield development, the gathering process plays an important role, which not only determines the overall level of oilfield development but also effectively improves the social and economic benefits of oil and gas enterprises. To this end, we collected a total of 1745 analytical records for the multi-programmed processes of fluid transport (gravity transport, vacuum transport, and evaporative transport) and established a knowledge map of industrial safety reports. For example, for fluid transport, Figure 5 shows the standardized industrial safety knowledge graph structure, and it is noteworthy that some nodes and relationships in the knowledge graph have been constrained by entity linking rules.

Safety-oriented knowledge-mapping applications, such as industrial safety knowledge-mapping visualization, industrial safety knowledge-mapping retrieval, and risk propagation reasoning, can explore and expand the value of industrial safety knowledge mapping and further improve its value to enhance the execution efficiency of industrial safety reports, which is important to improve the safety of the system. It can provide expandable practical applications for industrial engineering design and industrial safety integration, and the following are application-specific descriptions:

(1) Industrial safety knowledge graph visualization. The visualization process is shown in the Figure 6. The green circle is the asset entity, the blue circle is the cause entity, the red circle is the result entity, the purple circle is the suggestion entity, and the arrow indicates the relationship between various entities. The arrows between green and blue represent the cause composition relationship, the arrows between green and red represent the result composition relationship, the arrows between green and purple represent the

measure composition relationship, the arrows between blue and red represent the result relationship, and the arrows between red and purple represent the measure relationship. We take the nodes in Figure 6 as an example. In the process of a raw gas inlet, the raw gas enters the inlet cut-off valve magic Kui and the clear pipe acceptance device to the separator inlet. The industrial safety knowledge mapping uses the state 'not closed' (cause entity) corresponding to the asset 'receiving ball cylinder bypass valve' (asset entity) as the starting point for the hazard analysis and extends the consequences, 'the gathering of raw material gas causes fire and explosion hazards' (result entity). This is a very logical result. Through the above process, it is clear that industrial safety knowledge mapping can visually show that after the 'not closed' cause, it results in an 'explosion hazard'. This hazard process can be determined to take 'increase pressure low low interlock Shutdown' (suggestion entity) measures. Industrial safety knowledge-mapping visualization reduces the error rate of hazard detection and provides a reliable solution with greater completeness and safety;

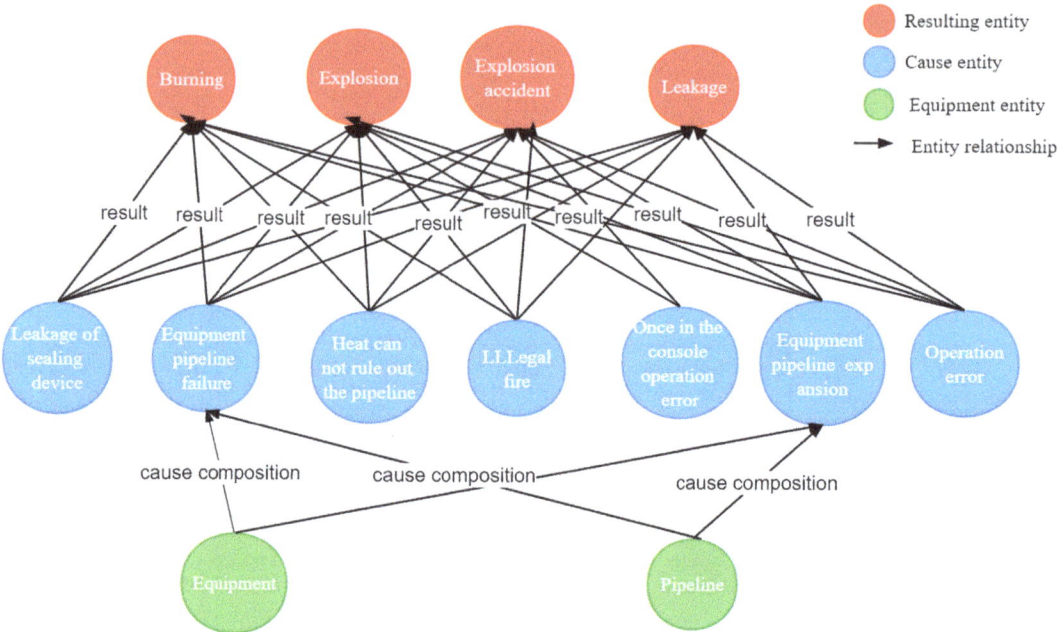

Figure 5. Standardized industrial safety knowledge graph structure.

(2) Industrial safety knowledge-mapping search. We need industrial safety knowledge maps that can be efficiently located and present us with relevant information. For example, when we retrieve an incoming valve set, its collector branch (operating pressure rise), cause status (false shutdown), and equipment assets (HH interlock, upper valve, and collector branch) can all be provided by the industrial safety knowledge map. The resulting process allows employees to more fully grasp the industrial safety knowledge mapping and become familiar with the corresponding requirements for process safety and the related operations;

(3) Auxiliary industrial safety reporting. When an accident occurs, operators can locate the consequences of a hazardous event and trace the cause of failure through industrial safety knowledge mapping based on abnormal phenomena to quickly make suggestions and effectively eliminate hidden dangers, which is of great significance to further improve the safety of the system;

(4) Hazard propagation reasoning. Omissions in industrial safety reports are inevitable. To further improve the industrial safety report, risk reasoning can be realized through industrial safety knowledge mapping to correct and make up for the industrial safety report. Industrial safety knowledge mapping can infer other possible propagation paths of accidents based on the paths between existing entities, which makes the whole safety protection process better and also assists experts in brainstorming to optimize industrial safety reports and achieve better knowledge accuracy.

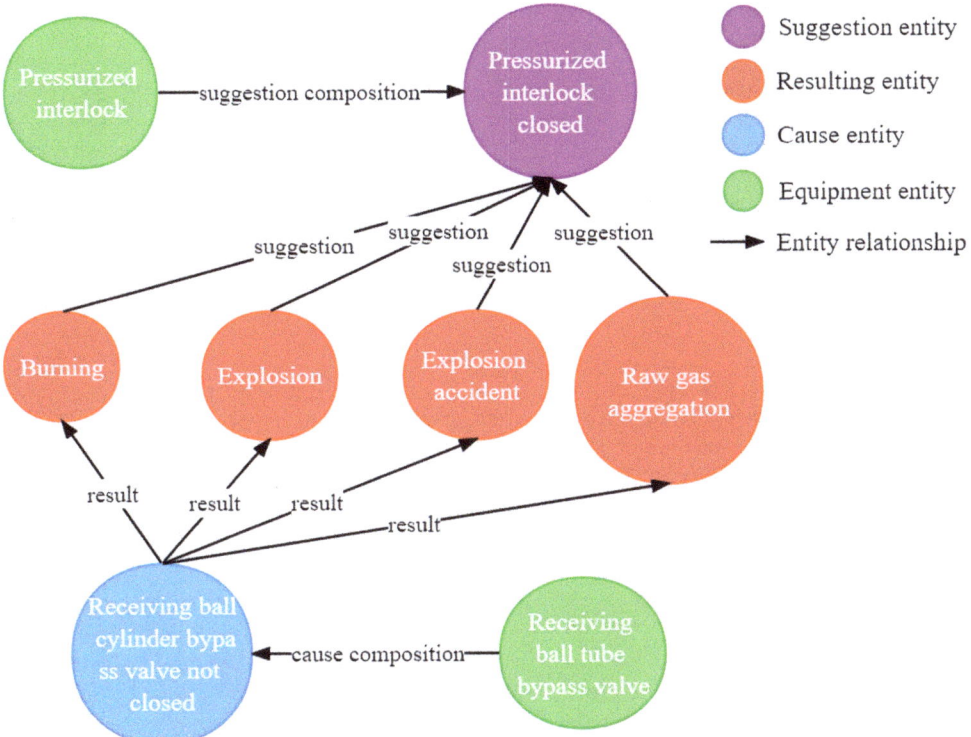

Figure 6. Content and structure display of safety knowledge map of oil and gas inbound module.

In conclusion, the industrial safety knowledge mapping constructed based on the INERM and its application liberate the safety reports and realize the reuse and motivation of industrial safety knowledge. The unified structure of industrial safety knowledge is an industrial safety engineering design practice [45], which expands the perspective of industrial safety engineering design and provides ideas for academic researchers. We also believe it can help realize intelligent and automated knowledge expression in industrial safety.

5. Conclusions

The industrial safety report, a central representative in industrial safety engineering, can optimize any scenario in a process industrial safety process and provide effective safety analysis decisions. It should be noted that the rich industrial safety knowledge contained in the industrial safety report template is not fully utilized. To effectively utilize the value of the industrial safety knowledge graph and optimize industrial safety reports, we build a new knowledge graph with industrial safety reports as the carrier.

Industrial safety knowledge mapping follows a knowledge-mapping-based approach. Specifically, firstly, in response to the dilemma of different expressions of industrial safety knowledge maps, a knowledge standardization framework is creatively developed to deconstruct and summarize industrial safety reports in a top-down manner. The industrial safety knowledge mapping contains the ontologies and relationships of industrial safety knowledge mapping, which can standardize industrial safety reports in various processes and unify the representation and integration of industrial safety knowledge mapping. Secondly, considering the special characteristics of industrial safety report texts, a deep learning-based information extraction model, INERM, is conceived by cleverly combining data science and deep learning to extract industrial safety knowledge graphs from industrial safety reports based on a structured framework of industrial safety knowledge, which realizes engineering design-oriented data science. Briefly, the INERM consists of a pre-trained model, a two-way long short-term memory network, a conditional random field, and a TFIDF. Finally, the industrial safety knowledge graph triad is constructed based on the industrial safety knowledge graph-structured framework and the INERM and is stored in the Neo4j graph database.

We have completed the example for oil and gas entry and exit stations. The industrial safety knowledge graph is an excellent example of combining artificial intelligence and industrial engineering, which can integrate and unlock the value of industrial safety knowledge graph reports in a feasible way. In addition, it is oriented to applications such as industrial safety knowledge graph visualization, industrial safety knowledge graph retrieval, and assisted industrial safety reports, which can develop the value of an industrial safety knowledge graph and further improve the execution efficiency of industrial safety reports, which is important for improving the system security which is of great significance. In addition, the development of targeted applications, such as question-and-answer systems, can also popularize safety knowledge and enhance the awareness of non-professionals.

In future work, we will further improve the scope of the abstraction of various industrial safety reports, such as the abstraction of deviations from HAZOP and the severity of the consequences of the PHA, and carry out tasks such as entity processing, entity linking, and knowledge fusion. All in all, shortly, we can foresee that the industrial safety knowledge graph will become more mature, providing added value to the daily practice of industrial safety and inspiring other researchers working on industrial safety engineering design and industrial knowledge graph design.

Author Contributions: Conceptualization, S.X. and Y.Y.; data curation, Z.Y., X.T. and Y.Y.; formal analysis, S.X. and Y.Y.; funding acquisition, L.S.; methodology, Z.Y.; project administration, S.X. and L.S.; resources, Z.Y. and X.T.; software, Z.Y., L.S. and X.T.; supervision, S.X., L.S. and Y.Y.; validation, Z.Y., S.X., L.S. and Y.Y.; visualization, Z.Y., L.S. and X.T.; writing—original draft, Z.Y. and X.T.; writing—review and editing, Z.Y. and X.T. All authors have read and agreed to the published version of the manuscript.

Funding: Funds required in this paper are provided by the Jiangsu Provincial Petrochemical Process Key Equipment Digital Twin Technology Engineering Research Center Open Project No. DTEC202103 and the Postgraduate Research & Practice Innovation Program of Jiangsu Province (No. KYCX22_3078).

Acknowledgments: Thanks to Shoukun Xu, Lin Shi, and Yang Yuan for their guidance on the experiment. Thank you Tan for providing the operational mechanism formula for the industrial equipment. Thanks to the tutor team for providing fund support.

Conflicts of Interest: The authors declare that the research was conducted in the absence of any commercial or financial relationships.

Abbreviations

The following abbreviations are used in this manuscript:

HAZOP	Hazard and Operability Analysis
PHA	Pre-Hazard Analysis
INERM	Industrial Safety Knowledge Extraction Model
BERT	Bidirectional Encoder Representation from Transformers
BiLSTM	Bidirectional Long- and Short-term Memory Network
JHA	Job Hazard Analysis
ET	Event Tree
AAS	Asset Administration Shell
NSP	NEST Sentence Prediction
CRF	Conditional Random Field
CDD	Common Data Dictionary
RNN	Recurrent Neural Network

References

1. Kang, J.; Guo, L. HAZOP analysis based on sensitivity evaluation. *Saf. Sci.* **2016**, *88*, 26–32. [CrossRef]
2. Flaus, J. Preliminary Hazard Analysis. In *Risk Analysis*; John Wiley & Sons, Inc.: Hoboken, NJ, USA, 2013. Available online: https://onlinelibrary.wiley.com/doi/pdf/10.1002/9781118790021.ch8 (accessed on 5 November 2022).
3. Baybutt, P. A critique of the Hazard and Operability (HAZOP) study. *J. Loss Prev. Process. Ind.* **2015**, *33*, 52–58. [CrossRef]
4. Cameron, I.; Mannan, S.; Németh, E.; Park, S.; Pasman, H.; Rogers, W.; Seligmann, B. Process hazard analysis, hazard identification and scenario definition: Are the conventional tools sufficient, or should and can we do much better? *Process. Saf. Environ. Prot.* **2017**, *110*, 53–70. [CrossRef]
5. Baybutt, P. Requirements for improved process hazard analysis (PHA) methods. *J. Loss Prev. Process. Ind.* **2014**, *32*, 182–191. [CrossRef]
6. Naderpour, M.; Lu, J.; Zhang, G. An abnormal situation modeling method to assist operators in safety-critical systems. *Reliab. Eng. Syst. Saf.* **2015**, *133*, 33–47. [CrossRef]
7. Paltrinieri, N.; Tugnoli, A.; Buston, J.; Wardman, M.; Cozzani, V. Dynamic Procedure for Atypical Scenarios Identification (DyPASI): A new systematic HAZID tool. *J. Loss Prev. Process. Ind.* **2013**, *26*, 683–695. [CrossRef]
8. Rodríguez, M.; de la Mata, J.L. Automating HAZOP studies using D-higraphs. *Comput. Chem. Eng.* **2012**, *45*, 102–113. [CrossRef]
9. Khan, F.I.; Abbasi, S. Towards automation of HAZOP with a new tool EXPERTOP. *Environ. Model. Softw.* **2000**, *15*, 67–77. [CrossRef]
10. Hu, J.; Zhang, L.; Cai, Z.; Wang, Y. An intelligent fault diagnosis system for process plant using a functional HAZOP and DBN integrated methodology. *Eng. Appl. Artif. Intell.* **2015**, *45*, 119–135. [CrossRef]
11. Feng, X.; Dai, Y.; Ji, X.; Zhou, L.; Dang, Y. Application of natural language processing in HAZOP reports. *Process. Saf. Environ. Protect.* **2021**, *155*, 41–48. [CrossRef]
12. Zeng, W. Research on building chemical safety knowledge graph based on Neo4j. *Heilongjiang Sci.* **2021**, *12*, 3.
13. Wang, Z.; Zhang, B.; Gao, D. A novel knowledge graph development for industry design: A case study on indirect coal liquefaction process. *arXiv* **2021**, arXiv:2111.13854.
14. Wang, J.; Zhang, W.; Wang, Y.; Sun, Z. Construction and inferential analysis of matter cognitive graphs for big data domains. *Chin. Sci. Inf. Sci.* **2020**, *50*, 15.
15. Chiarello, F.; Belingheri, P.; Fantoni, G. Data science for engineering design: State of the art and future directions. *Comput. Ind.* **2021**, *129*, 103447. [CrossRef]
16. Chhim, P.; Chinnam, R.B.; Sadawi, N. Product design and manufacturing process based ontology for manufacturing knowledge reuse. *J. Intell. Manuf.* **2017**, 905–916. [CrossRef]
17. Chiarello, F.; Melluso, N.; Bonaccorsi, A.; Fantoni, G. A Text Mining Based Map of Engineering Design: Topics and their Trajectories Over Time. In Proceedings of the Design Society: International Conference on Engineering Design, Delft, The Netherlands, 5–8 August 2019. Available online: https://www.researchgate.net/publication/334711416_A_Text_Mining_Based_Map_of_Engineering_Design_Topics_and_their_Trajectories_Over_Time (accessed on 25 March 2022).
18. Chiarello, F.; Cirri, I.; Melluso, N.; Fantoni, G.; Pavanello, T. *Approaches to Automatically Extract Affordances from Patents*; Cambridge University Press: Cambridge, UK, 2019; pp. 2487–2496. Available online: https://www.researchgate.net/publication/334711467_Approaches_to_Automatically_Extract_Affordances_from_Patents (accessed on 26 March 2022).
19. Khan, F.I.; Abbasi, S. Techniques and methodologies for risk analysis in chemical process industries. *J. Loss Prev. Process. Ind.* **1998**, *11*, 261–277. [CrossRef]
20. Devlin, J.; Chang, M.W.; Lee, K.; Toutanova, K. BERT: Pre-training of Deep Bidirectional Transformers for Language Understanding. 2018. Available online: https://arxiv.org/pdf/1810.04805.pdf (accessed on 1 April 2022).
21. Wang, Y.; Luo, S.; Yang, Y.; Zhang, H. Review of knowledge graph visualization. *J. Comput. Aided Des. Graph.* **2019**, *31*, 11. [CrossRef]

22. Gong, J.; Liu, J.; Zhao, B.-X.; Wu, H.-C. Knowledge-based automatic evaluation technique for pipeline layout. *Comput. Integr. Manuf. Syst.* **2014**, *20*, 2522–2531. [CrossRef]
23. Huijun, Z.; Shigang, W. Conceptual design of mechanical products based on multilayer reasoning mechanism. *J. Comput. Aided Des. Graph.* **1997**, *9*, 548–553. [CrossRef]
24. Cai, H.; He, Y.; Liu, H. Modeling and implementation of a design repository based on hierarchical semantic network. *Comput. Integr. Manuf. Syst.* **2005**, *11*, 73–78.
25. Guo, X.; Zhao, W.; Wang, J.; Wang, C.; Zhang, K.; Chen, C. Research on process design knowledge model and retrieval method for innovative design. *J. Mech. Eng.* **2017**, *53*, 80–86. [CrossRef]
26. Liu, H.; Du, J.; Bai, Y. Research on semantic modeling of manufacturing domain knowledge based on multidimensional ontology. *Manuf. Technol. Mach. Tools* **2019**, 140–146.
27. Bock, C.; Zha, X.F.; Suh, H.W.; Lee, J.H. Ontological product modeling for collaborative design. *Adv. Eng. Inform.* **2010**, *24*, 510–524. [CrossRef]
28. Huang, R.; Zhang, S.; Shi, Y.; Tao, J. Process language understanding and process semantic model construction for 3D reconstruction. *Aerosp. Manuf. Technol.* **2011**, 4. [CrossRef]
29. Zhou, B.; Bao, J.S.; Zhang, Q.W.; Liu, T.Y.; Liu, Y.H. A Knowledge Graph-Driven Method for Optimizing Equipment Resource Allocation. 2020. Available online: https://doc.taixueshu.com/patent/CN111191821A.html (accessed on 1 April 2022).
30. Wang, Z.; Zhang, B.; Gao, D. Text Mining of Hazard and Operability Analysis Reports Based on Active Learning. *Processes* **2021**, *9*, 1178. [CrossRef]
31. Wei, S.G.; Cai, B.; Gou, C.; Jian, W.; Wang, J. Research on reliability evaluation of high-speed railway train control system based on fault injection. In Proceedings of the International Conference on Environmental Science & Information Application Technology, Wuhan, China, 17–18 July 2010. Available online: http://en.cnki.com.cn/Article_en/CJFDTOTAL-TDTH201007003.htm (accessed on 7 February 2022).
32. Daramola, O.; Stålhane, T.; Omoronyia, I.; Sindre, G. Using Ontologies and Machine Learning for Hazard Identification and Safety Analysis. In *Managing Requirements Knowledge*; Maalej, W., Thurimella, A.K., Eds.; Springer: Berlin/Heidelberg, Germany, 2013; pp. 117–141. [CrossRef]
33. Qian, S.L.; Zhang, H.J.; Corporation, J.G.; University, H.N. The Research Development of Hazard and Operability (HAZOP) Analysis. *Shandong Chem. Ind.* **2013**, 2–5. Available online: http://en.cnki.com.cn/Article_en/CJFDTotal-SDHG201310020.htm (accessed on 5 November 2022).
34. Qin, Y.; Qi, X.; Wei, T.; Qingxiu, Y. Application of advance hazard analysis in natural gas boosting engineering. *Oil Gas Chem.* **2012**, *41*, 4.
35. Wei, L.; Yanping, W. protective layer analysis method. *Saf. Health Environ.* **2006**, 8–15. [CrossRef]
36. Li, Z. Application of HAZOP analysis method in natural gas distribution field stations. *Chin. Pet. Chem. Stand. Qual.* **2016**, *23*, 3. [CrossRef]
37. Lu, Y.H.; Zhang, L.; Tao, G.; Yu, Y.L. Risk Analysis of Cyclohexanone Production Unit Based on HAZOP-LOPA Coupled Phenol Hydrogenation. 2020. Available online: https://kns.cnki.net/KCMS/detail/detail.aspx?dbcode=IPFD&filename=ZKHJ202007001170 (accessed on 3 April 2022).
38. Imort, S. Product Lifecycle Management with the Asset Administration Shell. *Computers* **2021**, *10*, 84. [CrossRef]
39. Yue, L.; Liu, D.; Fang, Y. Asset management shell in Industry 4.0 components. *China Instrum.* **2017**, *13*, 6.
40. Dunjó, J.; Fthenakis, V.; Vílchez, J.A.; Arnaldos, J. Hazard and operability (HAZOP) analysis. A literature review. *J. Hazard. Mater.* **2010**, *173*, 19–32. [CrossRef] [PubMed]
41. Current, T. International Electrotechnical Commission-IEC. *Environ. Technol.* **2003**, *PER-7*, 27. [CrossRef]
42. Schuhmacher, M. Knowledge Graph Exploration for Natural Language Understanding in Web Information Retrieval. 2016. Available online: https://portal.dnb.de/opac.htm?method=simpleSearch&cqlMode=true&query=idn%3D1120302587 (accessed on 2 May 2022).
43. Vaswani, A.; Shazeer, N.; Parmar, N.; Uszkoreit, J.; Jones, L.; Gomez, A.N.; Kaiser, L.; Polosukhin, I. Attention Is All You Need. *arXiv* **2017**, arXiv:1706.03762.
44. Gers, F.A.; Schmidhuber, J.; Cummins, F. Learning to Forget: Continual Prediction with LSTM. *Neural Comput.* **2000**, *12*, 2451–2471. [CrossRef] [PubMed]
45. Calijorne Soares, M.A.; Parreiras, F.S. A literature review on question answering techniques, paradigms and systems. *J. King Saud Univ. Comput. Inf. Sci.* **2020**, *32*, 635–646. [CrossRef]

Disclaimer/Publisher's Note: The statements, opinions and data contained in all publications are solely those of the individual author(s) and contributor(s) and not of MDPI and/or the editor(s). MDPI and/or the editor(s) disclaim responsibility for any injury to people or property resulting from any ideas, methods, instructions or products referred to in the content.

Article

Task-Offloading and Resource Allocation Strategy in Multidomain Cooperation for IIoT

Zuojun Dai *, Ying Zhou, Hui Tian and Nan Ma

State Key Laboratory of Networking and Switching Technology, Beijing University of Posts and Telecommunications, Beijing 100876, China
* Correspondence: george.dai@bupt.edu.cn

Abstract: This study proposes a task-offloading and resource allocation strategy in multidomain cooperation (TARMC) for the industrial Internet of Things (IIoT) to resolve the problem of the non-uniform distribution of task computation among various cluster domain networks in the IIoT and the solidification of traditional industrial wireless network architecture, which produces low efficiency of static resource allocation and high delay in closed-loop data processing. Based on the closed-loop process of task interaction of intelligent terminals in wireless networks, the proposed strategy constructs a network model of multidomain collaborative task-offloading and resource allocation in IIoT for flexible and dynamic resource allocation among intelligent terminals, edge servers, and cluster networks. Considering the partial offloading mechanism, various tasks were segmented into multiple subtasks marked at bit-level per demand, which enabled local and edge servers to process all subtasks in parallel. Moreover, this study established a utility function for the closed-loop delay and terminal energy consumption of task processing, which transformed the process of multidomain collaborative task-offloading and resource allocation into the problem of task computing revenue. Furthermore, an improved Cuckoo Search algorithm was developed to derive the optimal offloading position and resource allocation decision through an alternating iterative method. The simulation results revealed that TARMC performed better than strategies.

Keywords: cross-domain; MEC; resource allocation; IIOT

1. Introduction

With the rapid development of advanced industrial manufacturing modes such as Industry 4.0, intelligent factory, and flexible manufacturing, communication technology and the manufacturing industry have become deeply integrated in recent years. Consequently, the digital and integrated industrial Internet of Things (IIoT) has emerged as a research hotspot [1–5]. However, the advantages of the three major application scenarios of 5G are incompatible and cannot coexist simultaneously. Moreover, the synchronous realization of ultralow closed-loop delay transmission, large connection, and large-bandwidth transmission is challenging for large-scale machine differentiated services. Therefore, further research is required to transform existing industrial wireless network architectures and resource allocation methods.

Currently, the mainstream wireless edge network adopts a centralized network mode on the terminal side, [6,7], and the information is transmitted between the nodes via the access edge server and cloud platform, which considerably increases the delay of data transmission between the nodes. For the large-scale wireless edge network, this rigid and centralized network mode poses problems such as high network-computation cost, serious resource conflict, and reduced network performance, which yields inferior scalability of the edge networks. This further raises the difficulty of supporting flexible, adaptive resource scheduling and ubiquitous computing functions of industrial edge networks. To support a large IIoT, the cluster domain network [8,9] contains numerous terminal nodes distributed in a certain region for constructing hierarchical networks using the clustering algorithm [10,11]. In addition, mobile edge computing (MEC) [12,13] extends cloud services to network edges that effectively coordinate the distributed edge resources. With the increasing performance requirements for computation-intensive and delay-sensitive loads in IIoT, cluster domain networks and MEC have emerged as potential solutions to accommodate complex IIoT applications for the integrated management of IIoT communications, sensing, and computing resources [14].

The traditional industrial wireless network based on the IEEE 802 protocol [15] can achieve only a 10 ms level delay in one-way communication transmission, which is vastly inadequate to achieve the performance requirements of IIoT. On one hand, the hierarchical network control mode relying on the core network yields low resource-management efficiency and does not fulfill the communication requirements of differentiated machine services. On the other hand, considering the extremely low delay requirements of closed-loop management for several IIoT applications in the manufacturing workshop, computing tasks require more fine-grained offloading strategies. To fulfill the demand for efficient interaction of information flow between massive machines in IIoT, the edge network should allow a portion of the computing tasks in mobile devices to be processed locally, and the remaining computing tasks are offloaded onto the server. According to the strict requirements for reliable real-time performance in industrial scenarios, computing tasks should be processed for real-time stored industrial data. Therefore, low-delay computing task-offloading methods and resource allocation strategies must be studied based on cluster domain network structure.

2. Related Work

In recent years, the study of computational offloading strategies has emerged as a research hotspot in the field of edge computing [16,17]. With various objectives, researchers have proposed several computational offloading strategies. To minimize task execution delay, Yang et al. [18] formulated a selection strategy for optimal offloading node as a Markov decision process and minimized the offloading delay by adopting a value iteration algorithm. Li et al. [19] studied a paradigm for dual computational offloading and proposes a hierarchical, cell-based distributed algorithm to obtain the optimal dual offloading scheme for implementing the overall delay minimization of task-offloading. Zhu et.al [20] studied the single-user multi-edge-server MEC system based on downlink NOMA to minimize task computation delay by jointly optimizing the NOMA-based transmission duration (TD) and workload offloading allocation (WOA) among edge computing servers. Luo et al. [21] proposed a self-taught-based distributed computational offloading algorithm to minimize its delay and information cost. Huang et al. [22] proposed an efficient multidevice and multi-BSs task-offloading scheme to minimize the delay of computational tasks. Gao et al. [23] proposed a two-stage computational offloading scheme to minimize task processing delay. Liao et al. [24] proposed a novel UAV-assisted edge computational framework that provided edge computational offloading based on the user distribution of time-varying hotspots to minimize average user delay. The current research primarily focuses on the simple network structure model, which is limited to the optimization of the one-way empty port-time delay that contradicts the closed-loop interaction characteristics of the information flow of the industrial intelligent machine network.

To minimize total energy consumption, Fang et al. [25] proposed a content-aware multi-subtask-offloading problem based on the individual features of subtasks with various delay requirements, under which the offloading decision and channel allocation were optimized. Aiming to obtain resource allocation and offloading decisions, Wu et al. [26] developed an efficient two-layer optimization algorithm for resolving the residual energy maximization problem. Chen et al. [27] formulated the offloading task as a stochastic optimization problem and proposed an energy-efficient dynamic offloading algorithm that minimized the energy consumption of task-offloading. In addition, Bozorgchenani et al. [28] modeled task-offloading in MEC as a constrained multi-objective optimization problem that minimizes both the energy consumption and task processing delay of the mobile devices. More recently, Zhang et.al [29] proposed an energy-saving algorithm based on deep reinforcement learning to optimize the overall energy cost in real-time multi-user MEC systems. However, the delay and energy consumption performance may bear distinct weight coefficients, for instance, the system focuses on the delay performance by increasing the delay weight, which consequently places higher requirements for optimizing and offloading the system task.

To reduce service response delay and energy expenditure, the user can opt to offload the task to the edge server or the cloud server for execution. Therefore, offloading schemes that combine delay demand and energy consumption demand should be considered. Lu et al. [30] designed a multitask-offloading policy that could handle dense offloading requests from various mobile devices to optimize the overall execution delay and energy consumption. Wang et al. [31] developed an efficient multi-objective evolutionary algorithm to solve the problems of minimizing the response time, minimizing the energy consumption, and minimizing the cost. Guan et al. [32] proposed a novel MEC-based mobility-aware offloading model to address the in-cloud offloading scheduling problem and the load between cloud sensing problems by offloading execution efficiency, task processing delay, and energy efficiency. Aiming to reduce system energy consumption as well as computational task delay, Chen et al. [33] proposed a robust computational offloading strategy with fault recovery capabilities in intermittently connected small cloud systems. Fang et al. [34] investigated the multi-user computational task offload problem in device-enhanced MEC based on the perspective of joint optimization of channel allocation, device pairing, and offload modes, considering the significance of delay and energy consumption to maximize the total offload benefit of all computationally-intensive users in the network.

The existing work mainly studies the offloading scheme of minimizing time delay, energy consumption or synthesis under the traditional industrial wireless network architecture, and solves some optimization problems of one-way air port delay and energy consumption under the simple network structure. However, the joint optimization of task-offloading delay and energy consumption can be realized only with the traditional network architecture. In case of multidomain network collaboration and extremely low closed-loop delay demand of IIoT, the utility aspect of network closed-loop delay and terminal energy consumption cannot still be effectively balanced. So, we developed an improved multidomain collaborative task-offloading mechanism to deeply analyze the impact of the multidomain resource linkage collaboration mode on the task-offloading process of intelligent terminals in the workshop in order to solve the problem of non-uniform distribution of task computation in the traditional hierarchical network and improve the utilization of idle resources in the full-domain network in the workshop. On the other hand, we established a utility function on task processing closed-loop time delay and terminal energy consumption to transform the multidomain collaborative task-offloading and resource allocation process into a task computation gain problem in order to solve the problems of low static resource allocation efficiency and high data processing closed-loop time delay in traditional industrial wireless networks. An improved Cuckoo Search algorithm is proposed to calculate the optimal offloading location and resource allocation decision to effectively weigh the network closed-loop delay and terminal energy consumption to improve the network communication performance of a flexible manufacturing workshop.

The primary contributions of this paper are summarized as follows:

(1) This study proposes a task-offloading and resource allocation strategy in multidomain cooperation (TARMC), to investigate the closed-loop process of intelligent terminal task interaction in wireless networks and the partial offloading mechanism of edge network for IIoT.

(2) A utility function was established for the closed-loop delay and terminal energy consumption of task processing to transform the multidomain collaborative task-offloading and resource allocation process into a task computing revenue problem.

(3) An improved Cuckoo Search algorithm was developed to compute the optimal offloading location and resource allocation decisions. In addition to strengthening

the network load balance, this algorithm effectively reduced the delay and energy consumption of task processing.

(4) An experiment was designed to compare TARMC, a genetic algorithm (GA) and simulated annealing algorithm (SA), to validate the optimization of delay and energy consumption in the multidomain collaboration method based on a real IIoT environment.

3. System Model

3.1. System Model

The TARMC network model comprises the terminal layer, network layer and resource management layer, as depicted in Figure 1. The terminal layer includes industrial intelligent terminals (e.g., robotic arms, AGV) with varying computing needs. In addition, it covers the corresponding application scenarios (e.g., industrial vision, AGV collaboration, and industrial detection), responsible for real-time local processing of computing tasks, establishing communication links with network layer equipment, and requesting collaborative task-offloading services. The set of industrial intelligent terminals is defined as $D = \{D_1, D_2, \ldots, D_i, \ldots, D_N\}$, which is responsible for offloading the task to the edge server on the router end. The network layer contains multiple routers with edge servers deployed around it, which is responsible for communicating and exchanging data with other cluster domain networks. This feature enables high real-time information interaction and multidomain collaborative task-offloading services for the terminal layer. The set of edge servers can be expressed as $S = \{S_1, S_2, \ldots, S_j, \ldots, S_J\}$ and is responsible for providing computing resources to complete the computing task. Furthermore, the resource management layer hosts a 5G intelligent control base station and cloud platform, which analyzes the computing requirements of various industrial terminals and offers resource allocation strategies to edge servers.

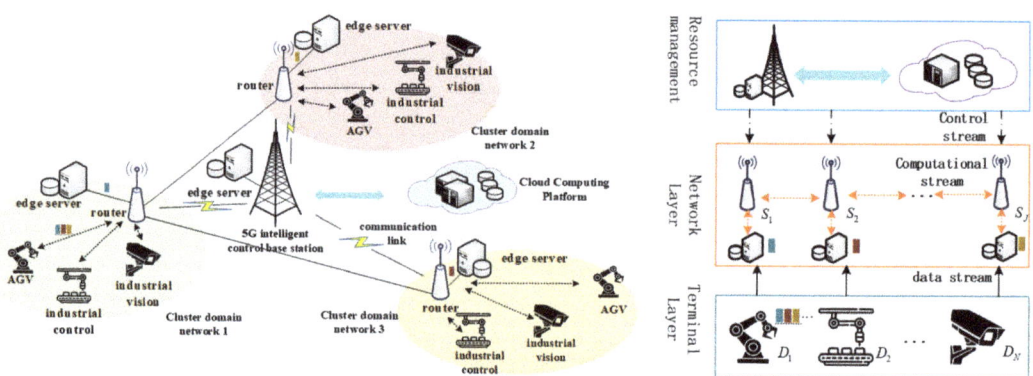

Figure 1. System model for task-offloading and resource allocation.

Upon assigning a computing task to the industrial intelligent terminal, a computing task service request will be uploaded, and the service demand will be reported by the 5G intelligent control base station through the access network. Thereafter, the edge server on the base station end receives the task request and sends a service response. The task is computed in the local processing if the industrial intelligent terminal can compute tasks within the scope of local computing power. In case the local computing power is insufficient, the 5G intelligent control base station offloads the task to an edge server installed in the remaining cluster domain networks within the communication range for processing. After processing, the calculation results will be fed back to each intelligent terminal. For non-real-time service requirements, the 5G intelligent control base station offloads the tasks to the cloud platform under a more accurate resource scheduling strategy and accessed from the cloud network.

The total frequency spectrum of the network system is segmented into orthogonal sub-channels, each with a bandwidth of B Hz. Under normal operation of the system, each industrial intelligent terminal provides a computing task for processing. Let us assume that the computing task quantity of the industrial intelligent terminal D_i is l_i, measured in Mbits; η_i denotes the ratio of output and input data for task D_i, i.e., the feedback received after task calculation is $\eta_i l_i$. The computing tasks of the industrial intelligent terminal D_i can be either locally processed or offloaded to the edge server for processing. b_i represents the local offloading ratio for an industrial intelligent terminal computing task, where ($b_i \in [0,1]$).

Subsequently, the industrial intelligent terminal forwards the computing task to the edge server on the 5G intelligent control base station for task-offloading, and the data require to be transmitted through the subchannel corresponding to the 5G intelligent control base station. According to [35], the uplink transmission rate from the industrial intelligent terminal D_i to the edge server S_j is expressed using Shannon's formula as:

$$r_{i,j} = B \log_2 \left(1 + \frac{p_i h_{i,j}^k}{N_0}\right) \quad (1)$$

where p_i denotes the transmission power of the industrial intelligent terminal D_i, $h_{i,j}^k$ represents the channel gain of the industrial intelligent terminal D_i and the edge server S_j on the sub-channel k. $h_{i,j} = \xi_0 d_{i,j}^{-\lambda} \sigma^2$, where ξ_0 is the path loss at a distance of one meter; $d_{i,j}^{-\lambda}$ symbolizes the propagation loss, d indicates the propagation distance, λ denotes the path loss exponent; σ^2 represents the Rayleigh fading parameters; N_0 indicates the noise power of Gaussian channel.

The computing resource allocated by the industrial intelligent terminal D_i for local processing of the computing task is denoted as (CPU cycles/second), and the CPU cycles required for processing 1 bit data is expressed as δ_{Local}. Thus, the delay in local task processing can be derived as

$$t_i^{local} = \frac{l_i b_i \delta_{Local}}{f_i} \quad (2)$$

If the power of the industrial intelligent terminal D_i at idle is P_i^{local}, the energy consumption of processing the calculation task can be locally evaluated as follows:

$$E_i^{local} = P_i^{local} t_i^{local} + \rho f_i^3 t_i^{local} \quad (3)$$

where $\rho f_i^3 t_i^{local}$ denotes the additional energy consumption during the terminal computing task, ρ indicates the CPU architecture constant and $\rho = 10^{-27}$. The industrial intelligent terminal D_i can process the computational tasks through collaboration between local computing and edge computing. If the industrial intelligent terminal D_i is processing a portion of the local computing tasks, all the remaining computing tasks are transmitted to the edge server S_j most proximate to the terminal, which schedules and assigns the remaining computing tasks to the other edge servers and jointly completes the task offload. As the edge servers communicate through a wired network, the transmission time is negligible, and further potential delays (e.g., packet preprocessing and queuing delays) can be neglected. The transmission delay generated when the smart terminal D_i transmits all the remaining computing tasks to the nearest edge server S_j can be derived as follows:

$$t_i^s = \frac{l_i(1-b_i)}{r_{i,j}} \quad (4)$$

Therefore, the transmission energy consumption of the computing task offloaded by D_i to S_j can be derived as follows:

$$E_{D_i S_j}^e = p_i t_i^s \quad (5)$$

The computing resource allocated by the edge server S_j to the industrial intelligent terminal D_i is f_j^i, the CPU of the edge server to process 1 bit data is δ_{MEC}, and the power required to perform the computing task is P_j^i. After offloading the task, multiple edge servers can perform the computing task, and the processing time of the computing task on the edge server S_j can be evaluated as follows:

$$t_{i,j}^m = \frac{\omega_{i,j} l_i (1-b_i) \delta_{MEC}}{f_j^i} \qquad (6)$$

where $\omega_{i,j}$ denotes the ratio of computing tasks on edge server S_j to total computing task of D_i offloaded to servers. Let us assume that the transmitting power of the edge server S_j to p_j. After processing the task, the multiple collaborative edge servers will feedback the results of the remaining tasks to the edge server S_j located near the intelligent terminal. Thus, the transmission delay occurring when S_j feeds back all the remaining task results to the terminal D_i can be expressed as follows:

$$t_i^c = \frac{(1-b_i) l_i \eta_i}{r_{i,j}} \qquad (7)$$

Therefore, if the intelligent terminal D_i receives the edge server S_j feedback result, the corresponding transmission energy consumption will be:

$$E_i^{offload} = p_i \cdot t_i^c \qquad (8)$$

Considering the simultaneous processing of the computing tasks on multiple edge servers, the industrial intelligent terminal D_i records the total processing duration of offloading the remaining tasks to the edge server for auxiliary computing process as T_i^m, and $T_i^m = \max_{j=1,2,...,M} t_{i,j}^m$. Therefore, in case the remaining computing task is offloaded to the edge server and the feedback data is received, the multidomain collaborative task-processing delay can be expressed as follows:

$$t_i^{offload} = t_i^s + T_i^m + t_i^c \qquad (9)$$

In case the industrial intelligent terminal D_i completes the corresponding computing task in local processing, it waits for the edge server to process together and provides feedback to D_i for the final result. In another case, if the industrial intelligent terminal D_i has not yet completed the local processing of the corresponding computing task, whereas the edge server has completed collaborative computing, the industrial intelligent terminal D_i receives the feedback of the final result after processing the local computing task. Therefore, the closed-loop time delay of the task processing at the industrial intelligent terminal D_i can be stated as follows:

$$t_i = \begin{cases} t_i^{offload}, & t_i^{local} < t_i^{offload} \\ t_i^{local}, & t_i^{local} \geq t_i^{offload} \end{cases} \qquad (10)$$

For the industrial intelligent terminal D_i, the total energy consumption is stated as follows

$$E_i = \begin{cases} E_i^{local} + E_{D_i S_j}^e + E_i^{offload}, & t_i^s + T_i^m < t_i^{local} \\ E_i^{local} + E_{D_i S_j}^e + E_i^{offload} + P_i^{local}(t_i^s + T_i^m - t_i^{local}), & t_i^s + T_i^m \geq t_i^{local} \end{cases} \qquad (11)$$

The total closed-loop time for task processing of all industrial intelligent terminals in the system can be expressed as:

$$T_{total} = \sum_{i=1}^{N} t_i \qquad (12)$$

The total power consumption of all industrial intelligent terminals to complete the task-offloading can be stated as

$$E_{total} = \sum_{i=1}^{N} (E_i) \qquad (13)$$

3.2. Optimization Objective

In practice, the delay and energy consumption performance can exhibit varying weight coefficients, for instance, the system improves the delay weight to focus on the delay performance when the AGV is included in route planning. Let us assume that the two weight coefficients are denotes as ω_T and ω_E, respectively. The impact of such delay and energy consumption on the performance of industrial intelligent terminals can be adjusted through ω_T and ω_E, and such a design can expand the applicability of the model. This study considers the premise of ensuring the energy consumption of all industrial intelligent terminals to complete task-offloading, minimizes the closed-loop delay of task processing, and obtains the optimal resource allocation strategy along with the computing task-offloading scheme of the edge server. The utility function is defined as follows:

$$f(b,f) = \frac{1}{N}\left(\sum_{i=1}^{N} \omega_T t_i + \sum_{i=1}^{N} \omega_E E_i\right) \qquad (14)$$

The optimization objective can be expressed as:

$$\begin{aligned}
&\min_{b,p,f} f(b,f) \\
&s.t. \, C1: b_i \in [0,1], \forall i \\
&\quad C2: 0 \leq f_i \leq f_{i,\max}, \forall i \\
&\quad C3: 0 \leq f_j^i \leq f_{j,\max}, \forall i \\
&\quad C4: t_i \leq t_{i,\max}, \forall i,j
\end{aligned} \qquad (15)$$

where constraint C_1 represents the range of offloading ratio for the industrial intelligent terminal computing task; C_2 indicates that the industrial intelligent terminals do not exceed the maximum allocated local computing resources; C_3 represents that the computing resources allocated to the edge server for industrial intelligent terminal tasks do not exceed the maximum allocated computing resources of the edge server; C_4 indicates the maximum value of the task calculation delay for the industrial intelligent terminal.

4. Improved Cuckoo Search Algorithm

Unlike the NP difficult problem under complete offloading mechanism, Equation (15) can be reduced to the ordinary combination optimization problem under partial offloading mechanism. To this end, an improved Cuckoo Search algorithm is proposed in this paper. In principle, the algorithm can weigh the number of local and global searches through adaptive discovery probability and step size, as well as conduct a local fine search representing the global optimal solution to improve the operation accuracy and search efficiency. The idea of a differential evolution algorithm is introduced to adjust, cross, and select the process of nest update position. By inheriting the optimal solution genetic information, the algorithm avoids intersection with the local optimal and converges speedily to provide the optimal resource allocation results.

Let us assume the nest location x_i^t of the i-th nest in generation t and M denotes the dimensionality, where $x_i^t = \{x_{i1}^t, x_{i2}^t, \ldots, x_{im}^t, \ldots, x_{iM}^t\}$. According to [36], the cuckoo's updated expression of the path and location for deriving a parasitic nest follows:

$$x_{i,m}^{t+1} = x_{i,m}^t + \alpha \cdot Rand \cdot Levy(\beta_1), \ i = 0, 1, 2, \ldots, J \tag{16}$$

where x_i^{t+1} denotes the new position of the i-th nest at nest position x_i^t in generation t after a global update. $x_{i,m}^t$ denotes the value of the i-th nest in the m-dimension in the nest position at generation t. α indicates a step factor and $Rand$ symbolizes a uniform distribution between $(0,1)$. $Levy(\beta_1)$ represents a random wandering process formed by the flight of cuckoo Levy, $Levy(\beta_1) \sim u = t^{-\beta_1}$, $(1 < \beta_1 \leq 3)$, where β_1 represents the impact factor, typically, $\beta_1 = 1.5$; According to the [36], the expression for the $Levy$ distribution is stated as follows.

$$Levy(\beta_1) = 0.01 \cdot \frac{u}{|v|^{1/\beta_1}} \cdot \left(x_{j,m}^t - b_{g,m}^t \right), \ j, g = 0, 1, 2, \ldots, J \tag{17}$$

where u and v both follow a normal distribution, i.e., $u \sim N(0, \sigma_u^2)$, $v \sim N(0, \sigma_v^2)$, $\sigma_u = \left\{ \frac{\Gamma(1+\beta_1) \cdot \sin(\pi \cdot \beta_1/2)}{\Gamma[(1+\beta_1)/2] \cdot \beta_1 \cdot 2^{(\beta_1-1)/2}} \right\}^{1/\beta_3}$, $\sigma_v = 1$.

$b_g^t = \left\{ b_{g,1}^t, b_{g,2}^t, \ldots, b_{g,m}^t \ldots, b_{g,M}^t \right\}$ denotes the current optimal solution space covered by the algorithm in the current search state, and if the current nest location corresponds with the optimal solution space, the magnitude of step adjustment is 0, i.e., $Levy(\beta_1) = 0$. In addition, the host bird of a parasitized nest will abandon the nest with an P_α probability of recognizing an egg parasitized by a cuckoo.

4.1. Adaptive Adjustment of Discovery Probabilities

In the original cuckoo algorithm, a given discovery probability is generally used to control the global search and preference random wandering process, which is conducive toward the balance between global and local search as the number of iterations increases. Thus, to improve the algorithm's search performance, this study applies dynamic discovery probability instead of fixed discovery probability P_α

$$P_\alpha = \begin{cases} \frac{1}{1+\frac{t_{it}}{T_{it}} \cdot e}, 0 < t_{it} \leq \beta_2 T_{it} \\ 1 - e^{\frac{t_{it}}{T_{it}} - 1} + \gamma \cdot \frac{t_{it}}{T_{it}}, \beta_2 T_{it} < t_{it} \leq T_{it} \end{cases} \tag{18}$$

where γ denotes the correction factor, generally, $\gamma = 0.1$, and β_2 indicates the trade-off factor, mostly, $0.5 \leq \beta_2 \leq 1$. This segmentation function represents a progressive decline in the probability of discovery P_α till the number of iterations t_{it} reaches $\beta_2 T_{it}$, and it is suitable for global searches over a large area with improved search efficiency. As the number of iterations t_{it} exceeds that of $\beta_2 T_{it}$, the probability of discovery decreases significantly, thereby enabling local search in a small area to improve the search accuracy.

4.2. Adaptive Adjustment of Step Size

Similarly, the step size of the Levy flight can be continuously decreased with the adaptive adjustment of the step-size factor in each iteration. Specifically, a larger step-size factor in the early iterations of the algorithm is conducive toward improving the global search capability of the algorithm and ensuring speedy convergence in the early stages of the algorithm. In the later stages of the algorithm iteration, the scope of the local search is narrowed by decreasing the step size for enhancing the local search performance of the algorithm.

$$\alpha = \beta_3 e^{(-\frac{t_{it}}{T_{it}} + 1)} \tag{19}$$

where β_3 denotes the correction factor, typically, $\beta_3 = 0.5$. In addition, after a global search in the Levy flight, certain solutions will further perform a local search to update the location, thereby retaining a more accurate set of solutions. During this local search, differential evolution of $x_{i,m}^t$ is performed by analyzing the differences between current and excellent individuals in the population to ensure that a great amount of genetic information from the excellent individuals is inherited by their offspring. The specific process is stated as follows.

4.3. Differential Evolution

First, the genetic information of multiple individuals can be obtained by mutating the individuals through a differential strategy, wherein the mutated individual $u_{i,m}^t$ is expressed as

$$u_{i,m}^t = x_{i,m}^t + \kappa \cdot \left(x_{p,m}^t - x_{q,m}^t \right), \ p,q = 0,1,2,\ldots,J \tag{20}$$

where κ denotes the scaling factor, $x_{p,m}^t$ represents the value in the m-th dimension of the nest position in generation t. After variation, individual $u_{i,m}^t$ retains an amount of information regarding maternal $x_{i,m}^t$, and, simultaneously, inherits information from individuals $x_{p,m}^t$ and $x_{q,m}^t$ to realize the transmission of the information between individuals. Thereafter, the candidate individual $v_{i,m}^t$ is generated by crossing over the maternal and intervariant information, thus ensuring that at least one set of individual information in the succeeding generation is contributed by the variant individual. The $v_{i,m}^t$ can be expressed as:

$$v_{i,m}^t = \begin{cases} u_{i,m}^t, & \alpha_2 \leq CR \text{ or } m = \beta_4 \\ x_{i,m}^t, & \text{otherwise} \end{cases} \tag{21}$$

where $CR \in [0,1]$ denotes the cross probability, $\alpha_2 = rand(0,1)$ represents the random number generated in $[0,1]$ interval, and $\beta_4 = unidrnd(M)$ indicates the random positive integer generated in $[1,M]$ interval.

Finally, the dominant relationship between individual $v_{i,m}^t$ and parent $x_{i,m}^t$ is determined by comparing the optimized objective function size, and a new generation of individual $x_{i,m}^{t+1}$ is generated to inherit the traits of excellent individuals in the succeeding generation.

$$x_{i,m}^{t+1} = \begin{cases} v_{i,m}^t, & T(v_{i,m}^t) < T(x_{i,m}^t) \\ x_{i,m}^t, & \text{otherwise} \end{cases} \tag{22}$$

In summary, the specific flow of the improved Cuckoo Search algorithm is stated as follows in Algorithm 1.

Algorithm 1 Improved Cuckoo Search Algorithm

InpuT: System parameters include set D of industrial intelligent terminal, set S of edge server, calculation task amount l_i of industrial intelligent terminal D_i and other indicators;
The cuckoo algorithm parameters include the nest position set $x_i^t = \{x_{i1}^t, x_{i2}^t, \ldots, x_{im}^t, \ldots, x_{iM}^t\}$, the maximum number of iterations t_{max}, etc.
Initialization: Initialize the nest position and other parameters to record the current optimal solution.
Output: begin
  1. **for** $t < t_{max}$ **do**
  2. Update Bird's Nest location according to Equation (16)
  3. Calculate and obtain the optimal solution according to Equation (15), and preserving the optimal solution space.
  4. Adaptive adjustment of discovery probability and step size according to Equation (18) and Equation (19)
  5. **if** $rand(0,1) > P_\alpha$ **then**
  6. Differential evolution according to Equations (20) and (21) and Equation (21) to locally update the nest position and obtain the optimal solution.
  7. **end if**
  8. **end for**
  9. Outputs optimal task-offloading and resource allocation results.
  10. **end**

Due to the combinatorial nature of the optimization problem, this paper first analyzes the time complexity of each embedded subprocess in the improved Cuckoo Search algorithm, and finally performs an overall analysis. Assume that the time to generate distributed random numbers is ξ_1, the population size is N, and the dimensionality of the problem is M. In the first iteration, the complexity of updating the positions of all nests is $O(\xi_1 + NM)$, the complexity of computing the optimal solution is $O(NM)$, the complexity of adaptively adjusting the discovery probability and step size is $O(1)$, and the complexity of the global search is $O(N)$. Because the discovery probability P_α changes adaptively, the number of populations in the differential evolution process also changes dynamically, the number of evolving populations is set to $P_\alpha \cdot N$, and the complexity of differential evolution is $O(P_\alpha NM)$, where $P_\alpha NM \in (0, NM)$. Therefore, the complexity of the improved Cuckoo Search algorithm after one iteration is $O(2NM) = O(NM)$ in the worst case. Moreover, we considered that the number of iterations of the algorithm cannot give a closed-form solution, this paper assumes that the maximum number of iterations is t_{max}. The complexity of the improved Cuckoo Search algorithm in the worst case is $O(t_{max}NM)$ when it iterating to the last convergence at same time. In addition, because the processes of global search and local search in this algorithm are jointly optimization, its convergence speed is fast, and we will verify the algorithm convergence by simulation in the next section.

5. Simulation and Results

An industrial manufacturing scenario within 300 m × 300 m area was simulated in MATLAB to cross-sectional to compare the performance of the TARMC strategy with those of GA algorithm [37] and SA algorithm [38]. The variations in closed-loop delay and endpoint energy consumption in processing tasks were obtained from simulations of non-cross-domain and cross-domain collaborative network architectures. In addition, we analyzed the impact of various resource allocation algorithms on the closed-loop delay and terminal energy consumption of task processing in case of interaction with multiple orders of magnitude of industrial smart terminals. The specific simulation parameters are summarized in Table 1.

Table 1. Simulation parameters.

Parameters	Numerical Values
Sub-channel bandwidth, B	1 MHz
Number of CPU cycles in industrial intelligent terminals, δ_{Local}	[500, 2000] cycles/bit
Number of CPU cycles for edge servers, δ_{MEC}	[500, 2000] cycles/bit
Industrial intelligent terminal idle operating power, P_i^{local}	0.3 W
Industrial intelligent terminal transmission power, p_i	1.3 W
Industrial Smart Terminal Computing Resources, $f_{i,max}$	4 GHz
Edge server computing resources, $f_{j,max}$	20 GHz
Channel gain, $h_{i,j}$	10^{-5}
Gaussian white noise, N_0	10^{-13} W

The trend of variations in the average closed-loop delay during processing tasks under the simulated resource allocation strategies is presented in Figure 2, where the horizontal axis represents the number of iterations and the vertical axis represents the average closed-loop delay of task processing. Furthermore, the plots with diamond, circular, star, vertical, triangular, and rectangular curves represent the TARMC strategy, TARMC strategy under non-cross-domain networks, GA strategy, and GA strategy under non-cross-domain networks, SA strategy, and SA strategy under non-cross-domain networks, respectively. As observed, the average closed-loop delay for processing tasks with TARMC, GA skimming, and SA strategies under cross-domain networks was much less than that of TARMC, GA and SA strategies under non-cross-domain networks. This is because the number and types of industrial terminals vary for each cluster domain network in the actual industrial production, and the corresponding task calculation quantity varies as well. If the task is calculated only in the current cluster domain network, the computational resource allocation of the global network in this industrial area is non-uniform, thereby resulting in low resource utilization and increased average closed-loop delay of task processing. A multidomain collaborative network enables cross-domain computing processing in performing tasks, which allocates numerous real-time tasks to cluster domain networks with more idle resources for collaborative computing. Thus, this feature reduces the task processing delay and diminishes the corresponding average closed-loop delay for task processing. In addition, the average closed-loop delay of processing tasks with the TARMC strategy is substantially less than that of the GA and SA strategies. This is because the TARMC strategy considers the task between large-scale industrial intelligent terminals, edge servers, and the cluster domain network communication interaction process according to the intelligent manufacturing workshop closed-loop control business requirements. In addition, it formulates the average closed-loop delay of task processing as an optimization function to ensure the communication performance of new IIoT networks, which effectively reduces the average closed-loop delay of task processing. However, the GA and SA strategies are based on a simple network model, considering the one-way empty port delay as the optimization goal and ignoring the impact of the task interaction between edge servers and cluster domain network on the overall delay. Thus, they are unable to satisfy the network requirements of intelligent manufacturing workshop, which increases the average closed-loop delay of task processing. As observed in Figure 2, the average closed-loop delay for task processing with TARMC strategy under multidomain synergy was 1.8401 s, whereas that for TARMC strategy under non-cross-domain networks was 2.6372 s, demonstrating an improvement of 30.2%. In addition, the average closed-loop delay in processing tasks with GA and SA strategies under multidomain collaboration was 3.2867 s and 2.0797 s, respectively, which corresponds to a performance improvement of 44.0% and 11.5% in comparison with the latter.

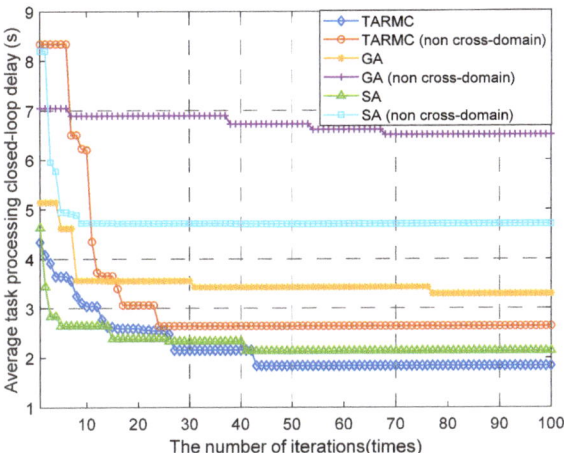

Figure 2. Variations in closed-loop delay of task processing under various resource allocation policies.

The trend of variations in average energy consumption between multiple resource allocation strategies is discussed herein. In Figure 3, the horizontal axis represents the number of iterations, and the vertical axis denotes the average energy consumption. Furthermore, the plots with diamond, circular, star, vertical, triangular, and rectangular curves represent the TARMC strategy, TARMC strategy under non-cross-domain networks, GA strategy, and GA strategy under non-cross-domain networks, SA strategy, and SA strategy under non-cross-domain networks, respectively. As observed, the average energy consumption of the TARMC, GA skimming and SA strategies under cross-domain networks is considerably less than the TARMC, GA strategy, and SA strategy under non-cross-domain networks. This is because the multidomain collaborative network can completely schedule the computing resources in the entire region, reduce the delay of industrial intelligent terminals in the local processing tasks, decrease the computing energy consumption of industrial intelligent terminals, and eventually, improve the average energy consumption of industrial intelligent terminals compared to the non-cross-domain network mode. In addition, the average energy consumption of the TARMC strategy is much less than that of the GA and SA strategies, as indicated in the figure. This is because the TARMC strategy can adaptively adjust the weight of the closed-loop delay and average energy consumption of task processing according to the requirements of the industrial intelligent terminal business, evaluate the priority of optimizing the average energy consumption, and thus, effectively reduce the average energy consumption. However, the GA and SA strategies only consider the impact of one-way air interface delay on the data processing process of industrial intelligent terminals, which inevitably sacrifices energy consumption in the optimization process, resulting in high average energy consumption. Moreover, as noted from Figure 3, the average energy consumption of the TARMC strategy under multidomain collaboration was 0.5091 J, whereas that under non-cross-domain networks was 1.2462 J, corresponding to an improvement of 59.2%. In addition, the average energy consumption of GA and SA strategies under multidomain collaboration was 1.3090 J and 0.9193 J, respectively, which improved by 61.1% and 44.6% in comparison to the latter.

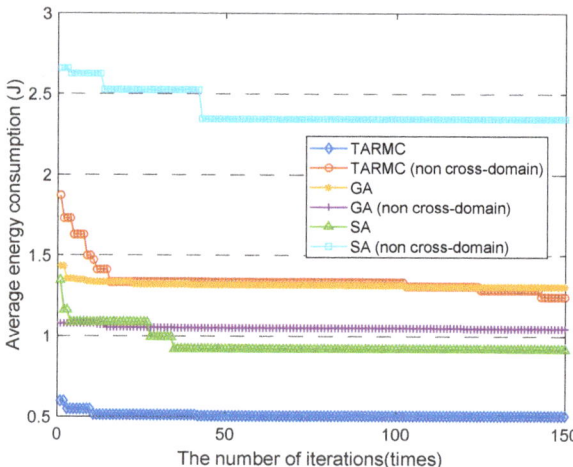

Figure 3. Average energy consumption of industrial intelligent terminals varies with resource allocation strategies.

The variations in delay of processing various tasks in multiple stages with several data sizes are plotted in Figure 4, wherein the horizontal axis represents the average size of the task data volume, and the vertical axis represents the delay. In the bar graph, the delay in task processing in various processes is stated as follows (from left to right): closed-loop processing, multidomain collaborative computing process, and local computing process. As observed from the figure, compared to the delay in the first two processes, the task exhibits the lowest processing delay during the local calculation process, and it gradually increases with the amount of task data, before eventually its convergence. This is because the local limited resources fail to execute the task of higher data volume. If the amount of data of the pending task attains the maximum limit of local computing processing, it will request multidomain collaborative processing instead of allocating new tasks to local processing. During this process, the delay in processing the task of local calculation gradually increases before stabilizing. Moreover, in the process of the multidomain collaboration task, the processing delay increases with the amount of data related to the task under process, and accordingly, the delay of the closed-loop process increases. Therefore, the processing delay in the calculation process is reasonably less than that of the other two processes, with a slow growth rate.

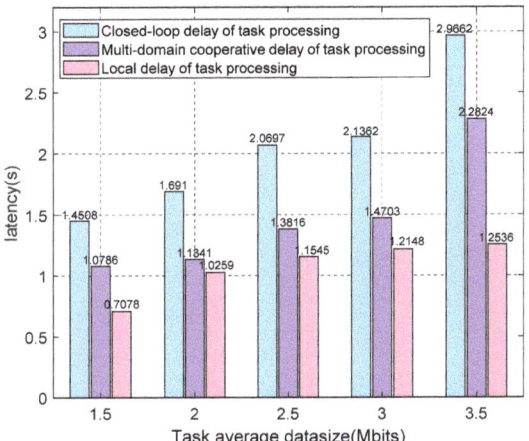

Figure 4. Variations in delay under various task processing stages for multiple task sizes.

This paper considered the energy consumption of industrial intelligent terminals at various stages of several task data sizes. In Figure 5, the horizontal axis represents the average size of task data volume, and the vertical axis represents energy consumption. In the bar chart, the energy consumption of industrial intelligent terminals in the closed-loop process of task processing, energy consumption in the process of multidomain collaborative computing, and energy consumption in the local calculation process are presented. As observed, the industrial intelligent terminal consumes the least energy in the multidomain collaborative computing process compared with that in the previous two processes, and the energy consumption of the industrial intelligent terminal in all processes increased with the task data volume. This is because the energy consumption of the industrial intelligent terminal in the process of multidomain collaborative computing primarily includes industrial terminal local computing after the end of standby energy consumption, transmit-and-accept-task data energy consumption, and local computing energy consumption. In the process of task computing and CPU computing energy consumption, task closed-loop process includes the energy consumption of the above-mentioned two processes. Owing to the extremely short time span of transmitting and receiving data, the process exhibits the lowest energy consumption, which often results in the lowest energy consumption in the domain collaborative computing process. Simultaneously, an increase in the amount of task data increases the time to transmit and receive the data, increases CPU computing time, the increases computing energy consumption, and eventually, increases energy consumption in all the processes.

The variations in delay of processing tasks at various stages for multiple industrial intelligent terminals is presented in Figure 6, where the horizontal axis indicates the number of industrial intelligent terminals, and the vertical axis represents the delay. In the bar graph, from left to right: delays of processing task in closed-loop process, the task during multidomain collaborative computing process, and the processing delay of task during local computing process. As depicted in Figure 6, the delay in processing tasks at various stages increases with the number of terminals. This is because the network task data doubles upon increasing the number of industrial intelligent terminals. In global network resources allocation, considering each task provides maximum delay and the network load should be balanced, the collaborative computing resources are allocated with several terminals to ensure the normal operation of various intelligent terminals, which increases the network delay.

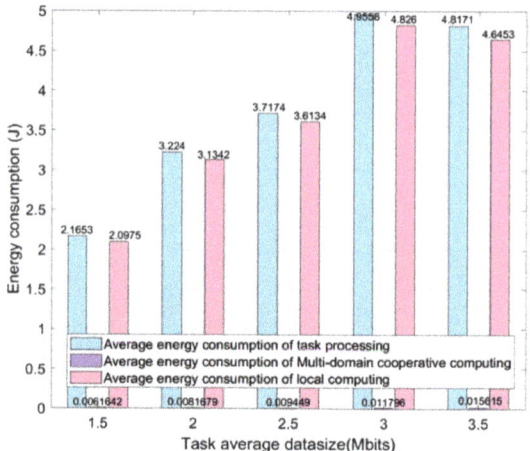

Figure 5. Variations in energy consumption of multiple task processing stages for various task sizes.

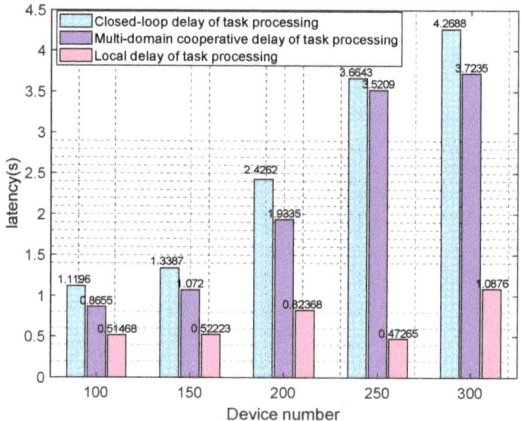

Figure 6. Delay variations in various task processing stages for multiple industrial intelligent terminals.

In this study, the energy consumption varied with the number of industrial intelligent terminals and the task processing was considered in multiple stages. In Figure 7, the horizontal axis represents the number of industrial smart terminals and the vertical axis represents energy consumption. In the bars graph, the energy consumption for various cases is stated as follows (from left to right): industrial intelligent terminal in the closed-loop process of task processing, the process of multidomain collaborative computing, and the process of local computing. As observed from the graph, the energy consumption of industrial intelligent terminals in the closed-loop process of task processing is not easily affected by the variations in the number of intelligent terminals and is minimized if the number of terminals reaches 150. This is because the proposed TARMC strategy can categorize various tasks into several subtasks with an extremely small volume of data. As the number of intelligent terminals increases, the amount of task data in the global network increases. However, the data amount of the segmented subtasks for multidomain collaborative computing remains negligibly small, and the impact of subtask data growth can be minimized by flexibly scheduling the global network computing resources. At this instant, the delays in processing and data of the industrial terminal transmission process are low, and the corresponding energy consumption is not easily affected by the growth of the number of intelligent terminals. In addition, as the improved Cuckoo Search algorithm of this strategy obtained a global approximate optimal solution through continuous iteration, the energy consumption fluctuated as the number of intelligent terminals increased, and it was minimized as the number of terminals reached 150.

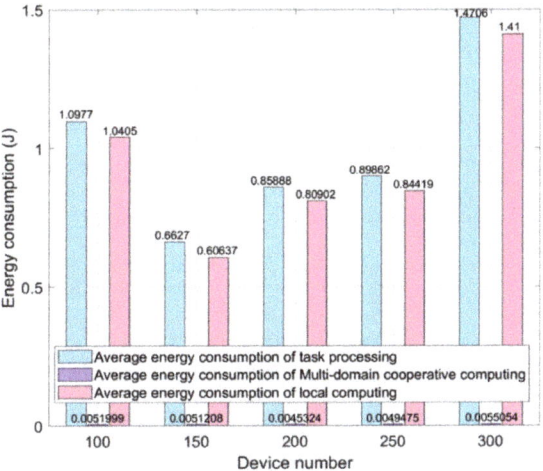

Figure 7. Variations in energy consumption across multiple task processing stages under various industrial intelligent terminals.

6. Conclusions

This study proposed a task-offloading and resource allocation strategy in multidomain cooperation for the IIoT. First, this strategy deeply examines the closed-loop process of information flow interaction between various layers of intelligent terminals in the wireless network, constructs a multidomain collaborative task-offloading and resource allocation network model for the IIoT, and efficiently allocates the resources between intelligent terminals, edge servers, and cluster domain networks according to the dynamic changes of the network load. Subsequently, various tasks are segmented and identified, enabling local and edge servers to process all subtasks in parallel. Simultaneously, the joint task-processing closed-loop delay and terminal energy consumption utility function of the intelligent terminal are developed around the machine, transforming the multidomain collaborative task-offloading and resource allocation process into the problem of task calculation revenue. Moreover, a modified Cuckoo Search algorithm was developed through the iterative alternating solution, which calculated the optimal offloading location and resource allocation decisions. The simulation results revealed that the TARMC strategy effectively improved the closed-loop delay and energy consumption of task processing compared with the GA- and SA-based resource allocation strategies. Furthermore, it verified that the delay and energy consumption optimization performance of multidomain collaborative methods is much higher than that of non-cross-domain methods. In future, we will continue to develop flexible manufacturing scenarios of the wireless-network resource-scheduling scheme, considering the workshop-level massive heterogeneous data information fusion method. In addition, the coupling correlation between the variations in physical environment and digital space should be further explored to improve the efficiency of multidimensional resource scheduling, enhance the overall real-time data interaction from factory production lines (businesses, control instructions, etc.), and increase production decision-making efficiency.

Author Contributions: Conceptualization, Z.D. and Y.Z.; methodology, Z.D. and Y.Z.; formal analysis, N.M. and H.T.; writing—original draft preparation, Z.D. and Y.Z.; writing—review and editing, Z.D. and Y.Z.; funding acquisition, N.M. All authors have read and agreed to the published version of the manuscript.

Funding: This research received no external funding.

Institutional Review Board Statement: Not applicable.

Informed Consent Statement: Not applicable.

Data Availability Statement: Not applicable.

Conflicts of Interest: The authors declare no conflict of interest.

References

1. Wu, Y.; Dai, H.-N.; Wang, H. Convergence of blockchain and edge computing for secure and scalable IIoT critical infrastructures in industry 4.0. *IEEE Int. Things J.* **2020**, *8*, 2300–2317. [CrossRef]
2. Chen, Q.; Xu, X.; You, Z.; Jiang, H.; Zhang, J.; Wang, F. Communication-Efficient Federated Edge Learning for NR-U based IIoT Networks. *IEEE Int. Things J.* **2021**. [CrossRef]
3. Jiang, T.; Zhang, J.; Tang, P.; Tian, L.; Zheng, Y.; Dou, J.; Asplund, H.; Raschkowski, L.; D'Errico, R.; Jamsa, T. 3GPP standardized 5G channel model for IIoT scenarios: A survey. *IEEE IEEE Int. Things J.* **2021**, *8*, 8799–8815. [CrossRef]
4. Goswami, P.; Mukherjee, A.; Maiti, M.; Tyagi, S.K.S.; Yang, L. A neural-network-based optimal resource allocation method for secure IIoT network. *IEEE Int. Things J.* **2021**, *9*, 2538–2544. [CrossRef]
5. Guo, B.; Liu, J.; Liu, S.; Wang, J.; Li, M.; Wang, C.; Yu, Z. CrowdIM: Crowd-Inspired Intelligent Manufacturing Space Design. *IEEE Int. Things J.* **2022**, *9*, 19387–19397. [CrossRef]
6. Chen, N.; Qiu, T.; Zhao, L.; Zhou, X.; Ning, H. Edge intelligent networking optimization for Internet of things in smart city. *IEEE Wireless Commun.* **2021**, *28*, 26–31. [CrossRef]
7. Wu, D.; Xu, Z.; Chen, B.; Zhang, Y.; Han, Z. Enforcing access control in information-centric edge networking. *IEEE Trans. Commun.* **2020**, *69*, 353–364. [CrossRef]
8. Ali, H.; Tariq, U.U.; Hussain, M.; Lu, L.; Panneerselvam, J.; Zhai, X. ARSH-FATI: A novel metaheuristic for cluster head selection in wireless sensor networks. *IEEE Syst. J.* **2020**, *15*, 2386–2397. [CrossRef]
9. Singh, J.; Yadav, S.S.; Kanungo, V.; Pal, V.; Yogita, Y. A node overhaul scheme for energy efficient clustering in wireless sensor networks. *IEEE Sens. Lett.* **2021**, *5*, 1–4. [CrossRef]
10. Rahman, G.M.; Wahid, K.A. LDCA: Lightweight dynamic clustering algorithm for IoTconnected wide-area WSN and mobile data sink using LoRa. *IEEE Int. Things J.* **2021**, *9*, 1313–1325. [CrossRef]
11. Al Khafaf, N.; Jalili, M.; Sokolowski, P. A novel clustering index to find optimal clusters size with application to segmentation of energy consumers. *IEEE Trans. Ind. Inf.* **2020**, *17*, 346–355. [CrossRef]
12. Abbas, N.; Zhang, Y.; Taherkordi, A.; Skeie, T. Mobile edge computing: A survey. *IEEE Int. Things J.* **2017**, *5*, 450–465. [CrossRef]
13. Mao, Y.; You, C.; Zhang, J.; Huang, K.; Letaief, K.B. A survey on mobile edge computing: The communication perspective. *IEEE Commun. Surv. Tutorials.* **2017**, *19*, 2322–2358. [CrossRef]
14. Liao, Y.; Shou, L.; Yu, Q.; Ai, Q.; Liu, Q. An intelligent computation demand response framework for IIoT-MEC interactive networks. *IEEE Networking Lett.* **2020**, *2*, 154–158. [CrossRef]
15. Liang, W.; Zhang, J.; Shi, H.; Wang, K.; Wang, Q.; Zheng, M.; Yu, H. An experimental evaluation of WIA-FA and IEEE 802.11 networks for discrete manufacturing. *IEEE Trans. Ind. Inf.* **2021**, *17*, 6260–6271. [CrossRef]
16. Liu, Y.; Peng, M.; Shou, G.; Chen, Y.; Chen, S. Toward edge intelligence: Multiaccess edge computing for 5G and Internet of Things. *IEEE Int. Things J.* **2020**, *7*, 6722–6747. [CrossRef]
17. Zhou, F.; Hu, R.Q.; Li, Z.; Wang, Y. Mobile edge computing in unmanned aerial vehicle networks. *IEEE Wireless Commun.* **2020**, *27*, 140–146. [CrossRef]
18. Yang, G.; Hou, L.; He, X.; He, D.; Chan, S.; Guizani, M. Offloading time optimization via Markov decision process in mobile-edge computing. *IEEE Int. Things J.* **2020**, *8*, 2483–2493. [CrossRef]
19. Li, Y.; Wu, Y.; Dai, M.; Lin, B.; Jia, W.; Shen, X. Hybrid NOMA-FDMA Assisted Dual Computation Offloading: A Latency Minimization Approach. *IEEE Trans. Network Sci. Eng.* **2022**, *9*, 3345–3360. [CrossRef]
20. Zhu, B.; Chi, K.; Liu, J.; Yu, K.; Mumtaz, S. Efficient Offloading for Minimizing Task Computation Delay of NOMA-Based Multiaccess Edge Computing. *IEEE Trans Commun.* **2022**, *70*, 3186–3203. [CrossRef]
21. Luo, Q.; Li, C.; Luan, T.H.; Shi, W.; Wu, W. Self-learning based computation offloading for internet of vehicles: Model and algorithm. *IEEE Trans. Wireless Commun.* **2021**, *20*, 5913–5925. [CrossRef]
22. Huang, J.; Wang, M.; Wu, Y.; Chen, Y.; Shen, X. Distributed Offloading in Overlapping Areas of Mobile Edge Computing for Internet of Things. *IEEE Int. Things J.* **2022**, *9*, 13837–13847. [CrossRef]
23. Gao, M.; Shen, R.; Li, J.; Yan, S.; Li, Y.; Shi, J.; Han, Z.; Zhuo, L. Computation offloading with instantaneous load billing for mobile edge computing. *IEEE Trans. Serv. Comput.* **2022**, *15*, 1473–1485. [CrossRef]

24. Liao, Z.; Ma, Y.; Huang, J.; Wang, J.; Wang, J. HOTSPOT: A UAV-assisted dynamic mobilityaware offloading for mobile-edge computing in 3-D space. *IEEE Int. Things J.* **2021**, *8*, 10940–10952. [CrossRef]
25. Fang, T.; Chen, J.; Zhang, Y. Content-Aware Multi-Subtask Offloading: A Coalition Formation Game-Theoretic Approach. *IEEE Commun. Lett.* **2021**, *25*, 2664–2668. [CrossRef]
26. Wu, M.; Qi, W.; Park, J.; Lin, P.; Guo, L.; Lee, I. Residual Energy Maximization for Wireless Powered Mobile Edge Computing Systems With Mixed-Offloading. *IEEE Trans. Veh. Technol.* **2022**, *71*, 4523–4528. [CrossRef]
27. Chen, Y.; Zhang, N.; Zhang, Y.; Chen, X.; Wu, W.; Shen, X. Energy efficient dynamic offloading in mobile edge computing for internet of things. *IEEE Trans. Cloud Comput.* **2021**, *9*, 1050–1060. [CrossRef]
28. Bozorgchenani, A.; Mashhadi, F.; Tarchi, D.; Monroy, S. Multi-Objective Computation Sharing in Energy and Delay Constrained Mobile Edge Computing Environments. *IEEE Trans. Mob. Comput.* **2021**, *20*, 2992–3005. [CrossRef]
29. Zhang, X.; Zhang, X.; Yang, W. Joint Offloading and Resource Allocation Using Deep Reinforcement Learning in Mobile Edge Computing. *IEEE Trans. Network Sci. Eng.* **2022**, *9*, 3454–3466. [CrossRef]
30. Lu, J.; Li, Q.; Guo, B.; Li, J.; Shen, Y.; Li, G.; Su, H. A Multi-task Oriented Framework for Mobile Computation Offloading. *IEEE Trans. Cloud Comput.* **2022**, *9*, 3454–3466. [CrossRef]
31. Wang, P.; Li, K.; Xiao, B.; Li, K. Multi-objective optimization for joint task offloading, power assignment, and resource allocation in mobile edge computing. *IEEE Int. Things J.* **2021**, *9*, 11737–11748. [CrossRef]
32. Guan, S.; Boukerche, A. A novel mobility-aware offloading management scheme in sustainable multi-access edge computing. *IEEE Trans. Sustainable Comput.* **2021**, *7*, 1–13. [CrossRef]
33. Chen, M.; Guo, S.; Liu, K.; Liao, X.; Xiao, B. Robust computation offloading and resource scheduling in cloudlet-based mobile cloud computing. *IEEE Trans. Mob. Comput.* **2020**, *20*, 2025–2040. [CrossRef]
34. Fang, T.; Yuan, F.; Ao, L.; Chen, J. Joint Task Offloading, D2D Pairing, and Resource Allocation in Device-Enhanced MEC: A Potential Game Approach. *IEEE Int. Things J.* **2021**, *9*, 3226–3237. [CrossRef]
35. Liu, X.; Zheng, J.; Zhang, M.; Li, Y.; Wang, R.; He, Y. A novel D2D–MEC method for enhanced computation capability in cellular networks. *Sci. Rep.* **2021**, *11*, 16918. [CrossRef]
36. Yang, X.S.; Deb, S. Cuckoo Search via Levey Flights. In *World Congress on Nature and Biologically Inspired Computing*; DEC 09-12: Coimbatore, India, 2009.
37. Aburukba, R.O.; AliKarrar, M.; Landolsi, T.; El-Fakih, K. Scheduling Internet of Things requests to minimize latency in hybrid Fog-Cloud computing. *Future Gener. Comput. Syst.* **2020**, *111*, 539–551. [CrossRef]
38. Liu, W.; Huang, G.; Zheng, A.; Liu, J. Research on the optimization of IIoT data processing latency. *Comput. Commun.* **2020**, *151*, 290–298. [CrossRef]

Disclaimer/Publisher's Note: The statements, opinions and data contained in all publications are solely those of the individual author(s) and contributor(s) and not of MDPI and/or the editor(s). MDPI and/or the editor(s) disclaim responsibility for any injury to people or property resulting from any ideas, methods, instructions or products referred to in the content.

Article

Assessing Waste Marble Powder Impact on Concrete Flexural Strength Using Gaussian Process, SVM, and ANFIS

Nitisha Sharma [1], Mohindra Singh Thakur [1], Raj Kumar [2,*], Mohammad Abdul Malik [3], Ahmad Aziz Alahmadi [4], Mamdooh Alwetaishi [5] and Ali Nasser Alzaed [6]

1 Department of Civil Engineering, Shoolini University, Solan 173229, Himachal Pradesh, India
2 Faculty of Engineering and Technology, Shoolini University, Solan 173229, Himachal Pradesh, India
3 Engineering Management Department, College of Engineering, Prince Sultan University, Riyadh 11586, Saudi Arabia
4 Department of Electrical Engineering, College of Engineering, Taif University, Taif 21944, Saudi Arabia
5 Department of Civil Engineering, College of Engineering, Taif University, Taif 21944, Saudi Arabia
6 Department of Architecture Engineering, College of Engineering, Taif University, Taif 21944, Saudi Arabia
* Correspondence: raj.me@shooliniuniversity.com

Citation: Sharma, N.; Thakur, M.S.; Kumar, R.; Malik, M.A.; Alahmadi, A.A.; Alwetaishi, M.; Alzaed, A.N. Assessing Waste Marble Powder Impact on Concrete Flexural Strength Using Gaussian Process, SVM, and ANFIS. *Processes* 2022, 10, 2745. https://doi.org/10.3390/pr10122745

Academic Editor: Xiong Luo

Received: 26 October 2022
Accepted: 16 December 2022
Published: 19 December 2022

Publisher's Note: MDPI stays neutral with regard to jurisdictional claims in published maps and institutional affiliations.

Copyright: © 2022 by the authors. Licensee MDPI, Basel, Switzerland. This article is an open access article distributed under the terms and conditions of the Creative Commons Attribution (CC BY) license (https://creativecommons.org/licenses/by/4.0/).

Abstract: The study's goal is to assess the flexural strength of concrete that includes waste marble powder using machine learning methods, i.e., ANFIS, Support vector machines, and Gaussian processes approaches. Flexural strength has also been studied by using the most reliable approach of sensitivity analysis in order to determine the influential independent variable to predict the dependent variable. The entire dataset consists of 202 observations, of which 120 were experimental and 82 were readings from previous research projects. The dataset was then arbitrarily split into two subsets, referred to as the training dataset and the testing dataset, each of which contained a weighted percentage of the total observations (70–30). Output was concrete mix flexural strength, whereas inputs comprised cement, fine and coarse aggregates, water, waste marble powder, and curing days. Using statistical criteria, an evaluation of the efficacy of the approaches was carried out. In comparison to other algorithms, the results demonstrate that the Gaussian process technique has a lower error bandwidth, which contributes to its superior performance. The Gaussian process is capable of producing more accurate predictions of the results of an experiment due to the fact that it has a higher coefficient of correlation (0.7476), a lower mean absolute error value (1.0884), and a smaller root mean square error value (1.5621). The number of curing days was identified as a significant predictor, in addition to a number of other factors, by sensitivity analysis.

Keywords: waste marble powder; flexural strength; support vector machines; Gaussian processes; ANFIS

1. Introduction

Cement, fine and coarse aggregates and water are the main ingredients of concrete. Every one of the components, with the exception of cement, is easily accessible in every region of the world. The only way to create cement is through the process of manufacturing it. The manufacture of cement results in the emission of carbon dioxide, which is harmful to the environment. Because of their extensive application, there is currently an increase in the overexploitation of several resources. As a result of industrialization and urbanization, concrete is used in a significant amount of construction projects, and the rising demand for the material will eventually lead to its depletion. If the waste material could meet the required criteria, then it could be used in the development of the infrastructure, which would make it economically viable [1,2]. The process of industrialization results in the production of a variety of hazardous wastes, the management of which can be accomplished by mixing these wastes into the fundamental components of concrete. There is a possibility that fly ash, silica fumes, and slag will raise the water demand of the concrete mix. This issue can be remedied by using a superplasticizer [3]. Waste marble powder (WMP) can be utilized in place of cement or fine aggregates as an alternative [4–6]. WMP is a potentially useful material that might be used to partially replace sand and cement. CaO, SiO_2, Al_2O_3, Fe_2O_3 are significant constituents, whereas MgO, SO_3, K_2O, and Na_2O are minor constituents. India produces the most marble waste throughout the mining process. The marble industry's waste can harm the environment and the economy if not properly managed. The demand for marble on the market is driven in part by its widespread application in ornamental settings. The production of marble results in the generation of a number of different chemical forms that are considered to be hazardous waste. The disposal of waste is not an efficient use of resources, and it also raises concerns for the environment. When appropriately integrated, the use of waste from industrial processes has the potential to reduce the amount of cement that must be added to concrete [7]. Marble sludge can be recycled and utilized as one of the primary components of concrete mix, which can subsequently be used as a building material or in the construction of road pavements, amongst other potential applications [8]. Soliman [9] found that as marble powder (MP) replaces cement in the nominal mix, the concrete strength decreases. Both the effect of substituting MP for cement (C) and the findings show that the tensile strength of WMP starts to decrease as the amount of WMP increases [10]. By replacing 10% of the cement with marble dust, Dhoka [11] noticed a 25% improvement in 28-day tensile strength compared to the composite samples. Many researchers use waste MP as a replacement of cement by weight [12–16]. In the experiment that was carried out by Kelestemur [14], on a concrete mix that contained various amounts of glass fiber, it can be seen that by adding marble dust, it achieves the highest CS. Workability was not affected by the capillarity properties of self-compacting concrete caused by the addition of waste marble dust as a cement replacement, but tensile strength was reduced as a result [15]. Uysal and Yilmaz [17] investigated the usage of lime, basalt, and MP as Portland cement substitutes. In addition, the tensile strength after 28 days was improved when both gravel and sand were used as a substitute [18]. It was determined that the utilization of MP as a filler was satisfactory [19]. According to the findings of the study, replacing sand with 10% mineral powder delivers the highest possible CS while maintaining a level of workability that is comparable to that of cement. MP offers good cohesiveness to mortar because of its fineness. MP can also be used as a substitute for SCC [20]. After 28 days of curing, Demirel [21] found that the porosity of the matrix began to decrease as the quantity of small particles in the matrix increased after being replaced with WMP. However, the CS rating improved. The mechanical and physical qualities of the concrete are altered when WMP is used as a filler ingredient in the production of SCC [22].

Waste marble powder (WMP) can be utilized in place of cement or fine aggregates as an alternative [5,6]. Researchers are currently employing methods of soft computing in an effort to find solutions to the problems [23–32]. The amount of cement, aggregates, water, admixtures, and waste products that are included in the mix are the primary factors that define the strength of the concrete. These elements can be incorporated into the model as input variables to facilitate more accurate forecasting of the ultimate outcome. In classic methodologies, the approaches of linear and non-linear regression are utilized the majority of the time in order to anticipate results. However, in recent years, techniques from the field of AI such as artificial neural networks (ANN), linear regression, group method of data handling (GMDH), random forest, and random tree (RT) have been utilized to estimate the concrete mechanical characteristics [33–38]. The majority of the research effort is being put towards attempting to forecast the mechanical characteristics of various concrete mixes. In order to accurately estimate the strength of no-slump concrete, a number of regressions, neural networks (NNT), and adaptive neuro-fuzzy inference system (ANFIS) models have been created [25,32]. These models use components of concrete as input parameters. The findings indicate that the NNT and ANFIS models are superior to the proposed standard regression models in terms of accuracy when it comes to forecasting the 28-day CS for non-slumping concrete. In Madandoust's [39] research, a neural network of the GMDH type was combined with ANFIS modelling to make a prediction about the strength of concrete made from cementitious components. During the course of the research, a genetic algorithm was utilized to construct a neural network of the GMDH variety. Input parameters consisted of things like ratios of length to diameter, core diameter, and other similar measurements in order to forecast the output strength. Ayat [40], in the year 2018, directed the study to analyses the affectability of the developed model to some basic factors influencing concrete CS. The goal of the investigation was to determine whether or not the constructed model is affected by these factors. It was found that the ANNs model that had been suggested was remarkable as a practical and very effective method for simulating the CS forecast of lime filler (LF) concrete. When it comes to forecasting the CS of concrete mixtures, tree-based models perform admirably.

In this paper, the effect of marble powder on flexural strength of concrete is demonstrated. Experimental investigations to study the effect of marble dust on flexural strength exploring possible reasons for the gain in strength have been conducted. Techniques from the field of soft computing have found widespread use in a variety of technical fields over the course of the past few decades. Fewer studies have been identified on the performance of soft computing techniques for predicting the FS of concrete mixtures that include waste MP. Some of the soft computing techniques that were utilized in this work are the Support Vector Machine (SVM), the Gaussian Process (GP), and the Adaptive Neuro-Fuzzy Inference System (ANFIS). The results were compared in order to identify the modelling strategy that proved to be the most reliable in predicting the FS of concrete mix includes waste marble powder. Additional sensitivity analysis was done to identify the most important input parameter.

2. Machine Learning Techniques

2.1. ANFIS

An artificial neural network that is built on the Takagi-Sugeno fuzzy inference system is called an adaptive neuro-fuzzy inference system (ANFIS). It wasn't until the early 1990s that the methodology was created. It offers the chance to use the benefits of both types of systems under a single framework because it combines neural networks and fuzzy logic concepts. Its inference system is made up of a collection of fuzzy IF–THEN rules with the capacity to approximate nonlinear functions through learning. As a result, ANFIS is regarded as a universal estimator. The best parameters acquired by genetic algorithm may be used to employ the ANFIS in a more efficient and optimal manner. Figure 1 presents the ANFIS architecture [41]. There are five layers in the ANFIS model. Each layer has its own set of nodes, which are specified by the node function. Layer one is the layer in which all of the nodes have a node function and are adaptive nodes. The second layer is where nodes multiply incoming signals, and the output is the sum of all the incoming signals. The firing strength of the ith rule is compared to the total firing strength of all node rules, which is the focus of Layer 3's calculation. Each node in layer 4 is responsible for calculating the contribution that the ith rule makes to the overall output. The signal node in layer 5 calculates the final output as the sum of all input signals.

Within the framework of this ANFIS system, the hybrid algorithm was implemented. The input and output membership functions of the ANFIS model each have their own unique shape. The 'trimf' membership function was chosen out of all the other MF's because it displays the lowest test error and the lesser value of mean absolute percentage error compared to the other membership functions. The 'trimf' membership function, which stands for 'triangular membership function,' also has incline and decline features with a specific value [42].

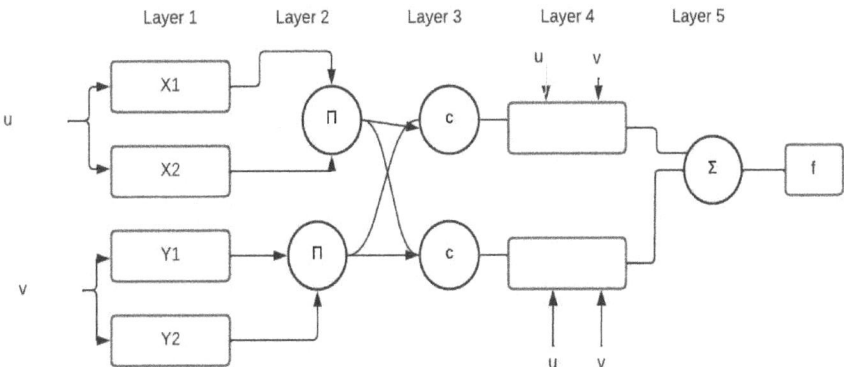

Figure 1. The architecture of ANFIS model.

2.2. Support Vector Machine (SVM)

Vapnik initially demonstrated the SVM in 1995. Researchers utilize this method to tackle categorization, prediction, and regression difficulties. It's a part of artificial intelligence (AI) [43,44]. SVM analysis involves training and testing data sets and input/output parameters. The optimal margin classifier is used in SVM analysis to segment the decision surface. The product of two vectors is determined using the kernel function approach. Fixed mapping is used to fit a non-linear kernel function in high-dimensional space after input data has been mapped using n-dimensional characteristics. When high-dimensional data is mapped using a kernel, the information separates linearly without altering the input space [44]. The input space is converted into a high-dimensional feature space via the kernel function, which enables non-linear relationships to be expressed in a linear fashion. The particular selection of a kernel function to map the non-linear input space into a linear feature space is highly dependent on the nature of the data, which refers to the type of underlying relationship that needs to be estimated in order to relate the input data with the desired output property. Finding such a kernel will be quite valuable. The Pearson VII Universal Kernel was utilized for use as the basis for the GP and SVM kernel function. The Pearson VII function offers outstanding flexibility and the opportunity to simply shift from a Gaussian into a Nonlinear peak shape and more by modifying its parameters. It also has the ability to transition from a Nonlinear peak shape to a Gaussian peak shape. As a result, the Pearson VII function can be utilized in place of a generic kernel [45].

2.3. Gaussian Processes (GPs)

Over the course of the last several years, a large amount of research and development effort has been concentrated on the study of machine learning as an area of study. The Gaussian process is a method for machine learning that involves performing analyses of models using kernels. It gives kernel machine novices hands-on experience [46,47]. Each finite random variable has a joint normal distribution. This collection is called a random variable ensemble. It is generally agreed that the mean function, which is represented by the symbol m(x), and the kernel function, which is represented by the symbol n(x,x'), are the two most important functions of the Gaussian process, which is represented by the symbol l (x).

2.4. Purpose of the Study

A comprehensive literature analysis found that fewer studies had utilized these modelling methodologies to assess the FS of concrete mixes including WMP. In civil engineering, their ability to predict the FS of concrete mixtures was evaluated using literature and lab data. In this paper, the effect of marble powder on flexural strength of concrete is demonstrated. Experimental investigations to study the effect of marble dust on flexural strength exploring possible reasons for the gain in strength have been conducted. The study's goal is to assess the flexural strength of concrete that includes waste marble powder using machine learning methods, i.e., ANFIS, Support vector machines, and Gaussian processes approaches. Other algorithms were also tested on the dataset used for the study in addition to GP, SVM, and ANFIS, but they showed a poor coefficient of correlation value for the dataset. Therefore, in place of other conventional methodologies, ANFIS, support vector machine, and Gaussian process methods were used to predict the flexural strength of concrete.

In order to determine which modelling technique was the most effective at predicting the FS of concrete mix, the results were compared. This was done so that the most dependable modelling strategy could be selected. Flexural strength has also been studied by using the most reliable approach of sensitivity analysis in order to determine the influential independent variable to predict the dependent variable.

3. Methodology

In order to accomplish the goal of the study, which was to predict the FS of concrete, the following approach was taken: data was gathered on the FS of concrete, and various forms of soft computing were utilized. It was important to collect adequate data for the purpose of predicting the FS, and this was accomplished by carrying out experimental study and data from previously published studies.

3.1. Experimental Investigation

Each of the 120 beam specimens measuring 700 mm × 150 mm × 150 mm provided the following information regarding the testing materials and procedures:

3.1.1. Aggregate

CA with nominal diameters between 10 and 20 mm was incorporated in the concrete mixture. The particle size distribution of the aggregate was graded [48]. The SG, crushing, and impact were found to be 2.61, 23.67, and 6.74 percent, respectively, by ASTM C-128 and ASTM C-127 [49,50]. The mechanical characteristics of FA and CA are shown in Table 1.

Table 1. Mechanical Characteristics of Fine and Coarse Aggregates.

Experiment	Unit	Observed Value	Permissible Limit	Standard
Impact test of CA	%	6.74	<10	[50]
Crushing value of CA	%	23.67	>45	[50]
SG of CA	gm/cm^3	2.61	-	
Apparent SG of CA	gm/cm^3	2.82	-	[49]
WA of CA	%	2.82	-	
SG of FA	gm/cm^3	2.47	-	
Apparent SG of FA	gm/cm^3	2.51	-	[49]
WA of FA	%	0.6	-	

3.1.2. Cement

Cement according to ASTM C-150 [51] Type-I cement was utilized in this study. Table 2 lists the mechanical characteristics of cement.

Table 2. Mechanical Characteristics of cement.

Test	Unit		Value	Permissible Limit	Standard
Fineness	%		5.77	<10	[52]
Consistency	%		32	>45	[53]
Soundness	mm		3.33	<10	[54]
SG	gm/cm^3		3.1	-	[55]
Setting Time	min	Initial	40	-	[56]
		Final	360	-	

3.1.3. Marble Powder

The Waste Marble Powder that was obtained came from its source, which was a marble company that was located locally. While Table 3 provides an explanation of the WMP's mechanical qualities, Figure 2 depicts the chemical analysis of the marble powder. An EDS analysis was carried out so that the elemental make-up of the WMP could be ascertained. The X-ray spectra, which can be seen in the image, are laid out with the energy, which is measured in keV, along the x-axis and the number of counts, which is measured along the y-axis. The information shown in Figure 2 makes it abundantly evident that Calcium and Oxygen have the highest weightage of all the elements.

Table 3. Mechanical Characteristics of MP.

Test	Unit	Value
Fineness	%	2.01
SG	gm/cm^3	2.44
Apparent SG	gm/cm^3	2.56
WA	%	1.96
Bulk SG	gm/cm^3	1.63

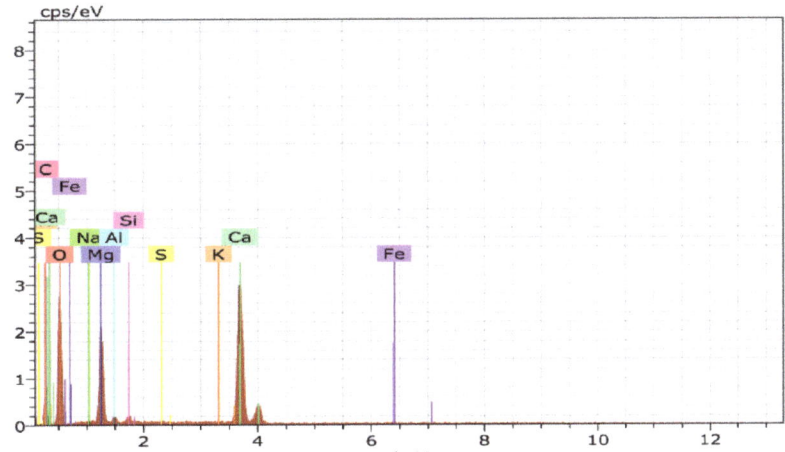

Figure 2. Chemical Analysis of Marble Powder.

3.1.4. Mix Design

When making batches, the amounts of C, FA, and MP that were specified were employed. Other components, such as CA and the ratio of water to cement, were always used in the same proportions throughout the process. Several unique sets of specimens, each of which had three beams, were manufactured as a part of the experiment. A total of one hundred and twenty beams were manufactured. The composition of the control specimens, as well as the composition of the specimens with 5, 10, 15, and 20% replacement by the weight of cement and sand, is detailed in Table 4.

Table 4. Mix Design.

Sr. No.	Mix-ID	Materials in kg/m³				
		Cement	FA	CA	Water	MP
1	M0	395.74	600.15	1103.09	217.65	0
2	A04	395.74	570.14	1103.09	217.65	30.00
3	A13	390.79	577.65	1103.09	214.93	27.44
4	A22	385.85	585.15	1103.09	212.21	24.89
5	A31	380.89	592.64	1103.09	209.49	22.34
6	A40	375.95	600.15	1103.09	206.77	19.78
7	B04	395.74	540.13	1103.09	217.65	60.01
8	B13	385.85	555.13	1103.09	212.21	54.90
9	B22	375.95	570.14	1103.09	206.77	49.75
10	B31	366.06	585.15	1103.09	201.33	44.68
11	B40	356.16	600.15	1103.09	195.89	39.57
12	C04	395.74	510.12	1103.09	217.65	90.02
13	C13	380.89	532.63	1103.09	209.49	82.35
14	C22	366.06	555.13	1103.09	201.33	74.69
15	C31	351.21	577.65	1103.09	193.16	67.02
16	C40	336.37	600.15	1103.09	185.00	59.36
17	D04	395.74	480.12	1103.09	217.65	120.03
18	D13	375.95	510.12	1103.09	206.77	109.80
19	D22	356.16	540.13	1103.09	195.89	99.58
20	D31	336.37	570.14	1103.09	185.00	89.43
21	D40	316.59	600.15	1103.09	174.12	79.14

M0 = control mix; (A represents 5% MP, B represents 10% MP, C represents 15% MP, D represents 20% MP) replacement.

ASTM D790 and ASTM C78 determine flexural strength using a two-point loading test. This method determines the flexural strength of hardened concrete test specimens by two-point loading [57,58]. Figure 3 shows a schematic of a flexural machine with two supports and two loads. Two supports considered as simply supported. The specimen's center was loaded and then two points until failure. The flexural test machine directly measured the load.

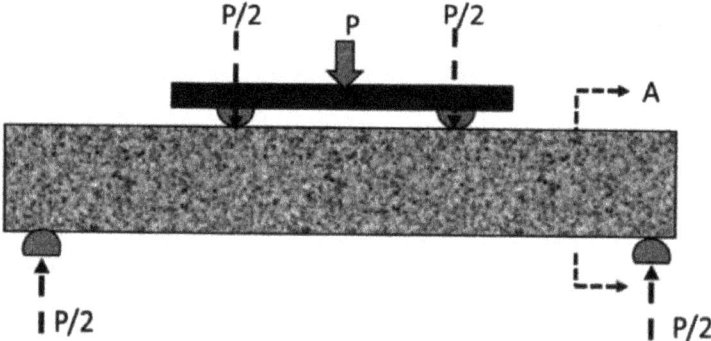

Figure 3. Experimental Setup for Flexural Strength [58].

3.1.5. Result and Discussion

The samples A04 and D40 that contained marble powder instead of sand and cement, respectively, showed an extra improvement in strength in the strength activity results as shown in Figure 4. After 28 days, the strength ratio for the samples was 15% and 3% higher, respectively, showing that a chemical reaction was occurring. The components with the biggest weightage, according to an EDS study, are calcium and oxygen in marble powder, which contribute to the increase in strength.

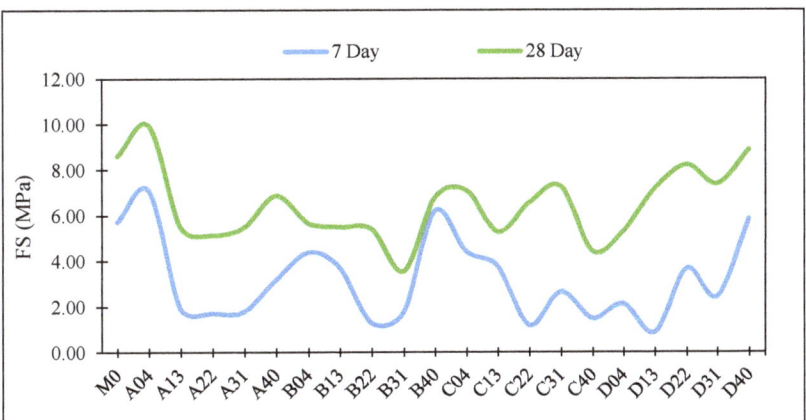

Figure 4. FS Results Based on Experimental Studies.

4. Statistical Analysis
4.1. Data Collection

The dataset is absolutely necessary for making an accurate prediction. Table 5 contains the range of the 202 observations that were gathered for this study from various sources, including the literature (82 readings), as well as laboratory data (120 readings). Table 6 contains detailed information regarding the observations that were analyzed as part of the investigation. After then, the 202 observations were divided into two subgroups at random, with a ratio of 70–30 for the training and testing subsets, respectively. In this study, FS served as the output variable, while ANFIS, SVM, and GP were the three methods that were employed to obtain the intended outcome. The input variables included C, FA, CA, w, MP, and CD. The software platforms that were used were MATLAB and Weka 3.9. In order to achieve the desired outcome, the researchers used independent variables including C, FA, CA, w, MP, and CD. In Table 7, the characteristics of the complete dataset, the dataset used for training, and the dataset used for testing are outlined. Consideration was given to the CC, MAE, RMSE, RAE, and RRSE when attempting to ascertain which model produced the most accurate results. These factors were helpful in determining which model was the most accurate. Better results are likely to have a higher CC value as well as a lower error value. Table 8 is a listing of the user-defined criteria that must be met when evaluating the FS of a concrete mixture using WMP. These user-defined optimal settings for various procedures are the product of a significant amount of research that were conducted. The effectiveness of each model was determined by the optimal configurations. Because the optimal parameters will have an effect on the performance of the model, it is essential that they be determined with extreme care. As a consequence of this, the example parameters were perfectly suitable for both the datasets used for training and for testing.

Table 5. Range of the dataset used.

Sr. No.	Independent Variable Range					Dependent Variable Range		Reference
	(kg/m³)					CD	FS (MPa)	
	C	FA	CA	W	MP			
1.	316.59–395.74	480.12–600.15	1103.09	174.13–217.66	0.00–120.03	7.00–28.00	0.71–11.73	Experimental Reading
2.	225.00–300.00	450.00	900.00	120.00	0.00–75.00	7.00-28.00	0.40–3.10	[59]
3.	383.00	273.00–546.00	1187.00	191.60	0.00–273.00	28.00	4.18–5.73	[60]
4.	340.00–400.00	672.00	1113.00	120.00–160.00	0.00–60.00	7.00–28.00	3.30–4.21	[61]
5.	240.00–300.00	312.30	1721.40	150.000	0.00–30.00	7.00–90.00	4.80–6.10	[62]
6.	270.20–337.80	741.40–927.00	1046.20	189.140–212.800	0.00–185.20	7.00–90.00	1.76–3.40	[63]

Table 6. Detail of dataset.

Sr. No.	1	2	3	4	5	6	Total
Author	Mansoor [59]	Anitha Selvasofia [60]	Sounthararajan and Sivakumar [61]	Ergun [62]	Kirgiz [63]	Experimental Readings	202
No. of observation	18	6	14	22	22	120	

Table 7. Characteristics of Datasets.

Dataset	Statistics	Minimum	Maximum	Mean	Standard Deviation	Kurtosis	Skewness
Total Dataset (202 observations)	C	225.00	400.00	345.23	48.54	−0.43	−0.89
	FA	273.00	927.00	556.21	132.14	0.59	0.12
	CA	900.00	1721.40	1149.32	209.67	3.40	2.07
	w	120.00	217.66	186.23	31.89	−0.32	−1.01
	MP	0.00	273.00	59.71	46.51	2.48	1.29
	CD	7.00	90.00	20.10	16.64	8.33	2.44
	FS	0.40	11.73	4.55	2.52	0.01	0.67
Training Dataset (142 Observations)	C	225.00	400.00	343.55	50.30	−0.60	−0.82
	FA	273.00	927.00	554.14	137.09	0.53	0.15
	CA	900.00	1721.40	1155.17	218.49	2.80	1.96
	w	120.00	217.66	185.80	32.29	−0.45	−0.95
	MP	0.00	273.00	59.21	48.52	2.95	1.44
	CD	7.00	90.00	21.05	18.62	6.82	2.39
	FS	0.40	11.73	4.59	2.62	0.04	0.75
Testing Dataset (60 Observations)	C	225.00	395.74	349.21	44.23	0.14	−1.05
	FA	312.30	834.30	561.10	120.60	0.81	0.05
	CA	900.00	1721.40	1135.46	188.16	5.90	2.46
	w	120.00	217.66	187.26	31.15	0.13	−1.17
	MP	0.00	185.20	60.89	41.72	0.34	0.73
	CD	7.00	28.00	17.85	10.34	−2.02	−0.05
	FS	0.71	10.31	4.46	2.27	−0.44	0.32

Table 8. Use Defined Parameters.

Model Used	User Defined Parameters
SVM	C = 1.5, PUK kernel O = 0.7, S = 0.7
GP	Noise = 0.1, PUK kernel O = 0.8, S = 0.8
ANFIS	Epoches = 10

Figure 5, show how distinct each data point's colors are. The color alterations on the pair charts depend on the output's level of intensity. Figure 5 shows how the color for flexure strength, which ranges from 0.4 MPa to 11.73 MPa, varies from blue to orange depending on the intensity of the output. As a result, each data point's color is unique for each variable and ranges from blue at 0.4 MPa to orange at 11.73 MPa. In addition, Figure 5 illustrates a pair plot that was created to visualize the given dataset and discover their relationship. Figure 5 depicts the complex relationship that exists between the flexural strength of concrete and the constituent elements of marble powder, curing days, water, and cement. As can be seen, an increase in the dependent variables such as cement, water, marble powder, and curing days has an effect on the FS of the concrete.

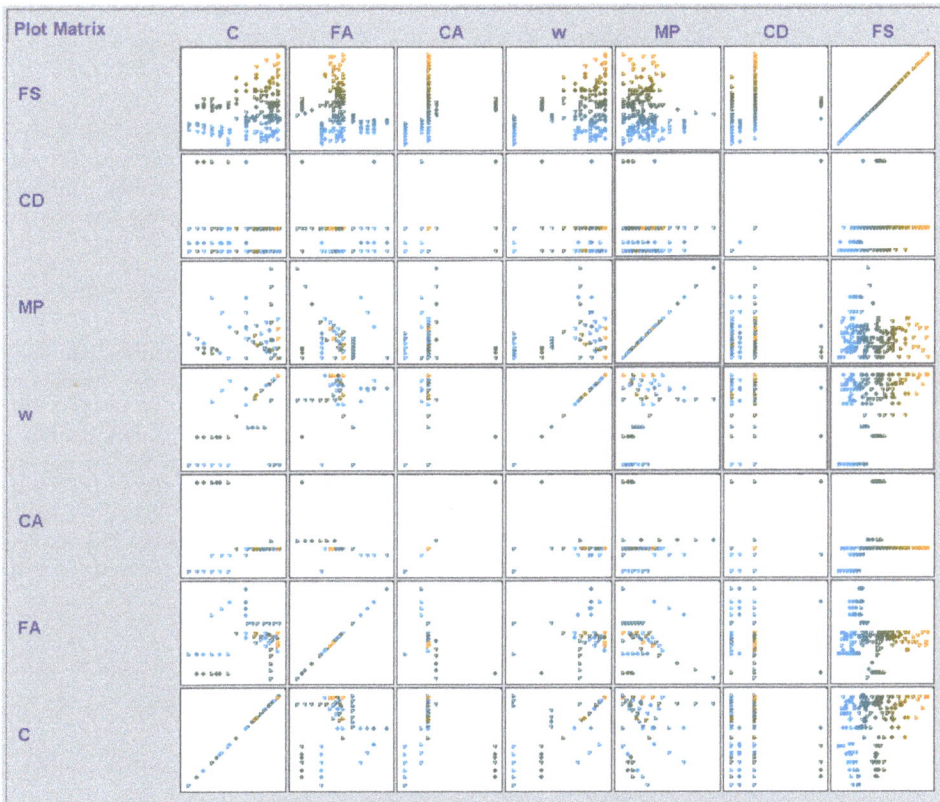

Figure 5. Pair Plot of all Variables.

4.2. Criteria for Evaluative Assessment

Using evaluating parameters ensures that algorithms perform to their greatest capacity. The CC, MAE, RMSE, RAE, and RRSE were used in this investigation.

$$CC = \frac{x(\sum_{i=1}^{x} OV) - (\sum_{i=1}^{x} O)(\sum_{i=1}^{x} V)}{\sqrt{[x \sum_{i=1}^{x} O^2 - (\sum_{i=1}^{x} O)^2]} \sqrt{[x \sum_{i=1}^{x} V^2 - (\sum_{i=1}^{x} V)^2]}} \quad (1)$$

$$RMSE = \sqrt{\frac{1}{x}\left(\sum_{i=1}^{x}(V-O)^2\right)} \quad (2)$$

$$MAE = \frac{1}{x}\left(\sum_{i=1}^{x}|V-O|\right) \quad (3)$$

$$RAE = \frac{\sum_{i=1}^{x}|O-V|}{\sum_{i=1}^{x}(|O-\overline{O}|)} \quad (4)$$

$$RRSE = \sqrt{\frac{\sum_{i=1}^{x}(O-V)^2}{\sum_{i=1}^{x}(|V-\overline{V}|)^2}} \quad (5)$$

O = Observed readings; $\overline{O}$ = the average of the Observed readings
V = Predicted readings; $\overline{V}$ = Predicted Values Average
x = the total number of readings.

The numbers assigned to the CC might range from minus one to plus one. The higher the CC number, the more favorable the outcomes are projected to be. Lower values of evaluation parameters such as RMSE, MAE, RAE, and RRSE, on the other hand, predict better outcomes; that is, if the computed error is low, it means that the output results will be better [64–70].

5. Findings and Discussion

5.1. ANFIS Based Assessment

Trial-and-error is used in the development of ANFIS-based models. Matlab can be used to predict FS. The model used in the study is triangular. The performance metrics for each membership function-based ANFIS model are listed in the later section. ANFIS model based on triangular membership function (MFs) predicts FS of concrete mix containing WMP. The CC values for training and testing were 0.8592 and 0.4687, respectively. The RMSE, MAE, RAE, and RRSE values were 1.3351 and 2.5116, 0.8487, 39.77% and 59.93%, respectively. Figure 6 illustrates observed and predicted ANFIS-based results for both phases. These numbers show how well the ANFIS trimf-based model predicts the FS of concrete mixes containing WMP. Reliable outcomes are predicted by a value that is closer to the line of perfect agreement [71–76].

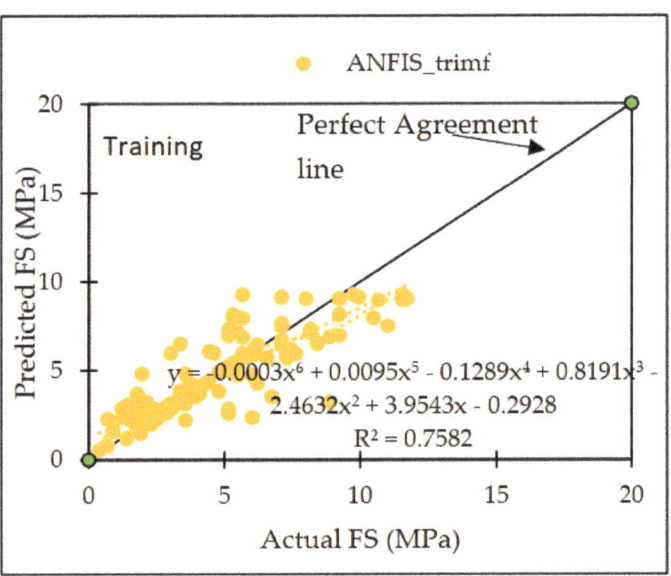

(a) Training

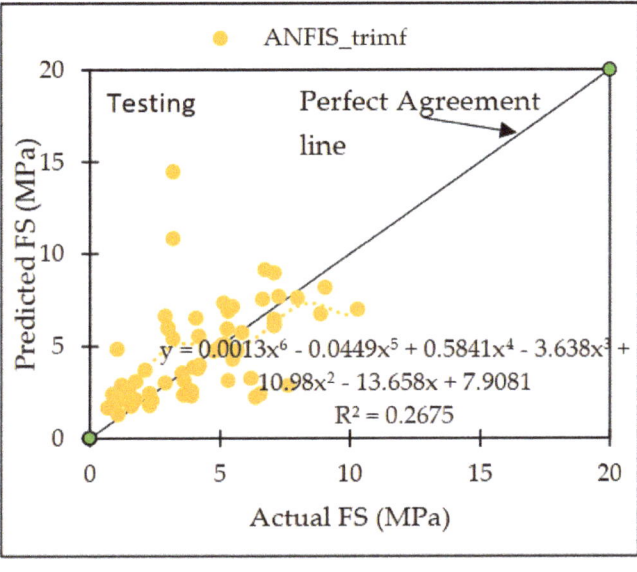

(b) Testing

Figure 6. The scatter graph shows observed and expected ANFIS FS values.

5.2. Support Vector Machine (SVM) Based Assessment

The Pearson VII function kernel, often known as the PUK kernel, is used in this model along with a number of user-defined parameters, such as C, omega (O), and sigma (S). The ideal method, which involved getting the maximum CC value while also minimizing the number of errors, was found after a substantial number of experiments were run [77–80]. The dataset that was used in this investigation yielded the most successful outcomes, with a c value of 1.5, O = 0.7, and S = 0.7, respectively. The performance metrics of the SVM are listed in Table 9, and it includes both the training and testing datasets. The RRSE was 50.88 percent during the training phase and 78.36 percent during the testing phase. The RAE was 31.49 percent during the training phase and 61.61 percent during the testing phase. The MAE was 0.6720 during the training phase and 1.1604 during the testing phase. The CC values were 0.8656 and 0.7020. A comparison of the actual and anticipated FS values of the concrete mix resulted in the creation of the agreement plot, which is depicted in Figure 7.

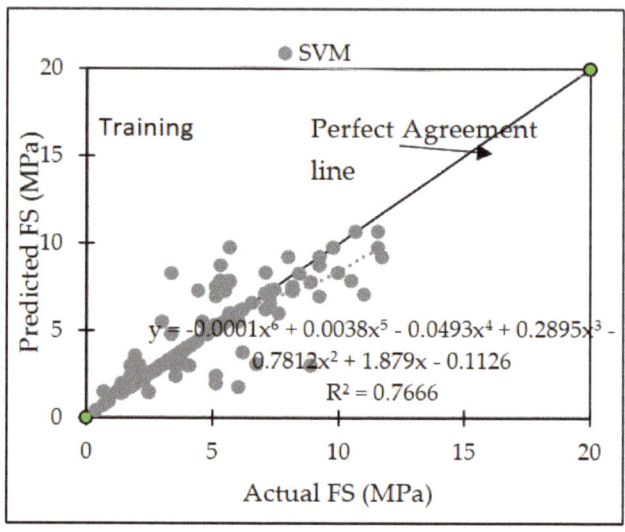

(a) Training

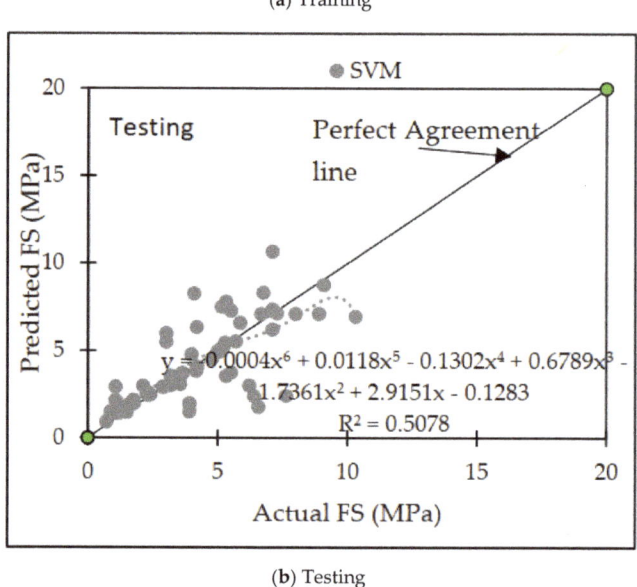

(b) Testing

Figure 7. The scatter graph shows SVM-predicted and observed FS values.

Table 9. Performances of SVM, GP, and ANFIS.

Machine Learning Techniques	CC	MAE	RMSE	RAE	RRSE
			Training		
GP	0.8967	0.7180	1.1563	33.64%	44.32%
SVM	0.8656	0.6720	1.3275	31.49%	50.88%
ANFIS_trimf	0.8592	0.8487	1.3351	39.77%	59.93%
			Testing		
GP	0.7476	1.0884	1.5621	57.79%	69.19%
SVM	0.7020	1.1604	1.7691	61.61%	78.36%
ANFIS_trimf	0.4687	1.6305	2.5116	86.99%	98.74%

5.3. Gaussian Processes (GPs) Based Assessment

The type of regression known as Gaussian Processes makes use of a Pearson VII function kernel, often known as a PUK kernel, together with specific user-defined parameters such as L, Omega (O), and Sigma (S). Numerous trials had to be conducted in order to find the optimal value, which was defined as the greatest CC value that could be achieved with the fewest errors [81–84]. With L values of 0.1, O = 0.8, and S = 0.8, respectively, the dataset employed in this experiment yielded the most effective findings. Table 9 can be accessed here and contains the performance metrics for the general practice training and testing datasets. The training and testing phases' respective RMSE values were 1.1563 and 1.5621, the training and testing phases' respective MAE values were 0.7180 and 1.0884, the training and testing phases' respective RAE values were 33.64 percent and 57.79 percent, and the training and testing phases' respective RRSE values were 44.32 percent and 69.19 percent. The actual FS of the concrete mix is compared to the projected FS in Figure 8, which illustrates the agreement plot.

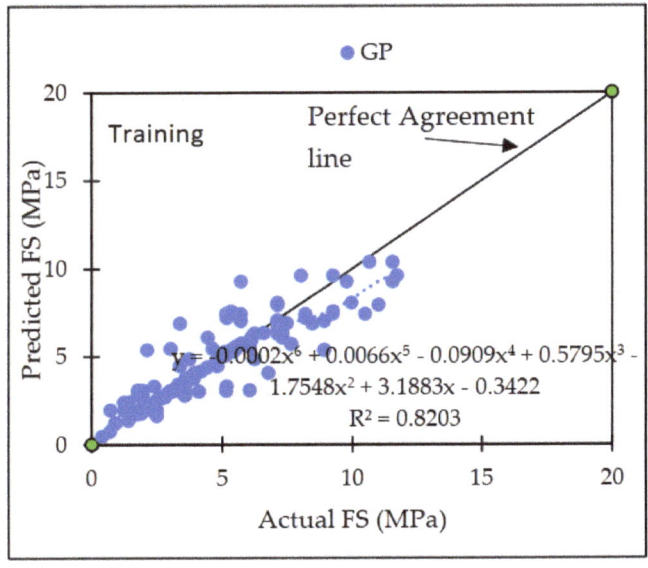

(a) Training

Figure 8. *Cont.*

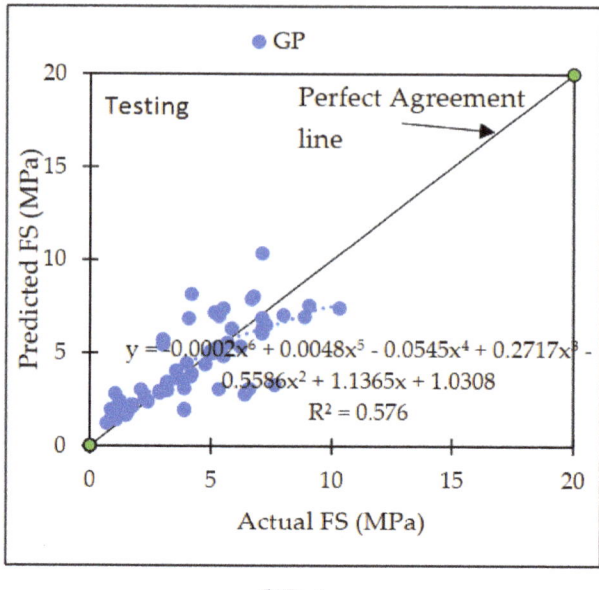

(b) Testing

Figure 8. The scatter graph displays the observed and GP-predicted FS.

6. Comparison

Throughout the course of this investigation, a variety of distinct strategies for machine learning were utilized. The GP model appears to outperform the others when these models are compared, both in terms of the training datasets and the testing datasets [65]. Both the training dataset and the testing dataset showed that the GP model had the greatest possible CC values of 0.8967 and 0.7476, respectively, for the testing dataset. Figure 9a,b illustrates the disparity that exists between the projected dataset and the actual dataset on which machine learning methods were performed.

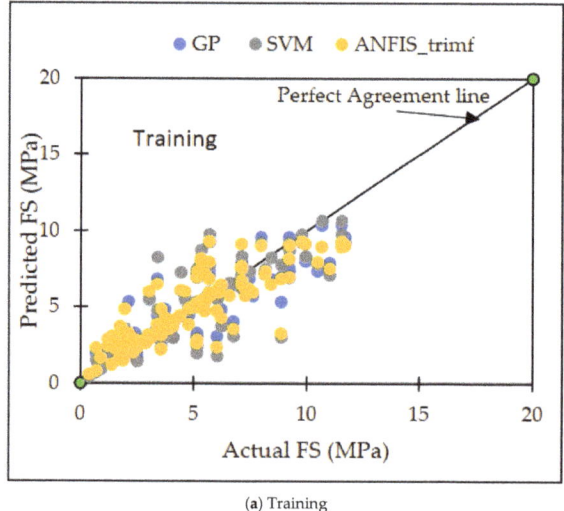

(a) Training

Figure 9. *Cont.*

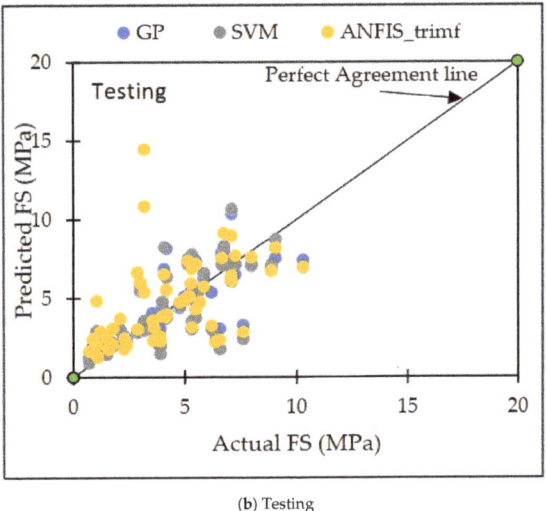

(b) Testing

Figure 9. The scatter plot shows observed and predicted values of FS from SVM, GP, and ANFIS.

GP model also had the lowest MAE (1.0884), RMSE (1.5621), RAE (57.79%), and RRSE (69.19%) for the testing dataset. These results can be seen in Table 9 and Figure 10.

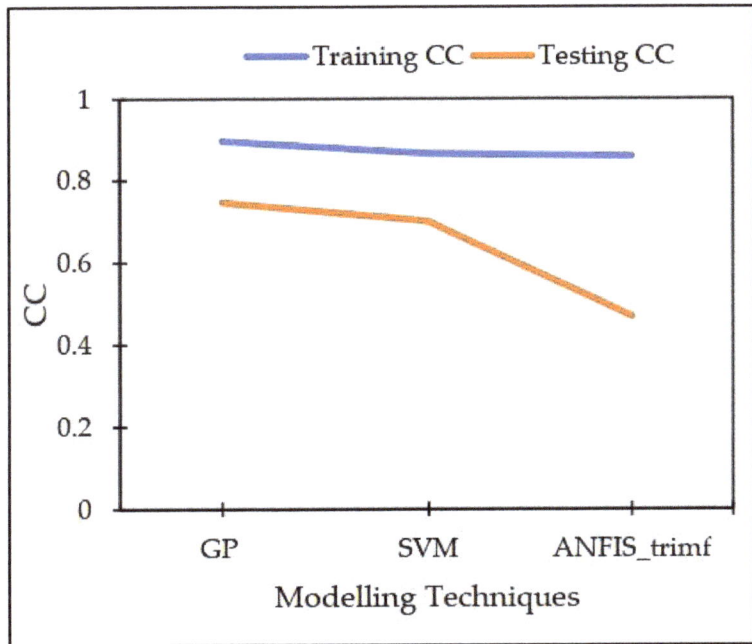

Figure 10. *Cont.*

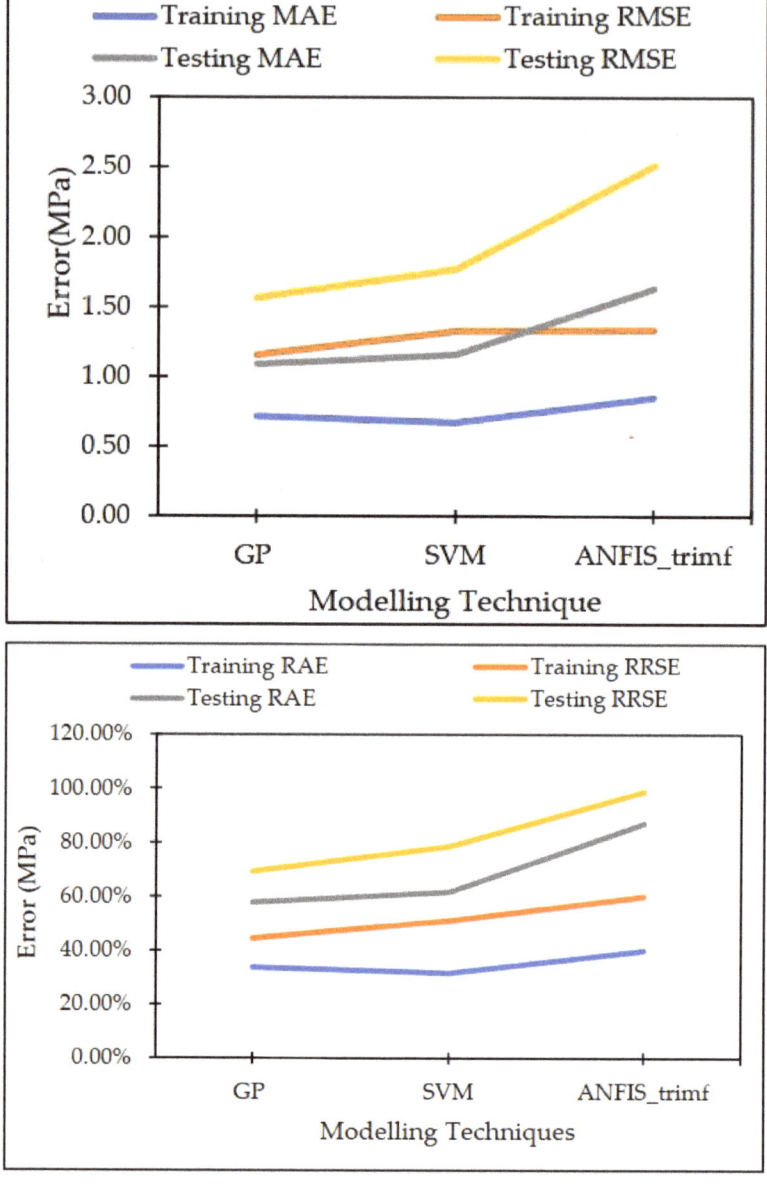

Figure 10. Performance Evaluation by Statistical Parameters.

In order to determine the FS of concrete mix that included MP, it was necessary to evaluate not only the actual value but also the quartile values of 25%, 50%, and 75% in addition to the actual value. Table 10 displays the findings obtained from the aforementioned assessments. Interquartile range (IQR) of GP is relatively near to IQR of the real data that was followed by ANFIS trimf, as can be shown in Figure 11 and Table 10, respectively.

Table 10. Statistics of observed and predicted output of testing dataset utilizing soft computing algorithms.

Output	Statistic Criteria	Actual	GP	SVM	ANFIS_Trimf
	Minimum	0.71	1.23	0.90	1.29
	Maximum	10.31	10.38	10.68	14.48
FS	1st Quartile	2.90	2.81	2.42	2.58
	Mean	4.46	4.50	4.41	4.83
	3rd Quartile	5.96	6.31	6.40	6.48
	IQR	3.06	3.50	3.98	3.90

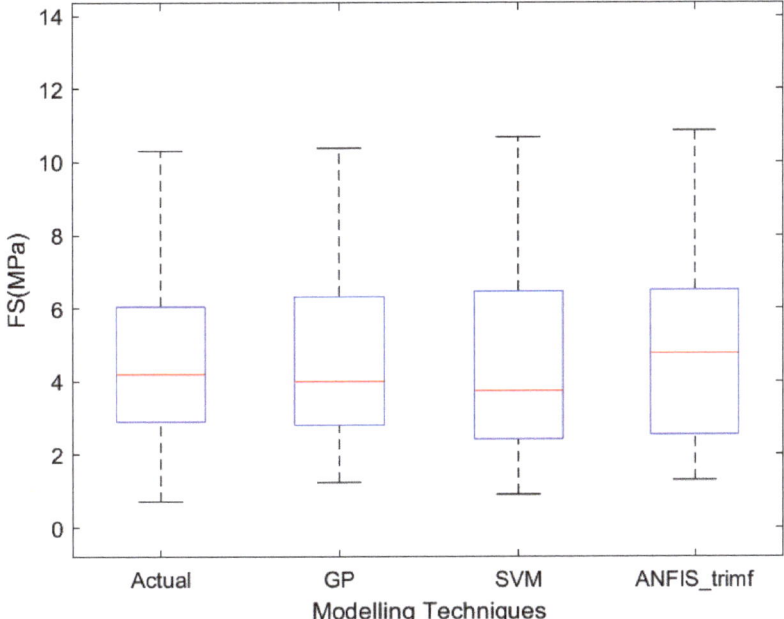

Figure 11. Box plots for all Testing Dataset models.

In addition, based on the examination of the data, the set of data has been separated into two groups, which are FS < 10 MPa and FS > 10 MPa. Table 11 and Figure 12 show the increasing trend in error with decreasing FS based on the modelling methodologies that were used, and they indicate that the error increases from 0.6411 to 1.3511 MPa for FS > 10 to FS < 10, respectively, for GP based model.

Table 11. Performances of SVM, GP, and ANFIS for FS < 10 MPa and FS > 10 Mpa.

	MAE	
	GP	SVM
FS < 10	1.3511	1.6208
FS > 10	0.6411	0.6647

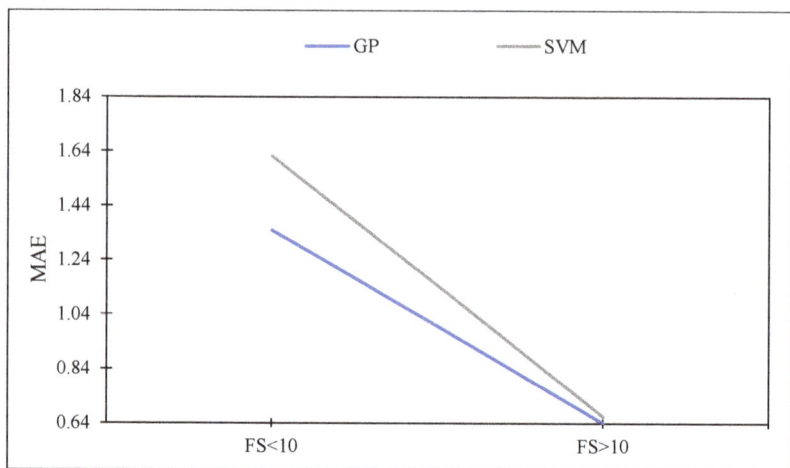

Figure 12. Relationship between Flexural Strength and MAE.

7. Sensitivity Assessments

The most important component of the input variable that affects the prediction of the FS of concrete mixes containing waste MP was identified as a possible variable using sensitivity analysis. It can be seen from Figure 4, which shows the experimental results, that curing days and the change in quantity of MP affects the concrete flexural strength of concrete. Further, sensitivity study was undertaken on the GP model because it performed the best among the other models for this dataset [85–87]. As shown in Table 12, this analysis involved changing the input combination and removing one input parameter one by one. For the purpose of determining which model performed the best, the study utilized statistical evaluation criteria such as CC, MAE, and RMSE. Table 12 indicates that one of the most important factors to consider when attempting to predict the FS of a concrete mixture is the number of curing days followed by the water. Figure 13 represents the relationship between removed parameter and the CC value based on the GP model. The following equation represents the best-fit model for independent variables:

$$y = -0.003x^5 + 0.0648x^4 - 0.5341x^3 + 2.0406x^2 - 3.4785x + 2.68 \tag{6}$$

where, x = independent variable, y = dependent variable

Table 12. GP-based sensitivity model results.

Removed Variable	GP Based Model		
	CC	MAE	RMSE
NIL (no parameter has been removed)	0.7713	1.2034	1.6713
CD	0.5441	1.5499	2.0857
w	0.7365	1.3137	1.8028
FA	0.7419	1.3177	1.7863
CA	0.7690	1.2135	1.6808
C	0.7641	1.2367	1.6909
MP	0.7774	1.1642	1.6194

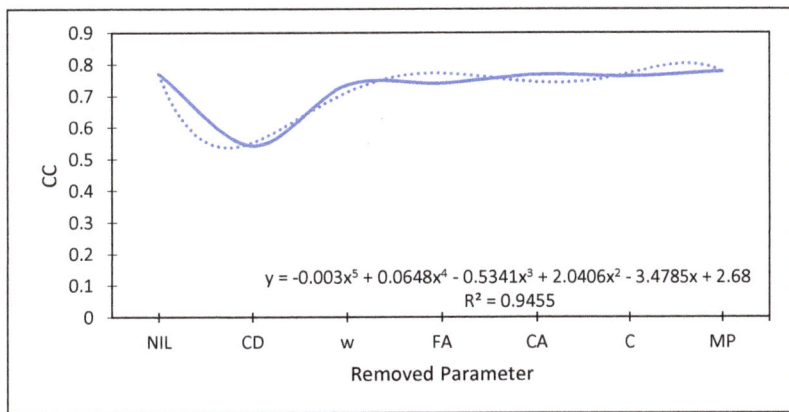

Figure 13. Relationship between Removed Parameters and CC Value Based on GP Model.

In addition, sensitivity analysis has been performed to check the sensitive variable when FS is divided into two parts, i.e., FS < 10 Mpa and FS > 10 Mpa. It can be seen from Table 13 that curing days has an influential effect on the flexural strength of the concrete with maximum MAE value, i.e., 4.8163 Mpa and 1.4743 Mpa for FS > 10 Mpa and FS < 10 Mpa, respectively. A gel is created during the pozzolanic reaction, which causes the FS to increase. Concrete can become stronger when the curing time is extended because it is a gradual process [66].

Table 13. GP-based sensitivity model results for FS < 10 and FS > 10.

Removed Variable	MAE	
	FS > 10	FS < 10
NIL (no parameter has been removed)	0.6411	1.3511
C	0.6378	1.0110
FA	0.6340	1.0131
CA	0.6411	0.9268
w	0.6379	1.0267
MP	0.6570	0.9492
CD	4.8163	1.4743

8. Conclusions

In this study, the algorithms that were used to predict the FS of concrete mixes that included WMP were compared using three different machine learning techniques. These techniques were ANFIS, SVM, and GP. The effectiveness of these models was assessed using the CC, MAE, RMSE, RAE, and RRSE metrics, respectively.

According to the results of the research, the GP model yields the most reliable predictions of the FS of concrete. This conclusion may be drawn from the data of the investigation. GP also predicts more accurate outcomes for the testing dataset than SVM, with corresponding CC values of 0.7476 and 0.7020, lower MAE values of 1.0884 and 1.1604, and lower RMSE values of 1.5621 and 1.7691, respectively.

The scatter plot demonstrates that the GP has the least error band width and is an important predictor of output. This is demonstrated by the fact that the GP has the smallest error band width. The amount of curing days that are subsequently followed by water is the most significant variable to take into consideration when attempting to estimate the FS of concrete. This is because, when compared to the other variables that are utilized as input for this data set, it is the most relevant variable.

Author Contributions: Conceptualization, N.S., M.A.M., A.A.A., M.A. and A.N.A.; methodology, N.S.; software, N.S.; validation, M.S.T.; formal analysis, N.S., M.A.M. and M.A.; investigation, N.S.; writing—original draft preparation, N.S.; writing—review and editing, M.S.T., M.A.M., A.A.A., M.A. and A.N.A.; visualization, N.S. and M.S.T.; Conceptualization, R.K.; methodology, R.K.; software, R.K., M.A.M., A.A.A., M.A. and A.N.A.; validation, R.K., formal analysis, investigation, R.K. All authors have read and agreed to the published version of the manuscript.

Funding: The authors acknowledge the support of Prince Sultan University for paying the article processing charges (APC) of this publication.

Institutional Review Board Statement: Not applicable.

Informed Consent Statement: Not applicable.

Data Availability Statement: Not applicable.

Acknowledgments: The authors would like to acknowledge the support received by Taif University Researchers Supporting Project number (TURSP-2020/240), Taif University, Taif, Saudi Arabia.

Conflicts of Interest: The authors declare no conflict of interest.

Abbreviations

CA	Coarse aggregate
CC	Coefficient of correlation
CS	Compressive strength
CD	Curing days
FA	Fine aggregate
FS	Flexural strength
GP	Gaussian Process
GMDH	Group method of data handling
MP	Marble powder
MAE	Mean absolute error
RAE	Relative absolute error
RMSE	Root mean squared error
RRSE	Root relative squared error
SG	Specific Gravity
SVM	Support vector machine
w	Water
WMP	Waste marble powder
WA	Water absorption

References

1. Eliche-Quesada, D.; Corpas-Iglesias, F.A.; Perez-Villarejo, L.; Iglesias-Godino, F.J. Recycling of sawdust, spent earth from oil filtration, compost and marble residues for brick manufacturing. *Constr. Build. Mater.* **2012**, *34*, 275–284. [CrossRef]
2. Cui, Y.; Liu, J.; Wang, L.; Liu, R.; Pang, B. A model to characterize the effect of particle size of fly ash on the mechanical properties of concrete by the grey multiple linear regression. *Comput. Concr.* **2020**, *26*, 175–183. [CrossRef]
3. Belaidi, A.S.E.; Azzouz, L.; Kadri, E.; Kenai, S. Effect of natural pozzolana and marble powder on the properties of self-compacting concrete. *Constr. Build. Mater.* **2012**, *31*, 251–257. [CrossRef]
4. Ghani, A.; Ali, Z.; Khan, F.A.; Shah, S.R.; Khan, S.W.; Rashid, M. Experimental study on the behavior of waste marble powder as partial replacement of sand in concrete. *SN Appl. Sci.* **2020**, *2*, 1554. [CrossRef]
5. Ashish, D.K.; Verma, S.K.; Kumar, R.; Sharma, N. Properties of concrete incorporating sand and cement with waste marble powder. *Adv. Concr. Constr.* **2016**, *4*, 145–160. [CrossRef]
6. Sharma, N.; Thakur, M.S.; Goel, P.L.; Sihag, P. A review: Sustainable compressive strength properties of concrete mix with replacement by marble powder. *J. Achiev. Mater. Manuf. Eng.* **2020**, *98*, 11–23. [CrossRef]
7. Agarwal, S.K.; Gulati, D. Utilization of industrial wastes and unprocessed micro-fillers for making cost effective mortars. *Constr. Build. Mater.* **2006**, *20*, 999–1004. [CrossRef]
8. Ahmed, K.; Nizami, S.; Raza, N.; Mahmood, K. Effect of micro sized marble sludge on physical properties of natural rubber composites. *Chem. Ind. Chem. Eng.* **2013**, *19*, 281–293. [CrossRef]
9. Soliman, N.M. Effect of using marble powder in concrete mixes on the behavior and strength. *Int. J. Curr. Eng. Technol.* **2013**, *3*, 1863–1870.

10. Shirule, P.A.; Rahman, A.; Gupta, R.D. Partial replacement of cement with marble. *Int. J. Adv. Eng. Res. Stud.* **2012**, *30*, 175–177.
11. Dhoka, M.C. Green Concrete: Using industrial waste of marble powder, quarry dust and paper pulp. *Int. J. Eng. Sci. Invent.* **2013**, *2*, 67–70.
12. Vaidevi, C. Engineering study on marble dust as partial replacement of cement in concrete. *Indian J. Eng.* **2013**, *4*, 14–16.
13. Aruntas, H.Y.; Guru, M.; Dayi, M.; Tekin, I. Utilization of waste marble dust as an additive in cement production. *Mater. Des.* **2010**, *31*, 4039–4042. [CrossRef]
14. Kelestemur, O.; Arici, E.; Yildiz, S.; Gokcer, B. Performance evaluation of cement mortars containing marble dust and glass fiber exposed to high temperature by using taguchi method. *Constr. Build. Mater.* **2014**, *60*, 17–24. [CrossRef]
15. Topcu, I.B.; Bilir, T.; Uygunoglu, T. Effect of waste marble dust content as filler on properties of self-compacting concrete. *Constr. Build. Mater.* **2009**, *23*, 1947–1953. [CrossRef]
16. Ashish, D.K. Feasibility of waste marble powder in concrete as partial substitution of cement and sand amalgam for sustainable growth. *J. Build. Eng.* **2017**, *15*, 236–242. [CrossRef]
17. Uysal, M.; Yilmaz, K. Effect of mineral admixtures on properties of self-compacting concrete. *Cem. Concr. Compos.* **2011**, *33*, 771–776. [CrossRef]
18. Hebhoub, H.; Aoun, H.; Belachia, M.; Houari, H.; Ghorbel, E. Use of waste marble aggregates in concrete. *Constr. Build. Mater.* **2011**, *25*, 1167–1171. [CrossRef]
19. Corinaldesi, V.; Moriconi, G.; Naik, T.R. Characterization of marble powder for its use in mortar and concrete. *Constr. Build. Mater.* **2010**, *24*, 113–117. [CrossRef]
20. Uysal, M.; Sumer, M. Performance of self-compacting concrete containing different mineral admixtures. *Constr. Build. Mater.* **2011**, *25*, 4112–4120. [CrossRef]
21. Demirel, B. The effect of using waste marble dust as fine sand on the mechanical properties of the concrete. *Int. J. Phys. Sci.* **2010**, *5*, 1372–1380.
22. Elyamany, H.E.; Abd Elmoaty, A.E.M.; Mohamed, B. Effect of filler types on physical, mechanical and microstructure of self compacting concrete and flow-able concrete. *Alex. Eng. J.* **2014**, *53*, 295–307. [CrossRef]
23. Sharma, N.; Thakur, M.S.; Upadhya, A.; Sihag, P. Evaluating flexural strength of concrete with steel fibre by using machine learning techniques. *Compos. Mater. Eng.* **2021**, *3*, 201–220. [CrossRef]
24. Thakur, M.S.; Pandhiani, S.M.; Kashyap, V.; Upadhya, A.; Sihag, P. Predicting Bond Strength of FRP Bars in Concrete Using Soft Computing Techniques. *Arab. J. Sci. Eng.* **2021**, *46*, 4951–4969. [CrossRef]
25. Sobhani, J.; Najimi, M.; Pourkhorshidi, A.R.; Parhizkar, T. Prediction of the compressive strength of no-slump concrete: A comparative study of regression, neural network and ANFIS models. *Constr. Build. Mater.* **2010**, *24*, 709–718. [CrossRef]
26. Sharma, N.; Upadhya, A.; Thakur, M.S.; Sihag, P. Comparison of Machine learning algorithms to evaluate Strength of Concrete with Marble Powder. *Adv. Mater. Res.* **2022**, *11*, 75–90. [CrossRef]
27. Sharma, N.; Thakur, M.S.; Sihag, P.; Malik, M.A.; Kumar, R.; Abbas, M.; Saleel, C.A. Machine learning techniques for evaluating concrete strength with waste marble powder. *Materials* **2022**, *15*, 5811. [CrossRef]
28. Yaswanth, K.K.; Revathy, J.; Gajalakshmi, P. Artificial intelligence for the compressive strength prediction of novel ductile geopolymer composites. *Comput. Concr.* **2021**, *28*, 55–68. [CrossRef]
29. Gholamzadeh-Chitgar, A.; Berenjian, J. Elman ANNs along with two different sets of inputs for predicting the properties of SCCs. *Comput. Concr.* **2019**, *24*, 399–412. [CrossRef]
30. Biswas, R.; Bardhan, A.; Samui, P.; Rai, B.; Nayak, S.; Armaghani, D.J. Efficient soft computing techniques for the prediction of compressive strength of geopolymer concrete. *Comput. Concr.* **2021**, *28*, 221–232. [CrossRef]
31. Kumar, A.; Rupali, S. Prediction of UCS and STS of Kaolin clay stabilized with supplementary cementitious material using ANN and MLR. *Adv. Comput. Des.* **2019**, *5*, 195–207. [CrossRef]
32. Chore, H.S.; Magar, R.B. Prediction of unconfined compressive and Brazilian tensile strength of fiber reinforced cement stabilized fly ash mixes using multiple linear regression and artificial neural network. *Adv. Comput. Des.* **2017**, *2*, 225–240. [CrossRef]
33. Sharma, N.; Thakur, M.S.; Upadhya, A.; Sihag, P. Evaluation of models by soft computing techniques for the prediction of compressive strength of concrete using steel fibre. In *Applications of Computational Intelligence in Concrete Technology*; CRC Press: Boca Raton, FL, USA, 2022. [CrossRef]
34. Poddar, A.; Kumar, A.; Kashyap, V.; Thapa, S. Data-driven modeling approach in model rainfall-runoff for a mountainous catchment. In *Modeling and Simulation of Environmental Systems*; CRC Press: Boca Raton, FL, USA, 2022; pp. 253–268.
35. Kashyap, V.; Poddar, A.; Kumar, N.; Rustum, R. A Comparative Study Using ANFIS and ANN for Determining the Compressive Strength of Concrete. In *Applications of Computational Intelligence in Concrete Technology*; CRC Press: Boca Raton, FL, USA, 2022; pp. 73–91.
36. Alyaseen, A.; Poddar, A.; Alissa, J.; Alahmad, H.; Almohammed, F. Behavior of CFRP-strengthened RC beams with web openings in shear zones: Numerical simulation. *Mater. Today Proc.* **2022**, *65*, 3229–3239. [CrossRef]
37. Alyaseen, A.; Poddar, A.; Almohammed, F.; Tajjour, S.; Hammadeh, K.; Alahmad, H. Compressive strength prediction and analysis of concrete using hybrid artificial neural networks. In *Applications of Computational Intelligence in Concrete Technology*; CRC Press: Boca Raton, FL, USA, 2022; pp. 285–303.

38. Alyaseen, A.; Poddar, A.; Almohammed, F.; Tajjour, S.; Hammadeh, K.; Alahmad, H. Predicting recycled aggregates compressive strength in high-performance concrete using artificial neural networks. In *Applications of Computational Intelligence in Concrete Technology*; CRC Press: Boca Raton, FL, USA, 2022; pp. 269–283.
39. Madandoust, R.; John, H.B.; Reza, G. Prediction of the concrete compressive strength by means of core testing using GMDH-type neural network and ANFIS models. *Comput. Mater. Sci.* **2012**, *51*, 261–272. [CrossRef]
40. Ayat, H.; Kellouche, Y.; Ghrici, M.; Boukhatem, B. Compressive strength prediction of limestone filler concrete using artificial neural networks. *Adv. Comput. Des.* **2018**, *3*, 289–302. [CrossRef]
41. Upadhya, A.; Thakur, M.S.; Sharma, N.; Sihag, P. Assessment of Soft Computing-Based Techniques for the Prediction of Marshall Stability of Asphalt Concrete Reinforced with Glass Fiber. *Int. J. Pavement Res. Technol.* **2021**, *15*, 1366–1385. [CrossRef]
42. Kumar, S.; Dhanabalan, S.; Narayanan, C.S. Application of ANFIS and GRA for multi-objective optimization of optimal wire-EDM parameters while machining Ti–6Al–4V alloy. *SN Appl. Sci.* **2019**, *1*, 298. [CrossRef]
43. Salcedo-Sanz, S.; Rojo-Alvarez, J.L.; Martinez-Ramon, M.; Camps-Valls, G. Support vector machines in engineering: An overview. *WIREs Data Min. Knowl. Discov.* **2014**, *4*, 234–267. [CrossRef]
44. Goh, A.T.C.; Goh, S.H. Support vector machines: Their use in geotechnical engineering as illustrated using seismic liquefaction data. *Comput. Geotech.* **2007**, *34*, 410–421. [CrossRef]
45. Abakar, K.A.A.; Yu, C. Performance of SVM based on PUK kernel in comparison to SVM based on RBF kernel in prediction of yarn tenacity. *Indian J. Fibre Text. Res.* **2014**, *39*, 55–59.
46. Rasmussen, C.E.; Williams, C.K.I. *Gaussian Processes for Machine Learning*; The MIT Press: Cambridge, MA, USA, 2006.
47. Deepa, C.; Sathiyakumari, K.; Preamsudha, V. Prediction of the compressive strength of high-performance concrete mix using tree based modeling. *Int. J. Comput. Appl.* **2010**, *6*, 18–24. [CrossRef]
48. ASTM D6913-04; Standard Test Methods for Particle Size Distribution of Soils. American Society for Testing of Materials: West Conshohocken, PA, USA, 1992.
49. ASTM C-128; Standard Test Method for Specific Gravity and Absorption of Fine Aggregate. Annual Book of ASTM Standards: West Conshohocken, PA, USA, 1992.
50. ASTM C 127; Test Method for Specific Gravity and Adsorption of Coarse Aggregate. Annual Book of ASTM Standards: West Conshohocken, PA, USA, 1992.
51. ASTM C150/C150M-21; Standard Specification for Portland Cement. ASTM International: West Conshohocken, PA, USA, 2021.
52. ASTM C184-94e1; Standard Test Method for Fineness of Hydraulic Cement by the 150-µm (No. 100) and 75-µm (No. 200) Sieves (Withdrawn 2002). ASTM International: West Conshohocken, PA, USA, 1994.
53. ASTM C187-16; Standard Test Method for Amount of Water Required for Normal Consistency of Hydraulic Cement Paste. ASTM International: West Conshohocken, PA, USA, 2016.
54. ASTM C151/C151M-18; Standard Test Method for Autoclave Expansion of Hydraulic Cement. ASTM International: West Conshohocken, PA, USA, 2018.
55. ASTM C188-17; Standard Test Method for Density of Hydraulic Cement. American Society for Testing and Material: West Conshohocken, PA, USA, 2009.
56. ASTM C191-19; Standard Test Methods for Time of Setting of Hydraulic Cement by Vicat Needle. ASTM International: West Conshohocken, PA, USA, 2019.
57. ASTM D790-10; Standard Test Methods for Flexural Properties of Unreinforced and Reinforced Plastics and Electrical Insulation Materials. ASTM International: West Conshohocken, PA, USA, 2007.
58. ASTM C78-10; ASTM International. Standard Test Method for Flexural Strength of Concrete (Using Simple Beam with Third-Point Loading). ASTM International: West Conshohocken, PA, USA, 2010.
59. Mansoor, J.; Shah, S.A.R.; Khan, M.M.; Sadiq, A.N.; Anwar, M.K.; Siddiq, M.U.; Ahmad, H. Analysis of mechanical properties of self-compacted concrete by partial replacement of cement with industrial wastes under elevated temperature. *Appl. Sci.* **2018**, *8*, 364. [CrossRef]
60. Anitha-Selvasofia, S.D.; Dinesh, A.; Sarath-Babu, V. Investigation of waste marble powder in the development of sustainable concrete. *Mater. Today Proc.* **2021**, *44*, 4223–4226. [CrossRef]
61. Sounthararajan, V.M.; Sivakumar, A. Effect of the lime content in marble powder for Producing high strength concrete. *J. Eng. Appl. Sci.* **2013**, *8*, 260–264.
62. Ergun, A. Effects of the usage of diatomite and waste marble powder as partial replacement of cement on the mechanical properties of concrete. *Constr. Build. Mater.* **2011**, *25*, 806–812. [CrossRef]
63. Kirgiz, M.S. Fresh and hardened properties of green binder concrete containing marble powder and brick powder. *Eur. J. Environ. Civ. Eng.* **2016**, *20*, 64–101. [CrossRef]
64. Nhu, V.H.; Shahabi, H.; Nohani, E.; Shirzadi, A.; Ansari, N.A.; Bahrami, S.; Miraki, S.; Geertsema, M.; Nguyen, H. Daily water level prediction of zrebar lake (Iran): A Comparison between M5P, Random Forest, Random Tree and Reduced Error Pruning Trees Algorithms. *Int. J. Geo-Inf.* **2020**, *9*, 479. [CrossRef]
65. Hoang, N.D.; Pham, A.D.; Nguyen, Q.L.; Pham, Q.N. Estimating compressive strength of high-performance concrete with gaussian process regression model. *Adv. Civ. Eng.* **2016**, *2016*, 2861380. [CrossRef]
66. Suthar, M. Applying several machine learning approaches for the prediction of unconfined compressive strength of stabilized pond ashes. *Neural Comput. Appl.* **2019**, *32*, 9019–9028. [CrossRef]

67. Afzal, A.; Khan, S.A.; Islam, T.; Jilte, R.D.; Khan, A.; Soudagar, M.E.M. Investigation and Back-Propagation Modeling of Base Pressure at Sonic and Supersonic Mach Numbers. *Phys. Fluids* **2020**, *32*, 096109. [CrossRef]
68. David, O.; Okwu, M.O.; Oyejide, O.J.; Taghinezhad, E.; Asif, A.; Kaveh, M. Optimizing Biodiesel Production from Abundant Waste Oils through Empirical Method and Grey Wolf Optimizer. *Fuel* **2020**, *281*, 118701. [CrossRef]
69. Afzal, A.; Saleel, C.A.; Badruddin, I.A.; Khan, T.M.Y.; Kamangar, S.; Mallick, Z.; Samuel, O.D.; Soudagar, M.E.M. Human Thermal Comfort in Passenger Vehicles Using an Organic Phase Change Material—An Experimental Investigation, Neural Network Modelling, and Optimization. *Build. Environ.* **2020**, *180*, 107012. [CrossRef]
70. Afzal, A.; Alshahrani, S.; ASobaian, A.; Buradi, A.; Khan, S.A. Power Plant Energy Predictions Based on Thermal Factors Using Ridge and Support Vector Regressor Algorithms. *Energies* **2021**, *14*, 7254. [CrossRef]
71. Afzal, A. Optimization of Thermal Management in Modern Electric Vehicle Battery Cells Employing Genetic Algorithm. *J. Heat Transf.* **2021**, *143*, 112902. [CrossRef]
72. Afzal, A.; Navid, K.M.Y.; Saidur, R.; Razak, R.K.A.; Subbiah, R. Back Propagation Modeling of Shear Stress and Viscosity of Aqueous Ionic—MXene Nanofluids. *J. Therm. Anal. Calorim.* **2021**, *145*, 2129–2149. [CrossRef]
73. Mokashi, I.; Afzal, A.; Khan, S.A.; Abdullah, N.A.; Bin Azami, M.H.; Jilte, R.D.; Samuel, O.D. Nusselt Number Analysis from a Battery Pack Cooled by Different Fluids and Multiple Back-Propagation Modelling Using Feed-Forward Networks. *Int. J. Therm. Sci.* **2021**, *161*, 106738. [CrossRef]
74. Elumalai, P.V.; Krishna Moorthy, R.; Parthasarathy, M.; Samuel, O.D.; Owamah, H.I.; Saleel, C.A.; Enweremadu, C.C.; Sreenivasa Reddy, M.; Afzal, A. Artificial Neural Networks Model for Predicting the Behavior of Different Injection Pressure Characteristics Powered by Blend of Biofuel-Nano Emulsion. *Energy Sci. Eng.* **2022**, *10*, 2367–2396. [CrossRef]
75. Veza, I.; Afzal, A.; Mujtaba, M.A.; Tuan Hoang, A.; Balasubramanian, D.; Sekar, M.; Fattah, I.M.R.; Soudagar, M.E.M.; EL-Seesy, A.I.; Djamari, D.W.; et al. Review of Artificial Neural Networks for Gasoline, Diesel and Homogeneous Charge Compression Ignition Engine: Review of ANN for Gasoline, Diesel and HCCI Engine. *Alex. Eng. J.* **2022**, *61*, 8363–8391. [CrossRef]
76. Bakır, H.; Ağbulut, Ü.; Gürel, A.E.; Yıldız, G.; Güvenç, U.; Soudagar, M.E.M.; Hoang, A.T.; Deepanraj, B.; Saini, G.; Afzal, A. Forecasting of Future Greenhouse Gas Emission Trajectory for India Using Energy and Economic Indexes with Various Metaheuristic Algorithms. *J. Clean. Prod.* **2022**, *360*, 131946. [CrossRef]
77. Sharma, P.; Said, Z.; Kumar, A.; Nižetić, S.; Pandey, A.; Hoang, A.T.; Huang, Z.; Afzal, A.; Li, C.; Le, A.T.; et al. Recent Advances in Machine Learning Research for Nanofluid-Based Heat Transfer in Renewable Energy System. *Energy Fuels* **2022**, *36*, 6626–6658. [CrossRef]
78. Sharma, J.; Soni, S.; Paliwal, P.; Saboor, S.; Chaurasiya, P.K.; Sharifpur, M.; Khalilpoor, N.; Afzal, A. A Novel Long Term Solar Photovoltaic Power Forecasting Approach Using LSTM with Nadam Optimizer: A Case Study of India. *Energy Sci. Eng.* **2022**, *10*, 2909–2929. [CrossRef]
79. Ziaee, O.; Zolfaghari, N.; Baghani, M.; Baniassadi, M.; Wang, K. A modified cellular automaton model for simulating ion dynamics in a Li-ion battery electrode. *Energy Equip. Syst.* **2022**, *10*, 41–49.
80. Taslimi, M.S.; Maleki Dastjerdi, S.; Bashiri Mousavi, S.; Ahmadi, P.; Ashjaee, M. Assessment and multi-objective optimization of an off-grid solar based energy system for a Conex. *Energy Equip. Syst.* **2021**, *9*, 127–143.
81. Sharifi, M.; Amidpour, M.; Mollaei, S. Investigating carbon emission abatement long-term plan with the aim of energy system modeling; case study of Iran. *Energy Equip. Syst.* **2018**, *6*, 337–349.
82. Zare, S.; Ayati, M.; Ha'iri Yazdi, M.R.; Kabir, A.A. Convolutional neural networks for wind turbine gearbox health monitoring. *Energy Equip. Syst.* **2022**, *10*, 73–82.
83. Sabzi, S.; Asadi, M.; Moghbelli, H. Review, analysis and simulation of different structures for hybrid electrical energy storages. *Energy Equip. Syst.* **2017**, *5*, 115–129.
84. Meignanamoorthy, M.; Ravichandran, M.; Mohanavel, V.; Afzal, A.; Sathish, T.; Alamri, S.; Khan, S.A.; Saleel, C.A. Microstructure, mechanical properties, and corrosion behavior of boron carbide reinforced aluminum alloy (al-Fe-Si-Zn-Cu) matrix composites produced via powder metallurgy route. *Materials* **2021**, *14*, 4315. [CrossRef]
85. Sathish, T.; Mohanavel, V.; Ansari, K.; Saravanan, R.; Karthick, A.; Afzal, A.; Alamri, S.; Saleel, C.A. Synthesis and characterization of mechanical properties and wire cut EDM process parameters analysis in AZ61 magnesium alloy+ B4C+ SiC. *Materials* **2021**, *14*, 3689. [CrossRef]
86. Chairman, C.A.; Ravichandran, M.; Mohanavel, V.; Sathish, T.; Rashedi, A.; Alarifi, I.M.; Badruddin, I.A.; Anqi, A.E.; Afzal, A. Mechanical and abrasive wear performance of titanium di-oxide filled woven glass fibre reinforced polymer composites by using taguchi and edas approach. *Materials* **2021**, *14*, 5257. [CrossRef]
87. Nagaraja, S.; Kodandappa, R.; Ansari, K.; Kuruniyan, M.S.; Afzal, A.; Kaladgi, A.R.; Aslfattahi, N.; Saleel, C.A.; Gowda, A.C.; Bindiganavile Anand, P. Influence of heat treatment and reinforcements on tensile characteristics of aluminium aa 5083/silicon carbide/fly ash composites. *Materials* **2021**, *14*, 5261. [CrossRef]

Applicability of Convolutional Neural Network for Estimation of Turbulent Diffusion Distance from Source Point

Takahiro Ishigami [1,2,*], Motoki Irikura [2] and Takahiro Tsukahara [1]

1 Department of Mechanical Engineering, Tokyo University of Science, Yamazaki 2641, Noda-shi 278-8510, Japan
2 Chiyoda Corporation, CGH 4-6-2, Minatomirai, Nishi-ku, Yokohama-shi 220-8765, Japan
* Correspondence: ishigami.takahiro@chiyodacorp.com; Tel.: +81-45-285-4495

Abstract: For locating the source of leaking gas in various engineering fields, several issues remain in the immediate estimation of the location of diffusion sources from limited observation data, because of the nonlinearity of turbulence. This study investigated the practical applicability of diffusion source-location prediction using a convolutional neural network (CNN) from leaking gas instantaneous distribution images captured by infrared cameras. We performed direct numerical simulation of a turbulent flow past a cylinder to provide training and test images, which are scalar concentration distribution fields integrated along the view direction, mimicking actual camera images. We discussed the effects of the direction in which the leaking gas flows into the camera's view and the distance between the camera and the leaking gas on the accuracy of inference. A single learner created by all images provided an inference accuracy exceeding 85%, regardless of the inflow direction or the distance between the camera and the leaking gas within the trained range. This indicated that, with sufficient training images, a high-inference accuracy can be achieved, regardless of the direction of gas leakage or the distance between the camera and the leaking gas.

Keywords: turbulence; passive scalar; machine learning; convolutional neural network; estimating diffusion source distance; leaking gas detection

1. Introduction

In petroleum and chemical plants, many measurement systems (mainly of the fixed-point type) are installed on piping and equipment to constantly monitor plant operations. Although the installation of numerous measurement systems enables closer data interval measurement, the balance between safety and economy dictates that an optimised number of instruments should be installed. In gas leak detectors, fixed-point sensors are installed according to laws and regulations. An alarm at preset gas concentrations indicates the measured values that are necessary for maintaining plant safety. In addition to the measured data, a detailed analysis of flow states based on these data enables us to understand the behavior of gas clouds in two or three dimensions, which is difficult using only fixed-point observations. This technology is expected to be useful for safe operations. In addition, as the diffusion of highly toxic substances is more dangerous when approaching a leak source, it is important to identify the leak source location based on the information from conventional gas leak detectors and analysis.

Against this background, to estimate the flow field using limited measurement data, the adjoint approach (data assimilation) has recently been studied to predict the initial turbulent flow conditions [1]. Wang et al. [2] stated that the data resolution in the streamwise or time direction should satisfy the criteria, based on the Taylor microscale in the streamwise direction. Tsukahara et al. [3] evaluated a simple method based on the Taylor diffusion theory for the turbulent transport of a passive scalar from a fixed-point source. As the Taylor diffusion theory is essentially based on the statistical properties of turbulence, their estimation from instantaneous information resulted in large errors. The time history of the source intensity, based on sensor measurements at different locations downstream from the source by adopting an adjoint approach or data assimilation, was estimated by Cerizza et al. [4]. They showed that the estimation performance remains an issue even with multiple sensors when the scalar source is located near the wall. However, owing to the strong nonlinearity of turbulence, several issues remain for the practical application of data assimilation, including numerical stability and quick prediction.

In addition, in rapidly predicting the source of mass diffusion, sequential unsteady three-dimensional simulations based on the convective diffusion equation and the Navier–Stokes equation, together with their associated equations, are not practically applicable, given the current computer performance and computational methods.

Therefore, we focused on the application of machine learning (deep artificial neural networks) for the quick estimation of physical quantities based on observed information. Fukami et al. [5] successfully reconstructed a three-dimensional eddy flow from limited pressure data by using machine learning. Several studies have applied machine learning to predict the concentration of air pollutants in urban areas [6], detect oil spills [7], and estimate the hazardousness of leaking gases [8]. Tan et al. [9] developed a sound-source localization model, which consisted of a convolutional neural network and a regression model. Their experiments in simulated acoustic scenarios showed that the proposed model effectively estimated the angles and distances even in multiple acoustic environments under different spatial conditions. Zhou et al. [10] proposed a gas identification framework based on a sensor array for high-temperature applications. They showed the enhanced accuracy and robustness of such a framework, compared with a multilayer perceptron and support vector machine. Shi et al. [11] proposed a hybrid probabilistic deep learning model to conduct a probabilistic real-time simulation of natural gas hydrate dispersion in a deep-water marine environment. Their advanced hybrid deep learning model with variation inference and physical constraint forecast spatiotemporal concentration evolution of natural gas, compared with the point-estimation deep learning model [12].

However, to the best of the authors' knowledge, diffusion source estimation using convolutional neural networks (CNNs) has not yet been examined. Focusing on gas measurement techniques, the background-oriented schlieren method [13] and imaging methods using infrared cameras [14,15] have been developed in recent years as imaging techniques for gas leaks.

Our previous study [16] demonstrated the feasibility of applying machine learning, specifically CNNs, to estimate the diffusion distance from a point source, based on two-dimensional, instantaneous images of diffused-substance distributions downstream from the source, which was photographed by the planar laser-induced fluorescence (PLIF) method. It was found that for dye diffusion from a point source in typical parallel-plate turbulence (i.e., turbulent channel flow), the distance from the downstream image to the upstream was estimated with more than 90% accuracy. However, the flow as a test platform was limited to a single condition in terms of the Reynolds and Schmidt numbers and to a wall-bounded, fully developed turbulence. In actual engineering plants, there are various turbulent flows due to the influence of wind condition and/or obstacles, such as piping and equipment. The resulting turbulent intensity affects the degree of scalar turbulent diffusion. Thus, the applicability of our method needs to be investigated with not only a specific turbulent intensity but also under various turbulent-intensity conditions. The Schmidt number is also a key parameter for the scalar diffusion in turbulent flow. The Schmidt number of the previous experimental data [16] should be as high as O(100), which would have resulted in scalar distributions with a strong effect of turbulent diffusion and worked well for image recognition. At low Schmidt numbers, the molecular diffusion should dissipate the effective information more rapidly. In such cases, potential features in the downstream scalar distribution are lost, and the estimation of an upstream diffusion source is expected to be difficult. Thus, studies at a lower Schmidt number for typical gas are necessary to confirm the applicability of our method. In addition, the test images of our previous study were based on the concentration distribution of a plane sliced from a certain cross-sectional area. In actual plants, the aforementioned infrared camera image is a distribution image in which the concentration is integrated along the viewpoint direction. In this image, it was assumed that small-scale concentration gradients and micro-scale fluid dynamics are not clearly captured by the integration, and relatively large-scale concentration distributions dominate the image. It is considered that the eliminated information for micro-scale fluid dynamics, which includes the scalar diffusion information, affects the inference accuracy. Therefore, the image simulating an infrared camera should be evaluated for the application.

In this study, we investigated the practical applicability of instantaneous diffusion source-location prediction using a CNN from leaking gas distribution images captured by infrared cameras. The images were obtained from direct numerical simulation of a turbulent flow with a typical Schmidt number of gas past a cylinder assuming gas leakage from surface on a piping. To consider the application in an actual plant, this study further investigated the effects of the direction in which the leaking gas flows into the camera's view and the distance between the camera and the leaking gas on the accuracy of inference. To investigate the effect of the direction of gas inflow into the camera view and the distance between the camera and the leaking gas on the accuracy of inference, we examined the effect of geometric changes (rotation, zoom-in, and zoom-out) on the generalization performance of a concentration distribution image in which the concentration is integrated along the viewpoint direction.

2. Methodology

To create the training images, an incompressible direct numerical simulation (DNS) was conducted using the commercial computational fluid dynamics simulation software STAR-CCM+ (ver. 2021, developed by SIEMENS, Munich and Berlin, Germany). The dimensionless governing equations are expressed as follows:
the continuity equation,

$$\frac{\partial u_i^*}{\partial x_j^*} = 0;$$

the Navier–Stokes equation,

$$\frac{\partial u_i^*}{\partial t^*} + u_j^* \frac{\partial u_i^*}{\partial x_j^*} = -\frac{\partial p^*}{\partial x_i^*} + \frac{1}{Re} \frac{\partial^2 u_i^*}{\partial x_j^* \partial x_j^*};$$

and the advection–diffusion equation,

$$\frac{\partial \phi}{\partial t^*} + u_j^* \frac{\partial \phi}{\partial x_j^*} = \frac{1}{Sc \cdot Re} \frac{\partial^2 \phi}{\partial x_j^* \partial x_j^*} + S_\phi;$$

where Re is the Reynolds number (defined later), t is the time, p is the pressure, and i is the direction of three-dimensional Cartesian coordinate system: $x_1 = x$, $x_2 = y$, and $x_3 = z$. Einstein's summation convention is used. S_ϕ is the passive scalar source term and ϕ is the scalar value. The symbol * indicates normalisation by u, ρ, and d.

The computational domain is shown in Figure 1a. An image of the passive scalar behavior is shown in Figure 1b. There was a background flow inlet at $x = -80$ with Re = 1000 (made dimensionless with cylinder diameter d, background flow velocity U, and kinematic viscosity ν). The cylinder was installed downstream at $80d$ from the background flow inlet ($x = 0$), and a certain amount of a passive scalar was continuously emitted from the source location, with an area of $0.01d^2$ at $y, z = 0$ on the cylinder surface. Training, validation, and testing images were obtained from a fully developed flow field. The same fluid and passive scalar flowed from the source at the volumetric background flow rate of $7 \times 10^{-3}\%$ and the Schmidt number of $Sc = 0.9$. The flow analysis meshes were approximately 9 million hexahedral meshes, and the wall meshes were set as $y^+ = 1.2$ in average (min: 0.04; max: 4.42). The Strouhal number of the Karman vortices generated in the wake of the cylinder was confirmed to be approximately 0.2, and the computational model was thus verified. It should be noted that the spatial-discretisation accuracy of a typical DNS is of the fourth order, and STAR-CCM+ has second-order accuracy [17–19]. In this case, although its accuracy was not fully verified as the DNS standards would require, reasonable results were nevertheless obtained, thus making this simulation method suitable for preparing image data for the objective of machine learning for relatively complicated shapes, similar to this study. Figure 2a shows the mean profile of concentration at $y = 0$ in the x direction at several points ($3d$, $9d$, $15d$, $21d$, $27d$, $33d$, and $39d$ from the source location), and Figure 2b denotes the root-mean-square of concentration for the same points as (a). It can be confirmed that the high-concentration passive scalar diffuses downstream, and the maximum value is near the center. The concentration becomes uniform along the x-direction, such that the concentration becomes completely uniform and no characteristic image of concentration is obtained. In this study, the concentration profile still existed at $39d$ downstream.

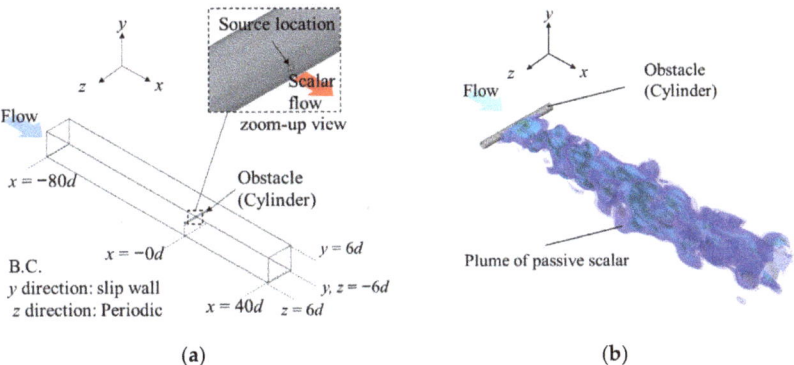

Figure 1. (a) Schematic for simulation model; (b) simulated plume of passive scalar.

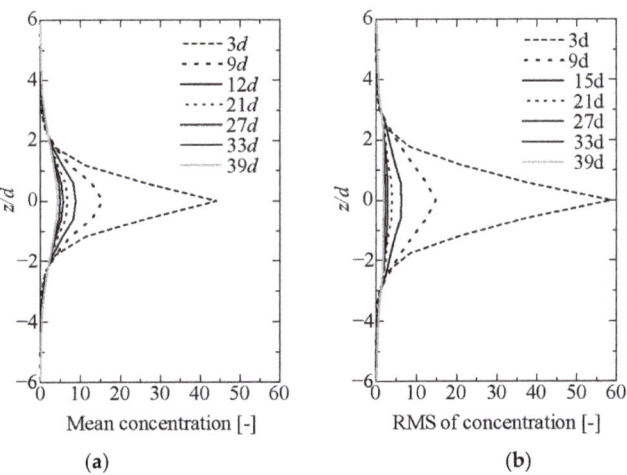

Figure 2. Concentration in the x direction at several points ($3d$, $9d$, $15d$, $21d$, $27d$, $33d$, and $39d$ from the source location): (a) mean profile of concentration at the plane $y = 6d$; (b) root-mean-square of the concentration at the plane $y = 6d$.

The image data used in this study were concentration distributions affected by the turbulent motion of the transport medium. These image data were prepared by the aforementioned DNS. Assuming that the infrared camera images for detecting leaking gas were realistic, the images were distribution images of $S_{integral} = \sum_{n=1}^{N_r} S_n \cdot V_n$, where Nr is the number of radial divisions, Sn is a scalar value, and Vn is the volume. Thus, the image is a distribution image, in which the concentration is integrated along the viewpoint direction. Figure 3a shows a conceptual diagram. In this image, it can be assumed that small-scale concentration gradients and microscale features of fluid dynamics are not clearly captured by the integration, and relatively large-scale concentration distributions dominate the image. As shown in Figure 3b, images were prepared for seven points with viewing angles of 60° and 90°, and viewpoints shifted downstream from the cylinder to $0d$, $6.5d$, $13d$, $19.5d$, $26d$, $32.5d$, and $39d$. Figure 3c shows the comparison between an infrared camera sample image [20] and CFD simulation image used in this study. Infrared camera and simulation images show the small-scale concentration gradients, but micro-scale fluid dynamics are not clearly captured. Figure 4 lists sample images for each class obtained from these viewpoints.

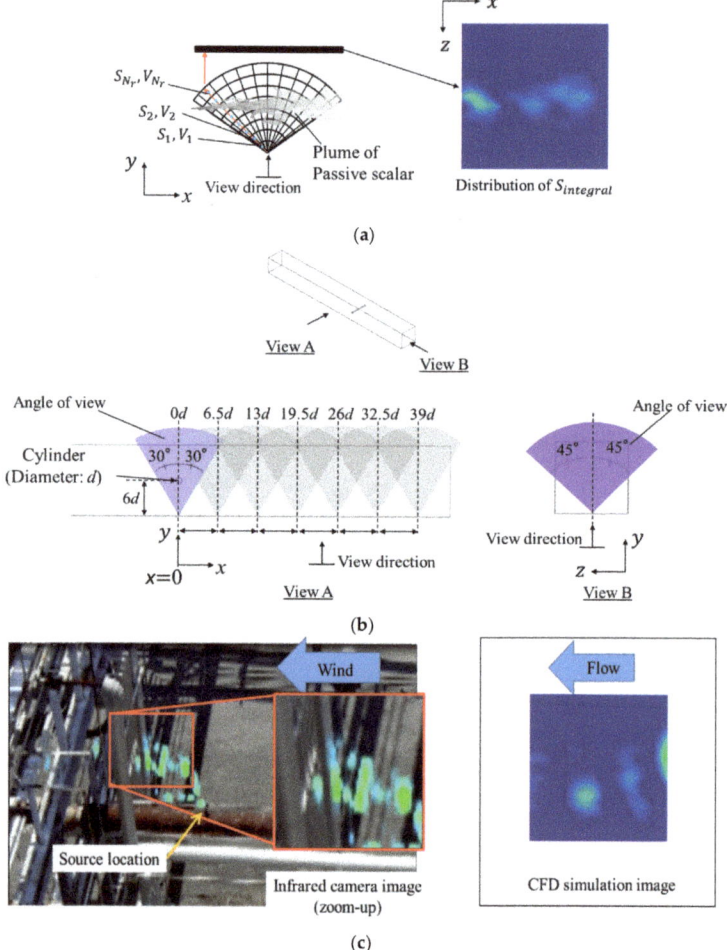

Figure 3. Scalar concentration images for machine learning: (**a**) conceptual diagram of distribution for $S_{integral}$: blue color indicates $S_{integral} = 0$ and red color indicates the highest passive scalar, which occurs at the source inlet; (**b**) angle of view for the image in x-y and y-z planes; (**c**) comparison of an infrared camera sample image [20] and a CFD simulation image.

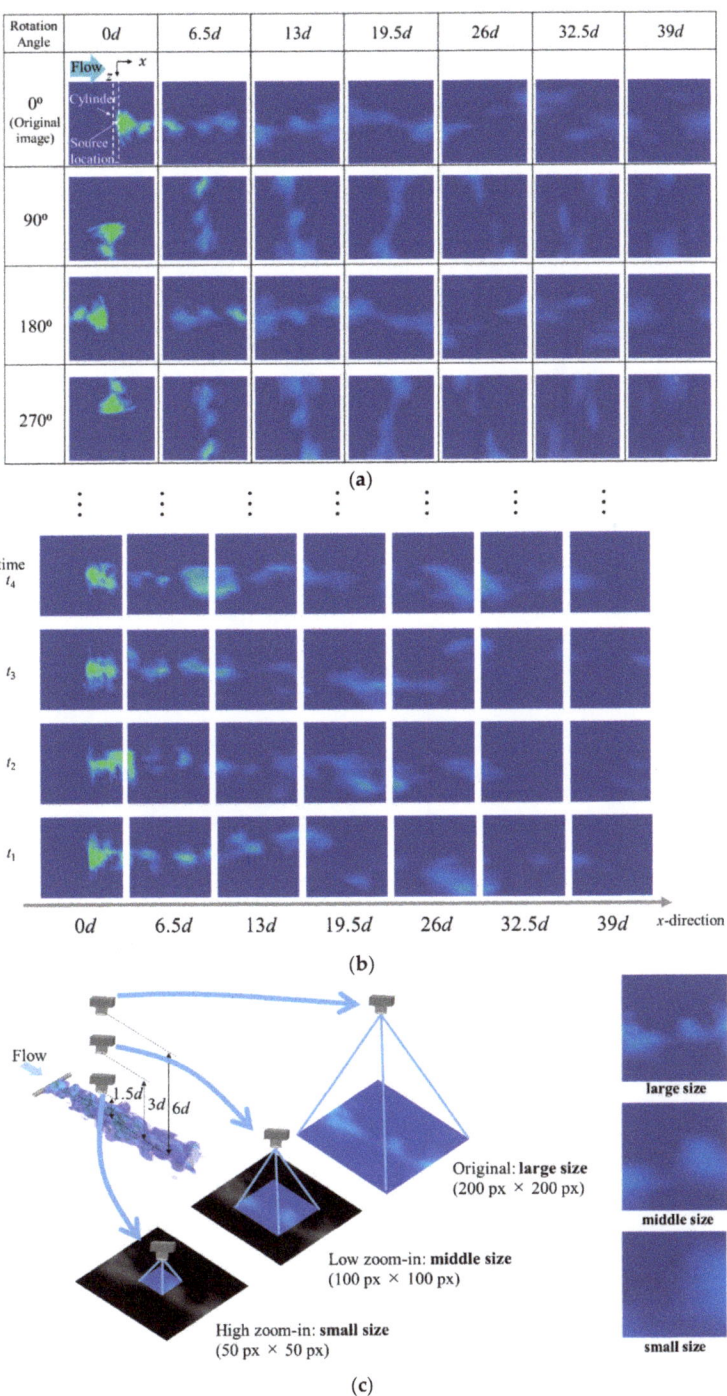

Figure 4. (a) Sample image for each class of machine learning and their rotated images; (b) sample images at different time instants; (c) conceptual diagram of each image size.

One image, as indicated in Figure 4a, has a resolution of 200 px × 200 px. Here, one pixel is equivalent to approximately 0.05d. To check the generalization performance for rotation, the original image was at 0°, and the images were rotated clockwise to 90°, 180°, and 270°, respectively (Figure 4a). The time interval between image acquisitions was longer than the turbulence time scale, so that a variety of scalar distributions were captured in images acquired under the same conditions, as shown in Figure 4b. This provides a dataset that is less prone to overlearning. The relative positions of the camera and the gas clouds are shown in Figure 4c. To simulate the difference in the relative positions of the camera and a gas cloud, images of different sizes were created using the original image. As shown in Figure 4c, low-zoom-in (100 px × 100 px) and high-zoom-in (50 px × 50 px) images were prepared for the original size (200 px × 200 px). Hereafter, these images are called "large size," "middle size," and "small size," respectively. Table 1 lists the learners selected for this study.

Table 1. List of the created learners.

Size	Training Image											
	Large				Middle				Small			
Rotation	0°	90°	180°	270°	0°	90°	180°	270°	0°	90°	180°	270°
Learner A	✓											
Learner B	✓			✓								
Learner C	✓	✓	✓	✓								
Learner D					✓							
Learner E	✓				✓				✓			
Learner F	✓	✓	✓	✓	✓	✓	✓	✓	✓	✓	✓	✓

We prepared 1800 training images, 600 validation images, and 100 testing images for each class to ensure that there was no duplication. A learner was created for each image to infer an unknown testing image for the evaluation. As previous research confirmed that Inception-ResNet-v2 [21] conducted inference with a high accuracy of at least 90% [16], Inception-ResNet-v2 was used in this study to conduct a classification problem using a CNN. The architecture of Inception-ResNet-v2 is presented in Appendix A. The input sequence, activation function, and hyperparameters were set according to the values from the existing literature, and each image was resized prior to entering the network to match the input image sequence size to that of the literature. The input image was a 24-bit red–green–blue (RGB) image, and the input array was resized to be (299 × 299 × 3), where the first and second elements signified the vertical and horizontal pixels, respectively, and the third element reflected the RGB configuration. Although not shown here, preliminary research confirmed that a smaller size of the input array, compared to that of the original image (200 × 200), leads to lower inference accuracy. The current array size to enter the network allows for high inference accuracy, as reported later. Adam was used as the solver of the gradient for the mini-batch in the network.

In this study, the accuracy rate Ac was used to evaluate the inference accuracy. Ac was obtained by setting the total number of data in each class as N_{di} ($i = 1, 2, \ldots,$ and 7) and the number of correct answers as N_{ci} ($i = 1, 2, \ldots,$ and N_{max}), and the accuracy rate at each position was set as $A_{ci} = N_{ci}/N_{di}$ or the accuracy rate for all cases was set as $A_{c\_total} = \sum_{i=1}^{7} N_{ci} / \sum_{i=1}^{7} N_{di}$.

3. Results

To check the generalization performance for the direction in which the leaking gas flows into the camera's view, four different rotated testing images were input to each learner: a learner trained by only 0° images (Learner A), a learner trained by only 0° and 270° images (Learner B), and a learner trained by all rotated images, i.e., 0°, 90°, 180°, and 270° (Learner C). Figure 5 shows the A_{c_total} for each learner. When the same image as the trained rotated image was used as the testing image for inference, it was confirmed that A_{c_total} was 100%. The applicability of this method to the immediate prediction of diffuse sources was confirmed by extracting the features of each location from the assumed infrared camera image.

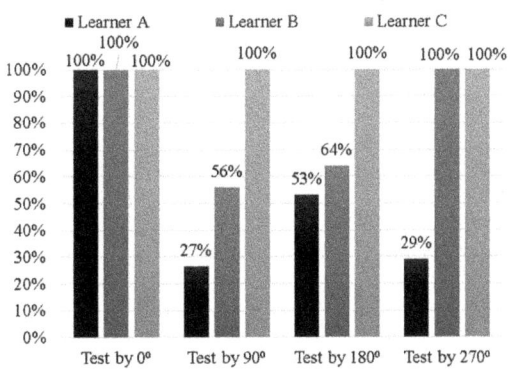

Figure 5. Accuracy of determination over seven classes for Learners A, B, and C by each testing image.

In contrast to Learner C, Learners A and B showed inference accuracies of 25% to 60% when the untrained rotated images were input. As CNN is robust to the parallel displacement of features by the pooling process, it was considered that the robustness to rotation was not very strong, and the reduction in inference accuracy for untrained rotated images was a reasonable result. It is known that turbulence has isotropic microscale regions, where microscale features eliminate anisotropy in fluid dynamics. It is difficult to extract rigorously the isotropic features because of the images in which the concentration is integrated along the viewpoint direction, leading to lower inference accuracy for rotational images. However, the learner that is trained with more variations in rotated images has a higher inference accuracy. For example, a learner created with images rotated by 0° and 270° (Learner B) obtained higher inference accuracy for angles (between 180° and 90°) than a learner trained only on images at 0° (Learner A). This result implies that a data augmentation method, such as rotation, successfully improves the inference accuracy for our approach without overfitting. When all rotation images (0°, 90°, 180°, and 270°) were trained (Learner C), it was confirmed that A_{c_total} was 100% correct, regardless of the rotation angle. This suggests that a deep architecture such as Inception-ResNet-v2 may result in a high inference accuracy, independent of the direction of gas cloud inflow, if training images from all angles are available.

To investigate the effect of the distance between the camera and diffused substances on inference accuracy, the dependence of the inference accuracy on the image size was determined, as shown in Figure 4c. Here, "middle size" images were used to create Learner D, and A_c in each class was estimated by using the input image sizes "large size" and "small size", which were different from the training images. The confusion matrices are shown in Figure 6a–c. For the middle-sized image, which had the same size as the training image, the accuracy was higher than 95% at all locations (Figure 6b), while for the large-sized image, the diffusion source distance tended to be underestimated upstream from the correct solution (Figure 6a). For small-sized images, the diffusion source distance was overestimated downstream from the correct solution (Figure 6c). This is consistent with the fact that the smaller the size of the image, the greater the diffusion of the substance in the longitudinal direction of the cylinder (z-direction) along the downstream direction; thus, the greater the diffusion of the substance, the smaller the size of the image. Conversely, in larger images, it was recognised that the substance was not diffused. From the results, the z-direction diffusion of the substances against the training image size was also inferred as a feature.

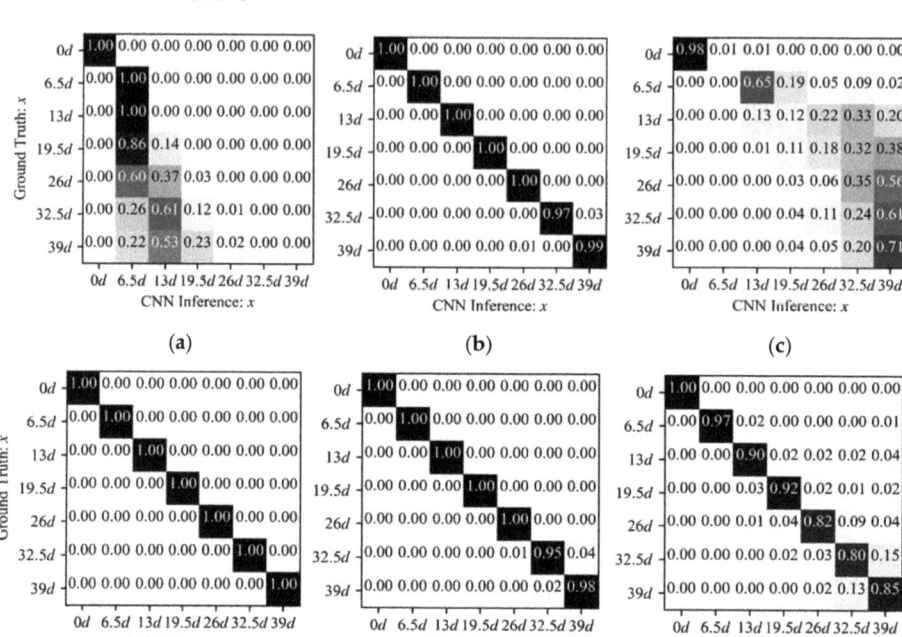

Figure 6. Accuracy of determination for image angle 0°: (**a**) Learner D tested by "large size" images; (**b**) same as (**a**), but tested by middle size; (**c**) same as (**a**), but tested by small size; (**d**) Learner E tested by "large size" images; (**e**) same as (**d**), but tested by middle size; (**f**) same as (**d**), but tested by small size.

A single trainee (Learner E) was created with all three sizes as training images, and the confusion matrix for each size is shown in Figure 6d–f. The inference accuracy was approximately 80% for small images at $26d$ downstream, and more than 90% for the other locations. This suggests that, similar to image rotation, if sufficient training images can be prepared for the image size, a high inference accuracy can be obtained for the application camera, regardless of the distance between the gas cloud and the camera. However, the slight drop in inference accuracy downstream from $26d$ for the small size may have occurred because the camera was significantly close (the gas cloud was magnified) and did not adequately capture the scale that is characteristic of turbulent mixing [10]. To confirm the characteristic scale in the $S_{integral}$ distribution, the autocorrelation coefficient, R_{BB}, for the x-direction of luminance relative to the image's center, is shown in Figure 7.

$$R_{BB}(\mathbf{r}) = \frac{\overline{B'(\mathbf{x})B'(\mathbf{x}+\mathbf{r})}}{\overline{B'(\mathbf{x})B'(\mathbf{x})}},$$

where **r** is a spatial two-point distance vector and $B(\mathbf{x})$ is the brightness fluctuation value of each pixel calculated from the image data of the distribution of $S_{integral}$. The overbar denotes the ensemble average. The fluctuating component $B'(\mathbf{x})$ denotes the brightness value of each pixel minus the average brightness, which was obtained in advance from all the image data points. As the autocorrelation coefficient is based on the image's center point, half of the image width pixels are at the edge of the image. Here, $R_{BB} \approx 0.2$ at 100 px downstream for the large size and $R_{BB} \approx 0.4$ at 50 px downstream for the middle size. However, for small sizes downstream from more than $13d$, $R_{BB} \approx 0.7$ at the edge of the image (25 px), which is relatively higher. This means that a small-sized image captured only a part of the fluid motion dynamics, but not all motions and, therefore, it is difficult to make inferences from such limited information. Therefore, a large-sized image that can capture the overall gas cloud is necessary to improve the accuracy of inference.

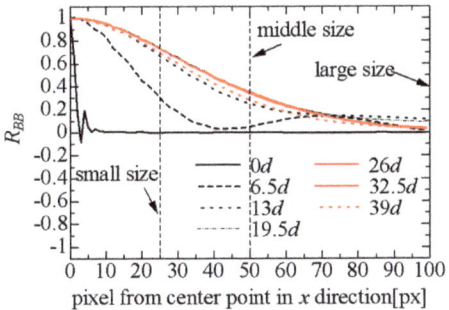

Figure 7. Autocorrelation coefficient of the brightness fluctuation value of each pixel, calculated from the image data of distribution for $S_{integral}$.

To improve the generalizability in both rotation direction and distance between the camera and leaking gas, a single trainee (Learner F) was created by training a total of 12 different images, where each image was a combination of four different rotation images (0°, 90°, 180°, and 270°), and three different image sizes: small, middle, and large. The A_{c_total} inferred for each of the 12 unknown images is shown in Figure 8. The accuracy rate exceeded 85%, regardless of image rotation and size. This indicated that when sufficient training images are prepared by data augmentation, the inference accuracy is high, regardless of the direction of the leaking gas flow into the camera's field of view or the distance from the camera.

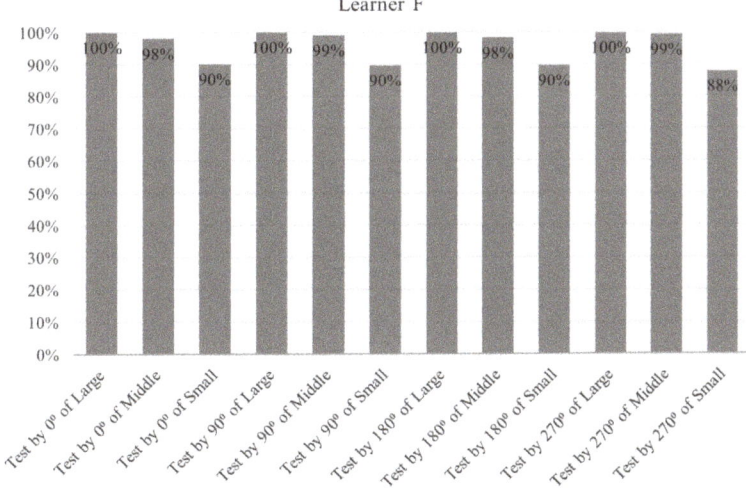

Figure 8. Accuracy of determination over seven classes for Learner F.

4. Conclusions

We investigated the applicability of CNNs for predicting the diffusion sources of turbulent substances using leaking gas detection images from infrared cameras. The image data prepared by DNS are concentration distributions affected by the turbulent motion of the transport medium. A concentration distribution image was used, in which the concentration was integrated along the view direction, assuming an actual camera image. In this image, the small-scale concentration gradients and small-scale features of fluid dynamics are difficult to capture clearly because of the integration along the view direction, and relatively large-scale concentration distributions dominate the image. The estimation of the distance from the leakage source was performed as a classification problem, divided into seven classes according to the distance downstream from the leakage source.

The effects of the direction in which the leaking gas flows into the camera's view and the distance between the camera and the leaking gas on the accuracy of the inference were examined. The images were prepared for data augmentation by rotating and scaling the original images. The inference accuracy for unknown images was examined.

For the rotated images, 100% accuracy was obtained for the same rotated image as the training image. However, for rotated images that were different from the training image, the inference accuracy was 25–60%, thereby resulting in poor generalization performance.

As CNN is robust to the parallel displacement of features by the pooling process, it was considered that the robustness to rotation was not very strong, and the reduction in inference accuracy for untrained rotated images was a reasonable result. It is known that turbulence has isotropic microscale regions, where microscale features eliminate anisotropy in fluid dynamics. It is difficult to extract rigorously the isotropic micro-scale features because of the images in which the concentration is integrated along the viewpoint direction, leading to lower inference accuracy for rotational images. However, when all rotation images (0°, 90°, 180°, and 270°) were trained, it was confirmed that A_{c_total} was 100% correct regardless of the rotation angle.

To investigate the effect of the distance between the camera and diffused substances on the inference accuracy, the inference accuracy for different image sizes was examined. For images that were different in size from the training image, the inference accuracy was lower, resulting in a poor generalization performance, similar to the image rotation case. However, it was found that a high inference accuracy could be obtained if the data were trained with all images, regardless of the distance between the gas cloud and the camera.

To improve the generalizability in both rotation direction and distance between the camera and leaking gas, a single trainer was created by training all images, and the inference accuracy exceeded 85%, regardless of the image rotation and size. This indicated that when sufficient training images are prepared by data augmentation, the inference accuracy is high, regardless of the direction of the leaking gas flow into the camera's field of view or the distance from the camera.

In the future, when the so-called digital twin is realized and training data can be obtained from the digital simulation data of the plant, many leakage scenarios can be run in such simulations, and a trainer can be created based on snapshot images obtained from camera arrangements in an actual plant. This study showed that a data augmentation method, such as rotation and image size, successfully improves the inference accuracy for our approach without overfitting. This implies that by utilizing data augmentation for image data, it may be possible to improve inference accuracy not only for a specific plant situation. For further practical applications for example, disaster prevention, pollution control, etc., the gas diffusivity caused by actual fluctuations in wind conditions should be considered.

Author Contributions: Conceptualization, T.I. and T.T.; methodology, T.I.; analysis, T.I.; investigation, T.I. and T.T.; writing—original draft preparation, T.I.; writing—review and editing, M.I. and T.T; visualization, T.I. All authors have read and agreed to the published version of the manuscript.

Funding: This work was partially supported by the Japan Society for the Promotion of Science (JSPS), Grant-in-Aid Scientific Research (S) and (A): Grant Number 21H05007 and 18H03758.

Institutional Review Board Statement: Not applicable.

Informed Consent Statement: Not applicable.

Data Availability Statement: Not applicable.

Conflicts of Interest: The authors declare no conflict of interest.

Appendix A

Architecture for Inception-ResNet-v2 is shown in Figure A1a. Inception-ResNet-v2 implements 164 layers by adopting residual inception blocks (Figure A1b), which was developed in ResNet (2015) [22] as the breakthrough. Three types of residual inception blocks (A, B, and C) were introduced, and multiple layers were created by repeating A, B, and C five, ten, and five times, respectively. With the residual inception block, efficient learning was possible, even in deep networks, via the dimensionality reduction given by inserting a 1 × 1 convolution layer, convolutions of different sizes in the branched network, and the operation of passing input directly to the next layer by shortcutting the bias.

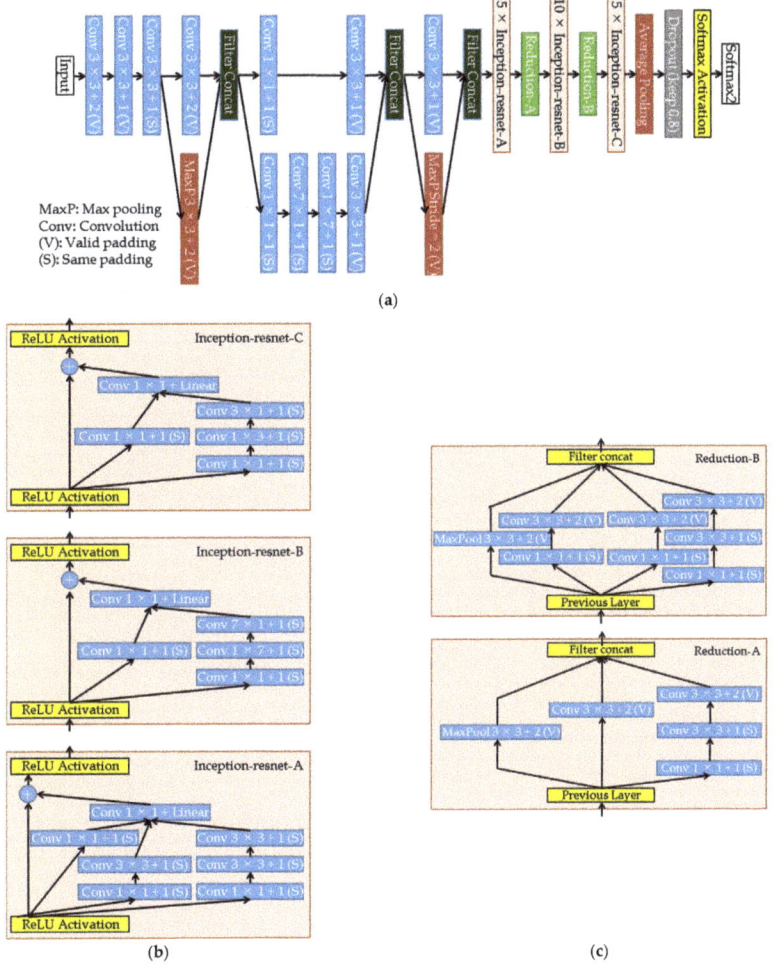

Figure A1. Schematic of Inception-ResNet-v2 architecture [22] referred to in our previous paper [16]: (**a**) overall network; (**b**) Inception-Resnet blocks: "-A" is repeated five times, "-B" is ten times, and "C" is five times; (**c**) Reduction-A and Reduction-B.

References

1. Zaki, T.A.; Wang, M. From limited observations to the state of turbulence: Fundamental difficulties of flow reconstruction. *Phys. Rev. Fluids* **2021**, *6*, 100501. [CrossRef]
2. Wang, M.; Zaki, T.A. State estimation in turbulent channel flow from limited observations. *J. Fluid Mech.* **2021**, *917*, A9. [CrossRef]
3. Tsukahara, T.; Oyagi, K.; Kawaguchi, Y. Estimation method to identify scalar point source in turbulent flow based on Taylor's diffusion theory. *Environ. Fluid Mech.* **2016**, *16*, 521–537. [CrossRef]
4. Cerizza, D.; Sekiguchi, W.; Tsukahara, T.; Zaki, T.A.; Hasegawa, Y. Reconstruction of scalar source intensity based on sensor signal in turbulent channel flow. *Flow Turbul. Combust.* **2016**, *97*, 1233. [CrossRef]
5. Fukami, K.; An, B.; Nohmi, M.; Obuchi, M.; Taira, K. Machine-learning-based reconstruction of turbulent vortices from sparse pressure sensors in a pump sump. *J. Fluids Eng.* **2022**, *144*, 121501. [CrossRef]
6. Qin, D.; Yu, J.; Zou, G.; Yong, R.; Zhao, Q.; Zhang, B. A novel combined prediction scheme based on CNN and LSTM for urban PM2.5 concentration. *IEEE Access.* **2019**, *7*, 20050–20059. [CrossRef]
7. Al-Ruzouq, R.; Gibril, M.B.A.; Shanableh, A.; Kais, A.; Hamed, O.; Al-Mansoori, S.; Khalil, M.A. Sensors, features, and machine learning for oil spill detection and monitoring: A review. *Remote Sens.* **2020**, *12*, 3338. [CrossRef]
8. Narkhede, P.; Walambe, R.; Mandaokar, S.; Chandel, P.; Kotecha, K.; Ghinea, G. Gas Detection and Identification Using Multimodal Artificial Intelligence Based Sensor Fusion. *Appl. Syst. Innov.* **2021**, *4*, 3. [CrossRef]
9. Tan, T.-H.; Lin, Y.-T.; Chang, Y.-L.; Alkhaleefah, M. Sound source localization using a convolutional neural network and regression model. *Sensors* **2021**, *21*, 8031. [CrossRef] [PubMed]
10. Zhou, K.; Liu, Y. Early-stage gas identification using convolutional long short-term neural network with sensor array time series data. *Sensors* **2021**, *21*, 4826. [CrossRef] [PubMed]
11. Shi, J.; Li, J.; Usmani, A.; Zhu, Y.; Chen, G.; Yang, D. Probabilistic real-time deep-water natural gas hydrate dispersion modeling by using a novel hybrid deep learning approach. *Energy* **2021**, *219*, 119572. [CrossRef]
12. Shi, J.; Xie, W.; Huang, X.; Usmani, A.; Khan, F.; Yin, X.; Chen, G. Real-time natural gas release forecasting by using physics-guided deep learning probability model. *J. Cleaner Prod.* **2022**, *368*, 133201. [CrossRef]
13. Raffel, M. Background-oriented schlieren (BOS) techniques. *Exp. Fluids.* **2015**, *56*, 60. [CrossRef]
14. Olbrycht, R.; Kałuża, M. Optical gas imaging with uncooled thermal imaging camera—Impact of warm filters and elevated background temperature. *IEEE Trans. Ind. Electron.* **2020**, *67*, 9824–9832. [CrossRef]
15. Campione, I.; Lucchi, F.; Santopuoli, N.; Seccia, L. 3D thermal imaging system with decoupled acquisition for industrial and cultural heritage applications. *NATO Adv. Sci. Inst. Ser. J. Eng. Appl. Sci.* **2020**, *10*, 828. [CrossRef]
16. Ishigami, T.; Irikura, M.; Tsukahara, T. Machine learning to estimate the mass-diffusion distance from a point source under turbulent conditions. *Processes* **2022**, *10*, 860. [CrossRef]
17. Shams, A.; Roelofs, F.; Komen, E.M.J.; Baglietto, E. Optimization of a pebble bed configuration for quasi-direct numerical simulation. *Nucl. Eng. Des.* **2012**, *242*, 331–340. [CrossRef]
18. Shams, A.; Roelofs, F.; Komen, E.M.J.; Baglietto, E. Quasi-direct numerical simulation of a pebble bed configuration. Part I: Flow (velocity) field analysis. *Nucl. Eng. Des.* **2013**, *263*, 473–489. [CrossRef]
19. Shams, A.; Roelofs, F.; Komen, E.M.J.; Baglietto, E. Quasi-direct numerical simulation of a pebble bed configuration. Part II: Temperature field analysis. *Nucl. Eng. Des.* **2013**, *263*, 490–499. [CrossRef]
20. Hioki, T.; Kato, M.; Ogiso, R. Visualization of leak for getting insight of appropriate judgement. *Health Saf. Environ. Asset Infrastruct. Gastech* 2017.
21. Szegedy, C.; Ioffe, S.; Vanhoucke, V.; Alemi, A. Inception-v4, Inception-ResNet and the impact of residual connections on learning. In Proceedings of the Thirty-First AAAI Conference on Artificial Intelligence, San Francisco, CA, USA, 23 June 2017; AAAI: Menlo Park, CA, USA, 2017; Volume 31, pp. 4278–4284. [CrossRef]
22. He, K.; Zhang, X.; Ren, S.; Sun, J. Deep residual learning for image recognition. In Proceedings of the IEEE Conference on Computer Vision and Pattern Recognition, Las Vegas, NV, USA, 27–30 June 2016; pp. 770–778.

Article

Research on Discrete Artificial Bee Colony Cache Strategy of UAV Edge Network

Yang Hong [1,2], Yuexia Zhang [1,3,*] and Shaoshuai Fan [3]

1 Key Laboratory of Modern Measurement & Control Technology, Ministry of Education, Beijing Information Science and Technology University, Beijing 100101, China
2 Key Laboratory of Information and Communication Systems, Ministry of Information Industry, Beijing Information Science and Technology University, Beijing 100101, China
3 State Key Laboratory of Networking and Switching Technology, Beijing University of Posts and Telecommunications, Beijing 100876, China
* Correspondence: zhangyuexia@bistu.edu.cn

Abstract: Unmanned aerial vehicle edge networks (UENs) can reduce the cache load of the core network and improve system performance to provide users with efficient content services. However, the time-varying characteristics of content popularity in UENs lead to a low accuracy of popularity prediction, and the capacity limitations of wireless channel conditions lead to a lower cache hit rate than the rates of traditional fiber-optic-based cache strategies. Therefore, this paper proposes the discrete artificial bee colony cache strategy of UENs (DABCCSU). First, the information–dynamics–dissemination model of UENs (IDDMU) is established to deduce the coupling relationship between the channel capacity and the service probability in IDDMU. The influence of the service probability change on the content dissemination process is discussed, and the content popularity in UENs is predicted by the state iteration matrix. Then, the discrete artificial bee colony cache (DABCC) optimization algorithm is proposed. The action function of the artificial bee colony is designed as a random action based on the historical cache strategy. The discrete cache strategy is used as an optimization variable, and the popularity prediction result obtained by IDDMU is used to maximize the cache hit rate. DABCC provides the optimal cache strategy for the UENs, and effectively improves the cache hit rate. The simulation result shows that the accuracy of DABCCSU in content popularity prediction is more than 90%, which achieves a good prediction effect. In terms of cache performance, the average cache hit rate of DABCCSU is 91.62%, which is better than the 51.09% of the Least Recently Used (LRU) strategy, 89.27% of the Greedy Algorithm (GA) and 54.26% of Binary Particle Swarm Optimization (BPSO). In addition, the cache hit rate of DABCCSU under different cache capacities is better than that of LRU, GA, and BPSO, showing a relatively stable performance. It shows that DABCCSU can achieve excellent content popularity prediction, and it can also maximize the cache hit rate under limited communication resources and cache resources to provide UENs with the optimal content cache strategy, and provides users with high-quality content services.

Keywords: UAV edge network; popularity prediction; cache strategy; artificial bee colony

Citation: Hong, Y.; Zhang, Y.; Fan, S. Research on Discrete Artificial Bee Colony Cache Strategy of UAV Edge Network. *Processes* **2022**, *10*, 1838. https://doi.org/10.3390/pr10091838

Academic Editor: Xiong Luo

Received: 23 August 2022
Accepted: 9 September 2022
Published: 13 September 2022

Publisher's Note: MDPI stays neutral with regard to jurisdictional claims in published maps and institutional affiliations.

Copyright: © 2022 by the authors. Licensee MDPI, Basel, Switzerland. This article is an open access article distributed under the terms and conditions of the Creative Commons Attribution (CC BY) license (https://creativecommons.org/licenses/by/4.0/).

1. Introduction

As the important technologies of the next generation communication network, edge networks (ENs) have attracted considerable research interest [1–7]. An edge network caches the content on the edge server and allows users to download interesting content from nearby edge servers. It can effectively cope with the rapid increase in wireless service loads, significantly reducing cache loads and service delays of the core networks, and solves the network congestion problem. Therefore, ENs have become a research hotspot in the field of next generation communication networks.

An unmanned aerial vehicle (UAV) [8,9] has excellent flexibility, mobility, and a unique line-of-sight (LOS) channel from which the UAV edge networks (UENs) [10,11] are derived.

The UENs uses the UAV as a flight relay-assist edge network, which can effectively reduce the cache load of the core network, improve the cache performance of the system, and provide users with efficient content services. The popularity-based edge cache [12–14] is a widely used cache method which uses a large amount of statistical data about content requests to predict content popularity and actively caches high-popularity content from the cloud database in the core network to meet the content needs of users. However, the content popularity changes dynamically with the passage of time. Most popularity-based cache strategies ignore the time variability of content popularity, which makes it difficult to describe the regularity of changes in content popularity. In addition, unlike the edge nodes of the traditional edge cache network that access the cloud database through optical fibers, data transmission between the UENs and the cloud database is realized through wireless communications. This reduced channel capacity seriously restricts the downlink rate between them, limits the content data transmission, and results in a decrease in the cache hit rate. Therefore, cache efficiency of the current popularity-based edge cache strategy is reduced by the limited content transmission between the UENs and cloud database caused by the wireless channel capacity and the low popularity prediction accuracy caused by the time-varying content popularity.

Content popularity prediction aims to improve the cache efficiency of the edge cache network. It needs to accurately capture the dynamic regularity of changes in content popularity. Many scholars have conducted research in related fields [15–20]. Sajad et al. [15] developed a probabilistic dynamics model for content popularity prediction considering the spatial–temporal correlation of content popularity. Kong et al. [16] proposed a popularity prediction method considering the contributions of different dynamic factors and a popularity prediction method based on pattern matching from the micro and macro levels. Fatma et al. [17] proposed a visual social convolutional neural network, which takes the social and visual features of image content into a unified network to predict its popularity. Li et al. [18] studied real data sets from social platforms and proposed a content popularity prediction method based on deep neural networks. Yan et al. [19] solved the content-popularity prediction problem based on the local and global user request states by a machine learning algorithm. Gao et al. [20] proposed the spatial–temporal heterogeneous bassmodel and feature-driven heterogeneous bassmodel to predict the popularity of a single tweet at the early and stable stages. However, studies noted above gave so much attention to content popularity prediction that the coupling relationship between the content popularity and content cache was ignored. Consequently, they have not solved the cache strategy optimization problem.

Currently, many scholars have considered the differences in content popularity and proposed some cache strategies based on content popularity prediction [21–26]. By discovering the correlation between content blocks in information-centric networks, Zhang et al. [21] proposed a block level cache and popularity prediction cache replacement method from the perspective of users. Gao et al. [22] proposed a reinforcement learning model to obtain a cooperative cache strategy based on maximum-distance-separable coding, which captured the time-varying regularity of content popularity. Ji et al. [23] studied the joint content cache and multihop delivery, introduced the distance-sensitive popularity parameter, and proposed a relay-assisted multihop routing algorithm. Liang et al. [24] considered multidimensional features such as historical and future popularity to predict content popularity, proposed a popularity prediction model based on multiheads attention, and then designed a cache strategy according to the prediction results. Chen et al. [25] proposed a popularity prediction framework based on weighted clustering to overcome the sparsity of user requests and considered the similarity of popularity evolution trends to improve cache performance. Liu et al. [26] built a popularity evolution model by analyzing the popularity characteristics of datasets, designed a data-driven popularity prediction method, and proposed a popularity-based eviction and prefetching algorithm to solve the problems of cache content and cache time. However, these studies did not consider the potential impact of wireless channel conditions on the content dissemination process or ignored the time variability of content popularity, which reduces the cache efficiency of the system.

This paper proposes a DABCCSU. This strategy studies the time-variability of content popularity in UEN based on the information dissemination dynamics model [27–29], which can effectively solve the problem of low popularity prediction accuracy caused by the time-varying of content popularity in the UENs. Working against the problem that the cache hit rate of the traditional cache strategy decreases due to the capacity limitation of the wireless channel condition, DABCCSU can maximize the cache hit rate based on popularity prediction of the contents to provide the UENs with the optimal cache strategy, thus improving cache performance. The specific contributions of this paper follow:

(1) An IDDMU is established. Based on this model, the content dissemination process in UEN is analyzed, and the influence of channel capacity on content dissemination results is discussed. Considering the heterogeneity of the dynamic equation, the iterative equation of the state transition is analyzed based on a single user perspective.

(2) A DABCC optimization algorithm is designed. Based on the traditional continuous artificial bee colony algorithm [30,31], the DABCC discretizes the feasible region and redesigns the action function of the artificial bee colony.

(3) A discrete artificial bee colony cache strategy of UEN is proposed. To predict the popularity of the cache content, the strategy obtains the state distribution of UEN users regarding the cache content that is acquired from the user-state iteration matrix of IDDMU. Then, the optimal cache strategy of UAVs is obtained by the DABCC optimization algorithm.

The rest of this paper is organized as follows: In Section 2, the system model is introduced. In Section 3, the cache optimization problem and DABCC algorithm are proposed. In Section 4, the performance of the DABCC algorithm is evaluated, and the simulation results and analysis are given. In Section 5, the conclusion of this paper is presented.

2. System Model

In this section, the channel capacity of UAVs in UEN is analyzed and the IDDMU is established. Then, based on IDDMU, the content dissemination process in UEN is discussed and the iterative matrix for predicting the popularity of cached content is derived.

2.1. UAV Edge Network

The UEN is shown in Figure 1, which includes the cloud database, M UAVs, and N users, where K contents are transmitted among users. The UAV set is represented by $S = \{s_1, s_2, \cdots, s_m, \cdots, s_M\}$, where s_m represents the m-th UAV. The cache capacity set of UAVs is $Ca = \{Ca_1, Ca_2, \cdots Ca_m, \cdots Ca_M\}$, where Ca_m represents the cache capacity of UAV s_m. The user set of the UEN is $U = \{u_1, u_2, \cdots, u_r, \cdots, u_R\}$, where u_r represents the r-th user in the UEN, and all users obey the Poisson distribution. Owing to power limitations, each UAV has a specific coverage. Users within the UAV's coverage are divided into a subset of U, and each user can only communicate with the UAV corresponding to the subset. Therefore, in this paper, the user set U is divided into M subsets $U_1, U_2, \cdots U_m, \cdots U_M$, where $U_m = \{u_{m,1}, u_{m,2}, \cdots, u_{m,n}, \cdots, u_{m,N_m}\}$ represents the user subset within the coverage of s_m, and $u_{m,n}$ represents the n-th user within U_m. It is assumed that the UAV set, and the user set in the UEN are stable, and the content set $F = \{f_1, f_2, \cdots, f_K\}$ is updated in real time. $f_k = \{\theta_k, L_k\}$ represents the k-th content, where $\theta_k \in (0,1)$ is the reject probability, which represents the average probability that the user is not interested in the content f_k, and L_k (bits) is the size of the content f_k.

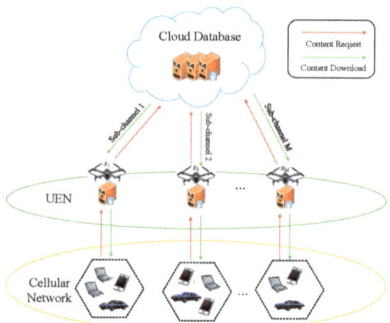

Figure 1. UAV edge network.

In the UEN, the cloud database stores all the contents. Any UAV can function as an edge server in the UEN and cache the high-popularity content from the cloud database according to the popularity prediction. Suppose that the channel capacity between any UAV and the cloud database is C_0. When user $u_{m,n}$ needs to download the content f_k of interest, if s_m has cached the content, $u_{m,n}$ directly downloads it from s_m. Otherwise, $u_{m,n}$ downloads content f_k from the cloud database. This paper mainly studies the cache strategy of the UAV edge server, thus it does not consider the case where users directly obtain content from the cloud database. The UAVs, which work in different frequency bands, update the cache contents from the cloud database in real time by wireless communication. One UAV communicates with the cloud database and all users under its coverage in the same frequency band. Different users covered by the same UAV use time-division duplexing (TDD) technology to communicate with the UAV. The frame structure of UEN is shown in Figure 2, in which the vertical axis shows the frequency band division of different UAVs, and the horizontal axis shows the frame of one UAV. $Frame\ j(j = 0, 1, 2 \cdots)$ is the j-th frame, and the frame length is Δt. Since the cache time of the UAVs and the download time of the users occupy the main part of a frame, the uplink time of the UAV and the user can be flexibly designed, which is not the focus of this paper. This paper mainly considers the downlink part of a frame. One frame is divided into sub-frame 1 and sub-frame 2, each of which is $\Delta t/2$ in length. Sub-frame 1 is divided into multiple time slots and one UAV transmits data to different users in different time slots. During sub-frame 1, users download content from the UAV based on interest, word of mouth, etc. During sub-frame 2, the cloud database predicts the popularity of all content according to the download requests of users in the UEN, designs a cache strategy based on the prediction results, and caches the relevant content to the UAVs. The UAVs in UEN work in different frequency bands and users communicate with UAV in TDD mode. Therefore, this paper ignores the interference between different UAVs and users covered by the same UAV. Assuming that the wireless channel between UAV and user is a LOS channel, the channel capacity is:

$$C_{m,n} = B_m \log\left(1 + \frac{P_m r_{m,n}^{-\xi}}{N_0}\right) \quad (1)$$

where B_m is the working bandwidth of s_m, P_m is the transmission power of s_m, $r_{m,n}$ is the spatial distance between s_m and $u_{m,n}$, N_0 is the Gaussian noise, and ξ is the path loss.

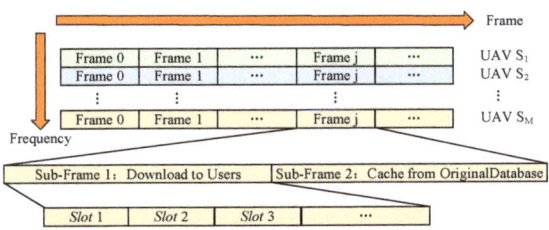

Figure 2. Frame structure of UEN.

2.2. Information Dissemination Dynamics Model of UEN

The IDDMU is shown in Figure 3. According to the user's behavior on the content f_k, the four states of the user regarding the content f_k in UEN are defined as follows:

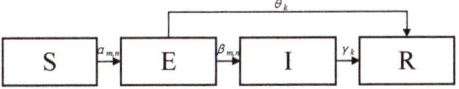

Figure 3. Information dissemination dynamics model of UEN.

S: Never informed on the content f_k. The user may receive recommendations from surrounding users at any time as a potential target.

E: Received the recommendation about content f_k from other users. In this state, there is a certain probability that the user is interested in the content f_k and downloads it from s_m, or is not interested in it and chooses to ignore it.

I: Interested in the content f_k. The user downloaded the content f_k from s_m and recommends it to the surrounding users.

R: Lost interest in content f_k. The user does not recommend content f_k to surrounding users.

$S_{m,k}(t)$, $E_{m,k}(t)$, $I_{m,k}(t)$, and $R_{m,k}(t)$, respectively, represent the number of corresponding state users regarding content f_k covered by s_m at time t, then $S_{m,k}(t) + E_{m,k}(t) + I_{m,k}(t) + R_{m,k}(t) = N_m$. According to the IDDMU, the dissemination dynamic equations of content f_k are obtained as follows:

$$\frac{dS_{m,k}(t)}{dt} = -\sum_{n=1}^{N_m} \alpha_{m,n} S_{m,k}(t) \frac{I_{m,k}(t)}{N_m} \quad (2)$$

$$\frac{dE_{m,k}(t)}{dt} = -\left(\theta_k + \frac{\sum_{n=1}^{N_m} \beta_{m,n}}{N_m}\right) E_{m,k}(t) + \sum_{n=1}^{N_m} \alpha_{m,n} S_{m,k}(t) \frac{I_{m,k}(t)}{N_m} \quad (3)$$

$$\frac{dI_{m,k}(t)}{dt} = -\gamma_k I_{m,k}(t) + \frac{\sum_{n=1}^{N_m} \beta_{m,n}}{N_m} E_{m,k}(t) \quad (4)$$

$$\frac{dR_{m,k}(t)}{dt} = \theta_k E_{m,k}(t) + \gamma_k I_{m,k}(t) \quad (5)$$

The specific definition of the transition probability in Equations (2)–(5) is as follows:

Contact Probability $\alpha_{m,n}$: indicates the probability that $u_{m,n}$ contacts with other users, calculated as:

$$\alpha_{m,n} = \delta \times \varphi_{m,n} \quad (6)$$

In Equation (6), δ is the average probability of successful communication between users and $\varphi_{m,n} = 1 - e^{-\lambda_R \pi R_{m,n}^2}$ is the probability of other users in the vicinity of $u_{m,n}$, where λ_R is the user density of the whole UEN, and $R_{m,n}$ is the communication range of $u_{m,n}$.

Service Probability $\beta_{m,n}$: To ensure that the content f_k can be well presented, the channel capacity between s_m and $u_{m,n}$ must meet certain requirements. Therefore, $\beta_{m,n}$ represents the probability that the channel capacity between the two meets the quality of service (QoS) requirements:

$$\beta_{m,n} = p(C_{m,n} \geq C_{m,n}^*) \tag{7}$$

where $C_{m,n}^*$ is the minimum channel capacity required for undistorted transmission between s_m and $u_{m,n}$.

According to Equations (1) and (7), the value of $\beta_{m,n}$ depends on the working bandwidth of s_m, the transmission power, and the space distance between s_m and $u_{m,n}$. The specific derivation process of the expression is as follows:

Substituting Equations (1)–(7), leads to:

$$p(C_{m,n} \geq C_{m,n}^*) = p\left(B_m \log\left(1 + \frac{P_m r_{m,n}^{-\xi}}{N_0}\right) \geq C_{m,n}^*\right) \tag{8}$$

Then, making certain transformations to the right side of the Equation (8) leads to:

$$p(C_{m,n} \geq C_{m,n}^*) = p\left(r_{m,n} \leq \left(\frac{P_m}{N_0\left(2^{\frac{C_{m,n}^*}{B_m}} - 1\right)}\right)^{\frac{1}{\xi}}\right) \tag{9}$$

All users in the UEN obey the Poisson distribution, thus Equation (9) can be expressed as:

$$p(C_{m,n} \geq C_{m,n}^*) = \frac{P_m^{\frac{2}{\xi}}}{R_m^2 N_0^{\frac{2}{\xi}} \left(2^{\frac{C_{m,n}^*}{B_m}} - 1\right)^{\frac{2}{\xi}}} \tag{10}$$

where R_m is the coverage range of the UAV s. Thus:

$$\beta_{m,n} = \frac{P_m^{\frac{2}{\xi}}}{R_m^2 N_0^{\frac{2}{\xi}} \left(2^{\frac{C_{m,n}^*}{B_m}} - 1\right)^{\frac{2}{\xi}}} \tag{11}$$

Reject Probability θ_k: indicates the average probability that the user is not interested in the content f_k.

Recovery Probability γ_k: indicates the average probability that users who have downloaded content f_k lose interest in it.

Considering the heterogeneity of ordinary differential equations (Equations (2)–(5)), it is difficult to calculate the specific result of the solution. Therefore, from the perspective of a single user, this paper defines $p_{k,n}^S(t)$, $p_{k,n}^E(t)$, $p_{k,n}^I(t)$, and $p_{k,n}^R(t)$ as the probability that $u_{m,n}$ is in corresponding states with respect to the content f_k at time t, and obtains the iterative equation of the state probability of $u_{m,n}$:

$$p_{k,n}^S(t+1) = \left(1 - p_{k,n}^I \alpha_{m,n}\right)^I p_{k,n}^S(t) \tag{12}$$

$$p_{k,n}^E(t+1) = \left(1 - \left(1 - p_{k,n}^I \alpha_{m,n}\right)^I\right) p_{k,n}^S(t) + (1 - \theta_k - \beta_{m,n}) p_{k,n}^E(t) \tag{13}$$

$$p_{k,n}^I(t+1) = \beta_{m,n} p_{k,n}^E(t) + (1 - \gamma_k) p_{k,n}^I(t) \tag{14}$$

$$p^R_{k,n}(t+1) = \theta_k p^E_{k,n}(t) + \gamma_k p^I_{k,n}(t) + p^R_{k,n}(t) \tag{15}$$

where l represents the degree of $u_{m,n}$. Converting Equations (12)–(15) into matrix form leads to:

$$\begin{pmatrix} p^S_{k,n}(t+1) \\ p^E_{k,n}(t+1) \\ p^I_{k,n}(t+1) \\ p^R_{k,n}(t+1) \end{pmatrix} = \begin{pmatrix} \left(1 - p^I_{k,n}\alpha_{m,n}\right)^l & 0 & 0 & 0 \\ 1 - \left(1 - p^I_{k,n}\alpha_{m,n}\right)^l & 1 - \beta_{m,n} - \theta_k & 0 & 0 \\ 0 & \beta_{m,n} & 1 - \gamma_k & 0 \\ 0 & \theta_k & \gamma_k & 1 \end{pmatrix} \begin{pmatrix} p^S_{k,n}(t) \\ p^E_{k,n}(t) \\ p^I_{k,n}(t) \\ p^R_{k,n}(t) \end{pmatrix} \tag{16}$$

The state iteration matrix $\mathbf{P}_{k,n}(t)$ is defined as:

$$\mathbf{P}_{k,n}(t) = \begin{pmatrix} \left(1 - p^I_{k,n}\alpha_{m,n}\right)^l & 0 & 0 & 0 \\ 1 - \left(1 - p^I_{k,n}\alpha_{m,n}\right)^l & 1 - \beta_{m,n} - \theta_k & 0 & 0 \\ 0 & \beta_{m,n} & 1 - \gamma_k & 0 \\ 0 & \theta_k & \gamma_k & 1 \end{pmatrix} \tag{17}$$

According to $\mathbf{P}_{k,n}(t)$, the proportion of $u_{m,n}$ in each state at time $t+1$ can be predicted as:

$$\mathbf{State}_{k,n}(t+1) = \sum_{n=1}^{N_m} \mathbf{P}_{k,n}(t) \mathbf{State}_{k,n}(t) \tag{18}$$

$$\mathbf{State}_{k,n}(t) = \left(p^S_{k,n}(t), p^E_{k,n}(t), p^I_{k,n}(t), p^R_{k,n}(t)\right)^T \tag{19}$$

Among the above four states, only $u_{m,n}$ in state E may apply to the UAV for downloading content f_k. Therefore, the cache strategy of UEN is obviously affected by $E_{m,k}(t)$ and $\beta_{m,n}$. Consequently, the prediction popularity of content f_k at time t is defined as:

$$D_{m,k}(t) = E_{m,k}(t) \times \frac{\sum_{n=1}^{N_m} \beta_{m,n}}{N_m} \tag{20}$$

3. Discrete Artificial Bee Colony Cache Strategy of UEN

Based on the content popularity analysis above, this section describes the cache strategy of the UEN and proposes a cache optimization problem. Then, aiming at the optimization problem, DABCCSU is proposed.

3.1. Content Cache

Considering that the content popularity differs among users under different UAV coverage, the UAVs have different cache strategy.

Suppose that $a_{k,m}(t)$ represents the cache of the content f_k by s_m at time t. If s_m caches the content f_k, then $a_{m,k}(t) = 1$, otherwise $a_{m,k}(t) = 0$. In different cases, s_m has the following four processing methods for content f_k:

(1) $a_{m,k}(t) = 1$ and $a_{m,k}(t-1) = 1$, s_m retains the content f_k.
(2) $a_{m,k}(t) = 1$ and $a_{m,k}(t-1) = 0$, s_m caches the content f_k from the cloud database.
(3) $a_{m,k}(t) = 0$ and $a_{m,k}(t-1) = 1$, s_m deletes the content f_k.
(4) $a_{m,k}(t) = 0$ and $a_{m,k}(t-1) = 0$, s_m does not process the content f_k.

Thus, the cache of all contents by s_m can be defined as a K-dimensional vector $\mathbf{A}_m(t) = [a_{m,1}(t), a_{m,2}(t), \cdots, a_{m,K}(t)]$.

In the ideal situation without considering constraint conditions such as cache capacity, the cache strategy of UAVs should contain all the content with non-zero popularity in the next frame. However, with the growth of content requirement in UEN, the limited cache capacity of UAVs cannot meet the cache capacity demand of the ideal cache strategy. Moreover, the backhaul capacity between UAVs and cloud database also causes UAVs to be unable to cache content at will. Therefore, this paper defines the cache hit rate of s_m as:

$$h_m(t) = \frac{\sum_{k=1}^{K} D_{m,k}(t) a_{m,k}(t)}{\sum_{k=1}^{K} D_{m,k}(t)} \tag{21}$$

As shown in Equation (21), $h_m(t)$ is actually the ratio of the user contentment of the cache strategy of s_m to the user contentment of the ideal cache strategy, where $\sum_{k=1}^{K} D_{m,k}(t) a_{m,k}(t)$ represents the user contentment of the cache strategy of s_m and is a value based on the weighted sum of popularity. Similarly, $\sum_{k=1}^{K} D_{m,k}(t)$ indicates the user contentment in the ideal situation. If and only if $a_{m,k}(t) = sgn(D_k(t))$, then $h_m(t) = 1$, where $sgn(\cdot)$ is the signum function.

3.2. Cache Optimization Problem

The cache strategy needs to meet the user's content requirements to the maximum extent, that is, to maximize the cache hit rate. The total cache hit rate of UAVs is given in Equation (22):

$$H(t) = \sum_{m=1}^{M} h_m(t) \tag{22}$$

The cache capacity of s_m is limited; as a result, it is impossible to cache all contents in the network at will:

$$\sum_{k=1}^{K} a_{m,k} L_k \leq Ca_m, m = 1, 2, \cdots, M \tag{23}$$

In addition, due to the limitation of channel capacity between the cloud database and the UAVs, it is difficult for s_m to achieve a sharp variation in the cache content within one frame. This is shown in Equation (24):

$$\sum_{k=1}^{K} a_{m,k}(t)(1 - a_{m,k}(t-1)) L_k \leq C_d \tag{24}$$
$$m = 1, 2, \cdots, M$$

where $a_{m,k}(t)(1 - a_{m,k}(t-1))$ processing methods for content f_k, and $C_d = \frac{1}{2} C_0 \Delta t$ represents the upper limit of bit data transmitted between the UAVs and the cloud database.

The cache optimization problem of the entire UEN can be obtained from Equations (22)–(24):

$$\max_{\mathbf{A}} H(t) \tag{25}$$
$$s.t. (23)(24)$$

where $\mathbf{A}$ is an M × K matrix, which represents the cache strategy of the entire UEN. Equation (23) represents the cache capacity constraint of the UAV, and Equation (24) represents the constraint of the channel capacity between UAVs and the cloud database.

3.3. Cache Strategy Optimization

The DABCCSU proposed in this paper includes two parts. First, based on the ID-DMU established in this paper, the content popularity prediction in UEN is obtained by the iteration matrix Equation (17), which was discussed in Section 2.2. Second, based on the prediction results, the DABCC algorithm is proposed to manage the cache optimization problem defined in Equation (25), and then the optimal cache scheme of the UEN is obtained.

The cache optimization problem Equation (25) proposed in this paper contains discrete variables. It is a non-convex integer non-linear programming (INLP) problem and also an NP-complete problem. An exact algorithm such as the enumeration algorithm can obtain the optimal solution of the problem, but its complexity is exponential. Heuristic algorithms such as simulated annealing algorithms can easily fall into local optimal solutions. Therefore, based on the traditional artificial bee colony algorithm, this paper proposes a discrete artificial bee colony cache (DABCC) optimization algorithm.

The cache optimization of UAVs is independent and simultaneous without influence on other UAVs. In other words, the cache strategy of one UAV is only constrained by channel conditions and the cache strategy in the previous frame. Based on this, the optimization problem Equation (25) can be decomposed into the cache optimization of a single UAV s_m, as given in Equation (26):

$$\max_{\mathbf{A}_m} h_m(t)$$
$$s.t. \sum_{k=1}^{K} a_{m,k} L_k \leq Ca_m \quad (26)$$
$$\sum_{k=1}^{K} a_{m,k}(t)(1 - a_{m,k}(t-1))L_k \leq \tfrac{1}{2}C_0 \Delta t$$

The optimization problem above can be transformed into a profitability function:

$$f_m(t) = h_m(t) - \lambda \max\left(\sum_{k=1}^{K} a_{m,k}(t)L_k - Ca_m, 0\right) \\ - \mu \max\left(\sum_{k=1}^{K} a_{m,k}(t)(1 - a_{m,k}(t-1))L_k - \tfrac{1}{2}C_0 \Delta t, 0\right) \quad (27)$$

where $\max(\cdot)$ is a comparison function that outputs the larger of the two parameters. λ and μ are regularization coefficients that are generally large numbers to ensure that the profitability of feasible solutions is greater than infeasible solutions, thus helping eliminate infeasible solutions in time.

The DABCC algorithm follows the definition of the traditional artificial bee colony algorithm and regards the feasible solution as the honey source. The total number of artificial bees is N_{Bee}, which is divided into leader bees, follower bees, and scouter bees. Generally, the number of leader bees and follower bees accounts for half, respectively, i.e., $N_{Bee}/2$. In some cases, scouter bees evolve from leader bees and follower bees. Specific definitions follow:

Honey Source: The honey collection coordinate of the artificial bee colony $Hb_j(j = 1, 2, \cdots, N_{bee}/2)$ represents the honey source of the j-th leader bee. The actions of the artificial bee colony are all centered on the honey sources. In fact, the honey sources are a series of K-dimensional vectors that represent the feasible solution of the optimization problem Equation (26). Artificial bees collect honey at the honey sources and constantly explore nearby honey sources. They compare the profitability of different honey sources by the profitability function and update the optimal honey source in real time. At the initial time, i.e., $t = 0$, since there is no reference honey source, the honey source coordinates are randomly generated:

$$a_{m,k}(t=0) = \begin{cases} 0, rand(0,1) < 0.5 \\ 1, otherwise \end{cases} \quad (28)$$

The honey source coordinates generated by Equation (28) are completely random, which increases the convergence time and calculation cost of the algorithm to a certain extent. Therefore, in the non-initial frame, the DABCC algorithm generates the honey source coordinates based on the cache strategy of the previous frame:

$$a_{m,k}(t) = \begin{cases} 1 - a_{m,k}(t-1), k = \hat{k} \\ a_{m,k}(t-1), otherwise \end{cases} \quad (29)$$

where $\hat{k}$ represents an integer randomly extracted from 1 to K. To ensure the difference between the honey source coordinates, this paper randomly extracts two different integers to execute Equation (29). In general, due to the constraint of channel conditions, the Hamming distance between the honey source generated by Equation (29) and the optimal honey source is smaller than that generated by Equation (28), which reduces the convergence time of the DABCC to a certain extent.

Leader Bee: A leader bee occupies a honey source, explores the nearby honey-source coordinates by the action function, and compares it with the best honey-source coordinates in its memory. When a honey source with a higher profitability is found, the leader bee updates memory and shares it with its follower bee. The leader bee will randomly compare the profitability of the honey source with another leader bee in one iteration. The action function of the leader bee is defined as $\varphi(Hb_j, Hb_{j'})$, where Hb_j and $Hb_{j'}$ represent the coordinates of the two paired bees; $\varphi(\cdot)$ retains the same components of the two honey sources and sets the different components to 1 in the form of roulette with the probability calculated by Equation (30):

$$Pr(k) = s_{m,k}(t) / \sum_{k=1}^{K} s_{m,k}(t) \quad (30)$$

where $s_{m,k}(t) = (D_{m,k}(t)/L_k)^Q$ and Q is the weight factor of a positive integer. When $Q = 1$, $s_{m,k}(t)$ represent the popularity gain of a unit content cache bit f_k. As Q increases, the content with the higher popularity gain of unit cache bit becomes more easily cached. The action function can effectively avoid the blind movement of the leader bee and makes it easier to move in the direction of high profitability.

Follower Bee: A follower bee follows a leader bee and explores the nearby honey source. When a better honey source is found by a follower bee, the optimal honey source of its paired leader bee is replaced and the two sides exchange roles. The follower bee selects whether to move using the probability shown in Equation (31). If the follower bee chooses to move, one component of its coordinate is randomly extracted and moved around based on Equation (29):

$$Pm_j = \hat{f}_j / \hat{f}_{max}. \quad (31)$$

where $\hat{f}_j$ represents the profitability of j-th leader bee and $\hat{f}_{max}$ represents the largest profitability of all leader bees. This action of follower bees reduces the calculation cost and ensures the exploration in the direction of high profitability.

Scouter Bee: When the optimal honey source of one leader bee and its follower bee do not change after a certain number of iterations, they are transformed into scouter bees to explore the honey source randomly generated by Equation (28) and redistribute to the leader bee and the follower bee to prevent the DABCC algorithm from falling into the local optimal solution.

The iterative process of DABCC algorithm is shown in Algorithm 1:

Algorithm 1 DABCC

Initialization: at initial time $t = 0$, obtain $\alpha_{m,n}$ of each user; obtain θ_k and γ_k of each content in the initial content set F. Calculate $\beta_{m,n}$ according to the channel conditions between s_m and u_m; Set N_{ite}, N_{lim}, N_{Bee}, λ and μ. Generate initial honey source $Hb_1 \sim Hb_{N_{Bee}}$ by Equation (28).
repeat:
  if $t \neq 0$
    Predict the popularity of content according to Equations (17)–(19).
    Detect $\hat{\alpha}_{m,n}$, $\hat{\theta}_k$, $\hat{\gamma}_k$ and $\hat{\beta}_{m,n}$;
    if $\hat{\alpha}_{m,n} \neq \alpha_{m,n}$ or $\hat{\theta}_k \neq \theta_k$ or $\hat{\gamma}_k \neq \gamma_k$ or $\hat{\beta}_{m,n} \neq \beta_{m,n}$
      Update relevant parameters.
    end
    if $\exists \hat{f}_k \notin F$
      add $\hat{f}_k$ to F.
    end
    Obtain $Pr(k)$ of each content by Equation (30).
  end
  Match the leader bees and follower bees randomly.
  for i = 1:N_{ite}
    for j = 1:N_{Bee}/2
      Leader bee Hb_j moves according to $\varphi(Hb_j, Hb_{j'})$.
      The follower bee explores the near honey source by Equations (29) and (31).
      Update the roles of leader bee and follower bee and the best honey source.
      Record the iterations N_{none} where the profitability has not improved.
      if $N_{none} = N_{lim}$
        Transform the leader bee and its follower bee into scouter bees for movement.
      end
    end
    Update the best profitability $\hat{f}_{max}$ and its honey source coordinate Hb_{max}.
  end
  Output the cache strategy $\mathbf{A}_m(t) = Hb_{max}$;
  $t = t + 1$;
until cache task finished.

In the initial frame, the DABCC algorithm initializes the parameters $\alpha_{m,n}$, θ_k, and γ_k of each content in the content set F and calculates $\beta_{m,n}$ according to the channel conditions of s_m. It then sets the iteration times of the algorithm N_{ite}, the maximum iteration times of artificial bees N_{lim}, the honey source dimension K, the punishment factor λ, μ, the number of artificial bees N_{Bee}, and the initial honey source $Hb_1 \sim Hb_{N_{Bee}}$. When the current frame is not the initial frame, the DABCC algorithm first predicts the popularity of the contents according to Equations (??)–(??), and then detects whether each parameter in the network changes to update it. Next, the DABCC algorithm adds the newly generated content to the content set and executes the action function of the artificial bee. Finally, the algorithm loops into the next frame until the whole cache task ends.

4. Results and Discussion

This section describes the simulation and performance evaluation for the proposed DABCCSU. In this paper, a 5 km ×5 km UEN is generated by MATLAB software to simulate the dissemination of 1000 contents, where users obey the Poisson distribution, and the communication range is 1 km. The generation and dissemination of contents happens randomly. θ_k and γ_k of each content are randomly generated between 0 and 1; $\delta = 0.8$ and $\alpha_{m,n}$ can be obtained by Equation (6). The path loss $\xi = 2$ and $\beta_{m,k}$ is fixed at 0.5 by Equation (11) to facilitate comparison. The parameters are shown in Table 1:

Table 1. Simulation parameters.

Parameter	Value
K	1000
θ_k, γ_k	Rand (0, 1)
$\beta_{m,n}$	0.5
$R_{m,n}$	1 km
ξ	2
C_d	1 Gbits
λ, μ	1×10^{12}
Q	1
N_{Bee}	100
N_{ite}	500
N_{lim}	10

4.1. Content Popularity Prediction by DABCCSU

The prediction results of content popularity by DABCCSU are shown in Figure 4, where the abscissa represents time and the ordinate represents popularity. The two curves are the predicted real content popularities. The sub-graphs (a), (b), and (c) correspond to the situation of UEN corresponding to the number of users N = 100, 300 and 500, respectively. In sub-graph (a), due to the small number of users, the dissemination of content shows randomness, that is, the popularity fluctuates in the early stage and there is a certain amount of error between the prediction result and the real popularity such that the average popularity prediction accuracy is 90.94%. The trend of prediction popularity curves in sub-graphs (b) and (c) is more obvious, and the error between the prediction result and the real popularity is less than sub-graph (a). The average popularity prediction accuracies in sub-graphs (b) and (c) are 92.57% and 93.34%, respectively. Compared with the predicted results of DABCCSU and the real popularity, both trends increase rapidly and then decrease to zero, which conforms to the dissemination content regularity in the network. Once the content is generated, it quickly attracts the interest of surrounding users, and the request for content increases significantly. As the content spreads to saturation, users gradually lose interest in the content, and the popularity of the content rapidly drops to zero. The increased number of users weakens the randomness of content dissemination, making the prediction results more consistent with statistical regularity. Therefore, with an increased number of users, the prediction results of DABCCSU are more accurate.

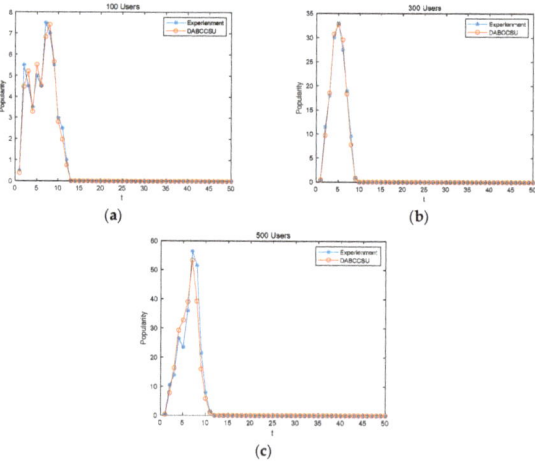

Figure 4. Prediction results of content popularity by DABCCSU: (a) 100, (b) 300, and (c) 500 users.

4.2. DABCC Optimization Algorithm

This paper compares the cache performance of the DABCC optimization algorithm with some common cache algorithms:

(1) Least Recently Used (LRU) Algorithm [32]: Its core idea is that if a content has recent high-frequency requests, it also has a greater probability of being requested currently. When the cache capacity is insufficient, content with a low historical request frequency is preferentially discarded.

(2) Greedy Algorithm (GA): The principle of the GA is to preferentially cache the content with largest $D_{m,k}(t)/L_k$ until the cache capacity or channel load reaches the upper limit.

(3) Binary Particle Swarm Optimization Algorithm (BPSO): BPSO is derived from the particle swarm optimization algorithm, and the value range of its particles is only 0 or 1. The number of iterations of the BPSO algorithm in this paper is set to 500 and the number of particles is set to 100. Other parameters are the same as DABCC.

This paper describes the cumulative cache hit rate of the DABCC and reference algorithm in different periods when K = 1000 and the content size is averagely distributed between 0 and 100 Mbits. Figure 5 shows four curves: the cumulative cache hit rates for the DABCC, LRU, GA, and BPSO algorithms, where the abscissa is the time period and the ordinate is the cache hit rate. According to Figure 5, the cumulative cache hit rate of the DABCC is 91.62%, which is much higher than 51.09% for LRU and 54.26% for BPSO and slightly higher than 89.27% for GA. This is because the LRU relies on the historical content request, which makes it difficult to capture the time-variant content popularity. Although the GA considers the time-variant problem of content popularity, it easily falls into the local optimal problem solution. The BPSO converges easily to the local optimal solution, and with the randomness of the search of the algorithm becoming stronger, the local search ability of the BPSO at the later stage of the iteration is weakened. The DABCC effectively avoids this dilemma, resulting in the best cache performance among the four algorithms.

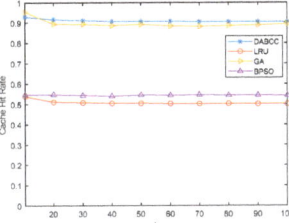

Figure 5. Cumulative cache hit rate.

In addition, this paper discusses the cache hit rate of each algorithm under different cache capacities, as shown in Figure 6. The abscissa represents the cache capacities, which are 0.5, 1, and 2 Gbits. The ordinate is the cache hit rate, and the bar graph represents the average cache hit rate of DABCC, LRU, and GA under different cache capacities. According to Figure 6, the average cache hit rate of the DABCC is higher than that of the other two algorithms regardless of the cache capacity, which conforms to the three algorithms analyzed in this paper. Under any cache capacity, the cache hit rate of the LRU algorithm is only slightly higher than 50%, and cache hit rate of BPSO is about 54%, which are far lower than the other two algorithms. In the case of 0.5 Gbits cache capacity, the DABCC can also achieve an average cache hit rate of 89.83%, which is better than GA's 58.64%. In the case of 2 Gbits cache capacity, the cache hit rate of the DABCC can reach 94.65%, which is slightly better than GA's 93.48%, indicating that the DABCC is more stable in different cache capacities. The LRU has a low cache hit rate because it is difficult to capture the time-variant popularity of the content. The BPSO has a low cache hit rate because of the randomness of particle motion and the lack of local exploration ability in the later stage.

The cache hit rate of the GA is seriously limited by cache capacity. In the case of low cache capacity, the cache hit rate is low owing to the large size content and limited cache capacity. As the cache capacity increases, these restrictions no longer affect the cache efficiency; thus, its cache hit rate can also reach a high level. The DABCC can flexibly design the cache strategy according to the cache capacity, to achieve the maximum cache hit rate under a limited cache capacity. Therefore, the cache hit rate of DABCC is the highest among the three algorithms.

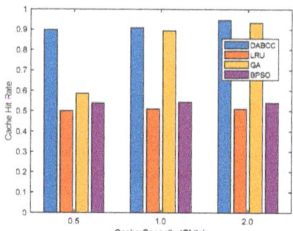

Figure 6. Cache hit rate under different cache capacities.

Figure 7 shows the cache hit rate of DABCC for different iteration times, where the abscissa is the value of N_{ite} and the ordinate is the cache hit rate. The five curves in Figure 7 represent the situation when N_{Bee} = 20, 40, 60, 80, and 100 respectively. It can be understood from Figure 7 that in the case of different N_{Bee}, the cache hit rate of DABCC gradually increases with the increase in the value of N_{ite}. When the value of N_{ite} is large, the cache hit rate tends to be flat. In addition, when N_{Bee} is low, the cache hit rate is significantly lower than when N_{Bee} is high. This phenomenon is in line with the expected results. With the increase in N_{ite}, DABCC gradually approaches the optimal solution, and the cache hit rate rapidly increases. When N_{ite} reaches a certain value, the cache hit rate rises slowly. Because the optimal cache strategy is obtained after a certain number of iterations, the increase in N_{ite} has little impact on the cache hit rate after that. The increase in N_{Bee} improves the efficiency of exploring honey sources in one iteration, resulting in a significantly lower cache hit rate when the N_{Bee} is lower than when N_{Bee} is higher under the same iteration number. Therefore, DABCC proposed in this paper can achieve a cache hit rate of more than 90% with limited N_{ite} and N_{Bee}, which proves DABCC has efficient cache performance.

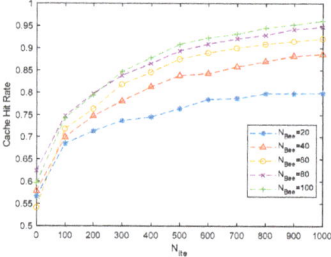

Figure 7. Cache hit rate of DABCC for different iteration times.

5. Conclusions

This paper proposes the discrete artificial bee colony cache strategy of UAV edge network (DABCCSU). The coupling relationship between the popularity and edge cache is derived according to the time-variant characteristics of content popularity in the UEN. In addition, DABCCSU also includes the DABCC optimization algorithm that maximizes the cache hit rate based on the content popularity prediction and provides an optimal cache strategy for the UEN. Simulation results show that the prediction accuracy of DABCCSU is over 90%, and the cache performance has an average cache hit rate of 91.62%, which is better than the LRU and GA strategies. In addition, DABCCSU has a more stable performance under different cache capacities. DABCCSU is expected to be widely used in UAV emergency communication networks or UAV networks in remote areas. In the future, on the basis of this paper, we will continue to study the cache strategy of UENs based on space–air–ground integrated networks, NOMA, intelligent reflect surface, and other technologies.

Author Contributions: Conceptualization, Y.H. and Y.Z.; methodology, Y.H. and Y.Z.; formal analysis, Y.H. and Y.Z.; writing—original draft preparation, Y.H. and Y.Z.; writing—review and editing, Y.H. and Y.Z.; funding acquisition, S.F. All authors have read and agreed to the published version of the manuscript.

Funding: This research was funded in part by a sub-project of the National Key Research and Development 2020 Plan (2020YFC1511704), Beijing Information Science and Technology University (2020KYNH212, 2021CGZH302), Beijing Science and Technology Project (Z211100004421009), and the Open Foundation of State Key Laboratory of Networking and Switching Technology (Beijing University of Posts and Telecommunications) (SKLNST-2022-1-16).

Institutional Review Board Statement: Not applicable.

Informed Consent Statement: Not applicable.

Data Availability Statement: Not applicable.

Acknowledgments: Great gratitude to Beijing Information Science and Technology University for providing an excellent experimental environment for the research reported in this paper.

Conflicts of Interest: The authors declare no conflict of interest.

References

1. Fu, Y.; Yu, Q.; Wong, A.K.Y.; Shi, Z.; Wang, H.; Quek, T.Q.S. Exploiting Coding and Recommendation to Improve Cache Efficiency of Reliability-Aware Wireless Edge Caching Networks. *IEEE Trans. Wirel. Commun.* **2021**, *20*, 7243–7256. [CrossRef]
2. Qiao, G.; Leng, S.; Maharjan, S.; Zhang, Y.; Ansari, N. Deep Reinforcement Learning for Cooperative Content Caching in Vehicular Edge Computing and Networks. *IEEE Internet Things J.* **2020**, *7*, 247–257. [CrossRef]
3. Zhu, X.; Jiang, C.; Kuang, L.; Zhao, Z. Cooperative Multilayer Edge Caching in Integrated Satellite-Terrestrial Networks. *IEEE Trans. Wirel. Commun.* **2022**, *21*, 2924–2937. [CrossRef]
4. Han, Y.; Ai, L.; Wang, R.; Wu, J.; Liu, D.; Ren, H. Cache Placement Optimization in Mobile Edge Computing Networks With Unaware Environment—An Extended Multi-Armed Bandit Approach. *IEEE Trans. Wirel. Commun.* **2021**, *20*, 8119–8133. [CrossRef]
5. Kwak, J.; Kim, Y.; Le, L.B.; Chong, S. Hybrid Content Caching in 5G Wireless Networks: Cloud Versus Edge Caching. *IEEE Trans. Wirel. Commun.* **2018**, *17*, 3030–3045. [CrossRef]
6. Sun, L.; Zhong, Z.; Qu, Z.; Xiong, N. PerAE: An Effective Personalized AutoEncoder for ECG-Based Biometric in Augmented Reality System. *IEEE J. Biomed. Health Inform.* **2022**, *26*, 2435–2446. [CrossRef] [PubMed]
7. Chen, S.; Yao, Z.; Jiang, X.; Yang, J.; Hanzo, L. Multi-Agent Deep Reinforcement Learning-Based Cooperative Edge Caching for Ultra-Dense Next-Generation Networks. *IEEE Trans. Commun.* **2021**, *69*, 2441–2456. [CrossRef]
8. Ji, J.; Zhu, K.; Niyato, D.; Wang, R. Probabilistic Cache Placement in UAV-Assisted Networks with D2D Connections: Performance Analysis and Trajectory Optimization. *IEEE Trans. Commun.* **2020**, *68*, 6331–6345. [CrossRef]
9. Zhang, M.; I-Hajjar, M.E.; Ng, S.X. Intelligent Caching in UAV-Aided Networks. *IEEE Trans. Veh. Technol.* **2022**, *71*, 739–752. [CrossRef]
10. Chai, S.; Lau, V.K.N. Multi-UAV Trajectory and Power Optimization for Cached UAV Wireless Networks with Energy and Content Recharging-Demand Driven Deep Learning Approach. *IEEE J. Sel. Areas Commun.* **2021**, *39*, 3208–3224. [CrossRef]
11. Luo, J.; Song, J.; Zheng, F.-C.; Gao, L.; Wang, T. User-Centric UAV Deployment and Content Placement in Cache-Enabled Multi-UAV Networks. *IEEE Trans. Veh. Technol.* **2022**, *71*, 5656–5660. [CrossRef]
12. Bharath, B.N.; Nagananda, K.G.; Gündüz, D.; Poor, H.V. Caching With Time-Varying Popularity Profiles: A Learning-Theoretic Perspective. *IEEE Trans. Commun.* **2018**, *66*, 3837–3847. [CrossRef]
13. Gao, J.; Zhang, S.; Zhao, L.; Shen, X. The Design of Dynamic Probabilistic Caching with Time-Varying Content Popularity. *IEEE Trans. Mob. Comput.* **2021**, *20*, 1672–1684. [CrossRef]
14. Sadeghi, A.; Sheikholeslami, F.; Giannakis, G.B. Optimal and Scalable Caching for 5G Using Reinforcement Learning of Space-Time Popularities. *IEEE J. Sel. Top. Signal Process.* **2018**, *12*, 180–190. [CrossRef]
15. Mehrizi, S.; Chatterjee, S.; Chatzinotas, S.; Ottersten, B. Online Spatiotemporal Popularity Learning via Variational Bayes for Cooperative Caching. *IEEE Trans. Commun.* **2020**, *68*, 7068–7082. [CrossRef]

16. Kong, Q.; Mao, W.; Chen, G.; Zeng, D. Exploring Trends and Patterns of Popularity Stage Evolution in Social Media. *IEEE Trans. Syst. Man Cybern. Syst.* **2020**, *50*, 3817–3827. [CrossRef]
17. Abousaleh, F.S.; Cheng, W.-H.; Yu, N.-H.; Tsao, Y. Multimodal Deep Learning Framework for Image Popularity Prediction on Social Media. *IEEE Trans. Cogn. Dev. Syst.* **2021**, *13*, 679–692. [CrossRef]
18. Li, G.; Liu, Y.; Ribeiro, B.; Ding, H. On New Group Popularity Prediction in Event-Based Social Networks. *IEEE Trans. Netw. Sci. Eng.* **2020**, *7*, 1239–1250. [CrossRef]
19. Yan, S.; Qi, L.; Zhou, Y.; Peng, M.; Rahman, G.M.S. Joint User Access Mode Selection and Content Popularity Prediction in Non-Orthogonal Multiple Access-Based F-RANs. *IEEE Trans. Commun.* **2020**, *68*, 654–666. [CrossRef]
20. Gao, X.; Zheng, Z.; Chu, Q.; Tang, S.; Chen, G.; Deng, Q. Popularity Prediction for Single Tweet Based on Heterogeneous Bass Model. *IEEE Trans. Knowl. Data Eng.* **2021**, *33*, 2165–2178. [CrossRef]
21. Zhang, Y.; Tan, X.; Li, W. PPC: Popularity Prediction Caching in ICN. *IEEE Commun. Lett.* **2018**, *22*, 5–8. [CrossRef]
22. Gao, S.; Dong, P.; Pan, Z.; Li, G.Y. Reinforcement Learning Based Cooperative Coded Caching Under Dynamic Popularities in Ultra-Dense Networks. *IEEE Trans. Veh. Technol.* **2020**, *69*, 5442–5456. [CrossRef]
23. Ji, Z.; Wu, S.; Jiang, C.; Wang, W. Popularity-Driven Content Placement and Multi-Hop Delivery for Terrestrial-Satellite Networks. *IEEE Commun. Lett.* **2020**, *24*, 2574–2578. [CrossRef]
24. Liang, J.; Zhu, D.; Liu, H.; Ping, H.; Li, T.; Zhang, H.; Geng, L.; Liu, Y. Multi-Head Attention Based Popularity Prediction Caching in Social Content-Centric Networking with Mobile Edge Computing. *IEEE Commun. Lett.* **2021**, *25*, 508–512. [CrossRef]
25. Chen, Q.; Wang, W.; Yu, F.R.; Tao, M.; Zhang, Z. Content Caching Oriented Popularity Prediction: A Weighted Clustering Approach. *IEEE Trans. Wirel. Commun.* **2021**, *20*, 623–636. [CrossRef]
26. Chen, B.; Liu, L.; Sun, M.; Ma, H. IoTCache: Toward Data-Driven Network Caching for Internet of Things. *IEEE Internet Things J.* **2019**, *6*, 10064–10076. [CrossRef]
27. Kang, H.; Sun, M.; Yu, Y.; Fu, X.; Bao, B. Spreading Dynamics of an SEIR Model with Delay on Scale-Free Networks. *IEEE Trans. Netw. Sci. Eng.* **2020**, *7*, 489–496.
28. Sun, L.; Wang, Y.; Qu, Z.; Xiong, N.N. BeatClass: A Sustainable ECG Classification System in IoT-Based eHealth. *IEEE Internet Things J.* **2022**, *9*, 7178–7195. [CrossRef]
29. Guizani, N.; Ghafoor, A. A Network Function Virtualization System for Detecting Malware in Large IoT Based Networks. *IEEE J. Sel. Areas Commun.* **2020**, *38*, 1218–1228. [CrossRef]
30. Karaboga, D. An idea based on Honeybee Swarm for Numerical Optimization. *Tech. Rep.-TR06* **2005**, *200*, 1–10.
31. Yu, Y.; Zheng, J.; Chen, S.; Yang, Z. Moving Target Imaging via Computational Ghost Imaging Combined With Artificial Bee Colony Optimization. *IEEE Trans. Instrum. Meas.* **2022**, *71*, 1–7. [CrossRef]
32. Kurniawan, F.S.; Yovita, L.V.; Wibowo, T.A. Modified-LRU Algorithm for Caching on Named Data Network. In Proceedings of the 2019 International Conference on Electrical Engineering and Informatics (ICEEI), Bandung, Indonesia, 9–10 July 2019.

Intelligent Facemask Coverage Detector in a World of Chaos

Sadaf Waziry [1], Ahmad Bilal Wardak [1], Jawad Rasheed [2,*], Raed M. Shubair [3] and Amani Yahyaoui [4]

1 Department of Software Engineering, Istanbul Aydin University, Istanbul 34295, Turkey
2 Department of Software Engineering, Nisantasi University, Istanbul 34398, Turkey
3 Department of Electrical and Computer Engineering, New York University (NYU), Abu Dhabi 129188, United Arab Emirates
4 Department of Software Engineering, Istanbul Sabahattin Zaim University, Istanbul 34303, Turkey
* Correspondence: jawad.rasheed@nisantasi.edu.tr

Abstract: The recent outbreak of COVID-19 around the world has caused a global health catastrophe along with economic consequences. As per the World Health Organization (WHO), this devastating crisis can be minimized and controlled if humans wear facemasks in public; however, the prevention of spreading COVID-19 can only be possible only if they are worn properly, covering both the nose and mouth. Nonetheless, in public places or in chaos, a manual check of persons wearing the masks properly or not is a hectic job and can cause panic. For such conditions, an automatic mask-wearing system is desired. Therefore, this study analyzed several deep learning pre-trained networks and classical machine learning algorithms that can automatically detect whether the person wears the facemask or not. For this, 40,000 images are utilized to train and test 9 different models, namely, InceptionV3, EfficientNetB0, EfficientNetB2, DenseNet201, ResNet152, VGG19, convolutional neural network (CNN), support vector machine (SVM), and random forest (RF), to recognize facemasks in images. Besides just detecting the mask, the trained models also detect whether the person is wearing the mask properly (covering nose and mouth), partially (mouth only), or wearing it inappropriately (not covering nose and mouth). Experimental work reveals that InceptionV3 and EfficientNetB2 outperformed all other methods by attaining an overall accuracy of around 98.40% and a precision, recall, and F1-score of 98.30%.

Keywords: deep learning; inappropriately wearing facemask; machine learning; mask detection

1. Introduction

For the past several years, the COVID-19 [1] pandemic has spread practically all over the globe, resulting in the world's most critical global health catastrophe that has had a huge effect on humanity and how we see the world and everyday lives [2]. Consequently, there are health procedures that must be followed to limit the transmission of coronavirus. A few of the norms are either staying at least 2 m apart from other humans or wearing a mask properly, particularly in public places [3]. In the chaos of the pandemic, there are many circumstances where wearing facemasks can contribute to controlling the transmission of COVID-19, such as migrants in refugee camps, workers taking subways, etc. Hence, authorities have consistently issued statements regarding COVID-19 international guidelines about contact and airborne precautions, including the consideration of utilization of facemasks as an adequate adoption in case of congested human chaos. As a result, it would be desirable if a system could automatically recognize a person who does not appropriately place the mask on his or her face or who does not wear any mask at all. On the other hand, this work employs hybrid deep and classical machine learning models to determine the face coverage area covered by facemasks in an image of a human. Figure 1 shows the workflow of the proposed scheme. In the first step, the proposed system removes duplicates, outliers, and unnecessary data. Next, it resizes the images according to the classification model. Lastly, it explores seven deep learning-based and two machine learning-based classifiers to classify the given image into four categories that include wearing a mask properly, mask not covering the nose, mask neither covering the nose nor mouth, and not wearing a mask at all.

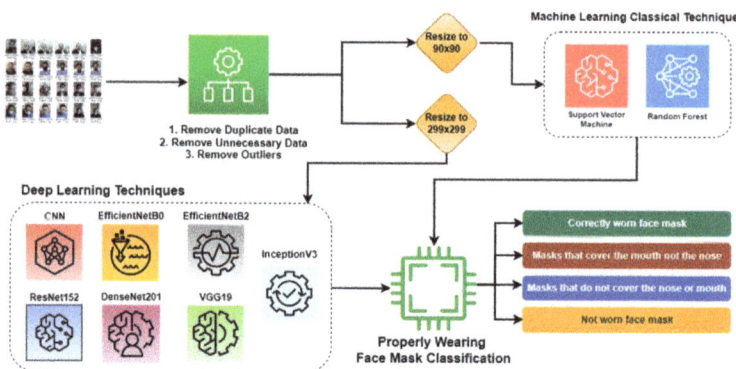

Figure 1. The overall workflow of the proposed system.

Deep neural networks are capable of performing computer vision tasks and performing cutting-edge image recognition [4] by taking an input image and distinguishing it by assigning priority, learnable weights, and biases to various sections of the image, for instance [5,6]. Furthermore, CNN [7] is often used to evaluate visual images and needs far less pre-processing than conventional classification techniques. However, classical machine learning algorithms such as RF, decision tree (DT), SVM, k-nearest neighbor (KNN), and many others also have a vast usage in image classification, such as COVID-19 and pneumonia classification systems in [8,9].

As facemask detection has become a critical area of study during the COVID-19 pandemic, numerous extensive studies have been conducted to address this issue using a variety of different techniques and strategies, such as the Spartan Face Detection and Identification System suggested in [10] employed CNN, AlexNet, and long-short-term-memory (LSTM) to handle the primary challenges of mask detection, classification of mask type, classification of mask placements, and identity recognition. Similarly, Ref. [11] proposes a real-time facemask detection model based on CNN, the computer vision technique, and MobileNet that runs in real-time and recognizes if a person is wearing a facemask; if not, it notifies higher authorities by text message.

To efficiently perform person detection, social distancing infringement detection, face identification, and facemask categorization on surveillance footage datasets, Ref. [12] presented YOLOv3, clustering of applications with noise based on density, a dual-shot face detector (DSFD), and a binary classifier based on MobileNetV2. Additionally, it included data augmentation strategies to address the community's data scarcity. To identify the facemask, Ref. [13] adopted a deep learning algorithm named YOLOv4 to identify the mask in the real-time scenario by deploying the equipment at Politeknik Negeri Batam, Indonesia.

Isunuri et al. proposed a MobileNet block for facemask identification that includes a global pooling [14]. Their proposed model flattens the feature vector using a global pooling layer and outperforms current models on publicly accessible facemask datasets in terms of critical performance metrics, parameter count, and training time. Yadav [2] proposed an efficient computer vision-based method for real-time automated monitoring of persons in public areas to detect both safe social separation and face coverings. He used the camera to watch activity and identify violations and developed the model on a raspberry pi4.

Table 1 outlines the techniques and algorithms used in prior facemask detection systems from the literature. Most of these facemask detection systems incorporated deep learning-based pre-trained or transfer-learning models. Moreover, according to our knowledge and research, the literature is full of systems that are capable to identify whether a person is wearing a mask or not; however, no study thus far determines the coverage of a facemask on a human face. The datasets used previously vary from one study to the next, and while the authors may have presented multiple conclusions based on a variety of datasets in a single piece of work, only one of those findings is disclosed.

Table 1. A summary of recent facemask detection studies.

Study	Method
[12]	MobileNetV2
[14]	MobileNet
[15]	Faster R-CNN
[16]	SSD and SSD-Mask algorithms
[17]	CNN and VGG16
[18]	MobileNet and OpenCV
[19]	SSD and MobileNetV2

In this paper, we compared CNN-, RF-, and SVM-based models and several deep learning pre-trained models (InceptionV3, EfficientNetB0, EfficientNetB2, DenseNet201, ResNet152, and VGG19) to detect whether people are wearing a mask or not and whether they are wearing it properly using face images with different types of facemask wearing. The study has the following major contributions:

- The proposed scheme checks whether the person wears a mask or not.
- It determines the coverage area of the facemask on the human face and classifies the facemask facial image into four categories: appropriately wearing a mask (covering both nose and mouth), partially wearing a mask (covering mouth but not nose), inappropriately wearing a mask (neither covering mouth nor nose), and not wearing a mask at all.
- The paper investigates state-of-the-art pre-trained models and analyzes the performance with traditional machine learning and deep learning models for facemask coverage.
- The study analyzes the performance of various models with several metrics, such as accuracy, F1-score, precision, and recall.
- The application of the proposed system ensures the mask fits and covers essential areas, including the nose, mouth, and chin.

The paper is organized as follows: Section 2 describes the explored hybrid deep and classical machine learning techniques, Section 3 presents a detailed discussion of the results, and the paper is concluded in Section 4.

2. Materials and Methods

The proposed facemask coverage detection scheme used in this study is divided into three stages: pre-processing of data, training the models, and facemask wearing classification. It utilizes several procedures during the pre-processing stage, including deleting duplicate data, removing extraneous data, and downsizing images to 299 × 299 for CNN and pre-trained models, and 50 × 50 for RF and SVM models. The data, which consist of images of people wearing facemasks, are fed into CNN, RF, SVM, and six pre-trained deep learning-based classifiers (InceptionV3, EfficientNetB0, EfficientNetB2, DenseNet201, ResNet152, and VGG19). The study carried out extensive experiments to fine-tune these models to properly determine whether a person is wearing a mask or not or wearing it properly.

2.1. Dataset

The dataset used to train the models comprises 40,000 images belonging to 4 distinct classes (ways of wearing the masks). Moreover, for better testing, we also used images from the downloaded dataset, a few of which are depicted in Figure 2, where persons are wearing masks in three different ways or not wearing a mask at all. The dataset was downloaded from a public repository [20]. After removing duplicate and unnecessary images, we were left with a total of 11,536 images for the 4 different types of masks worn: correctly worn masks that cover the nose and mouth, masks that cover the mouth but not the nose, masks that are worn but do not cover the nose and mouth, and faces without facemasks. Table 2 lists the further division of the dataset for each class. All images acquired in this repository use Toloka.ai's crowdsourcing platform and are verified by TrainingData.ru. To train and evaluate our models, we separated the dataset into training and test sets with 70/30 ratios. After successful training, the accuracy was computed using all images from the test dataset in each iteration.

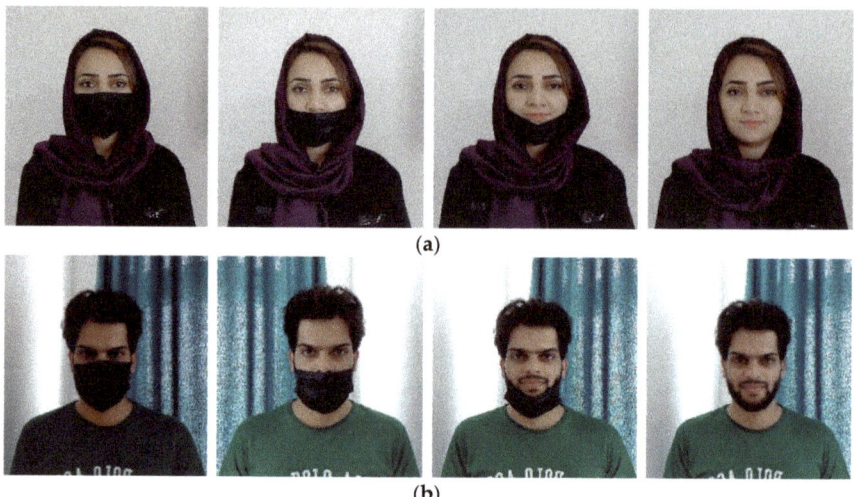

Figure 2. Sample of the unseen images in which persons are wearing a facemask in four different ways. (**a**) Images of a female covering her face using a facemask, and (**b**) images of a male covering his face using a facemask.

Table 2. A summary of the dataset used for facemask detection research.

Mask Wearing Type	No. of Images
Correctly worn masks	2884
Masks that cover the mouth but not the nose	2884
Masks that do not cover the nose or mouth	2884
Not wearing a mask	2884
Total	**11,536**
Training Set	**8075**
Test Set	**3461**

2.2. CNN Model Architecture

To identify the facemask and its coverage area, we constructed a CNN model that consists of three convolutional layers, three pooling layers, one dropout layer, one flattened layer, and a fully connected (dense) layer. However, each of the convolutional and pooling layers produced a three-dimensional (3D) form tensor as an output (height, width, channels). The max-pooling layer was then utilized to reduce the output volume's spatial dimensions. The dropout layer contributes to overfitting reduction by randomly changing input units to 0 at a frequency of the rate during the training period. The SoftMax layer normalizes the preceding layer's output to include the probability of the actual input image conforming to designated classes.

2.3. Machine Learning Classical Algorithms

To accomplish and test the facemask coverage categorization system using machine learning classical algorithms, we have fed our data to two classical algorithms: RF and SVM. The proposed scheme performed some pre-processing on the data before feeding it into these classifiers. This included resizing the data to a ratio of 50×50 and shuffling the data to rearrange the order in which the components appear. After that, it reshaped the value distribution by using the standard scaler to make the mean of the observed values equal to zero and the standard deviation equal to one. Each of these explored classical machine learning algorithms is briefly described below.

2.3.1. Random Forest

The RF approach [21] is an algorithm usually employed for supervised classification. It extends the idea of DTs and has been effectively utilized in a wide variety of scientific fields to reduce high-dimensional and multi-source data. Self-learning DTs are used by RF, based on a training dataset, and these trees automatically construct rules at each node. The RF is capable of effectively handling huge datasets to generate accurate forecasting that is simple to understand.

2.3.2. Support Vector Machine

SVM is a method that is widely used for pattern recognition and image categorization [22]. It does this by generating the most efficient separating hyperplanes on the premise of a kernel function. SVM offers two major benefits over other algorithms in terms of speed and performance with a small number of samples. This makes the approach ideal for classification tasks, where access to a dataset of just a few thousands of labeled samples is frequent.

2.4. Deep Neural Network Models

To perform facemask coverage categorization, we fine-tuned InceptionV3, EfficientNetB0, EfficientNetB2, DenseNet201, ResNet152, and VGG19 models. For these, the scheme used an input shape of (299, 299, 3) and added a final dense layer with four outputs and a SoftMax activation function since our data were separated into four classes. Each of these pre-trained models is briefly described below.

2.4.1. InceptionV3

The InceptionV3 [23] is a 48-layer deep learning model based on CNN used to classify images. The inceptionV3 model is an upgraded version of the InceptionV1 model, which was introduced in 2014 as GoogLeNet. It is a commonly used image recognition model with a demonstrated accuracy of more than 78.1% on the ImageNet dataset. Additionally, it is meant to work well under severe memory and computational resource constraints. The inception layer combines the 1×1, 3×3, and 5×5 convolutional layers, concatenating their output filter banks into a uniform output vector that serves as the subsequent stage's input.

2.4.2. EfficientNetB0 and EfficientNetB2

EfficientNet [24] is a scaling technique that uses a compound coefficient to scale all depth, resolution, and breadth parameters uniformly. The EfficientNetB0 base network is based on MobileNetV2's inverted bottleneck residual blocks, as well as squeeze-and-excite blocks, and consists of 237 layers composed of five modules. EfficientNets substantially outperform other convolutional networks in various tasks. AutoML MNAS created the baseline network, EfficientNetB0, and the subsequent networks, EfficientNetB1 through B7, by scaling up the baseline network. However, the most recent version of EfficientNet, EfficientNetB7, reached an unprecedented top 1 accuracy of 84.3%.

2.4.3. DenseNet201

DenseNet-201 [25] is a 201-layer CNN network. The pre-trained models are capable of accurately categorizing photos into 1000 different item categories. It is a dense convolutional network as it uses a technique that links each layer to every other layer using a feed-forward approach. DenseNets overcome the vanishing gradients issue, enhance feature reuse, and boost feature propagation, while needing much fewer parameters than general CNN networks, as they do not need to acquire any superfluous feature mappings.

2.4.4. ResNet201

ResNet is the abbreviation for the Residual Network. This breakthrough neural network was first reported by He, Zhang, Ren, and Sun in their 2015 computer vision study [26]. ResNet152 learns the residual representation functions rather than the signal analysis directly, resulting in an extremely deep network with up to 152 layers. ResNet uses skip connections (also known as shortcut connections) to fit input from one layer to another without modifying the input.

2.4.5. VGG19

Karen Simonyan and Andrew Zisserman, two academics from the University of Oxford, came up with the idea of the VGGNet design [27] in 2014. The VGG19 is a variation of the VGG network that has 19 weight layers. These weight layers are made up of a total of 16 convolutional layers, 3 layers that are completely linked, and 5 pooling layers. It has 2 fully connected layers, each with 4096 nodes, and one more fully connected layer having 1000 nodes to predict 1000 labels.

3. Results and Discussion

To obtain satisfactory results with the proposed CNN, RF, and SVM models for the detection of images of people wearing facemasks correctly, we performed several experiments and used a variety of hyperparameters to fine-tune these models. The hyperparameters for the models that performed better than the models with different hyperparameters are shown in Tables 3 and 4. Table 3 lists the hyperparameters for the proposed CNN model while Table 4 outlines the parameters of the RF model. The CNN model incorporates an Adam optimizer with 100 epochs, 120 batch sizes, and a learning rate of 0.000001. The RF model has a maximum depth of 3 with 20 estimators, as listed in Table 4.

Table 3. Hyperparameter tuning of the proposed convolutional neural network model.

Hyperparameters	Value
Optimizer	Adam
Number of epochs	100
Batch Size	120
Loss	categorical_crossentropy
Metrics	accuracy
Learning rate	0.000001

Table 4. Proposed random forest model hyperparameter tuning.

Hyperparameters	Value
Number of estimators	20
Criterion	entropy
Maximum depth	3

To evaluate the usefulness and effectiveness of the models, we used 8075 images of humans, with 4 different labels for the training and 4 metrics (f1-score, accuracy, precision, and recall) that were measured for each individual. Following the completion of the model training, each model was tested with 3461 test images as well as a few unseen data. The performance metrics obtained by each model on the test data are shown in Table 5.

Table 5. Performance analysis of explored models for facemask coverage classification.

Model	Accuracy %	Precision %	Recall %	F1-Score %
CNN	55.22	54.90	55.40	55.20
Random Forest	48.92	51.00	48.74	47.41
SVM	56.83	57.35	56.73	56.58
InceptionV3	**98.40**	98.30	98.30	98.30
EfficientNetB0	97.70	97.70	97.70	97.70
EfficientNetB2	98.35	98.30	98.30	98.40
DenseNet201	97.72	97.80	97.70	97.70
ResNet152	93.99	94.60	94.00	94.00
VGG19	24.65	31.20	25.00	24.60

Moreover, for better visual understanding, the study also plotted various performance curves. Thus, after successful training, the model computed the accuracy and loss using all images from the test dataset in each iteration. Figure 4 shows the visualization of both training and validation accuracy curves for each model (CNN, InceptionV3, EfficientNetB0, EfficientNetB2, DenseNet201, ResNet152, VGG19), whereas Figure 4 depicts training and testing loss curves for all exploited models.

It is worth noting that prior well-established studies majorly focused on detecting whether a person is wearing a mask or not. The majority of those used pre-trained deep learning networks and attained reasonable results at that time. However, only a few previously published studies in well-reputed journals attained an accuracy of more than 98% for the two-class classification task. Another study [28] also explored several pre-trained models, including InceptionV3, to handle a six-class classification problem for detection of the coverage area. They used a small dataset, and thus exploited the data augmentation technique, however they still just managed to achieve an accuracy of 83.4% on a test set that has less than a few hundred samples. However, they used a limited dataset, which may result in overfitting or underfitting issues. Contrarily, our study widened the approach by presenting a system for a four-class classification task and reasonably competes with prior studies, as shown in Table 6.

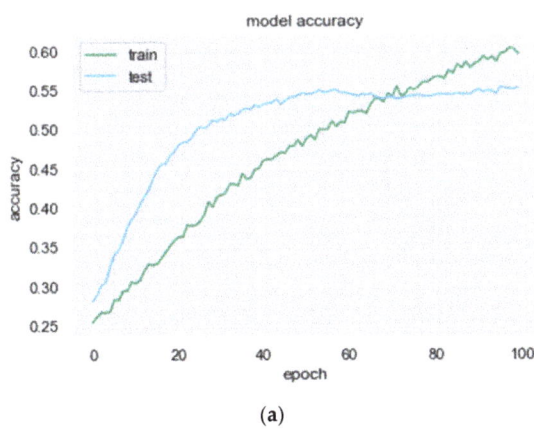

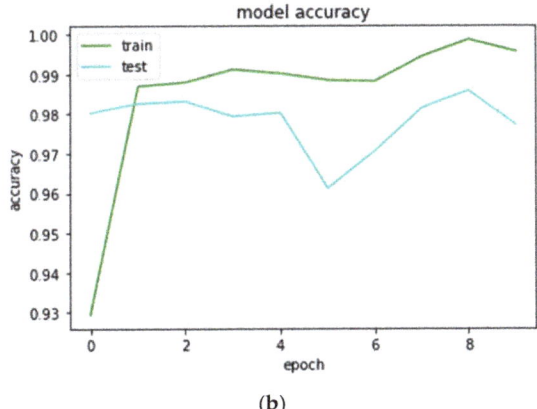

(a)

(b)

Figure 3. *Cont.*

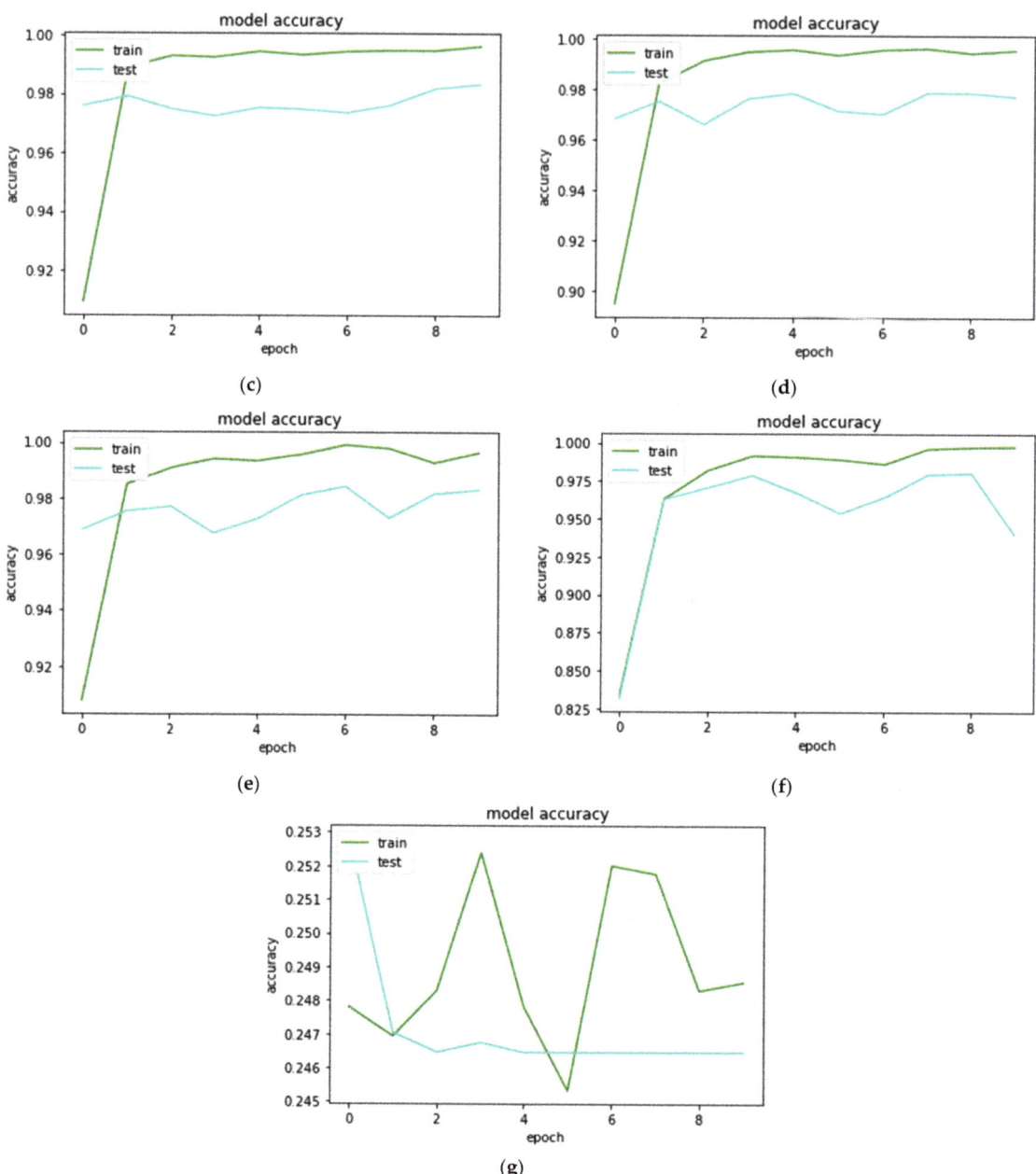

Figure 3. Training and validation accuracy curves of: (**a**) convolutional neural network, (**b**) DenseNet201, (**c**) EfficientNetB2, (**d**) EfficientNetB0, (**e**) InceptionV3, (**f**) ResNet152, and (**g**) VGG19 models, correspondingly, for the facemask coverage classification task.

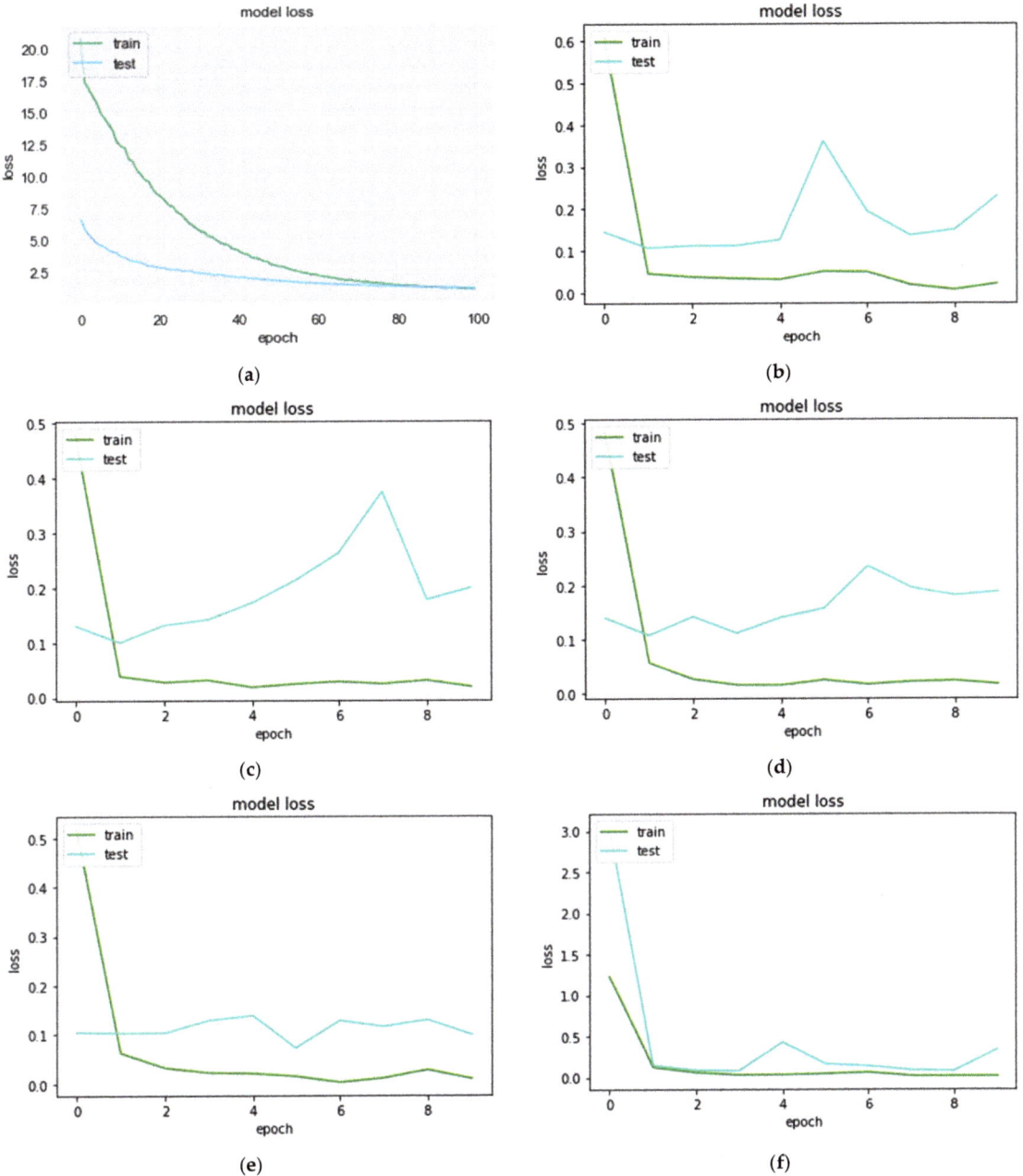

Figure 4. Cont.

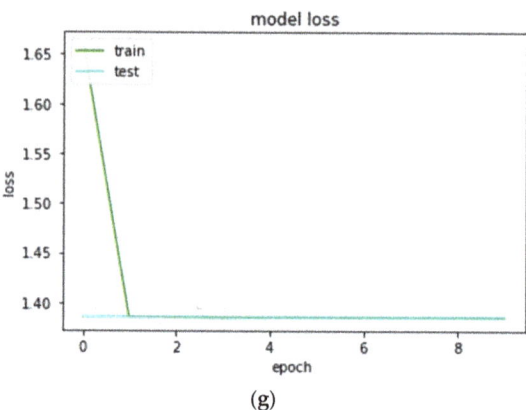

(g)

Figure 4. Training and validation loss curves of: (**a**) convolutional neural network, (**b**) DenseNet201, (**c**) EfficientNetB2, (**d**) EfficientNetB0, (**e**) InceptionV3, (**f**) ResNet152, and (**g**) VGG19 models, correspondingly, for the facemask coverage classification task.

Table 6. Comparative analyses of the proposed scheme with prior studies.

Study	Method	No. of Classes	Types of Detection	Result
[12]	MobileNetV2	2	mask/no mask	90.55%
[14]	MobileNet	2	mask/no mask	99.0%
[15]	Faster R-CNN	2	mask/no mask	73.0%
[16]	SSD and SSD-Mask algorithms	2	mask/no mask	86.3% and 88.2%
[17]	CNN and VGG16	2	mask/no mask	97.42% and 98.97%
[18]	MobileNet and OpenCV	2	mask/no mask	99.41%
[19]	SSD and MobileNetV2	2	mask/no mask	99.0%
[29]	ResNet50V2	2	mask/no mask	99.0%
[28]	VGG16	6	glasses/fit side/nose out/correct/bridge/no mask	83.4%
Proposed	InceptionV3	4	mouth-nose-chin covered/nose-chin covered/chin covered/no mask	98.40%

4. Conclusions

Humanity can be protected in a crisis such as the COVID-19 pandemic by properly wearing masks to minimize the virus transmission. Thus, ensuring the implementation of such rules requires widespread monitoring, but this can be achieved with help of intelligent systems and smart cameras. Therefore, this study proposed an intelligent facemask detection system. The proposed system is widened by analyzing facial features using classical machine learning classifiers and advanced pre-trained deep learning networks to predict whether a person is wearing a mask properly (fully), partially, substantially depleted, or not wearing one at all. The study investigated random forest (RF), support vector machine (SVM), convolutional neural network (CNN), and six CNN-based pre-trained networks (InceptionV3, EfficientNetB0, EfficientNetB2, DenseNet201, ResNet152, and VGG19). For this, 40,000 images were utilized to train and test these models. The dataset was split into training and test sets with 70/30 ratios. The experimental results revealed that VGG19 performed the worst, attaining an overall accuracy of 24.65% and F1-score of 24.60%, while InceptionV3 and EfficientNetB2 accomplished a remarkable performance by reaching an overall accuracy of 98.40% and 98.35%, and F1-scores of 98.30% and 98.40%, respectively. In the future, it is planned to investigate the performance of traditional machine learning classifiers on a given dataset when exploited along with computer vision and histogram analysis techniques.

Author Contributions: Conceptualization, J.R.; methodology, J.R. and S.W.; software, A.B.W., R.M.S. and A.Y.; validation, J.R., A.B.W., and A.Y.; formal analysis, J.R., S.W. and R.M.S.; investigation, J.R., S.W., R.M.S. and A.Y.; resources, J.R. and A.B.W.; data curation, J.R. and S.W.; writing—original draft preparation, J.R. and S.W.; writing—review and editing, J.R.; visualization, J.R., S.W., A.B.W., R.M.S. and A.Y.; supervision, J.R. All authors have read and agreed to the published version of the manuscript.

Funding: This research received no external funding.

Institutional Review Board Statement: Not applicable.

Informed Consent Statement: The dataset is publicly available, and no image was reproduced/published in this study from this dataset, and thus did not require informed consent. However, some external sample facial images of individuals (placed in this paper) were collected specifically for this study. Therefore, informed consent was obtained from all subjects involved in the study and written informed consent has been obtained from the individuals to publish this paper.

Data Availability Statement: This study did not generate any new datasets. The dataset used can be downloaded from a publicly available Kaggle repository [20].

Conflicts of Interest: The authors declare no conflict of interest.

References

1. Wang, C.; Horby, P.W.; Hayden, F.G.; Gao, G.F. A novel coronavirus outbreak of global health concern. *Lancet* **2020**, *395*, 470–473. [CrossRef]
2. Yadav, S. Deep Learning based Safe Social Distancing and Face Mask Detection in Public Areas for COVID-19 Safety Guidelines Adherence. *Int. J. Res. Appl. Sci. Eng. Technol.* **2020**, *8*, 1368–1375. [CrossRef]
3. Rasheed, J.; Jamil, A.; Hameed, A.A.; Al-Turjman, F.; Rasheed, A. COVID-19 in the Age of Artificial Intelligence: A Comprehensive Review. *Interdiscip. Sci. Comput. Life Sci.* **2021**, *13*, 153–175. [CrossRef] [PubMed]
4. Arora, D.; Garg, M.; Gupta, M. Diving deep in Deep Convolutional Neural Network. In Proceedings of the IEEE 2020 2nd International Conference on Advances in Computing, Communication Control and Networking, ICACCCN 2020, Greater Noida, India, 18–19 December 2020; pp. 749–751. [CrossRef]
5. Rasheed, J.; Waziry, S.; Alsubai, S.; Abu-Mahfouz, A.M. An Intelligent Gender Classification System in the Era of Pandemic Chaos with Veiled Faces. *Processes* **2022**, *10*, 1427. [CrossRef]
6. Rasheed, J.; Alimovski, E.; Rasheed, A.; Sirin, Y.; Jamil, A.; Yesiltepe, M. Effects of Glow Data Augmentation on Face Recognition System based on Deep Learning. In Proceedings of the 2020 International Congress on Human-Computer Interaction, Optimization and Robotic Applications (HORA), Ankara, Turkey, 26–28 June 2020; pp. 1–5. [CrossRef]
7. Albawi, S.; Mohammed, T.A.; Al-Zawi, S. Understanding of a convolutional neural network. In Proceedings of the 2017 International Conference on Engineering and Technology (ICET), Antalya, Turkey, 21–23 August 2017; pp. 1–6. [CrossRef]
8. Rasheed, J. Analyzing the Effect of Filtering and Feature-Extraction Techniques in a Machine Learning Model for Identification of Infectious Disease Using Radiography Imaging. *Symmetry* **2022**, *14*, 1398. [CrossRef]
9. Rasheed, J.; Shubair, R.M. Screening Lung Diseases Using Cascaded Feature Generation and Selection Strategies. *Healthcare* **2022**, *10*, 1313. [CrossRef] [PubMed]
10. Song, Z.; Nguyen, K.; Nguyen, T.; Cho, C.; Gao, J. Spartan Face Mask Detection and Facial Recognition System. *Healthcare* **2022**, *10*, 87. [CrossRef] [PubMed]
11. Suresh, K.; Palangappa, M.; Bhuvan, S. Face Mask Detection by using Optimistic Convolutional Neural Network. In Proceedings of the 6th International Conference on Inventive Computation Technologies, ICICT 2021, Coimbatore, India, 20–22 January 2021; pp. 1084–1089. [CrossRef]
12. Srinivasan, S.; Singh, R.R.; Biradar, R.R.; Revathi, S. COVID-19 monitoring system using social distancing and face mask detection on surveillance video datasets. In Proceedings of the 2021 International Conference on Emerging Smart Computing and Informatics, ESCI 2021, Pune, India, 5–7 March 2021; pp. 449–455. [CrossRef]
13. Susanto, S.; Putra, F.A.; Analia, R.; Suciningtyas, I.K.L.N. The face mask detection for preventing the spread of COVID-19 at politeknik negeri batam. In Proceedings of the ICAE 2020—3rd International Conference on Applied Engineering, Batam, Indonesia, 7–8 October 2020; pp. 1–5. [CrossRef]
14. Venkateswarlu, I.B.; Kakarla, J.; Prakash, S. Face mask detection using MobileNet and global pooling block. In Proceedings of the 4th IEEE Conference on Information and Communication Technology, CICT 2020, Chennai, India, 3–5 December 2020; pp. 1–4. [CrossRef]

15. Siradjuddin, I.A.; Muntasa, A. Faster Region-based Convolutional Neural Network for Mask Face Detection. In Proceedings of the 2021 5th International Conference on Informatics and Computational Sciences (ICICoS), Semarang, Indonesia, 24–25 November 2021; pp. 282–286. [CrossRef]
16. Xu, M.; Wang, H.; Yang, S.; Li, R. Mask wearing detection method based on SSD-Mask algorithm. In Proceedings of the 2020 International Conference on Computer Science and Management Technology, ICCSMT 2020, Shanghai, China, 20–22 November 2020; pp. 138–143. [CrossRef]
17. Negi, A.; Kumar, K.; Chauhan, P.; Rajput, R.S. Deep neural architecture for face mask detection on simulated masked face dataset against covid-19 pandemic. In Proceedings of the IEEE 2021 International Conference on Computing, Communication, and Intelligent Systems, ICCCIS 2021, Greater Noida, India, 19–20 February 2021; pp. 595–600. [CrossRef]
18. Nujella, R.B.P.; Sahu, S.; Prakash, S. Face-Mask Detection to Control the COVID-19 Spread Employing Deep Learning Approach. In Proceedings of the 2021 5th International Conference on Information Systems and Computer Networks (ISCON), Mathura, India, 22–23 October 2021; pp. 1–3. [CrossRef]
19. Gowri, S. A Real-Time Face Mask Detection Using SSD and MobileNetV2. In Proceedings of the 2021 4th International Conference on Computing and Communications Technologies (ICCCT), Chennai, India, 16–17 December 2021; pp. 144–148. [CrossRef]
20. Roman, K. 500 GB of Images with People Wearing Masks. Part 3 | Kaggle 2021. Available online: https://www.kaggle.com/datasets/tapakah68/medical-masks-p3 (accessed on 30 March 2022).
21. Sarica, A.; Cerasa, A.; Quattrone, A. Random Forest Algorithm for the Classification of Neuroimaging Data in Alzheimer's Disease: A Systematic Review. *Front. Aging Neurosci.* **2017**, *9*, 329. [CrossRef] [PubMed]
22. Thai, L.H.; Hai, T.S.; Thuy, N.T. Image Classification using Support Vector Machine and Artificial Neural Network. *Int. J. Inf. Technol. Comput. Sci.* **2012**, *4*, 32–38. [CrossRef]
23. Szegedy, C.; Vanhoucke, V.; Ioffe, S.; Shlens, J.; Wojna, Z. Rethinking the Inception Architecture for Computer Vision. In Proceedings of the IEEE Computer Society Conference on Computer Vision and Pattern Recognition, Las Vegas, NV, USA, 27–30 June 2016; pp. 2818–2826. [CrossRef]
24. Tan, M.; Le, Q.V. EfficientNet: Rethinking model scaling for convolutional neural networks. In Proceedings of the 36th International Conference on Machine Learning, ICML 2019, Long Beach, CA, USA, 9–15 June 2019; Volume 2019, pp. 10691–10700.
25. Huang, G.; Liu, Z.; Van Der Maaten, L.; Weinberger, K.Q. Densely connected convolutional networks. In Proceedings of the 30th IEEE Conference on Computer Vision and Pattern Recognition, CVPR 2017, Honolulu, HI, USA, 21–26 July 2017; Volume 2017, pp. 2261–2269. [CrossRef]
26. He, K.; Zhang, X.; Ren, S.; Sun, J. Deep residual learning for image recognition. In Proceedings of the IEEE Computer Society Conference on Computer Vision and Pattern Recognition, Las Vegas, NV, USA, 27–30 June 2016; Volume 2016, pp. 770–778. [CrossRef]
27. Simonyan, K.; Zisserman, A. Very deep convolutional networks for large-scale image recognition. In Proceedings of the 3rd International Conference on Learning Representations, ICLR 2015—Conference Track Proceedings, Online, 10 April 2015; pp. 1–14.
28. Tomás, J.; Rego, A.; Viciano-Tudela, S.; Lloret, J. Incorrect Facemask-Wearing Detection Using Convolutional Neural Networks with Transfer Learning. *Healthcare* **2021**, *9*, 1050. [CrossRef]
29. Sertic, P.; Alahmar, A.; Akilan, T.; Javorac, M.; Gupta, Y. Intelligent Real-Time Face-Mask Detection System with Hardware Acceleration for COVID-19 Mitigation. *Healthcare* **2022**, *10*, 873. [CrossRef]

Article

Lean Optimization Techniques for Improvement of Production Flows and Logistics Management: The Case Study of a Fruits Distribution Center

Ana P. Proença [1], Pedro Dinis Gaspar [1,2,*] and Tânia M. Lima [1,2]

[1] Department of Electromechanical Engineering, University of Beira Interior, Rua Marquês de D'Ávila e Bolama, 6201-001 Covilhã, Portugal; ana.proenca@ubi.pt (A.P.P.); tmlima@ubi.pt (T.M.L.)
[2] C-MAST—Center for Mechanical and Aerospace Science and Technologies, Rua Marquês de D'Ávila e Bolama, 6201-001 Covilhã, Portugal
* Correspondence: dinis@ubi.pt

Citation: Proença, A.P.; Gaspar, P.D.; Lima, T.M. Lean Optimization Techniques for Improvement of Production Flows and Logistics Management: The Case Study of a Fruits Distribution Center. *Processes* **2022**, *10*, 1384. https://doi.org/10.3390/pr10071384

Academic Editor: Xiong Luo

Received: 1 July 2022
Accepted: 13 July 2022
Published: 15 July 2022

Publisher's Note: MDPI stays neutral with regard to jurisdictional claims in published maps and institutional affiliations.

Copyright: © 2022 by the authors. Licensee MDPI, Basel, Switzerland. This article is an open access article distributed under the terms and conditions of the Creative Commons Attribution (CC BY) license (https://creativecommons.org/licenses/by/4.0/).

Abstract: The organizations of horticultural producers and, particularly, those that deal with extremely perishable endogenous fruits, such as peaches and cherries, have a greater need to optimize production flows and processes. A particularity of the horticultural industry is the short shelf life of raw materials and the seasonality of products. In this paper, optimization techniques are used to improve the production flows and the management of cold storage and distribution in a fruit central. The application of Lean tools allowed reducing the cycle time by 4.37 min and the lead time by 7.10 min of the whole process, i.e., a reduction of 35.5% and 10.6% of the cycle time and lead time, respectively, excluding the cold conservation operation. The study shows that it is possible to reduce, or even eliminate, waste throughout the process, reduce unnecessary movement, adapt the layout, maximize workspace, and level stocks, as well as greater supplier involvement in a continuous improvement approach. This approach can be outlined as a good practice for the optimization of productive flows and management logistics that may benefit productivity, energy efficiency, human resources distribution, food quality, and reduce food waste.

Keywords: agribusiness; optimization of the production flow; cold storage management; endogenous fruits; peaches; lean tools; 5S; Kaizen; Value Stream Mapping

1. Introduction

Over the past ten years, the approach to business management around the world has undergone a profound change. To combat the politico-economically unstable environment, organizations have sought to find new ways and means of responding based on knowledge, market research, and study, as well as creating and adapting to new work methodologies through metrics-driven management [1,2]. Organizational survival depends on the construction and integration of knowledge promoting adaptation and stimulation of the environment, as well as change through the firm's knowledge and practices [3].

The management of a firm requires access to information and efficient data management to monitor activities and evaluate the performance of the business processes. This analysis can be present in financial operations, customers, and products to obtain an analytical view of problems and opportunities [4].

Organizations are constantly looking for new ways to improve their performance, product quality and competitiveness [5]. In the agricultural sector, many innovations occur in the production process through improved production techniques. However, these can happen at any stage of the product and/or in certain processes in the supply chain [6]. In the last two decades, the development is quite remarkable. Although there is uneven development between different countries, which is reflected in differences in productivity between farms, it remains an issue that is grounded through structural adjustment [7].

Innovation can be interpreted as an opportunity for agricultural producers to do more and better with fewer resources. Better management of available resources and anticipation of problems can be reflected in increased productivity and consequently reduced costs. It also ensures long-term viability and reduces the negative environmental impacts of production, such as pollutants and waste. The existence of healthy, ecological, and sustainable food systems are fundamental principles to achieving the development of the chains [8].

Supply chain analysis provides a single, broad view of the entire supply chain, reveals opportunities for cost savings, and stimulates revenue growth. As well as increasing production efficiency and optimizing delivery time [9]. The competitive marketplace requires organizations to design reliable products that can be produced efficiently and quickly. In this quest to maximize the value and quality of the product that is offered to the customer, as well as to reduce lead times and costs, the Lean philosophy is an efficient alternative for continuous improvement [10]. Lean helps convert business inputs, such as people, machines, and raw materials, through value-adding processes. It can achieve the right results most effectively and efficiently by creating value for customers with fewer resources [3]. This philosophy seeks to simplify processes, eliminate waste, and use resources more efficiently in accomplishing tasks, as well as involving employees throughout the process, by creating value for customers and therefore value for the company [11].

Time is a key component that organizations can neither discard nor devalue. The expression "time is money" has gained more prominence these days, and in the industry, it isn't different. Time is precious and how organizations "spend" their time can determine their future success. It is up to top management to understand where time is spent and which activities may or may not add value, this way it will be possible to identify opportunities for improvement, saving time and consequently money [12].

Lean thinking can significantly improve many of the problems that agricultural organizations face daily such as long working hours, high staff turnover, repetition problems, breakdowns, waste, safety, and high costs are some of the factors usually identified.

This paper aims to learn how to identify waste, create employed and motivated teams, work more efficiently and productively, and solve problems quickly to save time and reduce costs, thus improving business performance and farm performance. The main objective is to support and boost the development of small organizations located in the interior of the country. These organizations are often conditioned and limited by agricultural policy issues, such as the lack of financial incentives (subsidies) from the State and European Funds, an aging population, and lack of unemployment, leading to very pronounced desertification [13]. This study will be carried out through the analysis of several studies carried out in the Agribusiness industry.

This article is organized into 5 chapters. Section 1 presents the contextualization of the work developed, the motivations for its realization, the defined objectives, the methodology used, and finally, the structure of this article is explained. In the Section 2, a theoretical framework of the Lean philosophy is presented, which includes its historical evolution, the definition of waste, its principles, and the main techniques, and tools. In the same chapter, examples of practical applications of Lean tools in Agribusiness are described. In Section 3, the company of the case study is presented and characterized, as well as the description of the entire production process and layout. The Section 4 aims to identify the Lean principles applied in the company, an initial survey is presented in which waste is identified and the respective proposals for improvement with the implementation of the 5S and Kaizen tools. In the final phase, the Value Stream Mapping tool is applied, which allowed the identification of the waste of resources along the production flow, a proposal for an adjustment to the current layout, as well as the definition of a new layout, and the reorganization of the cold rooms. In the Section 5, the conclusions and limitations of the study are presented, and proposals for future improvements that could be useful to the company in which the case study was carried out could be replicated in other companies in the same sector.

2. Literature Review

In this chapter a theoretical framework of the Lean philosophy is presented, including historical evolution, the definition of waste, principles, the main techniques, and tools.

In this paper, inductive and explanatory research is applied, focusing on the quantitative perspective. Inductive research aims to infer theoretical concepts and patterns from observed data, seeking to link ideas and identified factors to understand the causes and effects of phenomenon determination [14]. The literature review was conducted by searching and analyzing case studies published in scientific articles, books, scientific conference proceedings, and publications that fall within the scope of the research. At this stage, a thorough analysis was carried out to understand the results already produced and the type of instruments used to obtain them. The databases to be used to collect these documents were: Scopus, Web of Science, Science Direct, and IEEE Xplore. Based on the information collected and analyzed, a reflection was made on the optimization tools that can be applied to the case study.

2.1. The Origins and Evolution of Lean Management

The scientific organization of work led to the emergence of mass production. The standard times and the rationalization, standardization, and decomposition of work into tasks, in industrial terms, had Frederick Taylor as a great proponent of the scientific organization of work. Taylor emphasized the importance of the standardization of work, also known as Taylorism [15].

After the First World War large companies were created, mainly in the automobile industry, for example, the Ford Motor Company founded by Henry Ford. Ford chose to rationalize and control the assembly process and create a continuous flow throughout the whole process [16].

In parallel, Sakichi Toyoda, founder of Toyota Industries Corporation Ltd. developed the automatic loom, which was able to stop automatically when a thread breakage was detected. This led to the creation of the *Jidoka* concept, also defined as intelligent automation, which allowed the operator to control more machines during the manufacturing process [17].

In the 1980s Taiichi Ohno in collaboration with Shigeo Shingo developed the Toyota Production System (TPS). TPS is derived from the production process in the Japanese automobile industry, which aimed to improve and control production that was previously based on mass production. It was the result of innovative thinking forced to find a solution to resource scarcity and financial turbulence [18]. Lean began to gain greater prominence with the publication of the article "Triumph of the Lean Production System" in 1988 [19]. In 1990, the book "Machine That Changed the World" was published which revolutionized the perceptions of many scientists and professionals about the production process [20]. This book essentially introduced the term Lean to the world by describing Lean production [18]. Since then, the Lean philosophy has become a new management approach that has proven to be effective for the performance and management of organizations, both from a qualitative (e.g., employee satisfaction, commitment, safe and harmonious work environment) and quantitative point of view (e.g., improvements in processing, cycles and setup times, reduction of queues and defects) [21].

Despite the numerous definitions of Lean, it is important to understand that it is a business strategy and not a casual practice. Womack and Jones, in 1996, published a second book "Lean Thinking: Banish Waste and Create Wealth in your Corporation" [22], in which they presented the Lean philosophy based on five principles, seven wastes, and a set of extremely simple and powerful tools. The five fundamental principles of the Lean philosophy are [23]:

1. **Define value**—Identify how much the customer is willing to pay;
2. **Identify and map the value stream**—Identify the activities that create value and those that do not add value to the end customer;

3. **Create a flow that eliminates waste**—Ensure that what is flowing from the next steps occurs without interruptions or delays;
4. **Pull System**—Match customer demand and set up a downstream production system;
5. **Pursue perfection**—The vision to be achieved by using the previously listed principles together.

However, the five principles presented above have some shortcomings: only the customer value chain is considered (in fact, in an organization there are several value chains: one for each stakeholder), so the challenge is not in the creation of value, but in the creation of value [24]. Another constraint is that these tend to lead organizations into endless cycles of waste reduction ignoring the crucial activity of creating value through product, service, and process innovation. In this sense, two more principles were created with the aim of guiding the organization on the right path to excellence and extraordinary performance, they are: "Know the stakeholder" and "Always innovate" [24].

For Ohno [25], the Lean philosophy consists in improving processes through the removal of *Muda* (waste, e.g., everything that does not add value is waste and as such should be eliminated), *Muri* (excess or insufficiency, the organization should only do what is necessary when requested, based on a Pull system) and *Mura* (irregularity, it is eliminated by the standardization of work) in production [26]. The main objective is to achieve high-quality standards at low cost (reducing variability), with short lead times, eliminating waste of time and activities (*Muda* and *Muri*) [27].

Thus, being the whole basis of the Lean philosophy the elimination of waste, or elimination of *Muda*, it is also important to know how to identify them in the processes under study to achieve total quality [28]. Ohno [25] defined seven sources of waste as follows [16]:

1. **Overproduction**—More quantities are manufactured than are needed and ordered by customers. Unsold products may have to be discarded, which becomes expensive;
2. **Waiting time**—Usually caused by material waiting or shortages, idle or insufficient equipment capacity, and inefficient production order instruction;
3. **Stocks**—When stock is excessive, there is product degradation or damaged material, longer lead times in the production process, and high inventory holding costs can be associated;
4. **Movements**—Include any unnecessary movement of people, tools, or machines;
5. **Transport**—All unnecessary movements of resources that do not add value to the product are considered;
6. **Defective products**—This happens when the product does not comply with the minimum quality requirements. The definition of waste includes defects or quality problems. It also includes inspection costs, response to customer complaints, and rework. Human errors create defects;
7. **Over-processing**—This is related to excessive steps in manufacturing, e.g., doing more than is essential. Using more precision equipment than necessary or using components with capacity beyond what is needed can lead to exponential wear and tear of equipment and consequently a reduction in its useful life.

Initially, seven *Muda* were considered, e.g., seven possible sources of waste, but with the evolution of the Lean philosophy and knowledge of the production system, there are now eight, defined as the under-utilization of labor. This represents the existence of qualified labor that is not performing functions that correspond to their capacities, represents a waste of knowledge, but also a waste of capacity and creativity, since due to their qualifications, they could represent added value to the company, even with ideas for new methods of eliminating waste [27].

2.2. Lean Tools

This philosophy was not created overnight, nor was it developed by just Toyota. Lean has become internationally known and recognized, and has gradually developed, both conceptually and in fields of application other than production [28].

One of the ways to reduce the waste generated by organizations, and thus achieve greater competitiveness, productivity, and optimization of results is through the implementation of Lean philosophy and tools [29].

The diversity of Lean tools proves to have answers for the most diverse challenges, and companies are aware of this, adopting more and more methodologies and processes that aim to progressively reduce waste and adapt their production paradigm to what the market demands. It is up to each top management to survey the most important tools, and understand what they are, how they work, and how they can help the organization. Their evaluation and implementation can be key steps to success [29].

In this subchapter, some of the numerous Lean tools available are presented. Although there is a great variety and diversity of Lean tools, this article will focus on 5S methodology, Value Stream Mapping (VSM), and Kaizen.

2.2.1. 5S Methodology

5S is a Japanese organization methodology developed by Kaoru Ishikawa in 1950 [30]. This tool is governed by five distinct steps to organize, keep the place clean, and in this way increase productivity and standardize how tasks are executed [31].

It can be considered a systematic process, or a set of practical tools, that allows the organization of work areas, to eliminate or reduce waste in operations, improve hygiene, safety, ergonomics, and environmental conditions of workstations or areas of common use [32,33]. The main objective is to change attitudes and behaviors, eliminate waste and ensure competitiveness [33]. The name 5S has as acronyms five words, in Japanese, listed below:

- *Seiri* (Sense of use)—Is it useful?
  Identify objects, materials, and equipment at the workplace; List and separate by type, what is useful from what is useless; Mark what is not necessary; Eliminate or remove objects that are not necessary;
- *Seiton* (Sense of organization)—Is it easy to find? Define a place for each tool; Verify that each tool is in its place; Place the most frequently used tools at hand; Place identification labels (visual aids) on the tools and the respective place where they should be kept;
- *Seiso* (Sense of cleanliness)—Is the work area clean? Divide the workstation and assign a zone to each team member; Clean each zone of the workstation, as well as the surrounding area;
- *Seiketsu* (Sense of standardization)—What is the standard? Define a general standard/rule of tidiness and cleanliness for the workstation; Identify the visual aids and procedures, tidiness and cleanliness standards that work; Standardize throughout the factory the same type of equipment and workstations to ensure that the previous three steps are fulfilled;
- *Shitsuke* (Sense of discipline)—Is the standard respected? Practice the principles of organization, systematization, and cleanliness; Eliminate variability, e.g., always do it right the first time; Establish procedures for visual control (tidiness and cleanliness); Verify that actions and inspections are being carried out correctly; Develop a system of checklists and visual aids (colors, lights, direction indicators or charts).

An increasing number of companies are adding a sixth "S". The "S" of Safety is not independent, nor can it be dissociated from the previous ones, or any activity performed. For Jiménez et al. [34], this is a mandatory inclusion in the 5S method, not only because it will reduce and even eliminate the different risks that may exist in a workplace, but it also ensures that the work area complies with regulations, both regarding safety issues on the use of machinery and equipment and health. The main objective of 6S is to eliminate waste by controlling *Muda*, *Muri*, and *Mura*. This new methodology, 6S, forms the necessary and ideal basis for implementing a significant number of other Lean tools [34].

2.2.2. Value Stream Mapping (VSM)

Value Stream Management (VSM) is a simple, yet powerful and logical tool that allows an organization to identify wasted resources along the production stream [35]. It allows to analyze the current state and make a forecast for the future state. The goal of the current state is to map the existing state and find possible ways to implement Lean tools, reduce waste, align production, and demand, and develop action plans to arrive at a future state map [36].

The value stream is the set of value-added and non-value-added activities required to effectively transmit information since it allows the mapping of the processes involved, relates the processes, and allows the identification of which activities add value and which do not [30].

To simplify reading and interpretation, it presents a simple legend and basic icons (equipment, group work, departments or suppliers, and customers). In the definition and creation of these maps should be perceptible three sections [37].

In the first section, the process or production flow is represented, in which all tasks and sub-tasks are identified. The process flow is drawn from left to right and by reading it is possible to observe the main operations and secondary steps of the process, as well as tasks performed in parallel [38].

The communication section is included all kinds of information and communication, in-formal or formal, about the process and data transmission [38]. In this case, information can be read in both directions. In Lean, the information flow is as important as the material flow [30].

The time window section provides a visual representation of the timeline or timeline of the value stream. The upper part of the time scale represents the average time it takes for a component to move on to the next task (Production Lead Time). The lower part, on the other hand, represents the average time that each component takes to be worked on (Value Add Time) [38].

According to Dias et al. [39], the spaghetti diagram can be a complementary tool to the VSM. Similar to VSM, the spaghetti diagram allows the visualization of activities that do not generate value. This diagram is the visual representation that demonstrates the incidence of movements, number of movements, overlapping and crossing movements, and the features that happens due to the dispersion of all machines, which leads to the registration of movements that are often unnecessary [30].

2.2.3. Kaizen

Kaizen, meaning continuous improvement, is divided by the Japanese terms' *kai* and *zen* meaning change and improvement, respectively. Kaizen uses critical and analytical thinking to find solutions [29]. According to Otsuka and Ben-Mazw [40], Kaizen can be defined as activities that bridge the gap between the current state and the ideal state by solving problems or accomplishing tasks at an operational level. Thus, to be successful, an organization practicing kaizen must understand the current state, identify the ideal state, and have the will to bridge the gap between the two states [40]. Kaizen itself is about making small improvements that, as a whole, represent a big change, in a Leaner sense [30].

2.3. Examples of Practical Applications

The agri-food industry is of particular interest since it tries to deal simultaneously with a set of peculiar characteristics, often unseen in other industries (for example, the short shelf life of raw materials or seasonality of products) [41]. According to Lopes et al. [42], despite numerous successful applications in various sectors, the particular characteristics of the food sector may have led to resistance to changing companies' practices and the implementation of new management philosophies. For Pearce et al. [43], more recent studies highlight that rising food prices and increasingly limited agricultural production capacity are contributing to the renewal of processes in primary production, with an emphasis on sustainability. They also highlight the urgency in eliminating waste that is strongly aligned with the agricultural need to reduce operational waste, whether in the form of inefficient labor used, food waste, water, or energy [43]. Solano et al. [44], defend that the current conditions of agricultural production increasingly require an improvement of techniques and tools to improve the management quality and productivity in agriculture. This will allow for increased yields and work efficiency, and simultaneously minimize costs, waste, and balanced management of natural resources.

Studies such as Lehtinen and Torkko [45], Jiménez et al. [46], Dora et al. [47], Wesana et al. [48], Hmidach et al. [49], Rojas-Benites et al. [50], Somasundaram et al. [31], Farissi et al. [51], and Ali [52] proved that Lean practices are significantly beneficial through improvements such as: service and product value creation, production efficiency, increased employee involvement, team spirit, coordination between production and maintenance, and waste reduction, production cost reduction, optimization of storage area and stock control, and reduction of setup and lead time.

Ashraf et al. [53] through the implementation of 5S in a food and beverage industry (waters, juices, and lollipops) obtained a reduction in rejected products (19.4% to 13.3%) and an increase in productivity by 38.65%. Rojas-Benites et al. [50] tried to fight overproduction and immobilized products, and excess raw material. Using tools such as 5S and Kaizen, it was possible to reduce the 15.78% of immobilized stocks, which represented 8% of the annual turnover and to reduce waste by 9.56%. Jiménez et al. [46], through VSM, 5S, and Kaizen, achieved a reduction in stocks, a more adequate selection of relevant information, a 16% reduction in waste, and a decrease in lead time to 56%.

Considering the objective of this article, which consists of the implementation of Lean principles in an organization producing fruit to reduce waste, increase production efficiency, improve overall business performance, increase competitiveness and adaptability to demand, the following tools were selected: 5S, VSM and *Kaizen*. The selection criteria were the studies mentioned, the characteristics, limitations of the tools, and the respective constraints of the organization (size, human/financial resources).

3. Case Study

This study was conducted in a fruits distribution center. The organization was founded in 1982 by 25 producer members and markets fruit intending to promote Beira Interior and help small producers in the area to sell their products. Currently, 23 member producers and 18 non-member producers are still associated. It is a cooperative of certified producers that commercializes mostly peaches, apples, and pears of high quality from the Cova da Beira region, Portugal, an area of long tradition and great aptitude for fruit growing. It has a production area of about 160 hectares of orchards distributed by: 45 hectares of pear and apple and 110 hectares of stone fruits, of which peach. It also has cultivation areas located in the Cova da Beira region, in the counties of Fundão, Covilhã, Belmonte, Guarda and Sabugal. Other studies trying to improve productivity and sustainability, maintain the fruit quality, and characterize and reduce energy consumption were already developed in this distribution center [54–56].

Layout and Production Flow

An analysis of the production system was performed by representing the movements on the floor plan of the company's facilities. In the plant of the analyzed production lines were drawn that represent the movements during a certain period.

Figure 1 is represented the spaghetti diagram of the production flow from the moment of entry of the raw material in Warehouse 1 until the time of shipment.

Unnecessary movements were identified, as well as overlaps of different products and the crossing of raw material with the finished product. As illustrated in the figure, it is possible to observe that when the organization works with more than one type of fruit (for example, peach and apple) there is an overlap of several movements.

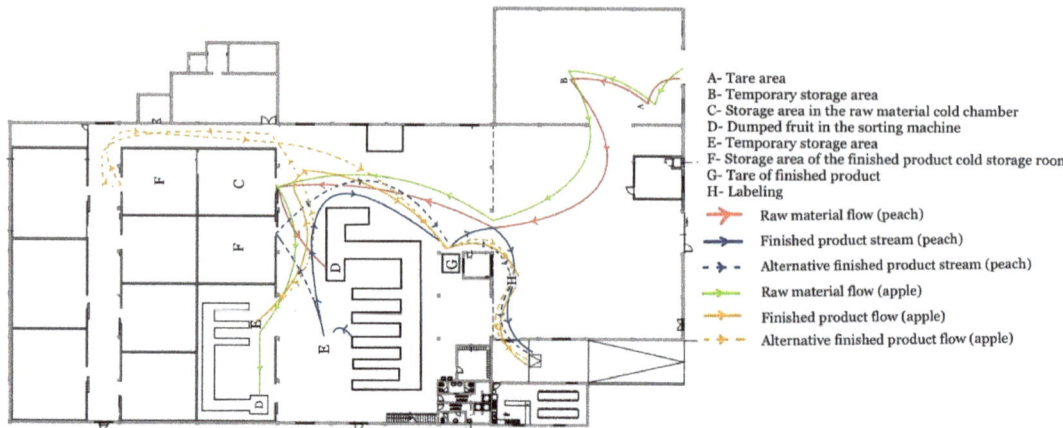

Figure 1. Spaghetti diagram of the production flow.

The whole process starts in the production field. Each producer is responsible for picking, collecting, and delivering the fruit to the premises. As a first step, the producer makes the delivery to Warehouse 1. In the area indicated A, the reception and control of technical requirements (e.g., weight, quantity, quality, and lot) is performed. Meanwhile, six random fruit samples are taken for quality control (penetrometer, °Brix, rottenness, stalk or stone condition, and taste). Afterward, the pallet boxes are temporarily stored in zone B until the person in charge has the availability to transport them to the cooling chambers located in Warehouse 2.

In Warehouse 2, considered the core of the whole production section, the fruit is stored in a controlled atmosphere in the cold chamber for raw materials (C) where the temperature varies between 1.6 °C and 7 °C, and which tries to respect the FIFO criterion (First In, First Out).

The pallet boxes are then dumped into the sorting machine (D) where the fruit is brushed and classified according to the caliber. The fruit falls along the lines and is sorted for packing into boxes. The boxes are placed on pallets in zone E, according to size, and transported to D to be weighed. When only one type of caliber is ordered, the remaining pallets are directed to chamber F, for finished products.

Finally, the pallets are again sent to Warehouse 1 where they are labeled and shipped (H). The expedition is carried out upon the arrival of the transport vehicles in appropriate conditions.

Warehouse 3 is only used when there is a larger production flow or when the organization works with different types of fruit, which need different storage conditions. In this case, the cold rooms are switched on and when there is more than one quality of fruit to be packed, the smaller sorting machine, located in warehouse 2, is used. This situation is quite recurrent in times of peak production. However, when there is only a small quantity of the other fruit being worked on, it is stored together with the remaining fruit in the same chamber F.

4. Discussion

4.1. Application of the Lean Philosophy

Implementing the Lean Philosophy allows to introduce systems and routines, save time, and provide a calm environment among employees. Lean tools involve all employees positively, through change, and in creating value for the customer. At the same time, it means that there will be fewer errors and more efficient and methodical workflows [2].

As mentioned before, Lean is based on five basic principles that are considered key elements of the Lean philosophy. In this subchapter, some of the principles will be presented and explained with application in the practical case.

4.1.1. Define Value

This principle aims to identify how much the customer is willing to pay. It is important to prioritize and identify where value exists. In this case study, value is created for the customer, since the customer can order according to the desired caliber and the variety of fruit required. The company offers a wide range of products from different producers.

4.1.2. Identify and Create a Flow That Eliminates Waste

The activities that create value and those that do not add value for the end customer should be identified. What does not add value for the customer may be considered waste and should be reduced or eliminated. An alternative used by the company is to sell fruits that do not comply with the stipulated quality requirements. This fruit is sent to partners who are responsible for reusing the fruit by transforming it into jams and juices. The concept of adding value can also be defined as a strategy to reduce losses.

It is also important to define a continuous flow, without interruptions to speed up production and reduce the waiting time between activities. In this case, sometimes there are long waiting times in the transportation of the raw material from reception to storage, as well as when the trucks arrive to ship the product. This long period can influence and accelerate the deterioration process of the fruit since it is at room temperature.

4.1.3. Pull System

Efficient stock management must match customer demand and define a downstream production system, e.g., produce only what is required in order not to create stocks. A particularity of the agri-food industry is the short shelf life of raw materials and seasonality of products. In the organization, one of the biggest difficulties faced is the control of raw material delivery by the producers. The producers deliver the raw material according to the maturation of the fruit, there is never an order to the supplier according to the needs of the organization. Given this limitation, at times of increased production flow, there may be an increase in stocks and difficulties in the organization of the cold storage rooms.

4.2. Improvement Proposals

In this subsection, the improvement proposals are presented with the practical application of the selected tools, Value Stream Mapping (VSM), 5S, and *Kaizen*. The main objective is the application of improvement proposals according to 5S, allied to *Kaizen*, and the identification of waste of resources along with the production flow (VSM) to organize the workplace and thus maximize efficiency and productivity.

4.2.1. Implementation of 5S and Kaizen

The 5S methodology can be extended to most work situations in a short period due to its simplicity. From raw material input to the final stage of shipping, activities were recorded and photographed to evaluate all processes. Each activity was evaluated separately to identify anomalies in production, such as tool movements, pallet arrangement, movements and changes of workers, changeover times, time spent on each activity, and use of work areas.

Figure 2 shows the layout of warehouses 1 and 2 with the respective constraints and bottlenecks identified. In summary, many of the problems mentioned are related to poor organization, layout not product-oriented, and unnecessary movements due to the dispersion of equipment.

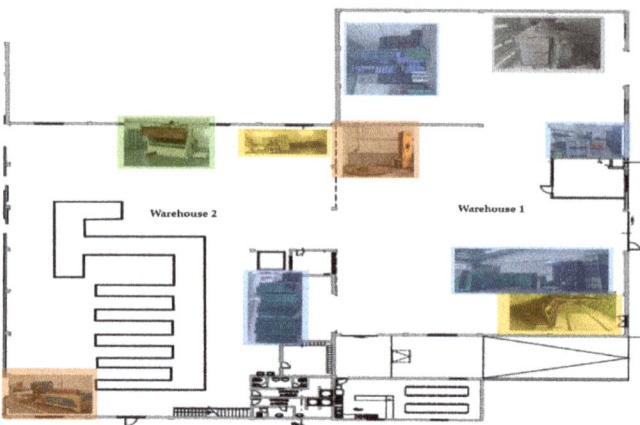

Figure 2. Distribution of machines in the facility.

As mentioned above, upon receipt in Warehouse 1, the pallet boxes with fruit are stored for an indefinite time at room temperature until they are transported to the cold storage rooms. In this same area several pallets, pallet boxes, and empty boxes of different sizes are also stored represented blue in the figure. If this material were removed, it would free up space and allow for a better organization at the time of unloading.

A similar situation occurs in the place where the shelf-life verification procedure is performed next to the small store. As can be seen in the figure, represented in blue, there are boxes and pallet boxes with fruit accumulated. Throughout the warehouse, there are more dispersed boxes that are often obstructing the movement of raw material, people, and stackers.

In this same reception area is located industrial washing equipment for plastic boxes, represented in gray. The final procedure of sanitizing the boxes is performed after the boxes return from customers. A proposal for improvement would be to move this equipment to another area and thus free up even more space.

There is also a large industrial washing machine for boxes (yellow) that is inactively located in the warehouse 1. The same happens with a sorting machine located in warehouse 2 that is no longer used (yellow). In addition to the equipment already mentioned, two packaging machines are no longer used. In the pictures, there is an automatic pallet packaging equipment (warehouse 1, orange) and a tubular net bag packaging machine (warehouse 2, orange). One suggestion would be to sell these machines, to maximize the storage and circulation space, as well as recover part of the money spent on the purchase and maintenance of this equipment.

In the main warehouse (2) there is a Hydrocooler for the fruit (green). Although the hydro-refrigeration is one of the most effective means of refrigeration, not only because it allows to maximize the shelf life, but also to guarantee the freshness of the fruit, the equipment in question is not used. This is refrigeration equipment with a closed circuit of cold water that allows decreasing the temperature of the pulp, eliminating the biological load, as well as to remove dust or garbage. This equipment was poorly structured, as it damages the fruit when the water cascades down. One of the proposals for improvement is to sell this equipment and buy one that is adequate or adapted to the needs.

Another situation that can be improved is the maintenance of the cleanliness of the workplace since there was an accumulation of leaves, dust, and peach hair near the calibration machine, as well as some pieces of fruit scattered around the factory floor. A proposal for improvement would be the creation of a daily hygiene control checklist. In this list, one or more employees responsible for cleaning the grading machine at the end of the day would be defined. This would be a preventive measure that would allow preventing the development of pests and/or microbiological niches, as well as prevent product contamination. It would also make it easier to clean, sanitize and preserve hygienic conditions during and after the maintenance of the grading machine.

The organization has track marks on the floor, but some are already barely visible due to wear and tear. Since there is a constant circulation of forklifts, the safety signs for the circulation routes must be visible, as well as the warning signs for forklift circulation. Thus, allowing the circulation and movement of workers under safe conditions. It is important to carry out continuous maintenance of the road markings. A proposal for improvement is the biannual maintenance and placement of signage.

As mentioned before, the company has several cold rooms, however only two are used, one for raw material and the other for the finished product. One of the recurring situations is the accumulation of stock at the time of seasonal peaks in the cold storage chamber for the raw material, which can reach up to 25 pallet boxes per day. The organization has no control over which days and quantities will be made available by the suppliers. Currently, the only person responsible for the storage creates lines of pallet boxes according to the day of entry and the producer. On days when the amount of fruit received is high, the person in charge distributes the pallet boxes by the cold chamber without any criterion. Despite trying to respect the FIFO criterion, many times it becomes complicated to respect and manage the organization of the cold chamber due to the great affluence of raw material. In extreme situations, it is necessary to mix the pallet boxes with the finished product. This situation occurs not only in this sector. Incorrect logistics practices using cold chambers are transversal to all the agri-food sector [57,58].

Another recurring situation is when, for example, the customer orders only pallets of one type of caliber, the other calibers must be stored in the cold stores until they are ordered by a future customer. Due to the unpredictability of deliveries, one improvement proposal is to connect one more of the available chambers. This would allow maximizing the working space and easier control and respect of the FIFO criterion. Another improvement proposal can be applied in both chambers, through the creation of floor markings. In the raw material chambers, it is suggested the separation of a variety of fruit and the day of the reception. Regarding the cold storage of packaged products, the separation can be carried out by creating areas inside the chamber according to the size and day of packaging. It is suggested that marks be applied on the floor to identify and separate the size and fruit that has been packed the longest is placed closest to the door. This allows any employee to easily identify the fruit that has to be shipped first and its respective caliber. This new way of organizing the spaces makes it easier to find and locate the desired fruit and to prepare the fruit in the chamber when it needs to be shipped.

In addition to the problems previously identified, other problems were perceived:

- Weak involvement of workers. The workers are neither motivated nor informed about the daily and global objectives of the company. To combat this demotivation and misinformation, the organization can give productivity bonuses. The organization can motivate workers with extra monetary compensation, such as for punctuality, attendance (e.g., no absences for two months in a row), and completion of previously established goals. The company would be able to motivate employees to be more productive in their daily tasks and to improve communication with their bosses.
- Lack of training of seasonal employees. It is suggested to invest in training and cooperation with more experienced employees.
- Existence of only two employees able to drive forklifts, the one responsible for unloading the goods when they arrive from the producer and the one responsible for production. When an employee is absent there is no substitute who can operate the forklifts and the work piles up. To mitigate this situation, we suggest the training of at least one more worker with a forklift driver's license, so that he can substitute whenever one of the employees is absent.

- Lack of employees, which can be overcome with a new distribution and attribution of tasks among the employees. On production lines, on the grading machine, it is suggested that more experienced employees be at the beginning of the line.
- Lack of monitoring after the initial implementation of the organization. The process was never reviewed and was rarely checked to ensure it was being followed. Whenever a new action plan is implemented, there should be periodic monitoring.
- Difficulty in performing equipment calibration and adjustments. It is suggested that a new product-oriented sorting machine be purchased, and that training be provided to the workers.
- Lack of a continuous improvement culture. The organization should promote the implementation of Lean tools with the full cooperation of all workers.

After the analysis of the current state of the factory floor, unused machines, pallet boxes, pallets, and boxes of different sizes stored in the warehouse were identified, which can be removed or reorganized in another suitable location, as well as the implementation of a cleaning routine of the workplace. One of the main problems identified was the inadequate planning of the layout and bad use of all the available areas. Thus, one proposal would be to improve the layout of the organization.

4.2.2. Implementation of Value Stream Mapping (VSM)

The VSM of the initial state was prepared to obtain a detailed view of the entire process. The collection of information for its elaboration was carried out through direct observation of all operations performed and dialogues with the workers who normally operate the machines and execute the tasks. The dialogue with the control and production manager was also fundamental for the collection and validation of data.

After defining the objectives and collecting all the necessary information and data for the preparation of the VSM of the current state, we processed an order of 516 kg of peach AA, which corresponds to a pallet with 72 boxes, over the phone. This is a frequent customer who orders weekly. The production control transmits the information verbally to the production manager, who transmits it to the person in charge. According to the customer's request, the person in charge checks if the ordered variety of fruit is in stock.

In this case, there is no contact between production control and the suppliers since they only deliver the fruit when it is ripe. A pallet box of fruit averages 320 kg, and in this case, two pallet boxes had to be processed to satisfy the customer's needs. Knowing that the utilization rate is on average 80%, e.g., two pallets (640 kg, 320 kg each one) will correspond to one pallet (516 kg). It is important to keep in mind that these are average values since when the peach is received all the calibers are mixed.

The employees work 8 h a day, 5 days a week with 15 min breaks both in the morning and the afternoon, which translates into an availability of 450 min per day.

The main activities, metrics, cycle time, lead time, availability, and a number of workers needed throughout the process were identified. Through observation, the activities were timed, the processing time for all operations was recorded, and the total average time for each operation and its standard deviation were calculated, as shown in Table 1.

At the moment of "Reception", it was considered the unloading time, weight, and data entry into the system. At this stage, all receiving activities are performed by a single worker, who at peak times is overloaded due to the high number of suppliers waiting to unload the raw material.

In the "Storage" were considered 1440 min, because the pallet boxes are piled up, and it is difficult to respect the FIFO criterion, and the organization chooses to keep the peach stored for one day since the storage time is determined by its state of ripeness.

In the "Brushing/Calibration" phase, the time from the moment the pallet boxes were picked from the cold storage, the unloading in the sorting machine until the fruit falls along the lines was considered. Greater dispersion of values was registered, since the fruit becomes stuck in the sorting machine due to the large turnout, and only one worker is available for all the tasks.

Table 1. Timing of sample processing.

Sample N°	Reception	Storage	Brushing/Calibration	Packing	Labeling	
1	4.73	1440.00	5.34	3.52	1.98	
2	6.31	1440.00	7.31	3.61	1.42	
3	5.01	1440.00	3.41	3.26	1.76	
4	5.24	1440.00	3.98	4.10	2.04	
5	6.43	1440.00	7.03	2.78	1.87	
6	8.35	1440.00	3.05	2.72	1.79	
7	6.17	1440.00	4.07	5.34	1.47	
8	5.97	1440.00	3.20	4.41	1.40	
9	7.13	1440.00	3.15	2.84	1.78	
10	7.94	1440.00	4.25	3.32	1.94	
Average time	6.33	1440.00	4.48	3.59	1.75	min
Standard deviation	1.20	0.00	1.57	0.83	0.24	min

In "Packing" a permanent employee was selected, and the time required to complete a box was recorded. Situations such as picking up the box and/or the cardboard base material from the box, as well as stopping duties to assist seasonal employees were some of the main constraints observed. Considering the constraints mentioned above, an average time of 3.59 min per box. Knowing that, on average, 8 employees operate, it is possible to make 8 boxes in 3.59 min. In this case, making a pallet with 72 boxes takes 32.31 min. Equation (1) is calculated the total average time to make a pallet. This value will be used in the cycle time of the actual production VSM since one pallet is processed instead of one box.

$$\text{Total average} = \frac{72 \text{ boxes} \times 3.59 \text{ min}}{8 \text{ boxes}} = 32.31 \text{ min} \quad (1)$$

In the last phase, "Labeling", an employee takes an average of 1.75 min to label each pallet.

According to Equation (2), the sum of cycle times or Value Add Time is given by:

$$\text{Cycle time} = 6.33 + 1440.00 + 4.48 + 32.31 + 1.75 = 1484.87 \text{ min} \quad (2)$$

After adding up the waiting times and the processing times for all operations, it is possible to calculate the total lead time. The lead time is calculated by summing the product of intermediate stocks and cycle time using Equation (3).

$$\text{Lead time} = \frac{2 \times 6.33}{0.9375} + 6.33 + \frac{2 \times 1440.00}{2} + 1440.00 + \frac{2 \times 4.48}{0.9375} + 4.48 + \frac{1 \times \frac{32.31}{0.9375}}{8} + 32.31 + \frac{1 \times 1.75}{0.9375} + 1.75 = 2954.11 \text{ min} \quad (3)$$

It is possible to conclude that the current state map has a lead time for the processing of an order of one pallet (516 kg) of 2954.11 min, which corresponds to 2.05 days. However, only 1484.87 min correspond to activities that add value, which represents 50.26% of the entire process. This means that the organization to meet the customer's needs is delayed by 2.05 days, e.g., it has to have the necessary quantities in stock, and this only happens when the suppliers deliver the ripe fruit.

In this case, the customer orders weekly, every 5 days. Considering that the month has an average of 22 working days, 4 weeks, the organization has 5.5 days to prepare an order. Considering that it takes 2.05 days to process an order for a pallet, which leaves only 3.45 days to respond to any adversities that may arise.

To aid the understanding of Value Stream Mapping, Figure 3 shows the symbology used in the VSM tool.

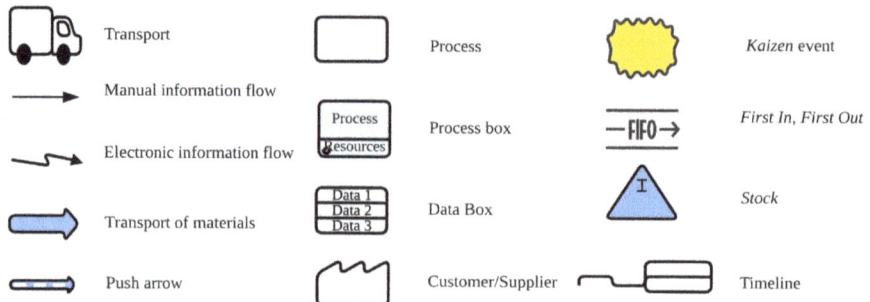

Figure 3. Symbology used in the VSM tool (Lucidchart, 2022).

Figure 4 shows the current VSM in which the previously mentioned order was processed.

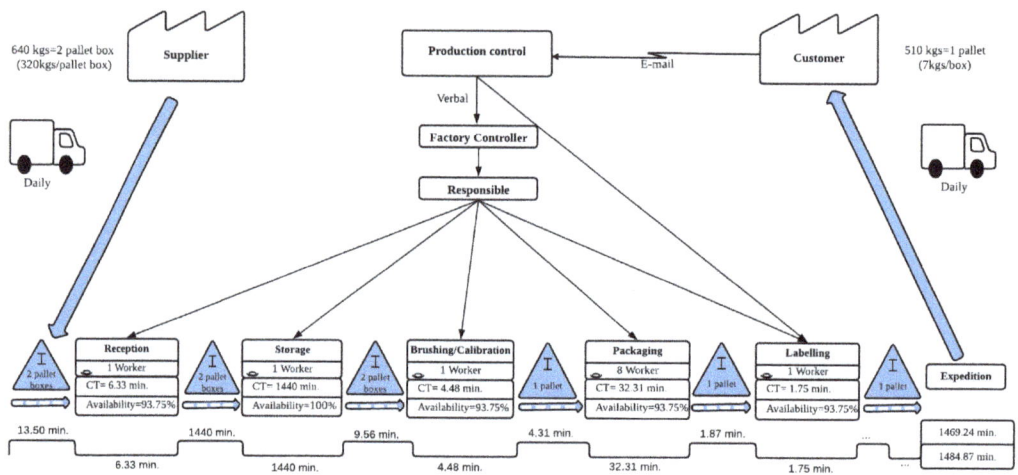

Figure 4. Current VSM of production.

After synthesizing the flow through the current VSM, the previously identified problems and constraints, as well as opportunities for improvement, were considered. Figure 5 shows the VSM with the improvement proposals.

The improvements identified were:

- Frequent communication between the company and the supplier, via telephone, to make a forecast every 2 weeks to know the state of ripeness of the fruit.
- Transport of the pallet boxes to the respective cold storage rooms immediately after receiving the raw material.
- Reorganization of the storage area inside the chambers, since sometimes they are accumulated without any criterion and consequently it becomes difficult to respect and comply with the FIFO criterion.
- Improvement of the labeling process, carried out manually, with the help of a label applicator.
- Reducing the cycle time of each of the activities and movements by changing the layout.

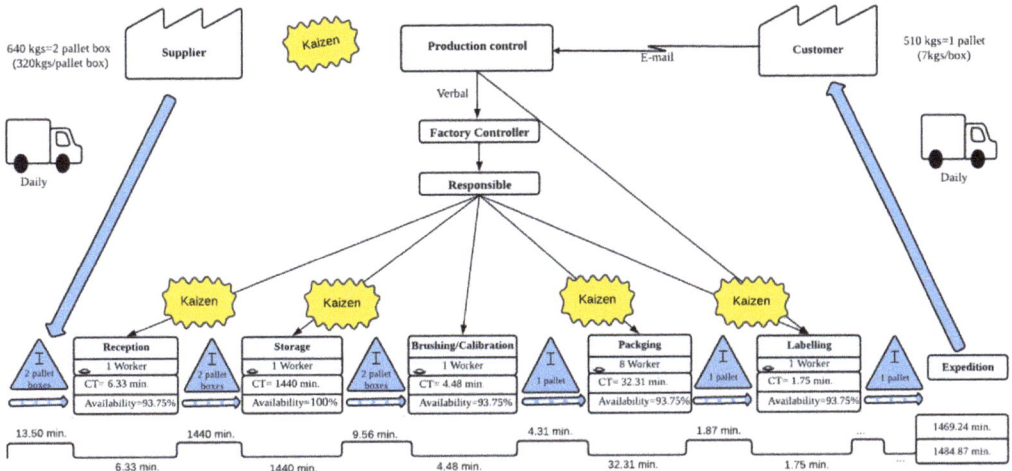

Figure 5. VSM with improvement proposal.

As mentioned earlier in the current VSM, about 49.74% is idle time, e.g., the product is waiting to be transported or is in steps that do not add value. If this time is reduced or even eliminated, several costs can be reduced.

The improvements identified will reduce the cycle times of each of the activities, except for "Storage", since the fruit has to be stored for 1440 min, e.g., one day. The "Receiving" activity will be reduced from 6.33 min to 6.00 min, by reducing unnecessary movements; the "Brushing/Crushing" activity will be reduced from 4.48 min to 4.00 min, by reducing unnecessary movements and reorganizing the layout and cold rooms; the "Packing" process will be reduced from 32.31 min to 29.30 min, by reorganizing the distribution of workers along the lines and improving the arrangement of materials (boxes and bases); finally "Labeling" will be reduced from 1.75 min to 1.20 min, with the help of a label applicator. Equation (4) presents the sum of the cycle times for the new VSM:

$$\text{Total average} = 6.00 + 1440 + 4.00 + 29.30 + 1.20 = 1480.50 \text{ min} \qquad (4)$$

Next, the lead time was calculated by summing the product of intermediate stocks with the cycle time, through the Equation (5).

$$\text{Lead time} = \frac{2 \times 6.00}{0.9375} + 6.00 + \frac{2 \times \frac{1440.00}{1}}{2} + 1440.00 + \frac{2 \times 4.00}{0.9375} + 4.00 + \frac{1 \times \frac{29.30}{0.9375}}{8} + 29.30 + \frac{1 \times 1.20}{0.9375} + 1.75 = 2947.01 \text{ min} \qquad (5)$$

With the improvements of the proposed new VSM, it will be possible to reduce 4.37 min in cycle time and the lead time of a pallet to 2947.01 min, 7.10 min less than the current VSM. In this case, it would take 2.04 days to process the 516 kg order. Although this is a negligible reduction, at the end of a month it will represent a total of 156.20 min and at the end of a year of operation, 1874.40 min, approximately 32 h, which is 8 h of work per day corresponds to 4 days, which in addition to the benefits inherent in better organization of space, incorporates a cost reduction.

It is suggested that the future VSM map be applied progressively in the short to medium term. Performance measurement and goal setting are important for the growth process, as it establishes a feasibility mindset in the team and leads to the successful implementation of the action plan. Next, a future vision of the most efficient value stream is presented through the representation of the future VSM illustrated in Figure 6.

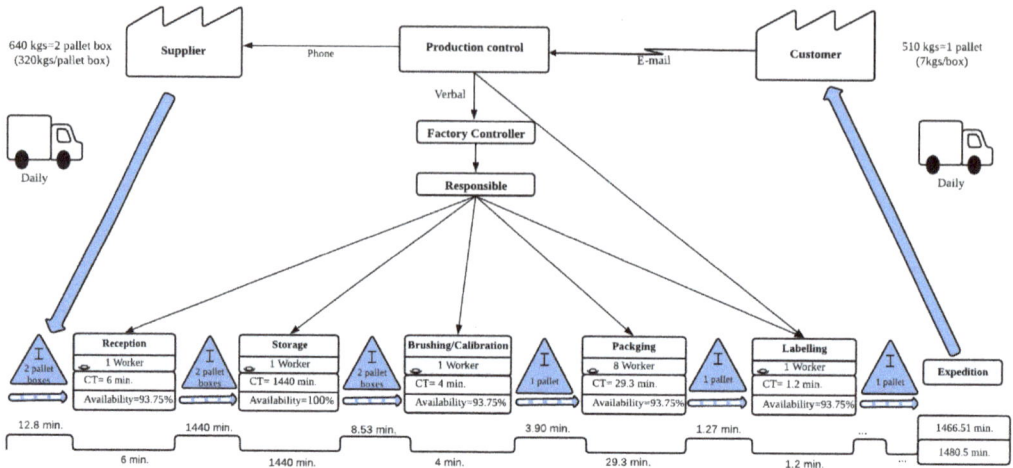

Figure 6. Future VSM.

4.3. Future Solution Proposals

In this subchapter, through the spaghetti diagram and the VSM, the proposals for improving the production layout of the agricultural company are presented, as well as the reorganization of the cold storage rooms.

4.3.1. Layout

One of the main problems identified was the poor management of available space by the organization, which has a large area. Situations such as the dispersion of machines, the overlapping of product movements, and disorganization in storage, since there is no area indicated for the storage of accumulated boxes, result in inefficient use of space, a situation that worsens in periods of seasonal peaks.

Figure 7 shows a proposal for a new layout. One of the main problems faced was to resize the largest sorting machine since it was only possible by eliminating production lines. The last line where the fruit considered "scrap" falls was removed. It is suggested that the warehouse where the smaller sorting machine is located be reused because previously this warehouse was cold storage and still has the same characteristics. This same space would be divided into two chambers of the same size, one for the raw material and the other for the finished product. The other two chambers would be adapted for the other classification machine as can be seen in Figure 7.

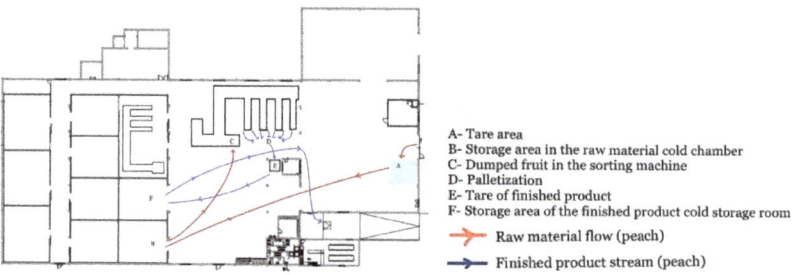

Figure 7. New layout.

This new layout will allow the finished product to be transported already packed in D, so that it can be weighed, and the "Labeling" process can then be carried out. After this process, the pallets would be forwarded to the cold storage chamber where they would be stored up to 10 min before the arrival of the transport.

Figure 8 illustrates the current layout with the proposed improvements. If the organization chooses to keep the same layout, it is suggested that the reception of the raw material is performed in another area designated as A. Subsequently, after the reception, the pallet boxes should be immediately transported to the chamber indicated as B. In D, it is suggested that whenever a pallet is finished, it should be directed to the cold storage chamber (E), and only removed no more than 40 min before dispatch so that the "Labeling" process can be carried out.

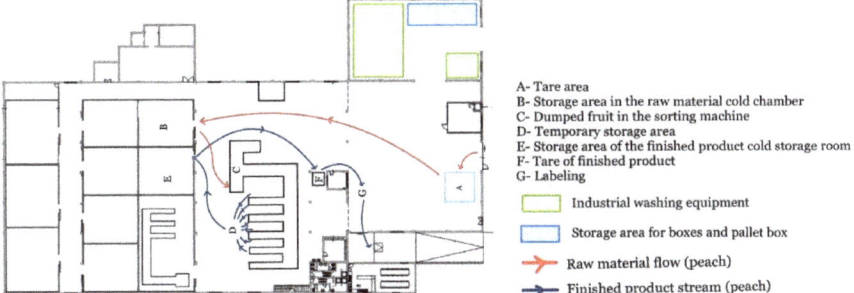

Figure 8. Current layout with proposals for improvement.

This new layout organization will maximize the use of space and organization indicated for the various boxes and pallet boxes spread throughout the warehouses.

4.3.2. Storage Area

Regardless of the layout chosen by the organization, another suggestion is the reorganization of the cold stores and the introduction of optical readers that allow not only to automate the process but also to control the entry and exit of stocks. By reading a bar-coded label, it would be possible to identify the pallet, which variety of fruit it contains, the lot number, the date of entry, and the producer. This data would be filled in at the reception of each pallet box.

In cold stores, by reading the barcodes, when it was necessary to load the pallet box into the sorting machine, it would be easily possible to identify the "latest" pallet box and thus respect the FIFO criterion.

A proposal for improvement would be to organize the cold rooms for the raw material and the finished product. It is known that the smallest chambers have an area of 85 m^2 and the largest, located in Warehouse 3, has 190 m^2.

Each pallet box has a dimension of 1200 × 1000 × 760 mm (0.912 m^3), that is, it occupies an area of 1.2 m^2 and in the chambers it is possible to overlap up to 13 pallet boxes. In the chambers, it will be necessary to take into consideration the circulation routes and the distance between pallet boxes. This distance is calculated by adding the external turning radius of the forklift, the distance between the forks and the front axle, the length of the forks with load, and the clearance, according to Equation (6):

$$\text{Width between pallet boxes} = 1.20 + 0.04 + 1.55 + 0.50 = 3.29 \text{ m} \quad (6)$$

The distance between the pallet boxes so that the forklift can be safely maneuvered is 3.29 m. In this sense, a new layout of the raw material chamber is proposed, as shown in Figure 9, which would allow the storage space to be optimized without endangering the safety of the workers.

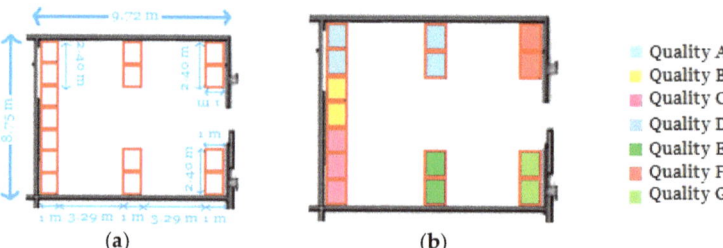

Figure 9. (a,b) New layout of the cold room for the raw material.

Knowing that the organization works with 7 varieties of peaches, one of the solutions would be to create parallel rows of 2 pallet boxes according to variety and day of entry into storage, represented in (b). This new arrangement would not only allow 182 pallet boxes to be placed in the chamber, organized according to quality and day of reception, but also allow any employee to easily identify which pallet should be loaded into the sorting machine. This process would be made easier with the help of the optical readers suggested above, and the FIFO criterion would be respected.

In relation to the empty pallets, each has a dimension of 1200 × 800 × 144 mm (1382 m^3). In this case, it is suggested that the storage be organized depending on the caliber, as illustrated in Figure 10.

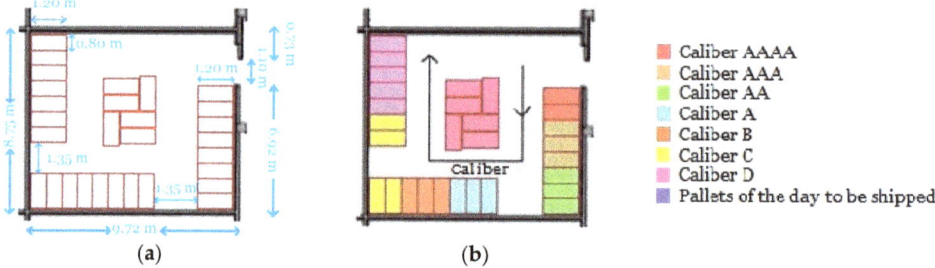

Figure 10. (a,b) New layout of the cold room for the finished product.

Since it is not possible to overlap the pallets, to facilitate circulation, it is suggested that the hand pallet truck be used with a distance of 1.35 m between pallets, as shown in (a). This would allow a larger maneuvering area and more storage. In (b) is also illustrated the distribution of the fruit size according to the new layout. To identify the caliber more easily, it is proposed that the pallets are placed from biggest to smallest size along the walls of the cold store. In the center can be placed the pallets that will be shipped on the day.

5. Conclusions

In recent decades, Lean has been an important catalyst for process organization and innovation in various industrial sectors. Despite successful applications in various industrial sectors, when it comes to the food and beverage industry, the application is more limited because it is a peculiar sector. The characteristics of this sector, such as the short shelf life of raw materials or seasonality of products, may have led to resistance to changing company practices and implementing new management philosophies such as LM [42]. LM implementation does not happen overnight. It needs time, stamina, focus on improving communication, and support from top management to make the change a reality. Continually increasing business competitiveness is vital to motivate change and sustain behaviors and attitudes, as well as by understanding and implementing Lean Thinking culture.

According to the authors, Pearce et al. [59], there is a dearth of studies investigating the application of Lean tools in the primary production segment of the agri-food supply chain. The application of Lean tools in the food processing industry has not received the same level of attention compared to traditional manufacturing industries. However, in 2021, the same authors Pearce et al. [43], point out that rising food prices and increasingly limited agricultural production capacity are contributing to process renewal in primary production with an emphasis on sustainability. They also highlight the urgency in eliminating waste that is strongly aligned with the agricultural need to reduce operational waste, whether in the form of inefficient labor used, food waste, water, or energy [43]. This idea was reinforced by the previously mentioned studies (Lehtinen and Torkko [45], Jiménez et al. [46], Dora et al. [47], Wesana et al. [48], Hmidach et al. [49], Rojas-Benites et al. [50], Somasundaram et al. [31], Farissi et al. [51], and Ali [52]) in which they proved that despite being a peculiar sector, the application of the Lean philosophy has grown exponentially. The excellent and promising results of the pioneering initiatives applied in Agribusiness demonstrate that this management philosophy can contribute to several fields of application, as well as allow the creation of synergies to enhance results and improve the management of available resources (financial and human).

It was concluded that the organization has a lead time of 2954.11 min, which corresponds to approximately 2.05 days. With the new VSM it would be possible to reduce the lead time to 2947.01 min, that is, 2.04 days. As well as reducing the cycle time from 1484.87 min to 1480.50 min. Although this is a slight reduction, it is quite significant after one year of operation, since it will allow the FIFO criterion to be respected and will allow the product to be sold in the order it was received, thus avoiding loss of product quality. If the cold conservation operation is excluded, the VSM application considers a reduction of 35.5% and 10.6% of the cycle time and lead time, respectively.

The application of Lean tools allows to reduce, or even eliminate waste throughout the process. Through the implementation of 5S, it is possible to reduce unnecessary movement, improve the layout and maximize workspace, level stocks, and motivate greater supplier involvement with a view to continuous improvement (Kaizen).

One of the main limitations was the seasonality and short shelf life of the product, which limited access to periodic data. As suggestions for future proposals regarding the subject under study, it is proposed:

- Installation of a pre-cooling area (Hydrocooler).
- Analysis of the feasibility of implementing Lean tools.
- Analysis of the feasibility of investing in a new sorting machine and defining a new product-oriented layout.
- Investing in Benchmarking allied to Industry 4.0 in the use of active and intelligent packing that allows the prolongation of the product's useful life.
- Marketing plans, with the creation of a website with essential information, increased presence in social networks, and presence in cultural events.
- Evaluation and study of ergonomic issues since it is repetitive work.

This study can be used as a reference for future work since Lean tools can be implemented individually, which facilitates the implementation process. This implementation can also be replicated especially in other companies in the same industry, due to the seasonal peculiarity of the products and short shelf life, which are often constrained and limited by a lack of financial and human resources.

Author Contributions: Conceptualization, P.D.G.; methodology, P.D.G. and T.M.L.; software, A.P.P.; validation, P.D.G. and T.M.L.; formal analysis, A.P.P. and P.D.G.; investigation, A.P.P.; resources, P.D.G. and T.M.L.; data curation, A.P.P.; writing—original draft preparation, A.P.P.; writing—review and editing, P.D.G. and T.M.L.; supervision, P.D.G. All authors have read and agreed to the published version of the manuscript.

Funding: This work was supported in part by the Fundação para a Ciência e Tecnologia (FCT) and C-MAST (Centre for Mechanical and Aerospace Science and Technologies), under project UIDB/00151/2020.

Data Availability Statement: The authors confirm that the data supporting the findings of this study are available within the article.

Acknowledgments: This work was supported in part by the Fundação para a Ciência e Tecnologia (FCT) and C-MAST (Centre for Mechanical and Aerospace Science and Technologies).

Conflicts of Interest: The authors declare no conflict of interest.

References

1. Hu, H.; Yin, M. Evolution of Business Intelligence: An Analysis from the Perspective of Social Network. *Teh. Vjesn.* **2022**, *29*, 497–503. [CrossRef]
2. Marques, P.A.; Carvalho, A.M.; Santos, J.O. Improving Operational and Sustainability Performance in a Retail Fresh Food Market Using Lean: A Portuguese Case Study. *Sustainability* **2022**, *14*, 403. [CrossRef]
3. Hartman, B.; Gerigscott, E. *The Lean Farm: How to Minimize Waste, Increase Efficiency, and Maximize Value and Profits with Less Work*; Chelsea Green Publishing: White River Junction, VT, USA, 2015.
4. Hocken, J. *The Lean Dairy Farm: Eliminate Waste, Save Time, Cut Costs-Creating a More Productive, Profitable and Higher Quality Farm*; John Wiley & Sons: Milton, Australia, 2019.
5. Hendriks, S.; Soussana, J.F.; Cole, M.; Kambugu, A.; Zilberman, D. *Ensuring Access to Safe and Nutritious Food for All through Transformation of Food Systems: A Paper on Action Track 1*; Center for Development Research (ZEF) in cooperation with the Scientific Group for the UN Food System Summit: Bonn, Germany, 2021. [CrossRef]
6. EC and DG for Agriculture and Rural Development. *EU Agricultural Outlook for Markets and Income 2020–2030*; Publications Office of the European Union: Luxembourg, 2020. Available online: https://data.europa.eu/doi/10.2762/252413 (accessed on 23 February 2022).
7. OCDE. Agricultural Productivity and Innovation. 2011. Available online: https://www.oecd.org/agriculture/topics/agricultural-productivity-and-innovation/ (accessed on 23 February 2022).
8. FAO. The Future of Food and Agriculture. 2017. Available online: https://www.fao.org/3/i6583e/I6583E.pdf (accessed on 23 February 2022).
9. Verano, T.D.C.; Medina, G.D.S.; Oliveira, J.R.D. Can Family Farmers Thrive in Commodity Markets? Quantitative Evidence on the Heterogeneity in Long Agribusiness Supply Chains. *Logistics* **2022**, *6*, 17. [CrossRef]
10. Kanchan, B.; Chandan, G.; Aslam, M. Implication of lean philosophies in signing supplier quality agreement: An empirical study. *Mater. Today* **2022**, *60*, 335–340. [CrossRef]
11. Hao, Z.; Liu, C.; Goh, M. Determining the effects of lean production and servitization of manufacturing on sustainable performance. *Sustain. Prod. Consum.* **2021**, *25*, 374–389. [CrossRef]
12. Verreydt, M.; Dewaelheyns, N.; Van, C. Time is money: An analysis of the time-to-failure in a flexible reorganization system. *Financ. Res. Lett.* **2022**, *46*, 102262. [CrossRef]
13. Oliveira, C.P.S.D. Agricultura familiar e desertificação: Estudos de casos nos distritos de Braga e da Guarda. Master's Thesis, University Institute of Lisbon, Lisbon, Portugal, September 2015.
14. Woiceshyn, J.; Daellenbach, U. Evaluating inductive vs. deductive research in management studies: Implications for authors, editors, reviewers. *Qual. Res. Organ. Manag. Int. J.* **2018**, *13*, 183–195. [CrossRef]
15. Liu, H. Digital Taylorism in China's e-commerce industry: A case study of internet professionals. *Econ. Ind. Democr.* **2022**, 0143831X211068887. [CrossRef]
16. Liker, J. *Toyota Way: 14 Management Principles from the World's Greatest Manufacturer*; McGraw-Hill: New York, NY, USA, 2020.
17. Glass, R.; Seifermann, S.; Metternich, J. The Spread of Lean Production in the Assembly, Process and Machining Industry. *Procedia CIRP* **2016**, *55*, 278–283. [CrossRef]
18. Tasdemir, C.; Gazo, R. A systematic literature review for better understanding of lean driven sustainability. *Sustainability* **2018**, *10*, 2544. [CrossRef]
19. Krafcik, J.F. Triumph of the Lean Production. *Sloan Manag. Rev.* **1988**, *30*, 41–52.
20. Womack, J.P.; Jones, D.T.; Roos, D. *The Machine That Changed the World: The Story of Lean Production-Toyota's Secret Weapon in the Global Car Wars That is Now Revolutionizing World Industry*; Rawson Associates: New York, NY, USA, 1990; pp. 17–70.
21. Danese, P.; Manfè, V.; Romano, P. A systematic literature review on recent lean research: State-of-the-art and future directions. *Int. J. Manag. Rev.* **2018**, *20*, 579–605. [CrossRef]
22. Womack, J.P.; Jones, D.T. *Lean Thinking: Banish Waste and Create Wealth in Your Corporation*; Simon and Schuster: London, UK, 1996.
23. Fowler, C.; Steffen, E.; Mentz, C. Using Lean Principles as an Implementation Strategy within the EBP Process. *J. PeriAnesthesia Nurs.* **2022**, *37*, 137–142. [CrossRef] [PubMed]
24. Pinto, P. *Pensamento Lean—A Filosofia Das Organizações Vencedoras*; Lidel Edições Técnicas: Lisbon, Portugal, 2009.
25. Ohno, T. *Toyota Production System: Beyond Large Scale Production*; Productivity Press: New York, NY, USA, 1988; pp. 1–44.

26. Cifone, F.D.; Hoberg, K.; Holweg, M.; Staudacher, A.P. Lean 4.0: How can digital technologies support lean practices? *Int. J. Prod. Econ.* **2021**, *241*, 108258. [CrossRef]
27. Alieva, J.; Haartman, R. Digital Muda—The New Form of Waste by Industry 4.0. *OSCM* **2020**, *13*, 269–278. [CrossRef]
28. Paladugu, B.; Grau, D. Toyota Production System-Monitoring Construction Work Progress with Lean Principles. *Encycl. Renew. Sustain. Mater.* **2020**, *5*, 560–565. [CrossRef]
29. Pinto, C.M.; Mendonça, J.; Babo, L.; Silva, F.J.; Fernandes, J.L. Analyzing the Implementation of Lean Methodologies and Practices in the Portuguese Industry: A Survey. *Sustainability* **2022**, *14*, 1929. [CrossRef]
30. Guzel, D.; Asiabi, A.S. Increasing Productivity of Furniture Factory with Lean Manufacturing Techniques (Case Study). *Teh. Glas.* **2022**, *16*, 82–92. [CrossRef]
31. Somasundaram, R.; Sundharesalingam, P.; Priya, P.V.; Renuka, P. Effectiveness of implementation of 5S tool in food industry during COVID-19. In Proceedings of the 2021 4th National Conference on Current and Emerging Process Technologies, Erode, India, 20 February 2021.
32. Willis, D. *Process Implementation through 5S: Laying the Foundations for Lean*; Productivity Press: New York, NY, USA, 2016.
33. Visco, D. *5S Made Easy: A Step-by-Step Guide to Implementing and Sustaining Your 5S Program*; CRC Press: Boca Raton, FL, USA, 2016.
34. Jiménez, M.; Romero, L.; Fernández, J.; Espinosa, M.M.; Domínguez, M. Extension of the Lean 5S Methodology to 6S with An Additional Layer to Ensure Occupational Safety and Health Levels. *Sustainability* **2019**, *11*, 3827. [CrossRef]
35. Castillo, C. The workers' perspective: Emotional consequences during a lean manufacturing change based on VSM analysis. *J. Manuf. Technol. Manag.* **2022**, *33*, 19–39. [CrossRef]
36. Zahoor, S.; Abdul-Kader, W.; Ijaz, H.; Khan, A.Q.; Saeed, Z.; Muzaffar, S. A Combined VSM and Kaizen Approach for Sustainable Continuous Process Improvement. *Int. J. Ind. Eng. Oper. Manag.* **2019**, *1*, 125–137. [CrossRef]
37. Waldron, K. *Handbook of Waste Management and Co-Product Recovery in Food Processing*; Woodhead Publishing: Sawston, UK, 2009.
38. Ikatrinasari, Z.F.; Kosasih, K.; Vizano, N.A. Value Stream Mapping (VSM) basic training to increase industrial productivity. In Proceedings of the 2019 International Conference on Community Development, Bandar Seri Begawan, Indonesia, 24–25 July 2019.
39. Dias, A.C.; Reis, A.C.; Oliveira, R.P.; Maruyama, Ú.; Martinez, P. Lean Manufacturing in healthcare: A systematic review of literature. *Rev. Prod. Desenvolv.* **2018**, *4*, 111–122. [CrossRef]
40. Otsuka, K.; Ben-Mazw, N. The impact of Kaizen: Assessing the intensive Kaizen training of auto-parts suppliers in South Africa. *S. Afr. J. Econ. Manag. Sci.* **2022**, *25*, 9. [CrossRef]
41. Muñoz-Villamizar, A.; Santos, J.; Grau, P.; Viles, E. Trends and gaps for integrating lean and green management in the agri-food sector. *Br. Food J.* **2019**, *121*, 1140–1153. [CrossRef]
42. Lopes, R.; Freitas, F.; Sousa, I. Application of Lean Manufacturing Tools in the Food and Beverage Industries. *J. Technol. Manag. Innov.* **2015**, *10*, 120–130. [CrossRef]
43. Pearce, D.; Dora, M.; Wesana, J.; Gellynck, X. Toward sustainable primary production through the application of lean management in South African fruit horticulture. *J. Clean. Prod.* **2021**, *313*, 127815. [CrossRef]
44. Solano, N.; Llinás, G.; Montoya-Torres, J. Towards the integration of lean principles and optimization for agricultural production systems: A conceptual review proposition. *J. Sci. Food Agric.* **2020**, *100*, 453–464. [CrossRef]
45. Lehtinen, U.; Torkko, M. The Lean Concept in the Food Industry: A Case Study of Contract a Manufacturer. *J. Food Distrib. Res.* **2005**, *36*, 57–67. [CrossRef]
46. Jiménez, E.; Tejeda, A.; Pérez, M.; Blanco, J.; Martínez, E. Applicability of lean production with VSM to the Rioja wine sector. *Int. J. Prod. Res.* **2012**, *50*, 1890–1904. [CrossRef]
47. Dora, M.; Van Goubergen, D.; Kumar, M.; Molnar, A.; Gellynck, X. Application of lean practices in small and medium-sized food enterprises. *Br. Food J.* **2014**, *116*, 125–141. [CrossRef]
48. Wesana, J.; Gellynck, X.; Dora, M.K.; Pearce, D.; De Steur, H. Measuring food losses in the supply chain through value stream mapping: A case study in the dairy sector. In *Saving Food*; Academic Press: Cambridge, MA, USA, 2019; pp. 249–277. [CrossRef]
49. Hmidach, S.; El Kihel, Y.; Amegouz, D.; El Kihel, B.; Regad, Y. Optimizing warehouse logistics flows by integrating new technologies: Case study of an agri-food industry. In Proceedings of the IEEE 2nd International Conference on Electronics, Control, Optimization and Computer Science (ICECOCS), Kenitra, Morocco, 2–3 December 2020.
50. Rojas-Benites, S.; Castro-Arroyo, A.; Viacava, G.; Aparicio, V.; del Carpio, C. Reduction of Waste in an SME in the Meat Sector in Peru through a Lean Manufacturing Approach Using a Model Based on 5S, Standardization, Demand Forecasting and Kanban. In Proceedings of the 7th International Conference on Industrial and Business Engineering, Macau, China, 27–29 September 2021.
51. Farissi, A.; Oumami, M.; Beidouri, Z. Assessing Lean Adoption in Food Companies: The Case of Morocco. *Int. J. Technol.* **2021**, *12*, 5–14. [CrossRef]
52. Ali, F.A. The role of lean manufacturing in adopting new products application study of a sample of employees of Alittihad Food Industries Co. Ltd. in babil governorate. *World Bull. Manag. Law* **2022**, *8*, 78–87. Available online: https://scholarexpress.net/index.php/wbml/article/view/679 (accessed on 22 May 2022).
53. Ashraf, S.R.B.; Rashid, M.M.; Rashid, A.H. Implementation of 5S methodology in a food & beverage industry: A case study. *Int. Res. J. Eng. Technol.* **2017**, *4*, 1791–1796. Available online: https://www.researchgate.net/publication/315697643_Implementation_of_5S_Methodology_in_a_Food_Beverage_Industry_A_Case_Study (accessed on 19 May 2022).
54. Rodrigues, C.; Gaspar, P.D.; Simões, M.P.; Silva, P.D.; Andrade, L.P. Review on techniques and treatments toward the mitigation of the chilling injury of peaches. *J. Food Process. Preserv.* **2020**, e14358. [CrossRef]

55. Gaspar, J.P.; Gaspar, P.D.; da Silva, P.D.; Simões, M.P.; Santo, C.E. Energy life-cycle assessment of fruit products-case study of Beira Interior's Peach (Portugal). *Sustainability* **2018**, *10*, 3530. [CrossRef]
56. Gaspar, P.D.; Silva, P.D.; Nunes, J.; Andrade, L.P. Characterization of the specific electrical energy consumption of agrifood industries in the central region of Portugal. *Appl. Mech. Mater.* **2014**, *590*, 878–882. [CrossRef]
57. Gaspar, P.D.; Carrilho Gonçalves, L.C.; Pitarma, R.A. CFD parametric studies for global performance improvement of open refrigerated display cabinets. *Model. Simul. Eng.* **2012**, *2012*, 867820. [CrossRef]
58. Nunes, J.; Silva, P.D.; Andrade, L.P.; Gaspar, P.D. Characterization of the specific energy consumption of electricity in the Portuguese sausage industry. *WIT Trans. Ecol. Environ.* **2014**, *186*, 763–774. [CrossRef]
59. Pearce, D.; Dora, M.; Wesana, J.; Gellynck, X. Determining factors driving sustainable performance through the application of lean management practices in horticultural primary production. *J. Clean. Prod.* **2018**, *203*, 400–417. [CrossRef]

Article

A Machine Learning Approach for Predicting the Maximum Spreading Factor of Droplets upon Impact on Surfaces with Various Wettabilities

Moussa Tembely [1,*], Damien C. Vadillo [2], Ali Dolatabadi [1] and Arthur Soucemarianadin [3]

[1] Department of Mechanical and Industrial Engineering, University of Toronto, Toronto, ON M5S 2E8, Canada; dolat@mie.utoronto.ca
[2] 3M Corporate Research Analytical Laboratory, Saint Paul, MN 55144, USA; dvadillo@mmm.com
[3] Univ. Grenoble Alpes, CNRS, Grenoble INP, LEGI, 38000 Grenoble, France; arthur.soucemarianadin@univ-grenoble-alpes.fr
* Correspondence: moussa.tembely@utoronto.ca or moussa.tembely@concordia.ca

Abstract: Drop impact on a dry substrate is ubiquitous in nature and industrial processes, including aircraft de-icing, ink-jet printing, microfluidics, and additive manufacturing. While the maximum spreading factor is crucial for controlling the efficiency of the majority of these processes, there is currently no comprehensive approach for predicting its value. In contrast to the traditional approach based on scaling laws and/or analytical models, this paper proposes a data-driven approach for estimating the maximum spreading factor using supervised machine learning (ML) algorithms such as linear regression, decision tree, random forest, and gradient boosting. For this purpose, a dataset of hundreds of experimental results from the literature and our own—spanning the last thirty years—is collected and analyzed. The dataset was divided into training and testing sets, each representing 70% and 30% of the input data, respectively. Subsequently, machine learning techniques were applied to relate the maximum spreading factor to relevant features such as flow controlling dimensionless numbers and substrate wettability. In the current study, the gradient boosting regression model, capable of handling structured high-dimensional data, is found to be the best-performing model, with an R2-score of more than 95%. Finally, the ML predictions agree well with the experimental data and are valid across a wide range of impact conditions. This work could pave the way for the development of a universal model for controlling droplet impact, enabling the optimization of a wide variety of industrial applications.

Keywords: drop impact; maximum spreading diameter; scaling laws; analytical models; machine learning

1. Introduction

The impact and spreading of droplets on a solid substrate is of paramount importance from a scientific and practical standpoint. Ink-jet printing, metal solidification, spray cooling, microfluidic systems, ice accretion, combustion, coating processes, and pesticide deposition are just some of the myriad of industrial and environmental applications that have spurred decades of research on drop impacts [1–7]. In each of these applications, the maximum spreading diameter is critical, whether it relates to a higher dot resolution in ink-jet printing or better surface coverage efficiency aiming at maximum coverage of the target materials with the minimum amount of liquid. In other extreme cases, superhydrophobic surfaces have been developed to limit the spreading diameter due to their enormous potential applications, such as anti-icing, drag reduction, self-cleaning, anti-bacteria, and corrosion resistance, to mention a few [8–10].

From a scientific point of view, many studies have been devoted to understanding the different phenomena happening after impact and which are controlled by a subtle interplay between inertia, viscosity, and capillary forces for drops smaller than the capillary length. According to the literature [1,11,12], the droplet impacting process can be divided into four phases: kinematic, spreading, relaxation, and wetting/equilibrium, with different outcomes. The outcomes are closely related to the kinematics and the interfacial properties of the liquid and the solid, the most important of the outcomes being deposition, receding contact line with break-up, splashing, and rebound, the latter being either partial or total [13–17].

Analytical models, which are further discussed in this paper, attempt to predict the maximum spreading diameter of droplet impingement using energy balance, momentum balance, and sometimes empirical considerations [18,19]. These models are crucial for understanding the underlying physics, as well as industrial applications. The kinetic energy, the surface energy, and the viscous dissipation of a droplet impacting on a solid surface must all be taken into account when analyzing the impact dynamics. It has been shown that drop impacts are best described and assessed when appropriate dimensionless groups are used. The Weber and Reynolds numbers are mostly employed in this regard. The Weber number $\left(We = \rho V_0^2 D_0 / \sigma\right)$ relates the inertia forces to the forces resulting from surface tension; it represents the ratio of kinetic energy to surface energy and is a measure of the deformability of the droplet. The Reynolds number $(Re = \rho V_0 D_0 / \mu)$ measures the ratio of inertia to viscosity, where V_0 and D_0 are the initial impact velocity and diameter of the liquid droplet, whilst ρ, σ, and μ are the density, surface tension, and viscosity of the fluid used for the experiments. Two other dimensionless numbers are also sometimes considered in the analysis, namely the Ohnesorge number $\left(Oh = We^{1/2}/Re\right)$ and the capillary number $(Ca = We/Re)$. It should be noted that these numbers are not independent of the first two (We, Re) but may be quite useful for scaling purposes and to better define regions of study and applications. Finally, another quantity of interest is β_{max}, the maximum spreading factor (or parameter). It serves to normalize the maximum deformation of the droplet and represents the ratio between the droplet's maximum spreading diameter (D_{max}) and its initial diameter (D_0).

Existing analytical models can be classified into two main categories: (i) β_{max} as a function of Re and We [17,20] and (ii) β_{max} as a function of Re, We, and θ [14,21], where θ could be the equilibrium contact angle or the advancing contact angle, with the latter being dynamic or not [22]. It is only when θ is introduced into the equations that the interactions between the solid and liquid are considered. Due to the difficulty in predicting the advancing dynamic contact angle theoretically, however, experimental data are often used instead. In this paper, some results from analytical models described above to those obtained using data-driven models are compared.

In view of the quantity of existing experimental results which have been generated over the years, of the various assumptions which are made to construct the models, and of the very large number of models, with some of them relatively specialized for certain fluids and operating conditions [23,24], it may be useful to consider whether one could not resort to some other technique to obtain the maximum spreading diameter. For instance, the lack of an analytical model can be circumvented if one applies machine learning (ML) or deep learning techniques able to unravel hidden interactions and to build a model directly from the experimental data [25]. The ML models in this work are applied in a supervised manner, which means that the data have to be prepared beforehand for a given target, which, in this paper, is the maximum spreading factor. As a result, the main aim of the present study is to investigate different tree-based machine learning models for the prediction of the maximum spreading factor of a single droplet onto a dry horizontal surface with various wettabilities. The simplicity of these models, relying on structured data, allows for better insight into the physics, unlike approaches such as deep learning applied on unstructured data [26,27]. The focus is essentially on the ensemble learning family of algorithms, which offer some of the most promising approaches in terms of prediction accuracy.

This paper's contribution is the development of a comprehensive ML approach for predicting the maximum spreading factors (β_{max}) over a wide range of impact conditions and machine learning models. Existing models do not address these issues and do not permit a direct comparison of β_{max} with empirical and energy models in the literature.

Current methods only predict the diameter after training on a subset of the diameter evolution or address the droplet impact classification problem [28,29].

This paper is organized as follows: Section 2 is devoted to the background on analytical models and scaling analyses which help to determine the maximum spreading diameter, and some of them will be used as benchmarks for comparisons later in the paper. Section 3 presents the machine learning methods used for regression, while Section 4 details the methodology and the results obtained, with special emphasis on the prediction of β_{max} for a large spectrum of dimensionless numbers and contact angles. Finally, Section 5 summarizes the main conclusions of this work and emphasizes the potentialities of machine learning methods in the analysis of heterogeneous data.

2. Prediction of the Maximum Spreading Diameter

2.1. Scaling Analyses and Analytical Models

Scaling laws between the maximum spreading factor (β_{max}) and the Weber (We) or Reynolds (Re) number have been proposed based on the type of force dominating the dynamics of drop impact. On one hand, for capillary-force-dominated spreading, one can obtain a scaling law of $\beta_{max} \propto We^{1/2}$ by energy conservation or as $\beta_{max} \propto We^{1/4}$ by using momentum conservation [17,30]. On the other hand, if the spreading is dominated by viscous force, then one obtains $\beta_{max} \propto Re^{1/5}$, whilst $\beta_{max} \propto Re^{1/4}$ when considering a balance of kinetic energy with viscous dissipation energy at initial and maximum spreading times [14]. It is noteworthy that Clanet et al. [17] proposed a model that fits well experimental data for impacts on superhydrophobic substrates and reads:

$$\beta_{max} = 0.9\, We^{1/4} \qquad (1)$$

The accuracy of the different estimations can be evaluated, in particular, on the basis of their ability to predict the maximum spreading factor, as performed by Clanet et al. [17], but only for a very specific type of substrate. In this context Laan et al. [31] explored the aforementioned scaling relations to enable universal scaling. The fact that no clear dependency on We or Re is found suggests that all three effects (inertia, capillarity, and viscosity) are important. By interpolating between $We^{1/2}$ and $Re^{1/5}$ using $\beta_{max} \propto Re^{1/5} f_{EC}\left(WeRe^{-2/5}\right)$, where f_{EC} is a function of the impact parameter $P = WeRe^{-2/5}$, Laan et al. [31] reach the following relation for the maximum spreading factor:

$$\beta_{max} = Re^{1/5}\, \frac{P^{1/2}}{(A + P^{1/2})} \qquad (2)$$

In the first category of models, which do not account for surface interactions, it is worth mentioning the semi-empirical correlation proposed by Roisman [20], based on a combination of scaling laws and experimental data fitting. This model has been extensively used in the literature for benchmarking but, however, fails for very low Weber impacts, whatever the wettability of the substrate, as well as for low-viscosity fluid drops landing on superhydrophobic substrates where the equilibrium contact angle θ_e is higher than $140°$.

In the category of models where the surface wettability is taken into account, one of the best known and abundantly cited is probably the one due to Pasandideh-Fard et al. [14], for which the maximum spreading factor is given explicitly:

$$\beta_{max} = \sqrt{\frac{We + 12}{3(1 - \cos\theta) + 4\left(\frac{We}{\sqrt{Re}}\right)}} \qquad (3)$$

In their work on carefully characterized substrates, Ukiwe and Kwok [18] concluded that the Pasandideh-Fard et al. model provided the best estimation, among a set of models, on their experimental data for β_{max}. This model was then modified to include different surface energy terms, resulting in new models [22].

2.2. Data-Driven Models

There are several traditional machine learning (ML) and deep learning methods, including decision trees [32], nearest neighbors, support vector machines, random forest, and many others [33]. Recently, neural networks [27] have shown significant potential in a wide range of applications [34–38]. Nevertheless, none of these models consistently outperform the other methods, and the performance of the model is data-dependent. Coming to the specific problem at hand, fluid dynamics presents challenges that differ from those commonly tackled in many applications of ML, such as speech and image recognition or even the control of manufacturing plants. The application of ML methods for characterizing drop impacts is rather limited, to the best of our knowledge. In 2018, Um et al. [39] proposed a new data-driven approach for modeling liquid splashes utilizing neural networks, which can learn to generate small-scale splash details using training data collected from high-fidelity numerical simulations. In the continuation of neural networks, Heidari et al. [28] present a method based on the NARX-ANN approach for predicting droplet spreading dynamics on a solid substrate. These types of neural networks seem to be particularly effective in predicting non-linear behavior [40], but, as usual with neural networks, the underlying phenomena are rather obfuscated. Moreover, Heidari et al. [28] do not conduct any comparisons with drop impact experiments performed on superhydrophobic substrates, making it difficult to determine if their neural network is equally effective regardless of the values of Weber, Reynolds, and contact angles, since it is found that superhydrophobic substrates have a peculiar behavior, as reported by [41]. Finally, Azimi et al. [29] utilized an approach based on machine learning to predict the behavior of impacting drops on hydrophobic and superhydrophobic surfaces. Their model, based on a random-forest approach, is used to predict drop behavior with high accuracy while aiming at finding those conditions favorable for producing a bouncing behavior upon drop impact for a wide range of Weber numbers and surfaces. Their results based on an ensemble method offer design criteria for superhydrophobic surfaces, so it is more of a classification problem than a regression one, as detailed in this paper.

3. Machine Learning Methods for Predicting Maximum Spreading Diameter
3.1. Multiple Linear Regression (MLR)

The first ML considered is a multiple linear regression (MLR), which involves predicting the target variable $F(x_i)$ (in our case, the maximum spreading factor) based on the p input features $x_1, x_2, \ldots x_p$ so that the following linear relation is satisfied:

$$F(x) = \alpha_0 + \sum_{i=1}^{p} \alpha_i x_i + \epsilon \qquad (4)$$

where α_i is the regression coefficient for the ith input feature x_i and ϵ represents the error. Using the set of observations compiled from our own experiments [22,42] and data from the literature (see below), the coefficients α_i can be computed using the least-squares approach by optimization.

3.2. Regression Tree (RT)

The regression tree (RT) method is a supervised nonparametric statistical method [43] that provides an alternative to parametric regression techniques, which typically need assumptions and simplifications to generate the described relationship. The main goal of a decision tree-based regression model is to predict the value of a target variable by learning simple decision rules based on the input data. To construct the regression tree, the entire dataset that represents the root node is recursively partitioned into more homogeneous groups, each of which is described by its own node. At the end of the splitting process, the resulting groups are known as leaves or terminal nodes. If the dataset is partitioned into M regions or homogeneous groups such as $R_1, R_2, \ldots R_M$, the system model can be expressed as:

$$F(x) = average(F(x_j)/x_j \in R_M) + \epsilon \tag{5}$$

where x_j corresponds to the input variables at jth observation while $F(x_j)$ represents target variables. Overall, Equation (5) illustrates that the predicted value can be computed based the average of $F(x_j)$ in region R_M with the associated error ϵ.

It should be mentioned that a small tree may not be able to capture a nonlinear relation, but a very large one can overfit with overly complex decision rules, which is more typical of the behaviour of a single tree. Consequently, tree size is a tuning parameter that can be adjusted in accordance with the data.

3.3. Random Forest (RF)

The random forest method comprises regression trees developed in a random manner. The purpose of the RF method is to build an ensemble of low-correlated regression trees and average them in order to address the weaknesses of decision trees and reduce variance, which is quite high in the case where a single tree is generated. The random forest method was first proposed by Breiman [44]. Randomization is applied in two processes to build low-correlated trees: each tree is formed using a random subset of observations and each node of a tree is split using a random subset of input features. RF can predict a new observation x by using a tree-based regression model in the forest to make new predictions $F_S(x)$ and then taking the average of the S prediction values as follows:

$$F(x) = \frac{1}{S}\sum_{s=1}^{S} F_s(x) + \epsilon \tag{6}$$

Thus, the random forest output is a meta-estimator that integrates the results of several predictions and many decision trees, with some adjustments that prevent overfitting and underfitting if sufficient trees are generated for a particular task.

3.4. Gradient Boost Regression Tree (GBRT)

Schapire [45] introduced the first boosting algorithm in 1990, followed by Freund and Schapire in 1996 with the AdaBoost method [46]. Boosting is a potent method for merging numerous base classifiers to create a group whose performance can be much superior to that of any base classifier. Boosting's central concept is to add new models to the ensemble sequentially but according to a predetermined pattern, as opposed to the random forest technique, in which trees are developed in parallel. At each successive iteration, a weak, base-learner model is trained relative to the error of the entire ensemble learned [47]. Gradient boosting, which was developed by Friedman [48], constructs the model in stages, such as in other boosting approaches, but generalizes weak learner models and optimizes the loss function based on gradient descent. As with the random forest method, it can be used for regression or classification problems and results in a lower variance than a single regression tree. The mathematical formulation for GBRT reads:

$$F(x) = \sum_{m=1}^{M} \gamma_m h_m(x) \tag{7}$$

where $hm(x)$ are the basis functions, which, in the context of boosting, are typically referred to as weak learners. GBRT employs small, fixed-size decision trees for weak learners. Numerous abilities of decision trees make them advantageous for boosting. GBRT constructs the additive model in forward stages [48] as follows:

$$F_m(x) = F_{m-1}(x) + \gamma_m h_m(x) \tag{8}$$

At each stage, the decision tree $h_m(x)$ is selected to minimize the loss function L, such as:

$$F_m(x) = F_{m-1}(x) + argmin \sum_{i=1}^{n} L(y_i, F_{m-1}(x_i) - h(x)) \qquad (9)$$

The initial model F_0 varies depending on the problem; for least squares regression, the mean of the target values is typically chosen, while the loss function is the mean squared error.

3.5. Data Description and Processing

The data that we use in this paper come from our own experiments [22,42], as well as quite a large number of experimental investigations which have been produced by different researchers over the past thirty years. Table 1 summarizes the provenance of the prominent data. The experimental results cover a large spectrum of Weber (0.2 to 802) and Reynolds numbers (8.7 to 14191), with drops impacting on substrates for which the equilibrium contact angle varies between 0 degree and 164 degrees.

Table 1. Selected experimental β_{max} and drop impact characteristics considered for ML models.

Investigation	Range of Weber Numbers	Range of Reynolds Numbers	Range of Equilibrium Contact Angles	Range of Values of Maximum Spreading Factors
Rioboo et al. [12]	36–614	20–10,394	0°–154°	1.4–5.4
Pasandideh-Fard et al. [14]	27–641	213–5833	20°–140°	2.15–4.4
Bayer et al. [15]	11.5	1078	10°–115°	2.1–2.5
Šikalo et al. [49]	50–802	27–12,300	0°–105°	1.7–5.2
Vadillo et al. and Vadillo [22,42]	0.21–12.4	39–2400	5°–160°	1.2 – 2.3
Roisman et al. [50]	0.88–7.9	400–1200	92°	1.2–1.5
Mao et al. [24]	11–511	1966–13,297	37°–97°	1.65–4.94
Kim and Chun [51]	30–582	3222–14,191	6.2°–87.5°	2.3–5.1
Antonini et al. [41]	33	3379	99°–164°	1.8–2.45

The dataset which has been constituted for this paper from various sources is probably one of the most extended reported in the literature on maximum spreading diameter. The detailed statistics on the dataset are shown in Table 2, with the number of data points(count), the minimum, mean, percentile, and the maximum of the different parameters describing the impact conditions. In addition, we represent various cross-plots between the dataset's variables in Figure 1. Finally, to apply the ML models, the collected data are subdivided into two independent and non-overlapping datasets: a training set of 70% and a test set of 30%. While the training set is used for regression analysis to predict maximum diameters, the test set is used for assessing prediction accuracy.

Table 2. Statistics on the test dataset.

	We	Re	θ_{eq}	β
count	204	204	204	204
mean	101.7	2551.3	49.7	2.5
std	170.1	3315.0	36.5	1.1
min	0.2	8.7	0.1	1.0
25%	10.6	140.3	16.0	1.6
50%	33.0	1046.3	48.5	2.2
75%	117.1	3392.8	77.0	3.2
max	802.0	14,191.0	164.0	5.4

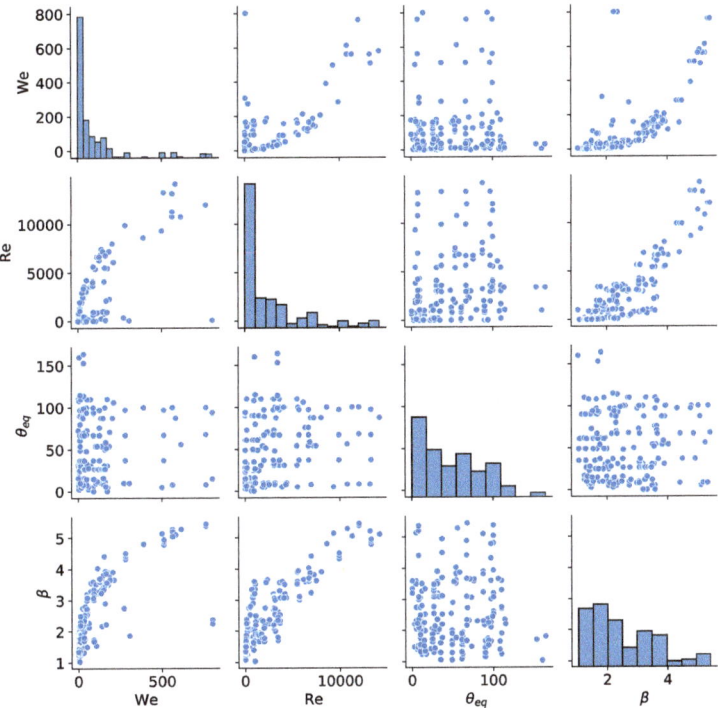

Figure 1. Exploratory analysis of the dataset based on the cross-plots of the different variables.

3.6. Feature Selection

As shown in Table 1, we have settled for the choice of Weber number (*We*), Reynolds number (*Re*), and equilibrium contact angle (θ_e) as features for the machine learning methods since these are the easiest to obtain when going through the different results reported in the literature. This does not mean, however, that other quantities such as surface tension, density of the fluid, and advancing and receding angles are unimportant, although some of them are present thanks to dimensionless numbers. To be practical, the point is that they are not mentioned in some papers, whilst all of them report the dimensionless flow numbers and the equilibrium contact angles of substrates used in the investigations.

3.7. ML Model Evaluation Metrics

To assess the performance of the different regression models, we use the R2-score between the actual (y_i) and predicted values ($\tilde{y}$), which measures the predictive capability of the ML model. This score can be defined as follows:

$$\text{R2-score} = 1 - \frac{\sum_{i=1}^{N}(y_i - \tilde{y}_i)^2}{\sum_{i=1}^{N}(y_i - \bar{y})^2} \qquad (10)$$

where $\bar{y} = \sum_{i=1}^{N} y_i / N$, with N corresponding to the number of samples. In addition, the mean absolute error (MAE) is computed as follows:

$$\text{MAE} = \frac{1}{N}\sum_{i=1}^{N}|y_i - \tilde{y}_i| \qquad (11)$$

Finally, we use randomized search and grid search to tune and set the hyperparameters of the different ML models.

4. Results and Discussion

4.1. Linear Regression Model (LRM)

After collecting and processing the data, we are in a position to test the accuracy of the data-driven models. A simple linear regression model constructs an optimized linear combination of the predictors variables, also known as features. The relatively strict assumption of a linear relationship makes it difficult to match with real-world problems, where many factors may contribute to the final result in a non-linear manner. One advantage of the multiple linear regression method is that it can be used to evaluate the contribution of each individual input variable to the target variable. The result of the model on estimating β_{max} is shown in Figure 2, with an R2-score of 78% and MAE of 0.41, highlighting the non-linearity, between the input features—chosen as Re, We, θ_e—and the target, β_{max}, which cannot be fully captured by the linear model.

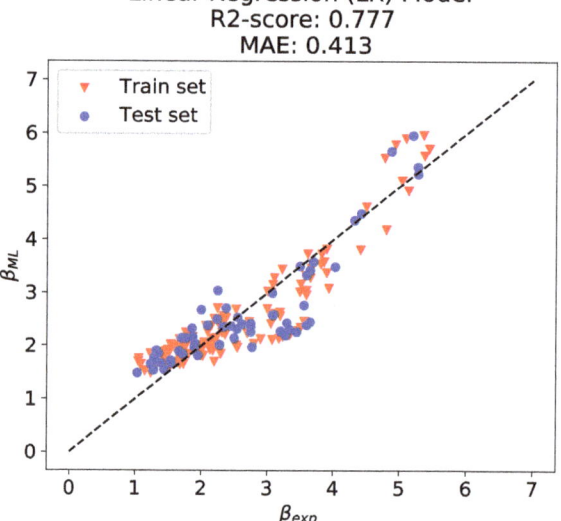

Figure 2. Linear regression model with three features.

4.2. Decision Tree (DT)

Due to their simplicity, practicality, and interpretability, decision trees have gained in popularity as a ML technique in recent years. In Figure 3, we find that the first split, at the level of the root node, is performed for a Reynolds number smaller than or equal to 3613. The mean maximum spreading factor value for the 142 samples, which concerns only the train set, in the root node is 2.44 and the mean squared error (MSE) is 1.16. The resulting tree is of quite small depth with only six leaves and is representative of the trees that will be used in the methods discussed later on. It should be emphasized that at such a low depth level, the highest MSE for a leaf is 0.13, so more than 10 times lower than the initial value, and the MSE could be as small as 0.04, i.e., more than 30 times smaller than the initial value. The regression tree seems to accommodate quite well for non-linearities that exist in the drop spreading phenomenon.

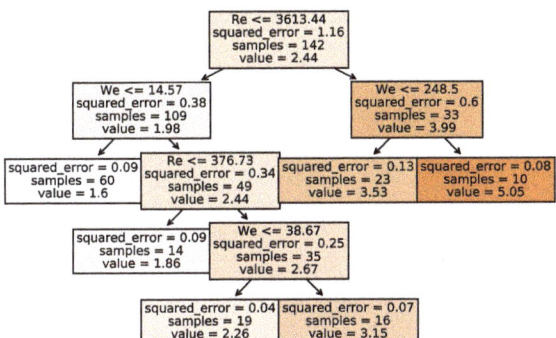

Figure 3. Decision tree graph for the maximum spreading factor.

4.3. Random Forest (RF)

As already explained, a single classification or regression tree is easy to obtain and its interpretability is straightforward, but one is confronted with the problem of high variance. As with the random forest approach, we plot β_{exp} vs. β_{ML} in Figure 4 below. It can be noted that there is a quantitative difference between the coefficients of determination found for the multiple linear regression and decision tree methods and the one for the random forest method (variation from 0.78 to almost 0.95), demonstrating the excellent non-linear mapping generalization ability of the latter method. We lose somewhat in terms of interpretability because of the number of trees which are grown, but we gain quite significantly in terms of prediction accuracy.

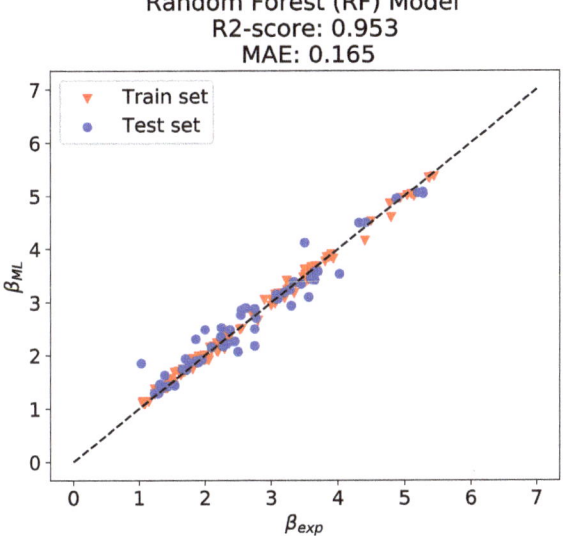

Figure 4. Experimental maximum spreading factor plotted against β_{max} given by the random forest method.

4.4. Gradient Boost Regression Tree (GBRT)

As a final method, we have chosen the gradient boost regression tree technique, which performs well, if not the best, on a variety of datasets. Instead of trees grown parallel, the trees are grown sequentially, correcting each time. As for the random forest method, there are a number of parameters which need to be tuned: (i) the number and depth of trees used in the ensemble, (ii) the learning rate, which should be a small number, used to limit how much each tree contributes to the ensemble, and (iii) random sampling such as fitting trees on random subsets of features and samples. One may note that the comparison (Figure 5) is slightly better than for the random forest method, which is a testimonial to the adequacy of this method to tackle highly non-linear problems, in line with results reported in the literature.

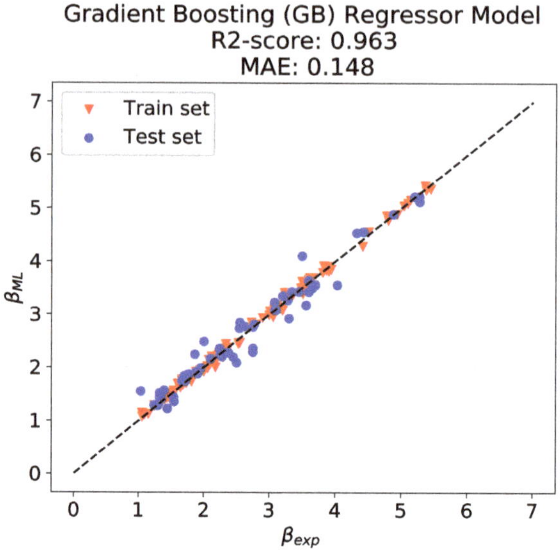

Figure 5. β_{max} experimental plotted against β_{max} given by the gradient boosting method.

Finally, we have added Table 3 summarizing the performance of the different ML models. We can observe that GBRT outperforms the other models in terms of both R2-score and MAE.

Table 3. Summary of the performance of the different models.

Evaluation Metrics	LR	RT	RF	GBRT
R2-score	0.777	0.885	0.953	0.963
MAE	0.413	0.308	0.165	0.148

4.5. Importance of Features

Since GBRT outperforms the different ML models tested, this technique has been used to determine the relevance of the input features controlling droplet impact on a flat surface. The result is shown in Figure 6, where the relevance of Re and We compared to θ_e is retrieved.

Finally, we provide the results of various models on the test set, hitherto unseen data (Table 4), including machine learning-based GBRT, the models of Pasandideh-Fard et al. [14], and Laan et al. [31]. The results, as shown in Figure 7, demonstrate that machine learning models can outperform existing models, paving the way for a data-driven approach to a better understanding and control of droplet formation and impact.

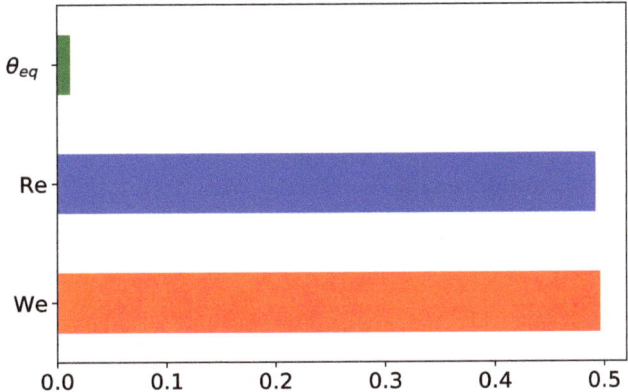

Figure 6. Feature importance as given by the GBRT.

Table 4. Statistics on the test dataset.

-	We	Re	θ_e
count	62	62	62
mean	122.7	2722.2	47.8
std	191.2	3394.8	39.1
min	0.2	8.7	0.1
max	802.0	13,297.2	160.0

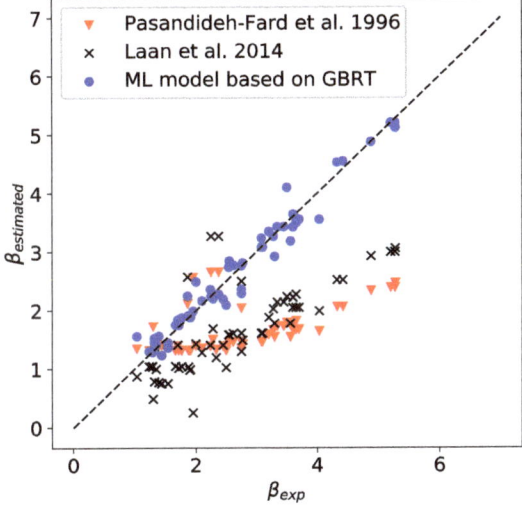

Figure 7. A comparative estimation of the maximum spreading factor based on machine learning, scaling, and analytical models. Pasandideh-Fard et al. [14], and Laan et al. [31].

5. Conclusions and Perspectives

The maximum spreading diameter of impacting drops plays a significant role in a number of industrial applications. Currently, there are three main methods for estimating the maximum spreading factor: (i) scaling law analyses, (ii) energy balance approach, and (iii) numerical simulation. In contrast, this paper offers a different approach to the issue. Indeed, recent advances in computing technologies have led to the development of an array of accurate and sophisticated machine learning techniques. In addition, the best machine learning technique cannot be determined beforehand, and numerous algorithms must be examined to determine their applicability for a particular task. This study compared the performance of commonly used scaling laws and analytical models to ensemble-based machine learning approaches, such as random forest (RF) and gradient boost (GB), which are both widely employed for prediction. We found that machine learning algorithms (RF and GB) that use decision trees as their base learners can predict experimental results of the maximum spreading factor more accurately than conventional methods. We posit that some of this improved estimation is due to hidden interactions (fluid properties fluctuations, substrate heterogeneities, experimental artifacts, and so on) that are not always completely controlled in experiments and are not accounted for in analytical models. Finally, the proposed machine learning models are highly versatile; they do not require any adjustable parameters and may be used to improve the interpretation of heterogeneous data, the detection of trends, and the performance of industrial processes involving droplet impact and spreading.

Author Contributions: Experimental Investigation, D.C.V.; Modeling, M.T.; Methodology, Conceptualization, Supervision, Writing and Editing M.T., D.C.V., A.D. and A.S. All authors have read and agreed to the published version of the manuscript.

Funding: This research received no external funding.

Institutional Review Board Statement: Not applicable.

Informed Consent Statement: Not applicable.

Data Availability Statement: The data that support the findings of this study are available from the corresponding author upon reasonable request.

Acknowledgments: D.C.V. thanks 3M Corporate Research for permission to publish this paper

Conflicts of Interest: The authors declare no conflicts of interest.

References

1. Yarin, A. Drop Impact Dynamics: Splashing, Spreading, Receding, Bouncing ... *Annu. Rev. Fluid Mech.* **2006**, *38*, 159–192. [CrossRef]
2. Josserand, C.; Thoroddsen, S. Drop Impact on a Solid Surface. *Annu. Rev. Fluid Mech.* **2016**, *48*, 365–391. [CrossRef]
3. Danzebrink, R.; Aegerter, M.A. Deposition of micropatterned coating using an ink-jet technique. *Thin Solid Film.* **1999**, *351*, 115–118. [CrossRef]
4. De Gans, B.J.; Duineveld, P.C.; Schubert, U.S. Inkjet printing of polymers: State of the art and future developments. *Adv. Mater.* **2004**, *16*, 203–213. [CrossRef]
5. Fedorchenko, A.I.; Wang, A.B.; Wang, Y.H. Effect of capillary and viscous forces on spreading of a liquid drop impinging on a solid surface. *Phys. Fluids* **2005**, *17*, 093104. [CrossRef]
6. Tembely, M.; Vadillo, D.; Soucemarianadin, A.; Dolatabadi, A. Numerical Simulations of Polymer Solution Droplet Impact on Surfaces of Different Wettabilities. *Processes* **2019**, *7*, 798. [CrossRef]
7. Gomaa, H.; Tembely, M.; Esmail, N.; Dolatabadi, A. Bouncing of cloud-sized microdroplets on superhydrophobic surfaces. *Phys. Fluids* **2020**, *32*, 122118. [CrossRef]
8. Liao, R.; Zuo, Z.; Guo, C.; Yuan, Y.; Zhuang, A. Fabrication of superhydrophobic surface on aluminum by continuous chemical etching and its anti-icing property. *Appl. Surf. Sci.* **2014**, *317*, 701–709. [CrossRef]
9. Bhushan, B.; Jung, Y.C. Natural and biomimetic artificial surfaces for superhydrophobicity, self-cleaning, low adhesion, and drag reduction. *Prog. Mater. Sci.* **2011**, *56*, 1–108. [CrossRef]
10. Yang, Z.; Liu, X.; Tian, Y. Hybrid Laser Ablation and Chemical Modification for Fast Fabrication of Bio-inspired Super-hydrophobic Surface with Excellent Self-cleaning, Stability and Corrosion Resistance. *J. Bionic Eng.* **2019**, *16*, 13–26. [CrossRef]
11. Rioboo, R.; Tropea, C.; Marengo, M. Outcomes from a drop impact on solid surfaces. *At. Sprays* **2001**, *11*, 155–165. [CrossRef]
12. Rioboo, R.; Marengo, M.; Tropea, C. Time evolution of liquid drop impact onto solid, dry surfaces. *Exp. Fluids* **2002**, *33*, 112–124. [CrossRef]
13. Chandra, S.; Avedisian, C.T. On the collision of a droplet with a solid surface. *Proc. R. Soc. A Math. Phys. Eng. Sci.* **1991**, *432*, 13–41. [CrossRef]
14. Pasandideh-Fard, M.; Qiao, Y.M.; Chandra, S.; Mostaghimi, J. Capillary effects during droplet impact on a solid surface. *Phys. Fluids* **1996**, *8*, 650–659. [CrossRef]

15. Bayer, I.S.; Megaridis, C.M. Contact angle dynamics in droplets impacting on flat surfaces with different wetting characteristics. *J. Fluid Mech.* **2006**, *558*, 415–449. [CrossRef]
16. Marengo, M.; Antonini, C.; Roisman, I.V.; Tropea, C. Drop collisions with simple and complex surfaces. *Curr. Opin. Colloid Interface Sci.* **2011**, *16*, 292–302. [CrossRef]
17. Clanet, C.; Béguin, C.; Richard, D.; Quéré, D. Maximal deformation of an impacting drop. *J. Fluid Mech.* **2004**, *517*, 199–208. [CrossRef]
18. Ukiwe, C.; Kwok, D.Y. On the maximum spreading diameter of impacting droplets on well-prepared solid surfaces. *Langmuir* **2005**, *21*, 666–673. [CrossRef]
19. Du, J.; Wang, X.; Li, Y.; Min, Q.; Wu, X. Analytical Consideration for the Maximum Spreading Factor of Liquid Droplet Impact on a Smooth Solid Surface. *Langmuir* **2021**, *37*, 7582–7590. [CrossRef]
20. Roisman, I.V.; Rioboo, R.; Tropea, C. Normal impact of a liquid drop on a dry surface: Model for spreading and receding. *Proc. R. Soc. A Math. Phys. Eng. Sci.* **2002**, *458*, 1411–1430. [CrossRef]
21. Choudhury, R.; Choi, J.; Yang, S.; Kim, Y.J.; Lee, D. Maximum spreading of liquid drop on various substrates with different wettabilities. *Appl. Surf. Sci.* **2017**, *415*, 149–154. [CrossRef]
22. Vadillo, D. Caractérisation des phénomènes Hydrodynamiques lors de l'impact de Gouttes sur Différents Types de Substrats. 2007. Available online: https://tel.archives-ouvertes.fr/tel-00178665/file/These_Vadillo.pdf (accessed on 15 April 2022).
23. Seo, J.; Lee, J.S.; Kim, H.Y.; Yoon, S.S. Empirical model for the maximum spreading diameter of low-viscosity droplets on a dry wall. *Exp. Therm. Fluid Sci.* **2015**, *61*, 121–129. [CrossRef]
24. Mao, T.; Kuhn, D.C.S.; Tran, H. Spread and rebound of liquid droplets upon impact on flat surfaces. *AIChE J.* **1997**, *43*, 2169–2179. [CrossRef]
25. Brunton, S.L.; Noack, B.R.; Koumoutsakos, P. Machine Learning for Fluid Mechanics. *Annu. Rev. Fluid Mech.* **2020**, *52*, 477–508. [CrossRef]
26. Tembely, M.; AlSumaiti, A.M.; Alameri, W. A deep learning perspective on predicting permeability in porous media from network modeling to direct simulation. *Comput. Geosci.* **2020**, *24*, 1541–1556. [CrossRef]
27. Hassantabar, S.; Wang, Z.; Jha, N.K. SCANN: Synthesis of Compact and Accurate Neural Networks. *IEEE Trans. Comput.-Aided Des. Integr. Circuits Syst.* **2021**. Available online: https://arxiv.org/abs/1904.09090v2 (accessed on 15 April 2022). [CrossRef]
28. Heidari, E.; Daeichian, A.; Sobati, M.A.; Movahedirad, S. Prediction of the droplet spreading dynamics on a solid substrate at irregular sampling intervals: Nonlinear Auto-Regressive eXogenous Artificial Neural Network approach (NARX-ANN). *Chem. Eng. Res. Des.* **2020**, *156*, 263–272. [CrossRef]
29. Azimi Yancheshme, A.; Hassantabar, S.; Maghsoudi, K.; Keshavarzi, S.; Jafari, R.; Momen, G. Integration of experimental analysis and machine learning to predict drop behavior on superhydrophobic surfaces. *Chem. Eng. J.* **2021**, *417*, 127898. [CrossRef]
30. Bartolo, D.; Josserand, C.; Bonn, D. Retraction dynamics of aqueous drops upon impact on non-wetting surfaces. *J. Fluid Mech.* **2005**, *545*, 329–338. [CrossRef]
31. Laan, N.; De Bruin, K.G.; Bartolo, D.; Josserand, C.; Bonn, D. Maximum diameter of impacting liquid droplets. *Phys. Rev. Appl.* **2014**, *2*, 044018. [CrossRef]
32. Salehi, H.; Burgueño, R. Emerging artificial intelligence methods in structural engineering. *Eng. Struct.* **2018**, *171*, 170–189. [CrossRef]
33. Touzani, S.; Granderson, J.; Fernandes, S. Gradient boosting machine for modeling the energy consumption of commercial buildings. *Energy Build.* **2018**, *158*, 1533–1543. [CrossRef]
34. Ha, S.; Jeong, H. Unraveling Hidden Interactions in Complex Systems With Deep Learning. *Sci. Rep. Nat.* **2021**, *11*, 12804. [CrossRef] [PubMed]
35. Yuan, X.; Li, L.; Shardt, Y.A.W.; Wang, Y.; Yang, C. Deep Learning With Spatiotemporal Attention-Based LSTM for Industrial Soft Sensor Model Development. *IEEE Trans. Ind. Electron.* **2021**, *68*, 4404–4414. [CrossRef]
36. Ou, C.; Zhu, H.; Shardt, Y.A.W.; Ye, L.; Yuan, X.; Wang, Y.; Yang, C. Quality-Driven Regularization for Deep Learning Networks and Its Application to Industrial Soft Sensors. *IEEE Trans. Neural Netw. Learn. Syst.* **2022**, 1–11. [CrossRef]
37. Zhu, H.H.; Zou, J.; Zhang, H.; Shi, Y.Z.; Luo, S.B.; Wang, N.; Cai, H.; Wan, L.X.; Wang, B.; Jiang, X.D.; et al. Space-efficient optical computing with an integrated chip diffractive neural network. *Nat. Commun.* **2022**, *13*, 1044. [CrossRef]
38. Luo, S.; Zhang, Y.; Nguyen, K.T.; Feng, S.; Shi, Y.; Liu, Y.; Hutchinson, P.; Chierchia, G.; Talbot, H.; Bourouina, T.; et al. Machine Learning-Based Pipeline for High Accuracy Bioparticle Sizing. *Micromachines* **2020**, *11*, 1084. [CrossRef]
39. Um, K.; Hu, X.; Thuerey, N. Liquid Splash Modeling with Neural Networks. *Comput. Graph. Forum* **2018**, *37*, 171–182. [CrossRef]
40. Lee, W.J.; Na, J.; Kim, K.; Lee, C.J.; Lee, Y.; Lee, J.M. NARX modeling for real-time optimization of air and gas compression systems in chemical processes. *Comput. Chem. Eng.* **2018**, *115*, 262–274. [CrossRef]
41. Antonini, C.; Amirfazli, A.; Marengo, M. Drop impact and wettability: From hydrophilic to superhydrophobic surfaces. *Phys. Fluids* **2012**, *24*, 102104. [CrossRef]
42. Vadillo, D.C.; Soucemarianadin, A.; Delattre, C.; Roux, D.C. Dynamic contact angle effects onto the maximum drop impact spreading on solid surfaces. *Phys. Fluids* **2009**, *21*, 122002. [CrossRef]
43. Eedi, H.; Kolla, M. Machine learning approaches for healthcare data analysis. *J. Crit. Rev.* **2020**, *7*, 806–811. [CrossRef]
44. Breiman, L. Random forests. *Mach. Learn.* **2001**, *45*, 5–32. [CrossRef]
45. Schapire, R.E. The Strength of Weak Learnability. *Mach. Learn.* **1990**, *5*, 197–227. [CrossRef]

46. Freund, Y.; Schapire, R.E. Experiments with a New Boosting Algorithm. In Proceedings of the 13th International Conference on Machine Learning, Bari, Italy, 3–6 July 1996; pp. 148–156. [CrossRef]
47. Natekin, A.; Knoll, A. Gradient boosting machines, a tutorial. *Front. Neurorobot.* **2013**, *7*, 1–21. [CrossRef]
48. Friedman, J.H. Greedy function approximation: A gradient boosting machine. *Ann. Stat.* **2001**, *29*, 1189–1232. [CrossRef]
49. Šikalo, Š.; Marengo, M.; Tropea, C.; Ganić, E.N. Analysis of impact of droplets on horizontal surfaces. *Exp. Therm. Fluid Sci.* **2002**, *25*, 503–510. [CrossRef]
50. Roisman, I.V.; Opfer, L.; Tropea, C.; Raessi, M.; Mostaghimi, J.; Chandra, S. Drop impact onto a dry surface: Role of the dynamic contact angle. *Colloids Surfaces A Physicochem. Eng. Asp.* **2008**, *322*, 183–191. [CrossRef]
51. Kim, H.Y.; Chun, J.H. The recoiling of liquid droplets upon collision with solid surfaces. *Phys. Fluids* **2001**, *13*, 643–659. [CrossRef]

Article

A Study of Text Vectorization Method Combining Topic Model and Transfer Learning

Xi Yang [1,2,*], Kaiwen Yang [1,*], Tianxu Cui [1], Min Chen [1] and Liyan He [1]

1. School of Information, Beijing Wuzi University, Beijing 101149, China; cuitianxubwu@163.com (T.C.); chenmincmark@163.com (M.C.); hly199808@163.com (L.H.)
2. School of Computer & Communication Engineering, University of Science and Technology Beijing, Beijing 100083, China
* Correspondence: yangxi@bwu.edu.cn (X.Y.); ykw1234@163.com (K.Y.)

Citation: Yang, X.; Yang, K.; Cui, T.; Chen, M.; He, L. A Study of Text Vectorization Method Combining Topic Model and Transfer Learning. Processes 2022, 10, 350. https:// doi.org/10.3390/pr10020350

Academic Editor: Mengchu Zhou

Received: 9 January 2022
Accepted: 6 February 2022
Published: 11 February 2022

Publisher's Note: MDPI stays neutral with regard to jurisdictional claims in published maps and institutional affiliations.

Copyright: © 2022 by the authors. Licensee MDPI, Basel, Switzerland. This article is an open access article distributed under the terms and conditions of the Creative Commons Attribution (CC BY) license (https:// creativecommons.org/licenses/by/ 4.0/).

Abstract: With the development of Internet cloud technology, the scale of data is expanding. Traditional processing methods find it difficult to deal with the problem of information extraction of big data. Therefore, it is necessary to use machine-learning-assisted intelligent processing to extract information from data in order to solve the optimization problem in complex systems. There are many forms of data storage. Among them, text data is an important data type that directly reflects semantic information. Text vectorization is an important concept in natural language processing tasks. Because text data can not be directly used for model parameter training, it is necessary to vectorize the original text data and make it numerical, and then the feature extraction operation can be carried out. The traditional text digitization method is often realized by constructing a bag of words, but the vector generated by this method can not reflect the semantic relationship between words, and it also easily causes the problems of data sparsity and dimension explosion. Therefore, this paper proposes a text vectorization method combining a topic model and transfer learning. Firstly, the topic model is selected to model the text data and extract its keywords, to grasp the main information of the text data. Then, with the help of the bidirectional encoder representations from transformers (BERT) model, which belongs to the pretrained model, model transfer learning is carried out to generate vectors, which are applied to the calculation of similarity between texts. By setting up a comparative experiment, this method is compared with the traditional vectorization method. The experimental results show that the vector generated by the topic-modeling- and transfer-learning-based text vectorization (TTTV) proposed in this paper can obtain better results when calculating the similarity between texts with the same topic, which means that it can more accurately judge whether the contents of the given two texts belong to the same topic.

Keywords: text vectorization; topic model; pretrained model; transfer learning

1. Introduction

In the Internet era, the interaction of online information is becoming more and more frequent, and the development of big data and the cloud computing technology promotes the dissemination of online information, which is a great driving force for the development of industries such as news media with information dissemination as the business core. Compared with the traditional paper media, online news is more timely because of the network as the communication media [1]. At the same time, because it is not limited by the printing layout, its communication quantity is often huge. For users who receive and browse news, a large number of fast updated online news cause them to enjoy the great convenience brought around by the fact that the Internet can retrieve information in seconds without the need to leave home [1]. However, in front of a large amount of information, how can they easily find other news with similar topics to expand their reading under the condition of browsing news in their field of interest, that is, the relevant recommendations? This is our consideration in modeling in this paper.

For the above scenarios, the traditional data processing methods are difficult to deal with. Therefore, it is necessary to adopt the machine-learning-assisted intelligent processing method to structurally operate the unstructured text data, and optimize the parameters of the model by analyzing the actual supply–demand relationship in the system. Therefore, we can obtain that for the currently browsed text data, finding other text data with high similarity is an effective method to solve the above problems. Because the text data cannot be directly used for modeling, it needs to be numerically processed [2,3], that is, the text vectorization operation [4,5], and then the generated vector, is used as the training data sample of the machine learning model. Text vectorization can be realized in two ways: one is the word vector, generated by taking the word as the basic unit [6], and the other is the paragraph vector, considering paragraph factors on the basis of word vector [7–9]. Word vector is a distributed representation of words, which aims to capture the syntactic and semantic information of words [10,11]. Before the text data is input into the network layer, it must be vectorized according to some method to become structured data. After the text is converted into word vector, the discrete symbols will be encoded according to the index to reduce the amount of parameters and improve the generalization ability.

In this paper, the text vectorization method combining topic model [12,13] and transfer learning [14,15] is studied. Firstly, the topic model is used to extract keywords from the text, to solve the problem of latent semantic mining which is difficult to solve by the traditional term frequency inverse document frequency method; then, the paragraph vector model is used to vectorize the text to solve the problem of mining the semantic relationship between paragraph and context that is difficult to solve by the word vector model. At the same time, the pretrained model is used for transfer learning to facilitate deeper feature learning of text data [16–18], so that the generated text vector can more accurately reflect semantic information.

The main contributions of this paper are as follows:

- The topic model keyword extraction method is introduced into the text vectorization operation.
- The text vector that can deeply reflect the semantic relationship is generated by transferring the pretrained model.
- The above text vectorization method is applied to the calculation task of text similarity.

The rest of this paper is organized as follows: Section 2 is the literature review; Section 3 introduces the materials and methods; in Section 4, a comparative experiment is designed. The text vectorization method used in this paper is applied to the calculation of text similarity, and compared with the text similarity calculated by the vector generated by traditional text vectorization, and the experimental results are analyzed; Section 5 is the conclusion.

2. Literature Review

We review the related literature from the following three aspects: text vectorization, topic model, and pretrained model for transfer learning.

The generation of word vector can be understood as encoding text data according to a certain model. Its development has roughly experienced several stages, such as one-hot representation [19], bag of words (BOW) [20,21], language model (LM) [22], word2vec [6], and so on. One-hot representation generates word vectors by binary coding, and each dimension only indicates whether the corresponding word in the dictionary is taken at the location. This method will not only bring dimensional disaster and lead to data sparsity, but also cause lack of feature extraction of text semantics; BOW replaces binary data with word frequency data on the basis of one-hot, but it still fails to solve the problems of dimension disaster and semantic loss; the LM model uses conditional probability to express the association between words in text sequence. The semantic representation method of the LM model is relatively primitive, so it has been developed to word2vec model. The word2vec model is composed of continuous bag of words model (CBOW) and skip-gram model. The word2vec model uses a structure similar to neural network to establish the relationship between words, but the model only focuses on the local semantic information and fails to combine the global information of the text. The vector of the same word is still the same in different contexts, that is, it cannot solve the problem of polysemy. As can be seen from the above, word vectors mostly focus on the semantic connection between words themselves or local words [10,11], so the information such as paragraphs and word order of the text can not be accurately extracted and fully utilized. Therefore, a paragraph vector model is proposed, that is, para2vec [7], sometimes referred to as doc2vec. Para2vec is an extension of word2vec [8,9]. When generating vectors, not only the context words but also the corresponding paragraph information are considered. Para2vec model consists of a distributed memory model (DM) and a distributed bag of words model (DBOW).

Text data is composed of a large number of sentences. In order to avoid the problem of dimension explosion, we cannot directly construct vectors with sentences as feature dimensions. Sentences can be regarded as a sequence of words [23], so we can extract the representative words, that is, keywords, and then generate vectors based on keywords by constructing certain models and algorithms. There are two kinds of text keyword extraction methods, one is the term frequency inverse document frequency (TFIDF) method based on frequency, and the other is the topic model method based on spatial mapping [12,13]. The TFIDF method measures the importance of a specific word in each sentence by two factors: term frequency, that is, the frequency of a word in the sentence, and inverse document frequency, that is, the reciprocal of the frequency of the sentence containing the above words. Although this method constructs the correlation between words and sentences, it only analyzes them from the perspective of frequency, and fails to construct the mapping relationship based on the understanding of text semantics. In order to extract keywords from text based on understanding semantic structure, the topic model method is proposed. The topic model is an unsupervised learning model for latent semantic mining and analysis of text data. Its core is to construct the mapping between sentence space and topic space and between topic space and word space by setting topic variables as intermediate variables. Using spatial mapping to analyze text semantics is not only conducive to clustering words to reduce redundancy, but also realizes dimension reduction operation, to better reflect the distribution features of words, topics, and sentences. The topic model is mainly composed of latent semantic analysis model (LSA) and latent Dirichlet allocation model (LDA). The core of LSA [24] is the operation of singular value decomposition of text matrix to generate the mapping relationship among words, topics, and sentences, that is, word space and sentence space are mapped to relatively lower dimensional topic space, respectively, to explore the latent semantic relationship [25–27]. Compared with LSA model, the LDA [28,29] model focuses on constructing the mapping relationship between the above three variable spaces from the perspective of probability distribution, to avoid the huge amount of matrix operation caused by singular value decomposition operation. By introducing the relevant theories of Dirichlet distribution and multinomial distribution [30,31], the LDA model can carry out latent semantic mining from the perspective of probability distribution [32–34].

By transferring the parameter information obtained from some large and general source tasks to the target task, transfer learning avoids the problem of starting from scratch every training [14,15]. In general, we often lack enough targeted datasets for training, so we can use the pretrained model trained by the general large dataset for transferring. In the field of natural language processing, the development of pretrained model has mainly experienced several stages, such as embeddings from language models (ELMo), generative pretraining (GPT), and bidirectional encoder representations from transformers (BERT). ELMo [35] first learns the word embedding of each word through the language model, and then dynamically adjusts the word embedding according to the context [36–38], which can solve the problem of polysemy and realize the function of semantic relationship judgment at the same time [39]. In terms of feature extractor, ELMo adopts the LSTM, but a new feature extractor transformer [40] was proposed later, and the feature extraction ability proved to be better than LSTM. Therefore, based on transformer as the feature extractor [41,42], GPT is proposed [43]. The model is first pretrained through the language model, and then fine-tuned to access the downstream tasks; however, the model is a one-way language model [44,45], that is, when predicting words in sentences, it only pays attention to the above without considering the following, so it is not comprehensive in semantic understanding. In order to consider the semantic information in two word order directions at the same time, BERT [16] is proposed. It is a two-way language model based on transformer. Through the training of large datasets, a general pre-trained model with strong transferring ability is obtained [46,47].

3. Materials and Methods

3.1. Word2vec

Word2vec is a word vector generation method based on word embedding. Its core idea is the distributed expression of words, which maps words to vectors with definable dimensions. Because the context of the current word is considered in the training process, a low-dimensional dense vector with semantic information can be generated.

Specifically, each statement in a text paragraph is essentially a word sequence, expressed as $d = \left[d^{(1)}, d^{(2)}, \ldots, d^{(j)}, \ldots, d^{(n)}\right]$, where $d^{(j)}$ represents the word at the current jth position in the sequence, and n is the sequence length, that is, the number of words contained. In order to obtain the word vector, we need to construct the mapping relationship between the current word and its context, that is, $d^{(i)} = f(d^{(j)}), i \neq j$, the mapping relationship is trained through the neural network structure, and the hidden layer weight obtained in the training process is the word vector. Word2vec consists of CBOW and skip-gram.

3.1.1. Continuous Bag of Words (CBOW)

CBOW constructs the mapping relationship between the two adjacent words before and after the current word as the context, that is, the current word is predicted by the context, that is, $d^{(j)} = f(d^{(j-2)}, d^{(j-1)}, d^{(j+1)}, d^{(j+2)})$. The specific structure of the model is shown in Figure 1a. The average value of the word vector of the context is input as the weight, and then converted into the conditional probability $p(d^{(j)} \mid d^{(j-2)}, d^{(j-1)}, d^{(j+1)}, d^{(j+2)})$ of the current word under the condition of the context through the softmax activation function, to realize the semantic association between the current word and the context.

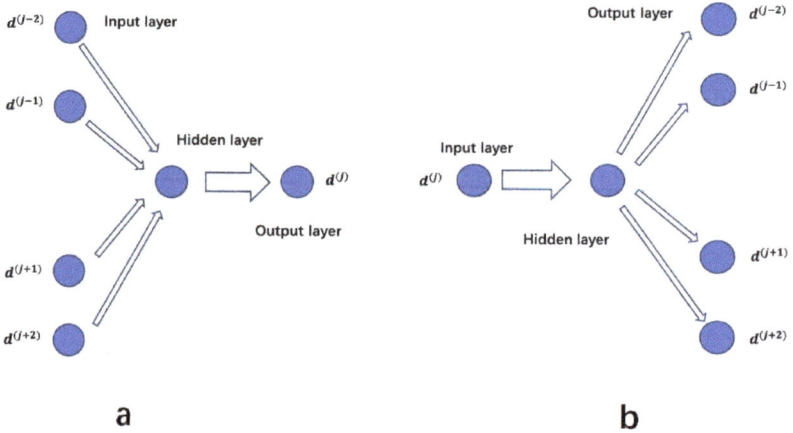

Figure 1. Word2vec ((**a**): CBOW (**b**): Skip-Gram).

3.1.2. Skip-Gram

Different from CBOW, skip-gram uses the current word to predict the context, and the scope of the context is definable. Its size of sliding window is called skip-window, as shown in Figure 1b. Letting the window size above and below be 2, respectively, and taking this as an example, the mapping relationship $d^{(j+c)} = f(d^{(j)}), c = \pm 1, \pm 2$ can be obtained. Then, similar to the training process of CBOW, feature extraction is carried out through the hidden layer, and finally probabilistic conversion is carried out through the softmax activation function to obtain the condition probability $p(d^{(j+c)} \mid d^{(j)}), c = \pm 1, \pm 2$.

3.2. Para2vec

Because the word2vec model does not consider paragraph factors in semantic learning, that is, the relationship between ordered clauses of a sentence, the para2vec model is proposed on this basis. The model mainly introduces a paragraph component with the same structure as the context component to predict the current word, namely the DM model, or the context is predicted by paragraph component, that is, the DBOW model.

3.2.1. Distributed Memory (DM)

DM is extended from CBOW. It also predicts the current word through context. On this basis, it adds paragraph ID and generates paragraph vector with the same structure as word vector. The paragraph component and context component are accumulated and connected together and sent to the network for training. Finally, it also uses softmax activation function for probabilistic conversion to obtain the conditional probability of the current word. In general, the DM model introduces word vector and paragraph vector into the process of semantic learning to predict the probability distribution of the current target word. The specific structure of the model is shown in Figure 2a.

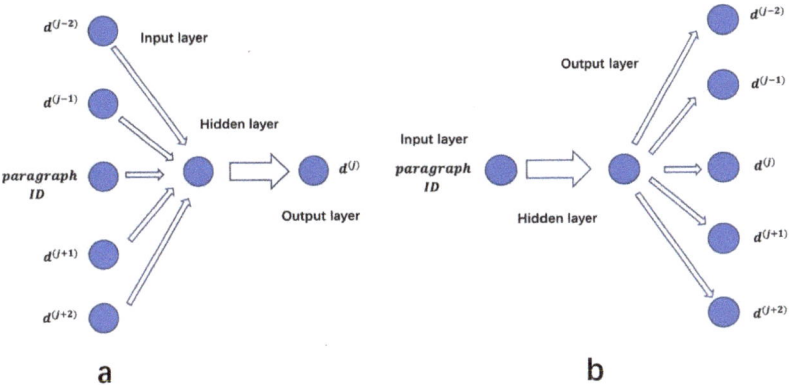

Figure 2. Para2vec ((**a**): DM (**b**): DBOW).

3.2.2. Distributed Bag of Words (DBOW)

DBOW is extended through skip-gram. It takes the context as the prediction target, and the range of the context to be predicted can also be determined by defining the size of the sliding window; the specific structure of the model is shown in Figure 2b. However, unlike skip-gram, DBOW does not directly use the current word, but takes the paragraph vector based on the paragraph ID as the input, and the predicted context word also comes from the inside of each input paragraph. Due to the two-way and orderly semantic relationship between input and output, such a para2vec learns not only semantic information, but also word order information.

3.3. Topic Model

Topic model is a kind of unsupervised learning model that analyzes text semantic information by constructing relationship mapping between sentence space, topic space, and word space.

Let the sentence space be D, in which each element d represents a sentence. The sentence can be regarded as a word sequence, so the sentence variable can be expressed as

$$d_i = \left[d_i^{(1)}, d_i^{(2)}, \ldots, d_i^{(j)}, \ldots, d_i^{(n_i)}\right] \quad i = 1, 2, \ldots, N, j = 1, 2, \ldots, n_i. \tag{1}$$

where $d_i^{(j)}$ represents the jth word in the ith sentence, N is the total number of sentence elements, and n_i is the total number of words in the ith sentence.

Let the topic space be T, where each element $t_k, k = 1, 2, \ldots, K$ represents the topic, and K is the number of types of topics.

Let the word space be W, where each element $w_v, v = 1, 2, \ldots, V$ represents a word and V is the number of types of words.

The distribution of each word in the sentence sequence is not random, but connected through the intermediate variable of topic. Because it is unobservable, it is called hidden variable, and the relative sentence variable and word variable are called observable variable. The goal of the topic model is to mine text semantic information by constructing the mapping relationship between the spaces of the above three variables. The common topic model consists of latent semantic analysis (LSA) and latent Dirichlet allocation (LDA).

3.3.1. Latent Semantic Analysis (LSA)

LSA is a topic model based on allocation matrix. Let the allocation matrix be $A_{N \times n}$, in which each element $a_i^{(j)}$ represents the word allocation probability at the jth position on the ith sentence. The allocation matrix can be expressed by the product of the allocation matrix $B_{N \times K}$ between sentence space and topic space and the $C_{K \times n}$ between topic space and word space, that is, $A_{N \times n} = B_{N \times K} \cdot C_{K \times n}$. Since the above distributions are hidden and cannot be solved directly, the singular value decomposition method is used to obtain the approximate estimates of $B_{N \times K}$ and $C_{K \times n}$.

3.3.2. Latent Dirichlet Allocation (LDA)

Because the singular value decomposition method used in LSA is mechanical matrix disassembly, it not only has a large amount of computation, but also does not consider the problem of probability distribution. LDA avoids the above defects. The model models each element in the sentence space, and then expands to the whole sentence space based on the principle of independent and identically distributed.

The specific modeling process is as follows:

The topic distribution of the sentence can be expressed as a parameter vector

$$\theta_i = [\theta_{i1}, \theta_{i2}, \ldots, \theta_{ik}, \ldots, \theta_{iK}], i = 1, 2, \ldots, N. \tag{2}$$

where each component θ_{ik} represents the distribution probability of the kth topic to which the ith sentence belongs. The parameter vector obeys the Dirichlet distribution, and its probability density function is

$$p(\theta_i \mid a) = \frac{\Gamma\left(\sum_k^K a_k\right)}{\prod_k^K a_k} \prod_k^K \theta_{ik}^{a_k - 1}. \tag{3}$$

where $a = [a_1, a_2, \ldots, a_k, \ldots, a_K], a_k > 0$ is distribution parameter.

Then, the topic distribution of the ith sentence is constructed by the multinomial distribution whose parameter is the parameter vector, and its probability density function is

$$p(t \mid \theta_i) = \frac{\left(\sum_k^K t_k\right)!}{\prod_k^K t_k!} \prod_k^K \theta_{ik}^{t_k}. \tag{4}$$

If each sample satisfies the principle of independent and identical distribution, the topic distribution $p(t \mid d_i)$ of the sentence can be randomly selected from the above distribution. The word distribution of the topic can be expressed as a parameter vector

$$\eta_k = [\eta_{k1}, \eta_{k2}, \ldots, \eta_{kv}, \ldots, \eta_{kV}], k = 1, 2, \ldots, K. \tag{5}$$

where each component η_{kv} represents the distribution probability of the vth word corresponding to the kth topic. The parameter vector obeys the Dirichlet distribution, and its probability density function is

$$p(\eta_k \mid b) = \frac{\Gamma\left(\sum_v^V b_v\right)}{\prod_v^V b_v} \prod_v^V \eta_{kv}^{b_v - 1}. \tag{6}$$

where $b = [b_1, b_2, \ldots, b_v, \ldots, b_V], b_v \geq 0$ is distribution parameter.

Then, the word distribution corresponding to the kth topic is constructed by using the multinomial distribution with the parameter vector as the distribution parameter, and its probability density function is

$$p(w \mid \eta_k) = \frac{\left(\sum_v^V w_v\right)!}{\prod_v^V w_v!} \prod_v^V \eta_{kv}^{w_v} \tag{7}$$

If each sample satisfies the principle of independent and identical distribution, the word distribution $p(w \mid t_k)$ of the topic can be randomly selected from the above distribution.

The symbolic representation is shown in Table 1 below, the probability distribution relationship between variables is shown in Figure 3, and the modeling process is shown in Algorithm 1.

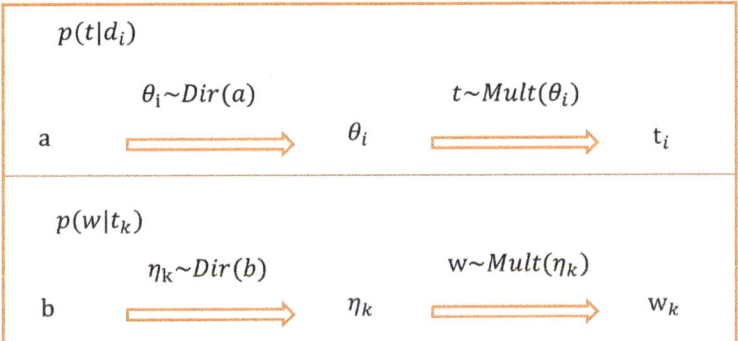

Figure 3. Probability distribution relationship between variables.

Table 1. List of mathematical symbols.

Symbol	Meaning
$d_i^{(j)}$	The component of the text sequence, which represents the jth word of the ith sentence
η_{kv}	Allocation probability when the kth topic corresponds to the vth word
b	Distribution parameters of Dirichlet distribution obeyed by η
$t_i^{(j)}$	The component of the topic sequence, which represents the topic corresponding to the jth word of the ith sentence
θ_{ik}	Distribution probability of the kth topic to which the ith sentence belongs
a	Distribution parameters of Dirichlet distribution obeyed by θ

Algorithm 1 Modeling based on LDA model.

Input: text set D; topic set T; word set W; parameters a, b of Dirichlet distribution; length n_i of each sentence $d_i \in D$.

Output: allocation θ_{ik} based on text-topic; allocation η_{kv} based on topic-word; probability density $p(t \mid \theta)$ of topic; probability density $p(w \mid \eta)$ of word; topic sequence t; sentence sequence d.

1: Initialize a and b to 1 respectively.
2: **for** each $d_i \in$ range (D) **do**
3:     **for** each $t_k \in$ range (T) **do**
4:         generate $\theta_{ik} \sim Dir(a)$ as $p(t \mid d_i)$.
5:     **end for**
6: **end for**
7: **for** each $i \in$ range (N) **do**
8:     **for** each $j \in$ range (n_i) **do**
9:         generate $t_i^{(j)} \sim Mult(\theta_i)$.
10:        generate $d_i^{(j)} \sim Mult(\eta_{t_i^{(j)}})$.
11:     **end for**
12: **end for**
13: **return** $\theta_{ik}, \eta_{kv}, p(t \mid \theta), p(w \mid \eta), \mathbf{t} = \left[t_i^{(j)}\right], \mathbf{d} = \left[d_i^{(j)}\right]$.

3.4. Pretrained Model and Transfer Learning

Pretraining means that when the model starts training, it does not need to initialize the parameters randomly from scratch, but initialize and then train on the basis of a set of model parameters that have learned a large number of general features in advance. BERT is a pretrained model. Through massive corpus training, word vectors with wide applicability are obtained. At the same time, it can be optimized in specific tasks, which greatly improves the experimental effect. The BERT model is a pretrained model based on multitask learning on the basis of bidirectional deep transformer. A major structural feature of BERT model is that it adopts a two-way self attention mechanism, which can take into account the context information in this encoder and left and right adjacent encoders at the same time.

The input layer of BERT consists of three layers, and the values of the three layers are added as the output of transformer. The token layer is used to embed word vectors, the segment layer is used to retrieve the sentences to which the word belongs, and the position layer is used to locate the position of the word in the word vector sequence. Taking Figure 4 as an example, when a piece of text data is input into the model, all words and the identification between internal segments are embedded through the token layer, so the composition of each word can be clearly distinguished in the token sequence. Then, the words and paragraph identifiers belonging to the same paragraph in the text are marked as the same category in the segment layer, that is, two sub-sentences in the sentence pair or multiple sub-sentences in the long sentence can be distinguished. Finally, in the position layer, each word and paragraph are identified and numbered consecutively as position embedding, which also provides a basis for the model to learn word order information.

With its strong transferring ability, BERT can adapt to the transfer learning of different downstream tasks. Therefore, it can be fine-tuned on the basis of the pretrained model, build word vectors in the way of transfer learning, improve the model performance and generalization ability, and reduce the demand for large-scale labeled data.

Figure 4. Input layer of BERT.

3.5. Text Similarity Calculation Based on Topic Modeling and Transfer-Learning-Based Text Vectorization (TTTV)

Deep learning involves a large number of operations. At the same time, the training of a neural network model also needs the supply of big data [48]. If the training task is initialized from scratch and solved iteratively every time, it will not only be inefficient, but also cause a waste of computing resources [49]. Therefore, this paper adopts the transfer learning method based on a pretrained model for training. The pretrained model was trained by large datasets, and we can directly use its corresponding structure and weight. In order to adapt to specific tasks, we can freeze some of its network layers, and then train the unfrozen parts on a small scale based on specific task datasets, and dynamically adjust the parameters to adapt to the characteristics of downstream tasks.

TTTV can be used to measure the similarity of texts with different contents belonging to the same topic. The first is keyword extraction. The text data is modeled by LDA belonging to the topic model, the mapping relationship among sentence space, topic space, and word space is constructed, and the number of keywords to be extracted is set. The P (precision), R (recall), and F1 (F1 measure) are used as measurement indicators, i.e.,

$$P = \frac{|T_1| \cap |T_2|}{|T_1|}. \tag{8}$$

$$R = \frac{|T_1| \cap |T_2|}{|T_2|}. \tag{9}$$

$$F1 = 2PR/(P + R). \tag{10}$$

where T_1 represents the extracted keyword set, and T_2 represents the keyword set marked by the original text. We comprehensively consider the above indicators and select the topic model parameters with the highest extraction performance for subsequent operations. After that, text vectorization is carried out, and the text vector is obtained through the transfer learning of the BERT model. We select the text vectors x_1 and x_2 generated by pairs of text data d_1 and d_2 belonging to the same topic but different contents, calculate their cosine distance, and define it as the similarity of the text to which they belong, i.e.,

$$\text{similarity}(d_1, d_2) \stackrel{\text{def}}{=} \text{cosine}(x_1, x_2) = \frac{x_1 \cdot x_2}{||x_1|| \cdot ||x_2||} \tag{11}$$

See Algorithm 2 for the specific process.

Algorithm 2 Text similarity based on TTTV.

Input: text set D; number K of keywords.
Output: similarity $(d_1, d_2); \forall d_1, d_2 \in D$.
 1: **for** each $d_i \in$ range (D) **do**
 2:     **for** each $k \in$ range (K) **do**
 3:         extract $keyword_k$ of d_i through LDA.
 4:     **end for**
 5:     generate vector x_i of text d_i.
 6:     based on set $\{keyword_k\}$ through BERT.
 7: **end for**
 8: $\text{cosine}(x_1, x_2) \leftarrow \frac{x_1 \cdot x_2}{||x_1|| \cdot ||x_2||}$.
 9: $\text{similarity}(d_1, d_2) \leftarrow \text{cosine}(x_1, x_2)$.
10: **return** $\text{similarity}(d_1, d_2)$.

---

4. Experiment

4.1. Experimental Environment and Data

The experimental environment is an Intel i7 processor with 16 GB memory, the programming language is Python, the Jieba is used for text word segmentation, and the Gensim is used for text vectorization training. The data used in the experiment is Sogou laboratory news dataset, including 18 subjects in international, sports, society, entertainment, and other fields, with a total of 1.02 GB news text data.

4.2. Experimental Setup and Analysis of Experimental Results

In this paper, cosine distance is used as the evaluation index to calculate the similarity between texts, to evaluate whether the vectors generated by different text vectorization methods can accurately judge whether the contents of any two texts belong to the same topic, and a comparative experiment is set up. In the keyword extraction stage, the traditional frequency-based TFIDF method and the topic model method used in this paper are used to extract the keywords of the text, to compare the impact of the extraction results on the performance of the final generated text vector. The topic model method can be compared in two cases: latent semantic analysis model (LSA) and latent Dirichlet allocation model (LDA). In the text vector generation stage, the word2vec method and the para2vec method are used for text vectorization, respectively. The word2vec method can be compared in the continuous bag of words (CBOW) model and skip-gram model, and the para2vec method can be compared in the distributed memory model (DM) and distributed bag of words model (DBOW). Finally, it is compared with the transfer learning method using the BERT model.

The experimental results are shown in Tables 2 and 3 and Figures 5–8. The first is text keyword extraction. We set the keyword extraction number to 3–18, respectively, and calculate the P (precision), R (recall), and F1 (F1 measure) to evaluate the extraction effect.

Table 2. Keyword extraction.

Method	K = 3			K = 4			K = 5			K = 6		
	P	R	F1	P	R	F1	P	R	F1	P	R	F1
TFIDF	0.67	0.11	0.19	0.75	0.17	0.27	0.80	0.22	0.35	0.83	0.28	0.42
LSA	0.67	0.11	0.19	0.50	0.11	0.18	0.60	0.17	0.26	0.67	0.22	0.33
LDA	0.66	0.11	0.19	0.75	0.17	0.27	0.60	0.17	0.26	0.67	0.22	0.33

Method	K = 7			K = 8			K = 9			K = 10		
	P	R	F1	P	R	F1	P	R	F1	P	R	F1
TFIDF	0.71	0.28	0.40	0.63	0.28	0.38	0.56	0.28	0.37	0.50	0.28	0.36
LSA	0.71	0.28	0.40	0.75	0.33	0.46	0.67	0.33	0.44	0.60	0.33	0.43
LDA	0.86	0.33	0.48	0.75	0.33	0.46	0.78	0.39	0.52	0.70	0.38	0.50

Method	K = 11			K = 12			K = 13			K = 14		
	P	R	F1	P	R	F1	P	R	F1	P	R	F1
TFIDF	0.45	0.28	0.34	0.42	0.28	0.33	0.46	0.33	0.39	0.50	0.39	0.44
LSA	0.55	0.33	0.41	0.50	0.33	0.40	0.46	0.33	0.39	0.43	0.33	0.38
LDA	0.82	0.50	0.62	0.75	0.50	0.60	0.77	0.56	0.65	0.79	0.61	0.69

Method	K = 15			K = 16			K = 17			K = 18		
	P	R	F1	P	R	F1	P	R	F1	P	R	F1
TFIDF	0.53	0.44	0.48	0.56	0.50	0.53	0.59	0.56	0.57	0.61	0.61	0.61
LSA	0.40	0.33	0.36	0.38	0.33	0.35	0.35	0.33	0.34	0.50	0.50	0.50
LDA	0.73	0.61	0.67	0.75	0.67	0.71	0.71	0.67	0.69	0.72	0.72	0.72

Table 3. Average text similarity.

Keyword Extraction	word2vec		para2vec		Pre-Trained
	CBOW	Skip-Gram	DM	DBOW	BERT
TFIDF	0.68	0.67	0.81	0.79	0.82
LSA	0.71	0.72	0.82	0.82	0.83
LDA	0.78	0.79	0.83	0.84	0.86

It can be seen from Figures 5–7 that in terms of extraction accuracy, when the keyword extraction number is less than or equal to six, the extraction precision of TFIDF method and LSA method shows an increasing trend, while the extraction precision of LDA method fluctuates but is relatively stable. When the keyword extraction number is located in [6,12] and [8,17], respectively, the extraction precision of TFIDF method and LSA method begins to decline, and the extraction precision of LDA method tends to be stable between 0.7–0.8. It can be seen that the method using non-LDA model is not suitable for the extraction of more keywords.

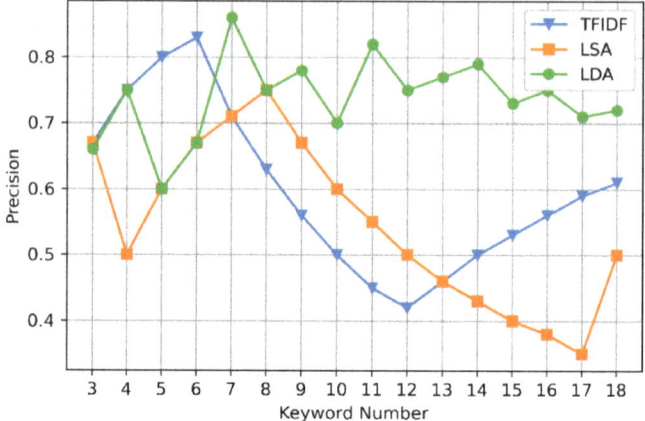

Figure 5. Experimental results of P.

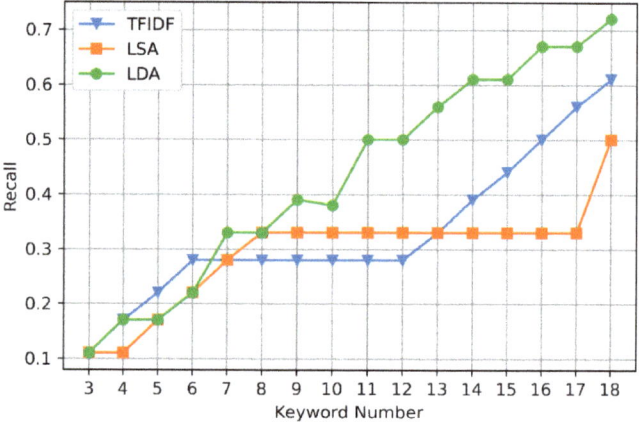

Figure 6. Experimental results of R.

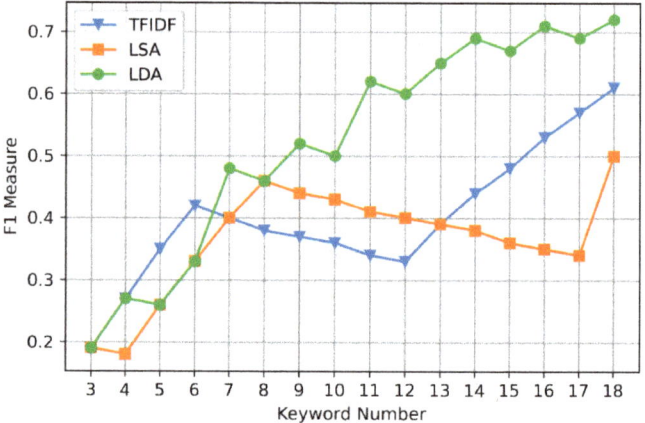

Figure 7. Experimental results of F1.

In terms of extraction recall, when the keyword extraction number is less than or equal to six, the extraction recall of each extraction method shows an increasing trend. When the keyword extraction number is located in the [6,12] interval and [8,17] interval, respectively, the extraction recall of the TFIDF method and the LSA method does not increase or decrease, indicating that the learning ability of non-LDA model for sample features is limited by local optimization. The recall of LDA extraction still shows a gradual upward trend.

Since it is not comprehensive to evaluate the extraction performance by precision or recall alone, the extraction performance can be comprehensively evaluated by its harmonic mean F1 measure. The F1 measure of the TFIDF method and the LSA method continues to decrease in [6,12] and [4,17], respectively, and the overall F1 measure is lower than that of the LDA method. Therefore, text keyword extraction is carried out through the LDA model, the extraction accuracy is high, and the performance is not easily affected by the change of the set number of keywords.

To sum up, we set the keyword extraction number to 18, then carry out the next vectorization operation, measure the similarity of paired text data belonging to the same topic but different contents in the dataset, and sum and average the similarity calculation results to obtain the average text similarity, as shown in Table 3 and Figure 8.

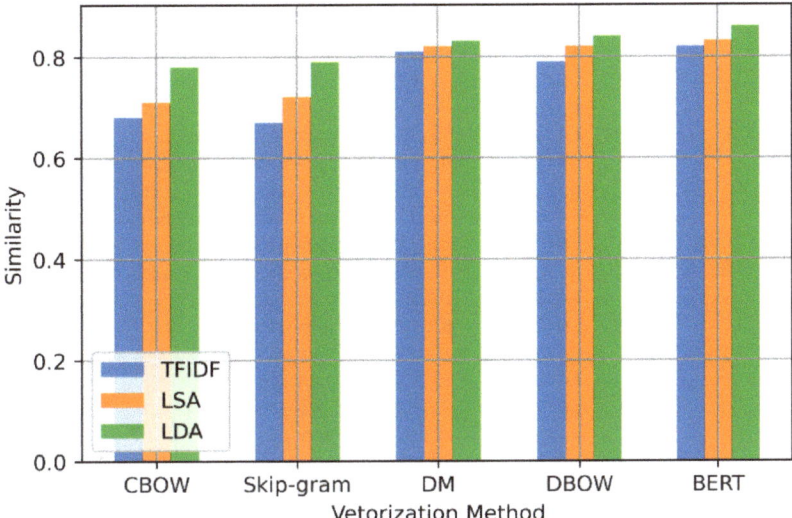

Figure 8. Comparison of text similarity calculation results.

Figure 8 lists five text vectorization methods: CBOW, skip-gram, DM, DBOW, and BERT. On the premise of three keyword extraction methods, TFIDF, LSA, and LDA, we measure the similarity of pairs of text data belonging to the same topic but different contents, and calculate the average text similarity.

It can be seen from the figure that for each vectorization model, the average text similarity calculated by the text vector generated on the premise of selecting LDA for keyword extraction is higher than that calculated based on TFIDF and LSA, respectively. This means that we can more accurately judge the text pairs with similar, or the same, topics. At the same time, we can see that the similarity judgment performance of the text vector generated by DM or DBOW is better than that calculated by CBOW or skip-gram method, which means that the para2vec method based on paragraph vector combined with word vector can grasp the text topic information more accurately than the word2vec method considering only word vector.

Compared with the word2vec method, both the para2vec method and the BERT method learn the semantic information in the text more effectively, so the performance is significantly improved when judging the text similarity. When comparing para2vec with BERT, it is found that although BERT improves the similarity results, the improvement range is not very large. This is because the BERT model is pretrained through a large amount of corpus, so it focuses more on the learning of general features, while para2vec is more suitable for the local feature learning of data with appropriate scale, but it is not good at learning general features. In other words, these two models have their own advantages and disadvantages, and the scalability brought by BERT with transfer learning will be an important aspect to make up for its shortcomings. In addition to the differences in model structure, another reason for this insignificant difference is that the dataset itself is relatively clustered and stored through similar topics, so it does not create a more general data distribution, that is, whether the texts of similar topics are clustered in the same round of tests is completely random. Therefore, the performance superiority of the model proposed in this paper is not obvious, although it does improve the experimental results.

Through comparison, the average text similarity results calculated by the text vector generated by the LDA topic model combined with the BERT pretrained model are higher than the above comparative experiments, that is, this method can judge the text pairs with similar, or the same, topics relatively more accurately.

5. Conclusions

In order to measure the similarity of text pairs with similar, or the same, topic in news texts, this paper proposes a text vectorization method combining topic model and transfer learning. The text data is transformed into vectors, and the cosine distance is used as the measurement index to calculate the similarity. By setting up comparative experiments, it is proved that this method can obtain higher results when calculating the similarity of text pairs with similar, or the same, topic, which means that it can more accurately judge whether the text pair belongs to the same subject.

There is still much room for improvement for such methods, such as considering the mapping relationship between vector dimension and semantic information, or adding additional feature weights to text paragraphs. This is also a collection of methods to be gradually improved in the next step, to facilitate more accurate semantic analysis and research of the text. In addition to the BERT model, there are many available pretrained models, such as RoBERTa [50], ALBERT [51], and SpanBERT [52]. Adding these models to the comparative experiment to study the performance differences in the process of transfer learning will become an entry point in our subsequent research.

Author Contributions: This paper was completed by five authors. Their contributions are as follows: Conceptualization, X.Y. and K.Y.; methodology, K.Y. and T.C.; software, X.Y. and K.Y.; validation, X.Y., K.Y. and T.C.; formal analysis, K.Y.; investigation, T.C.; resources, X.Y.; data curation, M.C. and L.H.; writing—original draft preparation, X.Y., K.Y., T.C. and L.H.; writing—review and editing, K.Y. and T.C.; visualization, K.Y. and L.H.; supervision, X.Y. and T.C.; project administration, M.C.; funding acquisition, M.C. and X.Y. All authors have read and agreed to the published version of the manuscript.

Funding: This paper was funded by National Natural Science Foundation of China (No. 61803035), Beijing Intelligent Logistics System Collaborative Innovation Center (No. BILSCIC-2019KF-08).

Conflicts of Interest: The authors declare no conflict of interest.

References

1. Jeffrey, C. South Online resources for news about toxicology and other environmental topics. *Toxicology* **2001**, *157*, 153–164.
2. Macskassy, S.A.; Hirsh, H.; Banerjee, A.; Dayanik, A.A. Converting numerical classification into text classification. *Artif. Intell.* **2003**, *143*, 51–77. [CrossRef]
3. Qi, D.; Liu, X.; Yao, Y.; Zhao, F. Numerical characteristics of word frequencies and their application to dissimilarity measure for sequence comparison. *J. Theor. Biol.* **2011**, *276*, 174–180.
4. Kang, X.; Ren, F.; Wu, Y. Exploring latent semantic information for textual emotion recognition in blog articles. *IEEE/CAA J. Autom. Sin.* **2018**, *5*, 204–216. [CrossRef]

5. Tan Z.; Chen, J.; Kang, Q.; Zhou, M.C.; Sedraoui, K. Dynamic embedding projection-gated convolutional neural networks for text classification. *IEEE Trans. Neural Netw. Learn. Syst.* **2021**, *99*, 1–10. [CrossRef]
6. Mikolov, T.; Chen, K.; Corrado, G.; Dean, J. Efficient estimation of word representations in vector space. *arXiv* **2013**, arXiv:1301.3781.
7. Le, Q.; Mikolov, T. Distributed Representations of Sentences and Documents. In Proceedings of the 31st International Conference on Machine Learning, Beijing, China, 21–26 June 2014.
8. Kim, D.; Seo, D.; Cho, S.; Kang, P. Multi-co-training for document classification using various document representations: Tf–idf, lda, and doc2vec. *Inform. Sci.* **2019**, *477*, 15–29. [CrossRef]
9. Gómez-Adorno, H.; Posadas-Durán, J.P.; Sidorov, G.; Pinto, D. Document embeddings learned on various types of n-grams for cross-topic authorship attribution. *Computing* **2018**, *100*, 741–756. [CrossRef]
10. Zhang, Y.; Xu, B.; Zhao, T. Convolutional multi-head self-attention on memory for aspect sentiment classification. *IEEE/CAA J. Autom. Sin.* **2020**, *7*, 1038–1044. [CrossRef]
11. Liu, H.; Chatterjee, I.; Zhou, M.C.; Lu, X.S.; Abusorrah, A. Aspect-based sentiment analysis: A survey of deep learning methods. *IEEE Trans. Comput. Soc. Syst.* **2020**, *7*, 1358–1375. [CrossRef]
12. Lan, D.; Buntine, W.; Jin, H. A segmented topic model based on the two-parameter poisson-dirichlet process. *Mach. Learn.* **2010**, *81*, 5–19.
13. Yang, Y.; Liu, Y.; Lu, X.; Xu, J.; Wang, F. A named entity topic model for news popularity prediction. *Knowl.-Based Syst.* **2020**, *208*, 106430. [CrossRef]
14. Buiu, C.; Dnil, V.R.; Rdu, C.N. Mobilenetv2 ensemble for cervical precancerous lesions classification. *Processes* **2020**, *8*, 595. [CrossRef]
15. Shin, S.J.; Kim, Y.M.; Meilanitasari, P. A holonic-based self-learning mechanism for energy-predictive planning in machining processes. *Processes* **2019**, *7*, 739. [CrossRef]
16. Devlin, J.; Chang, M.W.; Lee, K.; Toutanova, K. Bert: Pre-Training of Deep Bidirectional Transformers for Language Understanding. *arXiv* **2019**, arXiv:1810.04805.
17. Lai, P.T.; Lu, Z. Bert-gt: Cross-sentence n-ary relation extraction with bert and graph transformer. *arXiv* **2021**, arXiv:2101.04158.
18. Abdulnabi, I.; Yaseen, Q. Spam email detection using deep learning techniques. *Procedia Comput. Sci.* **2021**, *184*, 853–858. [CrossRef]
19. Boncalo, O.; Amaricai, A.; Savin, V.; Declercq, D.; Ghaffari, F. Check node unit for ldpc decoders based on one-hot data representation of messages. *Electron. Lett.* **2018**, *51*, 907–908. [CrossRef]
20. Wu, L.; Hoi, S.; Yu, N.; Declercq, D.; Ghaffari, F. Semantics-preserving bag-of-words models and applications. *IEEE Trans. Image Process.* **2010**, *19*, 1908–1920.
21. Lei, W.; Hoi, S. Enhancing bag-of-words models with semantics-preserving metric learning. *IEEE Multimed.* **2011**, *18*, 24–37.
22. Bengio, Y.; Ducharme, R.; Vincent, P.; Jauvin, C. A neural probabilistic language model. *J. Mach. Learn. Res.* **2003**, *3*, 1137–1155.
23. Ahn, G.; Lee, H.; Park, J.; Sun, H. Development of indicator of data sufficiency for feature-based early time series classification with applications of bearing fault diagnosis. *Processes* **2020**, *8*, 790. [CrossRef]
24. Deerwester, S.; Dumais, S.T.; Furnas, G.W.; Landauer, T.K.; Harshman, R. Indexing by latent semantic analysis. *J. Assoc. Inf. Sci. Technol.* **2010**, *41*, 391–407. [CrossRef]
25. Hofmann, T. Unsupervised learning by probabilistic latent semantic analysis. *Mach. Learn.* **2001**, *42*, 177–196. [CrossRef]
26. Ozsoy, M.G.; Alpaslan, F.N.; Cicekli, I. Text summarization using latent semantic analysis. *J. Inf. Sci.* **2011**, *37*, 405–417. [CrossRef]
27. Yong, W.; Hu, S. Probabilistic latent semantic analysis for dynamic textures recognition and localization. *J. Electron. Imaging* **2014**, *23*, 063006.
28. Blei, D.M.; Ng, A.Y.; Jordan, M.I. Latent dirichlet allocation. Advances in Neural Information Processing Systems 14. In Proceedings of the Neural Information Processing Systems: Natural and Synthetic, NIPS 2001, Vancouver, BC, Canada, 3–8 December 2001.
29. Kang, H.J.; Kim, C.; Kang, K. Analysis of the trends in biochemical research using latent dirichlet allocation (lda). *Processes* **2019**, *7*, 379. [CrossRef]
30. Chao, C.; Zare, A.; Cobb, J.T. Partial membership latent dirichlet allocation. *IEEE Trans. Image Process.* **2015**, *99*, 1.
31. Biggers, L.R.; Bocovich, C.; Ca Pshaw, R.; Eddy, B.P.; Etzkorn, L.H.; Kraft, N.A. Configuring latent dirichlet allocation based feature location. *Empir. Softw. Eng.* **2014**, *19*, 465–500. [CrossRef]
32. Jia, Z. A topic modeling toolbox using belief propagation. *J. Mach. Learn. Res.* **2012**, *13*, 2223–2226.
33. Zhu, X.; Jin, X.; Jia, D.; Sun, N.; Wang, P. Application of data mining in an intelligent early warning system for rock bursts. *Processes* **2019**, *7*, 155. [CrossRef]
34. Yao, L.; Huang, H.; Chen, S.H. Product quality detection through manufacturing process based on sequential patterns considering deep semantic learning and process rules. *Processes* **2020**, *8*, 751. [CrossRef]
35. Peters, M.; Neumann, M.; Iyyer, M.; Gardner, M.; Zettlemoyer, L. Deep Contextualized Word Representations. *arXiv* **2018**, arXiv:1802.05365.
36. Catelli, R.; Casola, V.; Pietro, G.D.; Fujita, H.; Esposito, M. Combining contextualized word representation and sub-document level analysis through bi-lstm + crf architecture for clinical de-identification. *Knowl.-Based Syst.* **2021**, *213*, 106649. [CrossRef]

37. Subramanyam, K.K.; Sangeetha, S. Deep contextualized medical concept normalization in social media text. *Procedia Comput. Sci.* **2020**, *171*, 1353–1362. [CrossRef]
38. Cen, X.; Yuan, J.; Pan, C.; Tang, Q.; Ma, Q. Contextual embedding bootstrapped neural network for medical information extraction of coronary artery disease records. *Med Biol. Eng. Comput.* **2021**, *59*, 1111–1121. [CrossRef]
39. Feng, C.; Rao, Y.; Nazir, A.; Wu, L.; He, L. Pre-trained language embedding-based contextual summary and multi-scale transmission network for aspect extraction—Sciencedirect. *Procedia Comput. Sci.* **2020**, *174*, 40–49. [CrossRef]
40. Vaswani, A.; Shazeer, N.; Parmar, N.; Uszkoreit, J.; Llion Jones, L.; Aidan, N.; Gomez, A.N.; Kaiser, L. Attention Is All You Need. In Proceedings of the 31st Conference on Neural Information Processing Systems, Long Beach, CA, USA, 4–9 December 2017.
41. Shan, Y.A.; Hl, B.; Sk, B.; Lx, A.; Jx, A.; Dan, S.B.; Lei, X.; Dong, Y. On the localness modeling for the self-attention based end-to-end speech synthesis. *Neural Netw.* **2020**, *125*, 121–130.
42. Mo, Y.; Wu, Q.; Li, X.; Huang, B. Remaining useful life estimation via transformer encoder enhanced by a gated convolutional unit. *J. Intell. Manuf.* **2021**, *2*, 1997–2006. [CrossRef]
43. Radford, A.; Narasimhan, K.; Salimans, T.; Sutskever, I. *Improving Language Understanding by Generative Pre-Training*; OpenAI: San Francisco, CA, USA, 2018.
44. Yao, C.; Cai, D.; Bu, J.; Chen, G. Pre-training the deep generative models with adaptive hyperparameter optimization. *Neurocomputing* **2017**, *247*, 144–155. [CrossRef]
45. Chan, Z.; Ngan, H.W.; Rad, A.B. Improving bayesian regularization of ann via pre-training with early-stopping. *Neural Process. Lett.* **2003**, *18*, 29–34. [CrossRef]
46. Sun, S.; Liu, H.; Meng, J.; Chen, C.; Yu, Y. Substructural regularization with data-sensitive granularity for sequence transfer learning. *IEEE Trans. Neural Netw. Learn. Syst.* **2018**, *29*, 2545–2557. [CrossRef] [PubMed]
47. Ohata, E.F.; Bezerra, G.M.; Chagas, J.; Neto, A.; Albuquerque, A.B.; Albuquerque, V.; Filho, P.P.R. Automatic detection of COVID-19 infection using chest x-ray images through transfer learning. *IEEE/CAA J. Autom. Sin.* **2021**, *8*, 239–248. [CrossRef]
48. Luo, X.; Li, J.; Chen, M.; Yang, X.; Li, X. Ophthalmic diseases detection via deep learning with a novel mixture loss function. *IEEE J. Biomed. Health Inform.* **2021**, *25*, 3332–3339. [CrossRef] [PubMed]
49. Luo, X.; Sun, J.; Wang, L.; Wang, W.; Zhao, W.; Wu, J.; Wang, J.H.; Zhang, Z. Short-term wind speed forecasting via stacked extreme learning machine with generalized correntropy. *IEEE Trans. Ind. Inf.* **2018**, *14*, 4963–4971. [CrossRef]
50. Liu, Y.; Ott, M.; Goyal, N.; Du, J.; Joshi, M.; Chen, D.; Levy, O.; Lewis, M.; Zettlemoyer, L.; Stoyanov, V. Roberta: A robustly optimized bert pretraining approach. *arXiv* **2019**, arXiv:1907.11692.
51. Lan, Z.; Chen, M.; Goodman, S.; Gimpel, K.; Sharma, P.; Soricut, R. Albert: A Lite Bert for Self-Supervised Learning of Language Representations. *arXiv* **2019**, arXiv:1909.11942.
52. Joshi, M.; Chen, D.; Liu, Y.; Weld, D.S.; Levy, O. Spanbert: Improving pre-training by representing and predicting spans. *Trans. Assoc. Comput. Linguist.* **2020**, *8*, 64–77. [CrossRef]

Article

Dynamic Prediction of *Chilo suppressalis* Occurrence in Rice Based on Deep Learning

Siqiao Tan [1,2], Yu Liang [2,3], Ruowen Zheng [2,3], Hongjie Yuan [1,2,*], Zhengbing Zhang [4,*] and Chenfeng Long [1,2,*]

1. Collage of Information and Intelligence, Hunan Agricultural University, Changsha 410128, China; tsq@hunau.edu.cn
2. Hunan Engineering Research Center of Rural and Agriculture Informatization, Changsha 410128, China; liangyu02@foxmail.com (Y.L.); zztzzlw@outlook.com (R.Z.)
3. College of Plant Protection, Hunan Agricultural University, Changsha 410128, China
4. Station of Plant Protection and Quarantine of Hunan Province, Changsha 410005, China
* Correspondence: JAYUAN@outlook.com (H.Y.); hnzb88@126.com (Z.Z.); elong@hunau.edu.cn (C.L.); Tel.: +86-158-0731-0801 (C.L.)

Citation: Tan, S.; Liang, Y.; Zheng, R.; Yuan, H.; Zhang, Z.; Long, C. Dynamic Prediction of *Chilo suppressalis* Occurrence in Rice Based on Deep Learning. *Processes* **2021**, *9*, 2166. https://doi.org/10.3390/pr9122166

Academic Editor: Xiong Luo

Received: 14 October 2021
Accepted: 17 November 2021
Published: 1 December 2021

Publisher's Note: MDPI stays neutral with regard to jurisdictional claims in published maps and institutional affiliations.

Copyright: © 2021 by the authors. Licensee MDPI, Basel, Switzerland. This article is an open access article distributed under the terms and conditions of the Creative Commons Attribution (CC BY) license (https://creativecommons.org/licenses/by/4.0/).

Abstract: (1) Background: The striped rice stem borer (SRSB), *Chilo suppressalis*, has severely diminished the yield and quality of rice in China. A timely and accurate prediction of the rice pest population can facilitate the designation of a pest control strategy. (2) Methods: In this study, we applied multiple linear regression (MLR), gradient boosting decision tree (GBDT), and deep autoregressive (DeepAR) models in the dynamic prediction of the SRSB population occurrence during the crop season from 2000 to 2020 in Hunan province, China, by using weather factors and time series of related pests. (3) Results: This research demonstrated the potential of the deep learning method used in integrated pest management through the qualitative and quantitative evaluation of a reasonable validating dataset (the average coefficient of determination R^2_{mean} for the DeepAR, GBDT, and MLR models were 0.952, 0.500, and 0.166, respectively). (4) Conclusions: The DeepAR model with integrated ground-based meteorological variables, time series of related pests, and time features achieved the most accurate dynamic forecasting of the population occurrence quantity of SRSB as compared with MLR and GBDT.

Keywords: *Chilo suppressalis*; meteorological data; time series analysis; DeepAR; deep learning; integrated pest management

1. Introduction

The *Chilo suppressalis* (striped rice stem borer, hereafter referred to as SRSB), the most widely distributed and destructive rice pest [1], is also the worst rice pest in China [2]. The larvae of SRSB eat rice stems, which leads to rice with dead hearts in the tillering stage, then forms white earheads during the heading stage, which can finally lead to rice with dead sheath [3] (Figure 1). Annually, China suffers severe rice yield reduction and economic losses from the SRSB pest [3–6]. This destruction is caused in part by the rapid proliferation of pests within pest populations, which makes it difficult for farmers to predict its outbreak. Continuously monitoring and accurately predicting the dynamic changes in the pest population during the crop growth period may be helpful for protecting rice from SRSB.

The insect population can be affected by many factors; both abiotic and biotic factors are believed to be responsible for changes in the insect population [1]. The effects of abiotic factors such as climate variables have been well-documented [7]. Therefore, an adequate early warning of an SRSB infestation combined with meteorological factors can support plant protection efforts. Apart from being threatened by SRSB, rice is also negatively affected by various pests such as the rice planthopper (hereafter referred to as RPH) and the paddy leaf roller (hereafter referred to as PLR). Thus, the species and the numbers of other pests in the region will also have effects on the population development trends for SRSB.

(a) Dead heart   (b) White heads   (c) Dead sheath

Figure 1. The main symptom in rice of damage by SRSB.

An agricultural pest prediction model is built on the pest occurrence mechanism, mathematical statistics, time series analyses, together with the critical factors affecting pest occurrence, which can provide information on pest occurrence, severity, and development trends. Differentiated by the principles of prediction methods, the current range of pest prediction models include statistical regression models, machine learning models, and deep learning models.

Statistical modeling for the early prediction of pest risks is one strategy that has been widely adopted [8], and whose essence is to ascertain the relationships between variables in the form of fitting equations. The predicting steps involve: performing a statistical analysis with the historical data on pests, extracting the relationship between the target pests y and a related factor x, establishing the mathematical equations, and then making a quantitative prediction of pests by means of these equations. This kind of prediction approach treats pest occurrence as a separate system, without considering the occurrence process and mechanism. The most commonly used approach is the multiple linear regression (MLR) model. The severe difficulty for statistical regression methods lies in choosing the relevant factor x; most researchers currently tend to build predicting models with relevant meteorological factors [9,10]. Some researchers have found that combining weather factors with other factors, such as variety, soil, fertilization, etc., can improve a model's prediction capability [11,12]. The statistical learning-based methods focusing on finding the linear relations between variables have high interpretability. However, most problems in real-life production show rich, non-linear links for which traditional statistical regression methods do not work.

The machine learning method has a strong predictive capability that automates the organization, fits the parameter adjustment model, obtains the optimal model to fit the current datasets, and predicts with the optimal model. The accuracy and speed of the machine learning method improve as the amount of data increases, which is what distinguishes it from traditional statistical regression methods. The machine learning method can also learn non-linear relationships; consequently, the machine learning-based regression analysis has become the mainstream in agricultural pest prediction, with support vector machines [13] and decision trees [10] as the two commonly adopted machine learning prediction algorithms. However, machine learning algorithms are so diverse that it is difficult for researchers to choose one for practical problems. Moreover, the pros and cons of machine learning algorithms also differ, such as the SVM being inefficient in processing large samples of data [14], while the performance of neural networks improves with an increase in data volume [15], but which also easily leads to higher computational costs and the overfitting of traditional neural networks [16].

Deep learning, a branch of machine learning, is an algorithm using the artificial neural networks as an architecture to characterize and learn data [17–21]. The algorithm is extensively applied in most traditional fields [22–25], and some progress has been made in the field of agricultural pest prediction in recent years [26]. With the reduction of hardware costs and the improvement of algorithms, deep learning-based methods will become a leading research topic for agricultural pest prediction.

Aiming at the prediction of SRSB occurrence in rice, and combining this with ground meteorological observation data and related pest time sequence data, this paper constructs a multi-dimensional dynamic probability prediction model based on the use of deep learning for time series analyses. The model presented in the paper is more applicable than the traditional pest prediction models and can realize a dynamic timing prediction of pests. The key works included in the paper are as follows: (1) investigating the relationships between ground meteorological data, related pests, and SRSB; (2) comparing the performances of the models using only meteorological variables to that of the models combining meteorological variables with the time series of related pests; (3) developing a deep learning-based dynamic probability prediction DeepAR model for the occurrence of SRSB; (4) evaluating the performance of the DeepAR model using the traditional MLR model and the machine learning GBDT model.

Our method is expected to lead to an improved method for the management of SRSB for following reasons:

(1) Our study suggests that combining related pest time series data with the ground meteorological data can improve the model's prediction accuracy as compared to previous studies using only the ground meteorological data;
(2) Combining weather and associated pest time series with deep learning-based DeepAR models can provide more accurate predictions than the traditional MLR and the machine learning GBDT. These findings could be utilized to support an integrated pest management (IPM) program to help farmers reduce the use of pesticides and minimize crop loss in rice paddy fields.

2. Materials and Methods

2.1. Study Areas

This paper mainly studied the dynamic population change of SRSB in Hunan Province, China, and the area selection was based on the following considerations:

1. Areas have a high number of insects;
2. Areas have a long history of rice cultivation;
3. Area characteristics can represent different regions in Hunan Province, China.

Based on these, A (Hongjiang), B (Yuangjiang), C (Dong'an), D (Linli), and E (Liling) were selected as the study areas (Figure 2). Hunan Province belongs to an area with the most extensive rice farming in China. The selected area has high temperatures and is rainy in summer and hot at the same time, which is suitable for the occurrence of SRSB.

2.2. Data Collection

2.2.1. Pest Data

The pest data came from the daily records of the rice pest light traps for major insect pests in the crop monitoring and early warning information system in Hunan Province, China. Pest species include 11 rice pests (Table 1), such as SRSB, RPH, and PLR. Adult pests were collected by a light trap set from 18:00 to 6:00 the next day, located in areas A (2000–2020), B (2000–2020), C (2000–2020), D (2000–2020), and E (2010–2020). Plant protection workers removed the insects from the traps every morning, and subsequently identified and counted them.

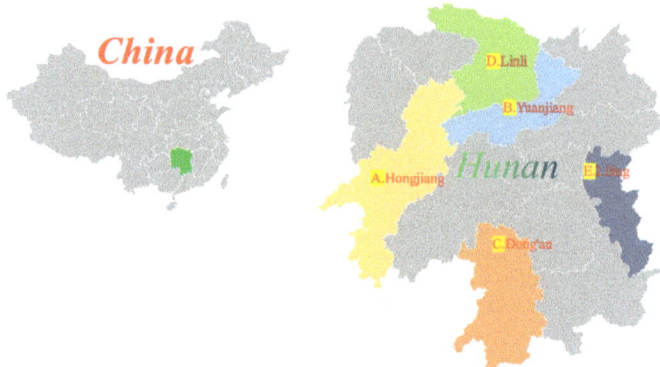

Figure 2. Locations of study areas and light traps.

Table 1. The main rice pests captured by the light traps.

Number	Name	Abbreviation	Latin Name
0	rice planthopper	RPH	-
1	paddy leaf roller	PLR	*Cnaphalocrocis medinalis*
2	striped rice stem borer	SRSB	*Chilo suppressalis*
3	pink sugarcane borer	PSB	*Sesamia grisescens*
4	yellow stem borer	YSB	*Scirpophaga incertulas*
5	rice green semilooper	RGS	*Naranga diffusa*
6	rice plant weevil	RPW	*Echinocnemus squameus*
7	rice water weevil	RWW	*Lissorhoptrus oryzophilus*
8	gall midge	GM	*Orseoia oryzae*
9	paddy armyworm	PA	*Mythimna separata*
10	-	Other *	-

* 'Other' is the sum of other species captured by our light traps apart from the rice pests shown (Numbers 0–9).

2.2.2. Meteorological Data

Meteorological data were obtained from the ground daily meteorological data downloaded by the National Meteorological Center, spanning the years 2000–2020, including 19 factors such as temperature, precipitation, and sunshine duration; the detailed information is shown in Table 2.

2.2.3. Time Features

As pest occurrence is a typical time series problem, it has prominent temporal characteristics. The extraction of the time characteristics of pest data facilitates the construction of more accurate predictive models. We extracted the time features, including years, seasons, months, weeks, weekdays, and days. Among these were March–May for spring, June–August for summer, September–November for autumn, and from December to the following February for winter. The weeks were composed of seven days as one week, with 52 weeks per year. Weekdays entailed the obtainment of working day information according to the Gregorian calendar, mainly considering that the acquisition of pest data required manual recording.

2.2.4. Data Preprocessing

The original pest data had some missing and outlier values. The missing values were interpolated using the average adjacent position interpolation method. We selected the five previous and five subsequent effective values of the missing fraction to calculate the arithmetic mean, and used this arithmetic mean to interpolate the missing part. The outliers were processed using the exponentially weighted averages method, and the exponentially weighted averages were defined as follows:

$$y_t = \frac{x_t + (1-\alpha)x_{t-1} + (1-\alpha)^2 x_{t-2} + \cdots\cdots + (1-\alpha)^t x_0}{1 + (1-\alpha) + (1-\alpha)^2 + \cdots\cdots + (1-\alpha)^t}, \quad (1)$$

where α is the smoothing factor ($\alpha \in (0, 1]$), y_t is the value after t moment smoothing, x_t is the value before t moment smoothing. In this paper, a sliding window with seven days as a window and one day as a step were established to smooth the pest data.

Table 2. Types and units of meteorological factors.

Number	Type	Abbreviation	Unit	Number	Type	Abbreviation	Unit
0	Temperature	TEMP	°C	10	Precipitation	PRCP	mm
1	Maximum temperature	Tmax	°C	11	Evaporation	EVP	mm
2	Minimum temperature	Tmin	°C	12	Atmospheric pressure	AP	pa
3	Average relative humidity	RH	%	13	Maximum atmospheric pressure	APmax	pa
4	Minimum relative humidity	RHmin	%	14	Minimum atmospheric pressure	APmin	pa
5	Wind speed	WDSP	m/s	15	Skin temperature	SKT	°C
6	Maximum wind speed	MXWDSP	m/s	16	Maximum skin temperature	SKTmax	°C
7	Maximum wind direction	MXWDD	16 directions	17	Minimum skin temperature	SKTmin	°C
8	Extreme wind speed	EXWDSP	m/s	18	Sunshine duration	SDD	H
9	Extreme wind direction	EXWDD	16 directions				

The meteorological data were processed in the same way. There were no meteorological stations in some parts of the study area. This paper used meteorological stations near cities and counties in the study area (Table 3).

Table 3. The study areas and the corresponding meteorological stations.

Number	Study Area	Meteorological Stations
0	Liling	Zhuzhou
1	Hongjiang	Zhijiang Dong Autonomous County
2	Dong'An	Lingling
3	Yuanjiang	Yuanjiang
4	Linli	Shimen

Some time series of related pests contain unique values. Unique values do not help with model construction. In addition, there is a collinearity relationship among some variables. Collinearity plays a consistent role in the process of model construction, where it raises the complexity of the model. Therefore, we removed the unique values and excess collinearity variables during the model construction. In this paper, high-quality pest variables, meteorological variables, and time datasets (Table 4) were constructed, laying the material basis for the subsequent analysis and prediction.

Table 4. Rice pests, weather, and time datasets.

Weather Variables		Time Series of Related Pests	Time Features
TEMP	EVP	RPH	Year
RH	AP	PLR	season
RHmin	PRCP	SRSB	month
WDSP	EXWDD	PSB	weeks
MXWDSP	EXWDSP	YSB	-
MXWDD	SDD	-	-
SKTmax	-	-	-

2.3. Methods

2.3.1. Datasets Preparation

To predict the SRSB, weather variables (including TEMP, RH, and PRCP) and the associated time series of related pests were included as input variables. Furthermore, the daily SRSB light trap catches were natural log-transformed before analysis to satisfy the regression hypothesis [27,28]. The SRSB light trap catches were treated as an output variable in all models and an input variable in the autoregressive model.

The datasets of all variables of crop seasons in E (Liling) from 2010 to 2019, and those of other study areas from 2000 to 2018 were used as training datasets. E (Liling) training datasets contained 3726 samples, and other study areas' training datasets contained 7013 samples. In Liling 2020, the remaining observations from other regions from 2019 to 2020 were used as test datasets to verify the model. We chose data from March to October to develop the models, as this period was commonly used to plan pest monitoring. All the details are summarized in Table 5.

Table 5. Details of the data used in model development.

Site	Place	Input Variable	Output Variable	Month (Yearly)	Training Data	Testing Data
A	Hongjiang	Weather variables, Time series of related pests, and Time features	Chilo suppressalis (SRSB)	March to October	2000 to 2018	2019 to 2020
B	Yuanjiang				2000 to 2018	2019 to 2020
C	Dong'an				2000 to 2018	2019 to 2020
D	Linli				2000 to 2018	2019 to 2020
E	Liling				2010 to 2019	2020

2.3.2. Model

Multiple Linear Regression (MLR)

Pearson correlation analysis was used to obtain the relationship between SRSB and meteorological data, associated pest time series, and time features. Taking the significant correlation coefficient (R) as the standard, we selected appropriate variables to develop the linear model of SRSB.

An MLR model using stepwise selection was established in three scenarios: (1) only meteorological variables were considered to estimate the maximum determination coefficient of the SRSB (the R square); (2) meteorological variables and time series-related pests were combined to estimate the maximum determination coefficient of the SRSB (the R square); (3) meteorological variables, time series-related pests, and time features were considered to estimate the maximum determination coefficient of the SRSB (the R square).

MLR is a statistical method of regression for analyzing the relationship of an individual dependent variable with two or more independent variables [29], which can be demonstrated as follows:

$$y = \alpha_0 + \alpha_1 x_1 + \alpha_2 x_2 + \cdots + \alpha_i x_i \cdots + \alpha_k x_k + \varepsilon, \tag{2}$$

Here y is the dependent variable, x_i is the independent variable, α_0 represents the intercept, α_i is the slope of x_i to y, ε is the residual. Stepwise regression can automatically select the most relevant independent variables when the number of independent variables is large and where it is noted possible to fit all potential models [30]. We used Python's statsmodels library to implement the MLR model.

Gradient Boosting Decision Tree (GBDT)

The GBDT or the Gradient Boosting Decision Tree, an ensemble model of an iterative decision tree algorithm proposed by Jerome Friedman in 1999, is a representative model of the ensemble method. GBDT takes the regression tree as a base learner, integrated gradient boosting algorithm [31].

To train the GBDT model, we used a grid search combined with a 5-fold cross-validation [32]. The GBDT model was parameter-optimized to obtain the best performing GBDT model under the current datasets. The training and test datasets contained all variables (meteorological, related pest, and time features). We selected the model with the highest R^2 as the best GBDT model, calculating and plotting the importance of the input variables. This model was developed using the LightGBM library of python.

DeepAR Model

DeepAR is a probabilistic prediction method based on auto-regression recurrent neural networks. The approach solves the prediction problem through deep neural network learning by combining the appropriate likelihood, using non-linear data transformation techniques. DeepAR takes advantage of LSTM-based recurrent neural network architecture [33,34]. It also builds on previous deep learning work on time-series data [35–37] to address the probabilistic prediction problem. Deep networks, allowing for more abstract data representation through more complex transformations [21], thus generally outperform shallow and broad neural networks.

DeepAR has the following advantages: First, it performs a probabilistic prediction of the sample using the Monte Carlo method and can calculate consistent quantile estimates across all sub-ranges in the predicted range. Secondly, the method does not assume Gaussian noise, but broad likelihood functions can be supported and allow users to select the parts most suitable for the statistical data properties. Once again, by learning from similar data, being able to provide predictions from data with little or no history is something that conventional one-dimensional predictions cannot do. Finally, DeepAR can understand seasonal behavior and complex dependencies with minimal human intervention [38].

Through the use of the deep learning DeepAR time series prediction model, combining the time series of related pests, meteorological variables, and time features to predict the daily capture of SRSB light traps produced training and test datasets that contained all variables (meteorological, pest, and time).

We used the Gluonts library based on the MXNet framework to build the DeepAR model of the rice SRSB, selected the negative binomial distribution as the likelihood function of the DeepAR model; all the other hyperparameters used the default hyperparameters.

2.3.3. Evaluation Metrics

Multiple metrics can be used to analyze the performance of our prediction, so we opted to use the top 4 most used metrics for time series forecasting. We used the Coefficient of Determination (R^2), Mean Absolute Error (MAE), Symmetric Mean Absolute Percentage Error (sMAPE), and Root Mean Square Error (RMSE) to evaluate the prediction model.

Coefficient of Determination (R^2)

R^2 was used to measure the proportion of various independent variables that independent variables could explain to judge the explanatory power of the regression model [39–41].

Suppose that a dataset includes $y_1, \cdots, y_n$ total n observations, the corresponding model of predicted values is thus $f_1, \cdots, f_n$. Defining the residual with $e_i = y_i - f_i$, the average observed value is calculated as follows:

$$y = \alpha_0 + \alpha_1 x_1 + \alpha_2 x_2 + \cdots + \alpha_i x_i \cdots + \alpha_k x_k + \varepsilon, \bar{y} = \frac{1}{n}\sum_{i=1}^{n} y_i, \tag{3}$$

The total sum of the square can thus be obtained with:

$$SS_{tot} = \sum_i (y_i - \bar{y})^2, \tag{4}$$

The sum of the squares of residuals can be calculated with the following formula:

$$SS_{res} = \sum_i (y_i - f_i)^2 = \sum_i e_i^2, \tag{5}$$

Thus, the determination coefficient can be defined as follows:

$$R^2 = 1 - \frac{SS_{res}}{SS_{tot}}, \tag{6}$$

The R^2 usually ranges from 0 to 1. The R^2 can be more truthful than *sMAPE*, *MAE*, *MAPE*, *MSE*, and *RMSE* in regression analysis evaluation [42].

Mean Absolute Error (*MAE*)

MAE refers to the meaning of the distance between the predictive model value f_i and the true value y_i of the sample. *MAE* is calculated as:

$$MAE = \frac{1}{n}\sum_{i=1}^{n} |y_i - f_i|, \tag{7}$$

Symmetric Mean Absolute Percentage Error (*sMAPE*)

sMAPE is an accuracy measure based on percentage (or relative) errors. It is usually defined as follows:

$$sMAPE = \frac{100\%}{n}\sum_{i=1}^{n} \frac{|f_i - y_i|}{(|f_i| + |y_i|)/2}, \tag{8}$$

Root Mean Square Error (*RMSE*)

RMSE is widely used to measure the differences between values predicted by a model and the values observed. It is defined as follows:

$$sMRMSE = \sqrt{\frac{1}{n}\sum_{i=1}^{n}(f_i - y_i)^2}, \tag{9}$$

In general, lower *MAE*, *sMAPE*, and *RMSE* are better than higher values, and all three metrics are non-negative. But for the R^2, higher is better.

3. Results

3.1. Relationship between Climatic Variables, Time Series of Related Pests, and Time Features, and the SRSB Light Trap Catch

The correlation coefficient (R) was calculated between the natural log-transformed SRSB light trap catch and the selected environmental variables (climatic variables, related pest, and time features), and the correlation coefficient (R) and sig. ($p > |t|$) were calculated for five study regions and then averaged (Table 6). Our results show that the SRSB light trap catch had a significant positive correlation with the RPH light trap catch (R = 0.458 ± 0.111, $p > |t|$), and had an extremely significant positive correlation with the PSB light trap catch (R = 0.271 ± 0.098, $p > |t|$), but had a significant negative correlation with AP (R= −0.445 ± 0.070, $p > |t|$) and the season (R = −0.247 ± 0.079, $p > |t|$). Meanwhile, it there was some correlation between the SRSB light trap catch and the TEMP, SDD, and PLR light trap catch, but not significant. Extremely significant and significant correlation variables were included in the linear and non-linear models to predict SRSB light trap catches.

3.2. Multiple Linear Regression Prediction

Using a stepwise selected MLR model, we combined meteorological, associated pest, and time features (Table 7). $Coef$ is the MLR model coefficient that indicates the contribution of each variable to the model. $std\ err$ is the standard error of the coefficient estimation. t and $p > |t|$ represent the effects of the independent variable on the dependent variable. The meteorological variable AP was significantly and negatively correlated with the SRSB light trap catch. Related pest RPH, YSB, and PSB with the light trap catch and the time variable season were negatively correlated with the SRSB light trap catch.

The use of meteorological variables (Model 1) alone explain approximately 35% (Adj.R^2 = 0.346) of the variability in the SRSB light trap catch; the model based on meteorological variables and related pest (Model 2) explains 39.9% (Adj.R^2 = 0.399) of the variability in the SRSB light trap capture; in comparison, a model based on meteorological variables, associated related pests, and time features (Model 3) could explain 40% (Adj.R^2 = 0.400) of the variability in the SRSB light trap catch. The variance inflation factor (VIF) for all the input variables was less than three, indicating no multiple collinearities among the variables. The adjusted R^2 selected the model combining meteorological variables, associated pests, and time features (Model 3) as the best model.

According to the results of the stepwise regression shown in Table 7, the prediction model of the Yuanjiang can be represented using the following regression equation:

$$ln(SRSB)535.9426 + (-45.5917 \times AP) + (0.1283 \times RPH) + (0.4709 \times PSB) + (2.1272 \times YSB) + (-0.005 \times Season), \tag{10}$$

The dependent variable $ln(SRSB)$ indicates the natural logarithm of the SRSB light trap catch. The independent variables AP, RPH, PSB, YSB, and $Season$ indicate the AP, RPH light trap catch, PSB light trap catch, YSB light trap catch, and Season, respectively.

The MLR model of the other SRSB light trap catch of the study area was obtained using the same method, and a summary of the MLR model for the training datasets of each study area is shown in Table 8. R^2 and Adj.R^2 represent the MLR fitting accuracy of the training datasets, and N represents the length of the training datasets. The results show that in different study regions, stepwise regression selected different independent variables.

Table 6. Pearson's correlation coefficient (R) between the natural log-transformed SRSB light trap catch and its associated pest, meteorological, and time features from March to October in the rice crop season.

Variable Types	External Variables	Correlation Coefficient (R)	Sig. ($p > |t|$)
Related pests	RPH	0.458 ± 0.111	0.008 ± 0.011 *
	PLR	0.368 ± 0.068	0.123 ± 0.179
	PSB	0.271 ± 0.098	0.000 ± 0.000 **
	YSB	0.086 ± 0.029	0.119 ± 0.265
Weather	TEMP	0.449 ± 0.046	0.213 ± 0.374
	RH	−0.031 ± 0.047	0.048 ± 0.235
	RHmin	−0.041 ± 0.064	0.082 ± 0.133
	WDSP	0.049 ± 0.136	0.052 ± 0.048
	MXWDSP	0.161 ± 0.083	0.121 ± 0.131
	MXWDD	0.086 ± 0.161	0.335 ± 0.364
	EXWDSP	0.175 ± 0.061	0.352 ± 0.355
	EXWDD	0.098 ± 0.155	0.334 ± 0.291
	SDD	0.282 ± 0.013	0.112 ± 0.174
	PRCP	0.091 ± 0.039	0.090 ± 0.121
	EVP	0.409 ± 0.033	0.073 ± 0.163
	AP	−0.445 ± 0.070	0.013 ± 0.029 *
	SKT	0.469 ± 0.050	0.208 ± 0.209
Time	Weeks	0.112 ± 0.042	0.562 ± 0.264
	Month	0.113 ± 0.041	0.477 ± 0.238
	Year	0.146 ± 0.087	0.191 ± 0.418
	Season	−0.247 ± 0.079	0.001 ± 0.001 *

** Extremely significant, * significant.

Table 7. Statistical diagnostics of the stepwise multiple linear regression models (taking the Yuanjiang SRSB as an example).

Model	Variables	Coef	Std Err	t	$p>|t|$	VIF < 3
Weather	Const.	708.1329	11.604	61.026	0.000	
	AP	−61.3799	1.007	−60.977	0.000	True
	N = 7013		R^2 = 0.347	Adj.R^2 = 0.346		
Weather and related pests time series	Const.	536.1561	13.543	39.591	0.000	
	AP	−46.4895	1.175	−39.568	0.000	True
	RPH	0.1205	0.006	19.113	0.000	True
	YSB	2.1725	0.194	11.182	0.000	True
	PSB	0.4584	0.043	10.694	0.000	True
	N = 7013		R^2 = 0.3998	Adj.R^2 = 0.399		
Weather, time series of related pests, and time features	Const.	535.9426	13.535	39.589	0.000	
	AP	−45.5927	1.210	−37.688	0.000	True
	RPH	0.1283	0.007	18.889	0.000	True
	YSB	2.1272	0.195	10.924	0.000	True
	PSB	0.4709	0.043	10.943	0.000	True
	Season	−0.0050	0.002	−3.067	0.002	True
	N = 7013		R^2 = 0.400	Adj.R^2 = 0.400		

The average coefficient of determination, minimum coefficient of determination, and maximum coefficient of determination of the MLR model based on the test dataset in the study areas (Linli, Liling, Yuanjiang, Dong'an, and Hongjiang) are $R^2_{mean} = 0.166$, $R^2_{min} = 0.083$, and $R^2_{max} = 0.312$, respectively.

3.3. GBDT Model Prediction

Based on the training dataset, the GBDT models from different study regions (Linli, Liling, Yuanjiang, Dong'an, and Hongjiang) yielded other results (R^2 = 0.420, 0.104, 0.639,

0.509, and 0.564, RMSE = 0.999, 1.799, 0.860, 1.078, and 0.733). Figure 3 shows the GBDT model input variable's importance in the natural log conversion ln (SRSB) light trap catch. The season is the least important input variable in the Yuanjiang GBDT model. Weeks and Year are the most important input variables in the GBDT model.

Table 8. Summary of the MLR model for the training datasets of each study area.

Variable \ Place	Yuanjiang (R^2 = 0.400, Adj.R^2 = 0.400, N = 7013)	Hongjiang (R^2 = 0.379, Adj.R^2 = 0.378, N = 7013)	Dong'an (R^2 = 0.398, Adj.R^2 = 0.398, N = 7013)	Linli (R^2 = 0.257, Adj.R^2 = 0.256, N = 7013)	Liling (R^2 = 0.359, Adj.R^2 = 0.358, N = 3726)
Const.	535.943	2.146	0.425	−0.489	−0.952
TEMP	0	0	0.071	0.494	0.701
RHmin	0	−0.412	0	0	0
AP	−45.592	0	0	0	0
RPH	0.128	0.209	0.258	0	0
PSB	0.471	0.759	0	2.123	0.430
YSB	2.127	−0.235	3.359	0.169	3.070
PLR	0	0	0	0.054	0.397
Season	−0.005	−0.134	−0.165	−0.159	−0.175
Weeks	0	−0.007	0	0	0
Month	0	0	−0.030	0	0

The average coefficient of determination, minimum coefficient of determination, and maximum coefficient of determination of the GBDT model based on the test dataset in the study areas (Linli, Liling, Yuanjiang, Dong'an, and Hongjiang) are R^2_{mean} = 0.500, R^2_{min} = 0.295, and R^2_{max} = 0.687, respectively.

3.4. DeepAR Model Prediction

DeepAR uses the previous time step value to set the current time step of the model. These values were available within the regulatory range during training and prediction. For the prediction range, the training and the forecast values must be distinguished. During projection, time-series values within the prediction range were not available because these were the results to be predicted. Therefore, the samples from the likelihood function (whose parameters were predicted in the previous step) were used as the input values for the current time step.

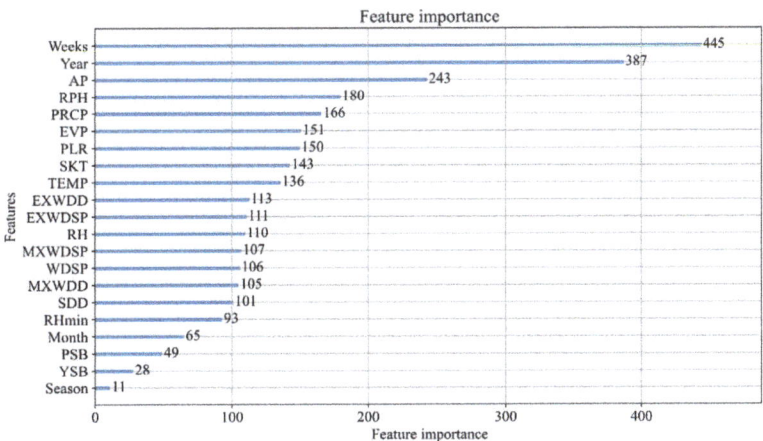

Figure 3. Variable importance derived from the GBDT model for natural log-transformed ln (SRSB) light trap catches in Yuanjiang.

Figure 4 shows the learning process of the DeepAR model [43], with the training process on the left and the prediction process on the right. After the training, the historical data $t < t_0$ were entered into the network to obtain the predicted initial hidden state $h_{i,t_0-1}t_0$, and then the prediction results were obtained using ancestral sampling. More specifically, at each time step, $t_0, t_0+1, \cdots, T$ could be randomly sampled to get $\bar{z}_{i,t}$, the $\bar{z}_{i,t}$ as a partial input for the next time step. In this way, a series of all sampling values from t_0 to T could be obtained on the time scale, and these sampling values could then be used to calculate the required target value.

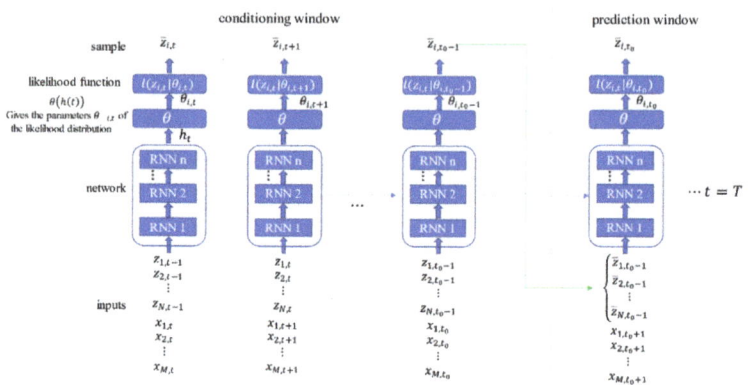

Figure 4. Forecasting process of DeepAR.

The average coefficient of determination, minimum coefficient of determination, and maximum coefficient of determination of the DeepAR model based on the test dataset in the study areas (Linli, Liling, Yuanjiang, Dong'an, and Hongjiang) are $R^2_{mean} = 0.952$, $R^2_{min} = 0.945$, and $R^2_{max} = 0.958$, respectively.

3.5. MLR, GBDT, and DeepAR Model Validation and Performance Comparison

Figure 5 compares the true and predicted values of the test datasets of the rice SRSB light trap capture after natural log transformation (ln) in different study regions under different models (traditional MLR model, machine learning GBDT, and deep learning DeepAR model).

We found that for all study regions, the MLR model could not correctly fit the actual values. Even negative predicted values were obtained for some periods (for example, in Hongjiang from December 2019 to January 2020), which have a large gap with the actual value. The GBDT model had good prediction results, although the prediction values in Hongjiang and Yuanjiang still could not accurately fit the actual values. However, the trend of the SRSB light trap catch was correctly reflected. It showed the upward and downward movement of the SRSB light trap catch in some periods (for example, in Hongjiang from April 2019 to October 2020, and in Yuanjiang from April 2019 to October 2020). The DeepAR model had the best predictions, and actual values could be accurately fitted in all study regions and periods.

The results show that the deep learning DeepAR model produced good predictions for all sites as compared to the traditional MLR model and the machine learning GBDT model.

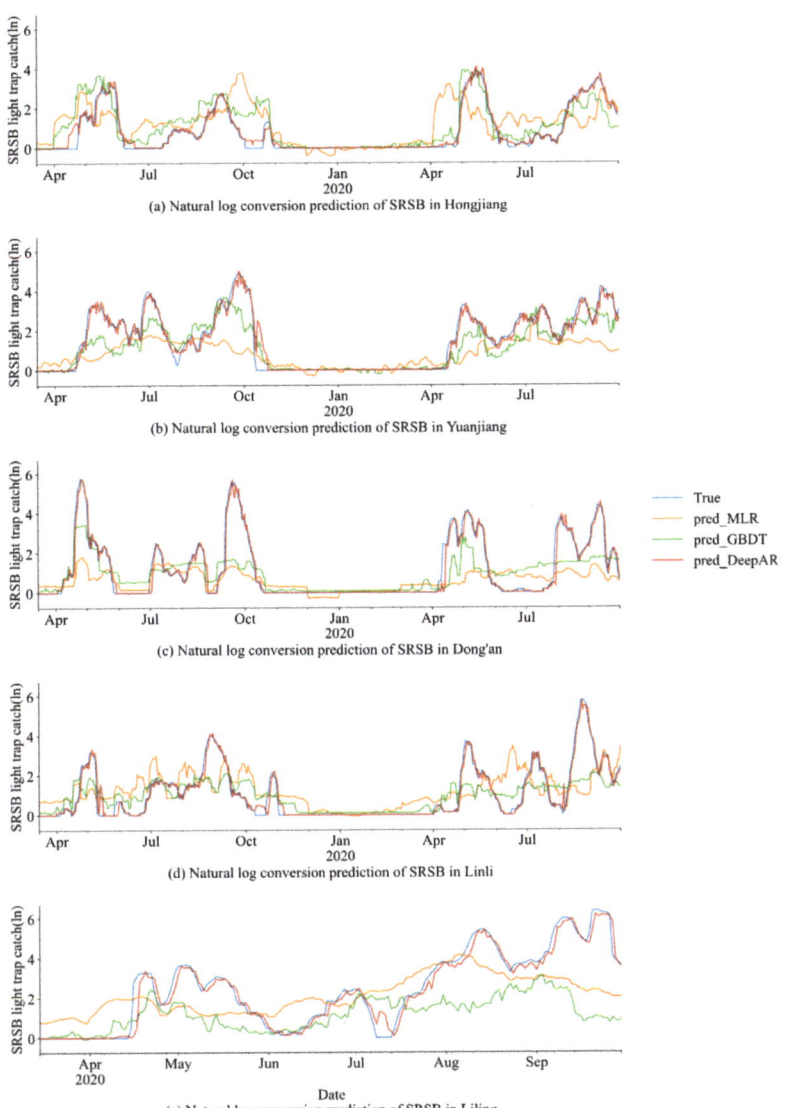

Figure 5. Predicted results of the SRSB light trap catches from the test datasets using the MLR, GBDT, and DeepAR models.

Figure 6 shows the comparison between the light trap catch of natural log-transformed SRSB populations as predicted by the MLR, GBDT, and DeepAR models, respectively. Compared to R^2 and RMSE, DeepAR models produced more accurate predictions than the MLR and GBDT models, and the GBDT was more accurate than the MLR. The R^2 values for DeepAR, GBDT, and MLR were 0.944–0.960, 0.295–0.687, and 0.083–0.312, respectively, and the RMSE values were 0.228–0.425, 0.733–1.271, and 1.158–1.576, respectively.

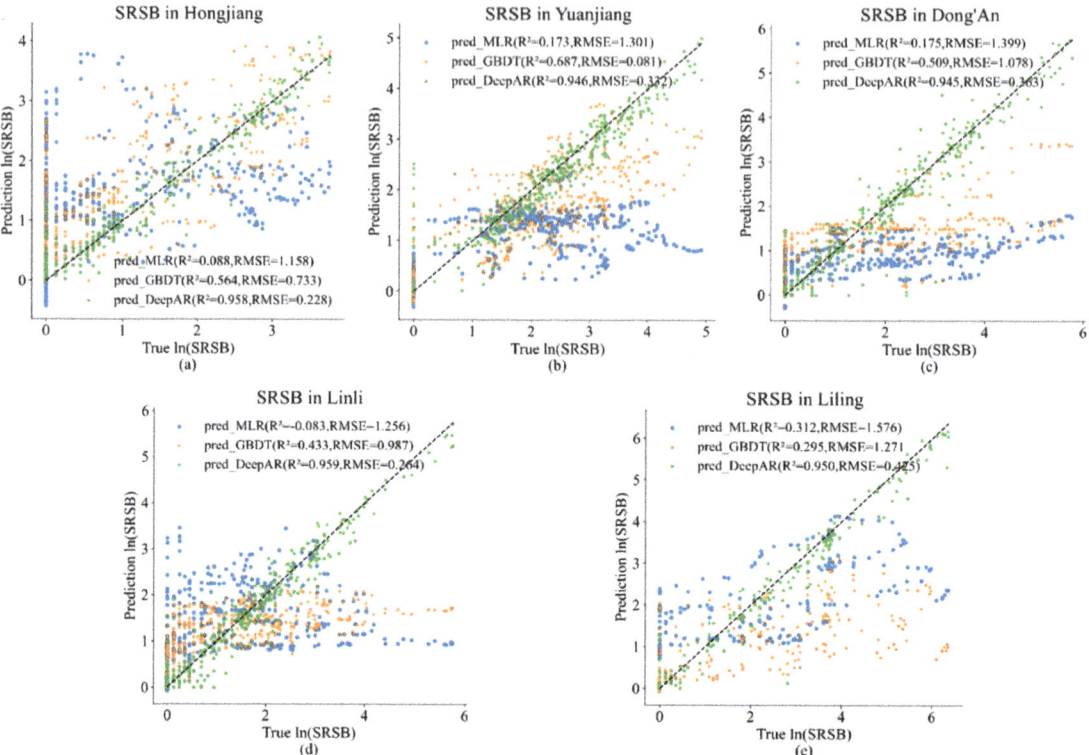

Figure 6. Actual versus predicted natural log-transformed ln (SRSB) in (**a**) Hongjiang, (**b**) Yuanjiang, (**c**) Dong'an, (**d**) Linli, and (**e**) Liling.

Figure 7 shows the performance of MLR, GBDT, and DeepAR in evaluating the indicators MAE, RMSE, sMAPE, and R^2 in different study areas. We found that the MLR model showed the worst performance in the SRSB light trap catches in Hongjiang, Yuanjiang, Dong'an, and Linli. The Liling GBDT model had the worst performance, probably the smallest sample of the datasets (compared to other study regions). The DeepAR model (MAE, RMSE, sMAPE, and R^2 were 0.125–0.245, 0.228–0.425, 0.360–0.657, and 0.945–0.959, respectively) had the best performance in all areas, outperforming the MLR (MAE, RMSE, sMAPE, and R^2 were 0.856–1.297, 1.158–1.576, 0.808–1.414, and 0.083–0.312, respectively) and the GBDT (MAE, RMSE, sMAPE, and R^2 were 0.494–0.981, 0.733–1.271, 0.003–1.296, and 0.295–0.687, respectively) models in terms of stability and accuracy.

In conclusion, it is feasible to predict the SRSB light trap catch using the deep learning DeepAR model.

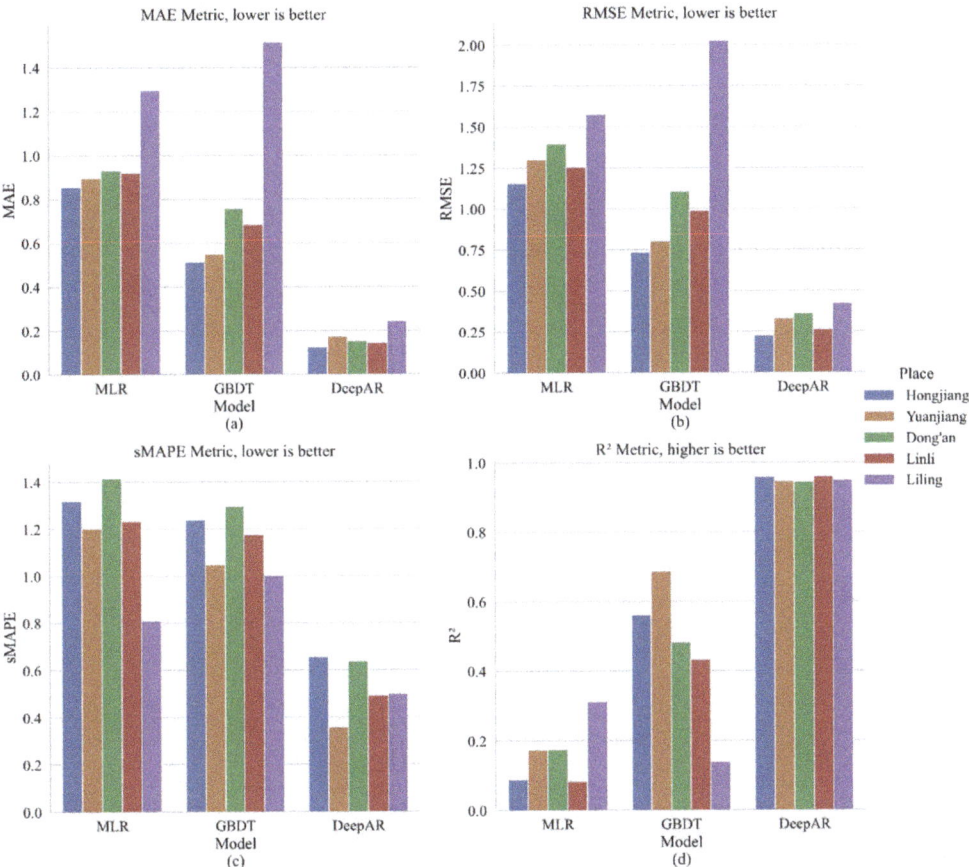

Figure 7. Predicted performance of MLR, GBDT, and DeepAR in different areas.

4. Discussion

Predicting pest populations helps specify pest management strategies, reduce the use of pesticides, and is an integral part of the successful implementation of IPM. For pest prediction models, weather variables such as temperature, humidity, rainfall, and sunshine duration are often used as abiotic predictors in model development [8–13,26]. We found that TEMP [1,7], RH, and SDD were positively associated with the SRSB light trap catch, while AP and PRCP were negatively associated with the SRSB light trap catch. WDSP, EVP, and MXWDSP were also associated with the SRSB light trap catch. Generally, when WDSP, EVP, and MXWDSP are moderate, the amount of SRSB is the highest.

The rice light trap was used to capture rice pests in order to study the relationship between them. We found a significant positive correlation between SRSB and RPH, and a highly significant positive correlation between SRSB and PSB. This indicates an interactional relationship between rice pests, which could be used to predict some areas with little or even no historical pest data, especially for migratory pests such as the *Spodoptera odorata*.

The stepwise multivariate regression model established in this study showed that the model which combined meteorological variables, associated pests, and time features (adjusted R^2 = 0.400) was more accurate than the model using meteorological variables alone (adjusted R^2 = 0.346).

The GBDT model is a suitable choice for predicting pest occurrence. Our study showed that the GBDT model produced more accurate pest predictions than the MLR model. The deep learning DeepAR model obtained the best predictions, probably because of the extended data cycles we used, and deep learning is known to perform well with large samples. Our study showed that the deep learning DeepAR model predicted the natural log-transformed SRSB light trap catch with an average accuracy of 95.2% (the average prediction accuracy of the MLR model was 16.6%, and that of the GBDT model was 50.0%), which has a good application value. Since the rice field is an open environment, the factors driving the growth of the SRSB population are variable. In addition to weather and pest-related factors, rice growth phenology, natural enemies, rice varieties, pest prevention, control information, and even farmer practices may affect population dynamics. The observed and predicted kurtosis differences in SRSB may be due to seasonality and changes in the surrounding environment. Rice-related pest factors with a larger area can be considered in future work.

5. Conclusions

In this study, we presented a prediction model for SRSB population occurrence in the Hunan Province of China by integrating time series variables of ground weather, the number of related pests captured by light traps, and the number of SRSB captured by light traps. The MLR, GBDT, and DeepAR models were constructed based on the abovementioned variables. MLR was used to study the predictive power of meteorological variables alone or combined with related pest and time variables. At the same time, the GBDT and DeepAR models were established to enhance the model prediction performance compared to MLR.

Based on the high correlation coefficient of the MLR model, the main features of the MLR model for the SRSB captured by the light trap in the research areas were selected as follows: Yuanjiang made use of AP, RPH, PSB, YSB, and Season; Hongjiang used RHmin, RPH, PSB, YSB, and Season; Dong'an used TEMP, RPH, YSB, and Season; Linli used TEMP, PSB, YSB, PLR, and Season; Liling used TEMP, PSB, YSB, PLR, and Season. The GBDT model performed better than the MLR model in four regions (Hongjiang, Yuanjiang, Dong'an, and Linli), and DeepAR performed better than MLR and GBDT in all areas.

In conclusion, deep learning-based DeepAR models can dynamically predict SRSB populations combined with the ground meteorological variables, associated pest variables, and pest variable-derived time variables, which can be applied to the timely management of crop pests after proper validation in different regions. We anticipate that these results can cooperate with an online rice pest monitoring and intelligent prediction system developed by the Hunan Provincial Department of Agriculture to support an effective early pest warning system.

Author Contributions: Conceptualization, Y.L. and S.T.; methodology, Y.L.; software, Y.L. and H.Y.; validation, Y.L., S.T. and H.Y.; formal analysis, Y.L.; investigation, Y.L.; resources, S.T., Z.Z. and C.L.; data curation, Y.L., R.Z. and H.Y.; writing—original draft preparation, Y.L., R.Z. and H.Y.; writing—review and editing, Y.L., C.L. and H.Y.; visualization, Y.L.; supervision, S.T. and C.L.; project administration, S.T.; funding acquisition, Z.Z. All authors have read and agreed to the published version of the manuscript.

Funding: This research was funded by the National Science Fund Project of China (31772157).

Institutional Review Board Statement: Not applicable.

Informed Consent Statement: Not applicable.

Data Availability Statement: The data presented in this study are available upon request from the corresponding author. The data are not publicly available due to privacy.

Conflicts of Interest: The authors declare no conflict of interest with respect to the research, authorship, and publication of this article.

References

1. Feng, Q.L. Physiology and interaction of insects with environmental factors. *J. Integr. Agric.* **2020**, *19*, 1411–1416. [CrossRef]
2. Sun, Y.; Xu, L.; Chen, Q.; Qin, W.; Huang, S.; Jiang, Y.; Qin, H. Chlorantraniliprole resistance and its biochemical and new molecular target mechanisms in laboratory and field strains of Chilo suppressalis (Walker). *Pest Manag. Sci.* **2018**, *74*, 1416–1423. [CrossRef]
3. Muralidharan, K.; Pasalu, I.C. Assessments of crop losses in rice ecosystems due to stem borer damage (Lepidoptera: Pyralidae). *Crop Prot.* **2006**, *25*, 409–417. [CrossRef]
4. Chen, M.; Shelton, A.; Ye, G. Insect-Resistant Genetically Modified Rice in China: From Research to Commercialization. *Annu. Rev. Entomol.* **2011**, *56*, 81–101. [CrossRef]
5. He, Y.; Zhang, J.; Gao, C.; Su, J.; Chen, J.; Shen, J. Regression analysis of dynamics of insecticide resistance in field populations of Chilo suppressalis (Lepidoptera: Crambidae) during 2002–2011 in China. *J. Econ. Entomol.* **2013**, *106*, 1832–1837. [CrossRef]
6. Wang, Y.N.; Ke, K.Q.; Li, Y.H.; Han, L.Z.; Liu, Y.M.; Hua, H.X.; Peng, Y.F. Comparison of three transgenic Bt rice lines for insecticidal protein expression and resistance against a target pest, Chilo suppressalis (Lepidoptera: Crambidae). *Insect Sci.* **2016**, *23*, 78–87. [CrossRef] [PubMed]
7. Qiang, C.K.; Du, Y.Z.; Yu, L.Y.; Qin, Y.H.; Feng, W.J. Effects of temperature stress on physiological indices of Chilo suppressalis Walker (Lepidoptera: Pyralidae) diapause larvae. *Chin. J. Appl. Ecol.* **2012**, *23*, 1365–1369.
8. Skawsang, S.; Nagai, M.; Tripathi, N.K.; Soni, P. Predicting Rice Pest Population Occurrence with Satellite-Derived Crop Phenology, Ground Meteorological Observation, and Machine Learning: A Case Study for the Central Plain of Thailand. *Appl. Sci.* **2019**, *9*, 4846. [CrossRef]
9. Aparecido, L.; Rolim, G.; De Moraes, J.R.D.S.; Costa, C.; Souza, P. Machine learning algorithms for forecasting the incidence of Coffea arabica pests and diseases. *Int. J. Biometeorol.* **2020**, *64*, 671–688. [CrossRef]
10. Holloway, P.; Kudenko, D.; Bell, J.R. Dynamic selection of environmental variables to improve the prediction of aphid phenology: A machine learning approach. *Ecol. Indic.* **2018**, *88*, 512–521. [CrossRef]
11. Narayanasamy, M.; Kennedy, J.; Geethalakshmi, V. Weather Based Pest Forewarning Model for Major Insect Pests of Rice—An Effective Way for Insect Pest Prediction. *Annu. Res. Rev. Biol.* **2017**, *21*, 1–13. [CrossRef]
12. Poggi, S.; Le Cointe, R.; Riou, J.; Larroudé, P.; Thibord, J.; Plantegenest, M. Relative influence of climate and agroenvironmental factors on wireworm damage risk in maize crops. *J. Pest Sci.* **2018**, *91*, 585–599. [CrossRef]
13. Gu, Y.H.; Yoo, S.J.; Park, C.J.; Kim, Y.H.; Park, S.K.; Kim, J.S.; Lim, J.H. BLITE-SVR: New forecasting model for late blight on potato using support-vector regression. *Comput. Electron. Agric.* **2016**, *130*, 169–176. [CrossRef]
14. Ni, T.; Zhai, J. A matrix-free smoothing algorithm for large-scale support vector machines. *Inf. Sci.* **2016**, *358*, 29–43. [CrossRef]
15. Feng, S.; Zhou, H.; Dong, H. Using deep neural network with small dataset to predict material defects. *Mater. Des.* **2019**, *162*, 300–310. [CrossRef]
16. Salman, S.; Liu, X. Overfitting Mechanism and Avoidance in Deep Neural Networks. *arXiv* **2019**, arXiv:1901.06566.
17. Bengio, Y. Learning Deep Architectures for AI. *Found. Trends Mach. Learn.* **2009**, *2*, 1–127. [CrossRef]
18. Schmidhuber, J. Deep learning in neural networks: An overview. *Neural Netw.* **2015**, *61*, 85–117. [CrossRef]
19. Bengio, Y.; Courville, A.; Vincent, P. Representation Learning: A Review and New Perspectives. *IEEE T. Pattern Anal.* **2013**, *35*, 1798–1828. [CrossRef] [PubMed]
20. Deng, L.; Yu, D. Deep Learning: Methods and Applications. *Found. Trends Signal Process.* **2014**, *7*, 197–387. [CrossRef]
21. Lecun, Y.; Bengio, Y.; Hinton, G. Deep learning. *Nature* **2015**, *521*, 436–444. [CrossRef] [PubMed]
22. Luo, X.; Li, J.; Chen, M.; Yang, X.; Li, X. Ophthalmic Disease Detection via Deep Learning with a Novel Mixture Loss Function. *IEEE J. Biomed. Health Inform.* **2021**, *25*, 3332–3339. [CrossRef]
23. Chen, M.; Li, Y.; Luo, X.; Wang, W.; Wang, L.; Zhao, W. A Novel Human Activity Recognition Scheme for Smart Health Using Multilayer Extreme Learning Machine. *IEEE Internet Things J.* **2019**, *6*, 1410–1418. [CrossRef]
24. Sun, J.; Luo, X.; Gao, H.; Wang, W.; Gao, Y.; Yang, X. Categorizing Malware via A Word2Vec-based Temporal Convolutional Network Scheme. *J. Cloud Comput.* **2020**, *9*, 1–14. [CrossRef]
25. Luo, X.; Sun, J.K.; Wang, L.; Wang, W.P.; Zhao, W.B.; Wu, J.S.; Wang, J.H.; Zhang, Z.J. Short-Term Wind Speed Forecasting via Stacked Extreme Learning Machine With Generalized Correntropy. *IEEE Trans. Ind. Inform.* **2018**, *14*, 4963–4971. [CrossRef]
26. Wahyono, T.; Yaya, H.; Haryono, S.; Saleh, A.B. Enhanced lstm multivariate time series forecasting for crop pest attack prediction. *ICIC Express Lett.* **2020**, *10*, 943–949.
27. Yan, Y.; Feng, C.; Wan, M.P.; Chang, K.T. *Multiple Regression and Artificial Neural Network for the Prediction of Crop Pest Risks*; Springer International Publishing: Cham, Switzerland, 2015; pp. 73–84. ISBN 1865-1348.
28. Yamamura, K.; Yokozawa, M.; Nishimori, M.; Ueda, Y.; Yokosuka, T. How to analyze long-term insect population dynamics under climate change: 50-year data of three insect pests in paddy fields. *Popul. Ecol.* **2006**, *48*, 31–48. [CrossRef]
29. Ghani, I.M.M.; Ahmad, S. Stepwise Multiple Regression Method to Forecast Fish Landing. *Procedia-Soc. Behav. Sci.* **2010**, *8*, 549–554. [CrossRef]
30. Amiri, S.S.; Mottahedi, M.; Asadi, S. Using multiple regression analysis to develop energy consumption indicators for commercial buildings in the U.S. *Energy Build.* **2015**, *109*, 209–216. [CrossRef]
31. Friedman, J.H. Greedy Function Approximation: A Gradient Boosting Machine. *Ann. Stat.* **2001**, *29*, 1189–1232. [CrossRef]
32. Picard, R.R.; Cook, R.D. Cross-Validation of Regression Models. *Publ. Am. Stat. Assoc.* **1984**, *79*, 575–583. [CrossRef]

33. Hochreiter, S.; Schmidhuber, J. Long Short-Term Memory. *Neural Comput.* **1997**, *9*, 1735–1780. [CrossRef]
34. Hochreiter, S.; Schmidhuber, J. LSTM can solve hard long time lag problems. In Proceedings of the 9th International Conference on Neural Information Processing Systems, Denver, CO, USA, 3–5 December 1996; pp. 473–479.
35. Graves, A. Generating Sequences With Recurrent Neural Networks. *arXiv* **2013**, arXiv:1308.0850.
36. Van den Oord, A.; Dieleman, S.; Zen, H.; Simonyan, K.; Vinyals, O.; Graves, A.; Kalchbrenner, N.; Senior, A.; Kavukcuoglu, K. WaveNet: A Generative Model for Raw Audio. *arXiv* **2016**, arXiv:1609.03499.
37. Zaremba, W.; Sutskever, I.; Vinyals, O. Recurrent Neural Network Regularization. *arXiv* **2014**, arXiv:1409.2329.
38. Salinas, D.; Flunkert, V.; Gasthaus, J.; Januschowski, T. DeepAR: Probabilistic forecasting with autoregressive recurrent networks. *Int. J. Forecast.* **2020**, *36*, 1181–1191. [CrossRef]
39. Draper, N.; Smith, H. *Applied Regression Analysis*, 2nd ed.; John Wiley: New York, NY, USA, 1981; ISBN 978-0-471-02995-3.
40. Glantz, S.A.V.; Slinker, B.K. *Primer of Applied Regression and Analysis of Variance*; McGraw-Hill: New York, NY, USA, 1990; ISBN 0070234078.
41. Carpenter, R.G. Principles and procedures of statistics, with special reference to the biological sciences. *Eugen. Rev.* **1960**, *52*, 172–173.
42. Chicco, D.; Warrens, M.J.; Jurman, G. The coefficient of determination R-squared is more informative than SMAPE, MAE, MAPE, MSE and RMSE in regression analysis evaluation. *PeerJ Comput. Sci.* **2021**, *7*, e623. [CrossRef]
43. Time Series Prediction—Telesens. Available online: https://www.telesens.co/2019/06/08/time-series-prediction/ (accessed on 21 September 2021).